Teaching Science for All Children

Ralph E. Martin, Jr.
Ohio University

Colleen Sexton
Ohio University

Kay Wagner

with

Jack Gerlovich

Allyn and Bacon
Boston   London   Toronto   Sydney   Tokyo   Singapore

Editor-in-Chief, Education: Nancy Forsyth
Editorial Assistant: Christine Nelson
Cover Administrator: Linda Dickinson
Composition Buyer: Linda Cox
Manufacturing Buyer: Louise Richardson
Production Coordinator: Deborah Brown
Editorial-Production Service: Woodstock Publishers Services
Text Designer: Glenna Collett
Cover Designer: Design Ad Cetera

The material in this book is based upon work supported by the National
Science Foundation under grant number 91–47392. Any opinions, findings,
conclusions, or recommendations expressed in this publication are those of
the authors and do not necessarily reflect the views of the Foundaton.

Library of Congress Cataloging-in-Publication Data

Teaching science for all children / Ralph Martin . . . (et al.)
    p.   cm.
    Includes bibliographical references and index.
    ISBN 0–205–14875–1
    1. Science—Study and teaching. 2. Science—Study and teaching
  (Elementary) 3. Activity programs in education. I. Martin, Ralph
E., 1951–   .
    Q181.T3534   1994   93–31546
    372.3'5044—dc20   CIP

Printed in the United States of America
10 9 8 7 6 5 4 3 2   98 97 96 95

DEDICATIONS

This book is dedicated, in part, to the memory of Elizabeth Barcikowski. Beth, as friend and former student, embraced practical hands-on minds-on learning with endless enthusiasm long before constructivism was fashionable as a term for describing what she did. Her enthusiasm persistently shaped new teachers. The after-school science enrichment program she developed continues serving with much success elementary children and college students alike, many years after her premature departure from East Elementary School in Athens, Ohio. Mrs. B, as her fourth grade students called her, inspired many of the scenarios of this book. She is featured in one specifically, which reveals her classroom ingenuity and her craft of successful questioning.

r. m.

To my former teachers who exemplified effective teaching and inspired me to follow in their footsteps.

c. s.

To my mentor and friend. Ditto.

k. w.

To the Elementary Science Methods students at Drake University who have been, and continue to be, inspirations for my science activity ideas, as well as enthusiastic supporters of hands-on, and often electronically delivered, quality science teaching.

j. g.

Contents

Part III   Science Teaching Methods

Part IV   Learning Activities and Teaching Materials to Meet the Goals of Elementary and Middle School Science

Part V   Appendixes

Science Lessons

SECTION III   Earth Science Activities   519

About the Authors

Ralph E. Martin, Jr. is a full professor at Ohio University in the School of Education. Throughout his years of teaching he has received more than 1 million dollars in grants for work in improving teaching and learning in elementary science and mathematics. He has served on Ohio commissions in science and vocational education to improve science education. He is presently active in the state science organization, Science Education Council of Ohio (SECO), and has been given the Service Award in Science Education. Presently, he serves as the Director for Southeast Ohio and serves on the state board of directors for SECO.

Dr. Martin has published several books, including *Introduction to Teaching* (1988) with co-authors George Wood and Ed Stevens, published by Allyn and Bacon.

Colleen Sexton has worked in preparing science teachers and promoting science education in a number of capacities. Dr. Sexton is involved in the Appalachian Distance Learning Project—a project which fiber optically links three third-grade classrooms, separated by over 150 miles. She has worked extensively with classroom teachers in helping them plan science lessons which take advantage of available technology.

For the past three years Dr. Sexton has worked with 43 elementary science teachers from 13 different school districts in southeast Ohio on an NSF-funded Lead Teacher Project. Dr. Sexton is also involved in a research project which is concerned with equity throughout Ohio's school districts.

Kay Wagner has 18 years of teaching experience and was Ohio's state science supervisor for five years. She was the Director of the Alliance Program for the Triangle Coalition for Science and Technology Education and is presently the Education Coordinator for the Science Applications International Corporation (SAIC) in support of the Office of Civilian Radioactive Waste Management of the U.S. Department of Energy.

Jack Gerlovich is Assistant Professor of Science Education at Drake University. He was the state science consultant for the Iowa Department of Education for 11 years. He is also the president and founder of JaKel, Inc., a science education safety company. His ten years of science teaching experience include junior high, high school, and college levels.

Dr. Gerlovich is a fellow at the American Association for the Advancement of Science and the Iowa Academy of Science. He is a member of the National Science Teachers Association (Board of Directors 1985–87), the Council of State Science Supervisors (National President 1985–87), and the National Academy of Applied Sciences (Board of Directors).

Dr. Gerlovich, a nationally renowned safety expert, has authored and coauthored 30 professional journal articles, eight state science publications, and developed books, software, and video products on the subject.

Preface

Learners may believe what they see, but they actually *understand* what they do. Understanding is easy to describe in theoretical terms, but is difficult to achieve with the limits and daily pressures of the classroom. Also, among science teachers the popular concept-turned-slogan of "hands-on" learning is often supported, but misunderstood. It is important that children's hands stimulate their senses, but it is, perhaps, more important that children's minds be strongly connected to what their hands *do*. Hands-on, minds-on learning can be effective, but only if *both* occur. Our book will help you to help learners make these important corrections.

Our mission, as science teachers, is to find effective ways to help learners construct their own understanding by connecting their many ideas into a fabric of concepts, attitudes, and skills that carries meaning for them personally and academically. Additional goals of this mission are to stimulate, among learners, an awareness of career opportunities, as well as to help children develop some understanding about the complex interrelationships among science, technology, and society.

The philosophy that guides our book is one of promoting the concept of *whole science* by making certain that the ideas, skills, and attitudes of science are all included in the experiences teachers offer learners. Whole science is based on the belief that knowledge exists only in the minds of learners after they have constructed it for themselves. The whole science approach was developed in our preservice teacher's courses at our universities several years ago. The methods were refined and expanded with recent funding from the National Science Foundation during the Lead Teacher Project at Ohio University. The project involved dozens of practicing elementary, middle school, and special education teachers who taught science. The Lead Teachers tested in their own classrooms and helped to improve the ideas and activities that are in this book. As leaders in science education reform, the teachers shared these same ideas and methods with hundreds of other teachers. All of the ideas, methods, and activities have been tested extensively; they can and do work if you are willing to accept as evidence significant and substantial gains in pupil science achievement, skills, and attitudes.

We have constructed our book to help you connect the important parts of science, first by helping you to understand the *wholistic* nature of science teaching, and later by helping you to develop your own impression about how learners construct their understanding. The science goals, planning techniques, and teaching approaches provided in our book support this conception of constructivism.

Our chapters contain some unique features. For example, on the first page of each chapter is a *concept map* (a type of flow-chart). A concept map is a picture of the main ideas we hope you obtain from the chapter and the relationships among those ideas. Read the map from box-to-box (top-to-bottom), noting the direction of the arrows and the linking words. Next, each chapter begins with a *scenario*. The scenarios are all factual, but have been changed for rather obvious reasons. Each scenario helps to create a vicarious experience through a short story related to the chapter. This experience, when combined with the map, should give you an advanced organizer (a mental framework) for understanding parts of the chapter that may be new or difficult to you. We hope these features help you to construct your own understanding of the material in our book.

Within each chapter we have added visuals—figures, tables, and photographs—to reinforce the ideas presented. Sometimes we include relevant exercises that you might want to try. One feature, "What Research Says," supplements the chapter with a brief authoritative report taken from the recent research. Another feature, "Teachers on Science Teaching," written by some of our finest teachers gives an applied view and describes classroom uses of the topics of the chapter. We close each chapter with a customary summary, which complements the concept map. *Discussion questions* and ideas for class *projects* are included; many of these are field-based to complement any early field experience or practice teaching that instructors may prefer. *Additional readings* contain annotations for further reading on the important topics of each chapter.

Please experiment with how you use this book because we have written each chapter to stand alone, even though we have organized this book in a linear way. In Part I we provide a foundation for science teaching in two chapters as we discuss the nature of science and learning. Then, in Part II, Chapters 3–5, we focus on the elementary and middle school science program by examining goals, planning and evaluation techniques, and historical influences on modern science programs. The goals we offer arose from extensive science education research. The goals are universal and are compatible with the recent reform efforts of states, science organizations, and the National Research Council.

Part III, Chapters 6–12, is devoted to a variety of teaching methods and teacher's skills. These chapters include: questioning, student-centered and inquiry instruction, direct instruction; teaching pupils who have special needs; classroom management; and locating and using important science teaching resources, as well as using technology to supplement the science program. Safe science teaching is featured throughout our book but is the primary focus of Chapter 11 with an option to purchase special science safety software that treats the needs of elementary and middle school science thoroughly.

Our book contains *58 complete lessons.* The lessons are contained in Part IV and are distributed among the expected science disciplines: life, physical, and earth. Our lessons contain more than *150 different activities* that are constructed in a very powerful way—a way to encourage the highest level of student hands-on/minds-on activity, and a way to stimulate high levels of concept formation. Our plans are consistent with how children construct their own understanding and with "constructivist" teaching practices. We use the 4–E learning cycle of Exploration, Explanation, Expansion, and Evaluation. The lessons have been classroom tested by our own undergraduate,

and graduate students and the Lead Teachers previously mentioned.

All chapters and activities are supported by several unique appendixes located in Part V. These are written for preservice and inservice teachers who want to locate effective science resources or entire science curriculum projects, and want to become involved in networks or alliances of science teachers through state or federal agencies.

Of course, at all times we encourage you to try in your own way the ideas in our book. If you do, you will be learning about teaching science as we advocate for teaching children by constructing *your* own understanding. So you see, we hope you will believe the ideas and information that you see in this book, but, more importantly, we hope that you will try each idea and learn to understand the complexity and rewards of effective science teaching from what you *do.*

ACKNOWLEDGMENTS

No book is ever written alone. In addition to our author team, many important persons supported the project and turned the dreams and ideas into a reality. Indeed it is an understatement to say we are grateful to those many talented persons who include:

Nancy Forsyth, Editor-in-Chief, Education, and her able assistant Christine Nelson, whose beliefs in our book yielded first-class treatment at every stage of the publishing process. Deborah Brown, Production Administrator; Barbara Gracia, *Woodstock Publishers Services;* and Ellen Mann, Marketing Manager oversaw the details—the creative and the tedious. Karen Stone's keen eye, as copy editor, shaped a complex manuscript to fit the wonderful design developed by Glenna Collett. Illustrations by Cindy Parman and Guy Stuart provide the correct concrete visuals for our abstract ideas.

Other research support and assistance has been provided by Mindy Cisneros, Rhonda Elahee, Christine Kilgore, and Holly Larson during the years it took to write this book. Without them the task would have been much more difficult.

Our special thanks go to the reviewers who offered substantial suggestions that helped to shape our book. They are:

Joel E. Bass, Sam Houston State University; Herbert Cohen, Arizona State University; Frances Lawrenz, Minneapolis, Minnesota; Robert Miller, Eastern Kentucky University; John A. Novak, Eastern Michigan University; Frances H. Squires, Indiana University Southeast.

We want to acknowledge and thank the following teachers who contributed essays for "Teachers on Science Teaching:"

Najwa Abdul-Abdul-Tawwab, Oliver Wendell Holmes, Dorchester, Massachusetts;

Earnestine Blakley, Bessie Ellison Elementary, St. Joseph, Missouri;

Michael E. Cawthra, Kyffin Elementary School, Golden, Colorado;

Phyllis A. Frysinger, Miami View Elementary, Charleston, Ohio;

Terry L. Kluesner, Erin Elementary School, Hartford, Wisconsin;

Kathryn C. Marshall, Hopkinson, Philadelphia, Pennsylvania;

Johanna Ramsey, Marion Elementary School, Marion, New York;

Michael S. Roberts, Hollister School District, Hollister, California;

Charlotte Schartz, Kingman Middle School, Kingman, Kansas;

Ursula Sexton, Green Valley Elementary School, Ramon, California;

Mary Ann Sloan, Paumanok Elementary School, Dix Hills, New York;

Barbara J. Smith, Wainwright Elementary, Houston, Texas.

Too numerous to mention here, forty-two Lead Teachers worked with us for three years to develop some of the material in this book. Their practical uses and suggestions provided invaluable tips for which we are immensely grateful.

We also acknowledge and express appreciation for several ideas offered by Piyush Swami, science educator at the University of Cincinnati. He helped to shape some early drafts of a manuscript, which eventually evolved into this text.

Finally, we give our gratitude to our spouses and children for their encouragement and support, especially during the tense moments that always accompany such a large project. Knowing that we could help our children's teachers gave inspiration and helped to shape our mission. There will always be a special place in our hearts for Marilyn, Jennifer, Jessica, Jonathan, Tim, Sarah, Celeste, Carl, Cade, Kara, Pat, Jacque, and Kelly.

PART ONE

The Nature of Science and Learning

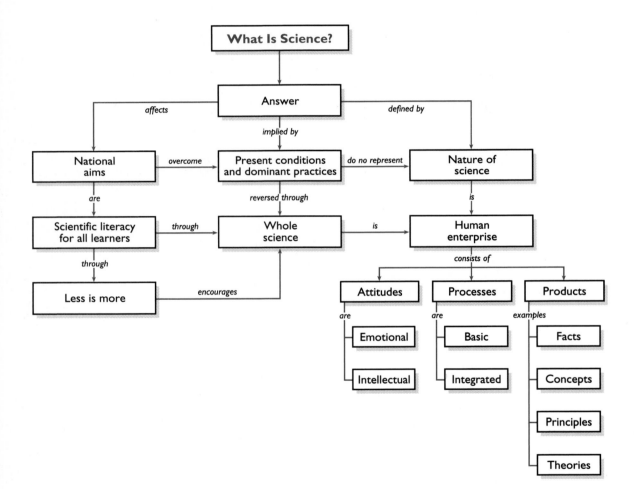

What Is Science?

"I'm not looking forward to this term," Betty confided to a friend. When asked to explain, she shared her discomfort with science and all of its dreaded memories: difficult word lists, endless definitions, and reading, reading, reading during her elementary and middle school years—that is, when science was taught, and that didn't seem very often. In high school, Betty remembered studying creepy things like insects and snakes. Other experiences stood out in Betty's mind, too, like smelly, gooey dissections, memorization of the Periodic Table, and difficult metric and English measurement conversions. All her teachers had seemed to suggest that science was important, but Betty had never understood why. "Why do I need to learn this?" Betty had often asked.

Still, Betty's friends, parents, and advisor urged her to give the science methods course a fair chance. "Maybe you'll learn something," they usually said. After a couple of classes in the methods course Betty was about to believe they were correct.

The professor had begun with activities that had required some simple observations and predictions. Each prediction was tested by what had seemed like trial and error. Then a challenge had been given: Find several ways to light some small bulbs with minimal equipment. From there the class had moved on to building simple circuits. Any scientific terminology had always been introduced after Betty was familiar with the equipment and its operation.

Today's class was her biggest challenge so far. Betty had accumulated the odd assortment of materials: a cardboard tube, a bottle cap, paper fasteners, a paper clip, batteries, a couple of short wires, and a flashlight bulb. How would she ever figure out how to make a flashlight? Oh well, she would try—that was all her professor asked besides today's objective. That required practical application of what she had learned: Construct a flashlight and show him that it worked at least one time.

Minutes seemed like hours, and Betty felt pressure that goes with being the last one to finish. "I did it!" She couldn't help herself. Her shout attracted the attention of the whole class, and now the professor was approaching her work station. His serious puckered concentration turned into a broad grin and his wink assured Betty that he understood the sweet feeling of success.

"That's what science is all about," he whispered to Betty as he turned to the class and asked, "What are your feelings, what caused them, and what have you learned?" Betty's classmates offered comments that confirmed her own positive feelings. They agreed that the positive feelings were caused by the experiences of discovery and achievement, and that it is important for children to have the same feelings about learning.

"In this course we are going to explore ways to offer the same types of experiences to children," Betty's professor continued. "I think the best place to start is at the beginning, considering what you've told me about your prior experiences with science and your impressions of it. Think about what we have been doing and answer this question: 'What is science?' Once we know the answer answer to this question, we can make real progress in learning ways to teach science."

INTRODUCTION

Betty's view of science influenced her initial performance in her classes. The same can happen to you. But there is more. Our perceptions influence our teaching decisions and what we expect from our students. This is why it is important to begin with a view of science in this course: It becomes a foundation for building our understanding about science and for determining our teaching mission.

This chapter helps to build a foundation for teaching science. To begin this foundation, we introduce you to:

1. The present conditions of science learning and teaching,
2. The nature of science,
3. The concept of whole science and its essential parts,
4. The aims of modern science education.

WHERE IS ELEMENTARY SCIENCE?

"In the curriculum!" might be your answer to this seemingly silly question. But the actual profiencies of our children make this question a serious one. In international comparisons, U.S. elementary (fourth-grade) youth rank ninth out of twelve countries. In biology, the most popular high school course, U.S. students rank last. The good news is that there are no substantial gender differences in the test scores for elementary children in the United States, although a gap appears and widens as children progress through school.[1] The 1990 National Assessment of Educational Progress (NAEP) reports that:

- About two thirds of our eighth graders and one third of our fourth graders demonstrate an understanding of basic information in the physical sciences and ecological principles, with just a beginning ability to interpret experimental results.
- Across grades 4, 8, and 12 there are large differences in the proficiency levels between whites and minority students.
- Students from advantaged urban communities perform better than disadvantaged students.
- Several factors in students' home environments are related to their science proficiencies, including the amounts and types of reading materials available, the presence of both parents in the home, and the amount of time spent watching television.
- At the fourth-grade level, fewer than half the schools give science priority status; science receives only slightly better treatment at the other grade levels in the study.
- Most fourth-grade students report that they like science, but interest declines as students progress through school.[2]

Now let us examine Table 1.1, which reports the percentage of students in the tested grades who performed at each of the four different levels during a national assessment. Level 200 means that the students are able to show that they have developed some level of understanding simple scientific principles. At level 250, students can interpret simple tables and make inferences about the outcomes of experiments; students show whether they can apply what they have learned. Level 300 indicates that students can evaluate the appropriateness of the design of an experiment and that they have more skill in applying what

TABLE 1.1   Percentage of Students at or Above the Four Proficiency Levels on the National Assessment of Educational Progress Science Scale

		Percentage of Students at or Above		
	Level	Grade 4	Grade 8	Grade 12
Understands simple scientific principles	200	85	94	99
Applies general scientific information	250	31	64	84
Analyzes scientific procedures and data	300	1	18	45
Integrates specialized scientific information	350	0	1	9

Source: The 1990 Report Card, U.S. Department of Education, 1992, p. 28.

they have learned. Level 350 requires that students use detailed scientific knowledge to infer relationships and draw scientific conclusions.

The assessment included a national sample of 6,500 students at each of grades 4, 8, and 12 from public and private schools. What the students knew and could do was determined through multiple-choice and constructed-response questions. Constructed-response questions required students to write an explanation, provide a drawing, graph information, and so on. Proficiency levels could range from 0 to 500, but too few students scored beyond 350 to make reporting those results worthwhile.[3]

A very large portion of our students do very well with level-200 questions. However, ask them to apply information, and the performances drop off extensively, especially for our elementary children. Very few of our nation's students

WHAT DO YOU THINK?

Table 1.1 shows the percentages of students who scored at or above the four proficiency levels for each grade level tested in the 1990 National Assessment of Educational Progress. Challenge yourself to go beyond the simple level by trying to apply what you have learned in science and mathematics classes to the data revealed in the table. For example:

- What general problem does the table reveal to you?
- How would you graph the data to show the story of the results? Show your graph here.
- What patterns do you detect in the data?
- Why do you think each pattern occurs?

can integrate special science information in ways that permit them to draw meaningful conclusions. Why is this? Perhaps it is because of the limited way science is viewed in many schools. Let us investigate the nature of science to see if we can uncover part of the solution to our nation's teaching and learning problems and to understand Betty's experiences from our chapter scenario.

THE NATURE OF SCIENCE

The word *science* originates from the Latin word *scientia*, meaning *knowledge*, as in possessing knowledge instead of misunderstanding or being ignorant. In fact, one of the authors distinctly remembers having to memorize a definition from a junior high textbook (long since forgotten along with most everything else in it) that defined science as "an organized body of knowledge." Following that we memorized steps of the scientific method: (1) identify the problem, (2) examine the data, (3) form a hypothesis, (4) experiment, and (5) make a conclusion. But a text definition or memory exercise is helpful only to a point in learning *about* science, its nature, and its implications for society. Unfortunately, a definition does not always help answer a question like Betty's: "Why do I need to learn this?" Such a narrow, incomplete definition also gives an insufficient impression of what and how science should be taught for maximum effect.

Consider Betty's recollections of her classroom experiences with science and the influence those experiences had on her. It seems fair to assume that Betty's teachers carried an image and feeling about science. Betty's teachers' images formed their beliefs and affected their teaching of science. Their teaching influenced Betty's beliefs. When Betty teaches, she will continue the cycle by influencing her own students' beliefs. Perhaps this is not a desirable picture when you consider the influence Betty could have had on children *before* she acquired new impressions about science.

Throughout much of recorded history, science usually had two classical functions. First, science was for pure intellectual study, and its primary aim was "satisfy the needs of the mind and not those of the body; it appeals to nothing but the disinterested curiosity of mankind."[4] This image of science contrasts rather sharply with a second function of science, "as a body of useful and practical knowledge and method for obtaining it."[5] These functions fall short of fulfilling the needs of modern science.

It is rather easy to get the impression that the purpose of science is to provide us with information and mental exercises. This impression is consistent with learning science by reading and writing about it. Unfortunately this view is not complete, does not provide an accurate impression of what science actually is, and does not answer Betty's question in our opening scenario: *Why* does Betty have to learn science?

How does a child receive information, construct knowledge, and gain meaning from what is accumulated? Both of the above views of science do offer us some useful clues for answering this question. The first view highlights the assumption that human curiosity is important. The second view reminds us of the skills that are needed for learning: skills for acquiring useful information that has practical value and carries real meaning for learners, meaning that is constructed from the learners' experiences.

Science is a human construct and a human activity. Children in particular are naturally curious. Their curiosity motivates them to discover new ways to use this powerful key for unlocking the mysteries of their world. Therefore, when we consider what science is and make decisions about what and how to teach children, three parts of what science actually is must be remembered and put to use:

- Science encourages humans to develop positive attitudes and their powerful curiosity.
- Science requires that humans use their curiosity to construct new ways of investigating and to process information.
- Science consists of the meaning and information humans construct for themselves to benefit their everyday living.

The new things children learn tend to stimulate curiosity further. When children are given a complete experience with all that science is—whole science—a science cycle is established and continues to build its own momentum. (See Figure 1.1.) Or, put in simpler terms, whole science consists of three parts: development of children's *attitudes,* development of their *process skills,* and their construction of useful ideas, *products.* Children's experiences can stimulate their

OPENING OUR EYES

The April 9, 1990, *Newsweek* contained an enlightening article, "Not Just For Nerds—How to Teach Science to Our Kids." An excerpt helps to make our point about the problem of misunderstanding science and teaching it improperly.

Science is simply a way of looking at the world. At root, it consists of asking questions, proposing answers, and testing them rigorously against the available evidence. As the popular astronomer Carl Sagan wrote recently, "Science invites us to let the facts in, even when they don't conform to our preconceptions. It counsels us to carry alternative hypotheses in our heads and see which best match the facts." For all the natural forces it explains, science is a course in analytical thought.

Unfortunately, few American students ever get to taste real science, for few of the nation's schools teach it. All parties now seem to agree that American science education serves not to nurture children's natural curiosity but to extinguish it with catalogs of dreary facts and terms. "The questions we're all interested in concern the universe we live in, the way our bodies work, what the mind is, how all things are integrated," says Stephen Toulmin, a physicist turned philosopher at Northwestern University. As most of us know firsthand, those aren't the kinds of questions that kids are encouraged to ponder. Instead, says Toulmin, "we teach them to solve differential equations, to handle test tubes without breaking them."

Source: Excerpted from *Newsweek,* April 9, 1990, pp. 52–53.

FIGURE 1.1 The Science Cycle Children receive a whole science experience when they are immersed in *all* of science's parts. The synergy among the parts makes science whole.

CHILD'S EXPERIENCE UNIVERSE

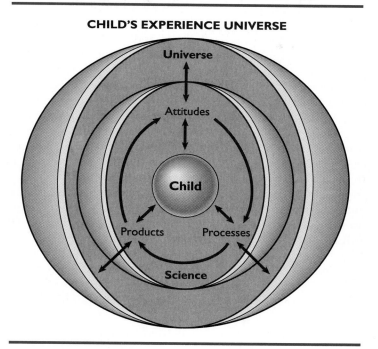

curiosity (or attitudes), which can motivate them to develop new process skills; these are used to construct the products of science. Successful learning enriches the experience universe and stimulates further inquiry. We provide children with a whole science experience when they are immersed in *all* of science's parts.

THREE PARTS OF SCIENCE

Again whole science consists of three parts: development of children's attitudes, development of their process skills, and children's construction of useful ideas, or science products.

Attitudes

What Are Attitudes? Attitudes are mental predispositions toward people, objects, subjects, events, and so on. In science, attitudes are important because of three primary factors.[6] First, a child's attitude carries a mental state of readiness with it. With a positive attitude, a child will perceive science objects, topics, activities, and people positively. If he or she is unready or hesitant, for whatever reason, a child will be less willing to interact with people and things associated with science. Realize, though, that this readiness factor occurs unconsciously in a child, without prior thought or overt consent.

Second, attitudes are not innate or inborn. Contemporary psychologists maintain that attitudes are learned and are organized through experiences as children develop.[7] Furthermore, a child's attitude can be changed through additional experiences.

Third, attitudes are dynamic results of experiences that act as directive factors when a child enters into new experiences. As a result, attitudes carry an emotional and an intellectual tone, both of which lead to making decisions and forming evaluations. These decisions and evaluations can cause a child to set priorities and hold different preferences. In our chapter scenario, Betty is an example. Her attitude toward science and the way she values it appear to shift from a negative to a neutral or perhaps even a positive viewpoint. In time, with continued positive experiences and adjustments in her attitude, Betty may become more open to science, think differently about it, and accumulate more useful ideas and skills—all products of her learning. But all of this begins with her attitude. Attitudes influence how people respond.

Emotional Attitudes.   Young children's attitudes, so it seems, are more emotional than intellectual. Curiosity, the natural start of it all, may be accompanied by perseverance, a positive approach to failure (or accepting not getting one's own way all the time), and openness to new experiences or even other people's points of view (such as tolerance for other children's ways of playing a favorite game). These are fundamental attitudes, useful for building

Positive attitudes help children succeed in science.

TABLE 1.2   Attitudes of Young Scientists

Emotional

From children's natural curiosity for learning and acquiring new experiences, we can encourage them to further develop:

- more curiosity
- perseverance
- a positive approach to failure
- open-mindedness
- cooperation with others

Intellectual

From children's positive learning experiences we can encourage them to further develop:

- a desire for reliable sources of information
- skepticism; a desire to be shown or to have alternative points of view proven
- avoidance of broad generalizations when evidence is limited
- tolerance for other opinions, explanations, or points of view
- willingness to withhold judgment until all evidence or information is found or examined
- refusal to believe in superstitions or to accept claims without proof
- openness to changing their minds when evidence for change is given and openness to questions about their own ideas

the other specific scientific attitudes that are necessary for success and the continuation of the science cycle.

Intellectual Attitudes.   Attitudes based on intellect or rational thought develop simultaneously with science process skills (the second part of science) and with the discovery or construction of useful science ideas (the third part of science). Teacher guidance, learning materials that can be manipulated, and interactive teaching methods help encourage formation of intellectual attitudes. Examples include skepticism and the development of a desire to follow procedures that increase objectivity. (See Table 1.2.)

Importance of Attitudes.   Young children have positive attitudes toward science and display many of these attitudes as they explore and interact with age-mates. However, over time these initial positive attitudes decline. For example, 67 percent of third graders in a study responded "Yes" to this question: "When you have science in school, do you like it?"[8] The children also expressed considerable interest in science (78 percent), believed that what they learn in science is useful out of school (67 percent), and believed that knowing a lot about science would help them when they grow up (71 percent).[9] This attitude de-

WHAT RESEARCH SAYS

Attitudes and Science Teaching

The importance of attitudes was recognized in science teaching and learning in the 1960s. The Educational Policies Commission issued a document titled *Education and the Spirit of Science.* The writers urged schools to promote "understanding of the values on which science is everywhere based. . . .We believe that the following values underlie science:

1. Longing to know and to understand
2. Questioning of all things
3. Search for data and their meaning
4. Demand for verification
5. Respect for logic
6. Consideration for premises
7. Consideration of consequences

"Commission members believed that the values of science are the most complete expression of one of the deepest of human values—the belief in today and assume a lower level of rigor for elementary children,

this is one way to justify the importance of developing a scientific attitude in children. Other reasons have been offered during more recent years: such attitudes help students have a better understanding of the nature of science by encouraging them to act out roles similar to those of scientists, and it is important for all students to become rational thinkers. What does this imply for science teachers?

"First, the science teacher is the key person for successful promotion of positive attitudes and affective attributes in children. Therefore, the science teacher must have a good knowledge of the nature of science and must be a good role model. Students must be enabled to perform experiments and solve problems that require use of the thinking skills involved in scientific inquiry."

Source: Compiled from Patricia Blosser, Bulletin Editor, Attitude Research in Science Education, Columbus, OH: ERIC/SMEAC, 1984, pp. 2–3.

clined when seventh graders (53 percent) and twelfth graders (49 percent) were asked about the usefulness of science.[10]

Children can develop appreciation for the role science plays in their daily lives and realize its utility when attitudes and practical value become teaching goals. Consider, for example, the influence science has on the food we eat, the clothing we wear, our use of leisure time, the forms of entertainment we enjoy, and the higher quality of life its technology provides us. Is there any career that is unaffected by science? Appreciation for science and recognition of its value accumulate as the intellectual attitudes of science are emphasized. Guide children through the science process skills—ways of doing and learning science—to stimulate and develop the intellectual attitudes.

Science Process Skills

Perhaps you learned something in your science classes called the *scientific method.* Does the term sound familiar to you? Do you know what it means? It is one thing to list several words or steps, but it is another to understand the intention and meaning of the methods of science and to be able to use them productively.

Have you ever used the methods of science outside of a science class? We believe you have, even if you think you have not. The methods of science actually consist of two factors: (1) a way of thinking critically and creatively, and (2) the *processes* one follows when solving problems. What sets scientists apart from the rest of us might only be the level of skill they have developed to solve their problems.

The mission of elementary and middle school science is not to persuade all children to become scientists. The mission is to help make science more accessible to *all* children. One way this can be done is to help children discover how science can be important to them. Therefore, let us consider the process skills rooted in science that young children must develop and the ways children can use these skills to solve their own problems of learning and life.

Learning How to Learn.   Some people refer to developing science process skills as "learning how to learn." Children learn how to learn by thinking critically and using information creatively. Children continue to learn how to learn

> when making discriminating observations, when organizing and analyzing facts and concepts, when giving reasons for expecting particular outcomes, when evaluating and interpreting the results of experiments, and when drawing justifiable conclusions. [Also, children] . . . should be able to predict what will happen when the conditions of a phenomenon in nature are changed.[11]

Types of Process Skills.   In science, the ways of thinking, measuring, solving problems, and using thoughts are called *processes*. *Process skills* describe the types of thinking and reasoning required. Science process skills may be divided into two types: basic skills and integrated skills.[12] Table 1.3 suggests the grade levels at which these skills are appropriate.

Basic Skills.   If children show that they can observe, classify, communicate, measure, estimate, predict, and infer, they are showing understanding of basic science processes.

Observation is the primary way children obtain information, and this does not mean that they benefit solely from watching someone else and listening to what others think. Children observe by using all their senses. For example, how do you observe a concert? Can you close your eyes now and recreate a concert you have attended by recalling how your senses were stimulated? Can you see the lights and special effects? Can you smell the odors unique to the crowd and those special effects? Can you feel the vibrations of the bass and drums? Can you hear the music and vocals—really hear them with all of their rhythm? Can you taste the popcorn or the Milk Duds? Teachers stimulate useful observation through the five senses when they ask children questions that cause them to identify properties of objects, changes, and similarities and differences; and to determine the difference between an observation and an inference. An example of an observation could be: *The object is hard, gray, round, and the size of a*

TABLE 1.3   Science Process Skills

Basic skills can be emphasized at the primary grades and then serve as a foundation for using the integrated skills at the intermediate grades and higher.

					Grades				
Basic Skills	*K*	*1*	*2*	*3*	*4*	*5*	*6*	*7*	*8*
Observation	X	X	X	X	X	X	X	X	X
Classification	X	X	X	X	X	X	X	X	X
Communication	X	X	X	X	X	X	X	X	X
Measurement	X	X	X	X	X	X	X	X	X
Estimation	X	X	X	X	X	X	X	X	X
Prediction	X	X	X	X	X	X	X	X	X
Inference	X	X	X	X	X	X	X	X	X
Integrated Skills	*K*	*1*	*2*	*3*	*4*	*5*	*6*	*7*	*8*
Identifying				X	X	X	X	X	X
Controlling Variables				X	X	X	X	X	X
Defining Operationally				X	X	X	X	X	X
Hypothesizing				X	X	X	X	X	X
Experimenting				X	X	X	X	X	X
Graphing				X	X	X	X	X	X
Interpreting				X	X	X	X	X	X
Modelling				X	X	X	X	X	X
Investigating				X	X	X	X	X	X

baseball. Instruments such as thermometers, volt meters, balances, and computers help to add precision to observations.

Classification requires that children organize their observations in ways that carry special meaning. Teachers can encourage children to classify when they ask them to group objects by their observed properties and/or to arrange objects or events in a particular order. An example is: *Placing all rocks of the same size, color and hardness into the same group.*

When *communication* is emphasized, children use language (spoken, written, and symbolic in many forms) to express their thoughts in ways that others can understand. Development of useful communication skills is encouraged by teachers who ask children to define words and terms operationally, to describe objects and events as they are perceived, and to record information and make data tables, graphs, and models to show what they have found. An example is: *Describing an observed change in a river over time by speaking, writing, or showing in a graph or data table.*

Measurement enhances thinking by adding precision to observations, classifications, and communications. Children can be encouraged to measure by using tools like rulers, meter sticks, balances, graduated cylinders, calibrated liquid containers, clocks, calculators, computers, electrical instruments, and even arbitrary units such as marbles, paper clips, and so on to measure quantity or distance. An example is: *Using a meter stick to describe the height of a child*. (Note: The metric system is *the* system in science.)

Estimation involves using judgment to approximate an amount or a value. The estimate is based on knowledge of measurement, but not direct measure. Estimation is useful for quick observations for which precision is not necessary. An example of an estimate could be: *I think the chair is about one meter high*, or *the glass looks like it has about 300 milliliters of water in it*.

Predictions refer to types of thinking that require our best guesses based on the information available to us. Meteorologists, for example, predict the weather. Their predictions are made in advance of the weather's actual occurrence and are based on accumulated observations, analysis of information, and prior experience. Similarly, children can be encouraged to make predictions before they carry out an act, such as grouping different objects into classifications based on a prediction concerning whether or not they will float when placed in water. A teacher can stimulate predictive thinking by asking children to review the observed properties of objects or events and asking them to tell what they think will happen when a change of some sort is made, such as our sink-or-float example above. Another example is: *Predicting the size and shape of an ice cube after heating it for ten minutes*.

Inferences are conclusions about the cause of an observation. Consider the sink-or-float example again. Children may observe that all light-weight objects from their collections float in water and infer that light weight was the cause of floating. Of course, this could be disproved by items not included in the children's limited collection of objects. Therefore, it is necessary to help children make better inferences by guiding their thinking in ways that (1) help them make conclusions, (2) about an observation, (3) based on the prior knowledge they have. Another example of an inference is: *Saying a person is happy because she smiles and hums a song*.

Integrated Science Process Skills.   Integrated science process skills rely on the students' capabilities to think at a higher level and to consider more than one thought at a time. Just as the word *integrated* implies, several of the basic process skills can be combined for greater power to form the tools used to solve problems. As the basic skills are prerequisites for integrated skills, the latter are the skills necessary to do science experiments. These skills consist of identifying and controlling variables, defining operationally, forming hypotheses, experimenting, interpreting data, forming models, making graphs, and investigating.

Identifying and controlling variables requires students to identify aspects of an experiment that can affect its outcome and to keep constant as many as

William E. Mills

Observation is a basic science process.

possible, while manipulating only the aspects or factors (variables) that are independent. Example: *Varying only the amount of fertilizer used on similar plants while keeping soil type, amount of sunlight, water, and temperature the same.*

Defining operationally occurs when children use observations and other information gained through experience to describe or label an object or event. Example: *An acid is a substance that changes bromethymol blue indicator from blue to yellow.*

Forming hypotheses is important for designed investigations and is similar to prediction, but more controlled and formal. Hypothesizing is using information to make a best educated guess about the expected outcome of an experiment. An example could be: *The more fertilizer is added to plants, the greater their growth.*

Experimenting requires using many thinking skills to design and conduct a controlled scientific test. This consists of asking a research question, forming a hypothesis, identifying and controlling variables, using operational definitions, conducting the experiment, and interpreting the data. An example could be: *The entire operational process of investigating the effects of amounts of fertilizer added to plants of the same type.*

Graphing makes it necessary for students to convert measurements into a diagram to show the relationships among and between the measures. An example could be from the experiment above: *Constructing a graph to show the heights of the plants, experimental and control, for each day (or week) of the experiment.*

Interpreting data requires that students collect observations and measurements (data) in an organized way and that they draw conclusions from the information obtained by reading tables, graphs and diagrams. An example: *Reading information in a table or graph about the growth of plants in the experiment described above and forming conclusions based on the interpretation of the data.* The interpretation could help to "prove" that *more fertilizer added to plants causes greater growth.*

Forming models requires that students create an abstract (mental) or concrete (physical) illustration of an object or event. An example could be: *A model that shows the best amount of fertilizer to use on a plant and the consequences of using too little or too much.*

Investigating is a complex process skill that requires students to use observations, to collect and analyze data, and to draw conclusions in order to solve a problem. Applying our plant experiment example further: *Complete an investigation to evaluate the fertilizer dosage model as a way of deciding upon a plant feeding routine for the class's garden.*

Importance of Process Skills. Basic science skills help children to expand their learning through experience. They begin with simple ideas, and then those ideas compound and form new, more complex ideas. All ideas are valuable because they have the potential to help children to become better decision makers, consumers, citizens, and problem solvers. Emphasis on science process skills helps children discover meaningful information and accumulate knowledge by constructing their understanding within and beyond the science classroom.

Science Products

Importance of Science Products. Children construct important ideas and discover much for themselves when they use the skills of science. Children gain knowledge by accumulating and processing information and by forming concepts about their natural world, human use of natural resources, and the impact of this use on society. Children also discover, in time, that knowledge provides power and carries with it a responsibility for its proper use. Perhaps most important, children can understand that much of science is tentative, has changed over time, and is subject to future change. Knowledge in science is not absolute, and research findings may be interpreted differently by different people, depending on their values and experiences.

Types of Science Products.   The information and ideas of science are often referred to as *products*. That is because new discoveries that add to the base of scientific information are the products of experimentation. An interesting thing about products, though, is that new discoveries often lead to more questions, more experiments, and more new discoveries. Indeed, the solutions to scientific problems can create new problems. The science cycle moves under its own momentum, propelled initially and again later sustained by human curiosity and a desire to explain natural phenomena. The effect is an exploding accumulation of new information. The science products consist primarily of facts, concepts, principles, and theories. (Figure 1.2)

Facts are specific, verifiable pieces of information obtained through observation and measurement. For example, let us say that during a class project Betty observes over the course of two weeks that she produces an average of one kilogram of solid waste each day: cans, bottles, paper, plastic, and so on—a fact of her living habits.

Concepts are abstract ideas that are generalized from facts or specific relevant experiences. In Betty's case, her class project may help her form concepts that her habits of consumption yield considerable solid waste over a period of time. Since she believes her habits are typical of other young adults, she

FIGURE 1.2   Products of Science   The knowledge of science is a product of a hierarchy of facts and ideas.

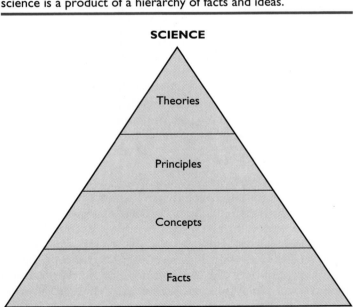

Children construct the products of science for themselves.

also forms a conception of how much solid waste a number of people generate within a specific amount of time. Concepts are single ideas that may become linked to form more complex ideas.

Principles are more complex ideas based on several related concepts. To continue with Betty's example, she might declare that "The reason people recycle solids is because they create a lot of waste." Betty's principle is based on three concepts: creation, waste, and recycling.

Theories consist of broadly related principles that provide an explanation for a phenomenon. The purpose of a theory is to provide a best explanation based on evidence. Theories are used to explain, relate, and predict. After some added observation and consideration, Betty may theorize that commercial marketing practices and convenience packaging are responsible for much of the Eastern United States' landfill problems. She may use her theory to urge lawmakers to develop regulations and to persuade city leaders to establish recycling programs to ease the pressures on their landfills.

WHAT IS WHOLE SCIENCE?

Science has three distinct and interrelated parts: attitudes, processes, and products. Science is a human endeavor and is affected by human character and ambition. Attitudes motivate humans to engage in the processes of science, the thinking and problem-solving skills necessary for constructing ideas and for making discoveries. Attitudes, process skills, and products are the three key concepts of whole science.

The synergy that arises from essential science experiences produces a whole greater than the sum of its independent parts. Emphasizing any one of the parts at the expense of the others encourages children to form inaccurate and incomplete conceptions of science. How else could a child ever learn that science is tentative and not absolute, that science is evidence oriented, that science is speculative and creative? This understanding of science is possible only if science is learned wholistically through thoughtful and appropriate experiences rather than learned by rote as a collection of facts and names to be memorized.

Although the procedures of science can appear very precise, as in Figure 1.3, the means of making scientific discoveries are far from perfect. After each new hypothesis or investigation, a considerable amount of reflective processing can cause scientists to revise their thinking. We must also remember that science can be affected by human desires, emotions, and disappointments. Consider, for example, what is probably the most scientifically and technologically advanced invention of the twentieth century, the United States' space shuttle. This reusable spacecraft resulted from human desire for a system capable of carrying large payloads and teams of astronaut/researchers into space and back with a reasonable turnaround time. Its systems are too numerous and too complex for any one person to design, construct, and maintain. Scores of scientific and engineering teams and thousands of technicians worked for many years to develop the prototype and then to refine additions to the shuttle fleet. During the years of development and testing, emotions ranged from high to low spirits, yet there was always optimism. The 1986 explosion of the shuttle *Challenger* and the loss of its crew was devastating. Yet human perseverance emerged from the sadness and disappointment, and engineers, scientists, and technicians were able to resolve the problem. Curiosity, perseverance, and the skills to press onward toward greater discoveries and accomplishments are what whole science is all about.

THE AIMS OF MODERN SCIENCE EDUCATION

The aims of modern science education exceed the simplicity of understanding the three parts of science. The primary aim is to provide pupils with experiences that will help them become *scientifically literate*. Literacy is more than commanding a list of ideas and demonstrating selected skills. Modern views of scientific

FIGURE 1.3   A Diagram of a Scientist's Way: Methods of Intelligence

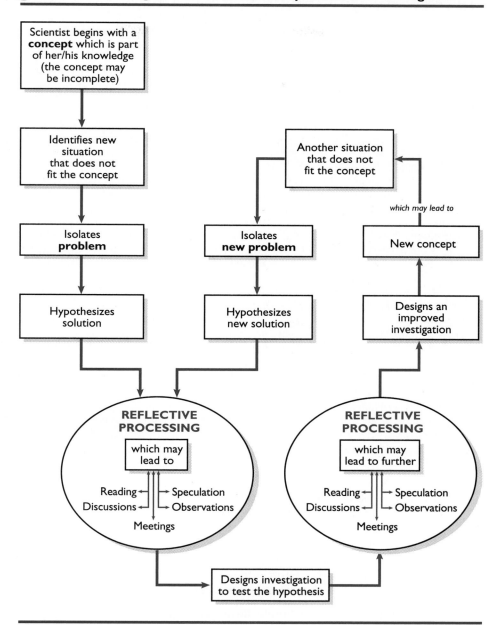

Source: Adapted from Paul F. Brandwein, *Substance, Structure and Style in the Teaching of Science* (New York: Harcourt Brace Jovanovich, 1971).

TEACHERS ON SCIENCE TEACHING

How Do Science and Real Life Connect?

By Phyllis Frysinger
Grades 7 and 8 Science Teacher, Miami View Elementary, South Charleston, Ohio

Remember the first time you learned that spiders have book lungs, sponges have spicules, oak trees have inadequate abscission layers, and two round bacteria existing together are called diplococci? I thought that was really interesting, too, and I couldn't wait to tell kids all of this neat stuff. Today I find myself presenting discovery lessons on the value of spiders, natural carnivores, as possible best controllers in soybean fields; that strong sponge spicules will reap havoc on populated beaches; that oak trees that keep their leaves longer will also lose more water in the fall; and I don't teach that diplo-coccus business, but rather demonstrate the subtlety of bacterial contamination.

Today's students are much more demanding that you as a teacher have a justification as to why you are teaching what you are. Be prepared: If you are using a text, don't try to cover all of Chapter 2 by Friday. Instead, sit down, read Chapter 2, and pretend that there is a student sitting beside you asking, "Why do we have to know this?" If you can't come up with an answer, then leave it out. Develop a list of outcomes or test objectives that you want to obtain from material to be studied. Give this list to the students at the beginning,

develop a way to teach each of your objectives, and show them how you plan to present each of these goals. If you cannot come up with a way to teach a particular goal or objective without standing in front of the class and telling them about it, then leave it out.

Once you have decided what is important and how you are going to teach it, sit down and write the evaluation for the chapter. Yes, right now, not the night before so that you only have time to reproduce it. This way you can justify in your own mind how you will evaluate an objective or your evaluation technique. Newer evaluation techniques are being proposed, and I have used all sorts of things through the years. You will, too, if you keep up with the times.

Oh yes, keeping up with the times. This does not mean doing the Lombada while you are dissecting a frog, but developing viable alternatives to dissection in general. I still use dissecting and have even developed anatomy lessons to use with my eighth-grade earth science classes.

By promoting science as an important part of the life of students, you will promote a positive attitude toward science and encourage students to

literacy include mathematics as well as technology and the social sciences as well as the natural sciences.

Science for All Americans (Project 2061) is a significant report and curriculum effort based on many years of collaboration among several hundred scientists, mathematicians, engineers, physicians, philosophers, historians, and educators. This effort offers a comprehensive and valid view of modern scientific literacy, the prime aim of science teaching. We learn from this report that

> the scientifically literate person is one who is aware that science, mathematics, and technology are interdependent human enterprises with strengths and limitations; understands key concepts and principles of science; is familiar with the natural world and recognizes both its diversity and unity; and uses scientific knowledge and scientific ways of thinking for individual and social purposes.[13]

develop science skills they will use for the rest of their lives.

To be more specific, I am now teaching in a multidisciplinary situation with a pod scheduled time in which three teachers have all of the seventh-grade students in the morning and all of the eighth-grade students in the afternoon. During this time we teach science, English, and literature.

Recently we presented a lesson in which the science classes had been working on chemical reactions. We had mixed together several chemicals including starch, sucrose, ovalbumin, ethyl buterate, and triglycerides to note a chemical reaction. The product was a cake. In literature class the students were reading *A Christmas Carol*, by Charles Dickens. In a combined class we mixed the ingredients for a traditional plum pudding, noting the chemical ingredients and the importance of accurate measurement, as in the science class. The English teacher made the point that there were no plums in the plum pudding and discussed the origin of the word. The literature teacher reflected Mrs. Cratchit's anxiety over the preparation.

After the concoction was properly steamed and the traditions closely followed, including the stirring and wish making by each student, the pudding was flamed with orange extract and we all enjoyed the feast.

With this approach, the students were presented the opportunity of learning the importance and the interrelationship of each of the disciplines involved. There really was an answer to "Why do we have to know this?" We write journals each day, and it was certainly rewarding to note the number of times that we read "I'm going to take this recipe home and make plum pudding for my family." When the students want to take your lesson home and share it with others, then you know that you have taught science.

One more thing: Don't forget to join all the professional organizations that are available, and participate in them. You will not only learn the latest that is available in your field, but will also have a great deal of support in your professional years. That's how I ended up taking physics almost thirty years after I entered the classroom when I don't even teach physical science.

We must expand our vision of science when we take on this aim. Our national vision is to "make our students first in the world in math and science achievement (by the year 2000)"[14] and to develop a system of science education that prepares students to be informed and active participants in civic life, citizens who are productive workers and lifelong learners. The vision sees in the future a better informed citizenry that helps to maintain a strong democracy, strengthens our country's economy, and maintains excellent standing in science and technology.

The National Science Education Project (coordinated by the National Research Council of the National Academy of Sciences and the National Academy of Engineering) advocates a less-is-more philosophy for developing science curriculum, teaching approaches, and appropriate forms of assessment. These standards support practical learning experiences and problem-solving opportunities for children. The standards are based on a wholistic view of science. These standards can help us progress toward our national aims and to do our part, as teachers, to fulfill the national vision. Forthcoming chapters describe specific goals for science teaching and methods for the covering-less-but-doing-and-learning-more philosophy that undergirds the goals.

This chapter has introduced you to some of the problems observed in elementary science, described a wholistic view of science, and outlined the aims of modern elementary science. The remaining chapters will help you to understand and to practice *whole science*.

ABOUT THIS BOOK

We realize that these words are typically placed in a book's preface. We also realize that eager learners often skip the front material in favor of digging into the ideas quickly, and we have added several words here to help you do that. Let us consider two factors: (1) how we have designed this book and its features to assist your access to the ideas, and (2) an alternative route through the text.

First, each of our chapters contains some standard features. The first page of each chapter is a *concept map* (you might call it a flow chart); concept maps are explained in the chapter on planning, Chapter 4. A concept map is a picture of the main ideas we hope you will obtain from the chapter and the relationships among those ideas. Read the map from box to box, noting the direction of the arrows and the linking words. The text of each chapter begins with a *scenario*. The scenarios are all factual, but have been changed for rather obvious reasons. The scenario helps to create a vicarious experience through a short story; this, when combined with the map, should help you to create a mental framework for understanding those parts of the chapter that may be new or difficult.

Within each chapter we have added figures, tables, and photographs to reinforce the ideas presented; sometimes we include relevant exercises that you might want to try. One different feature is *What Research Says*. This material supplements the chapter's text with a brief authoritative report on recent research. Of course we close each chapter with the customary summary that complements the concept map. *Discussion questions* and ideas for *class projects* are included; many of these are field based to complement any early field experience or practice teaching your professor may ask you to do. *Additional readings* contain suggestions for further reading on the important topics of each chapter.

One other feature we have added is *Teachers on Science Teaching*. This gives a practicing teacher's view on the chapter's topic, with real applications described.

The last section of this book contains sixty *complete science lesson plans* distributed among the life, physical, and earth science disciplines. Our plans contain 150 different activities and are constructed in a very powerful way—a way to encourage the highest level of student physical and mental activity and to stimulate high levels of pupil achievement. Our plans are consistent with how children construct their own understanding of science.

The second factor we want you to notice is that we have written this book in a linear way. We provide a foundation for science teaching in two chapters as we discuss the nature of science and learning. Then in Chapters 3 through 5 we focus on the elementary science program by examining goals, planning, and historical influences on modern science programs.

Our next section (Chapters 6 through 12) is devoted to a variety of teaching methods and teacher skills. These chapters include questioning, student-centered instruction, inquiry instruction, direct instruction, special needs, management, safety, and locating important teaching resources.

Often teachers and professors prefer a different approach, given the press of time and other factors. In that case, you might consider this approach:

1. Study Chapter 1 to understand our text's philosophy. Then explore contemporary theorists' preferred perspectives on how children learn science. Chapter 2 will also introduce you briefly to teaching approaches.
2. You may wish to select some science plans from the last section of our book and try teaching children or your peers. Specific teaching approaches can be studied and used from Chapters 7 and 8.
3. If planning becomes too challenging, you might want to jump back to Chapter 4 for an explanation of the techniques we recommend, and then perhaps to Chapter 3 if you want to explore science goals and outcomes.
4. Questioning, in Chapter 6, is an important skill that you may wish to develop as you teach.
5. As you encounter the need to understand and to promote student diversity, Chapter 9 should be helpful.
6. As needed, Chapter 10 can provide ideas on classroom management; Chapter 11 discusses safe science teaching; and Chapter 12, as well as our lesson plans, can help you to locate appropriate teaching materials and resources.

Of course, at all times we encourage you to try the ideas your own way. If you do, you will be learning about teaching science the way we advocate for the children you will teach: by constructing *your* own understanding.

CHAPTER SUMMARY

Whole science is more than knowledge and scientific names and facts. This chapter has shown that assumptions about science that focus only on treating it as a body of knowledge are incomplete and incorrect. Science *is* possible because it is inherently human. Human attitudes provide the curiosity to begin its study, the perseverance to continue, and the necessary qualities for making informed judgments. Science process skills make it possible for children to accumulate the factual information they use to construct concepts, form scientific principles, and comprehend theories. Children are able to construct their own understanding when encouraged to explore, to question, and to seek.

Science has the most impact on children when they value it and learn it wholistically. Children value science when they find uses for it and enjoy its pleasures. Elementary science programs, science teaching practices, and assessment techniques must provide experiences that will help children to value and use science by making important discoveries for themselves. How children construct ideas and learn is a topic explored in Chapter 2.

DISCUSSION QUESTIONS AND PROJECTS

1. Think back to your elementary and middle school years. What do you remember about your science classes? How do your memories compare with those of your classmates? In what ways do your recollections represent whole science?

2. To what extent did your teachers teach science according to our definition? What do you remember about the emphasis given to attitudes, thinking skills, and science information? Why do you think your teachers emphasized (or did not emphasize) each of these parts?

3. Consider the case made for the science cycle in this chapter. Do you agree or disagree with it? State your reasons.

4. Think about developmental differences observed between first-, third-, and sixth-grade students. In each grade, how much emphasis do you think should be given to emotional and intellectual attitude development? Give reasons for your answer.

5. Review the differences between basic and integrated science process skills. Describe the connection between these skills and the types of science information children are expected to learn.

6. How much instructional time do you believe should be devoted to science? How should that time be used to emphasize attitudes, process skills, and information? Give reasons for your answers.

7. The attitudes we carry with us are linked to experiences we have accumulated over time. Both help us form images that we treat as our independent sense of reality. Sometimes these images represent widely recognized stereotypes. For example, when you hear the word *scientist*, what image comes to mind? Draw a picture of a scientist.

8. Compare your picture of a scientist with other class members' pictures. Classify them according to such features as age, gender, amount and types of hair, eyeglasses, lab coat, laboratory apparatus, appearance (weird, out of control, and so on), and so on. Tally the features and compute percentages to develop a class profile of a scientist. Treat this as a pretest and do the exercise again at the end of the course to look for any possible differences in stereotypes.

9. Try a version of the projects described above with elementary school children. How do their pictures compare with your own or those of your college class? Develop a summary of the children's views and speculate about reasons.

NOTES

1. Educational Testing Service, *A World of Differences: An International Assessment of Mathematics and Science* (Princeton, NJ: Center for the Assessment of Educational Progress, 1989), p. 36.

2. Educational Testing Service, *National Assessment of Educational Progress* (Washington, DC: U.S. Department of Education, 1992), pp. 3–5.

3. Ibid., p .8.

4. Norman Campbell, *What Is Science?* (New York: Dover Publications, 1953), p.1.

5. Ibid.

6. Ralph E. Martin, Jr., *The Credibility Principle and Teacher Attitudes Toward Science* (New York: Peter Lang, 1984) pp. 13–14.

7. J. D. Halloran, *Attitude Formation and Change* (Great Britain: Leicester University Press, 1970) and S. Oskamp, Attitudes and Opinions (Englewood Cliffs, NJ: Prentice Hall, 1977).

8. Ina V. S. Mullis and Lynn B. Jenkins, *The Science Report Card: Elements of Risk and Recovery* (Princeton, NJ: Educational Testing Service, 1988), p. 126.

9. Ibid., p. 126.

10. Ibid., p. 127.

11. Edward Victor, *Science for the Elementary School* (New York: Macmillan, 1985), p. 17.

12. H. J. Funk, J. R. Okey, R. L. Fiel, H. H. Jaus, and C. S. Sprague, *Learning Science Process Skills* (Dubuque, IA: Kendall/Hunt Publishing Company, 1985).

13. F. James Rutherford and Andrew Ahlgren, *Science for All Americans* (New York: Oxford University Press, 1990), p. ix.

14. *America 2000: An Education Strategy*, National Education Goal no. 4 (Washington, DC: U. S. Department of Education, 1991).

ADDITIONAL READINGS

If you are interested in learning more about some of the topics raised in this chapter, consider the following sources.

Carl J. Sindermann, *The Joy of Science* (New York: Plenum Press, 1985). The author accumulated many case histories from scientists over the years and used them to provide an inside look at the reasons for successful careers in science.

The 1990 Science Report Card (or latest available version), prepared by the Educational Testing Service for the Office of Educational Research and Improvement of the U.S. Department of Education, March 1992. The wealth of demographic and example test items contained in this source is guaranteed to expand your vision of the conditions of science education and the means to determine what our youth know and can do.

F. James Rutherford and Andrew Ahlgren, *Science for All Americans* (New York: Oxford University Press, 1990). This remake of the 1989 edition from the American Association for the Advancement of Science puts the complete vision of scientific literacy in terms the lay person can fully comprehend.

Robert M. Hazen and James Trefil, *Science Matters: Achieving Scientific Literacy* (New York: Doubleday, 1991). This is a unique source with a compelling introduction on scientific literacy. This book can be used as a primer to help you understand the most fundamental concepts the authors believe are necessary for modern science.

Carol Minnick and Donna Alvermann (eds.), *Science Learning Processes and Applications* (Newark, DE: International Reading Association, 1991); and Karen Ostlund, *Science Process Skills: Assessing Hands-On Student Performance* (Menlo Park, CA: Addison-Wesley Publishing Company, 1992). These are two fine sources for obtaining practical ideas to help you promote science process skills in your classroom.

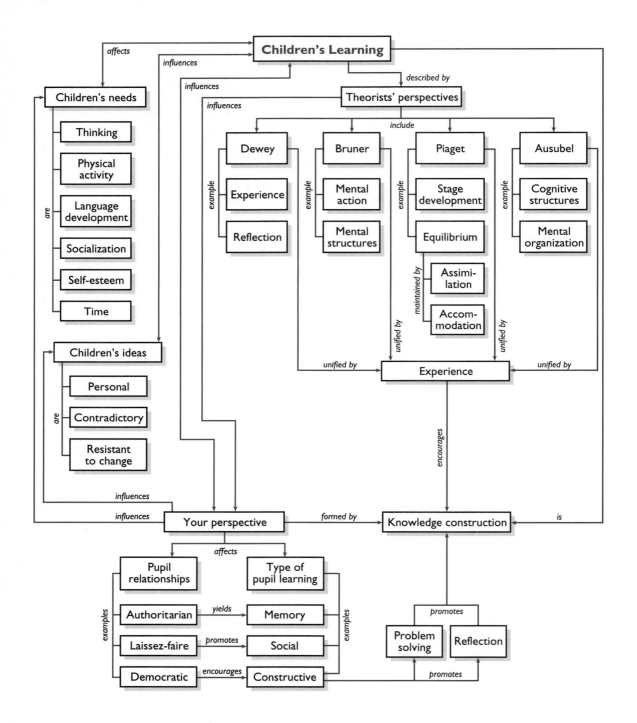

How Do Children Learn Science?

Vera's teaching methods were consistent. In math, she presented the topic, demonstrated models, explained the functions and steps to follow by giving examples, and involved some of the children in board work. Drill and practice came next. These were followed by assigned seat work, which was reviewed the first thing during math time the following day.

In science, Vera explained the point, provided a demonstration, and gave her pupils step-by-step instructions for doing the corresponding activity. Each learner followed her recipe, and her methods were similar for all subjects.

Vera was frustrated. The children only seemed to do well at recalling what they had memorized. They returned to their own ideas when confronted with a problem or question that was not an exact replica of what they had studied in class. Learning appeared to be superficial, and retention was elusive. What could Vera do to develop deeper, lasting understanding?

Vera decided to try a new learning opportunity for herself. She viewed her learners through new eyes as she considered different perspectives on how children learn; she tried different teaching approaches. Vera avoided her own demonstration and recipe instructions this time. Instead she distributed the materials for the science lesson *first:* clay, scissors, cardboard, rulers, string, and so on. She asked small groups of children to work together in teams to design and construct a landscape—any type of landscape *they* chose.

The groups did not begin smoothly, perhaps because the children were not accustomed to such vague instructions. However, the puzzled expressions and occasional off-task behavior associated with the new-found freedom quickly subsided as Vera maintained consistent contact with each group and asked such guiding questions as "How else could you do that?" or "What other features could you add?" or "Where have you seen landscapes like this?" Vera also displayed unique examples for other groups to examine.

After a bit more exploration, Vera challenged each group to draw two-dimensional maps of their three-dimensional landscapes. This proved difficult until the concepts of *contour* and *interval* were constructed. Soon each group was applying basic math and measurement skills to construct a contour map of its own landscape to scale. Later, the children successfully took real contour maps and recreated landscapes they had never visited, again to scale. Still using traditional testing, Vera seemed to notice a deeper understanding in the children's learning. When she asked questions or when the children wrote answers on her tests, the responses were more detailed and more thoughtful.

INTRODUCTION

How did you learn science? Was it similar to Vera's typical way of teaching it? Was your experience based on the teacher's instructions and explanations, vocabulary development, and memorization? Or was your experience more like an adventure, where the exact steps to follow were as unknown as the consequences of your decisions? Did your teachers emphasize the facts, symbols, labels, and formulas of science? Or were the general ideas—concepts—developed in a way that helped you to discover the connections among the many ideas and fields of science?

How you view science and how children learn share related consequences. If you view science as a discrete body of information to be learned, you will probably bring that assumption to your teaching, which will be much like Vera's routine. If, after reading Chapter 1, you view science as a dynamic opportunity to help children develop essential attitudes, skills, and ideas that can benefit each of them, you will likely bring that assumption to your teaching, which may resemble Vera's experimental approach. Your present view of how children learn has been shaped by your teachers, and in turn your beliefs will affect the children you teach. With a little imagination you can see the repeating cycle.

Vera's routine methods did not produce the results she wanted. She decided to experiment with her methods and in doing so, challenged and adapted her beliefs about learning. In this chapter we challenge you to:

1. Consider the role that children's prior ideas play in their learning.
2. Identify what children need to help them become self-motivated and to sustain independent learning.
3. Examine the dominant contemporary perspectives on learning.
4. Explore how your view of learning is related to your teaching.

HOW DO CHILDREN'S IDEAS INFLUENCE THEIR LEARNING?

Rosalind Driver and her fellow researchers have studied this question extensively. Consider the following classroom example involving two 11-year-old students.

Tim and Ricky are studying the way a spring extends as they add ball bearings to a plastic drinking cup that is attached to and hangs from the spring, which is suspended from a clamp on a stand. Ricky carefully adds the bearings

Children form their own science ideas through direct experience.

William E. Mills

one at a time and measures the change in the length of the spring after each addition. Tim watches and inquires, "Wait a moment. What happens if we lift up the spring?" Ricky clamps the spring higher on the stand, measures its stretched length, and continues after he is satisfied that the length of the spring is the same as before the change in position. An observer asks Tim for the reasons behind his suggestion. Tim picks up two bearings, pretends they are pebbles, and explains his idea about weight changing as objects are lifted higher.

> This is farther up and gravity is pulling it down harder the farther away. The higher it gets the more effect gravity will have on it because if you just stood over there and someone dropped a pebble on him, it would just sting him, it wouldn't hurt him. But if I dropped it from an aeroplane it would be accelerating faster and faster and when it hit someone on the head it would kill him.[1]

Tim's idea is not scientifically correct. The object's weight does not increase as height changes. However, the idea is not irrational if you consider Tim's reasoning: He seems to be referring to what scientists call gravitational potential energy. The ideas children bring with them often influence what and how they learn.

What Do We Know About Children's Ideas?

Children bring many ideas to class. Their ideas represent the interpretations they have formed about the dilemmas and phenomena the children have encountered, as in Tim's example. Many of these experiences occur out of school and are not connected to formal teaching. Children's ideas arise from everyday experiences including play, conversations, and events observed through the media. The recent research on children's ideas reveals three important factors. Children's ideas are very personal constructions, the ideas may seem incomplete or contradictory, and the ideas are often very stable and highly resistant to change.[2]

Children's Ideas Are Personal.   Have you ever been with a group of your friends and witnessed a remarkable event such as a concert, athletic event, or auto accident? Or have you participated in a heated debate about a topic important to you? How did your perceptions of the facts or the event compare with those of your friends? Was there complete agreement on each detail? "No" is not an unusual answer. Consider the children in a class, each participating in the same science activity. It is likely that the children will report diverse perceptions of what happened during the activity. Each child has seen and experienced the activity, but each has internalized the experiences in his or her own way. Our perceptions and descriptions depend as much on our original ideas as they do on the nature of the new experience or lesson. All readers do not receive exactly the same message, even from written words.

Learners construct their own meanings. Constructed meanings are based on new experiences that are accumulated and compared with and processed from old ideas. The preexisting ideas are the basis for observing, classifying, and interpreting new experiences. In this way, each learner, even a very young one, continually forms and reforms hypotheses and theories about natural phenomena. We call upon the mind's existing ideas to help us understand new experiences.[3] What is remarkable is that even though ideas are constructed independently, the general interpretations and conclusions are often shared by many.[4]

A Child's Individual Ideas May Seem Contradictory.　Natural science is blessed with many intriguing discrepancies. Touch the flat bottom of an uncoated paper cup with a candle flame, and predictably, the paper burns after a brief time. But add water to a cup and the cup will not burn even when heated by a stronger source for a much longer time. This challenges the mature mind to identify a coherent reason that explains the behavior of the candle and cup under all circumstances. The younger mind may see no problem and simply use another, even contradictory, explanation, unconcerned that the explanation is inconsistent with what was previously said. As Driver reminds us:

> The same child may have different conceptions of a particular type of phenomenon, sometimes using different arguments leading to opposite predictions in situations which are equivalent from a scientist's point of view, and even switching from one sort of explanation to another for the same phenomenon.[5]

A child does not have the same need for coherence as an adult or a scientist, nor does a child have a mental model to use to unify a range of different perceptions that relate to the same event. Furthermore, a child usually does not see the need for a consistent view. The constructed ideas work quite well for the child in his or her classroom practice, even though the ideas may be based upon prior false conclusions.

Children's Ideas Resist Change.　It is not simple for teachers to change children's incomplete or flawed ideas about scientific events and phenomena. Additional activities, comparative discussions, and even direct teacher explanations may not cause children to modify their ideas. Changing ideas is slow, and the necessary changes may never be complete. Children may simply realize that they are to provide a certain correct answer to a teacher's questions, but choose to turn off the academically correct in favor of the previous independent ideas once the test is over. Counter evidence presented to the child seems to make no difference. Interpretations often are based on prior ideas. Personal, if contradictory, ideas have tremendous stability and endurance.[6]

WHAT DO CHILDREN NEED TO HELP THEM LEARN?

We must concern ourselves with more than what happens in the learner's mind. Stimulating learning in science, or any other subject, is a complex mission. Compare two age groups of children: primary and middle school. The physical, intellectual, social, and emotional differences are obvious. Younger children tend to be much smaller with less developed muscle structures, are less social, and are more prone to spontaneous emotional outbursts. As children become older and more experienced, their interest in their peers increases, they become less reliant on concrete objects and more capable of abstract reasoning, and their speech and language patterns become more complex.

Change and development happen over time. While their bodies are maturing and becoming stronger through exercise, children's minds, emotions, and self-confidence also develop through the exercise afforded by useful experiences. Children need experiences that will help develop their thinking, afford considerable activity, stimulate language, and help them develop social skills and self-confidence. Children need time for all of these changes to occur.

Thinking

Younger children benefit from using their five senses extensively. Talking at and showing children pictures of mammals, for example, provides less stimulation than giving them time to smell, touch, hear, and observe the movements of classroom pets. Imagine teaching children about foods that are salty, sweet, sour, or bitter without letting them taste! Stimulate many of the senses to overcome the limits imposed on children by just listening. Older youths benefit from the stimulation too, even though they are more capable of mental reasoning. Do you recall the difficulties prior ideas bring to new learning?

Physical Activity

Middle school children may be able to sit still for rather long periods of time, but young children cannot. Indeed, very young children may actually get more tired if they have to sit still for long. Martha Denckla, a professor of neurology and pediatrics, explains that this difference is related to development of the brain: "The frontal lobe, the part of the brain that applies the brakes to children's natural energy and curiosity, is still maturing in 6–9 year olds. As the lobe develops, so does 'boredom tolerance.'"[7] Purposeful physical activity helps to provide the experiences that are essential for thinking and language development.

Language

Children learn to develop and use language by talking, not by learning isolated skills. Reasoning and expression are developed through child–child and child–adult conversations. Encourage communication of ideas first; then worry over spelling and grammar. Again, class experience affords abundant opportunities to develop language and thinking patterns. Acquire the experience first, then develop the language from it.

Socialization

Social development is related to academic success. Children who are socially maladjusted and cannot get along with their peers often do poorly in school and may eventually drop out. Children tend to do better in school when they work in groups and cooperate with others. Some educators claim that *relationships* should be the first of the three Rs.[8] Science provides abundant opportunities for children to cooperate and develop relationships through group activities and projects.

Self-Esteem

Younger and older children struggle to meet the teacher's adult expectations and in doing so, learn to judge themselves in relation to others. The unfortunate aspect to this is that young children have not yet learned to distinguish between

WHAT RESEARCH SAYS

Brain-Based Learning

Much has been written about hemispheric brain dominance, and these ideas have influenced our views on learning and teaching even though they do not apply to normal learners. While it is true that our brains benefit from abundant varieties of stimulation, prescriptions are difficult and risky because we are still learning how our brains function. Researchers Renate and Geoffrey Caine have summarized several important principles from the brain-based research on teaching and learning that may help you to find effective ways to stimulate learning. The principles include:

- Previous experiences and meaning affect how the brain processes new experiences and organizes new knowledge
- Our emotions and our learning share an important relationship
- Learning is more than exercising the brain like a muscle: It is a true physiological experience that involves a sophisticated set of systems
- Our brain processes and organizes many stimuli and ideas at the same time, even though we may focus only on one thing at a time
- The significance of subject matter content depends on how our experiences are arranged and fit into patterns

- Our brains process peripheral stimuli consciously and unconsciously
- Parts and wholes are processed simultaneously by our brains, not separately or in isolation in a particular hemisphere
- We possess spatial memories that help us to retrieve experiences rapidly and easily; for example, we might have a detailed memory of an important event even though we made no special attempt to memorize details
- We need more practice to recall facts and to establish a level of skill when these facts are not embedded in our spatial memories
- Our brains respond positively to problems and challenges, but are less effective under duress

Sam Crowell, an educator, describes these principles of learning in a way that is closely compatible with our contemporary views on learning. He says that learning is complex, interrelated, unified, and emergent.

Sources: Renate Nummela Caine and Geoffrey Caine, *Teaching and the Human Brain* (Alexandria, VA: Association for Supervision and Curriculum Development, 1991); and Sam Crowell, "A New Way of Thinking: The Challenge of the Future," *Educational Leadership*, September 1989, pp. 60–63.

effort and ability. If trying hard to accomplish a task results in failure, a child is likely to conclude that he or she will never be able to succeed. Cooperation, rather than competition, may inflate self-esteem while it deflates feelings of incompetence.

Time

We cannot create more time. But we can decide how to allot the time we have. The fact is that young children need time to grow, mature, and develop the thinking and communication skills, socialization, and self-esteem they need for productive learning. Piling on more challenges for younger children or accelerating the classroom pace will not help them develop into well adjusted, creative, and critically thinking youth. Developmental differences observed during the primary years often wash out around the fourth grade if the children have been exposed to useful experiences through heterogeneous groups during their early years.

The many needs of children are a part of their learning environment. Attend to the needs and the learning will follow as children become self-motivated and confident and as they develop the capability to think more abstractly and to communicate their ideas. Successes that arise from fulfilled needs help children to develop and sustain the capability to learn more independently.

WHAT ARE THE DOMINANT CONTEMPORARY PERSPECTIVES ON LEARNING?

Learning has been an important field of inquiry for philosophers and of experimentation for psychologists. The nature of experience and the role it plays in learning have often been debated. Let us briefly visit the perspectives of several theorists to examine the nature and role of experience.

John Dewey

John Dewey—philosopher, psychologist, and theorist—exerted considerable influence on education at the turn of the twentieth century. Dewey's ideas are still at the forefront of the progressive movement in American education. Dewey believed that thinking and learning evolved in humans because they serve a vital function. Originally, thinking and learning served practical functions, such as helping humans survive by avoiding and escaping danger. Now thinking and learning help humans to foresee serious problems and to plan for them before they occur.[9]

Dewey advocated physical and mental learning for children. He believed that students learn best when they have to solve problems that are meaningful to them. Dewey championed the notion of mentally active, hands-on learning (we now call it *hands-on, minds-on* learning). He believed that children learn effectively through personal struggles in which they must investigate, accumulate ideas, process information, and put ideas to practical use.[10] Dewey believed

**FIGURE 2.1   Learning Model Based on Dewey's
Theories**   Worthwhile problems form the motivation and substance of learning for children.

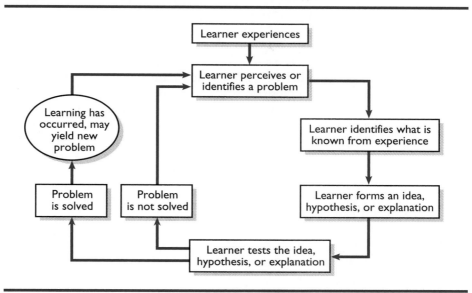

we learn by doing and reflecting on what we do. Often the process unfolds like this scenario (which is illustrated in Figure 2.1):

> Thinking always gets started when a person genuinely feels a problem arise. Then the mind actively jumps back and forth—struggling to find a clearer formulation of the problem, looking for suggestions and possible solutions, surveying elements in the problematic situation that might be relevant, drawing on prior knowledge in an attempt to better understand the situation. Then the mind begins forming a plan of action, a hypothesis about how best the problem might be solved. The hypothesis is then tested; if the problem is solved, then according to Dewey something has been learned.[11]

In Dewey's view, we use a version of the scientific method as we process ideas and try to solve our problems. The foundation of Dewey's view is the need for direct, rich, meaningful experience for *each* learner. What is *meaningful* interests and meets the needs of the learner, and is not that meaning given or assigned by the teacher, or that meaning contained in any particular textbook. Dewey also emphasized the role of community in education. He argued that students should not be isolated from each other and that socialization was important to assure purposeful activity. Further, Dewey urged educators to consider that the best way to learn a new idea was through normal communication processes with others.

Jerome Bruner

Educational psychologist Jerome Bruner's views on learning became widely studied in 1959 during the early years of the United States' response to the Soviet Union during the space race. Bruner supported *inductive learning,* in which teaching began with the specific experiences of the learner and then built upon them to the general idea or concept of the subject. Bruner claimed that the learner is not merely a seated listener. He believed that children learn best if their minds act on what is being learned and that this mental action can occur through listening, speaking, reading, seeing, and thinking.

Bruner encouraged induction (Figure 2.2) as one way to promote active learning and as a way to form and understand concepts. Induction consists of a series of steps beginning with each child exploring the topic in his or her own way, accumulating a variety of impressions and ideas. As an example, reconsider the chapter scenario. Providing minimal instructions, Vera encouraged each group to construct a landscape. Next, Vera used guiding questions to help the children explore their landscapes and identify the outstanding features. Then Vera helped the children to construct the general ideas of the lesson: contour and interval. In Bruner's system, the meaning is further clarified through teacher examples and then generalized into a concept statement, principle, rule, or formula. In our example, Vera had the children expand their understanding of the lesson's concepts by applying them to new situations—the development of contour maps and new landscapes recreated from real contour maps. Firsthand experience was the specific point of departure for the lesson, and developing the concept was the generality. The generality arose from students' experi-

FIGURE 2.2   Inductive Learning Model

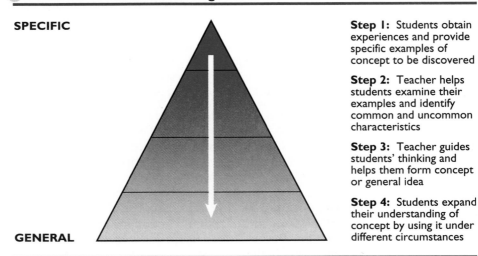

SPECIFIC

GENERAL

Step 1: Students obtain experiences and provide specific examples of concept to be discovered

Step 2: Teacher helps students examine their examples and identify common and uncommon characteristics

Step 3: Teacher guides students' thinking and helps them form concept or general idea

Step 4: Students expand their understanding of concept by using it under different circumstances

ences, by making thoughtful comparisons, and by finding regularities and irregularities in their experiences. Bruner urged teachers to provide children with specific activities to help them see the underlying concepts, relationships, and patterns in science.

Bruner was deeply concerned with how learning in science could be made more meaningful. He advocated teaching in a way that helped students to form mental structures and to grasp the structures of a discipline such as science. He wrote:

> Grasping the structure of a subject is understanding it in a way that permits many other things to be related to it meaningfully. To learn structure, in short, is to learn how things are related. . . . In order for a person to be able to recognize the applicability or inapplicability of an idea to a new situation and to broaden learning thereby, he must have clearly in mind the general nature of the phenomenon with which he is dealing.[12]

Jean Piaget

Trained as a biologist, Jean Piaget (1896–1980) developed a theory of cognitive development that dominated for several decades our view of how children learn science. Not a learning theorist, Piaget described a process by which knowledge accumulates in a learner's mind when mental structures are formed.

If you have completed a course in educational psychology or child development, you may be familiar with Piaget's developmental stage theory. The stages are linked to probable age ranges and are labeled Sensorimotor, Preoperational, Concrete Operational, and Formal Operational. Young school children usually fit the preoperational stage description, while most elementary and middle school youngsters fit the descriptions of the concrete and formal operations stages, with many affected by the gradual transition between the two stages.

Preoperational Stage.   Children who think preoperationally may be five to seven years old and not capable of reversing their thinking. In Piaget's classic experiment, a child believes that a ball of clay patted into a sausage shape has more or less clay than the original ball. Children have difficulty seeing that there is no difference in the amount. Young children tend to be intuitive, egocentric, not rational, and not logical; they may confuse play with reality.

Concrete Operations.   Thought becomes internal, rational, and reversible during this stage. Children at this stage interact well with real objects, not abstract ideas. Children who process events concretely develop the ability to classify and conserve, and they develop some ability to engage in if–then hypothetical thinking.

Formal Operations.   During early adolescence, perhaps from age 11 onward, children tend to develop the capability to think more formally, more abstractly.

They can consider many alternatives to a problem and can begin to identify the important variables that influence the outcomes of science activities and experiments. The ability to think about one's own thinking—metacognition—opens wonderful worlds of self-reliance and creativity.

The different stages are used to describe developmental differences among learners and to show progressive mental maturation through the experiences that each learner must process in his or her own mind. For educators, Piaget's work has been helpful in designing learning experiences that are most developmentally appropriate and that afford abundant opportunities for pupil success.

The stage progression portion of Piaget's theory implies that no person skips a stage and that learning is developmental; individuals may take different lengths of time and need different experiences to complete their development. Mental development does not merely click into place with a passing birthday. Indeed, learners differ in capability, most likely due to variations in their physical and mental experiences. Researchers in the United Kingdom and the United States report experimental results that cause them to question the absolute validity of the stage development and progression portion of Piaget's theory.[13] Perhaps Piaget's most important contribution to our quest to understand learning is his description of a process through which each individual experiences stimuli and uses them to produce meaning.

Physical Knowledge.   Physical knowledge is formed from external observations and interactions with the physical world. Referring back to the Tim and Ricky scenario, each child observed a change in the length of the spring as each ball bearing was added to the cup. They could not have known the stretchiness of the spring and the firm, rolling weight of the bearings except through physical contact with the objects.

Logicomathematical Knowledge.   A more sophisticated type of knowledge, logicomathematical knowledge, is created when a learner establishes mental relationships between objects. Tim observed a type of cause-and-effect relationship about the length of the spring as more bearings were added; he formed a connection, albeit not completely correct, between the weight of the bearings and the distance the spring stretched away from the cup. Tim's mistake may have been due to a mental assumption that the bearing-and-spring experience was like pebbles being dropped first from the room's ceiling and then from an aircraft. The relationship existed in Tim's mind and was not based on direct physical knowledge.

External and Internal Knowledge.   In Piaget's theory, knowledge comes from two sources: external and internal. Physical knowledge is often external, and logicomathematical knowledge is internal. These sources of knowledge help each learner to form mental schemes or constructions. Schemes are mental images constructed by organizing observations, behaviors, or thoughts into patterns. Piaget offers three other concepts to help us understand the complexity of forming schemes while learning: equilibration, assimilation, and accommodation.

Equilibration. According to Piaget's theory, learning is an active mental process in which each learner must construct knowledge by interacting with the environment and by resolving the cognitive conflicts that arise between what is expected and what is observed.[14] Each new interaction or conflict creates a dilemma in each learner's mind about how to maintain mental equilibrium.

Equilibration is a process by which each learner compensates mentally for each dilemma. Each new attempt at restoring equilibrium helps to create a higher level of functional equilibration; higher mental structures are formed. (See Figure 2.3.) However, equilibrium is not a static point at which the mind rests as if on a balance beam. Instead, equilibration is like a cyclist maintaining dynamic balance with each new challenge on the touring course. "The brain is continually seeking to impose order on incoming stimuli and to generate models that lead to adaptive behavior and useful predictions."[15]

FIGURE 2.3 Equilibration Model Based on Piaget's Theory
Disequilibrium occurs in each learner's universe of experiences and causes an attempt to restore equilibrium through assimilation and accommodation.

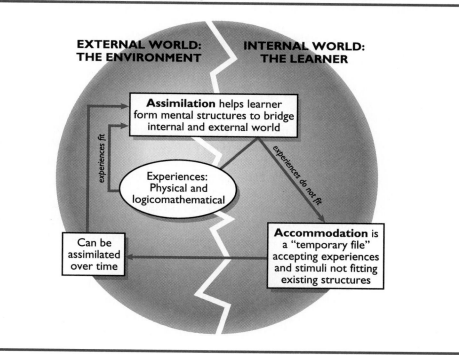

TEACHERS ON SCIENCE TEACHING

How Can You Teach Skills Now, Content Later?

By Charlotte Schartz
Grade 6 Mathematics and Science Teacher, Kingman Middle School, Kingman, Kansas

The year is 1977 and it's time for sixth grade science class. There will be a unit on, let's say, the cell. We'll do lots of worksheets, with a large amount of reading. I'll lecture, assigning much vocabulary to memorize, and maybe I'll do a demonstration or two. The students are listening, I think. Individual seat work is the norm. Talking to your neighbor is out. I am on stage telling them what to learn, what to memorize. The emphasis is on content.

That was then, this is now, and I'm learning. My evolving theory on how an adolescent learns is based on a conglomeration of articles that I have read, behaviors that I have observed, and experiences that I have had. I believe that students learn in inconsistent surges. Their rate of content absorption is in proportion to their social, emotional, and hormonal situation at any given moment.

I am becoming more and more convinced that middle school students learned before they got

to me, and they'll learn more at a later stage in their lives. But right now, they have more important things on their minds, like what to wear, who's going with who, why Susie didn't smile today, or why she smiled at someone else. They are distracted by the unpredictable changes associated with unstable families, economic conditions, and so on. The plant or animal cell just can't compete. And after visiting with the teachers at the senior high, I learned that when they introduce that same cell, they start from the beginning, assuming that most 15- to 16-year-olds will not remember too much from middle school anyway.

I used to spend so much time on content. That's what the experts said was right at the time, I guess. . . . That was then, this is now, and I'm learning.

My teaching style has changed. I'm trying to match it to something unknown, unpredictable,

Assimilation.   Assimilation is one way the mind may adapt to the learning challenge and restore equilibrium. If the stimulus is not too different from previous experiences and mental actions, it may be combined with or added to existing mental structures, like filing a new letter into a preexisting folder containing the same or similar information.

Accommodation.   On those occasions when no preexisting mental structures (or file folders) are available to assimilate, the mind must adapt by changing or adding to its mental structures. This process of adaptation is called accommodation. The learner's thinking is adapted to accommodate the dilemma.

In practice, assimilation and accommodation are related and do not occur in isolation; each process complements the other. A rational, thinking learner is mentally active. Always losing equilibrium and trying to restore it, the learner develops structures through the continuous interaction between the person and the external world. Again, rich, stimulating experiences—physical and mental— feed the learner's development.

inconsistent: a middle school student. If they aren't physically, emotionally, or socially able to learn and apply a bunch of big words mingled with abstract ideas and global concepts, then I must focus on something more concrete, like the skills that a scientist will need. In my classroom, we make observations, measure, keep records, analyze our data, make comparisons, predict based on patterns, and draw conclusions. During a project such as the design of a controlled experiment with bean seeds, my youngsters are expected to use all of the above. They work with their cooperative learning team to make their own observations, taking their own measurements, keeping their own records. They feel more of an ownership and involvement than if I had just told them about when someone else grew beans. (It's also safer to express an opinion, make a suggestion, or verbalize a revelation while working in a small group instead of in front of the whole class.) Now, are they ready to go out into the world as master bean growers? No, even though some relatively thorough content did get slipped in. But they will have practiced some useful scientific skills, constructed some important science concepts, and developed a greater ability to think, along with some critical social skills. They have a greater chance of remembering something they did rather than something they heard about. And who knows if there will even BE bean farms in fifty years?!? Look what happened to the four food groups! I do feel certain however, that the skills of doing science will endure. People will still have to observe, predict, compare, keep records, and so on; people will still have to think and solve problems.

David Ausubel

David Ausubel, an educational psychologist, provides a useful perspective on learning. He is not preoccupied with the stage limitations described by Piaget. Ausubel, with further support from Joseph Novak's research, offers a teaching procedure for helping learners to form appropriate cognitive structures: "[Cognitive development] is dependent on the framework of specific concepts and integrations between these concepts acquired during the life-span of the individual."[16]

Ausubel maintains that each learner organizes and structures his or her own knowledge. Furthermore, this knowledge is structured as a framework of specific concepts. Ausubel values verbal learning and believes it is most efficient for students after ages 11 or 12. Ausubel concedes that before this age, direct experiences benefit younger learners when they have considerable time to manipulate objects. He believes, however, that eventually pupils learn to relate new knowledge to relevant existing concepts in their mental structures. Ausubel declares that "[the] most important single factor influencing learning is what the learner already knows. Ascertain this and teach him [or her] accordingly."[17]

Advance Organizer.   What can a teacher do if it is not possible to determine what a learner already knows? A teacher may try to set the learner's mind so that it is ready to receive new ideas and so that it has put into place a framework for accepting these new ideas by relating them and forming the proper mental structures. The technique used for this is called an *advance organizer.* An organizer is abstract and general; it encompasses the ideas of the lesson and is provided before the lesson begins; it is not the actual lesson itself. We use two features in this text as organizers: concept maps and scenarios to help you visualize the general ideas of each chapter.

Consider the efficacy of an organizer this way. Students return to you after lunch or recess. Where are their minds: on you and the lesson you wish to teach or on what they have just been doing? Learning is most efficient and effective if students' minds can be properly focused and can begin to think about the concepts of the lesson before they experience the material. How can you help make the material meaningful and stimulate your learners' minds so that they are active and receptive? Consider two examples.

Example 1: Expository Organizer.   "Today we are going to study photosynthesis. Photosynthesis is the process by which plants use chlorophyll and convert the sun's energy into chemical energy that is stored until it is needed." The generality of this statement ensures that students would have some basic idea of the relationship between plants, the sun, and producing and storing energy, but would not understand any of the specific processes by which chemical energy is produced or used. The organizer is given to the learners through teacher exposition lecture.

Example 2: Comparative Organizer.   "Today we are going to test our mousetrap machines to see how long they operate and how far they travel, and to compare how long it would take to travel a greater distance in these machines. We need to know how to solve motion problems to do this. Motion problems involve time, rate of speed, and distance. For example, today I had to solve a motion problem in getting to school. I needed to know when to leave home so I could get to school by 7:30 A.M. Knowing that I live 10 miles from school and figuring that I could travel 35 miles per hour, I estimated that 20 minutes would be enough time. Bus lines, airlines, and railroads have to solve problems like this all the time. What are some examples of motion problems you have had to solve?" In this example, students have some idea how the problem can be solved and why this type of problem is important, but they have not yet been taught how to solve the problem. The lesson will provide the details and the students should be able to fit the information into its proper place in a mental scheme of concepts. Comparative organizers are used with relatively familiar material so that new concepts are integrated properly with similar concepts already in the learners' cognitive structures.

Model of Instruction.   Ausubel believes, as Bruner does, that structured concepts, such as those for a discipline like science, can be taught to students. He regards the human mind as a system for receiving, processing, and storing information. Ausubel advocates learning new ideas by relating them to available concepts or anchoring ideas.[18]

Ausubel's Advance Organizers help learners link new ideas with existing concepts or newly provided anchoring ideas. Organizers fit well in a direct instruction method called *deductive teaching,* the opposite of Bruner's inductive teaching. A direct approach is similar to the standard method Vera used in the opening scenario of our chapter before she began to make changes. Vera did not use an advance organizer. (Refer to Figure 2.4.)

FIGURE 2.4   Advance Organizers and Deductive Teaching: Teach from the General to the Specific
An organizer helps to provide a foundation or a mental scaffolding before the teacher presents the abstraction or generality of the lesson (1), then proceeds to clarify key terms (2), provide examples (3), and have students work with specific examples (4).

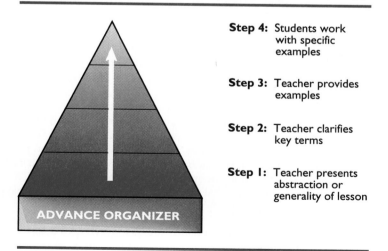

Step 4: Students work with specific examples

Step 3: Teacher provides examples

Step 2: Teacher clarifies key terms

Step 1: Teacher presents abstraction or generality of lesson

ADVANCE ORGANIZER

Constructivism: A Synthesis of the Most Promising Perspectives on Learning

In Transition.   The ancient Chinese are credited with a proverb that goes like this: "I hear and I forget; I see and I remember; I *do* and I *understand*." A lot of wisdom is packed into these three phrases. One type of sensory experience alone is insufficient when we strive for understanding. Experience requires substantial stimulation of all senses and each child's mental processes if meaningful learning is to happen.

Childhood educators Connie Williams and Constance Kamii recommend that we strive to accomplish three things when we encourage children toward understanding:

- Use or create learning circumstances that are indeed meaningful to the learners,
- Encourage children to make real decisions,
- Provide children opportunities to refine their thinking and deepen their understanding by exchanging views with their peers.

Williams and Kamii remind us that what is important is "the mental action that is encouraged when children act on objects themselves."[19] The prevailing view of how children learn captures this intent: How can teachers stimulate the mental action necessary for children to construct ideas?

Constructivism Defined.   "Constructivism is a theory that assumes knowledge cannot exist outside the bodies of cognising beings. . . . Knowledge is a construction of reality."[20]

Constructivism emphasizes the importance of each pupil's active construction of knowledge through the interplay of prior learning and newer learning. Connections are sought between the prior and newer learning; the connections are constructed by the learners for themselves. Researchers and theorists maintain that the key element of constructivist theory is that people learn by actively constructing their own knowledge, comparing new information with their previous understanding and using all of this to work through discrepancies to come to a new understanding.[21] For example:

> In their early experiences of the world, pupils develop ideas which enable them to make sense of the things that happen around them. They bring these informal ideas into the classroom and the aim of science education is to give pupils more explanatory power so that their ideas can become useful concepts. Viewed from this perspective, it is important that we should take a pupil's initial ideas seriously so as to ensure that any change or development of these ideas . . . becomes "owned" by the pupil.[22]

Consider the possible vast difference between a scientist's ideas and those of a child. A scientist's perspective might be that "A plant is a producer." In contrast, a child's perspective might be that

A plant is something that grows in a garden. Carrots and cabbage from the garden are not plants; they are vegetables. Trees are not plants; they are plants when they are little, but when they grow up they are not plants. Seeds are not plants. Dandelions are not plants; they are weeds. Plants . . . have multiple sources of food. Photosynthesis is not important to plants.[23]

Some concepts are correct but not inclusive. Other concepts are incorrect and merit thoughtful attention and eventual correction.

Constructivism is a synthesis of several dominant perspectives on learning. It is not entirely new. Contemporary researchers from Great Britain, Australia, New Zealand, and the United States have updated the theories and methods to capture the synergy of legendary psychologists, philosophers, and researchers such as those whose ideas were presented earlier in this chapter. Important contributions to constructivist theory include Dewey's notion of the nature and importance of direct experience; Bruner's encouragement of appropriate mental action built from specific experiences; Piaget's cognitive development and processing view; and Ausubel's emphasis upon the formation of mental structures. The research evidence in favor of the efforts of constructivism is compelling. Constructivist views strongly influence the whole language movement in English, the standards of the National Council of Teachers of Mathematics (from which the national science standards are influenced), and the recommendations

Knowledge is a construction of reality.

William E. Mills

of the National Research Council and the National Center for Improving Science Education (upon which the national standards in science education are based).

A Constructivist Model.   Constructivism strives toward a deeper understanding. Frontal teaching—telling and showing students all kinds of things—is minimized. According to Eleanor Duckworth of the Harvard Graduate School of Education, all people ever have is their own understanding, and you cannot make them believe anything unless they construct it for themselves. Some of the greatest gains from constructivist approaches have occurred in the teaching of mathematics. Martin Simon, a mathematics researcher and educator at Pennsylvania State University, maintains that giving students the ideas impairs "the robustness of what students learn, their depth and breadth of understanding, and their self-confidence."[24] As an alternative, students can be encouraged to learn by reinventing the wheel for themselves—not a particularly time-efficient approach, but it *is* effective: retention is greater and understanding is deeper. The learner does the discovering by forming mental connections; the teacher mediates the learning environment.

There is a downside of which we must be aware: Not all student constructions are equally valid, and simply voting on what is right does not make it so. At times like this a teacher may feel compelled to step in and correct the record. This can be fine, but beware the tendency to do too much telling. Instead, try an approach like the one shown in Figure 2.5. Provide an opportunity for children to explore and be directly involved in manipulating objects; ask questions and

FIGURE 2.5   A Constructivist Learning and Teaching Model

TEACHER'S ACTIVITY

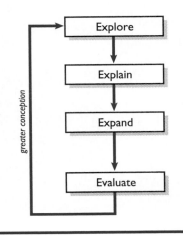

Provide opportunities for students to explore through all appropriate senses and to be fully involved. Encourage group cooperation during investigations; encourage questions.

Interact with children to discover their ideas. Question to cause them to reflect. Help them use ideas formed from exploration to "construct" concepts and meaning sensible to them.

Help children develop their ideas further through additional physical and mental activity. Help them refine their ideas and expand their repertoire of science process skills. Encourage communication through group cooperation and broader experience of nature and technology.

Evaluate conception by examining changes in children's ideas and by their mastery of science process skills. Use hands-on assessment, pictorial problem-solving, and reflective questioning. Encourage children's interest in the ideas and reasoning of others.

encourage children to ask useful and productive questions themselves. Help children to construct best explanations from their direct experiences by finding out their ideas and encouraging them to reflect on similarities and differences, to construct connections among and between their ideas. Encourage children to expand on their ideas by using them in other settings, such as the natural world and technology, and to develop process skills to enhance their thinking. Try to evaluate children's thinking by assessing any change in their ideas and process skills. Also encourage children to evaluate ideas by helping them to become interested in the explanations of others.

Constructivist Teaching. *Constructivism* is becoming a popular catchword in education. Teachers may mistakenly believe they are already using constructivism. (Try your hand at Figure 2.6 to be certain.) While it is true that hands-on science, mathematics manipulatives, and process writing share some common intentions with constructivism, applying constructivist research is much more difficult. The constructivist teacher must fill many roles, but largely functions as a facilitator of knowledge construction. Young children can be encouraged to construct their own understanding if you perform these roles:

- *Presenter*—not a lecturer, but one who demonstrates, models, and presents activities to groups of children and options to individuals so that direct pupil experiences are encouraged in an ongoing fashion
- *Observer*—one who works in formal and informal ways to identify children's ideas, to interact appropriately, and to provide learning options
- *Question Asker and Problem Poser*—one who stimulates idea formation, idea testing, and concept construction by asking questions and posing problems that arise from observation
- *Environment Organizer*—one who organizes carefully and clearly what children are to do, while allowing sufficient freedom for true exploration; one who organizes from the child's perspective
- *Public Relations Coordinator*—one who encourages cooperation, development of human relations, and patience with diversity within the class, and who defends this practice and educates others outside the class about the benefits for children of this approach
- *Documenter of Learning*—one who satisfies the accountability expectations and gauges the impact of these practices on each learner in terms of knowledge construction and science skill development
- *Theory Builder*—one who helps children to form connections between and among their ideas and to construct meaningful patterns that represent their constructed knowledge[25]

Intermediate and middle school children can benefit from these same roles, particularly if cognition is elevated to a stimulating and challenging level that is developmentally appropriate.

FIGURE 2.6   Does Your Teaching Support Constructivism?   Use this continuum to determine the extent to which you are supporting constructivism.

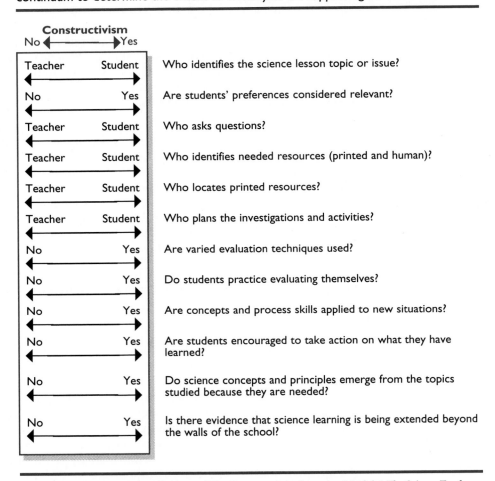

Constructivism No ← → Yes	
Teacher ← → Student	Who identifies the science lesson topic or issue?
No ← → Yes	Are students' preferences considered relevant?
Teacher ← → Student	Who asks questions?
Teacher ← → Student	Who identifies needed resources (printed and human)?
Teacher ← → Student	Who locates printed resources?
Teacher ← → Student	Who plans the investigations and activities?
No ← → Yes	Are varied evaluation techniques used?
No ← → Yes	Do students practice evaluating themselves?
No ← → Yes	Are concepts and process skills applied to new situations?
No ← → Yes	Are students encouraged to take action on what they have learned?
No ← → Yes	Do science concepts and principles emerge from the topics studied because they are needed?
No ← → Yes	Is there evidence that science learning is being extended beyond the walls of the school?

Source: Adapted from Robert E. Yager, "The Constructivist Learning Model," *The Science Teacher,* September 1991, p. 56.

HOW IS YOUR VIEW OF LEARNING RELATED TO YOUR SCIENCE TEACHING?

Your beliefs about how children learn will influence how you choose to plan, teach, and evaluate learning. In short, the role you define for yourself is based on your learning beliefs. This self-defined role places limits on the possible relationships you may have with your science pupils.

Possible Science Teaching Relationships

In his book *Learning Theories for Teachers,* Morris Bigge[26] describes three typical types of relationships based on the teachers' beliefs about how children learn. These types seem to capture the essence of different teacher views converted into classroom practice; we have witnessed each in elementary and middle school science classrooms. Which type of science teacher do you prefer to be?

Authoritarian Teacher.   Firm, centralized control is evident in this classroom. The teacher makes the significant decisions by doing all the planning for the class and issuing instructions. Student thinking is limited to teacher decisions; students are viewed as passive, and the teacher is the active agent. A pleasant teacher will take the edge off this type of classroom with friendliness and warm feelings expressed for the children. However, control is maintained and conformity is expected; learning often is devoted to recall through reading, recitation, and worksheets.

Laissez-Faire Teacher.   This type of classroom is the other extreme. A laissez-faire teacher does not go with the flow, but rather lets it (the flow) happen without leadership. Students essentially are permitted to follow their own initiatives, deciding what to do and how to do it. Teacher direction-giving and planning are absent. Students may develop social skills and determine what are adequate standards.

Democratic Teacher.   The teacher becomes the group leader; work is done cooperatively by the teacher and the students. The analogy Bigge offers compares the teacher to the head scientist in a laboratory. The teacher's role is to lead the students into the study of important topics and problems. The atmosphere is composed of give and take, flexibility, and compromise; all ideas are respected; each person is accountable to the others. Ideas are based on evidence, and insight is generated through cooperation and teamwork. Critiques are evident and expected as teacher's and students' ideas are all subject to proof, analysis, and revision. Teacher and students learn together, even though the teacher may be an expert or an authority. A democratic teacher usually emphasizes purposeful science experiences and cooperative, constructive behavior.

What Type of Learning?

Preparation for the complexities of the twenty-first century requires problem-centered learning. Each student must be able to develop understanding and to refine his or her thinking through reflection. The quality and quantity of what children learn is inseparable from experience. A democratic view of learning and science teaching will help children learn to construct their own knowledge, understand how it changes and grows, and see that knowledge is open to interpretation. Good thinking is difficult to encourage among students, and it is even more complex for teachers to understand. Constructivist teaching and learning approaches can help children to develop

> intellectual habits of curiosity, inquiry, persistence, and carefulness . . . [as well as] to discern the difference between relevant and irrelevant information and reliable and unreliable sources and to detect the purposive and the accidental fallacies that occur when others seek to influence their thinking.[27]

Our next chapter describes science program and teaching goals that help children advance their learning toward this aim. Subsequent chapters provide planning and teaching techniques that are consistent with these goals as well as the means for developing teaching skills that are consistent with this chapter's foundation on how children learn science.

CHAPTER SUMMARY

We have taken an approach in this chapter that is different from what you might find in other texts on teaching science. We assume you have completed a course in psychology or educational psychology, perhaps even a course in child development. Therefore, rather than revisit the depths of some theories you may have studied, we visit the prime ideas behind the theories from the perspective of a practicing teacher. How can we take some of the dominant ideas or perspectives on learning and use them to teach science better?

No perspective on learning is complete without considering the prior ideas of children. These ideas are very personal, may be contradictory when examined under a variety of circumstances, and are stubbornly rooted in children's minds—their ideas are resistant to change, a big challenge for teachers.

Children's learning needs must be considered and assimilated into a teacher's perspective on learning. As children develop over time, their needs change. Their exact cognitive capabilities are dynamic rather than static. Children need extensive experiences to stimulate their senses and to effect thinking. Physical activity is especially important for younger children, and men-

tal and physical activity are interrelated when it comes to learning. Language has no automatic meaning for children, since words have no inherent value; this makes an emphasis on word recognition and memorization meaningless. However, language constructed from experience has meaning that represents the physical and mental action children understand. A child's social development is related to academic success. Group work and tasks that require cooperation help a child to learn. Self-esteem is still another need for effective learning. And all of these needs must be attended to over time. The time factor is variable for children, since maturation and development occur at different rates.

Experience is the one factor that unites the dominant perspectives on how children learn science. But not all experiences are equivalent, and experience alone is insufficient. Theorists advocate several approaches for stimulating mental action and learning in conjunction with experience. John Dewey emphasized the role of reflection and problem solving; Jerome Bruner placed a premium upon conceptualization; Jean Piaget described a biological process of learning that is dependent upon dynamic equilibrium maintained through cognitive assimilation and accommodation through experience; David Ausubel recommended a way to build desired cognitive structures.

Constructivism is the contemporary concept we use to think about a child learning. This perspective focuses on the child and what the child does during learning. The focus of this perspective is on the notions that knowledge cannot exist outside the mind of a learner, it cannot be directly transferred, and it must be each learner's construction of reality. The teaching recommendations offered should help you to construct appropriate roles for yourself. If you follow these recommendations, you will find yourself covering less and guiding more, and your students learning more in the deepest sense

of the words. The chapter ends with a philosophical look at the relationship between your views on learning and the type of science teacher you may become. We challenge you to envision the type of learning you want for children.

So, how do children learn science? Looking back, we helped you answer this question for yourself, and in the course of considering the question and the chapter's material, you began to develop a philosophy of science teaching. Combined with your emerging view of what science is and why it is important, this chapter completes our foundation for science education before introducing you to teaching goals, techniques for planning instruction, and different skills and approaches for effective science teaching.

DISCUSSION QUESTIONS AND PROJECTS

1. In what ways do children benefit from learning through experience? What types of materials or problems do you think are developmentally appropriate for young children? for the intermediate grades? for middle school youth? What similarities and differences do you detect when you compare the materials and problems you favor for each group?

2. How might Piaget's notion of assimilation and accommodation be included in the perspectives of Dewey, Bruner, and Ausubel?

3. As may be revealed by their prior ideas, how might children's science misconceptions affect how you teach? What kinds of things could you do to learn about these prior ideas and to identify misconceptions?

4. Select any science concept. How would you teach it using the different approaches of Dewey, Bruner, Piaget, and Ausubel? How similar or dissimilar is your approach to the recommendations for constructivist teaching and learning?

5. Select several science concepts. Interview several children, perhaps from different age groups, to determine their ideas about the concepts. What are their misconceptions? What similarities or differences do you detect across the age groups you have selected? How do you think you could attempt to correct those misconceptions? What perspectives on learning could you use to help you with this task?

6. Prepare a lesson that attempts to teach a particular science concept. What teaching and learning recommendations do you plan to use to help your learners be successful? Videotape your lesson as you teach it. Analyze the tape. How consistent were you in using the recommendations you selected? What do you plan to do to become the type of science teacher you prefer? What are your specific goals and action plan for accomplishing your goals?

NOTES

1. Rosalind Driver, Edith Guensne, and Andree Tiberghien, *Children's Ideas in Science* (Milton Keynes, England: Open University Press, 1985), pp. 1–2.

2. Ibid.

3. Wynne Harlen, *The Teaching of Science* (London: David Fulton Publishers, 1992), p. 11.

4. Rosalind Driver, *The Pupil as Scientist?* (Milton Keynes, England: Open University Press, 1983).

5. Driver, p. 3.

6. Ibid., p. 4.

7. Martha Denckla as quoted in Barbara Kantrowitz and Pat Wingert, "How Kids Learn," *Newsweek*, April 17, 1989, pp. 53–54.

8. Lillian Katz in Barbara Kantrowitz and Pat Wingert, "How Kids Learn," *Newsweek*, April 17, 1989, p. 55.

9. D. C. Phillips and Jonas F. Soltis, *Perspectives on Learning* (New York: Teachers College Press, 1992), p. 38.

10. John Dewey, *Experience and Education* (New York: Macmillan, 1938).

11. Phillips and Soltis, p. 39.

12. Jerome Bruner, *The Process of Education* (New York: Vintage Books, 1963), pp. 7, 18.

13. Driver, pp. 52–58.

14. Ibid., p. 52.

15. Robert E. Yager, "The Constructivist Learning Model," *The Science Teacher,* September 1991, p. 54.

16. Joseph Novak, "An Alternative to Piagetian Psychology for Science and Mathematics Education," *Studies in Science Education,* (1978), 5, 1, pp. 1–30.

17. David P. Ausubel, *Educational Psychology: A Cognitive View* (New York: Holt, Rinehart and Winston, 1968), preface.

18. Bruce Joyce and Marsha Weil with Beverly Showers, *Models of Teaching* (Boston: Allyn and Bacon, 1992).

19. Connie K. Williams and Constance Kamii, "How Do Children Learn by Handling Objects?" *Young Children,* November 1986, p. 26.

20. Kenneth Tobin, "Social Constructivist Perspectives on the Reform of Science Education," *Australian Science Teachers Journal,* Vol. 36, No. 4, p. 30.

21. Support for this claim can be found in several sources, including Susan Loucks-Horsley (Ed.), *Elementary School Science for the '90s,* (Andover, MA: The NETWORK, 1990); Wynne Harlen, *The Teaching of Science,* (London: David Fulton Publishers, 1992); Penelope Peterson and Nancy Knapp, "Inventing and Reinventing Ideas: Constructivist Teaching and Learning in Mathematics," in Gordon Cawletti, (Ed.), *Challenges and Achievements of American Education* (Alexandria, VA: Association for Supervision and Curriculum Development, 1993); and Robert E. Yager, "The Constructivist Learning Model," *The Science Teacher,* September 1991, pp. 52–57.

22. National Curriculum Council, *Science: Non-Statutory Guidance* (London: NCC, 1989), A7, paragraph 6.2.

23. Roger Osborne and Peter Freyberg, *Learning in Science: The Implications of Children's Science* (Portsmouth, NH: Heinemann, 1985) as reported in Susan Loucks-Horsley (Ed.), *Elementary School Science for the '90s,* (Andover, MA: The NETWORK, 1990), p. 49.

24. ASCD *Update,* March 1992, Vol. 34, No. 3, p. 4.

25. Christine Chaille and Lory Britain, *The Young Child as Scientist* (New York: HarperCollins, 1991), p. 54.

26. Morris L. Bigge, *Learning Theories for Teachers* (New York: Harper and Row, 1976).

27. Ibid., p. 337.

ADDITIONAL READINGS

If you are interested in learning more about some of the topics raised in this chapter, consider the following sources.

Renate Nummela Caine and Geoffrey Caine, *Making Connections: Teaching and the Human Brain* (Alexandria, VA: ASCD, 1991). In this book for teachers, the authors describe the most recent synthesis from brain research.

Christine Chaille and Lory Britain, *The Young Child as Scientist* (New York: HarperCollins, 1991). This delightful, practical book for teachers of young children takes a constructivist perspective.

John Dewey, *Experience and Education* (originally published in 1938 by Kappa Delta Pi). This classic is a concise statement that describes Dewey's complex views on the nature and importance of experience and solving meaningful problems.

Jerome Bruner and Helen Haste, *Making Sense: The Child's Construction of the World* (New York: Metheren, 1987). The authors provide us with a more detailed look at how children construct meaning.

David Ausubel, *Education Psychology: A Cognitive View* (New York: Holt, Rinehart and Winston, 1968). In this classic study, Ausubel affords us a deeper look at his use of advance organizers for encouraging mental processing.

Joseph Novak and D. Bob Gown, *Learning How To Learn* (London: Cambridge University Press, 1984). This book explores in depth the ways to help learners develop mental structures through concept mapping and Vee-maps.

Jean Piaget, *To Understand Is to Invent* (New York: Penguin Books, reprinted from earlier translations in 1976). This is Piaget's essay on how the learner must invent meaning independently for understanding to occur.

D. C. Phillips and Jonas F. Soltis, *Perspectives on Learn-*

ing (New York: Teachers College Press, 1991). This primer is especially reader friendly; the prime perspectives on learning from ancient Greece to modern times are reviewed in a contemporary context.

Anita Woolfolk, *Educational Psychology* (Boston: Allyn and Bacon, 1993). This is perhaps the most comprehensive text available on learning from an educational psychology perspective.

PART TWO

The Science Program

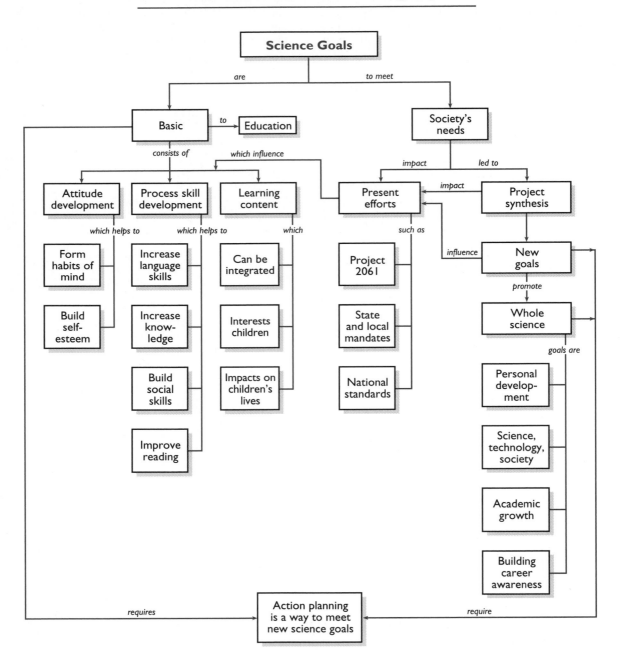

What Are the Goals for Elementary and Middle School Science?

B eing an experienced principal did not make this part of his job any easier. Mr. Caid always felt some personal loss when any one of his teachers left for another opportunity. However, the chance to interview new teacher candidates always encouraged him because the newer generation of teachers was becoming more sophisticated, but not necessarily a good fit for his school's science program. Mr. Caid had invested time and energy to help the school's teachers make their home away from home an exciting place. Calling their school a zoo was a compliment, not an insult. All the classrooms and offices had live plants and animals, and each hallway supported a different living theme. Science was emphasized and was used as a way of promoting social studies, mathematics, reading, and language. Indeed, education was alive in the school and was made as real as possible.

Pride ran high, and it was important to maintain the proper mix of teachers to support the school's vision. Mr. Caid was hopeful that the next candidate would be a good fit, especially for the science program they were all so proud of. After a brief guided tour and warm-up chat, the interview began.

Mr. Caid: Kara, would you please tell me what you think our most important goals should be for science?

Kara: Well, as you know, I'm not a science specialist.

Mr. Caid: The position doesn't call for a specialist, Kara. We're proud of our science program and want all teachers to support it. So, what do you think you would try to accomplish in science if we hired you?

Kara: I think a good science program should be more than science. I like to think in terms of what I would like children to be able to do.

Mr. Caid: Such as?

Kara: I would like children to learn that even *they* are responsible, in some small ways, for what happens to our environment. That even *they* should think about it. So I guess that means they should be able to think and solve problems. And I guess they should understand that something like science is both good and potentially bad if misused. I would like the children in my class to be curious, aware, and even skeptical from time to time. I don't want them to depend on me for the right answer, but to learn how to figure out some things for themselves. I think this will be especially important when they grow up and have to solve serious problems for themselves. So I guess what they do in science should carry over to the other subjects.

Mr. Caid: How would you teach, Kara, to make your goals happen?

Kara: Obviously, the children need to *do* science. I think *hands-on* is more than a slogan. I want children to get their minds involved in what they're doing. One way of doing that is to make the learning real. For example, I would try to help the children develop a knowledge of the working world: how their clothes are constructed, what the differences are among fabrics and comfort, why it's important to cook certain foods in particular ways, why they need to brush their teeth, and why some plants grow better in some environments than in others. I would want the students to see examples of how science is used by society and the problems as well as the good that causes. Also, I would like children to understand that science is an important career, but that it is also important to many other careers.

Mr. Caid: Kara, what you have described sounds like what most people would call a basic education. Is this what you really mean?

INTRODUCTION

Mr. Caid raises a fair question. Does any one subject in the elementary or middle school curriculum hold dominion over the others, and can it lay claim to being more important? Or, as in Kara's description of her preferred goals in science, is it realistic to see science as broad enough to cover so much? We try to respond to these questions in this chapter by dividing it into two parts: First, an examination of the belief that science is a basic part of the school curriculum, and second, an exploration of goals that can benefit any science program. The chapter concludes with the preliminary steps for selecting goals and building your science program through action planning.

IS SCIENCE A BASIC?

Not long ago the standard refrain in education said the basics were readin', 'ritin', and 'rithmetic. You have heard them called the 3 Rs. We know this view is simply too narrow to provide an education that will help our youngsters survive in a complex world with wonders of technology and sophisticated social, economic, and political problems. Tomorrow's leaders and policy makers must know more, have a different world view, and possess an impressive array of skills. What are the basics for education in modern society?

Good question. Almost everyone who is anyone has an opinion; often it supports a special interest. You know our special interest is science. So let us defer to an organization that has attempted to answer the question without bias.

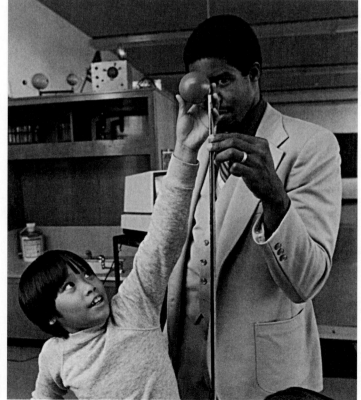

William E. Mills

Science helps improve our lives.

The Council for Basic Education is a group of prestigious educators who are committed to a basic education for *all*. The council maintains that emphasis must be placed on the *intellectual disciplines* and defines them as English (which must consist of reading, writing, speech, and literature), mathematics, *science*, history, geography, government, foreign language, and the arts. The Council urges that each pupil develop thinking skills and positive attitudes toward learning.[1] As the Chinese proverb says: "Teach a person how to fish, feed the person for a lifetime." The Council's recommendation is to promote basic skills that develop the attitudes, skills, and knowledge for *lifelong learning:* Teach a person how to learn, and the person will learn for a lifetime.

Science, then, is a basic; perhaps we could call it the *fourth R.* Whole science provides much more than the content or products of science: It provides opportunities to develop thinking skills and ways to acquire and process information, and it provides opportunities to develop positive attitudes toward learning.

What Is Basic About Science Attitudes?

Positive attitudes such as persistence, curiosity, humility, and a healthy dose of skepticism motivate a learner to approach a task or problem—to be interested enough to find out for him- or herself. An interesting relationship exists among attitudes, interests, achievement, and perception of one's successes. The saying

FIGURE 3.1   Importance of Basic Science Attitudes: Building a Learner's Self-Esteem

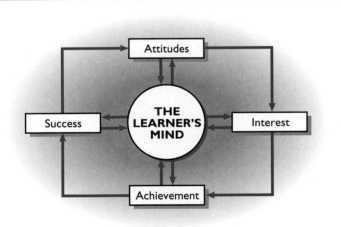

Source: Adapted from Benjamin Bloom, *Human Characteristics and School Learning,* (McGraw-Hill, 1979).

that "success breeds success" sums up the relationship, and anyone who has ever persisted with a problem long enough to solve it knows the sweet feeling of achievement—that can-do attitude that accompanies success. Figure 3.1 demonstrates the interactions of attitudinal factors. According to Benjamin Bloom's research, the relationship appears to be cumulative. As children develop more positive attitudes and more interest in science and other subjects, their achievements increase. This stimulates a feeling of success and helps to develop a higher level of self-esteem. The cycle is cumulative, building on its own momentum. Put simply: *What the mind can perceive and believe, it can achieve.*

So what is basic about science attitudes? They have impact on much more than science. Science attitudes

- promote creativity,
- encourage creative writing,
- are the foundation of good health habits,
- develop mathematical skills,
- provide experiences that can be the inspiration for art and music,
- develop reading and social studies skills.[2]

The attitudes we associate with the business of science are essential for all of the major subject and skill areas in the school curriculum. This relationship helps to classify science as a basic of schooling and to make it integral for the creative and critical thinking and problem solving learners must do in and out of school.

What Is Basic About Science Processes?

The processes of science are the skills by which observations are made and meaning is constructed. Processes can provide the type and quality of the science experience that helps children expand and improve their thinking.

Considerable research over the past twenty years urges that science processes be emphasized on an equal level with science content.[3] Why? Because the processes of science are considered lifelong learning skills. Processes also support the other subject areas typical of schooling. Observing, classifying, measuring, recording, identifying and controlling variables, inferring, predicting, and so on are examples of the processes; these skills are helpful to thinking and are interrelated with the other subject areas.

Process skills have tremendous carryover value in and out of school. Process skills are also vital to adult living; they are the mechanisms by which we identify, explore, and solve problems. Whether the adult mission is to improve or improvise on a recipe, determine the cause of a blown fuse or tripped circuit breaker, troubleshoot the cause of a car's failure to start, plan the best route to run a new line for an extension telephone, identify evidence and separate it from opinion while listening to a political candidate, or determine how to thread a sewing machine, we use the processes of science to solve the problem.

Skills Important to Science and Reading

The skills of science and reading are remarkably similar because they share information-processing procedures. When children are doing science, following scientific procedures and thinking as scientists, they are developing skills that are necessary for effective reading.* A creative planner can have students working on science and reading skills simultaneously. Science experiences can help preschool children develop their intellect and get an early start on fundamental reading skills. Primary students can become motivated through science activities and their natural interests to work on otherwise less exciting tasks like vocabulary development, word discrimination, and comprehension. Intermediate and middle school youth develop their abilities to identify and control variables, make meaningful conclusions, and communicate ideas clearly, as shown in the following table.**

*Michael Padilla, Denise Muth, and Rosemary Lund Padilla, "Science and Reading: Many Process Skills in Common," in Carol Minnick Santa and Donna E. Alvermann, *Science Learning: Processes and Applications* (Newark, DE: International Reading Association, 1991), pp. 14–19.

**The comparisons are drawn from Glenda S. Carter and Ronald D. Simpson's "Science and Reading: A Basic Duo," *The Science Teacher,* March 1978, p. 20, and from Ronald Simpson and Norman Anderson's Science, *Students and Schools: A Guide for the Middle and Secondary School Teacher* (New York: John Wiley and Sons, 1980).

Science Skills	Reading Skills	Examples
Observation	Discrimination of shapes, sounds, syllables, and word accents	Break words in syllables and list on chalkboard. Class pronounces new words aloud. Teacher mispronounces some words and rewards students who make corrections.
Identification	Recognition of letters, words, prefixes, suffixes, and base words	Select a common science prefix, suffix, or base word, define it and list several words in which it may be used. Examples: kilo (1000): kilometer, kilogram, kiloliter
Description	Isolation of important attributes and characteristics Enumeration of ideas Use of appropriate terminology and synonyms	Ask students to state the purpose of an activity. Construct keys for student rock collections, etc. Play vocabulary games. Use characteristics to identify an object or animal.

Science Skills	Reading Skills	Examples
Classification	Comparisons and constrasts of characteristics Arranging ideas and ordering and sequencing information Consideration of multiple attributes	List in order the steps of a mealworm's metamorphosis. Construct charts that compare and constrast characteristics. Put concepts in order.
Investigation design	Question asking Investigating possible relationships Following organized procedures	Have students use library resources and design an experiment from an outline. Write original lab reports. Outline facts and concepts.
Data collection	Note taking Using reference materials Using different parts of a book Recording information in an organized way Being precise and accurate	Prepare bibliographies from library information. Use tables of contents, indexes, and organizational features of chapters. Use quantitative skills in lab activities. Have students compare and discuss notes.
Interpretation of data	Recognition of cause-and-effect relationships Organization of facts Summarizing new information Variation of reading rate Thinking inductively and deductively	Discuss matters that could affect the health of an animal. Teach students to preview and scan printed text. Have students organize notes in an outline. Have students construct concept maps, flow charts, and new arrangements of facts.
Communication of results	Using graphs Arranging information logically Sequencing ideas Describing clearly	List discoveries through a time line. Ask for conclusions from graphed data or tables and figures. Describe chronological events.
Conclusion formation	Generalization Critical analysis Identification of main ideas Establishing relationships Using information in other situations	Ask "What if?" questions. Have students scrutinize conclusions for errors. Use case studies to develop conclusions through critical thinking.

The following represents a widely held view of why the processes are basic to a complete education.

> The crucial tools of today's human living include not only the familiar three Rs, but also those skills that allow us both to adapt ourselves to our environment— to live with uncertainty and tolerate ambiguity—and to adapt our environment to ourselves—to analyze, synthesize, and hypothesize. These process-oriented basics cut across subject matter lines to give the person a capacity for response in a range of situations.[4]

Science process skills are basic to learning. These skills emphasize thinking, investigating, and problem solving. Children can learn to develop these skills if *you* choose to emphasize them. At least one study has found that hands-on, minds-on science programs that emphasized the development of process skills had an impact on the rest of the school curriculum. This is the evidence cited:

- increased language skills and general knowledge,
- development of measuring skills,
- increased understanding of mathematics concepts and number skills,
- improved social studies skills,
- improved visual perception skills,
- suitable substitution as a reading-readiness program for preschool and early primary grade children.[5]

The accountability movement makes the process skills of science an imperative. Some standardized tests measure the processes of learning—classification, interpretation of information, prediction, evaluation. Even reading tests like those contained within the *Iowa Test of Basic Skills* are designed to measure such skills as making predictions, determining cause and effect, making inferences, classifying information, and using time sequences: science process skills. (See What Research Says.) The new generation of science tests adds urgency to treating the processes as basics that are useful across the curriculum. These tests require multiple mental operations and applications of problem-solving skills. Emphasizing the processes helps the student to prepare for testing, regardless of the test's content.

What Is Basic About Science Content?

In a word, interest. Children are naturally interested in science and associated science topics. Surveys done in elementary schools show that children choose science a majority of the time when they are given lists of school topics to choose from. Parents report, too, that their children list science as one of their favorite school subjects.[6]

Like you, children cannot escape the importance of science; it affects every aspect of their lives. However, the intent of science content is that it be a means, not an end. If science content is applied to real circumstances, it can help children to become responsible consumers and to see how learning science will benefit them. Recommendations from organizations like the National Science Teachers Association urge that children have daily opportunities to relate science to their own lives and that science study not be limited only to science time. The knowledge, attitudes, and skills of science can be used to enrich other school experiences. Times for reading, art, music, social studies, writing, mathematics, discussion, physical education, and so on can be used to deepen children's understanding of science. Indeed, programs that emphasize science's relationships with other areas of the curriculum are encouraged. This, then, brings forth an important question: What should be the goals of science?

WHAT ARE THE GOALS FOR EFFECTIVE SCIENCE TEACHING?

Science teaching goals may be provided by your state curriculum or by major science improvement efforts such as those sponsored by the National Science Foundation (NSF), the American Association for the Advancement of Science (AAAS), the National Science Teachers Association (NSTA), or the National

---

EXERCISE 3.1

What Is the Relationship Between Science and Other School Subjects?

We have listed below some common topics in science that you may be asked to teach. Science has considerable potential for integration with other subject or skill areas. How could you help make this integration work for you? Try to list several subjects into which the science topics could be integrated and exchange your ideas with your classmates to develop a resource file of ideas.

Science Topic	Related School Subject/Topic	Science Topic	Related School Subject/Topic
simple machines	_____	energy	_____
growth	_____	plants	_____
nutrition	_____	animals	_____
weather	_____	space	_____
electricity	_____	life cycles	_____
sound	_____	senses	_____
color	_____	adaptations	_____

Research Council. Modern goals respond to urgent needs and are based on the knowledge of what works. In this chapter we present three sources of elementary and middle school science teaching goals that are important for their contemporary breadth and depth: *Project 2061* of the American Association for the Advancement of Science; the *National Science Education Standards* of the National Committee on Science Education and Assessment; and *Project Synthesis* of the NSF.

Project 2061

The American Association for the Advancement of Science (AAAS) commissioned a comprehensive initiative to improve science education called *Project 2061*—named for the year Halley's Comet will reappear.[7] Project 2061 recommends several principles for effective science instruction. Guided by the National Council on Science and Technology Education, the project relies on scientists, engineers, and mathematicians to provide ideas used by the project staff and consultants. Teams of consultants and reviewers consist of scientists, teachers, educators, historians, philosophers, and others who use science and reflect on its place in human affairs. Project 2061 is built upon eleven important guiding principles. Each principle suggests some elements that should be included in the new goals for science instruction. They address the following ideas:

- What science students should know must be carefully identified.
- Effective science instruction must encourage student diversity and serve the needs and interests of all students with a common core of knowledge and experiences.
- Students should learn science concepts rather than a list of science topics.
- Learning outcomes should be accomplished through appropriate teaching practices that begin with questions and phenomena that interest children and should be directed toward helping them find out how things work.
- The science curriculum should be selective and relevant and should not try to cover the full spectrum of the sciences.
- Science should be integrated with other subjects (such as mathematics and the humanities) when integration will *not* make learning science substantially more difficult.
- Science learning goals should be more generic without reference to a specific science course.
- Students must learn that science is tentative, not absolute, and that it is evidence oriented, speculative, and creative.
- Science curricula should include content that deals with social issues and technology when possible.
- Science taught in school should be based on explicitly stated educational criteria.[8]

National Science Education Standards

The National Research Council (NRC) coordinated the development of the national standards for K–12 science education with final standards published in 1994. More than 150 documents from professional organizations, states, and

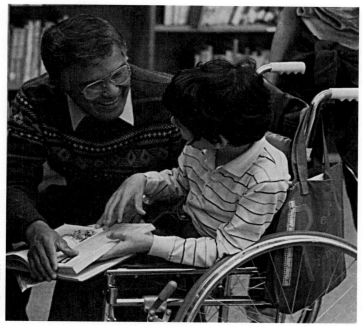

William E. Mills

Modern science includes all children.

other countries were examined, and ideas were transformed into standards. On a national level, this is a difficult task. Preliminary standards include the following goals to prepare students who understand

- and who can use a limited number of the basic concepts of science and the fundamental principles, laws, and theories that represent the body of scientific knowledge;
- the modes of reasoning of scientific inquiry, and who know how use them;
- the nature of science and its ways of knowing;
- the history of scientific development, the relationship of science to technology, and the historical, cultural, and social contexts in which the relationship is embedded.[9]

These broad goals may be addressed through school science programs if science instruction provides experiences that

- are personally and socially relevant to the child;
- include a wide range of knowledge, methods, and approaches so that students can analyze personal and societal issues critically;
- encourage students to think and act in ways that reflect their understanding of the impact science has on their lives, society, and the world;
- encourage students to appreciate science;
- help students develop an appreciation for the beauty and order of the natural world.[10]

Project Synthesis

The principles that guide Project 2061 and the National Standards arose from the findings of another significant science education endeavor, *Project Synthesis*.[11] The National Science Foundation (NSF) supported $2 billion worth of programs and courses developed in mathematics and science during the 1960s and 1970s. Major social and political pressures removed adequate levels of funding for science education during the mid-to-late 1970s. Teachers and citizens concluded that federal funds had been wasted and, in the wake of mixed research reports, that the programs had not accomplished what they were designed to do. It was in this setting that the National Science Foundation responded to Congressional pressure and awarded contracts in 1976 for several landmark studies of science education.[12]

Consensus within and among the Project Synthesis research groups yielded several general conclusions about the status of science education. For the most part, these conclusions are still accurate today, based on examinations of curriculum materials, courses offered, characteristics of teachers, teaching methods used, and student performance. These conclusions are:

1. Science education at all levels is given a low priority when compared with the importance of language arts, mathematics, and social studies. School systems generally do not support science.
2. Textbooks dominate science teaching and learning and limit what can be accomplished.
3. School science programs generally emphasize preparing students for the next grade level of study or for college.
4. Teachers become the curriculum to the extent that they decide what will be taught or studied from texts. Therefore, teachers determine many of the goals of science education. These goals are often incongruent with the national agenda and with what works in elementary science education.[13]

These general conclusions led researchers and science educators to proclaim that existing science programs did not serve the majority of children well. In fact, many existing programs served only about one out of every ten pupils well. Their primary goal was to recruit students into science careers. These conclusions helped to set new goals for science teaching.

GOALS AND OUTCOMES FOR ELEMENTARY AND MIDDLE SCHOOL SCIENCE

The extensive bases of research and recommendations help us set new goals for effective elementary science instruction. These goals provide a foundation for planning and influence the new science improvement initiatives that arise from national organizations and states. The goals we have set are designed to accommodate the new national standards by clustering the standards into groups of related individual outcomes. These outcomes conveniently cluster around four broad goals for science teaching that are similar to those revealed in Project Synthesis. They indicate an era of new conceptualization for science and what students are expected to do, and new emphases for teaching it. These goals are described below.

Goal I:

Science Must Enhance Each Learner's Personal Development.   Science education should help learners use science to improve their own lives and to learn how to cope with an increasingly technological world.

This goal focuses on ways to enhance each student's curiosity, honesty, imagination, self-confidence, and ability to be persistent, make decisions, cope with changes, examine values, reason logically, and practice the ethics of science. This goal reflects the many ways science and technology affect one's life. Included are the attitudes and abilities one needs to become a responsible consumer, to maintain a healthy body, and to use science in making daily decisions and solving daily problems.

Goal II:

Learners Must Understand the Interrelationships of Science, Technology, and Society.   The science curriculum must prepare students to function as informed citizens and to deal responsibly with science-related social and technological issues. Opportunities must be provided for students to develop a greater ability to understand the impact science has on social issues and the way science shapes our expectations about responsible citizenship: personal interaction with the environment, responsible consumerism, respect for environmental order and aesthetics, and so on.

In addition, this goal teaches that technology and science are worthy human endeavors, that there are distinctions between them, and that students must recognize their impact on the future of society.

Goal III:

Science Must Develop Each Learner's Academic and Process Skills.   The science curriculum must provide all students opportunities to acquire the academic knowledge and skills they need to solve personal problems and to continue lifelong learning. Therefore, emphasis must be given to improving children's thinking skills. The science program must also prepare students who are likely to pursue science and science-related careers with the fundamental knowledge and skills necessary to support further education in their career fields.

This goal concentrates on what children need to become scientifically literate. The curriculum must include the knowledge, concepts, principles, and ideas of science, as well as the attitudes, values, and ethics of science, and critical thinking and problem-solving skills.

Goal IV:

Science Must Help to Expand Each Learner's Career Awareness. Science education should give *all* students an awareness of the nature and scope of the science- and technology-related careers that exist. The science curriculum must provide opportunities for children to develop an awareness of how important science is to different occupations and professions. This goal helps students realize that science is relevant to all fields of employment. It also includes development of positive attitudes toward science-related careers and an awareness that these careers provide occupational opportunities for women, minorities, and the handicapped. Some examples could include the many careers in research, engineering, laboratory technology, equipment design, and computer programming; they could include jobs in which people apply scientific knowledge, in such fields as agriculture, nutrition, medicine, sanitation, conservation, and so on.

TEACHERS ON SCIENCE TEACHING

What Are the Goals of Elementary and Middle School Science?

By Terry L. Kluesner
Erin Elementary School, Hartford, Wisconsin

"Thank you for making science interesting," was a comment I heard this past fall during Parent/Teacher Conferences from a mother of a sixth grader. It was especially gratifying for me to hear because I feel the most important goal of a middle school science program is to develop and maintain within students an interest in the field and study of science. My hope is that this interest is carried into high school, where they will take more than the required science courses. This kind of preparation would not only give students a broader choice in their higher education goals, but ultimately, if the interest is carried into adulthood, produce more scientifically literate adults able to make knowledgeable decisions in this increasingly technological world.

How does a teacher develop interest in science? In the past, many people interpreted this as making science fun. *Hands-on* became the catchphrase, and students began manipulating just about anything the teacher could get his or her

hands on without any real information being gained. I do believe my classes are often fun, but when fun becomes the priority, it is possible that the thought processes of science get abandoned. I believe students will be interested in science only when they see it as worthwhile to them, when they feel a part of the learning, and when the information gained holds some meaning for them. The key to this is to have students actively involved, not only with their hands but with their minds as well.

Before conducting any investigation or hands-on experiment, students must be given enough pertinent background knowledge about a subject so they can generate informed hypotheses. They must have a reason to carry out the experiment: Why would the students need to or want to find out the kind of information you're asking them to find? Once the experiment is completed, students must be asked to organize the data into tables and graphs as well as to make some sort of meaningful interpretation or conclusion from the data. Only when

Students should become informed about the contributions people in such careers make to society as well as the specific educational preparation, interests, attitudes, and abilities associated with each career. Students must realize that science, mathematics, language arts, and social studies are interrelated, and they should understand the interrelationships of science, technology and society.

The new goals, we have found, are comfortable guides for teachers who have limited time for planning and limited curriculum experience. The outcomes associated with these goals can be added to the present program or selected lessons. Through expansion techniques described throughout this chapter, your planning can turn a program of limited impact into an effective program of science instruction. The philosophy of these goals and outcomess also transfers well to new national and local initiatives, should you be employed by a school involved in those efforts. We begin by examining the specific outcomes.

students are asked to engage in scientific reasoning will they see how the information they collected is relevant to them.

Problem solving is intertwined throughout this whole learning process. Students must not only be able to perform canned experiments the teacher sets up, but must be able to figure out how to answer questions and solve problems of their own. What variables would they manipulate, control, and measure? Students need to be given opportunities to practice designing their own experiments. These may be formal written plans on topics such as plant propagation or more spontaneous, creative experiments, such as trying to design a catapult that is capable of flinging a 2 cm by 2 cm piece of potato into a 1 meter square target from a distance of 4 meters.

One of the things I do in my classroom throughout the year to maintain interest is to run contests. These contests most often require the use of problem solving. The contests range from the very simple, such as the Egg Drop Contest and the Mealworm Race, to the complex, such as the Straw Bridge Contest and the Hot-Air Balloon Contest. Toward the end of the year I hold a science fair in which students in grades 6, 7, and 8 compete for gold, silver, and bronze medals at each grade level. I realize there is controversy over the competition aspect of contests and a science fair, but I find that when it is not used excessively, it is a great motivator as well as a lesson on the competitive nature of scientists in the business world.

In summary, I believe the major goals of any school science program must be to develop and maintain interest in science and include

- the learning of basic science knowledge and concepts,
- active participation by students,
- opportunities for hands-on learning,
- opportunities for problem solving,
- scientific reasoning development.

Science goals focus on the learner, society, technology, and careers.

New Outcomes for Effective Science Instruction

Outcomes provide direction and help to clarify what teachers and students are expected to accomplish. These outcomes can help teachers plan for effective instruction, help school administrators maintain clear expectations for children's learning and teachers' professional development, and help science program committee members write clear and comprehensive outcome statements for locally developed curricula.

The outcome statements that follow can help organize an entire K–12 science program. Variations in state recommendations and each local school district's philosophy may require different degrees of emphasis on particular outcomes between grade levels. Differences can also be caused by diverse community expectations and student characteristics. However, the intent is that *each outcome* be accomplished for *each child* by the time the student completes the school science experience. Also, it seems improbable that each outcome can be addressed in every lesson or unit. But a majority of the outcomes listed for each goal should be included within each grade level of every science course in the program. As a result, it is possible that some outcomes will take on a first level of importance while others will assume lower levels of importance within any given lesson or unit.

The four goals described in this chapter reflect an interpretation of outcomes science educators at the national level believe are important for science teaching. The order in which the outcomes are presented and the number of outcomes listed for each goal should not suggest their relative importance. The names of these goals have

TABLE 3.1   The Four Goals of Science Instruction with Outcomes for Effective Science Instruction

---

Goal 1: Personal Development
The children will:

(1.1) understand and use new ideas and scientific information to improve their lives.

(1.2) develop skills to support scientific inquiry.

(1.3) develop problem-solving skills needed to respond to a changing society and environment.

(1.4) develop a positive attitude toward science that will encourage continued interest and learning.

(1.5) develop the attitudes and skills they need to become responsible consumers.

Goal 2: Science, Technology, and Society Interrelationships
The children will:

(2.1) understand the interactions of science, technology, and society.

(2.2) recognize that the solution to one problem can create new problems and that decisions must consider the possible consequences for other community members.

(2.3) recognize that data may be interpreted differently by different people depending on their values and experiences.

(2.4) recognize how the advancement of science and technology has changed the lives of people in local, national, and global communities.

(2.5) possess a sense of custodianship (collective responsibility for the environment over a period of time) as the need for conservation increases.

Goal 3: Academic Growth
The children will:

(3.1) develop a knowledge and understanding of scientific principles and concepts.

(3.2) develop attitudes, values, and ethics of science to use as a basis for science-related decisions.

(3.3) learn to think critically, creatively, and rationally so that they can solve problems and promote lifelong learning.

(3.4) develop process skills so that they can think scientifically.

(3.5) develop psychomotor skills so that they can properly manipulate equipment and instruments.

Goal 4: Career Awareness
The children will:

(4.1) realize that science and technology are relevant to all fields of employment.

(4.2) develop an awareness of the occupational and professional opportunities in science for women, minorities, and the handicapped.

(4.3) develop an awareness of the science requirements for occupations and professions.

(4.4) recognize that scientists and technicians possess a full range of personal characteristics and should not be stereotyped.

(4.5) develop effective and positive work habits related to science.

(4.6) become informed about the contributions scientists make to society.

been adapted from the labels provided by Project Synthesis and are shown in Table 3.1.[14] Related outcomes are clustered under each goal.

How important are these goals, and how much should they be emphasized in the science curriculum? Public perceptions may help answer these questions. Surveys of citizens' groups across twenty-two states in 1982 and 1984 reveal some interesting public perceptions. Table 3.2 and Figure 3.2 suggest that societal and career awareness goals have become more important, while personal and academic goals may need less emphasis. Public opinion will continue to affect trends. These future trends will continue to influence the importance teachers choose to give each goal. Meanwhile, each goal must be given serious consideration as you determine the amount of classroom emphasis that is necessary to fulfill the school district's science program philosophy and program outcomes.

Forming an Action Plan

Taking the Steps.   Let us assume you accept and understand the goals recommended for science teaching. What is your first step for using the goals? You need an action plan. Action plans differ from teacher lesson plans because they build a large view of the teacher's science-teaching mission. An action plan consists of several steps that are followed to identify and make necessary changes. These steps are shown in Figure 3.3 and are described below. They will help you develop your own science program for those occasions when no curriculum guide or science program exists to help you.[15]

Step 1. Understand or determine the *purpose* of the science program and identify the science *topics* you will teach.

Address the purposes and topics by writing appropriate goals. Consider the recommendations of professional organizations and those taken from profes-

TABLE 3.2   Comparison of the Importance of the Goals at K–9 Grade Levels, 1982–1984*

		Percent That Is Important			
		Personal Development	*Societal Issues*	*Career Awareness*	*Academic Preparation*
K–3	1982	51	8	1	40
	1984	38	15	10	37
4–6	1982	45	9	2	44
	1984	33	19	14	34
7–9	1982	38	15	10	37
	1984	25	21	20	34

*n = 5,400 in 1982
n = 8,291 in 1984

FIGURE 3.2 Citizen Groups' Perceived Importance of Science Goals Differences in percentages show the amount of emphasis that citizens believe the science outcomes should receive in a school science program.

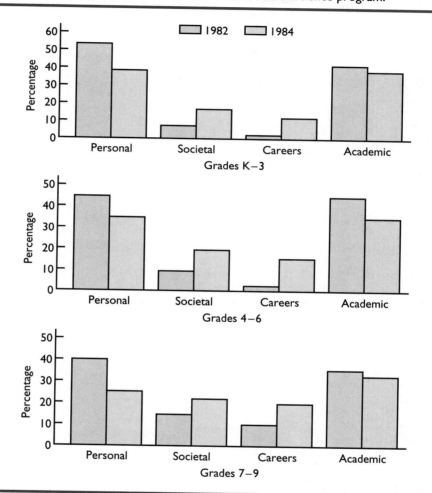

Source: Alfred F. Pogge and Robert E. Yager, "Citizen Groups' Perceived Importance of the Major Goals for School Science," *Science Education,* 71, 2, p. 224, 1987.

sional reading when developing or selecting goals. Make a list of the major learning goals. The four science goals and outcomes can help (see Table 3.2).

Step 2: Identify those student *outcomes* that are important in the achievement of each of these broad goals.

Come up with examples of things children are expected to learn if the goals are to be met. Try to turn these into specific objectives. (The next chapter expands on lesson planning.)

Step 3: Identify the available teaching resources and select appropriate activities.

Identify all useful resources and weed out the least effective ones. You might try using the CD-ROM *Science Helper*, which is described in Chapter 12. Select or design activities that will help children reach the outcomes or objectives you have set.

Step 4: Evaluate progress.

Decide what you will do to help your students accomplish the broad and specific goals you have selected for them. The most important curriculum decisions are made by teachers and become evident in the learning activities they use. Evaluate your students' progress appropriately and adjust your instruction as needed.

Less Is More.   Effective science instruction depends on your ability to see a big plan and to identify the important ideas you will teach. Your action plan becomes this big plan—a vision for what and how your students will learn. You need to know how your ideas and preferences fit into this big plan when you set out to help children make mental connections between many separate ideas. We suggest you be guided by the educational maxim *less is more.* Covering less, but doing it better, yields more opportunity for children to

FIGURE 3.3   Action Planning Steps

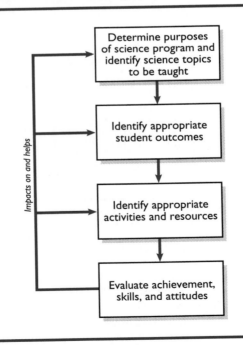

science, develop skills, and form appropriate attitudes. Strive to help children connect the ideas of science through their own experiences so that they understand and appreciate the importance of science in their daily lives and the potential science offers for their futures. Concept mapping is one approach that promises to help teachers help children make these connections efficiently and effectively. This is shown in the next chapter.

CHAPTER SUMMARY

Part of the answer to the question "What are the goals for science teaching?" lies in the belief that science is a basic and must achieve its proper place in the school curriculum. When science is regarded as a discrete unit of study, this defeats the concept of the basics that are necessary for an effective education. Science can, however, help learners to develop important attitudes that foster useful problem-solving and thinking skills and high self-esteem. The attitudes typically arise from successes children experience while they are developing many skills. In science we call these *process skills* (described in Chapter 1). Through processes, children achieve such important outcomes as improved language, social, and reading skills, and new levels of knowledge. Knowledge acquisition is the focus of many subjects, and in science, this is one desired outcome. Even so, the knowledge gained in science is viewed as a route to other destinations. Children can integrate the science content they learn with other subject and skill areas. Children tell us that they are interested in science, and we know that it can have a tremendous impact on their lives.

The potential positive impact of science requires four important goals for teaching it. These goals address the personal improvements and benefits children can expect from the attitudes, skills, and content of science. Other goals build the learners' awareness of careers, for scientists and nonscientists alike, and illuminate the interrelationships among science, technology, and society. Academic growth is a goal that makes clear the need to press beyond memorizing mere lists of facts. These goals are consistent with the efforts of science organizations and the national standards.

Less is more is more than a slogan in science education. This phrase represents a philosophy and aim of delving more deeply and purposefully into what children learn. More content is not the express purpose of delving; acquiring more enriching experiences—mentally, physically, socially, and attitudinally—provides the *more*. To achieve this *more*, we as teachers must choose our goals and establish outcomes care-

DISCUSSION QUESTIONS AND PROJECTS

1. What principles guide your views on teaching and learning? Combine your beliefs into a philosophy statement and write it down. Now compare your philosophy with the goals and outcomes of science education given in this chapter. How does your own philosophy compare? How do your ideas compare with those of others in your class?

2. Imagine that you are preparing for an interview with a school principal or a director of personnel. You have heard that this question will be asked: "What are your top four or five goals for teaching science in ____ grade?" How would you answer this question?

3. Survey your state department of education,

school district, and science professionals to compile a list of the main goals for elementary or middle school science education. How does this list compare to the goals or recommendations of the National Research Council, Project 2061, and our four goals and outcomes?

4. Examine several popular elementary science texts and/or school science programs. How have the goals we have recommended been used?

5. How can you act on the science outcomes by building them into your lessons? Examine how we have used the outcomes in our lesson plans located in the last section of this book. What other suggestions do you have for using the outcomes?

NOTES

1. Kenneth R. Mechling and Donna L. Oliver, *Science Teaches Basic Skills*, Handbook 1 (Washington, DC: National Science Teachers Association, 1983), p. 2.

2. Ibid., pp. 14–34.

3. Ibid., p. 9.

4. Mario D. Fantini, "The Right to Quality Education," *Educational Leadership*, January 1980, p. 325.

5. William K. and Mary K. Esler, *Teaching Elementary Science* (Belmont, CA: Wadsworth Publishing Company, 1981) p. 5.

6. Mechling and Oliver, p. 5.

7. American Association for the Advancement of Science, *Science for All Americans: A Report on Literacy Goals in Science, Mathematics, and Technology* (Washington, DC, 1989).

8. F. James Rutherford and Andrew Ahlgren, "Rethinking the Science Curriculum," in Ronald S. Brandt, ed.,*Content of the Curriculum* (Alexandria, VA: Association for Supervision and Curriculum Development, 1988), pp. 75–90.

9. National Research Council, *National Science Education Standards: A Sampler* (Washington, DC: National Research Council, November 1992), p. 6.

10. Ibid., p. 7.

11. Rutherford.

12. Norris Harms, "Project Synthesis: Summary and Implications for Teachers," in Norris C. Harms and Robert E. Yager, eds., *What Research Says to the Science Teacher*, vol. 3 (Washington, DC: National Science Teachers Association, 1981), pp. 114–117.

13. Pertinent studies include: Iris R. Weiss, *Report of the 1977 National Survey of Science, Mathematics, and Social Studies Education*, SE 78–72, prepared for the National Science Foundation Directorate for Science Education, Center for Educational Research and Evaluation, (Research Triangle Park, North Carolina, March, 1978); Stanley L. Helgeson, Patricia E. Blosser, and Robert W. Howe, *The Status of Pre-College Science, Mathematics and Social Science Education: 1955–1975* (The Center for Science and Mathematics Education, Ohio State University, Columbus, OH, 1977); Robert E. Stake and J. Easley, *Case Studies in Science Education, Volumes I and II* (Center for Instructional Research and Curriculum Evaluation, University of Illinois, Urbana-Champaign, 1978); and David Holdzkom and Pamela B. Lutz, eds., *Research Within Reach: Science Education* (Research and Development Interpretation Service, Charleston, WV, 1984).

14. Kay Wagner, ed., *New Dimensions in Science Education* (Columbus, OH: Ohio Department of Education, 1989). The authors contributed to the development of the goals adapted from Project Synthesis that appear in Chapter 6 and acknowledge their appreciation for permission to use these materials in a modified form as presented in this chapter.

15. Ibid.

ADDITIONAL READINGS

If you are interested in learning more about some of the topics raised in this chapter consider the following sources.

Carol Minnick and Donna Alvermann, *Science Learning* (Newark, DE: International Reading Association, 1991). The authors emphasize the basic and integrated science process skills as an important aspect of learning to read.

F. James Rutherford and Andrew Ahlgren, *Science for All Americans* (New York: Oxford University Press, 1990). Written in a layman's language, this book contains a complete description of the content and type of science teaching the authors envision.

The *2061 Today* newsletter is also available. Write to 2061 Today, American Association for the Advancement of Science, 1333 H Street NW, Washington, DC 20005.

Kenneth R. Mechling and Donna L. Oliver, *Science*

Teaches Basic Skills (Washington, DC: National Science Teachers Association, 1983). This book was written with the elementary school principal in mind and is part of a five-handbook series. We referred to the good-sense, practical reports of the research in this chapter. This source contains abundant examples in great detail.

Victor M. Showalter, *Conditions for Good Science Teaching* (Washington, DC: National Science Teachers Association, 1984). The conditions necessary for teaching science K–12 are discussed. The format of this booklet permits easy self-appraisal.

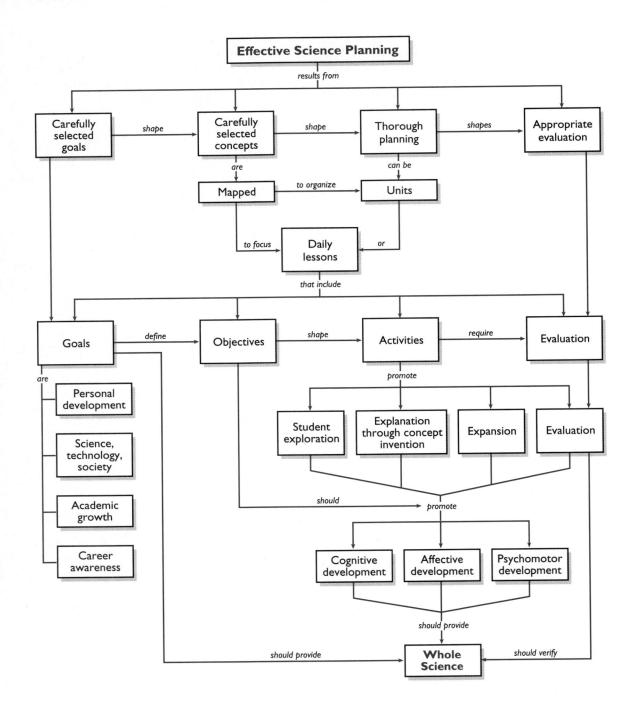

Planning:
How Can You Plan
Effective Science Instruction?

CHAPTER

4

W illiam Philips, an earth-science teacher, discovered some interesting but depressing facts about what his students knew about science—or rather, what they really did not understand. What was most troublesome was what his students thought they knew without realizing they were incorrect: their misconceptions. These are his words:

> Misconceptions are rarely expressed aloud or in writing and, therefore, often go undetected. Twenty years ago, shortly after I began teaching science, I encountered an outrageous misconception (or so it seemed at the time). While I was using a globe to explain seasonal changes, one very attentive eighth grader raised her hand and asked, "Where are we?" Thinking she wanted to know the location of our

school, I pointed to Delaware and resumed my lecture. She immediately stopped me with another question. "No. I don't mean that. I mean, do we live inside the Earth or outside it?" The question caused several students to laugh, but most appeared to be waiting for an answer. It was all I could do to hide my astonishment.[1]

INTRODUCTION

Philips cites a survey in which second-grade teachers estimated that 95 percent of their students knew the earth is a sphere.[2] Later the teachers conducted interviews with the children and discovered that the students actually believed the earth is flat. Misconceptions are common, and once formed, they are held a long while. Misconceptions are linked to intuitive ideas or beliefs that children acquire before they begin school learning. It is not unusual for students to progress through school providing correct answers when the teachers ask for them, but believing otherwise, much like the second graders mentioned above. When students give science facts correctly to questions and on tests, it does not mean they have replaced the misconceptions they formed much earlier.

Examples of misconceptions Philips uncovered are given in Table 4.1. Misconceptions seem to occur as students construct knowledge; they may be linked to incomplete or insufficient experiences, faulty explanations, and misperceived meanings. Joseph Novak, professor of science and education, reminds us that students

TABLE 4.1   Common Earth Science Misconceptions

More than ten years' worth of research on misconceptions yielded the following list for children. Adults often harbor the same misconceptions.

The earth is sitting on something.	Rain comes from clouds' sweating.
The earth is larger than the sun.	Rain falls from funnels in the clouds.
The earth is round like a pancake.	Rain occurs when clouds are shaken.
We live on the flat middle of a sphere.	God and angels cause thunder and lightning.
There is a definite up and down in space.	Clouds move because we move.
Astrology is able to predict the future.	Clouds come from somewhere above the sky.
Gravity increases with height.	Empty clouds are refilled by the sea.
Gravity cannot exist without air.	Clouds are formed by vapors from kettles.
Any crystal that scratches glass is a diamond.	The sun boils the sea to create water vapor.
Coral reefs exist throughout the Gulf of Mexico and the North Atlantic.	Clouds are made of cotton, wool, or smoke.
Dinosaurs and cavemen lived at the same time.	Clouds are bags of water.
Rain comes from holes in clouds.	

Source: These misconceptions are excerpted from the list provided by William C. Philips in "Earth Science Misconceptions," *The Science Teacher*, February 1991, pp. 21–23.

Direct experiences help to reduce misconceptions.

must construct new meaning from the foundation of the knowledge they already possess.[3] This means that we as teachers cannot afford to overlook student misconceptions, because of the negative learning cycle caused by misunderstanding the simplest point. Novak also states that students can only create new meaning by constructing new propositions, linked concepts that are usually formed through discovery learning.

Planning, then, carries the burden of providing clear, representative experiences and follow-up discussion. These can be used to refute students' misconceptions and to build a correct understanding. This chapter is devoted to the elements of planning for effective science instruction. In this chapter we

1. illustrate the importance, methods, and uses of concept mapping;
2. describe the elements and techniques of planning science units and lessons;
3. survey several approaches for evaluating students' science learning, skills, and attitudes.

CONCEPT MAPPING

Concept mapping is one of the most promising developments in education. In this section, we explain why concept maps are essential tools for planning and teaching and how you can use concept maps to improve science instruction to avoid some misconceptions. Concept mapping may be new to you. It is a recent development that is becoming more widely used as constructivist learning models are more accepted in science education.

Concept mapping is perhaps the most important recent innovation to help children produce meaningful learning in classrooms. Maps provide concrete visual aids to help organize information before it is learned (see, for example, the discussion of David Ausubel's ideas in Chapter 2). Science textbooks are beginning to use concept mapping among the end-of-chapter activities. Teachers who have used concept maps have found that they give them a logical basis for deciding what main ideas to include in or delete from their plans and science teaching. Concept maps can be developed for an entire course, one or more units, or even a single lesson. We use maps to introduce you to each chapter's dominant ideas and to illustrate the relationships among the chapter's concepts.

Necessary Definitions

Some definitions must be provided before we can proceed. Bear in mind the fundamental purpose of education: to help students find new meaning in what they learn. We refer to this as *meaningful learning*. David Ausubel contrasts meaningful learning with rote learning, which is the result of many disjointed lessons. Concept maps use three types of knowledge: facts, concepts, and generalizations.

Meaningful Learning.   Meaningful learning implies that as a result of instruction, individuals are able to relate new material to previously acquired learning. This means that learners see new knowledge in light of what they already know and understand; hence they find new meaning. Knowledge continually grows, but in a fashion that encourages connections with what learners already know. If these connections are missing, learners may regard the ideas they are taught as useless abstractions that only need to be memorized for a test.

As an example, learning that electricity flows through a circuit can be meaningful for children if they are able to see (with a teacher's guidance) that this idea applies to their previous understanding about how and where electricity is used. (Refer to Figure 4.1.) Children may have previously believed that electricity comes from the wall where an electric switch or outlet is located. When someone turns the switch on or plugs an appliance into the outlet, the electricity flows to a lamp or an appliance. A teacher would facilitate learning by helping children understand that electricity indeed flows through the switch or comes out of the outlet, but also that there are continuous electric wires between the electric pole outside the house and the switch or outlet inside the house, and between the switch or outlet and the appliance. Unless children are able to see these connections between the existing

FIGURE 4.1 **Example Concept Map**

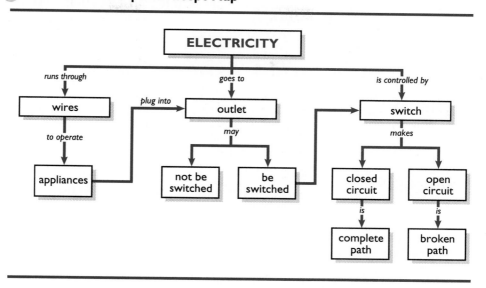

knowledge and the new, they are likely to regard this generalization about electricity as an abstraction, or something to memorize without exactly knowing its importance.

Rote Learning. Memorization without understanding and without a connection to the previous knowledge is called *rote learning.* Rote learning promotes memorization of facts; meaningful learning promotes conceptual understanding.

Facts. A *fact* is a singular occurrence that happens in the past or present and that has no predictive value for the future. Thus, the information that you are now reading in this book at a specific time of day is a fact, just as a statement about what you ate for lunch or dinner yesterday is a fact. These facts may be completely isolated events that give no indications about your study or eating habits. On the other hand, if you regularly read your science methods book at the same time, or if you consistently eat salad for lunch and chicken or fish for dinner, then these seemingly isolated facts have much in common with your similar actions at other times.

Concepts. Common attributes between facts can be described and named. The name given represents a *concept.* Interestingly, your behavior today or yesterday can be described by a single word or brief phrase. Words such as *preparation* and *follow-up* or a phrase like *nutritious diet* are examples of concepts based on an accumulation of facts. The definitions of these concepts may include descriptions

TEACHERS ON SCIENCE TEACHING

How Can You Create Learning Opportunities?

By Mike Roberts
Grade 1 Teacher, Hollister School District, Hollister, CA

When I was a student teacher, my master teacher made available to me a space in which to save some of the materials I used in her second-grade classroom. Here I saved all the odds and ends for which I had no other place. Eventually this collection included many objects that were useful for creating science activities.

One day a boy brought an old fifth-grade science textbook into school. He had found many activities in it that he desperately wanted to do. I told him to select one we could do with the things we had on hand. He selected a wind speed indicator made from a paper plate, paper cups, a pin, tape, and a pencil—all things readily available from the box of extra materials. We constructed it, and he made many more with his friends.

There were several lessons here for me. First, children have a very good idea of what they want to learn about. Second, they can figure out how to create something from the available material. Third and most important, it is very important to keep a significant amount of stuff around for children to use.

Since then I have tried to ensure that somewhere in the room there are materials that students can use in their own fashion. I collect everyday materials because science is a curricular area that requires that students investigate their everyday world and inquire about its workings. That's all well and good, but there are also practical questions. How does a teacher plan for something like this? How does a teacher set up a classroom for this kind of activity? What are the rest of the students doing while several are messing about with a box of interesting materials? How do we meet students' needs?

Here are some of the ways I dealt with these issues, and I am sure other teachers are inventing different ways also. First, collect things that you suspect may be useful: paper tubes, plates, cups, string, wire, batteries, lights, switches—the list goes on and on. These things are supposed to be in your science kits, but in my experience they have been used up and not replaced. If you do have a pristine kit, then you will be expected to replace what is used. I found it best to collect my own. I don't spend a lot of money. Most of this can be salvaged from the refuse of daily life.

Second, I arranged my school day to accommodate a free time that allows activities that give the students a chance to use materials with my supervision. I try to encourage, question, and challenge. I try not to direct. I know everyone won't choose every activity every day. The material at hand will allow the students to negotiate and discuss the use of whatever is available.

The goal of our educational system is to engage young minds in activities that lead them to experiment. As they become more aware of their world, they are encouraged to explore and then use their new knowledge to construct a more complete understanding. More understanding means more use of the knowledge and more questions.

I haven't written a lesson plan here, but I've described a plan for creating learning opportunities. This is how I as a teacher place the materials in the room and how I build in opportunities for students to explore them. This way they learn to question each other and me and to experiment and thereby construct a better understanding of their world.

such as "you read your textbook before and after the science methods class," or "you try to eat foods that are low in calories, fat, and cholesterol." A concept covers a broader set of events than a singular occurrence that might happen at random. Therefore, concepts by their nature are abstract. Other examples of concepts are computer, animal, mineral, vegetable, food chain, magnets, solution, conservation, and buoyancy. All require that we know the definition to understand the meaning. In fact, most words in the dictionary represent concepts. All learners, especially young children, need to experience many examples of singular occurrences or facts before they can develop the abstract understanding necessary for conceptualization. But once they learn the concept, they do not need to learn isolated facts that are subsumed in it. They can reconstruct these facts when they need them.

Generalizations. *Generalizations* are broad patterns between "two or more concepts that . . . have predictive value."[4] Generalizations are rules or principles that contain more than one concept and that have predictive value. Thus, a statement such as "like poles in magnets repel each other and opposite poles attract" is a generalization, and it can predict what would happen if two magnets were brought next to each other. Learners must know the concepts of *magnets, poles, attraction,* and *repel* before they can fully understand the meaning of the generalization.

What Are Concept Maps?

Concepts are abstract ideas. Concept maps, on the other hand, are concrete graphic illustrations that indicate how a single concept is related to other concepts in the same category (see Figure 4.2). As you begin to learn about concept maps, you may

FIGURE 4.2 Concept Map: AIR

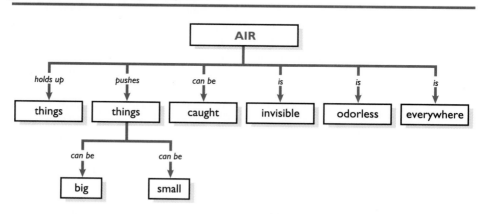

Source: Represents concepts found in the first-grade text (Addison-Wesley, publisher) described by John R. Staver and Mary Bay in "Analysis of the Conceptual Structure and Reasoning Demands of Elementary Science Texts at the Primary (K–3) Level," *Journal of Research in Science Teaching,* 1989, 26, 4, p. 334. Reprinted with permission of John Wiley & Sons, Inc. © 1989.

prefer to think of them as sophisticated planning webs that reveal what concepts children must learn and how the concepts must be related. Curricula are primarily designed to teach concepts that students do not already know. Therefore, teaching and learning will be greatly enhanced if we know which concepts should be included and which need to be excluded from instructional programs.

Concept maps show relationships among different smaller and larger concepts. By looking at a concept map, and considering the level of the children's abilities and other instructional factors, you can make a decision about the scope of the concepts you need to cover in an instructional program. Joseph Novak states that

> a good curriculum design requires an analysis first of the concepts in a field of knowledge and, second, consideration of some relationships between these concepts that can serve to illustrate which concepts are most general and superordinate and which are more specific and subordinate.[5]

A concept map's visual illustration of main ideas is the primary advantage it provides over other ways of planning instruction. A concept map shows hierarchical relationships: how various subordinate concepts are related to the superordinate concepts. A relationship can descend several levels deep in the hierarchy of concepts. The relationship between superordinate and subordinate concepts is shown in Figure 4.3. We have also used concept maps throughout this book to show which concepts are included in each chapter and to represent the connections between the individual concepts that make up the meaning of each chapter. Please note, though, that concept maps are unique constructions created by individual learners. Indeed, maps that represent the same material can be drawn differently to reflect the specific visions of their creators.

A concept map is different in several ways from the outline or table of contents generally found at the beginning of a book. First, outlines do not show any definite relationships between concepts; they simply show how the material is organized. Concept maps, on the other hand, show a definite relationship between big ideas and small ideas, thus clarifying the difference between details or specifics and the big idea or superordinate concept. This can be helpful when a teacher must decide how much emphasis to give to specific facts as compared to concepts in a lesson.

The second difference is that concept maps provide visual imagery that can help students to recall information and see relationships between concepts. Outlines do not provide such imagery. Outlines do serve a useful function: They indicate a sequence of different steps. Concept maps, on the other hand, show "hierarchies of ideas that suggest psychologically valid sequences."[6] These hierarchies may not match the linear sequence, or outline, that a teacher has decided to use for a presentation.

Third, concept maps can show interrelationships between ideas, or *cross-links*. These help to "tie it all together," as students often remark.

Why Should Concept Maps Be Developed?

Concept maps help teachers understand the various concepts that are embedded in the larger topic they are to teach. This understanding improves teacher planning

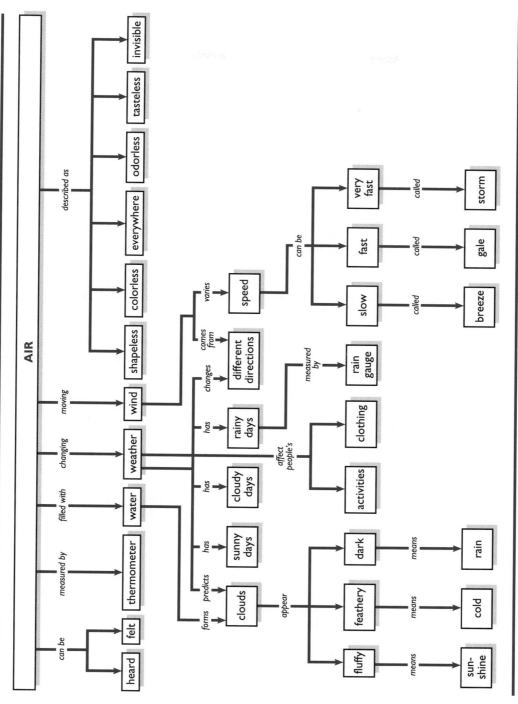

FIGURE 4.3 Expanded Concept Map of AIR

The figure shows the relationship of several levels of subordinate concepts as provided by John R. Staver and Mary Bay, in "Analysis of the Conceptual Structure and Reasoning Demands of Elementary Science Texts at the Primary (K–3) Level," *Journal of Research in Science Teaching*, 1989, 26, 4, 339. The researchers examined the contents of the Merrill first grade science text. Reprinted with permission of John Wiley & Sons, Inc. © 1989.

and instruction. Since the science knowledge domain is vast, and most of us have acquired it in pieces at different stages, we are not likely to see the important connections between the separate ideas we teach. As an exercise, mapping provides us with an opportunity to express our present understanding about various concepts and to show relationships with other similar and dissimilar concepts. Ultimately, the larger topic or unit (superordinate concept) is hierarchically arranged. This arrangement shows facts at the bottom and subordinate concepts arranged in relationships with each other in the body of the map (see, for example, the details of Figures 4.1 through 4.3). Our experience with hundreds of teachers and students has convinced us that they gain new insight from developing concept maps when they structure what they know around a superordinate concept. This observation is also supported by Novak and Gowin: "Students and teachers often remark that they recognize new relationships among concepts that they did not before."[7]

Concept mapping is one of the most crucial steps to take while deciding what to include in a curriculum, unit, or lesson plan. Clear mapping may help to avoid student-formed misconceptions. Without concept maps, teachers choose to teach what they can remember or what they prefer. The topics they select in this manner may be appropriate at times, especially for teachers who have had previous successful experiences with the material, but this process opens a major psychological flaw in the process of curriculum development and lesson planning. The concepts or topics chosen may be so disconnected from each other that learners are baffled and see no connections themselves. Learners may also fail to receive new meaning because they cannot link the new material with what they have previously learned. As a result, learners may resort to memorizing isolated facts, treating the experiences and ideas with less thought than we prefer. This mental inaction would defeat the modern science goal of developing new habits of the mind.

While some things must be memorized, sustained memorization has questionable value in science. Taking the time to identify concepts yields clear science topics and helps to determine which topics are worth learning. Mapping concepts suggests specific objectives that we as teachers must establish for pupils. Concept maps can help you see the logic of the relationships among specific concepts. Once you see this logic, you then can decide how much depth or breadth to include in your lessons so that students will see the same conceptual relationships. These decisions consist of choosing the proper activities and learning aids as well as selecting the appropriate type of pupil evaluation.

You can also use concept maps to organize the flow of the classroom lessons. We have used concept maps as advance organizers to focus students' attention and guide them along to seeing a bigger picture and for use as a mental scaffolding for organizing their thoughts and discoveries. You can use concept maps as road maps to indicate the direction in which instruction is to proceed in your classroom—up, down, and across the map. Students can be shown concept maps several times during instruction so that they can see what has been covered and how it fits with the rest.

Another way you can use concept maps is for student evaluations. For example, display large pieces of newsprint in a conspicuous place and use them daily to show the science ideas students have learned and how these ideas interrelate. This daily effort is an example of *formative evaluation*. You could ask intermediate and middle school children to develop maps at the end of instruction to reflect what they understand, a process called *summative evaluation*.

Steps for Developing a Concept Map

A concept map can be developed for the entire course for a year or semester, or for a single unit, or even for a single lesson. Figure 4.4 shows the relationship of concepts in a concept map. The following steps work for all concept maps:

1. List on paper all of the concepts (names of topics) that pertain to a general area you will teach. Only the names are needed at this stage. No descriptions are necessary. For example, let us say you have examined your next science chapter or module and have listed the following topics: air, weather, clouds, storms, and effects of weather.

2. Note any specific facts (examples) that are either essential for students to learn or that you find especially interesting. The facts and examples you list might include: air moves, measurements are used to track air movement, moving air causes weather, weather can be helpful or harmful, and weather helps us decide what clothes to wear.

3. From the list of concepts, choose what you find as an overarching concept (superordinate), and place it at the top of the paper. (You may want to use a large sheet of newsprint or other suitable drawing paper.) You decide that the overarching concept is *weather*. It seems that all other ideas relate to it. Satisfied, you now line up the other concepts by going to step four.

4. Arrange the first level of subordinate concepts underneath the superordinate concept. Generally, this stage requires the use of propositions or linking words like *provides, types, contains, can be,* and so on to develop the appropriate connections between subordinate concepts. Refer to the second line of circles in Figure 4.4. (The first level of subordinate concepts is known by another term, *coordinate concepts,* because they link or coordinate the superordinate concept and the subordinate concepts found lower in the hierarchy. Each coordinate concept is related to the same superordinate concept, but it is distinctly different from other concepts arranged at that level of the hierarchy.)

5. After the first level of coordinate concepts has been identified, start arranging other subordinate concepts that are directly related to the level above. Similarly, you can develop further hierarchies by going down several levels. You will find that specific facts will be examples of certain individual subordinate concepts that will most likely be at the bottom of the hierarchy. See, for example, in Figure 4.3 that *clouds* is a subordinate concept that is connected to coordinate concepts of *water* and *weather,* and the concepts *fluffy, feathery,* and *dark* are connected to *clouds* to show other subordinate concepts in the hierarchy; each concept relates back to the superordinate concept *air*.

FIGURE 4.4   Concept Map for Concept Maps

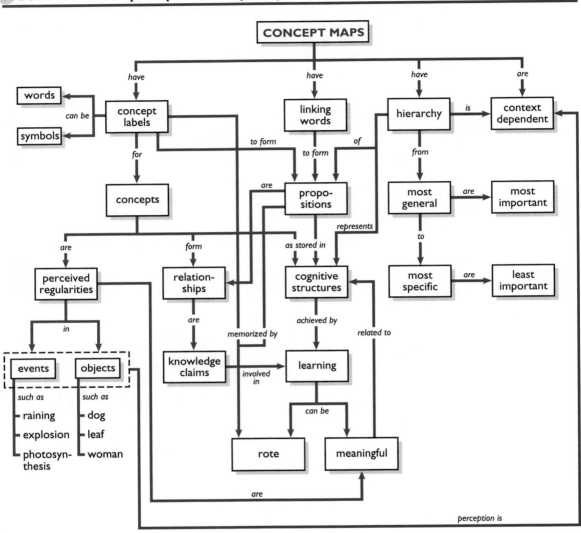

Source: Joseph Novak, "Clarify with Concept Maps," *The Science Teacher*, October, 1991, 46. Reprinted with permission. Copyright © 1991 by the National Science Teachers Association, 1742 Connecticut Avenue, NW, Washington, DC 20009.

6. Draw lines to show relationships among the subordinate, coordinate, and superordinate concepts. The entire hierarchy should resemble a pyramid. Write linking words (propositions) on the lines to show relationships between concepts. These relationships form principles. Refer to Figure 4.4 and notice the connecting lines with propositions—for example, *can be, as stored, have,* and so on.

7. After the entire map has been developed, you can mark or circle certain subordinate concepts that are particularly appealing for your learners or are at the appropriate difficulty level. These would generally constitute your course or unit for the given time period.

There are two mistakes you need to avoid. First, try to minimize jumping around the entire map; try not to select topics without a strong rationale. The strongest reason for selecting a topic should rest on the knowledge the children acquired earlier. During the appropriate phases of your instruction (called *concept invention* and *expansion,* which are explained later in this chapter), you need to help children link the new concept with previous learning.

Second, we suggest that the number of specific details you teach needs to be balanced in terms of how well they contribute to overall conceptual development. Remember, the factual information sits at the bottom of the map, and your purpose is to have children understand what rests at higher levels of the map. Teaching factual information alone does not help children to develop concepts at a higher level unless you make specific attempts to move up the hierarchical ladder.

PLANNING INSTRUCTION

Plan instruction to suit children's needs. One reason for effective planning is to avoid or overcome children's science misconceptions. Steve Rakow, editor of *Science Scope,* the journal for middle school science teachers, offers a planning strategy for overcoming the troublesome problem of student misconceptions. The strategy involves first determining where the students are and then building meaningful experiences from that level. His steps are given in Table 4.2.

Preschool and primary grade children learn or retain little without manipulating real objects. Early childhood educators Connie Williams and Constance Kamii remind us that "young children think better when they act on objects."[8] Handling science objects with skillful teacher guidance helps young minds to grow. In contrast, typical learning devices such as worksheets do not do much to advance children's thinking, and young children cannot think very well at all when they are required to sit silently. Table 4.3 summarizes Williams and Kamii's recommendations for encouraging young children's thinking and learning. These recommendations are also useful for intermediate and middle school youth. Setting appropriate instructional goals is the first step in planning effective science instruction.

Setting Goals

Goals state expectations for teachers and students. They also represent the general purpose of a lesson and can be used to identify the topic of study. For example, a teacher may ask: "What do I want to emphasize in this unit or accomplish during this lesson?" or "How can I help children learn to think?" or "What are the three most important things I want students to learn in this science lesson?"

Goals vary in the amount of time they require to achieve. They may be designed for an entire year, a semester, a week, or just a single day.   It

TABLE 4.2   Six Steps to More Meaning

How might teachers help children avoid some common misconceptions? Certain strategies may help to make planning and teaching more effective. The following strategies are based on David Ausubel's research and represent how to organize children's minds and teach them to form and link correct conceptions. These strategies are recommended:

1. Test the students before a lesson to determine what they recall from prior experiences. Tests should not be limited to paper and pencil, but can be in the form of interviews, pupil demonstrations, and tape-recorded student explanations.
2. Identify any science misconceptions and address them directly. Confront incorrect thinking with a correct explanation.
3. Begin with what the students know and help the entire class identify how new information and experiences relate to previous learning.
4. Begin with the general, broad ideas and work your way down to the specific details of the concept.
5. Help students to see how concepts relate to others and how several may interrelate. Concept mapping is a way to make this type of thinking more concrete.
6. After the lesson, try to determine how well the students have assimilated the ideas by asking them to explain relationships and connections. Capable students may be asked to make their own concept maps.

Source: These recommendations are adapted from the strategies provided by Steven Rakow in "Six Steps to More Meaning," *Science Scope,* October 1992, pp. 18–19.

is also possible to evaluate goals, which helps teachers and schools to demonstrate accountability.

There are three fundamental types of goals—cognitive, affective, and psychomotor. These are often referred to as the three *domains* of learning.[9]

Cognitive Domain. *The cognitive domain* is emphasized much of the time in traditional classrooms. In fact, some researchers estimate that 80 to 90 percent of a child's school time is spent learning in the cognitive domain.[10] This domain has six levels. The *knowledge* level (recall of information) is the simplest. When children can describe what they see, hear, or read in their own words and their own ideas, they demonstrate that they *comprehend.* When children can use what they have learned in a different situation, they demonstrate the *application* level. *Analysis* is more difficult because learners have to break the whole down into its many parts, as in finding out why an electric circuit does not work. Children think and learn at the *synthesis* level when they put together many parts to form a new, unique whole, as in suggesting a new way to solve an old problem. *Evaluation* is regarded as the highest level of thinking, and it can often be stimulated simply by asking, "Why?" or "How?" as follow-up questions to students' observations and suggestions.

TABLE 4.3 How to Encourage Children's Thinking and Learning

1. Use or create situations that are personally meaningful to children. Meaning develops within children's minds based on prior experiences. Concept mapping can be used to help children form useful mental frameworks for organizing classroom experiences.
2. Provide opportunities for children to make decisions. Decisions will often be based upon observations they collect and classifications they form. Making decisions will strengthen their thinking skills and mental frameworks.
3. Provide opportunities for them to exchange viewpoints with their peers. Children can develop objective thinking habits if they are required to examine other viewpoints. Egocentrism will fade.

Source: Adapted from Connie K. Williams and Constance Kamii, "How Do Children Learn by Handling Objects?" *Young Children*, November 1986, pp. 23–26.

Useful science goals involve the cognitive, affective, and psychomotor domains of learning.

Affective Domain.   *The affective domain* refers to emotional aspects of learning, such as attitudes, values, and ethics. According to David Krathwohl,[11] simple awareness is the lowest level of affective behavior, called *receiving*. *Responding* is the next level, at which children show overt involvement, such as choosing and doing a science activity without a teacher's encouragement. *Valuing* is shown in a child's behavior and signifies that which is prized or cherished. The next level is called *organization*. At this level a child will pull together differences in values and find a way to resolve any conflicts between them. A willingness to compromise is regarded as evidence of organization. *Characterization by a value or value complex* is the highest level of the affective domain. When learners act consistently within their value systems in predictable situations, they demonstrate evidence of this level.

Psychomotor Domain.   *The psychomotor domain* is linked to development of children's motor skills and physical coordination. This domain has seven levels.

TABLE 4.4   New Science Goals and the Domains of Learning

Goals may be selected for the particular domain they nurture. The following science goals (formulated from the science program outcomes in Chapter 3) are listed with the domains they support. Some goals can sustain more than one domain, depending on what you emphasize.

Cognitive Domain
  The children will:
  (1.1) understand and use new ideas and scientific information to improve his or her life.
  (1.2) develop problem-solving skills necessary to respond to a changing society and environment.
  (2.1) understand the interactions of science, technology, and society.
  (2.2) recognize that the solution to one problem can create new problems and that decisions must consider the possible consequences for other community members.
  (2.3) recognize that data may be interpreted differently by different people depending on their values and experiences.
  (2.4) recognize how the advancement of science and technology has changed the lives of people in local, national, and global communities.
  (3.1) develop a knowledge and understanding of scientific principles and concepts.
  (3.3) learn to think critically, creatively, and rationally so that he or she can solve problems and promote lifelong learning.
  (3.4) develop process skills so that he or she can think scientifically.
  (4.1) realize that science and technology are relevant to all fields of employment.
  (4.2) develop an awareness of the occupational and professional opportunities for women, minorities, and the handicapped in science.
  (4.3) develop an awareness of the science requirements for occupations and professions.
  (4.4) recognize that scientists and technicians possess a full range of personal characteristics and should not be stereotyped.
  (4.6) become informed about the contributions scientists make to society.

Perception originates in the brain and must occur if students are going to be aware of such attributes as left-right, up-down, rows-columns, foreground-background, and so on. *Set* illustrates physical readiness to perform a task, such as properly grasping forceps before beginning to move masses on a balance. *Guided response* is a behavior directed by a teacher. A child follows a sequence of instructions properly, such as the correct way to grasp a clamp, pick up a test tube, and move it to a new location. *Mechanism* is the label used when a child no longer has to think through each mechanical step as it is done; the task appears to be done automatically. *Complex overt response* is a more complicated extension of the mechanism level. *Adaptation* is shown when children can adapt their physical performance to the situation's demands. *Origination* is demonstrated when children create new movements to fit particular learning requirements. Often this level of the psychomotor domain is referred to as a student's *style*. Overall, science goals represent all domains.

Goals can be teacher constructed or selected from the school's program goals. In the absence of clear science goals, you may prefer to make your selections from

---

Affective Domain
The children will:
- (1.3) develop the attitudes and skills necessary to become a responsible consumer.
- (2.2) recognize that the solution to one problem can create new problems and that decisions must consider the possible consequences for other community members.
- (2.3) recognize that data may be interpreted differently by different people depending on their values and experiences.
- (2.4) recognize how the advancement of science and technology has changed the lives of people in local, national, and global communities.
- (2.5) possess a sense of custodianship (collective responsibility for the environment over a period of time) as the need for energy and natural resource conservation increases.
- (3.2) develop attitudes, values, and ethics of science to use as a basis for science-related decisions.
- (4.4) recognize that scientists and technicians possess a full range of personal characteristics and should not be stereotyped.
- (4.5) develop effective and positive work habits related to science.

Psychomotor Domain
The children will:
- (1.2) develop problem-solving skills needed to respond to a changing society and environment.
- (3.4) develop process skills so that he or she can think scientifically.
- (3.5) develop psychomotor skills so that he or she can properly manipulate equipment and instruments.

those goals and outcomes offered in Chapter 3. Outcomes are goals that have been made more specific to accomplish particular learning needs, school aims, or to develop specific concepts. See Table 4.4 for examples of science goals that fit into the three learning domains.

Developing Objectives

Objectives are more narrowly focused than goals and consist of the many smaller steps you take to accomplish a goal. Objectives are descriptions of what you the teacher expect your students to *do.* This last word is important. Objectives make clear the particular expectations teachers have for their students; objectives use key *action words*—verbs—to describe what students will do to satisfy the teacher that they are meeting the goals or fulfilling the desired outcome. Objectives are beneficial because they help sequence instruction properly, suggest appropriate learning activities and resources, and specify the appropriate evaluation procedures.

Different kinds of objectives exist. The type recommended in this chapter may be called a *performance* or *behavioral objective.* Named after its intention, a performance objective is a statement that describes what students are expected to be able to do. This type of objective has four parts and can be remembered by the letters A, B, C, and D.

A is the **audience** (class, group, or child) for whom the objective is intended.
B is the **behavior** that a teacher expects from the children.
C is the **conditions** that are necessary for the learning to take place (such as the prerequisites, prior activity, arrangements, or support materials that are needed).
D is the **degree** or minimum level of student performance that shows that the children have completed the objective satisfactorily.

For example, "Given plastic drinking straws, straight pins, thread, tape, modeling clay, paper clips, and metal washers (conditions), each fourth-grade child (audience) will build (behavior) a structure that is at least 30 centimeters tall, uses at least three triangles, and supports at least ten washers without falling down (degree)." This type of objective could support academic growth goal number 3.5 found in Table 4.4 under the psychomotor domain. This same objective could reinforce learning from the other two domains, depending on the behavior that a teacher chooses to emphasize.

The behavior stated in a goal must follow a precise rule: The behavior must be observable or measurable. For example, verbs like *appreciate, desire, feel, know, like,* and *understand* are too general to use in an objective, yet these verbs are fine when used in a goal, because a goal *is* more general. Verbs like *build, classify, measure* and *match* are much more precise, and the teacher can measure or observe accomplishment; there is no need to make assumptions about whether or not a child has done them. Lists of science process skills are rich sources of verbs for your objectives. Table 4.5 provides some brief examples of attitude and thinking skills that are appropriate for objectives.

TABLE 4.5   Science Attitude and Process Skill Objectives

Include in your unit and lesson planning the development of proper scientific attitudes and process skills. The following are brief examples.

To develop the necessary *scientific attitudes,* children should be given learning experiences in which they are expected to:

- use their curiosity to help them make observations
- persevere when given a difficult task to complete
- demonstrate a positive outlook when they fail
- remain open minded when presented with alternatives or conflicting points of view
- cooperate with others
- seek reliable sources of information
- be skeptical about questionable information

- avoid broad generalizations when evidence is limited
- tolerate other people's opinions and viewpoints
- withhold judgment until all evidence or information has been examined
- question superstitions and unsubstantiated claims
- change their minds when evidence no longer supports the prior conclusion or idea

To develop the necessary *scientific process skills,* children should be given learning experiences in which they are expected to:

- observe
- classify
- communicate
- measure
- predict
- infer

- identify and control variables
- form operational definitions
- design and conduct experiments
- interpret data
- reach and defend conclusions

Selecting or Developing Unit Activities

Goals and objectives provide the expectations for a unit plan; proper learning activities provide the means. Researchers of mental development and cognition provide important suggestions for teachers that are helpful when selecting or developing learning activities. Planning by concept mapping and by objectives avoids the fill-up-the-empty-bag approach that is common among beginning teachers. This approach is often chosen because of the need to fill a certain amount of time that has been set aside for science—just to keep the children busy and orderly. To help children develop their thinking skills and learn meaningful science, select or plan activities used for instruction so that you can:

1. Provide a variety of activities for learning. Activities that provide children opportunities to experience and manipulate real objects are essential. Stress direct physical and mental involvement for children in primary and intermediate grades. All children must be given opportunities to explain what they experience and to communicate to others in written and spoken language. All learning activities should be expanded to address as many of the goal clusters as possible.

2. Use specialized vocabulary and introduce concepts *after* children have gained first-hand experiences with the object or concept. As a general rule, teachers should *talk less* and *involve students more.* One way of doing this is to *tell less* and *ask more.* Questions are great devices for encouraging children to use their minds. Chapter 6 is devoted to the uses of questions.

3. Interact with children and have them interact with each other. Questions stimulate interaction and interaction encourages thinking. Ask children to describe what they have done or observed. Encourage children to ask each other questions about their experiences and to ask *why?* questions.

4. Focus learning experiences so that children are encouraged to discover concepts. Focusing on concepts, the main ideas behind learning, helps children learn connections more easily and removes the learning barrier of disconnected facts. The next section of this chapter tells more about doing this.

A unit plan consists of goals, objectives, and learning activities. Two types of goals are included: global goals or outcomes selected from visionary science groups and national recommendations that guide the elementary science program (such as those provided here and in Chapter 3) and goals set by the teacher or the school that guide the unit itself. Objectives are smaller, specific statements of what students will do. Learning activities consist of descriptions of what teachers and students will do; they are selected to fulfill the objectives. When the learning activities have been completed, the objectives will have been met, and when the objectives have been met, the unit goals will have been achieved. In turn, when the unit goals have been achieved, meaningful progress will have been made toward accomplishing the science program goals.

FIGURE 4.5   Concept Map: Relationships Among Science Program Goals, Unit Plans, Lesson Plans and Evaluation

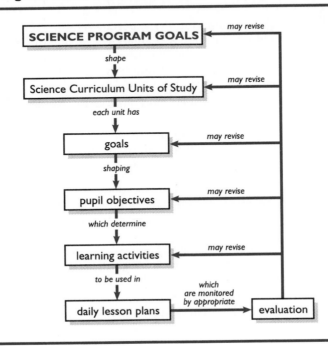

FIGURE 4.6   A Unit Planning Format

Unit Title: The Human Body

Grade Level: K–2

Science Program Goals	Science Unit Goals	Student Objectives	Learning Activities	Evaluation
1.1 The children will understand and use new ideas and scientific information to improve their lives.	The children will understand the importance of maintaining a clean body to prevent disease.	The children will: 1. communicate why they should wash daily. 2. infer how keeping a clean body can prevent disease. 3. demonstrate proper dental care.	1. Wash hands before eating. 2. Dentist or hygienist to demonstrate and discuss proper care. 3. Collect and display pictures to show proper dental care. 4. Match vocabulary words to hygiene	Practical handwashing and tooth-brushing test. Attitude and process skills observation checklists. Match pictures and words on worksheet.
2.4 The children will recognize how the advancement of science ahd technology has changed the lives of people in local, national, and global communities.	The children will understand the effects of unsanitary conditions on the health of a community.	The children will: 1. infer how diseases are transmitted. 2. observe proper hygiene in public facilities. 3. describe the reasons for and demonstrate the correct way to use a public facility.	1. Discuss how disease is transmitted. 2. Discuss how to prevent disease. 3. Experiment with soap, oil and dirt. 4. Collect pictures or objects used to clean kitchen, bathroom, etc.	Student interviews. Observation in washrooms. Attitude and process skills observation checklists.
3.1 The children will develop a knowledge and understanding of scientific principles and concepts.	The children will understand the general framework of the human body and how it can be kept healthy and strong.	The children will: 1. describe the function of the human skeleton. 2. discuss ways to care for and maintain a healthy body. 3. describe the functions of basic human organs.	1. Construct layed model of body with skin, organs, skeleton, etc. 2. Discuss skeleton and organs. 3. Survey class to find out whose relatives have had organs removed. 4. Discuss how broken bones heal.	Human body project. Student presentations of projects and descriptions of good health practices. Attitude and process skills observation checklists.
4.6 The children will become informed about the contributions scientists make to society.	The children will learn about the health professions.	The children will: 1. identify and name major occupations related to health care. 2. describe specific health care services received by individuals in the class or family.	1. Construct collage of health care professionals. 2. Provide hats of health care uniforms for students to wear while they discuss the activities of the professional.	Attitude and Observations checklists. Observe attitudes while wearing hats. Discuss sex-role stereotypes. Practical test over collage via student interviews re: occupations.

Note: *Conditions* should be stated contingent on the learning environment and the sequence of instruction. The *degree* of expected student performance must be set by each teacher (if not preset by the curriculum) according to student abilities. It must correlate with the method selected for evaluation.

Figure 4.5 shows the relationships among the parts of the unit plan, and Figure 4.6 provides a process for organizing goals, objectives, and activities into a useful unit plan. This process can be used by individual teachers, groups of teachers, curriculum supervisors, and administrators to develop science curriculum materials that are consistent with the four goals and science outcomes recommended for effective instruction. This process helps to ensure that a teacher develops a continuum of related parts while planning, instead of merely filling a block of time. The format in Figure 4.6 helps you to plan a science unit that identifies the important goals, objectives, and learning activities. It helps children to make important connections as they learn. To use the format

1. Enter the unit title.
2. Enter the grade level or group.
3. Take science program goals from those shown in Table 4.4.
4. Set your expectations or unit goals. Each should contribute to the continuum of the science program and emphasize concept development.
5. Determine the student objectives, which indicate the specific attitudes, thinking skills (or science processes), and/or science content concepts students are to demonstrate upon completion of the unit.
6. Plan your activities, learning experiences that contribute to one or more of the student objectives and that form the substance of the daily lesson plan. Activities should provide experiences and knowledge for concept development.
7. Select evaluation techniques to measure accomplishment of the objectives and progress made toward goals, and for purposes of revising the plan.

PLANNING THE LESSON

Effective science lessons are planned to provide important student experiences. Lessons that provide meaningful experiences are often student centered and afford children many opportunities to organize experiences and information into concepts. Once formed, these concepts must be applied to the children's world. This application expands the depth of learning and addresses the goal clusters for personal development; promotes learning about the interrelationships of science, technology, and society; contributes to greater academic growth; and helps expand career awareness.

The lesson planning format given in this chapter closely follows the original format of the Science Curriculum Improvement Study (SCIS; see Chapter 5), which is credited with the greatest gains in student science achievement when compared to any similar experimental science program. SCIS has contributed important gains in process skill development as well as improved pupil attitudes toward science.[12] This planning technique has been modified to reflect constructivist learning expectations and to emphasize appropriate student evaluation. The approach is simple and thorough and has considerable potential to effect improvements in children's learning. Our technique is based upon a planning and teaching method called a

FIGURE 4.7 The Planning and Learning Cycle

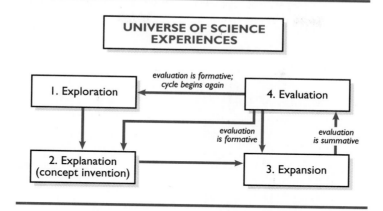

learning cycle (see Figure 4.7). A detailed description of the teaching method is given is Chapter 7. The elements of planning are given here.

The four phases of the science planning and learning cycle provide most of the structure for planning an effective science lesson. Once you identify the concept that is to be learned, you can structure the learning activity to take advantage of the learning cycle. Then you can add descriptions of the proper ways to evaluate what the children learn.

The *4 E approach* is recommended: Exploration, Explanation, Expansion, and Evaluation. The following questions should help you plan for each step of the learning cycle as you write the lesson plan. The parenthetical remarks suggest the aspects of science and teaching strategies that may be used. A sample science learning cycle lesson plan is shown in Exhibit 4.1.

Step 1: Planning for Student Exploration. Children must have concrete materials and experiences if they are to learn concrete concepts. Abstract concepts are largely inappropriate, even with concrete materials, until around age 15 for most pupils. Use these guiding questions:

- What do I want the children to learn? (goals, objectives, attitudes, processes, products)
- What concepts will be invented? (science products)
- What activities must the children do to find and to construct the needed data? (processes, information, answers to questions)
- What kinds of records should the children keep? (process skills)
- What kinds of instructions and encouragement will the children need? (attitudes)

Effective lessons require many interesting resources.

Teachers need to direct the children's activities and suggest what kinds of records they should keep. *They should not tell or explain the concept.* State the instructions succinctly, even in the form of objectives. Plan this step carefully so that it is student centered and student-activity based.

Step 2: Planning for Explanation.   The main purpose of this phase is to reach mental equilibrium through accommodation, as described in the theory of Jean Piaget (see Chapter 2). Equilibrium is reached when a new concept is formed and/or linked to previously understood related concepts. Here students must focus on their primary findings from exploration, and the teacher must help them by introducing proper language or concept labels. This step was originally called *concept invention.* The teacher's task is to lead students through a discussion so that students can discover the concept by inventing it for themselves. The teacher's technique is to question skillfully so that students use the experiences of their explorations to construct scientific meaning. The teacher acts as a facilitator and introduces any special vocabulary that must accompany the concept. Plan this step carefully so that it does not become completely teacher centered; your lectures must be minimal. Use these questions as you plan for this part of your lesson:

- What kinds of information or findings are students expected to provide? (products, process skills)
- How will the students' findings from the exploration phase be reviewed and summarized? (teacher questioning, pupil discussion, graphing, board work)

- How can I use the students' findings and refrain from telling them what they should have found, even if they are incorrect or incomplete? (teacher questioning, guided construction, attitudes)
- What are the proper concept labels or terms that must be attached to the concept? (products)
- What reasons can I give the students if they ask me why the concept is important? (teacher exposition, lesson expansion)

The last question automatically leads to the next phase: *Expansion.*

Step 3: Planning for Expansion. The purpose of this phase is to help students organize their thinking by applying what they have just learned to other ideas or experiences that relate to the lesson's concept and to help the students to expand their ideas. It is very important to use the language of the concept during the expansion-of-the-idea phase. Plan this phase for student involvement. Consider using these questions:

- What previous experiences have the children had that are related to the concept? How can I connect the concept to these experiences? (new activities, questioning)
- What are some examples of how the concept encourages the children's personal development, investigation of science-technology-society relationships, academic growth, and career awareness? (address science goals again, emphasize science attitudes)
- What questions can I ask to encourage students to give examples of the concept's importance, how it is used, the problems it solves, the problems it causes, and the careers influenced by it? (questioning, guided discussion)
- What new experiences do the children need in order to expand on the concept? (processes, attitudes, activities)
- What is the next concept related to the present one? How can I encourage exploration of the next concept? (products, processes)

Step 4: Planning for Evaluation. The purpose of this phase is to go beyond standard forms of testing. Learning must occur in small increments before larger leaps of insight are possible. Your evaluation can be planned in terms of outcomes and pupil objectives. Several types of measures are necessary to form a wholistic evaluation of the students' learning and to encourage conceptual understanding as well as process skill development. Figure 4.8 reflects the need for continual evaluation, not just end-of-chapter or end-of-unit testing. Evaluation can occur at any point in the lesson. Consistent evaluation can help to reveal misconceptions before they become deeply rooted. Ask yourself:

- What key questions should I ask to encourage deep exploration? (processes, attitudes)
- What questions can I ask to help students think about their data in an effort to construct realistic concepts? (processes)

- What questions will expand conception and achieve several science goals or outcomes? (processes, products)
- What behavior (mental, physical, attitudinal) can I expect from the students? (attitudes, processes)
- What hands-on assessments can the students do to demonstrate the basic skills of observation, classification, communication, measurement, prediction, and inference? (processes)
- What assessments can students do to demonstrate the integrated skills of identifying and controlling variables, defining operationally, forming hypotheses, experimenting, interpreting data, and forming models?
- What pictorial assessments can students do to demonstrate how well they can *think* through problems that require both knowledge and the integration of ideas? (products)
- What reflective question assessments will indicate how well the students recall and use what has been learned? (products)

HOW CAN YOU EVALUATE STUDENT LEARNING?

Children learn more and better when we focus clearly on the learning outcomes and objectives we want them to achieve, because planning, teaching, and evaluation go hand in hand.[13] Next we explore these connections.

Limits and Purposes of Tests

Typical forms of evaluation, such as standardized tests and teacher prepared paper-and-pencil multiple choice or true-false tests, have severe limits. True, they are easy to use and grade. However, their formats limit what they can evaluate; their almost exclusive focus on facts omits coverage of deductive reasoning, scientific process skills, and affective factors of learning. Indeed, facts are necessary, and children cannot do much science or effectively reason scientifically without a solid factual base. Children may be able to memorize the facts, however, without having any idea about how to apply them. Being able to identify or describe a scientific procedure or apparatus on paper does not mean a child knows when that procedure is appropriate or how to properly use the apparatus. Consider the following test items, which are similar to those used by the National Assessment of Education Progress (NAEP).[14]

1. [The child is given a picture of four animals; one is a bird and the other three are mammals.] Which one of these animals is not a mammal?
2. Which of the following is used to measure temperature? Feet, degrees, centimeters, minutes, calories
3. Mary and Jane each bought the same kind of rubber ball. Mary said, "My ball bounces better than yours." Jane replied, "I'd like to see you prove that."

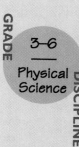

GRADE

3–6

Physical Science

DISCIPLINE

Batteries and Bulbs—Simple Circuits

Concept statement to be invented
Main idea—a *circuit* is a pathway electricity follows from the power source to the bulb and back to the power source.

Secondary concepts that are important for expansion
Open or closed circuit, series circuit, parallel circuit, switch, filament, insulation, conductor.

Attitudes to emphasize
Curiosity, open-mindedness, perseverance, positive approach to failure, cooperation.

Materials needed
Dry cells, wires, flashlight bulbs, bulb holders, switches, wire strippers, screwdrivers, scissors, aluminum foil, paper clips, paper fasteners, masking tape, small pieces of cardboard.

⊃ **Safety precautions:** limit the number of dry cells the students connect to five in the same circuit to limit shock potential and to preserve light bulbs.

1. EXPLORATION: What process skills will the children use?

(Observation, predictions, classification)

What will the children do?
Teacher's instructions: Using only the three pieces of equipment given to you, light the bulb. Once you are successful, find three other ways to light the bulb. You can use only the three pieces of equipment you have been given. Carefully draw a picture of each method you use to try to light the bulb. Label your drawings *will light* and *will not light*. Be certain to show exactly where your wire is touching and how your bulb is positioned with the battery.

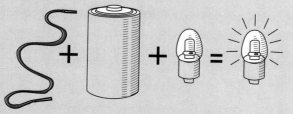

2. CONCEPT INVENTION: What is the main idea? How will the main idea be identified?

Concept: *circuit*.

Have students draw their pictures on the chalkboard. Use your finger to trace the pathway that electricity from the battery flows through when the bulb lights and when it does not light. This path is called a *circuit*. Tell them that a *circuit* is a pathway electricity follows from the power source to the bulb and back to the power source. Show the children that contact with the bulb must be made in two specific places. The path must be complete from the battery, through the bulb, and back to the battery for the bulb to light. A key question to ask: "In how many places must metal touch the bulb for it to light?" The answer is "two": the side and bottom conductors of the bulb must be included in the circuit.

EXHIBIT 4.1 A Sample Lesson Plan Based on the Planning and Learning Cycle

3. CONCEPT EXPANSION: What process skills will the students use?

(Making predictions, classifying, controlling variables)

How will the concept be applied and expanded?
Challenge the students to light more than one bulb, combine batteries for more power, and add additional equipment such as a bulb holder, a switch, and more wires. Ask what happens to other bulbs when one is unscrewed. Make a circuit so all bulbs go out when one is unscrewed: a series circuit. Make a circuit so the other bulbs remain lighted when one bulb is unscrewed: a parallel circuit or a separate series circuit; look carefully.

Why is the concept important for personal development?
Include science goals and outcomes fully in your expansion; the numbers in parentheses refer to the science outcomes shown in Chapter 3 and goals in Table 4.3.

1. Name some devices you use that require an electrical circuit. (1.1)
2. What type of circuit is needed? (1.1)
3. What would your life be like without electricity controlled by circuits? (1.2)

Why is the concept important for science, technology, and society?
A set of car headlights is one example of a specific circuit used for safety purposes. When one light burns out or is broken, the others remain lighted.

1. What are other examples in which the type of circuit used is important for safety or convenience? (2.2)
2. A flashlight uses a simple series circuit and is an example of technology. How has the simple flashlight improved or affected your life? your community? the world? (2.4)

Why is the concept important for academic growth?
Expansion concepts include complete and incomplete circuits, open and closed circuits, series and parallel circuits. Identify new concepts in new lessons, such as resistance, cell versus battery, electromagnetism. Use the idea of a circuit to make a flashlight out of these materials: cardboard tube, wire, two D-cell batteries, flashlight bulb, paper clip, two paper fasteners, bottle cap, tape (3.1, 3.3, 3.5).

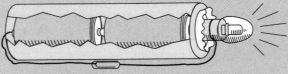

Why is the concept important for career awareness?
  1. Thomas Edison experimented thousands of times before he successfully found a material suitable as a filament that could be used to complete the circuit in a light bulb. How would our world be different today if Edison had never succeeded? (4.6)
  2. Who needs to know about circuits? Name careers and have students identify those careers that they previously did not know about that rely on some knowledge of electrical circuits. (4.1)

EXHIBIT 4.1 (Cont'd) A Sample Lesson Plan Based on the Planning and Learning Cycle

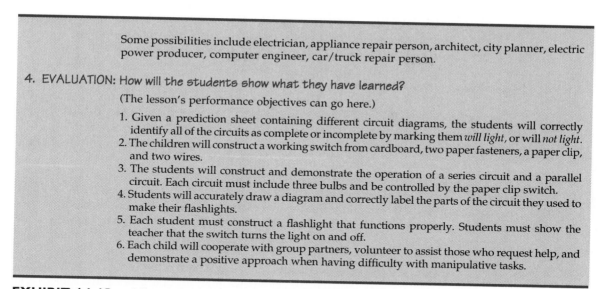

Some possibilities include electrician, appliance repair person, architect, city planner, electric power producer, computer engineer, car/truck repair person.

4. EVALUATION: How will the students show what they have learned?

(The lesson's performance objectives can go here.)

1. Given a prediction sheet containing different circuit diagrams, the students will correctly identify all of the circuits as complete or incomplete by marking them *will light*, or will *not light*.
2. The children will construct a working switch from cardboard, two paper fasteners, a paper clip, and two wires.
3. The students will construct and demonstrate the operation of a series circuit and a parallel circuit. Each circuit must include three bulbs and be controlled by the paper clip switch.
4. Students will accurately draw a diagram and correctly label the parts of the circuit they used to make their flashlights.
5. Each student must construct a flashlight that functions properly. Students must show the teacher that the switch turns the light on and off.
6. Each child will cooperate with group partners, volunteer to assist those who request help, and demonstrate a positive approach when having difficulty with manipulative tasks.

EXHIBIT 4.1 (Cont'd)   A Sample Lesson Plan Based on the Planning and Learning Cycle

What should Mary do?

a. Drop both balls from the same height and notice which bounces higher.
b. Throw both balls against a wall and see how far each ball bounces off the wall.
c. Drop the two balls from different heights and notice which bounces higher.
d. Throw the balls down against the floor and see how high they bounce.
e. Feel the balls to see which is harder.

The first item asks for a factual answer that could be memorized. The second item also requires a factual answer, but a student could answer correctly without ever having had science, since everyday experience could prevail. Even though the third item is more complex, as a teacher you could find it difficult to determine why a pupil gave a wrong answer, since there is no way to evaluate the child's reasoning with this format. Benjamin Bloom sums up the emphasis of traditional testing practices: "Teacher-made [and standardized] tests are largely tests of remembered information. . . . [It] is estimated that over 90 percent of test questions the U.S. public school students are now expected to answer deal with little more than information."[15] Bloom claims that instructional material and classroom teaching rarely rise above the lowest level of his taxonomy for the cognitive domain—the *knowledge* level. In response, science testing is receiving a great deal of attention, and alternate forms of elementary and middle school science assessments are being developed.

Types of Science Evaluation Tools

Science evaluations should include measures of subject matter learned and process skills developed as well as teacher observations of the students' developing scientific attitudes. The objectives you plan for children to accomplish influence what you teach and what your pupils learn. Your planned objectives represent learning outcomes. Figure 4.8 shows a relationship between the types of evaluation techniques outcomes and learning. The more Xs shown, the better the evaluation tool for the outcome sought.

With some careful thought and planning your teacher-made evaluations can avoid the trap Bloom describes. In the rest of this chapter we describe procedures, provide tips, and share some examples of how your teacher-made tests, records, and observations can provide more meaningful evaluations, which will also help to improve your planning and instruction.

Teacher-Made Written Tests.   Teacher-made written tests should contain some factual items and should probe the processes students use to solve problems. Avoid formats that require children to select a single correct answer, because some problems have several acceptable answers. Encourage students to sort through information and make decisions.

There are three basic types of teacher-made written tests: multiple choice, supply items, and essay. *Multiple-choice tests* often provide four or five choices and require children to select the single best answer to the question. Some principles to keep in mind when constructing this type of test include

- focus a single item on a single learning outcome,
- state the stem of the item in simple, clear language,
- state the stem in the positive and underline any negative wording,

FIGURE 4.8   Relationship of Evaluation Techniques to Learning Outcomes

Outcomes	Teacher-Made Tests		Teacher Observation	Teacher Records
	Written Tests	Practical Tests	Observations, Discussions, Interviews	Written Work, Science Projects
Science Products	XX[a]	X	XX	X
Process Skills	X	XXX	XXX	XX
Scientific Attitudes	X	X	XXX	XX

Source: Based on Elizabeth Meng and Rodney L. Doran, ". . . About Appropriate Methods of Assessment," *Science and Children,* September 1990, p. 42.

[a]More Xs indicate a greater likelihood of the learning outcome desired.

WHAT RESEARCH SAYS

Questions to Ask About Tests

Here are some questions the National Center for Improving Science Education suggests that teachers ask when they evaluate the quality of a science test:

1. Are there problems that require students to think about and analyze situations?
2. Are the levels of thinking and analysis developmentally appropriate for the children?
3. Does the test feature sets of problems that call for more than one step in arriving at a solution?
4. Are problems with more than one correct solution included?
5. Are there opportunities for students to use their own data and create their own problems?
6. Are the students encouraged to use a variety of approaches to solve a problem?
7. Are there assessment exercises that encourage students to estimate their answers and check their results?

8. Is the science information that is given in the story problem and elicited in the answer accurate?
9. Is there an opportunity for assessing skills (both in the use of science tools and in science thinking) through some exercises that call for hands-on activities?
10. Are there exercises included in the overall assessment strategy that need to be carried out over time?
11. Are there problems with purposely missing or mistaken information that ask students to find errors or critique the way the problem is set up?
12. Are there opportunities for students to make up their own questions, problems, or designs?

Source: Adapted from Senta A. Raizen and Joyce S. Kaser, "Assessing Science Learning in Elementary School: Why, What, and How?" *Phi Delta Kappan,* May 1989, p. 721.

- if a single answer is intended, make certain it is clearly best,
- make all answer choices parallel with the stem and grammatically correct,
- use distractors that appear possible to the uninformed,
- vary the length and order of the correct answers.

Supply item tests include true-false, matching, and fill-in-the-blank formats. With the exception of true-false formats, supply item tests minimize student guessing and encourage children not to limit their thinking to a brief list of possibilities. You can easily identify misconceptions and partial understanding of the material with a supply item test.

Your *true-false tests* will improve if you

- include one idea in each statement,
- word items so they can be judged as absolutely true or false, not both or some of each,
- keep the wording brief and use simple language,
- avoid negative statements or double negatives,
- avoid words like *always, never, sometimes,* and so forth.

For the best *matching tests*

- keep the list of items brief and use short responses,
- provide more responses than needed or permit some responses to be used more than once to help encourage pupil discrimination,
- specify in your directions that responses may be used more than once and that all responses might not be needed.

Fill-in-the-blank tests will be improved if you

- word the item so that only a single word or a brief predictable answer is needed,
- use complete and direct questions,
- require that answers provide the main idea or concept,
- avoid giving extraneous clues or using distractors.

Essay questions require children to demonstrate, in their own words, their level of understanding of a topic by organizing ideas, processing information, and communicating thoughts. Essay questions excel at revealing student misconceptions, and they almost completely prevent guessing. They are more time consuming to grade and may represent your subjective views if you have not carefully organized your thoughts and expectations. Bear in mind that essay tests may be unfair to some children who have difficulty expressing themselves in writing or who have disabilities. Your essay tests can be improved if you

- provide specific, well-defined convergent questions rather than broad divergent questions,
- make clear your expectations about length, spelling, and detail,
- compose a master list of elements you expect to be included in the answer; this list can help you grade the responses more fairly.

Practical Tests.   Practical tests are hands-on and may be given individually or to student groups. This type of test requires students to observe and manipulate materials. An individual child may orally give answers to an observer, such as a teacher or an aide, whereas group practical tests almost always require that students read instructions, do a task, and give a written response. Some science educators[16] believe that practical tests show better than other tests what children know and can do and that practicals are fairer because they are not so dependent on reading and writing. Student guessing is almost completely prevented, children can ask for clarification, and the format is flexible. Children appear to enjoy the practical test format and score better than on written tests. Some examples of tasks that could be included on a practical test:[17]

- Describe and explain color change of bromthymol blue solution after you blow air through a straw.
- Cite at least three similarities and differences between two plastic animal specimens.
- Determine if four objects are electrical conductors by testing them in a battery and bulb circuit.

- Predict and measure the temperature of the mixture of equal amounts of hot and cold water.
- Observe and explain the dissolution of coffee crystals in water.
- Determine which seeds contain oil by rubbing them on paper.

Practical tests do have limits. They require materials, space, and time to prepare and clean up. They take longer to do and, especially if done individually, require a trained observer or prepared observation guide for recording student responses.

Teacher Records and Observations. Tangible records can reveal a lot about what students know and can and cannot do. Useful records can include the successes and difficulties a child has with homework assignments and notations about the quality of a completed science project, written report, class notes, activity data sheets, and so on. Your teacher records are important because they can reveal the interplay between factual information and how well children understand and use the scientific concepts. Emphasis on practical application encourages hands-on, minds-on interaction and helps to address the personal dimension of the science program. Figure 4.9 shows a record-keeping system a teacher might use to complement the sample lesson plan on basic electricity. This type of record keeping is useful because

FIGURE 4.9 Student Progress Report

Student's Name: Raul
Lesson or Unit: Basic Electricity

Concept Number	Description of Activity or Skill	Teacher Rating Low 12345 High	Teacher Comments
1	Open circuit using one bulb, wire, and dry cell	5	Was the first to do it in group
2	Closed circuit using same materials	3	Had difficulty, needed my help
3	Closed circuit with bulb socket	4	Easily done after I helped with clips
4	Series circuit, 2 or more bulbs	5	Done independently
5	Parallel circuit	2	Having difficulty, made 2 series circuits
6	Short circuit	4	
7	Use a knife switch	5	Easily done
8	Make a paper clip switch	5	Concept easily shown
9	Construct a flashlight	4	No circuit trouble, difficulty with bulb connections only

FIGURE 4.10   Class Record-Keeping System

Unit: Basic Electricity

Children's Names	Concept, Skill, or Activity Number											Comments
	1	2	3	4	5	6	7	8	9	10	11	
Emerson												
Frankie												
Jaclyn												
Jenny												
Jessie												
Jon												
Marilyn												
Tim												

Note: This format is easily managed by a spreadsheet program available for all popular microcomputers.

it helps to focus a teacher's observations of a child on the concepts and processes to be learned. Figure 4.10 shows a generic form suitable for an entire class. It may be used as a checklist to keep track of who has and has not demonstrated mastery of the concepts or preferred science skills.

The types of records shown in Figures 4.9 and 4.10 require systematic teacher observation. Systematic observation is another source of information that is helpful to meaningful evaluation. Teachers always make observations, but systematic observation goes beyond being aware that Emily is interested in birds, Joel asks questions all the time, and David creates messes. Systematic observation is illustrated in this example:

> A teacher divides the class into working groups to figure out a way to test the strength of different brands of paper towels. As the children work on the problem, the teacher walks about the room, listens carefully to the questions the children ask each other, and observes how they approach the task. The teacher notes who does nothing, who appears to have difficulty, who has trouble measuring, who asks the most interesting questions, and who offers the most interesting ideas.

Systematic observation is guided by a structure; the teacher's observations are focused on specific tasks. These tasks include trying to determine how well the children demonstrate their understanding of the science ideas, how well the children use the science process skills, and what types of scientific attitudes the children

FIGURE 4.11   Recording Science Process Skills*

Directions: Circle the number which best represents skill level you have observed. Number 1 means *having difficulty*, 2 means *fair*, 3 means *good*, 4 means *outstanding*.

Name	Observation	Classification	Communication	Measurement	Prediction
Sam	1 2 3 4	1 2 3 4	1 2 3 4	1 2 3 4	1 2 3 4
Wanda	1 2 3 4	1 2 3 4	1 2 3 4	1 2 3 4	1 2 3 4
Herman	1 2 3 4	1 2 3 4	1 2 3 4	1 2 3 4	1 2 3 4
Kara	1 2 3 4	1 2 3 4	1 2 3 4	1 2 3 4	1 2 3 4

*The process skills can be changed and the form expanded to address better the science skills your lessons emphasize.

demonstrate. (See Figure 4.11 for an example of a way to evaluate students' science skills.)

Science learning improves when student attitudes are positive.[18] There are dramatic differences between traditional science classrooms and exemplary ones where teaching and assessment involve all learning domains. Positive attitudes about science greatly influence students' achievement levels and process skills, as is shown by research on exemplary science classrooms.[19] These results are now prompting teachers to question their old view that attitudes are inconsequential. Figure 4.12 shows one way you can evaluate and record the levels of your students' science attitudes.

FIGURE 4.12   Evaluating and Recording Science Attitudes

Check those attitudes or record the number of times each student demonstrates the desired scientific attitudes during the observation period.

Name	Is curious	Cooperates	Persists	Is open-minded	Safely uses materials
Celeste	✓✓✓	✓✓	✓	✓	✓
Jen	✓	✓✓✓✓	✓	✓✓✓	✓✓✓
Jessie	✓✓✓✓	✓✓✓	✓✓✓✓✓	✓✓	✓✓✓
Jon	✓	✓✓✓	✓✓	✓✓	✓✓
Sara	✓✓	✓✓	✓✓✓	✓✓✓✓	✓✓✓✓

CHAPTER SUMMARY

All effective science instruction has a common goal—helping children develop their ability to think and to avoid science misconceptions. Instruction must be planned carefully to accomplish this goal. The first step is to select proper goals and use them for more effective planning. Concept mapping, writing objectives, introducing the concept, expanding the concept, and evaluating learning are necessary steps for effective planning and teaching strategies for instruction.

Concept mapping helps you to build a vision for an entire course and a smaller part of that course, the traditional unit of instruction. The science learning cycle is an ideal process for planning and teaching lessons. The 4-E learning cycle—Exploration, Explanation, Expansion, and Evaluation—is a planning tool that promotes the modern goals of elementary science teaching.

Traditional forms of tests do not capture the essence of science and are not always accurate indicators of what children really learn. Teacher records and observations may play an important role in evaluating what children learn more accurately and more wholistically.

DISCUSSION QUESTIONS AND PROJECTS

1. Contemporary movements in education usually embrace the preference for students to demonstrate learning outcomes. Performance or behavioral objectives may be used for this purpose. What advantages or disadvantages do you see with this type of objective?

2. Some teachers say it is nearly impossible to write behavioral objectives for the affective or psychomotor domains. Do you agree? Why? Prepare examples that support your answer.

3. Examine a textbook or science module and teacher's manual for any grade level you choose. Construct a concept map for the material you select. State your opinion about how the printed materials' organization helps make connections between associated concepts.

4. Prepare a unit plan for science teaching. First map the concepts you wish to teach, and then use the unit planning format demonstrated in this chapter to organize the unit. What new science education goals are you able to address?

5. Prepare a lesson plan using the 4-E approach. How many learning activities do you have and where do they fit into the cycle? What science goals do you pursue? How do you evaluate student's learning?

6. Construct appropriate ways to evaluate the children's science knowledge, skills, and attitudes for your plans in #4 and #5.

NOTES

1. William C. Philips, "Earth Science Misconceptions," *The Science Teacher*, February 1991, p. 21.
2. Ibid., p. 21.
3. Joseph Novak, "Clarify with Concept Maps," *The Science Teacher*, October 1991, p. 45.
4. Paul D. Eggen and Donald P. Kauchak, *Strategies for Teachers* (Englewood Cliffs, NJ: Prentice Hall, 1989). This book contains excellent definitions and examples within pages 43–62.
5. Joseph D. Novak, *A Theory of Education* (Ithaca, NY: Cornell University Press, 1979), p. 86.
6. Ibid., pp. 78–83.
7. Joseph Novak and D. Bob Gowin, *Learning How to Learn* (New York: Cambridge University Press, 1986), p. 17.
8. Connie K. Williams and Constance Kamii, "How Do Children Learn by Handling Objects?" *Young Children*, November 1986, pp. 23–26.
9. See, for example, Benjamin S. Bloom, et al., *Taxonomy of Education Objectives: The Classification of Education Goals*, Handbook I, *Cognitive Domain* (New York: Longman, 1956); David Krathwohl (ed.), *Taxonomy of Educational Goals*, Handbook II, *Affective Domain* (New York: Longman, 1964); E. J. Simpson, *The Classification of Educational Objectives in the Psychomotor Domain*, vol. 3 (Washington, DC: Gryphon House, 1972).
10. David Jacobsen, Paul Eggen, Donald Kauchak, and Carole Dulaney, *Methods for Teaching: A Skills Approach* (Columbus, OH: Charles E. Merrill Publishing Company, 1985).
11. David Krathwohl (ed.), *Taxonomy of Educational Goals*, Handbook II, *Affective Domain* (New York: Longman, 1964).
12. See the studies reported by James A. Shymansky,

William C. Kyle, Jr., and Jennifer M. Alport, "How Effective Were the Hands-On Science Programs of Yesterday?" *Science and Children,* November/December 1982, pp. 14–15; and Ted Bredderman, "Activity Science—The Evidence Shows It Matters," *Science and Children,* September 1982, pp. 39–41. The effects of these studies were described in Chapter 3.

13. Senta A. Raizen and Joyce S. Kaser, "Assessing Science Learning in Elementary School: Why, What, and How?" *Phi Delta Kappan,* May 1989, pp. 718–722.

14. Ibid., p. 718.

15. Benjamin S. Bloom, "The 2 Sigma Problem: The Search for Methods of Group Instruction as Effective as One-to-One Tutoring," *Educational Researcher,* vol. 13, 1984, pp. 4–16.

16. Elizabeth Meng and Rodney L. Doran, ". . . About Appropriate Methods of Assessment," *Science and Children,* September 1990, pp. 42–45.

17. Rodney L. Doran, ". . . About Assessment," *Science and Children,* May 1990.

18. Robert E. Yager and John E. Penick, "New Concerns for Affective Outcomes in School Science," *Educational Leadership,* October 1987, p. 93.

19. Ibid.

ADDITIONAL READINGS

If you are interested in learning more about some of the topics raised in this chapter, consider the following sources.

Patricia Blosser, *Science Misconceptions Research and Some Implications for the Teaching of Science to Elementary School Students,* a newsletter research report (No. 1, 1987) available through the ERIC Clearinghouse for Science, Mathematics, and Environmental Education, 1200 Chambers Road, Third Floor, Columbus, OH 43212.

Charles Ault, "Intelligently Wrong: Some Comments on Children's Misconceptions," *Science and Children,* May 1984, pp. 22–24.

Joseph Stepans and Christine Kuehn, "What Research Says: Children's Conceptions of Weather," *Science and Children,* September 1985, pp. 44–47.

Jerry J. Herman, *Developing an Effective Elementary Science Curriculum* (West Nyack, NY: Parker Publishing, 1969). Although dated, Herman's book reports an extensive case study of an approach used to develop a science curriculum with the Lakeview School District of St. Clair Shores, Michigan. Herman takes the practitioner's approach in describing all the variables that impact on curriculum. The book contains practical examples and useful procedures.

John W. Renner and Edmund A. Marek, *The Learning Cycle and Elementary School Science Teaching* (Portsmouth, NH: Heinemann, 1988). This book is organized around three phases of the learning cycle. Detailed sample learning cycle plans are given for grades K–6. Examples include lessons in the biological, earth, and physical sciences, as well as special lessons for kindergarten children.

Debra L. Seabury and Susan L. Peeples, *Ready-to-Use Science Activities for the Elementary Classroom* (West Nyack, NY: The Center for Applied Research in Education, 1987). Included are more than 175 reproducible activity pages that cover six interdisciplinary teaching units: plants, animals, the human body, geology, weather, and space. Activities can accommodate many of the science goals encouraged in this chapter and can be adapted to the learning cycle lesson planning format.

Marvin N. Tolman and James O. Morton, *Life Science Activities for Grades 2–8, Earth Science Activities for Grades 2–8,* and *Physical Science Activities for Grades 2–8* (West Nyack, NY: Parker Publishing, 1986). Nearly 500 science activities are included in these three books. The concept/skills index in each book makes it simple to identify the science concepts for each activity and to see the big picture necessary for concept mapping a course or unit. Each activity may be easily adapted for the learning cycle.

Science Scope, vol. 15, no. 6, March 1992. This issue provides a special supplement on science assessment. Numerous ways to evaluate student learning are amply illustrated and include classroom-tested examples of portfolios, group assessment, concept mapping, performance-based assessment, and scoring rubrics.

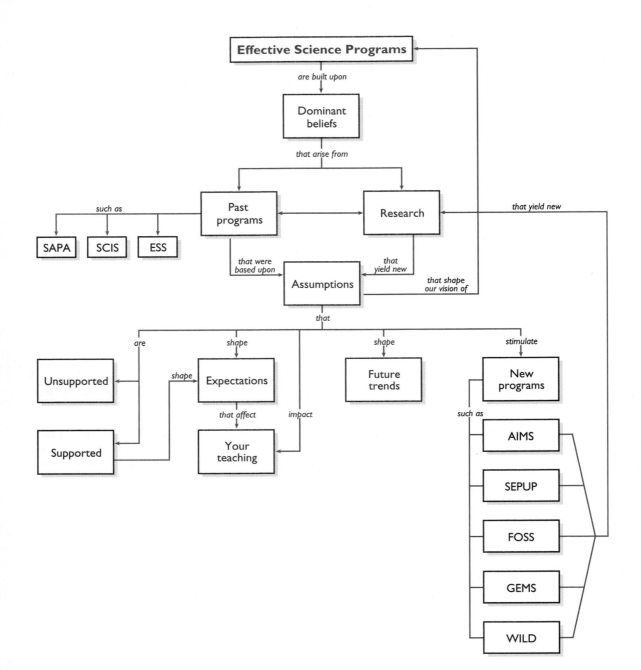

What Are the Characteristics of Effective Elementary and Middle School Science Programs?

J ennifer Emerson had divided the science methods class into research teams. Their purpose was to pick any elementary school science topic and locate all the materials available on that topic in the lab, library, and college curriculum collection. The team members were to examine and compare the materials, classify them by intended purposes, and then use their findings to speculate about what makes an effective science lesson. They were told to be prepared to generalize beyond single lessons because the class would attempt to identify the characteristics of an effective science program. The groans that were prompted by the need to include text and nontext publications of the last thirty years subsided when Professor Emerson demonstrated the speed and ease of *Science Helper*, the CD-ROM system containing hundreds of government-sponsored lessons from experimental science programs.

Professor Emerson reconvened the class and asked the groups to report. She listed the features the students found most often among the materials: objectives, suggested teaching methods, materials needed, background information, illustrations, assessment devices, and ideas for extending the activities. Some older materials and many newer lessons contained references to conceptual frameworks, skills to be developed, ideal group sizes, key vocabulary, lesson rationales, competencies, and subjects with which the lessons could be integrated. When she asked for the groups' ideas about effective programs, she received such replies as: "They emphasize subject matter most and produce higher test scores," "Effective programs are those that children like," and "You can tell the program is effective if more children take science in high school and if more want to enter scientific careers." These replies fell short of Dr. Emerson's hopes, so she guided the class into a discussion of the assignment, pressed them to give specific examples of what they found, and repeated the assignment's central question: What makes an effective science program?

The students' thinking expanded a bit with the observation that some materials prepared in the last decade have features that resemble those of the experimental programs of the 1960s, but that the newer science textbooks seem to contain several features not found in science textbooks of the earlier era. Still, Professor Emerson sensed frustration. Her suspicion was confirmed when one brave soul, Jonathan, asked, "I don't understand why you had us look at out-of-date materials. Why did you have us do this assignment? Don't the developers and publishers agree on what's best, and shouldn't we always just try to use the most recent materials?"

INTRODUCTION

We are likely to repeat mistakes of the past if we are ignorant of history. Looking back, we see considerable similarity among the recommendations that arose from several science education reports during the mid-1940s, again during the late 1950s and early 1960s, and still again during the late 1980s and early 1990s. Calls for more intellectual rigor, increased standards, elevated expectations, improved student discipline, increased classroom time on task, improved test scores, and enhanced teacher subject expertise often make up the substance of these reports, but different approaches were used in attempts to fulfill the recommendations. Indeed, devoting more time to intellectual subject matter in science is a common and worthwhile goal, but when it is the only expectation it falls short of fulfilling the larger goal of more effective science programs. The key to effective science instruction is selecting and using hands-on activities effectively with the proper mix of science content and processes.

Present calls or mandates for improved pupil achievement and recommendations for producing these improvements may be naïvely based on uninformed right/wrong perspectives. These perspectives might rest upon faulty assumptions about what should be taught and learned and about how youngsters learn and should be taught. But what role are you expected to play? You will be involved, at some point in your career, with science program development. More immediately, your concern is probably for selecting the best materials available to plan and teach effective lessons. Can you afford to ignore the lessons of the past? This chapter provides a foundation that can help define what is best and help you form a rationale for what you choose to do.

This chapter

1. describes dominant beliefs about science education in the past
2. describes several model elementary science programs that have been influential in shaping modern elementary science curricula and research on effective teaching practices
3. reviews the effects these model programs had on children's science achievement, skills, and attitudes
4. exposes false assumptions about learning and teaching science and reveals assumptions that shape new science curricula
5. offers recommendations for an effective elementary science program

DOMINANT BELIEFS IN SCIENCE EDUCATION

Quality and *excellence* are two widely held goals for education in general. The elementary science program must have high quality and demonstrate excellence in its curriculum and teaching. Critics and supporters agree on these goals, but they by no means agree on the direction the program ought to take, the science subject matter that is most worth knowing, or the conditions that best foster that knowing.[1] As an example, consider these conflicting beliefs about science education:

- Science is structured and consists of a body of well-known facts, concepts, principles, and theories that are useful to all and that should be learned by everyone.
- Science is a way of doing and learning from doing.
- Science is important for its own sake; therefore, everyone needs to learn about science.
- Everyone is affected by science; therefore, everyone needs to learn science.
- To be most useful, science must be relevant; therefore it must be taught so that it can be understood and useful to those who learn it.

Which of these beliefs appear compatible to you, and which appear to conflict? Why is it that experts' beliefs openly conflict?

Let us take a brief look back in time to understand the importance of the issues surrounding these beliefs as well as how they affect the answer to the main question that guides this chapter: What are the characteristics of effective elementary science programs?

CHANGES OVER TIME: LEGACY OF THE PAST

Biology, Chemistry, Physics, and *Earth Science* are common school science curriculum labels. Even within general science and elementary science courses these labels persist as topics or units of study. They arose from their parent scientific research disciplines, which were popular during the 1800s. However, since about 1900 these disciplines of study have not accurately represented the important areas of science. Thousands of diverse scientific journals now report experimental findings from a countless number of new fields of science and technology. Distinctions among the different fields of science are now made more by the type of problem being researched than by the discipline being served.[2] Today there is simply too much—too many facts of science to be learned in a school science program. The amount of scientific information continues to double about every five years. Then what should be taught? At times this question has been answered with an issues-and-problems approach.

A specific problem in science education has always been to resolve the issue of how the schools could best prepare "citizens to live in a culture most often

Past programs prepared children to become scientists.

William E. Mills

described in terms of achievements in science and technology."[3] In the 1930s and 1940s, elementary schools tried to resolve this issue by teaching in a "prescribed authoritative manner almost exclusively through single-author textbooks."[4] Basically, science was a reading program that covered a large body of information and used the subtle but powerful force of conformity and consensus to control the direction of American society and to aid citizens as they tried to adjust to society's new directions. The important facts, concepts, and theories of science that were taught were based on the consensus of specialists. Specialists told previous generations of teachers what was important to know and teach.

Teacher emphasis on pupil conformity and learning science by reading is still highly visible today. Another emphasis from the past that is still widely supported is the cry to get back to basics, with emphasis on reading, writing, and arithmetic. This chant began after World War II for the same reasons that it can be heard today: a perceived overall low quality of high school graduates as shown by their falling achievement scores and poor job skills, and the need for our citizens to keep pace with scientific and technological breakthroughs of other advanced countries.[5] Ironically, this last need makes the study of science a basic need for all, a basic subject in the school curriculum, as described in Chapter 3.

MAJOR ELEMENTARY SCIENCE PROGRAM MODELS: LOOKING BACK FOR THE SOURCE OF WISDOM

Efforts began earlier, but it was the launching of the Soviet satellite Sputnik in 1957 that caused the most serious attempts at science curriculum reform. During the twenty-five years after Sputnik, $2 billion was spent to support mathematics and science education in elementary and secondary schools. The main goal then, as many believe it should be now, was to prepare future scientists and engineers, mostly out of a concern for our national defense. As important as this goal is, we now know that defense issues rise and fall in urgency and that "This is a goal that is appropriate for only 3 percent of high school graduates, and a goal where we have traditionally spent 95 percent of our time, efforts, resources and attention."[6]

The Alphabet Soup

The decade after Sputnik is known for its alphabet soup elementary science programs (see Table 5.1). Three programs developed during that decade are worth mentioning now because of their goals, their effects on children's learning, and the eventually improved quality of modern textbooks and other curriculum materials. Several of the assumptions the programs were based on have been supported over time by a growing body of research, while other assumptions have fallen from favor. The programs we refer to here are known as SAPA, SCIS, and ESS.

Science—A Process Approach (SAPA), Science Curriculum Improvement Study (SCIS), and the Elementary Science Study (ESS) were regarded as innovative programs in their day. Designed and field tested during the 1960s and then

TABLE 5.1   Examples of Alphabet Soup Elementary Science Programs

SAPA (Science—A Process Approach), American Association for the Advancement of
  Science Commission on Science Education, 1963
COPES (Conceptually Oriented Program in Elementary Science), 1967
ESSP (Elementary School Science Project), University of California, Berkeley, 1962
E-SSP (Elementary-School Science Project), University of Illinois, 1963
ESSP (Elementary School Science Project), Utah State University, 1964
ESS (Elementary Science Study), 1964
IDP (Inquiry Development Program), 1962
MinneMAST (Minnesota Mathematics and Science Teaching Project), 1966
SSCP (School Science Curriculum Project), 1964
SCIS (Science Curriculum Improvement Study), 1961
SQAIESS (Study of a Quantitative Approach in Elementary School Science), 1964
USMES (Unified Sciences and Mathematics for Elementary Schools), 1973
WIMSA (The Webster Institute for Mathematics, Science and the Arts), 1965

Source: Information excerpted from Paul DeHart Hurd (ed.), *New Directions in Elementary Science
Teaching,* (Belmont, CA: Wadsworth Publishing, 1968). Note that dates given are approximate
beginning dates for each program.

revised during the 1970s, these experimental programs had several features in
common:

- The programs were developed by teams of scientists, psychologists, educators,
  and professional curriculum specialists rather than written by single authors or
  single expert specialists.
- Federal funds were widely available for development, research, field testing,
  dissemination, and teacher inservice training.
- Each project was developed from particular assumptions about learning. These
  were drawn from prominent theories and used to form a specific framework for
  each project. Behavioral and cognitive-development psychology had major
  influences.
- Each project was developed from what were assumed to be the ways children
  learned best. Specific teaching approaches were emphasized and were used to
  help children to learn the ways and knowledge of science and to develop the
  attitudes of scientists.
- Active pupil learning was assumed to be very important. Each project provided
  hands-on learning experiences for all children because it was assumed that
  manipulatives helped children learn best.
- The projects did not provide a standard textbook for each child. In fact, a
  workbook for recording observations was as close as some children came to
  anything that resembled a text.
- There was no attempt to teach all that should be known about science. Specific
  science processes or content areas were selected for each project, thus narrow-
  ing the field of topics to a specialized few.

FIGURE 5.1   Structure and Emphasis Comparisons of Landmark Elementary Science Programs

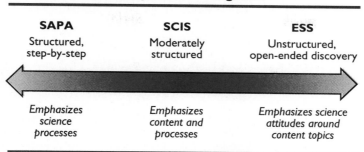

SAPA	**SCIS**	**ESS**
Structured, step-by-step	Moderately structured	Unstructured, open-ended discovery

Emphasizes science processes — *Emphasizes content and processes* — *Emphasizes science attitudes around content topics*

Each program is available from Delta Education, P.O. Box 915, Hudson, NH 03051. Phone: 1-800-258-1302.

- Attention was given to the basic ideas of science, the concepts and theories, with the intention of increasing the number of citizens who would seek careers in science and engineering.
- The programs were conveniently packaged. Equipment was included with curriculum materials. This made the programs easier to use and reduced teacher preparation time by eliminating the need to gather diverse equipment.
- Mathematical skills were emphasized. The programs were more quantitative than qualitative. Emphasis was placed on student observation, careful measurement, and the use of appropriate calculations to form ideas or reach conclusions.
- Science was taught as a subject by itself and was not associated with social studies, health, or reading. At times, science was treated as a pure subject that was believed to have inherent value for all children.
- The teacher's role changed. Teachers used such less direct methods of teaching as inquiry, and functioned as questioners, guides for students, and avoided lecturing or more didactic forms of direct instruction. The teacher was *not* to be an expert who spoke what children should memorize.

SAPA, SCIS, and ESS are landmark elementary science programs, still available today. As shown in Figure 5.1, they differ essentially on two factors: first, the amount of structure or flexibility each contains in its design for classroom use, and second, the emphasis each gives to science content, attitudes, or thinking processes. Let us explore each program briefly to understand better the legacy that has brought positive influences to the options available in elementary science education today.

Science—A Process Approach (SAPA)

SAPA's Prime Assumptions.

Children need to learn how to *do* science, and this means acquiring the skills essential to learning and understanding science information. These knowledge-

Effective programs promote scientific inquiry.

acquiring skills are called cognitive [thinking] skills or process skills and are similar to the procedures used by scientists to acquire new knowledge. Process skills may be compared to the program [of] a computer. Computers are incapable of handling information without a program to provide directions; the human mind does not cope effectively with incoming information in the absence of learning strategies (a program).[7]

The American Association for the Advancement of Science's Commission on Science Education assumed that a sequential program was necessary for developing a child's intellect. In 1963, a team of scientists, psychologists, elementary teachers, and curriculum specialists developed plans and materials for trial versions of what became Science—A Process Approach. The program is based upon two assumptions: first, that prepared materials must consider the intellectual development of the child, and second, that a total program must use a sequential approach for the long-range development of the child's intellectual skills.

The first assumption worked well. Materials that were developed on the child's ability level were appropriate. Incremental advances in the complexity of the materials seemed to help children develop intellectually. However, the long-term sequential approach proved too rigid to use without difficulty in schools where children attend school irregularly or transfer in mid-year.

Description of SAPA.   SAPA is the most structured of the three programs we explore here. Its structure arises from behavioral psychology. The underlying psychological assumptions were first, that any skill can be broken down into smaller steps, and second, that children need to learn lower level skills before they can learn more advanced skills. Predictably, the original version of SAPA developed into a set of skills to be mastered through a complex, highly structured hierarchy (see Figure 5.2) and step-by-step teaching.

Skill development takes precedence over science subject matter in SAPA. Even after revision and the development of SAPA II, the content of science is only important as it serves as a vehicle for developing thinking processes. The complex task of inquiry, therefore, is broken into a series of smaller, easier-to-acquire skills. All skill development is expected to arise from a child's direct experiences performing prescribed learning tasks, usually with concrete manipulable objects. Hands-on learning involves children in doing science the way many scientists say they do it themselves—carefully planned step-by-step procedures.

SAPA process skills are divided into two types: *basic* and *integrated* skills. In the primary grades (K–3) children develop these basic process skills: observing, using space/time relationships, classifying, using numbers, measuring, communicating, predicting, and inferring. In the intermediate grades (4–6) children use the basic process skills as a foundation for developing more complex skills: controlling variables, interpreting data, formulating hypotheses, defining operationally, and experimenting.

The knowledge explosion in the sciences helps SAPA justify its approach; it is a unique program that emphasizes science skills over content. Creators of SAPA believe that it is impossible for individuals, including scientists, to keep up to date in all the sciences and that it is also unrealistic to expect children to learn everything about science. SAPA's intention is to equip each child with the thinking skills that can be used to solve problems they find in the future.

SAPA is a complete K–6 program. The learning activities in the revised SAPA II are packaged in a series of 105 ungraded learning modules, with approximately fifteen modules per traditional grade level. Each module is devoted to a specific skill. SAPA II arose in 1975 from extensive field testing, program evaluation, and materials revisions, and it is an improvement over the original design. Clusters of modules help teachers overcome the rigid sequence of skills used in the original flow chart approach (Figure 5.2). SAPA II strives to reflect important changes in

FIGURE 5.2   SAPA Then and Now

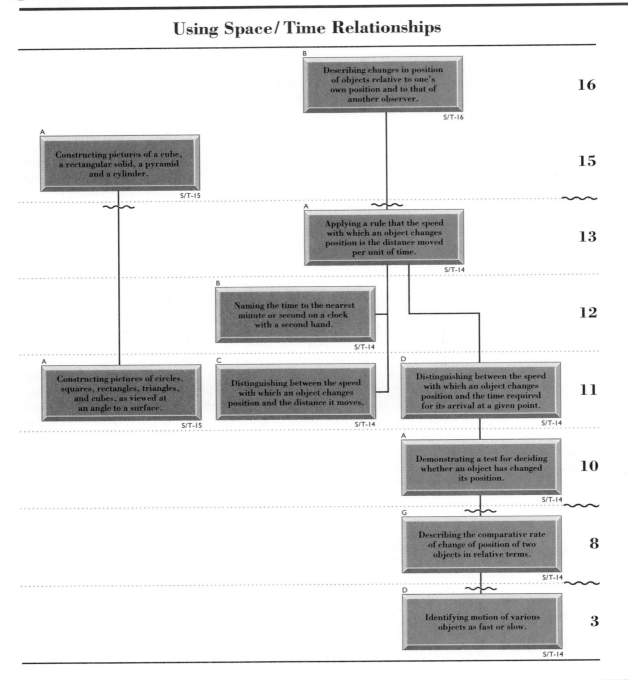

Using Space/Time Relationships

B
Describing changes in position of objects relative to one's own position and to that of another observer.
S/T-16

16

A
Constructing pictures of a cube, a rectangular solid, a pyramid and a cylinder.
S/T-15

15

A
Applying a rule that the speed with which an object changes position is the distance moved per unit of time.
S/T-14

13

B
Naming the time to the nearest minute or second on a clock with a second hand.
S/T-14

12

A
Constructing pictures of circles, squares, rectangles, triangles, and cubes, as viewed at an angle to a surface.
S/T-15

C
Distinguishing between the speed with which an object changes position and the distance it moves.
S/T-14

D
Distinguishing between the speed with which an object changes position and the time required for its arrival at a given point.
S/T-14

11

A
Demonstrating a test for deciding whether an object has changed its position.
S/T-14

10

G
Describing the comparative rate of change of position of two objects in relative terms.
S/T-14

8

D
Identifying motion of various objects as fast or slow.
S/T-14

3

Science... A Process Approach
Planning Chart

| IX | X | XI | XII |

Module 32
Classifying/d
Terrarium

Separating living organisms into categories. Construct-ing a simple classification system and demonstrating its use. Placing new organ-isms in the appropriate categories of an established classification system.

PREMOD: 16

Module 39
Measuring/g
Solids, Liquids, and Gases

Measuring the volume of liquids using metric units. Naming a substance as being a solid, a liquid, or a gas. Describing a substance as a solid, a liquid, or a gas by using various physical characteristics, such as shape and appearance.

PREMODS: 17, 23, 32

Module 42
Classifying/e
Sorting Mixtures

Demonstrating a specified method for classifying the components of a mixture by size. Ordering the compo-nents of a mixture by size. Ordering the components of a mixture by volume or weight.

PREMODS: 26, 39

Module 41
Measuring/h
Temperature and Thermometers

Demonstrating how to use a thermometer to measure the temperature of a gas or liquid, and naming temperature in degrees Celsius. Using a thermo-meter to measure tempera-ture change, and naming initial and final tempera-tures in degrees Celsius.

PREMODS: 21, 27, 30

Module 31
Communicating/d
Life Cycles

Describing an animal according to several of its characteristics. Describing the changing characteristics of a young animal as it grows from one stage to another.

PREMOD: 16, 28

Module 36
Observing/l
Animal Responses

Describing the kinds of locomotion characteristic of animals having various shapes and appendages. Identifying an animalÕs response to an identified stimulus.

PREMOD: 31

Module 43
Communicating/e
A Plant Part That Grows

Distinguishing between a developing new plant and the original plant it is growing from. Describing vegetative growth qualitatively. Describing the techniques used to produce growth from plant parts other than seeds.

PREMOD: 36

Module 33
Inferring/a
What's inside?

Distinguishing between state-ments that are observations and those that are explana-tions of observations, and identifying the explanations as inferences. Constructing inferences in terms of likeli-hood rather than certainty.

PREMOD: 18

Module 40
Inferring/b
*How certain can you be?
Shake and Peek*

Describing new observations that are needed to test an inference. Identifying obser-vations that support an infer-ence. Distinguishing between an inference that accounts for all of the observations and one that does not.

PREMODS: 29, 33

Module 35
Using Space/Time/f
Symmetry

Identifying objects that have line or plane symmetry. Demonstrating that some objects can be folded or cut in one or more ways to produce matching halves. Identifying and describing bilateral symmetry.

PREMOD: 12

Module 45
Using Space/Time/g
Lines, Curves, and Surfaces

Identifying, naming, and constructing straight and curved paths on plane and curved surfaces. Determining whether a surface is a plane surface. Identifying linear and circular motion.

PREMODS: 27, 35

Determining Sequences Within the Program

One convenient order for using the modules is the *numerical sequence* with which they are coded. If that order is followed, children will have the opportunity to develop skills in a sequence in which success is highly probable. Frequently it is necessary or desirable to alter the sequence when several teachers share materials, weather conditions interfere, or other scheduling problems arise. It is not necessary to use the modules in numerical sequence so long as the children have mastered the prerequisites before a module is begun.

science education, is more flexible than the original design, reflects a greater emphasis on environmental topics, and attempts more pupil individualization. Students have no books, yet spirit masters for dittoes are available; modular teacher guides are used in place of a teacher's textbook guide.

Each learning module has the same features and structure (Figure 5.3). The cover of each module presents the specific process skill that is emphasized within. The module title identifies the science content selected, and behavioral objectives specify what each child should be able to do at the end of the module. The sequence chart inside the cover shows the relationship and fit of the module's objectives with those of related modules (refer to Figure 5.2). A complete rationale justifies the purpose and describes the benefits of the module's activities for children and their intellectual development. The instructional procedure gives an overall introduction and describes each specific learning activity. Materials needed are listed with each activity, and modules contain about three to six activities. Each module contains a section, generalizing the experience, for extension of the learning activities. Evaluation is emphasized strongly in SAPA. An appraisal section describes class performance options for evaluation, and the competency measure section fully describes evaluation tasks that can be used with individual children. Specific questions and suggested answers are given. Competency measure tasks are keyed to the specific module objectives.

SAPA Program Effects.   Did SAPA make a difference? James Shymansky et al.[8] and Ted Bredderman[9] say "yes." Shymansky specifically reports that students learning science in the SAPA program outperformed children who learned from traditional science programs by 7 statistically significant percentile points on measures of achievement. (Traditional programs were defined as those whose development followed pre-1955 models, emphasized the information of science, and used laboratory activities to verify or to supplement lessons.) This difference may not seem great, but take a closer look: Let us suppose that two classes of elementary students take the same standardized achievement test in science and all differences are controlled except the program that they learn science from. One class learns from the traditional textbook approach that is designed to teach science facts through reading and memorization; the other class learns from another program—SAPA— that does not stress facts or science information, but instead focuses on doing science and developing thinking skills. The result? Let us say that the average student score from the traditional science program class is at the fiftieth percentile on a test designed to measure knowledge of science facts. Then by comparison, the average student in the SAPA class achieves at the fifty-seventh percentile on the same test— a distinct and significant achievement gain. The SAPA students knew more facts.

SAPA has several other factors going for it even more important than the performance of the average children from our example. In each case, these findings arose from research and careful study; the findings are real, not imagined. SAPA students scored 15 percentile points higher than non-SAPA students on measures of attitude toward science. On tests of process skills, SAPA students scored 36 percentile points higher than children from traditional programs. In such other areas as related study skills (reading and mathematics), creativity, and Piagetian tasks, SAPA children scored higher by 4, 7, and 12 percentile points respectively. Many of the assumptions that undergird SAPA appear to produce differences, just as its developers envisioned.

Science Curriculum Improvement Study (SCIS)
SCIS's Prime Assumptions.

> In a world where there is so much to learn and know, concepts provide an intellectual economy in helping to organize large amounts of information. [T]his is the way concepts serve scientists and it is also the way concepts can improve children's learning. There is too much to be known, even by children, to expect it can be learned by rote and as isolated facts. But a large amount of information can be organized into a few concepts. Systems of related concepts can then be built to form principles or rules whereby children are able to interpret and explain new observations and experiences. . . . One advantage of having children form concepts is that new information can be more easily related to that already known. The result is the likelihood that both the new information and related concept will have greater meaning, and understanding will be increased. If on the other hand, new information cannot be brought into an organized form, there is a likelihood that the new information will confuse rather than aid understanding. . . . [E]ach new relevant observation acquires meaning because it becomes associated with many previous experiences.[10]

The Science Curriculum Improvement Study (SCIS) was developed to help elementary school children form a broad conceptual framework for understanding science. Teams of scientists, educators, and psychologists began work in 1961 to produce the first of what eventually became three SCIS versions: SCIS and SCIIS were developed by the same team and SCIS II by another; the related versions are described here and are generically called SCIS.

The conceptual curriculum is organized around the structure of science as scientists see it. Specific concepts are chosen for their wide application and potential usefulness in each child's future. The unique challenge of SCIS is to provide a program that will help children explore science, guide children's thinking, and help children to form concepts and link them together within SCIS's conceptual structure.

Description of SCIS. SCIS is a sequential program that emphasizes both process and content, making SCIS rather middle of the road according to Figure 5.1. The instruction in SCIS is less structured than in SAPA. Specific teaching approaches complement the program's intention: to reach pupils at their current level of development as they form the intended science concepts.

The original version of SCIS introduced concepts that were new to elementary science. These concepts were linked together to form such units of study as properties, relativity, systems, interactions, variation and measurement, and ecosystems.

FIGURE 5.3 Excerpts from a SAPA II Module

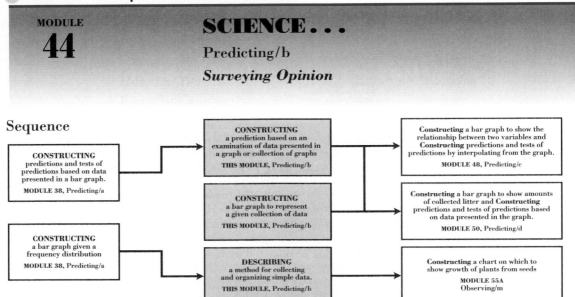

MODULE

44

SCIENCE...

Predicting/b

Surveying Opinion

Sequence

CONSTRUCTING
predictions and tests of
predictions based on data
presented in a bar graph.
MODULE 38, Predicting/a

CONSTRUCTING
a bar graph given a
frequency distribution
MODULE 38, Predicting/a

CONSTRUCTING
a prediction based on an
examination of data presented in
a graph or collection of graphs
THIS MODULE, Predicting/b

CONSTRUCTING
a bar graph to represent
a given collection of data
THIS MODULE, Predicting/b

DESCRIBING
a method for collecting
and organizing simple data.
THIS MODULE, Predicting/b

Constructing a bar graph to show the
relationship between two variables and
Constructing predictions and tests of
predictions by interpolating from the graph.
MODULE 48, Predicting/c

Constructing a bar graph to show amounts
of collected litter and Constructing
predictions and tests of predictions based
on data presented in the graph.
MODULE 50, Predicting/d

Constructing a chart on which to
show growth of plants from seeds
MODULE 55A
Observing/m

Rationale

It is essential that contributing evidence upon which a prediction is based be collected, organized, and recorded in a clear and usable way. The activities in this module provide children with experience in making predictions based on a survey of children in the school, thus using the childrens natural interest in collecting, interviewing, and surveying.

You must be sure to point out carefully the limitations on the dependability of predictions based on an opinion survey. Emphasize that accurate predictions are difficult in the early phases of the survey, and are impossible if they are based on only small bits of information. As more data are added, trends or patterns are often noticeable. These trends can be used to make more reliable predictions...

Because favorite kinds of snacks are the subject matter of this module, the results of the surveys are unpredictable and may vary considerably with locale, time of year, the childrenOs previous experience, and other factors. Remember that although the children will be very much interested in the results of the survey, these results are merely a means to an end. The objective is to provide experience in making predictions based on available evidence...

In *Activity 3*, the children survey other groups in the school. Take advantage of the excitement that such surveys create and the opportunity they provide for improvement of communication skills, but be sure to plan the surveying procedures carefully with the other teachers involved...

Vocabulary: predict, prediction, survey, opinion, tally, poll, polling

Instructional Procedure

Ask the children what the word predict means to them. They may have several suggestions. For example, they may recall that when they studied *Shadows, Using Space/Time Relationships e, Module 29*, they were asked to predict the two-dimensional shapes of the shadows of a three-dimensional object...

The children should also recall the predictions they made from the bar graphs they constructed in *Using Graphs, Predicting a, Module 38*.

Perhaps some child will mention that the weather man predicts the weather. Another may recall a time of national elections when there were predictions about which candidate would win. Remind them that predicting is telling what you think is going to happen based on experience.

If possible, bring periodical or newspaper examples of polls that have been taken. A copy of a survey made within the school would be useful too. Discuss the value of surveys. Use questions as these: What is an opinion? What is a survey? How is the information obtained when we survey opinion? Suggest that the class make its own survey...

Materials: Surveys, several examples from periodicals or newspapers.

Activity 1

Give each child a piece of paper and a pencil. With no preliminary discussion ask the children to write down the names of three of their favorite kinds of snacks. Be sure that they do this independently. Then collect their papers.

Tell the children that you have just taken a *poll* of their favorite snacks. Ask which snack the children think was named the most times. After several children have expressed their ideas, ask why they think a particular snack was the most popular. Suggest that their ideas are largely guesses because, at this point, they have little or no evidence to use as a basis for making predictions...

Materials: Writing paper, 1 sheet for each child, Pencils, 1 for each child

A Process Approach II

Objectives   At the end of this module the child should be able to:

1. **Describe** a method for collecting and organizing simple data.
2. **Construct** a bar graph to represent a given collection of data.
3. **Construct** a prediction based on an examination for the data presented in a graph or collection of graphs.

Activity 2

Ask the children for their ideas about organizing the data so that each child can have a copy of the results. There should be a number of suggestions. Try to accept one of them.

If the children do not suggest a feasible plan, use the following procedure. Give each child one paper marked during the previous activity, a clean sheet of paper, and a pencil. Call on the children to read from their marked papers. When a snack is first mentioned, tell everyone to write it down and put a tally mark next to it; each time it is mentioned again, have everyone put another mark next to the snack. Several children will probably have listed specific candy bars, flavors of ice cream, and so forth. Have the children tally all such listings under general headings, such as "candy" and "ice cream." Some children may list two items such as "cookies and milk." In this case put one tally next to "cookies" and another next to "milk…"

For the purpose of discussion, ask the children to imagine that milk was named more often than any other kind of snack, and that it was listed 20 times. Also ask them to imagine that candy was named 6 times and ice cream was mentioned 4 times. Figure 1 shows how these data may be graphed…

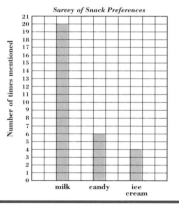

Survey of Snack Preferences

Generalizing Experience

Some children may be much more interested in this series of activities than are others. You should provide opportunities for the most interested children to continue with the surveys and to report the tallies to the others in the room…

Ask the children to make additional surveys about snack preferences. For example, have them ask a teenager, their mother or father, or some other friend to list three favorite kinds of snacks. You will get greater cooperation from the parents if you send a note with the child describing the project and the importance of the information. The children should get data from the same number of adults as there are members in their room. Tell the children that they should make their predictions beforehand and discuss the reasons for them. Then have them make the tabulation and discuss the results. If you find that more practice in graphing is desirable, you could have the children graph these data before they discuss the results…

Appraisal

Divide the children into two groups, each containing about the same number of boys and girls. Ask everyone to write on a piece of paper the names of their three favorite flavors of ice cream. Have the children in one group tabulate their own data, and ask the other group to do the same. Be sure the groups do not overhear each other's results…

Competency Measure

Task 1 (Objective 1): Say to the child, *In planning for the school picnic, the P.T.A. members want to get an idea of how many hamburgers, hot dogs, and cold-meat sandwiches to make. Tell me how they could get the information they need.* The child should describe a method of surveying some of the children in the school.

Task 2 (Objective 2): Say, *A poll in Miss Brown's room of 30 children gave the following data abut preferences: hamburgers, 15 children; hot dogs, 10 children; cold-meat sandwiches, 5 children.* Give the child the data on a piece of paper or write the information on the chalkboard. Then give him a piece of graph paper and say, *Make a graph showing the number of times each kind of food was chosen.* The child should include the following entries on the graph: a proper title that identifies the subject of the graph, a scale of numerals on the vertical number line, the name of the teacher whose children were surveyed—perhaps included in the title, the proper labeling of the horizontal base line and vertical number line, bars drawn to the correct height to show the number of choices. If the child makes any errors in constructing the graph, correct them before continuing.

Task 3 (Objective 3): Ask the child, *Could you use your graph to predict exactly how many times hamburgers would be chosen by the children in another room?* The child should indicate that an exact prediction probably cannot be made.

Task 4 (Objective 3): Show the child the two picture cards of graphs—one showing a graph that represents the choices made by the children in Mr. Smith's room, the other showing a graph that represents the choices made by the children in Miss Jones' room. Read the labels below the horizontal base line of each graph. Say, *Look at the three graphs—the one you made and the two I have just given you. Make a prediction about which kind of food the children in Mrs. White's class will select most often.* The child should say, "Hamburgers."

Task 5 (Objective 3): Ask, *Why did you make that selection?* The child should identify a pattern that supports his or her answer.

Understanding these concepts yielded the primary goal of SCIS: scientific literacy. The program is divided into two parts: a physical/earth science sequence and a life/earth science sequence. Each grade level's program contains concepts and essential processes prerequisite for study at the next grade level (see Figure 5.4).

The SCIS concepts represent different levels of abstraction. For example, the first level pertains to matter, living things, variation, and conservation of matter. The second level includes concepts of interaction, causal relations, relativity, and geometric relations. The third level concepts pertain to energy, equilibrium, steady state, and the behavior, reproduction, and speciation of living things. These concepts are somewhat complex when compared to simpler collections of facts; therefore, in SCIS instruction receives special attention.

SCIS gives children direct, concrete experiences. The teacher's role is to help children acquire and use their observations to form the broad conceptual ideas of science—to guide, not to tell. The instructional method has three distinct phases and is known as the *learning cycle*.[11]

- Phase 1, *exploration* in an activity-oriented setting, permits the children to explore the learning materials or phenomena.
- Phase 2, *invention,* does not leave children to their own devices, but guides them toward the concepts by gathering their observations and using them to invent ideas that help the children organize and understand their experiences.

FIGURE 5.4   SCIIS Structure and Sequence of Units

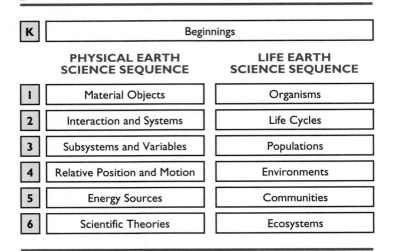

K	Beginnings	
	PHYSICAL EARTH SCIENCE SEQUENCE	**LIFE EARTH SCIENCE SEQUENCE**
I	Material Objects	Organisms
2	Interaction and Systems	Life Cycles
3	Subsystems and Variables	Populations
4	Relative Position and Motion	Environments
5	Energy Sources	Communities
6	Scientific Theories	Ecosystems

Source: Delta Education, Inc. Hudson, NH 03051. Reprinted by permission of copyright holder.

- Phase 3, *application*, helps the children discover relationships and broaden their experiences by giving them opportunities to use the newly formed concepts in new contexts.

Although most of the attention is given to academic skills through concept formation, SCIS also gives attention to student attitudes and thinking skills. The skills developed in the program are similar to those developed in SAPA: Students carefully observe, record their observations, make comparisons, recognize similari-

---

TEACHERS ON SCIENCE TEACHING

How Can You Create an Effective Science Program?

By Earnestine Blakley
Grade 3 Teacher, Bessie Ellison Elementary School, St. Joseph, MO

My science classes are all about hands-on, minds-on, and problem-solving experiences. In all situations, I challenge my students to think and to interact with the physical world around them. They realize that science is discovery; it's excitement; it's magic; and it's fun!

An effective science program should offer youngsters the opportunity to experiment with the natural world around them. Students should be permitted to discover facts rather than having mounds of isolated data thrust upon them. Science teaching and learning should be a time of movement and interaction.

Science in my classroom is a high-energy period of thinking, manipulating, and problem solving. When I was teaching a unit on gas, the students created carbon dioxide by mixing baking soda and vinegar. The trapped gas they created was used to blow up a balloon. First I gave the students a 16-ounce beverage bottle (remember to use safety goggles in case the bottle breaks). They placed four tablespoons of vinegar inside the bottle. Next, they funneled two tablespoons of baking soda into a balloon. Then they carefully placed the mouth of the balloon over the opening of the bottle so that the baking soda would not escape. Finally, they raised the balloon to an upright position so that the baking soda could flow into the vinegar in the bottle. Their eyes widened with amazement as they watched the balloon expand. I then began to ask cause-and-effect questions: What happened and why?

After the discussion and questions, I posed another problem. I asked the students what would happen if we used a 2-liter bottle and added the same amount of vinegar. We would use the same amount of baking soda and the same size balloon. The only change would be the size of the bottle. The students made their predictions, and I recorded their responses on the chalk board. We then proceeded with the experiment. Afterward, we used a tape measure to measure the size of each balloon. From the comparison, we concluded that the balloon attached to the 2-liter bottle was slightly smaller. We discussed possible reasons for the difference in size.

Learning science will never be dull as long as youngsters can predict, observe, measure, compare, manipulate, and interact with the world around them. With such experiences, the students will treasure fond memories of science throughout their lives.

ties, use measurements, and develop vocabulary as they discuss their experiences and form meaningful concepts.

Each grade level of SCIS is packaged conveniently, and most grades have two modular kits, one for physical science and one for life science. Each kit contains all the equipment and materials needed for teaching the specific unit and accommodates classes of up to thirty-two children. Materials are carefully selected to provide the specific experiences each child needs to form the selected concepts; some materials are consumable and need regular replacement. Print materials include wall charts, game boards, card decks, and visual transparencies. Student manuals (record books) are provided for each grade level except kindergarten, which does not use the learning cycle. Children use the manuals to record their observations and complete investigations that help to evaluate their progress. An evaluation packet is provided for each unit and helps the teacher determine each child's concept formation, skill, and attitude development. Living materials are needed for approximately half of the school year; these materials are provided for a fee at the time specified by the teacher. Extending Your Experiences (EYE) cards for concept expansion, review, remediation, and special projects can be used with individual children, small groups, or an entire class.

The teacher's guide is exceptionally well organized. Guides contain a concise lesson plan, the synopsis, lists of materials, background information, tips for advance preparation, specific teaching suggestions, helpful illustrations, descriptions of optional activities, and descriptions of ways to do concept and process evaluation. All of these materials are packaged with a complete kit for every unit (see Figure 5.5).

SCIS Program Effects.   What kinds of effects did SCIS have on children? Again, we can look to James Shymansky and his fellow researchers for some answers. In achievement tests, students in SCIS programs scored 34 percentile points above children from traditional science programs. Of the three programs we describe in this chapter, SCIS had the greatest effect on pupil achievement, outdistancing SAPA and ESS by 30 and 27 percentile points respectively.

Concurrently, SCIS produced gains of 21 percentile points in science process skills and 34 percentile points in children's creativity when compared to traditional programs. Smaller improvements were measured in pupil attitudes, related study skills such as reading and mathematics, and Piagetian tasks. An unexpected benefit of SCIS is reported by John Renner: The first-grade unit, material objects, was compared to a commercial first-grade reading readiness program. Children in the experimental group studied material objects without reading readiness, and children in the control group studied traditional reading readiness materials without material objects. Both groups were equivalent and were pretested with the Metropolitan Reading Readiness Test and then posttested six weeks later. The SCIS experimental group outscored the control group in all areas—word meaning, listening, matching, alphabet, numbers, and total score—except copying.[12] Apparently the thinking skill development in the SCIS program was much more potent

FIGURE 5.5 SCIIS Teacher's Guide Kit

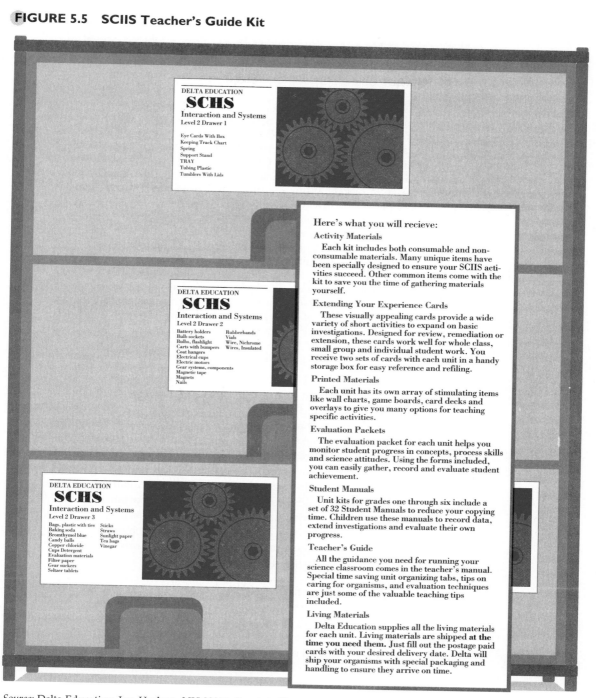

than direct reading readiness instruction. The assumptions that SCIS developers made about children's learning appear to be valid, given the extent of gains in achievement, process skills, and other important aspects of learning.

The Elementary Science Study (ESS)

ESS's Prime Assumptions.

> The central question is whether whatever a child learns is more meaningful and is retained longer if he works his own way through a topic [discovery] or if it is taught him by assertion. Proponents of the discovery approach cite the following values in its favor: (1) Children are motivated by the satisfaction they receive from finding out things for themselves, and satisfaction is recognized as an important attitude in stimulating learning; (2) since children are more personally involved with information and ideas in a discovery approach, deeper understanding of subject matter results and forgetting is reduced; (3) discovery procedures help children develop strategies of inquiry, or process skills. . . ; and (4) transfer of learning is improved.
>
> [Discovery in ESS means that] children explore freely with the materials of a topic until they begin to ask questions of their own. These questions form the basis for further investigation. Teacher direction is at a minimum and the pupils are permitted to pursue their own lines of inquiry in a capitalization on the natural curiosity and ability of children to profit from self-directed experiences. Given this freedom, each child can delve into features of a problem that are interesting and important to him. Discovery learning in this approach is seen as increasing motivation and improving the intuitive meaning of observations.[13]

The developers of ESS believed that the elementary school should provide children with abundant time to explore and to examine relationships between humans and the physical and living world. Terms like *free discovery* and *guided discovery* arose from the teaching methods used with ESS. David Hawkins, developer of ESS, used the term *messing about* to describe the class time students should spend in unguided exploration activities—the initial learning phase of ESS. Developers believed that learning must provide children with interesting and enriching experiences and that abundant, varied activities must be available. A number of psychologists supported the ESS goals by stressing the importance of free, unstructured periods of exploration during the initial phases of learning. Also, psychologists affirmed that children learn at different rates, have different interests, and learn different things from the same learning activity. These views support the notion that learning must be individualized—a feature of ESS.

Description of ESS.   The main goal of ESS for teachers is to provide them with a wide variety of learning materials, which are packaged into unit booklets. Some topics stress experiences with skills fundamental to learning, such as weighing, graphing, and using instruments, while other topics emphasize science concepts. All have been field tested and revised during development so that they continue to motivate children and foster positive attitudes toward science.

ESS originally contained fifty-six different units with a suggested range of grade levels. Now about thirty-eight different units are in print (see Figure 5.6 for some examples). Each unit takes several weeks to complete and contains material useful for a K–9 science program. Although no prepackaged course of study exists, the units can be easily adapted to fit most existing curricula. Each unit stretches across a range of grade levels and can be used in any sequence, unlike SAPA and SCIS. Each unit strives to develop science concepts and thinking skills simultaneously. The rationale is that children acquire mental strategies for organizing their observations as they form science concepts based on those same experiences. This belief is consistent with Piagetian developmental psychology and the learning theory of Jerome Bruner.

The questions children ask are highly valued in ESS. In fact, this is the main intent of the ESS materials—that children will raise all kinds of questions about their experiences and try ways to work with the materials that have not been preplanned by the teacher. As a consequence, teachers have to expect that children will talk with other children as they compare observations and form explanations about what they experience.

ESS has a flexible structure and emphasizes attitudes as the discovery method is used by children to learn science content. The kits consist of low-cost materials and provide the kinds of direct experiences favored by program developers. As the units vary, so do the kits. Some kits are meant for entire classes of thirty students, but most are for smaller numbers: groups of about six, or individual students for certain activities (see Figure 5.7). Each kit and teacher's guide can be purchased separately, giving more freedom and flexibility when selecting curriculum materials for the science program than either SAPA or SCIS. Some ESS units may be used by purchasing only the teacher's guide without the expense of a commercial kit.

A teacher's guide accompanies the pupil kit. The guide contains background information and teaching tips that are suggestions rather than specific directions. Notes on classroom management share examples of the kinds of questions that teachers could ask children and examples of the kinds of answers children may give or the types of questions children may ask. Other suggestions help the teacher become a guide or advisor of inquiry rather than a provider of information. This teacher role assures that the responsibility for learning is shifted to the child, as each is stimulated to devise her or his own way of acquiring and making meaning out of information from the exploration (see Figure 5.8).

ESS has no student textbooks. Worksheets, pictures, and supplementary brief booklets, called *readers*, accompany some of the units, while brief film loops provide learning experiences not easily acquired otherwise. There is considerable variation among the many ESS units, but this variation serves a fundamental purpose: to promote unguided exploration that motivates children to pursue topics of interest. ESS assumes that this kind of experience will help each child develop useful learning skills and that knowledge gained from this approach is meaningful and long lasting.

FIGURE 5.6   ESS Scope and Sequence Chart

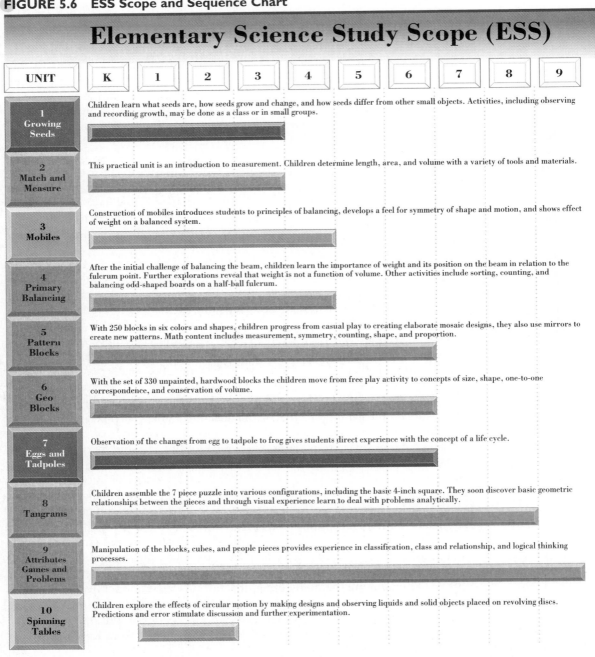

Elementary Science Study Scope (ESS)

UNIT	K	1	2	3	4	5	6	7	8	9

1 Growing Seeds — Children learn what seeds are, how seeds grow and change, and how seeds differ from other small objects. Activities, including observing and recording growth, may be done as a class or in small groups.

2 Match and Measure — This practical unit is an introduction to measurement. Children determine length, area, and volume with a variety of tools and materials.

3 Mobiles — Construction of mobiles introduces students to principles of balancing, develops a feel for symmetry of shape and motion, and shows effect of weight on a balanced system.

4 Primary Balancing — After the initial challenge of balancing the beam, children learn the importance of weight and its position on the beam in relation to the fulcrum point. Further explorations reveal that weight is not a function of volume. Other activities include sorting, counting, and balancing odd-shaped boards on a half-ball fulcrum.

5 Pattern Blocks — With 250 blocks in six colors and shapes, children progress from casual play to creating elaborate mosaic designs, they also use mirrors to create new patterns. Math content includes measurement, symmetry, counting, shape, and proportion.

6 Geo Blocks — With the set of 330 unpainted, hardwood blocks the children move from free play activity to concepts of size, shape, one-to-one correspondence, and conservation of volume.

7 Eggs and Tadpoles — Observation of the changes from egg to tadpole to frog gives students direct experience with the concept of a life cycle.

8 Tangrams — Children assemble the 7 piece puzzle into various configurations, including the basic 4-inch square. They soon discover basic geometric relationships between the pieces and through visual experience learn to deal with problems analytically.

9 Attributes Games and Problems — Manipulation of the blocks, cubes, and people pieces provides experience in classification, class and relationship, and logical thinking processes.

10 Spinning Tables — Children explore the effects of circular motion by making designs and observing liquids and solid objects placed on revolving discs. Predictions and error stimulate discussion and further experimentation.

Source: Delta Education, Inc. Hudson, NH 03051. Reprinted by permission of copyright holder.

Scope and Sequence Chart

UNIT	K	1	2	3	4	5	6	7	8	9

11 Brine Shrimp
This durable organism provides children with concrete evidence of a life cycle and effects of environmental conditions on living things.

12 Printing
Through the handling of individual letters and formulation of words in the type holders, children learn the basics of printing. They also develop an appreciation of the printed word as a means of communication.

13 Structures
Students build structures with materials chosen to create structural problems. They learn to deal with properties such as size, strength of materials, and design configuration.

14 Sink or Float
Students discover that buoyancy of an object is a property of both the object and the liquid. Investigations involve different materials and shapes placed in liquids of varying densities.

15 Clay Boats
Children discover how to make clay float, and develop predicting, weighing, and measuring skills while learning about volume displacement and buoyancy.

16 Drops, Streams & Containers
Children observe characteristics of common liquids when these liquids are poured into one another or dropped on different surfaces. New ways to transfer liquids are developed.

17 Mystery Powders
Through use of scientific method, students progress from identification of harmless, common white powders to more advanced analysis of properties.

18 Ice Cubes
Activities with ice introduce the students to the effects that heat, insulation, shape, and conductivity have on melting rates. Thermometers are used to measure freezing and melting points.

19 Rocks and Charts
Children discover the many individual characteristics of a mineral which make it different from others. Rock sorting and chart making develop useful classification skills.

Physical Science	Life Science	General Skills	Earth Science	Math

FIGURE 5.7   ESS Pupil Kits

GROWING SEEDS: Exploration of Simple Plants ▶

Students study to determine if they are seeds. This is accomplished through external and internal observation, and planning. Growth rate is recorded on graphs. *Grades K–3 (6–8 week program)*

◀BALLOONS AND GASES: Introduction to Common Gases

An introduction to Common Gases. The generating of common gases allows students to discover some properties of gases and to differentiate between one gas and another. Students work with simple acids, bases, and bromothymol blue, or color indicator. "Mystery" gases are introduced by the teacher and the students attempt to identify them using their previous experiences.   *Grades 5–8 (1–22 class sessions)*

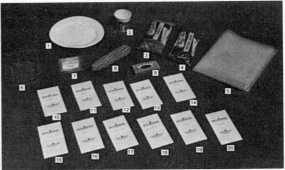

◀EGGS & TADPOLES: Observing a Frog's Life Cycle

Students observe a frog develop from egg through various tadpole states and, with great care, even to a young frog. The students will answer many of their questions through observation and group discussions. *Grades K–6 (3 week to 6 month program)*

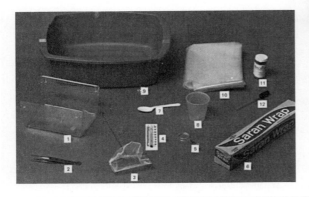

ESS Program Effects.   ESS strives to help children learn science and thinking skills through positive attitudes. Does this work? Again we can refer to the report of James Shymansky and his fellow researchers.[14] Yes, to an extent ESS is successful. Achievement gains were less than with SCIS and SAPA, yet children who learned science by ESS did outperform their age-mates in traditional science programs by an average of 4 percentile points. Attitude improvements were impressive: average ESS scores were 20 percentile points above the averages of children from traditional programs, by far the largest advance of the three programs we compare in this chapter. Substantial increases in creativity and process skill development were shown by 26 and 18 percentile point gains, while completion of Piagetian tasks was 2 percentile points above those of traditional programs. Achievement gains were not as great as the theoretical assumptions of ESS might suggest, yet these assumptions were not completely wrong given the other substantial gains children made from the ESS program.

SAPA, SCIS, and ESS have shown some superior characteristics and effects when compared with traditional science programs. Yet each program is based on a different design and a different teaching approach, and for different reasons. Developers of the programs made different assumptions, but shared some in common as well. What are the characteristics of effective science teaching that should be included in a science program?

WHAT WORKS?

Take a look in a large number of elementary classrooms where science is taught and what do you see? Perhaps you observe what Donald Wright reports: "Fifty to 80 percent of all science classes use a single text or multiple texts as *the* basis for instruction. . .for students, knowing is more a function of reading, digesting, and regurgitating information from the textbook or lab manual than it is of analyzing, synthesizing, and evaluating."[15]

Hands-on, minds-on learning makes the difference.

FIGURE 5.8   Excerpts from an ESS Teacher's Guide

Part 1: Simple Circuits

Beginning Circuits

Before Starting to Teach

Materials you will need:
2 8-inch pieces of #20 bare copper wire
2 8-inch pieces of #22 plastic-covered copper wire
3 #48 (PB) bulbs
3 D batteries
1 wire stripper

The following suggestions will guide your initial exploration. If you take enough time to try your own ideas as well, you will be ready for the variety of ideas your students are sure to propose.

Try to light one of the bulbs, using a piece of bare wire and a battery. Some people have taken 20 minutes to light the bulb the first time, so do not worry if yours does not light right away. See how many different ways you can devise to make the bulb light. It is helpful to make sketches of your various attempts, including those that do not work.

Using the plastic-covered wire, light a bulb. You will have to remove the covering from the ends. The wire stripper is designed to remove the plastic cover without cutting the wire. You can adjust the knob so that the wire opening will cut only the plastic.

Stripper

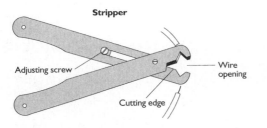

Place the wire in the opening and close the handles; then pull the stripper toward the end of the wire, so that it strips off a piece of the covering.

Now try some connections using a battery, a bulb, and two wires. You may find some surprises. For example, you know that the bulb in *A* below will light, but what will happen when you add another wire, as in *B* or *C*?

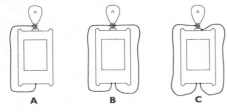

In the Classroom

Materials you will need for each child:Ê
1 8-inch piece of #22 plastic-covered copper wire
1 #48 (PB) bulb
1 D battery

For each group:
1 wire stripper

To have available:
extra supplies of the above materials

It is suggested that the students work in groups of two to four. Although they don't need to share equipment for the initial activity, they will soon need to do so.

Each student should have a box or paper bag in which to keep his materials at the end of each class period. It has worked well for children to keep the materials originally passed out to them for the duration of the unit. They use these materials, as well as others to be distributed later, continually. Whether or not the children take equipment home to work with is up to you.

LEAD-OFF QUESTION
Can you make the bulb light with one battery and one wire?

Some children will take 20 minutes to light the bulb, while others will take only five. Once one child in a class manages to make the bulb light, his method catches on quickly. Probably only five or six will light the bulb on their own. The rest will follow a neighbor's lead.

As the bulbs are lighted, assure the children that there are different ways to light bulbs, and have them look for more. Invite them up to the chalkbaord to draw the various ways they have tried. Ways in which the bulb does not light are just as important and should be drawn on the board, too.

It is extremely important to give children this time for free investigation with the equipment, so that they can pursue whatever questions occur to them. Their questions at this early stage will provide good leads for later work. After doing these first experiments, some children may bring household bulbs into the class. One such class connected seven batteries to a 50-watt bulb and still saw no light. Then a girl felt that the bulb was warm; they added another battery or two and were rewarded by a slight glow. One battery was removed, and the bulb dimmed. The class then went on to compare the number of batteries required to light bulbs of various sizes.

FOLLOW-UP QUESTION
How many different ways can you light the bulb?

ACTIVITIES CHILDREN MAY TRY
• Using two or more batteries, light the PB.
• Find out how many bulbs can be lit with one battery.
• Find out how brightly a bulb will shine when three, four, or eight batteries are used.
• Find out how many batteries it takes to burn out a bulb.
• Use plastic-covered wire, light a PB.
• Use more wire to see if a PB will still light.

- Find out which will wear out first, if contact between a battery and a PB is maintained for a long time. How long does it take?
- Attach a wire from one end of the battery to the other. See how the battery feels after five minutes in this situation and after an hour.
- See if the battery will light a bulb after an hour.

Note: When investigating the different ways that will light the bulb, children often discuss the question, "Does turning the battery around make another way?" The fact that a battery works both ways is an exciting discovery to many.

POSSIBLE DISCUSSION QUESTIONS

After three or four sessions with these materials, the children will be ready to come together as a class to share their experiences. One way to begin such a discussion is to draw some circuits on the board and ask if the class can predict whether the bulbs in the arrangements will light. Below are examples of some circuits you may want to discuss.

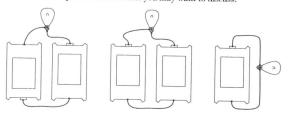

Will these bulbs light? Why?

Let the children discuss all their ideas. Have them try out each new circuit with the equipment to verify their predictions. Perhaps some students will want to make generalizations about the features of those circuits in which the bulb lights and those in which the bulb does not light.

What did you find out in the last few lessons?

You'll find that many children will have forgotten some of their work because they did not keep a record of it. They should now see the need for simple notes and diagrams.

How many ways did you find to make the bulb light?
Does the bulb have to be touching the battery?
Does the wire have to be wrapped around th bulb?
What special places must be touched on the bulb for it to light?
Can you make a "rule" about lighting the bulb?

Be prepared for a variety. Give each child who has something to say a chance to be heard.

Teaching Background

Since this is the initial section of the unit, it has been designed to open the way to many later areas of investigation. The general background presented here is, therefore, intended to suggest ways in which you can help children both to go further and to understand where they are going.

A bulb can be lit essentially in four ways, using one wire and one battery. (Actually, turning the wire around could be considered to be creating new ways, too.)

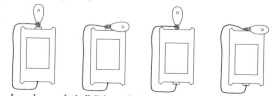

In each case, the bulb lights with the same brightness. Asking a child about the brightness of different arrangements helps him to see that brightness is a way to tell something about a circuit.

Since the battery lights the bulb with equal brightness, regardless of which way it is facing in the circuit, children may wonder why some batteries are marked with a "+" (positive) and a "–" (negative) at the top and the flat end respectively. If the bulb can't tell one end from the other, why do we bother about designating the poles positive and negative? This question will be answered when the children start working with more than one battery. At that time, the students will see that with two or more batteries in a circuit, the direction of each is important.

The "flow" of electricity usually comes up sooner or later. Does the electricity "flow" in circits from the positive to the negative end of the battery or vice versa? This is a very difficult question to answer experimentally. It is further complicated by the fact that when different materials are used in circuits, different things happen. Students who are quick to explain simple circuits in terms of a particular direction of flow might profit from a question such as: "Are you sure? What difference would you notice if the flow were actually the reverse?" Since the students have noticed that the bulb works equally well on both ends of the battery, they should begin to realize that the particular direction of electricity flow doesn't matter in this situation.

When students start lighting more than one bulb with one battery, or one bulb with more than one battery, a great many possibilities for further investigation emerge.

The changes in brightness of the bulb can be accounted for, if you recognize that the bulb is acting like a meter, giving a measure of how much or how little of "something" is in the wire. If children can group the results of their experiments in such a way that they see relationships between, and common elements in, activities that dim and activities that brighten a bulb, they are on the way to understanding what is happening.

Predicting Sheet 1

Prediction Sheet 1 illustrates twelve situations closely related to many of the activities your children may have investigated in the first section.

After a child has thought about each circuit and marked the sheet accordingly, discuss some of his predictions with him. What reasons are given for a particular answer? When a child predicts incorrectly or cannot describe a convincing basis for his prediction, recommend that he test his prediction by making the circuit. He may then be able to give a clearer explanation for some results.

Furthermore, you may have an impression that a direct, authoritative, prescriptive approach with the same pace for everyone and where the 3 Rs are emphasized is actually the best way to teach science. As added support for this view you could refer to the fact that the three NSF-sponsored programs we have just mentioned have never been used by more than 30 percent of the school districts in the United States; also, only 7 percent of K–6 teachers have ever attended an NSF-sponsored meeting.[16] Certainly if the government spent millions to develop these programs, they would be used if they actually worked, right? Wrong.

What the three programs we compare all have in common is a hands-on curriculum and teaching approach. Despite what is widely believed and practiced, the hands-on, minds-on learning approach is superior to the traditional approach. James Shymansky and his colleagues tell us that synthesis of the abundant research shows conclusively that children in a hands-on science program achieve more, like science more, and improve their problem-solving skills more than children who learn from traditional textbook-based programs;[17] the hands help the minds grow. These conclusions endured resynthesis even though original statistics have been revised to yield results of greater precision.[18] (See Table 5.2.)

Ted Bredderman adds support to this view. Bredderman's research is provided as a part of *Project Synthesis*, a massive research effort funded by the National Science Foundation to determine the effects of past experimental programs so that present and future science education goals could be revised. Bredderman's research collected the results from sixty studies that involved 13,000 students in 1,000 elementary classrooms over fifteen years. He analyzed the results of these studies carefully through meta-analysis procedures to sort out conflicting findings reported in the literature. His conclusion clearly shows what works:

TABLE 5.2 Performance Improvement for Students in Classrooms Using ESS, SCIS, or SAPA as Compared to Students in Traditional Classrooms

Performance Area	*Percentage Points Gained*		
	ESS	*SCIS*	*SAPA*
Achievement	4	34	7
Attitudes	20	3	15
Process Skills	18	21	36
Related Skills	*	8	4
Creativity	26	34	7
Piagetian Tasks	2	5	12

* No studies reported

Source: This table is from James A. Shymansky, William C. Kyle, Jr., and Jennifer M. Alport, "How Effective Were the Hands-On Science Programs of Yesterday?" *Science and Children* (November/December 1982), p. 15.

. . . with the use of activity-based science programs, teachers can expect substantially improved performance in science process and creativity; modestly increased performance on tests of perception, logic, language development, science content, and math; modestly improved attitudes toward science and science class; and pronounced benefits for disadvantaged students. . . .[19]

Hands-on, minds-on learning makes the difference. Exploring, investigating, and discovering are essential to meaningful learning and effective science teaching. When children solve problems and make discoveries, they are actually learning how to learn. Jerome Bruner points out the benefits for children as they make discoveries through active learning:

- Children's intellectual potency is increased; their powers of thinking improve.
- Children's rewards for learning shift from those that come from the teacher or someone else to those that are found inside themselves from the satisfaction they feel.
- Children learn the procedures and important steps for making discoveries and find ways to transfer these to other learning opportunities.
- What children learn takes on more meaning, and they remember it longer.[20]

While all three example programs surveyed here report successes, they also have limitations. From the research that has been synthesized it seems prudent to mix emphases on science content and process skills for the most potent teaching and learning combination. Yet researchers like Ted Bredderman and James Shymansky and his colleagues warn us against abandoning the present traditional textbook-based program in complete favor of SAPA, SCIS, ESS, or the like. Instead, they recommend incorporating the useful methods and materials into existing science programs as a step toward improvement.

What are we to do? First, realize that some of the effective alphabet soup science programs remain. Several schools still use SAPA, SCIS, and ESS. Parts of these can be added to existing school programs to provide children with more hands-on learning opportunities. Next, be aware that there have been substantial improvements in recent editions of texts and that new generations of curriculum supplements have been developed. These supplements may be available through your university or state department of education. Both of these types of resources have capitalized on several features that made the alphabet soup programs successful. For example, we find more frequent use of student learning activities, better organization of teaching materials, and convenient packaging of curriculum materials; we can attribute these improvements to the effects of the hands-on, minds-on programs.

What science should be taught largely remains an unresolved issue. Several initiatives, such as the National Science Foundation's Project Synthesis, the American Association for the Advancement of Science's Project 2061, the National Science Teachers Association scope and sequence project, and the National Research Council's National Standards have produced useful materials to help resolve this issue; many state curricula pursue it as well. We now know that if the elementary science

Criteria for Excellence in K–6 Science Programs

All citizens need

science competence to make the most of their individual potential, and to cope with an increasingly technical world. And as participants in a democratic society, individuals must be prepared to make informed, responsible decisions about science-related social issues. Moreover, as the pace of change accelerates, new careers are being created almost daily, as diverse as the interests and aptitudes of students themselves. Alerting students to the ever-widening range of opportunities in careers related to science and technology, teaching science for life, and teaching science for citizenship: these are the three challenges the Project [Search for Excellence in Science Education, SESE] poses to the science programs of today and tomorrow.*

SESE consists of a network of fifty-two state committees that meet each year to nominate the very best science programs for a national award. A national panel of judges screens the states' nominations and then selects six to thirteen programs that most closely achieve the ideal. In reality, no program ever meets all the criteria for excellence. Just the same, the criteria set the direction for the future of science education. An effec-

tive and exemplary elementary science program meets the following criteria:

Students

- Demonstrate effective consumer behavior.
- Acquire good health habits.
- Understand the relationship between people and their environments.
- Use scientific resources to solve problems.
- Realize that science is hard work and that the resolution of one problem can cause other problems.

Curriculum

- Emphasizes hands-on learning for all students through a planned, sequential program.
- Uses well-defined objectives that are demonstrated through effective teaching.
- Uses evaluation for periodic review and ongoing assessment of science content, teaching, and learning.
- Provides information and experiences that students can use in their everyday lives.
- Provides useful guidelines for teacher planning and science activities.

program is to serve *all* children well, specific assumptions must guide program development and science teaching. Science must be taught so that children receive direct, hands-on experiences from their learning and expand their thinking skills. Furthermore, the subject matter must provide opportunities for children to develop personally; to learn about the many interrelationships among science, technology, and our society; to grow academically; and to be exposed to scientific careers.

Each elementary science program can evolve from its present condition to a level where relevant learning opportunities are provided for all children. The following list of assumptions and supported research is associated with effective science programs. The list is gleaned from research supported by the National Science Foundation and the National Science Teachers Association's recommendations for exemplary elementary science programs. These assumptions reveal some

Instruction

- Has an adequate budget and administrative guidance.
- Offers realistic problem-solving activities for students.
- Provides enough materials for every student to benefit from direct experiences and experiments.
- Exceeds state and national minimum class time expectations (number of minutes in science per week).
- Integrates the subject matter of science into other subject areas regularly.

Teachers

- Understand and use the goals of the school science program.
- Seek new ideas and experiment with new teaching methods.
- Provide varied experiences for children within the subject matter, science processes, and other aspects of science.
- Provide learning experiences from various fields of science (life, physical, and environmental), as well as from technology, the community, and larger social problems.
- Encourage students to think and solve problems by using their science experiences.

The criteria are predictions of the future. How these criteria may be articulated can be found in the many classrooms of people who are committed to excellence. These teachers are talented, dedicated, and generous individuals who have developed and who guide programs that really work. The Search for Excellence in Science Education program selects new recipients of the prestigious award each year. Check with the National Science Teachers Association, your state NSTA-affiliated organization, or your state department of education to see which elementary programs in your area have received the award.

Source: Quote taken and other portions excerpted from *Criteria for Excellence* (Washington, DC: National Science Teachers Association, 1987), pp. 4–7. Copyright 1987. Reprinted with permission.

of the impact of historically significant science programs and predict the future trends science programs will face. We suggest that you keep these assumptions handy and let them help you plan more effective science instruction as well as advise your school principal or curriculum committee.

Supported Assumptions About Effective Elementary Science Programs

1. National Science Foundation experimental elementary science programs and sponsored new approaches to teacher preparation have been successful, even though a low percentage of schools (30 percent) have used the programs and an even smaller percentage of teachers (7 percent) have received direct training.

2. Effective elementary science programs keep pace with changes in science, society, knowledge, and trends in schooling.

3. Most current elementary school science programs do not serve all children well. Effective programs have meaning for diverse audiences.

4. Effective science programs strive to promote children's personal development; to help children explore the interrelationships among science, technology, and society; to continue academic preparation; and to build career awareness.

5. Effective programs have no single author, but are developed by teams with teacher involvement. Extensive classroom testing and program revision are necessary and must be done frequently.

6. Children learn successfully in different ways; multiple views on learning add diversity and help to balance the effective science program.

7. Programs that emphasize conceptual learning appear to be most effective overall and produce the greatest and most enduring gains in achievement.

8. Multiple teaching methods are useful, and hands-on learning opportunities are necessary for all children. Overall, guided discovery methods and learning cycles are useful methods for helping children learn science concepts.

9. What is taught—the substance of science—must be useful and relevant for each child.

10. Packaging the program is helpful and reduces teachers' preparation time. New generation science curriculum supplements have several common features that add impact to the materials: They define purposes or objectives, give background information, list materials needed, state procedures for teaching, identify essential vocabulary, offer ideas for evaluation or lesson expansion, and so on.

11. The nature of science makes it possible to integrate topics into other subject lessons. Science's diversity enriches other parts of the elementary curriculum and adds to its power as a basic subject.

12. A less direct, teacher-as-guide instructional role is effective because students are encouraged to assume a greater amount of responsibility for their own learning.

13. Conceptual learning takes time and should not be rushed; effectiveness rather than time efficiency should be the driving force of the curriculum.

14. Children in hands-on, minds-on science programs achieve more, like science more, and improve their problem-solving skills more than children who learn from traditional textbook-based programs. Innovative newer generations of science texts incorporate many of the features of the effective experimental programs.

15. Effective science programs promote children's intellectual development by improving their thinking.

16. Materials and learning activities must match the child's level of development to have the greatest impact.

17. Children receive intrinsic rewards from the personal discoveries they make through first-hand learning experiences with manipulatives.

18. The science they learn from effective programs helps children transfer their learning to other circumstances better, get more meaning, and remember what they learn longer.

THE NEXT GENERATION

Lessons from the past have helped to improve the wonderful new resources available to teachers. This exciting era of curriculum and program development has helped to renew interest in science. Science programs are attempting to keep pace with changes in the fields of science and technology and to investigate the impact of each on our society through the eyes and experiences of children.

New Science Programs

New programs strive to serve the interests and needs of all children, not only an intellectual elite. New programs often emphasize conceptual development, use multiple teaching methods to fill multiple student interests, and incorporate multiple views on human diversity. The direct and sustained involvement of classroom

New science programs provide a variety of experiences to help children understand their complex worlds.

teachers is one of the greatest factors that shape new science programs. Attempts are made to match the child's level of development to appropriate learning experiences. Classroom testing the materials helps to limit flaws and apply the supported assumptions about effective science programs.

While there are numerous small-scale efforts, space only permits a sample of the larger efforts to be mentioned below. Chapter 12 and Appendix A contain additional references to several wonderful new science programs.

AIMS.   *Activities to Integrate Mathematics and Science* publishes elementary and middle school curriculum materials that integrate mathematics and science for grades K–9. These materials are provided in easy-to-use teacher manuals that have been produced and classroom tested by teachers. Workshops and seminars are available through the AIMS organization, based in Fresno, California. Titles include *Floaters and Sinkers, Jawbreakers and Heart Thumpers, Glide into Winter with Math and Science, Pieces and Patterns,* and *The Sky's the Limit!* Some are available in Spanish.

Explorations in Science.   For grades 6 through 9, this program uses CD-ROM and computer network technology to teach physical, life, and earth science. Computers simulate laboratories and learners complete hands-on activities to form scientific concepts and to develop thinking skills. The computers simulate experiments that are dangerous, expensive, or time consuming. The program is provided by Jostens Learning Corporation in San Diego, California.

FOSS.   *Full Option Science System,* of the Lawrence Hall of Science in Berkeley, California, is distributed by the Encyclopaedia Britannica Educational Corporation. For grades 3 through 6, student equipment kits and print materials are accompanied by some of the most innovative assessment alternatives we have seen. Children do science, construct concepts, and perform direct evaluation exercises in the areas of life, physical, and earth science and scientific reasoning and technology.

GEMS.   *Great Exploration in Math and Science* is designed for students in grades K through 12. Science and mathematics are integrated in twenty-four different teacher activity publications and student project booklets. Available through the Lawrence Hall of Science in Berkeley, California, topics include *Animals in Action, Bubbleology, Buzzing a Hive, Crime Lab Chemistry, Fingerprinting, Mapping Fish Habitats, Oobleck,* and *Vitamin C Testing.*

Kids-Net.   *National Geographic Kids Network* of Washington, DC, involves children in a nationwide computer network; learners collect data in their home environments and send it to the national server. Sharing information helps children to make comparisons and discover concepts about water quality and rain, for example, on a national and global scale. Learners are linked with practicing scientists.

Project WILD and Aquatic.   Two different versions of a great idea, these projects emphasize wildlife and aquatic life respectively. Interdisciplinary and for grades K through 12, the materials accommodate major school subjects and skills areas by involving children in direct and simulated wildlife experiences. The purpose is to increase awareness first, then to build toward making personal decisions and taking responsible human actions. The teacher-designed materials make it easy to bring outdoor wildlife concepts into the classroom. Students love the outdoor action sections. The activity guides are available only through training sessions. Information can be obtained by contacting Project WILD, P.O. Box 18060, Boulder, Colorado 80308-8060.

Project Learning Tree.   In intent *PLT* is similar to *WILD* and *Aquatic.* The obvious difference is the emphasis on plant life, beginning with single tree concepts for young children and building to forest and forestry issues for older children. The K–12 program has an exceptionally thorough concept outline, which also progresses from awareness to responsible action. Information about Project Learning Tree is available from the American Forest Council, 1250 Connecticut Avenue NW, Washington, DC 20036.

SS&C.   *The Scope, Sequence and Coordination Project* of the National Science Teachers Association is working to develop, field test, and distribute new curricula for grades 7 through 12 that dismantle the layer-cake approach to learning science. Discrete courses in biology, chemistry, physics, and so on are being replaced by an approach that provides science for all students every year. All disciplines of science are thoroughly integrated, eliminating separate courses and disconnected concepts.

SEPUP.   *Science Education for Public Understanding Program* is developed and provided by the Lawrence Hall of Science in Berkeley, California. The materials exist in modules. The original program, CEPUP, emphasized chemical education; new modules address physical, earth, and life sciences as well as science processes. SEPUP emphasizes an integrated approach to teaching issues-oriented science. SEPUP kits are designed for children in grades 6 through 8 and address topics like pollution, household chemicals, waste, and chemicals in foods. Yearlong SEPUP courses for grades 7 through 10 strive to make science concepts relevant to the real world.

CHAPTER SUMMARY

This chapter explores many assumptions that are made while forming an answer to the principal guiding question: What are the characteristics of effective elementary science instruction? A broad view is taken by examining assumptions that undergird landmark experimental programs

tested extensively in elementary schools. The characteristics of these effective older programs provide a foundation for learning and practicing techniques of effective instruction.

The historical sense of this foundation can help you separate the gimmicks from today's genuine improvements. At times the assumptions are explicit; at other times we find subtle hidden assumptions that tend to reveal themselves as we probe into past events and future recommendations for science education.

The primary concept of this chapter is that effective elementary science programs are built upon dominant beliefs that arise from the past and effectiveness research. Assumptions change as some fall from favor or are proven wrong; new ones are added to reflect changes in the knowledge base and different priorities. Assumptions help guide changes in science programming and impact upon your teaching by stimulating changes in science materials as well as by setting new expectations for the present and identifying future trends.

The chapter concludes with a brief answer to the question "What works?" The answer is drawn from recent program evaluation research and the National Science Teachers Association's criteria for program excellence. The planning techniques, sample lessons, and teaching strategies of subsequent chapters arise from supported assumptions about effective elementary science programs.

DISCUSSION QUESTIONS AND PROJECTS

1. What is your current position on what an effective elementary science program should contain? How would you defend your position to a teacher or school administrator who holds an opposing view?

2. Examine copies of several different science textbooks for the same grade level. What evidence do you find that shows inclusion of the criteria for effective programs?

3. Refer to the assumptions about elementary school science summarized at the end of this chapter. How could you use these assumptions to form a philosophy of science teaching? What is your philosophy?

4. Which would you believe, the research findings and criteria for effective programs such as those from sources cited in this chapter, the opinions of several teachers, or a report made by a presidential advisory committee? Why?

5. Examine a school's course of study or curriculum guide for elementary or middle school science. Identify the assumptions about effective science programs and compare them to those stated at the end of this chapter. Report your comparison.

6. Use the assumptions about elementary science programs to develop a survey, and then use the survey to interview several elementary teachers, principals, scientists, parents, and so on. What do you conclude about the accuracy of different people's assumptions?

7. Examine samples of SAPA, SCIS, and ESS materials and compare them with current elementary science textbooks and supplementary curriculum materials such as Project WILD, Outdoor Biology Instructional Strategies, Project Learning Tree, FOSS, SEPUP, Project AIMS, and others. How do the older experimental elementary science programs compare with the newer generation of textbooks and teaching materials? What features are similar? Why?

NOTES

1. Paul DeHart Hurd, "Perspectives for the Reform of Science Education," *Phi Delta Kappan* (January 1986), pp. 353–358.

2. Ibid., p. 354.

3. Ibid., p. 355.

4. Naama Sabar, "Science, Curriculum, and Society: Trends in Science Curriculum," *Science Education* 63, 2 (1979), pp. 257–269.

5. Ibid., p. 258.

6. Robert E. Yager, "The *Major* Crisis in Science Education," *School Science and Mathematics* 84, 3 (1984), p. 196.

7. Paul DeHart Hurd (ed.), *New Directions in Elementary Science Teaching* (Belmont, CA: Wadsworth Publishing Company, 1968), 11–12.

8. James A. Shymansky, William C. Kyle, Jr., and Jennifer M. Alport, "How Effective Were the Hands-On Science Programs of Yesterday?" *Science and Children* (November/December 1982), pp. 14–15.

9. Ted Bredderman, "Activity Science—The Evidence Shows It Matters," *Science and Children* (September 1982), pp. 39–41.

10. Hurd, 1968, pp. 9–10.

11. Robert Karplus, "The Science Curriculum Improvement Study—Report to the Piaget Conference," *Journal of Research in Science Teaching* 2 (1964), pp. 236–240.

12. John W. Renner and Edmund A. Marek, *The Learning Cycle and Elementary School Science Teaching* (Portsmouth, NH: Heinemann Educational Books, 1988), pp. 193–196.

13. Hurd, 1968, pp. 18–19.

14. Shymansky et al.,

15. Donald Wright, "A Report on the Implications for the Science Community of Three NSF-Supported Studies of the State of Precollege Science Education," in Herbert A. Smith (ed.), *What Are the Needs in Precollege Science, Mathematics, and Social Science Education? Views from the Field* (Washington, DC: National Science Foundation SE 80-9, 1980), p. 144.

16. Iris R. Weiss, *Report of the 1977 National Survey of Science, Mathematics, and Social Studies Education,* SE 78-72, prepared for the National Science Foundation Directorate for Science Education (Research Triangle Park, NC: Center for Educational Research and Evaluation, March 1978).

17. Shymansky et al.

18. James Shymansky, Larry Hedges, and George Woodworth, "A Reassessment of the Effects of Inquiry-Based Science Curricula of the 60s on Student Performance," *Journal of Research on Science Teaching,* 27, 2 (1990), pp. 127–144.

19. Bredderman, pp. 39–41.

20. Jerome Bruner, "The Act of Discovery," *Harvard Educational Review,* vol. 31, 1961, pp. 21–32.

ADDITIONAL READINGS

If you are interested in learning more about some of the topics raised in this chapter, consider the following sources:

Patricia E. Blosser, "What Research Says: Improving Science Education" (*School Science and Mathematics,* 86, 7, November 1986, pp. 597–612). Dr. Blosser draws on her access to extensive information from the ERIC Clearinghouse for Science, Mathematics, and Environmental Education to identify past and present trends and issues for reform of science education. She provides a succinct historical account of the evolution of science education, lists the barriers to improvement, and reports the researched effects of various programs. Blosser confirms the need to teach science interactively.

Kenneth R. Mechling and Donna L. Oliver, *What Research Says About Elementary School Science* (Washington, DC: National Science Teachers Association, 1983). This is Handbook IV from the "Project for Promoting Science Among Elementary School Principals," which was funded by the National Science Foundation. Although written for school principals, this particular handbook is also valuable for teachers who want to get the facts from research and avoid the myths that surround the purposes and practices of elementary science. Oliver is a former elementary school teacher who brings practical experience to the "Recipe for Success" section.

Norris C. Harms and Robert E. Yager, *What Research Says to the Science Teacher,* vol. 3 (Washington, DC: National Science Teachers Association, 1981). Used extensively for portions of this chapter, this book provides the source recommendations attributed to Project Synthesis. We highly recommend that you read parts I, II, V, VI, VII, and VIII.

Criteria for Excellence (Washington, DC: National Science Teachers Association, 1987). Among other program areas, this compact book provides specific criteria for exemplary programs in K–6 science, middle/junior high science, science-technology-society, environmental education, inquiry science, science teaching, and career awareness. The writing is straightforward, and descriptions are complemented with lists of school programs that have received national recognition for excellence in science programs and teaching.

Ronald J. Bonnstetter, John E. Penick, and Robert E. Yager, *Teachers in Exemplary Programs: How Do They Compare?* (Washington, DC: National Science Teachers Association, 1983). This is one of a series of monographs devoted to excellence in science teaching. It is peppered with profiles and statistics about effective science teachers. The conclusion is that "teachers in programs which stand out as different are themselves different from teachers in general." (p. 30)

PART THREE

Science Teaching Methods

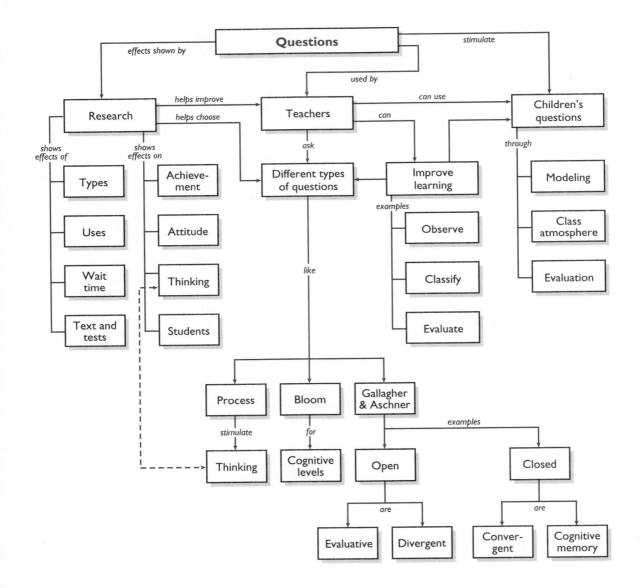

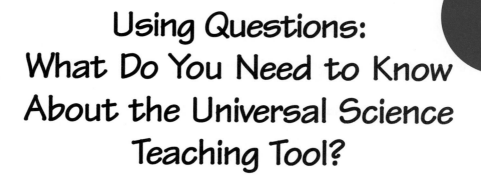

Using Questions:
What Do You Need to Know
About the Universal Science
Teaching Tool?

Mrs. Barcikowski extended warm greetings to each as the children came running into the lab. A table in the middle of the room was piled with rocks of many different types, colors, shapes, and sizes. Each child was encouraged to pick up several samples and look at them carefully. The children rubbed the samples, held them up to the light, and used magnifying glasses to make closer inspections. The room was buzzing with activity, including the predictable horseplay of a few, and the buzz was punctuated with the exclamations of scientific discoveries. All the while, Mrs. B expressed her interest by asking many different questions that helped the children sharpen their observations.

Then she had the children gather around her on the piece of old carpet. When all were seated, Mrs. B began making conversation with such casual questions as "How many of you have a hobby? How 'bout your parents or brothers or sisters? What are some of your hobbies?"

After a moment of listening and encouraging, Mrs. B said, "It seems that many of you collect different things for a hobby. Right?" Smiles and nodding heads gave her an entry. "I do too. In fact one of my favorite things to do on vacation is to look for unusual rocks to add to the collection I've been sharing with you today. Would you like to see one of my favorites?" Holding up a smoothly polished quarter-sized sample for all to see, and passing around others for them to hold, Mrs. B said, "We've been studying the concept of *properties* for many of our lessons. Let's use properties to help us study rocks. What kinds of properties do you observe in this rock?" The children's observations were accepted with encouragement and occasional praise. Another key question Mrs. B asked was "What other rocks from our pile seem like this one?" After noticing variety in the color, size, and shape of the other samples, a child pointed out that some of them were more different than alike. "True," Mrs. B confirmed. "I guess we need to focus a bit. What property appears to be the same in each of the samples?"

"Crystals?" offered a child.

"That's right! This type of rock is known especially for its crystals. What kind of rock do you think this is?" Mrs. B waited patiently and she reminded the children to refer back to their observations while they tossed ideas around among themselves. She watched them closely and then invited Elizabeth, who seemed unsure, to venture a guess.

"Well, it looks kinda milky so I guess it's called . . . a 'milk rock?'" asked Elizabeth as she groped for an answer. The other children laughed, but Mrs. B reminded them to be polite; then she smiled as she saw how a connection could be made.

"I know you go to the grocery with your parents. What sizes of containers does milk come in?"

Elizabeth thought to herself: gallon? half gallon? Somehow those didn't seem right. Then an idea came to her. "A quart rock?" Elizabeth hesitantly asked.

"Good try. Almost, Elizabeth, just one more letter," encouraged Mrs. B as she wrote the word *quart* on the lap chalk board and held it up for all to see. "Let's add a zzz sound to this and see what we have. *Q-u-a-r-t-z.* What does that spell, Elizabeth?"

"Quartz!" exclaimed Elizabeth, with emphasis on the z.

"Now everyone," encouraged Mrs. B.

For the next several seconds, the class spelled and pronounced the new word like cheerleaders. Then Mrs. B referred them back to the samples and continued her questions, always waiting patiently, encouraging, and building on the children's ideas. She paused periodically to add a point or two of her own. By the lesson's end the children had learned that quartz is a common mineral found in rocks and comes in many different colors. When polished smooth, quartz may be used in jewelry as a semiprecious stone, and quartz crystals are used to manufacture prisms, lenses, watches, computer chips, and other electronic gadgets. They even learned that the scientific name is silicon dioxide, SiO_2.

INTRODUCTION

Questions are tools for planning, teaching, thinking, and learning. What do you know about classroom uses of questions and your own questioning skills? It is typical for teachers to use questions intuitively or even out of habit. Some may even achieve satisfactory results. Yet research suggests that many teachers do not realize that modest improvements in their questions can result in considerable gains for their students. In science, the students' questions play an important role in their learning; they need to be encouraged. The mission of this chapter is to:

1. Raise questions about questions and report the effects that questions have on children's achievement, attitudes, and thinking skills;
2. Explore the different types and uses of questions;
3. Investigate how questions can be used;
4. Offer some suggestions you can use to monitor and improve your own questions.

QUESTIONS ON QUESTIONS

What is a question? We use questions often, but do you know much about their proper uses and effects? This part of the chapter raises seven important questions about questions. Try answering them from what you already know. Then read on to check your answers. How well informed are you about this most potent teaching tool?

- What kinds of questions do teachers ask and what kinds of answers do they require?
- Why do teachers use questions?
- How do questions affect students?
- How are teacher questions and student answers related?
- How do teachers use questions to involve *all* students?
- What is wait-time and why is it important?
- What types of questions are used most in elementary science books and tests?

What Kinds of Questions Do Teachers Ask and What Kinds of Answers Do They Require?

Research verifies that elementary teachers use questions more than any other teaching strategy. For example, one study reports that third-grade teachers asked reading groups a question every 43 seconds,[1] while another study found that teachers ask as many as 300 to 400 questions each day; the average is 348.[2] Most of these questions seem to be asked in a rapid-fire question-answer pattern. The

FIGURE 6.1   What Is a Question?

A question is an interrogative sentence that asks for a response. A question is expressed in simple, clear, straight-forward language that students can understand. A good question stimulates thinking and should be adapted to the age, abilities, and interests of the students.

A good question is one that is appropriate and is used for a specific purpose. Questions are used:

- to find out what is not known or to find out whether someone knows
- to motivate
- to provide drill and practice
- to help students organize thinking
- to develop an ability to think
- to interpret meaning
- to emphasize a point
- to show relationships

- to establish cause and effect
- to discover interests
- to help develop appreciation
- to provide review
- to reveal thinking processes
- to diagnose learning difficulties
- to evaluate
- to give practice
- to permit expression

Four type of questions:

1. Memory questions establish or review the facts.
2. Convergent questions have one correct answer and require reasoning.
3. Divergent questions have several answers and help to promote possibility thinking and creativity.
4. Evaluative questions promote decision making and defensible judgments.

How do you use questions?
How do you use children's questions?

pattern and extent of question use appears to have changed little for more than fifty years, with teachers asking about 93 percent of all questions and giving children little time to respond or opportunity to ask their own questions.[3] The questions' effectiveness is limited by this type of use.

Abundant use of questions would suggest considerable room for variety, but is this true? No. The questions teachers usually ask require factual answers and low levels of thinking. Knowledge and comprehension levels make up at least 70 per-cent of the questions, while questions that require application, analysis, synthesis, or evaluation thinking are used much less often.[4]

Why Do Teachers Use Questions?

According to Mary Budd Rowe,[5] a science educator, teachers use questions for three main purposes:

- to *evaluate* or to find out what the pupils already know;

- to *control* the functions of the classroom: inquisition used as a classroom management strategy or to reduce off-task behavior;
- to *instruct* children by suggesting resources and procedures, focusing observation, pointing out differences and discrepancies, and so on.

Questions have other uses as the stock in trade of teachers, and the potential far exceeds the three fundamental uses Rowe details. See Table 6.1.

How Do Questions Affect Students?

The questions teachers choose and use can influence children in three areas: attitudes, thinking, and achievement.

How Do Questions Influence Students' Attitudes? Attitudes influence how students participate, think, and achieve. Students with positive attitudes tend to look more favorably on a subject, teacher, or method of teaching. Children with negative attitudes often link them to a subject, school experience, or teacher and tend to resist and perform poorly. From his research, William Wilen[6] concludes that teacher use of questions plays an important part in shaping children's attitudes, thinking, and achievement. "Students must develop positive attitudes toward higher-level questioning if instructional approaches such as inquiry are to be effective,"[7] Wilen writes.

How Do Questions Influence Students' Thinking? Hilda Taba discovered that the questions teachers used influenced the children's levels of thinking. Teachers expected children to think at a certain level (according to Bloom's taxonomy of the cognitive domain), composed and used questions for the expected level, and then received responses from students that matched their expectations.[8] Teachers can

TABLE 6.1 How Can Teachers Use Questions?

- To arouse children's interest and motivate participation
- To determine children's prior knowledge before a lesson begins
- To determine students' thoughts and other information essential to a problem before it is explored
- To guide children's thinking toward higher levels
- To discipline disruptive students by asking them to explain their behavior
- To provide listening cues for students with difficulties and to focus inattentive students' attention
- To diagnose students' strengths and weaknesses
- To help children develop concepts or see relationships between objects or phenomena
- To review or summarize lessons
- To informally check students' comprehension
- To evaluate planned learning outcomes, such as performance objectives

What other uses can you add to this list?

and do control the thought levels of students.[9] In fact, Gallagher and Aschner report that a mere 5 percent increase in divergent questioning can encourage up to a 40 percent increase in divergent responses from students.[10] Divergent thinking is important for problem-solving tasks and for learning that requires creativity. Also, high-level questions help students to evaluate information better and improve their understanding of lower-level facts.[11]

How pupils think must match the requirements of teachers' methods if students are to become confident learners. The questions children ask are indicators of the thinking they are doing and of the impact of your questions. Dorothy Alfke gives us this recommendation to help children improve their thinking through questioning:

> Inquiry learning must involve questions **asked by, meaningful to, and potentially productive for** the learners. . . . Young people must ask the kinds of questions which lead them back to doing something with the materials in order to derive answers. They need to ask the kinds of questions they can get answers to. . . . [If] learning how to learn, inquiry learning, and conceptual learning are high in your value system, develop the skill of asking operational questions in your classes. Listen to the kinds of questions your children are asking as they interact with new observations of science phenomena. Listen also to the questions you, as a teacher, are asking your students, because your questions have a heavy influence on the kinds of question patterns your students are developing.[12]

Even young children can learn to change their thinking behavior. For example, second-grade nonnative speakers of English learn to modify their own thinking and question-asking strategies when they are exposed to proper question-

Appropriate questions can improve children's attitudes, thinking, and achievement.

ing and reinforcement.[13] Iva Brown sums up best the importance of questioning on pupil thinking:

> The key to successful classroom experiences with hands-on science activities is clearly the use of questioning in the instructional process. Without well-thought-out questions in the lesson, manipulative activities may soon deteriorate into rather meaningless messing around.[14]

Questions can make the difference between learning from *meaningful* manipulation of materials and *meaningless* messing around. This belief is based on a process-product model of classroom learning, in which specific teaching behaviors provide useful pupil learning experiences. The product of this process is pupil achievement (see Figure 6.3). This model suggests that "increases in the quantity and quality of pupil behaviors should result in concomitant increases in pupil achievement."[15] The assumed increases are attributed to the quality of verbal interaction. For example, teachers and students are reported to talk about 71 percent of the time in activity-based classrooms, compared to 80 percent of the time spent talking in nonactivity-based classrooms. In average activity-based elementary science classrooms, 29 percent of the questions are at a high level, while only 13 percent of teachers' questions are high level in average nonactivity-based classrooms.[16]

How Do Questions Influence Students' Achievement? Do the changes in verbal interaction make a difference? Apparently, yes. The studies here are limited, but the results show that a teacher's questions can produce pupil achievement superior to levels attributed to written questions found in textbooks and on worksheets.[17] Some earlier studies appear to conflict with this conclusion.[18,19] However, more recent studies suggest that key ingredients of effective verbal interaction may have been missing in the earlier research. For example, Kenneth Tobin describes increased achievement for middle school students in science when teachers redirected questions, used probing strategies, and used wait-time to increase student discourse and reaction.[20] Higher-level questions seem to stimulate greater science achievement when combined with a longer wait-time.[21]

How Are Teacher Questions and Student Answers Related?

Raising the level of questions is all well and good, but it only makes a difference if students actually think and respond on the same level as that required by the questions used. Is this what happens?

Greater use of higher-level questions may be a significant difference between hands-on science learning and traditional teaching, according to Ted Bredderman. He reports a direct relationship between the level of questioning and the level of response in elementary science lessons. Bredderman observed specially trained teachers (such as reading teachers trained in the SCIS program) raising the level of questioning in reading lessons. His research suggests that questioning levels "can be raised through activity-based science training, which could have the effect of raising the cognitive level of classroom discourse and could result in increased achievement."[22] Other researchers found that higher-level questions had a positive influence on the language development of young children and on skills such as analytical thinking.[23] What is the general conclusion? There is a positive relationship between higher-level questions and higher-level student answers.[24] We recommend using more advanced questions to obtain more thoughtful answers from children.

How Do Teachers Use Questions to Involve All Students?

Exemplary teachers treat different pupils equitably and are capable of adapting instruction according to student needs, including the levels of questions they use. How equitable is the questioning treatment that is found in typical elementary classrooms?

Studies done in urban classrooms show that teachers call on students whom they perceive as high achievers more frequently than on students they perceive as low achievers. Also, teachers are less likely to react to the responses received from low achievers: 3 percent fail to react to high achievers and 18 percent fail to provide feedback to low achievers. When high achievers hesitate to answer, they are given more time to think. Low achievers receive less and often no time, perhaps out of regard for the students' feelings. High achievers also receive more opportunities to exchange ideas with teachers at higher thought levels. Similar data show questioning differences between Caucasian and African-American students, with African-American males most deprived of opportunity.

What is the relationship between where a student sits in a classroom and the number of opportunities the student receives to answer questions? In a study of first-, sixth-, and eleventh-grade classrooms with traditional seating arrangements of rows facing the teacher's desk, the students most likely to be asked questions were seated in a T shape with the top of the T across the front of the room and the stem of the T down the middle (see Figure 6.2). Certainly the shape was not always perfect, yet there were distinct areas in the back of the classrooms along the sides where students were seldom involved in questioning and instructive verbal interaction.[25] Who sits in these areas most often? Who needs more opportunities, feedback, and encouragement? Answer: lower-achieving students.

What Is Wait-Time and Why Is It Important?

Pause for a few seconds and think about what happens when you are the student and a teacher asks you a question. Unless you have memorized the answer, you must decode the meaning of the question (no small task if it is unclear or if multiple questions are used); think "What do I know?" about the question's possible answer; ask "How can I say the answer without sounding foolish?"; actually form the answer; and then give the response to the teacher. All of these steps take time, as suggested by Figure 6.3.

Wait-time is defined in different ways, but usually two types of wait-time are recognized. *Wait-time 1* refers to the length of time a teacher waits for a student to respond. *Wait-time 2* is the length of time a teacher waits after a student has responded before the teacher reacts to what was said.

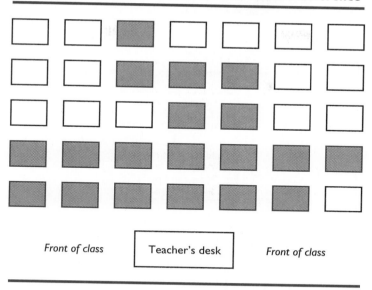

FIGURE 6.2   Where a Child Sits Can Make a Difference

Front of class   Teacher's desk   *Front of class*

How long do teachers typically wait? Mary Budd Rowe[26] first researched this topic and reported an average for wait-time 1 of about one second. Wait-time 2 was equally short, with teachers often only parroting the students' answers or providing very low-value feedback, such as "Okay," "Uh-huh," or "Good." Many teachers wait about one second for students to respond without any adjustment for the difficulty of the question and then almost immediately react to what the students have said without giving the response much thought. "Evidently students are expected to respond as quickly to comprehension questions as they are to knowledge-level questions," and teachers believe they can accurately predict what students will say.[27] Under what conditions do you think wait-times of one second or less *are* appropriate?

There is a growing list of advantages we can expect from increasing the length of our wait-times. Kenneth Tobin reports increases in the length of student responses, increases in student achievement, and changes in teacher discourse. Teachers tend to "probe and obtain further student input rather than mimicking pupil responses."[28] Yet there is a possible threshold effect; a certain optimal length of wait-time exists depending upon the type of question, advises Joseph Riley II.[29] Tobin and Capie[30] recommend an overall wait-time of about three seconds with an approximate mix of 50 percent lower-level questions and 50 percent higher-level questions to produce optimal pupil responses. They advise us to establish the facts first in order to give the students something worthwhile to think about before we build on the base of knowledge by using higher-level questions. Tobin even

FIGURE 6.3   Questioning Map: Children Need Time to Think   What Happens After a Child Is Asked a Question?

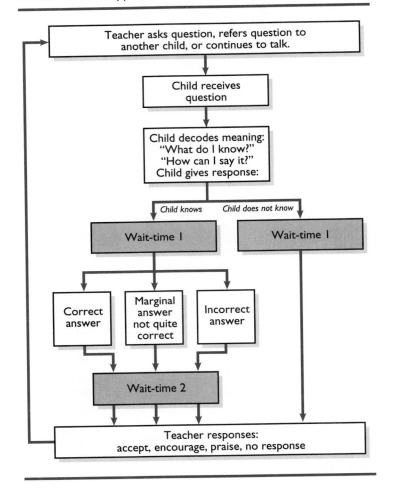

suggests that an effective strategy is to ask the question, wait, call on a student to answer, wait, then redirect the question or react accordingly (see Figure 6.4).

Some teachers encourage cooperative types of learning by using the *think-pair-share* approach. A teacher asks the question and waits; students think about possible answers for ten to twenty seconds; students then pair up and compare answers. A student pair is then asked to share its answer with the class.

Students might find the waiting time awkward at first and misinterpret your intentions. We have had considerable success with children by telling them about wait-time and why we are going to use it, then cueing them to think before

FIGURE 6.4   A Whole Class Questioning Strategy   There are times when questions should be used with the whole class. This questioning strategy can maximize student involvement.

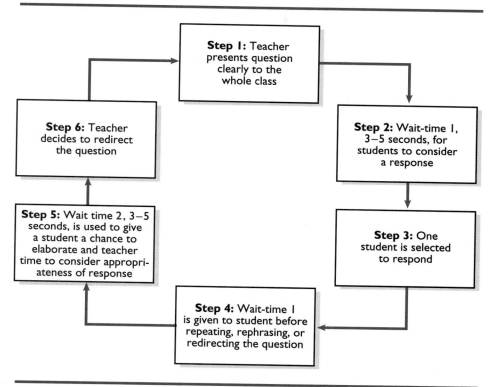

Step 1: Teacher presents question clearly to the whole class

Step 2: Wait-time 1, 3–5 seconds, for students to consider a response

Step 3: One student is selected to respond

Step 4: Wait-time 1 is given to student before repeating, rephrasing, or redirecting the question

Step 5: Wait time 2, 3–5 seconds, is used to give a student a chance to elaborate and teacher time to consider appropriateness of response

Step 6: Teacher decides to redirect the question

Source: This strategy is based on the research of Kenneth Tobin as reported in "Effects of Extended Wait-Time on Discourse Characteristics and Achievement in Middle School Grades," *Journal of Research in Science Teaching,* vol. 21, no. 8 (1984), pp. 779–791.

responding. Try waiting at least three seconds before you respond, and you may discover the benefits reported by Mary Budd Rowe:[31]

- Student responses can become 400 to 800 percent longer.
- The number of appropriate but unsolicited student responses increases.
- Failure of students to respond decreases.
- Children's confidence levels increase.
- Students ask more questions.
- Low achievers may contribute up to 37 percent more.
- Speculative and predictive thinking can increase as much as 700 percent.
- Students respond and react more to each other.
- Discipline problems decrease.

What Types of Questions Are Used Most in Elementary Science Books and Tests?

Textbooks have a profound impact on curriculum, teachers, and instruction because student texts and teacher guides often determine the level of questions used. Questions, as we have learned, influence the extent of thinking and learning that takes place. Low-level questions have been consistently used in textbooks for several school subjects, but high-level questions have seldom been found. For example, of more than 61,000 questions from history textbooks, teacher guides, and student workbooks, more than 95 percent were devoted to recalling facts.[32] Another researcher found that only nine out of 144 lesson plans in the teacher guides from the basal readers of four major publishers contained questions distributed over Bloom's various cognitive levels.[33] Overall, series of elementary science textbooks are no better, but recent improvements are encouraging. Excellent resource experiment books are also available; they pose questions based on the science processes (see Exercise 6.1).

These findings also raise concern for tests and the printed materials they represent. What types of test items are provided? Tests supplied by text publishers appear to be devoted to low levels of thought as well. Gregory Risner studied the cognitive levels of questions demonstrated by test items that accompanied fifth-grade science textbooks. Rated on Bloom's taxonomy, Risner found about 95 percent of the test questions devoted to knowledge or comprehension, about 5 percent used for application, and 0.2 percent used for evaluation;[34] analysis and synthesis questions were neglected completely. All types of questions are important, but consistent overuse of any one type can limit learning. You must be able to identify questions necessary for stimulating desired levels of thought and then build those questions into your teaching.

WHAT ARE THE DIFFERENT TYPES OF QUESTIONS?

Many innovative scientists would never have made their most important discoveries had they been unable to think divergently in their pursuit of the new. Through thinking nontraditionally and divergently, scientists like Copernicus, Galileo, Pasteur, and Salk discovered solutions, formulated theories, and made discoveries that revolutionized the modern world. The need for divergent thinking did not die with their achievements.[35]

These scientists learned to think divergently—broadly, creatively, and deeply about many possibilities. They learned how to ask the right questions at the right time. "Wrong questions tend to begin with such innocent interrogatives as why, how, or what."[36] Jos Elstgeest provides an excellent example in this brief story:

I once witnessed a marvelous science lesson virtually go to ruins. It was a class of young secondary school girls who, for the first time, were let free to handle batteries, bulbs, and wires. They were busy incessantly, and there were cries of surprise and delight. Arguments were settled by "You see?" and problems were

Using Questions in Science Classrooms

One function of teaching science is to help children develop higher levels of thinking. To do this you must facilitate better communication with and among your students. One way to encourage communication is by asking questions. "Teacher questions can serve a variety of purposes," such as

- Managing the classroom ("How many of you have finished the activity?")
- Reinforcing a fact or concept ("What name is given to the process plants used to make food?")
- Stimulating thinking ("What do you think would happen if. . . ?")
- Arousing interest ("Have you ever seen such a sight?")
- Helping students develop a particular mind-set ("A steel bar does not float on water; I wonder why a steel ship floats?")

Science teachers are concerned about helping students to become critical thinkers, problem solvers, and scientifically literate citizens. If we want students to function as independent thinkers, we need to provide opportunities in our science classes that allow for greater student involvement and initiative and less teacher domination of the learning process. This means a shift in teacher role from that of information-giver to that of a facilitator and guide of the learning process.

Central to this shift in teacher role are the types of questions that teachers ask. Questions that require students to recall data or facts have a different impact on pupils than questions which encourage pupils to process and interpret data in a variety of ways.

The differential effects of various types of teacher questions seem obvious, but what goes on in classrooms? In one review of observational studies of teacher questioning, spanning 1963–1983, it was reported that the central focus of all teacher questioning activity

appeared to be the textbook. Teachers appeared to consider their job to be [seeing] that students have studied the text. Similar findings have been reported from observational studies of teachers' questioning styles in science classrooms. Science teachers appear to function primarily at the "recall" level in the questions they ask, whether the science lessons are being taught to elementary students or secondary school pupils.

Why doesn't questioning behavior match educational objectives? One hypothesis is that teachers are not aware of their customary questioning patterns. One way to test this hypothesis is to use a question analysis system.

You can do several things if you want to improve your questioning behavior by using a wider variety of questions. First,

> locate a question category system [you] can use comfortably and then apply it, during lesson planning and in post-lesson analysis. Because of the variety of things that go on during a lesson, a post-lesson analysis is best accomplished by tape-recording the lesson or at least those parts of the lesson containing the most teacher questions.

Are the kinds of questions you ask different? What kinds of teacher-student interaction patterns seem to exist? Are some patterns of interaction more effective than others? Compare your written and oral questions. Do they accomplish what you intend? If you use a variety of oral questions to promote different levels of thinking, quiz and test questions should do the same. Students quickly figure out what you value and then strive for it.

Source: Excerpted from Patricia Blosser, "Using Questions in Science Classrooms," in Rod Doran (ed.), *Research Matters . . . To the Science Teacher*, vol. 2, 1985 (ERIC document no. 273490).

Questions can encourage children to develop science process skills.

solved with "Let's try!" Hardly a thinkable combination of batteries, bulbs, and wires was left untried. Then in the midst of the hubbub, the teacher clapped her hands and, chalk poised at the blackboard, announced: "Now, girls, let us summarize what we have learned today. Emmy, what is a battery?" "Joyce, what is a positive terminal?" "Lucy, what is the correct way to close a circuit?" And the "correct" diagram was deftly sketched and labeled, the "correct" symbols were added, and the "correct" definitions were scribbled down. And Emmy, Joyce, and Lucy and the others deflated audibly into silence and submission, obediently copying the diagram and the summary. What they had done seemed of no importance. The questions were in no way related to their work. The rich experience with the batteries and other equipment, which would have given them plenty to talk and think about and to question, was in no way used to bring order and system into the information they actually did gather.[37]

Elstgeest defines *good questions* as those taking a first step toward an answer, like a problem that actually has a solution. The good question stimulates, invites the child to take a closer look, or leads to where the answer can be found. The good question refers to the child's experience, real objects, or events under study. The good question invites children to show rather than say an answer. Good questions may be modeled after the science process skills in which children are asked to take a closer look and describe what they find. Try matching the questions and skills in Exercise 6.1.

There are several additional ways to classify questions. When presenting information from the research on questions, we have often referred to Bloom's taxonomy of the cognitive domain. It is possible to write questions for each level of the taxonomy. See Figure 6.5 for examples.

- *Knowledge-level* questions request the memorized facts.
- *Comprehension-level* questions stimulate responses of memorized information in the students' own words.
- *Application-level* questions cause students to use information while thinking about how to put what they have learned to use in a new context.
- *Analysis-level* questions require that students break down what they know into smaller parts to look for differences, patterns, and so on.

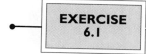

**EXERCISE
6.1**

Science Process Questions*

The questions below are representative of those found in books for children. Use these science processes to label the questions: observing, communicating, hypoth-esizing/experimenting, measuring, comparing/contrasting, and generalizing/predicting.

Process	Question
_____	1. Which plants seem to be sturdier: ones left in sun or ones left in shade?
_____	2. Most rain in clouds comes from the ocean; why doesn't it rain over the ocean and nowhere else?
_____	3. Which plant do you think will grow better?
_____	4. Do the creatures react to such things as light or shadows or an object in their path?
_____	5. What was the temperature?
_____	6. Which length works best?
_____	7. What can you move with the air you blow through a straw?
_____	8. Which seeds stick to your clothes as you walk through a weedy field?
_____	9. What happens to the number of breathing movements as the temperature drops?
_____	10. How long does the solution bubble?

*For a complete discussion, see Sandra Styer, "Books that Ask the Right Questions," *Science and Children* (March 1984), pp. 40–42. See page 186 for answers to Exercise 6.1.

FIGURE 6.5 Bloom's Taxonomy of the Cognitive Domain

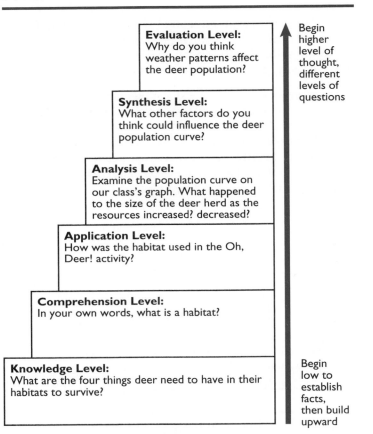

Source: The taxonomy used in this figure originated in Benjamin S. Bloom (ed.), *Taxonomy of Educational Objectives, the Classification of Educational Goals, Handbook I: Cognitive Domain* (New York: Longman, 1956).

- *Synthesis-level* questions stimulate children to consider variety, new ideas, or original possibilities.
- *Evaluation-level* questions require children to make choices and provide reasons.

Educators often disagree about the level at which a question is written. This can make Bloom's taxonomy difficult to use, but it is worth learning. Spreading your questions across the taxonomy's range can make you a more effective teacher.

Gallagher and Aschner offer a simple and useful method for classifying questions.[38] This method has four types of questions that address all of Bloom's levels and incorporate the science processes. The simplicity of this method makes

TABLE 6.2 Levels of Thinking Questions Require

Question Type	Level	Type of Thinking Expected
Closed Questions	Low	Cognitive memory operations Convergent operations
Open Questions	High	Divergent thinking operations Evaluative thinking operations

Source: A comparison of Gallagher and Aschner's questions as adapted from Patricia Blosser, *How to Ask the Right Questions* (Washington, DC: National Science Teachers Association, 1991), p. 4.

it useful for all subject areas. Table 6.2 provides a level-of-thinking context, and Figure 6.6 provides examples of the following kinds of questions:

- *Cognitive memory questions* require students to recall facts, formulas, procedures, and other essential information. This is similar to Bloom's knowledge and comprehension levels and helps students establish the facts before moving toward higher levels. Memory questions also assist observations and communication.
- *Convergent thinking questions* cause students to apply and analyze information. To do this successfully, children must have a command of cognitive memory types of information. Convergent questions assist in problem solving and are useful for the basic science processes: measuring, communicating, comparing, and contrasting.
- *Divergent thinking questions* stimulate children to think independently. Students are given little teacher structure or prior information; they are encouraged to do possibility thinking by combining original and known ideas into new ideas or explanations. Questions of this type require synthesis thinking and promote creative problem solving and the integrated science processes (hypothesizing and experimenting).
- *Evaluative thinking questions* cause students to choose, judge, value, criticize, defend, or justify. Often the simple question "Why?" or "How?" propels thinking to this level after students are asked simple choice or yes-no types of questions. Processes stimulated by evaluation questions include making predictions, reaching conclusions, and forming generalizations.

Science for many children, unfortunately, may be an exercise in closed thinking, in which memory and convergent questions are emphasized. Children are prodded to seek the so-called right answer or verify the correct results. Teachers should use both open and closed types of questions. Open questions are those that encourage divergent and evaluative thinking processes. Because they are traditional and expedient, closed questions have been used by most teachers. Yet there is a danger associated with overuse of closed questions. "Convergent questions

FIGURE 6.6   Composing the Correct Level of Question: Higher Levels of Thought

QUESTION CATEGORY			SAMPLE QUESTION PHASES
Evaluative Thinking	**Bloom's Evaluation Level:** • Make choices • Form values • Overlap critiques, judgments, defenses	**How and Why Reasonings:** • Choose, appraise, select, evaluate, judge, assess, defend, justify • Form conclusions and generalizations	• *What do you favor...?* • *What is your feeling about...?* • *What is your reason for...?*
Divergent Thinking	**Bloom's Synthesis Level:** • Develop own ideas and information • Integrate own ideas • Plan, construct, or reconstruct	**Open-ended Questions for Problem Posing and Action:** • Infer, predict, design, invent • Hypothesize and experiment • Communicate ideas	• *What do you think...?* • *What could you do...?* • *How could you design...?* • *What do you think will happen if...?*
Convergent Thinking	**Bloom's Application and Analysis Level:** • Uses of logic • Deductive and inductive reasoning • Construct or reconstruct	**Closed Questions to:** • Focus attention, guide, encourage measurement and counting, make comparisons, take action • Use logic, state relationships • Apply solutions • Solve problems • Hypothesize and experiment • Communicate ideas	• *If "A", then what will happen to "B"...?* • *Which are facts, opinions and inferences...?* • *What is the author's purpose...?* • *What is the relationship of "x" to "y"...?*
Cognitive Memory	**Bloom's Knowledge and Comprehension Level:** • Rote memorization • Selective recall of facts, formulas, instructions, rules, or procedures • Recognition	**Managerial and Rhetorical Questions:** • Simple attention focusing, yes-no responses **Information:** • Repeat, name, describe, identify, observe, simple explanation, compare	• *What is the definition of...?* • *What are the three steps in...?* • *Who discovered...?* • *In your own words, what is the meaning of...?*
Intended mental activity →			Key function or science processes ←

sacrifice the potential for many students to be rewarded for good answers, since their focus is a search for one right or best answer."[39] Because science is a creative process, much more divergent thinking must be encouraged. Try your hand at classifying convergent and divergent questions in Exercise 6.2, and experiment with both while you teach. Be advised that there are risks for teachers who use divergent or open-ended questions.

> The risks for the teachers who practice divergent question-asking should not be underestimated: an open-ended question can alter the day's schedule, spark discussion on topics the teacher may not be prepared for, and shift the teacher's role from guardian of known answers to stimulator of productive (and often surprising) thinking. But they are risks well worth taking.[40]

There are risks associated with using *any* type of question. What can you do to limit the risks? How can you learn to use questions more effectively?

WHAT ARE THE KEYS TO EFFECTIVE QUESTIONING?

Plan specific questions.[41] Take the time to write specific questions before you teach. List six to eight key questions that cover the levels of thinking you wish to promote, and then use the questions as a guide for what you teach. The questions should help establish the knowledge base of information and then help build toward higher levels. Avoid yes-no questions unless that is your specific purpose; instead, focus the questions on the lesson topic by building toward the objectives. Open-ended questions can stimulate exploration, and convergent questions can focus concept invention. Both, along with evaluation questions, can contribute to expansion of the lesson's main idea. Pay attention to the types of questions used in children's books, and then select books and materials with many different types and supplement with your own questions for special purposes.

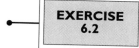

**EXERCISE
6.2**

Identifying Convergent and Divergent Questions

Convergent questions mean to elicit the single best answer, while divergent questions encourage a wide range of answers without concern for a single correct answer. Use the letters C and D to classify the following questions:

_____ 1. What kinds of food make your mouth water?

_____ 2. What name do we call the spit in your mouth?

_____ 3. What is another name for your esophagus?

_____ 4. How many intestines does your body have?

_____ 5. How many weights do you think you can add to your structure before it falls down?

_____ 6. Are you kept warm by radiation, conduc-

tion, convection, or all three?

_____ 7. Why does sound travel faster through solids and liquids than it does through air?

_____ 8. What kinds of uses does a balloon have?

_____ 9. How does electricity work?

_____ 10. How do you use electricity?

Check your answers with those at the end of the chapter. How well do we agree? What makes it difficult for you to classify questions?

See page 187 for answers to Exercise 6.2.

Ask your questions as simply, concisely, and directly as possible. Make your purpose clear, and use single questions. Build upon previous questions once they have been answered, and avoid multiple, piggy-backed questions. These confuse children and indicate that the question is not well defined in the teacher's mind.

Ask your question before selecting who should answer. This helps keep all children listening and thinking. Pause briefly after asking the question so all children can think about it. Then select an individual to respond. Give both high and low achievers a chance to answer, and try to provide equal and genuine feedback. Involve as many different types of children as possible, volunteers and nonvolunteers as well. A total class shouting out answers could create discipline problems. Limit rapid-fire, drill-and-practice questions to times when specific facts need to be gathered or reviewed. Avoid parroting the students' answers, but do try to use the students' ideas as much as possible.

Practice using wait-time. Wait-time 1 is often one second or less. Practice waiting at least three seconds for students to respond to most questions, especially if students are exploring or trying to expand upon the lesson's main idea. Wait-time gives the children opportunities to think, create, and demonstrate more fully what they understand. Higher-level questions may require a wait-time longer than three seconds.

Wait-time 2 may need to be longer than wait-time 1. Mary Budd Rowe believes this wait-time is more important, especially when the occasion calls for critical or creative thinking. Quality and quantity of student responses increase, low achievers respond more, and the teacher has more time to think carefully about the questioning sequence.

Listen carefully to your students' responses. Encourage students nonverbally and verbally without overkilling with praise. Make any praise or encouraging remarks genuine. Check to make certain the children's responses match the level intended by your questions, and prompt them if the level is not appropriate. Do not always stop with the right answer: Probing benefits students who are partially correct and helps them construct a more acceptable answer. As a general rule, do not move on to another student before giving the first student a chance to form a better answer. This is a great opportunity to gather clues about students' misconceptions, incomplete information, or limited experiences. A brief questioning sequence may be all that is needed to overcome important learning problems.

Try using more questions to produce conceptual conflict. Piaget's research suggests that learners should be in a state of mental disequilibrium to help them adapt or add new mental constructions to their thinking.

What do you think will happen if . . . ?

If this happened to *x*, then what could happen to *y*?

How would you . . . ?

What evidence do you have to support . . . ?

What other ways are possible to . . . ?

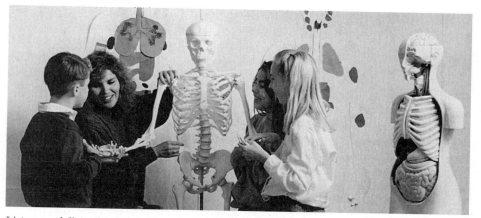

Listen carefully, ask concise, direct questions, practice wait-time, and match the level of the questions to the level of the child.

How can you explain . . . ?

What do you think causes . . . ?

Talk less and ask more, but make your questions count. Ask, don't tell. Use questions to guide and invite your students to tell you. Work with students by exchanging ideas instead of conducting an inquisition. Try to make discussions more conversational by asking students to share thoughts and react to each other.

Try to use questions that yield more complete and more complex responses. Given consistently adequate wait-time, students should give longer and more thoughtful answers. The effectiveness of any specific question you use is never any greater than the answer you are willing to accept. Establish a base of information first; then build on it by asking questions that require more complex answers. Ask students who give short, incomplete answers to contribute more.

Ask different types of questions to encourage all children. Some children seem unprepared for or incapable of answering high-level questions. If this is the case, try beginning your questions at a low level before attempting a higher level; build upward. Recalling information with frequent low-level questions for review, recitation, and drill helps children experience success, develop confidence, and establish a reliable foundation to build higher thinking upon. But do not let your questioning stagnate. Begin with closed questions to establish a firm footing and then move on to more open-ended questions. Use divergent and evaluative questions less often initially, and increase their use over time if your students have difficulty responding as you desire.

Children who have already had more successful and satisfying school experiences are eager and appear more capable of responding to higher levels of questions sooner. Reflective discussions that mix convergent, divergent, and evaluative questions can form a strategy for critical and original thinking. Yet despite the type of student, several studies show that lower-level questions promote greater achievement gains for all primary children when learning basic skills.

Several learning theorists and researchers remind us about differences in how primary and upper elementary children think. Each group processes information differently because of differences in mental development. Yet appropriate experiences can help mental development reach its full potential. Questions related to the processes of science provide the momentum for this development.

For younger children in primary grades (ages 5 to 10), use questions to stimulate

- observation of basic properties,
- classification based on similarities and differences,
- communication to show thoughts and increase the value of the experience as well as to develop cooperation and interpersonal relations,
- measurement, using numbers and time,
- prediction to form guesses based on what is known,
- inferences for attempting explanations and expanding thinking.

For older children in upper elementary grades (ages beyond 11), use questions that will help them

- identify and control variables,
- form operational definitions based on verified information,
- form and test hypotheses to reach conclusions,
- experiment to test ideas and eliminate guesses and inferences,
- interpret data from experiments,
- form models to explain occurrences or represent theories.

Finally, determine whether the children are providing answers equal to the level of your questions. To do this you will need to monitor your questions and your students' responses.

HOW CAN YOU IMPROVE YOUR QUESTIONING?

You can improve your questioning with training and practice. One way to improve is to videotape or tape-record a lesson in which you use questions, play back the recording, identify the questions, and analyze them. Observation instruments or checklists such as those in Table 6.3 can be used. A more informative approach is to structure your observation and analysis around your questions. For example:

- How often did you use cognitive memory questions?
- How does this amount compare to your uses of convergent, divergent, and evaluative questions?
- How are your questions phrased? Do you avoid yes-no questions as much as possible?

- How do you know your questions are on the appropriate level for your students?
- What evidence did you find indicating that you adjust questions to the language and ability levels of the children?
- Are your questions distributed among all children regardless of ability, gender, socioeconomic status, and where they are seated?
- How often do you call on nonvolunteers? How do you decide which nonvolunteer to call upon?
- How often do you use probing to encourage students to complete responses, clarify, expand, or support a decision?
- How long do you wait? How do you use wait-time? What benefits do you receive from using wait-time? How does your use of wait-time 1 compare with wait-time 2?
- How well do the written questions on your plan match the verbal questions you use in class? Do your test questions represent the same levels as questions used in class?
- How often do children ask questions? What types of questions do they ask? Under what circumstances do they ask questions?

TABLE 6.3   Effective Questioning Checklist

Do you

_____ 1. use broad or narrow questions to accomplish your objectives?
_____ 2. avoid yes-no questions unless that is your intention?
_____ 3. avoid repeating student answers?
_____ 4. encourage students to ask questions?
_____ 5. expand on students' ideas?
_____ 6. not stop the discussion after receiving the right answer?
_____ 7. use wait-times of at least three seconds?
_____ 8. avoid asking multiple questions?
_____ 9. avoid answering your own questions?
_____ 10. ask students to clarify, summarize, and review material?
_____ 11. avoid repeating your questions?
_____ 12. rephrase misunderstood or unclear questions?
_____ 13. call on volunteers and nonvolunteers?
_____ 14. ask questions at different levels?
_____ 15. talk less and ask more?
_____ 16. use good grammar on a level understood by the children?
_____ 17. encourage student-to-student discussion?
_____ 18. not use questions to punish or embarrass students?

Source: Adapted from Iva D. Brown, "Topic 4: Teacher Questioning Techniques," *Staff Development Project—Science Grades K–6* (Jackson, MS: Mississippi Association for Teacher Education, 1986), ERIC Document no. ED 285726, p. 159.

WHY USE CHILDREN'S QUESTIONS?

The children's questions worry me. I can deal with the child who just wants attention, but because I've had no science background I take other questions at face value and get bothered when I don't know the answer. I don't mind saying I don't know, though I don't want to do it too often. I've tried the let's-find-out-together approach, but it's not easy and can be very frustrating.[42]

Why Bother with Children's Questions?

"Can one black hole swallow another?"
"Why do fireflies light up?"
"How does a steel ship float when it weighs so much?"
"Why are soda cans shaped like a cylinder and not a rectangle?"[43]

Children's questions give precious insight into their world and illustrate topics of interest. Their questions can surprise teachers who might underestimate the ability of particular children and may suggest that certain children have more ability than is evident from their reading and written work. The questions children ask also give a guide to what they know and don't know, and when they want to know it. These questions give clues about what science content is understood and the level of concept development—if we are willing to listen closely. Questions could also indicate an anxious child, or simply reveal a habit formed by one who has been reinforced to ask questions.[44]

Children's questions can be used to develop interesting problems for science inquiry and to encourage the useful habit of reflection.

Questions help children focus and gain knowledge that interests them. Incessant "Why?" questions can be a method of gaining attention, but unlike the 2-year-old, the school age child who asks "Why?" reveals an area where understanding is lacking and is desired. Questions help young children resolve unexpected outcomes or work through problem situations; they can also be a way of confirming a belief. Children's questions also help them learn more quickly. "When they are following their own noses, learning what they are curious about, children go faster, cover more territory than we would ever think of trying to mark out for them, or make them cover."[45]

Encouraging children to ask questions develops a useful habit: reflection. Habits take time to form, and question-asking is a habit that can enrich a school's curriculum. Time spent in contemplation helps form this habit. Asking oneself questions and hazarding guesses about their answers stimulate creative thinking, provide a means for solving critical problems, and can help a child learn "to find interest and enjoyment in situations that others would see as dull or boring."[46]

How Can You Stimulate Children's Questions?

Four factors stimulate children to ask questions. If you want children to ask more questions, you should provide adequate stimulation, model appropriate question asking, develop a classroom atmosphere that values questions, and include question asking in your evaluations of children.

Stimulation.   Direct contact with materials is a first step. What kinds of materials stimulate curiosity in children and provide them opportunities to explore? The best indicator is the materials children bring in spontaneously. The children's sharing has a built-in curiosity factor and requires little effort to conduct discussion; simply invite them to share and ask questions. The mind *will* be on what the hands are doing.

Modeling.   Teacher question asking is modeling. Children must be shown how to ask good, productive questions. Showing genuine enthusiasm and consideration for what interests others can show children how to do the same. Consider some of the following as ways to bring this modeling into the routine of your classroom.[47]

Share collections and develop classroom displays, much as Mrs. B did in our opening scenario. Link these activities to regular classwork and organize them around key questions. Use one of the question classification systems described earlier in this chapter to help you ask questions at many different levels. Invite children to share their own collections and create class displays while building questions into the discussion the children share with classmates.

Establish a problem corner in your classroom or use a "Question of the Week" approach to stimulate children's thought and questions. These approaches can be part of regular class activity or used for enrichment. Catherine Valentino's Question of the Week materials could be a good place to start until you acquire enough ideas of your own. Consider one of her examples, "I Lava Volcano," a photo of an erupting volcano, which asks these questions: "Do volcanic eruptions serve any useful purpose? Over millions of years, what changes would occur on the earth if all volcanic activity suddenly stopped?"[48] Valentino's full-color weekly posters and questions stimulate curiosity and inquiry. The materials are published by Dale Seymour Publications.

TEACHERS ON SCIENCE TEACHING

How Do Questions Create Independent Thinkers?

By Ursula M. Sexton
Grades 1–5, Green Valley Elementary School, Danville, CA

I moved away from pouring information, most of which students forgot, to facilitating discussions, providing opportunities for explorations and ways to assess our progress and goals. I guess you could say I've gone from being an informational witness to becoming a thinking coach.

I am now defining my teacher role as one who provides the means for my students to make connections of big ideas; to guide them through process-oriented activities; to demonstrate circumstances that would otherwise be dangerous, foreign, or inaccessible to them; and to be the listener and facilitator. It works best when they are given situations, open-ended explorations, dynamic roles, and the tools or options to build, to research, to communicate, and to share their thinking. I tell my students our most used questions are "Why do you think so?" and "How can you support it?" and "What do you mean by that?" and "How does it work and why?" and "What do you think would happen if. . . ."

Some ideas that foster a climate not only for higher thinking questions and answers, but for inclusion of all students are:

• Set the stage like a mystery scene, in which students are given the clues, and they need to prove that these clues are valid to solve the mystery, or they need to use them to find further clues (process skills). They share with the class their approaches and solutions, back them up, and record them on graphs, videotape, illustrations, journals, or portfolios.

• Provide scenarios to visualize, to make mental images, or think of characteristics by which they could describe an object, animal, plant, place, person, or situation. We make and write brainstorm umbrellas of big ideas for categorization, such as color, weight, time, location, traits, extinct or not, parts, functions, habitats, means of survival, and so on, and hang them around the room for reference.

• Give plenty of opportunities and different materials and means to classify and label their sorting. This one is especially dear to me, because it was my wake-up call to learn to encourage and understand the children's thinking. One day my little first-grade scientists were reviewing the process of classification by sorting ourselves into three groups. Silently I would point to a child and direct him or her to an assigned area in the classroom, within clear sight of the rest of the class. To play, they could not call out the answer to the rule or pattern being sorted, but had to point to the team they thought they belonged to, once they studied it and recognized the rule. If they were correct, they would stand with the team. If not, they would remain seated for a later turn. At the end, everyone was standing in one of the teams. As I inquired what their team characteristic or pattern was, most children called out what I, as the chooser, had thought for the rule. "We all have turtlenecks," called one. "We all have collars," said the others. Finally, in the third team,

Prepare lists of questions to investigate with popular children's books. Encourage children to add their own questions to the list.

Use questions to organize any teacher-made activity cards that children may use independently. Encourage children to think of their work as an investigative mission and to see themselves as clue seekers.

the speaker said, "We all have jackets." At that moment, one of the girls in the middle team said, "I thought I was here because we all have red and none of the other teams do." Indeed, she was right! So I decided to capitalize on the thought and asked the rest of the class, "Can you think of any other ways by which we all might be sorted while in the teams we are now?" Oh! it was just wonderful to hear their reasoning! They were very proud of themselves. These are the circumstances that teachers need to act upon repeatedly throughout the day and not in isolated instances. Becoming aware of them takes a little self-training and practice.

- "What ifs. . . ?" are just wonderful, open-ended questions that can be connected to real-life circumstances.
- Have a discovery corner with manipulatives and questions promoting scientific processes.
- Have the children design new questions to go along with the discovery corner boards for another class to try out.

One of the most important elements of science instruction is the teacher's attitude toward science. Your own attitude toward learning will be the underlying gift you pass on to your kids. If and when you need to be the guide, do it with enthusiasm. Facilitate in a motivating, nonthreatening, and enthusiastic manner. If you were asked to write a newspaper advertisement for a science classroom guide and facilitator, what would you write? Check how this description matches the way you teach in the classroom. Take notes on your style if you need to focus more in this direction. You'll probably be pleasantly surprised to see how much you really do to foster the children's previous knowledge and their questions. When you introduce new concepts, ask yourself, "New to whom? to a few? how new? new to me? What questions might they have that will definitely show growth when we are done learning about it? What am I learning from this process?" Listen to their discussions and their questions; take notes. Make comments, bring out onto the light awesome and small achievements, discoveries, questions that foster further questioning. With ownership of their thinking processes, they'll become independent thinkers. For assessment, remember that tests are merely a reflection and a tool to tell how well you've conveyed a message and how well they have received it. That is why assessment should be ongoing, by observation, cooperation, participation, and communication.

I have learned so much from my students' attitudes about learning, their questions, their inquisitiveness or lack of it, and their experiences. The gifts they bring on their own are assets to all. It is because of them that I enjoy teaching. They challenge me on a daily basis. I grow with them on a daily basis.

Classroom Atmosphere.   Richard Suchman believes children inquire only when they feel free to share their ideas without fear of being censored, criticized, or ridiculed.[49] Successful teachers listen to children and do not belittle their curious questions. Establish an atmosphere that fosters curiosity by praising those who invent good questions; reinforce their reflective habits. You can provide opportunities for questions by:

- using class time regularly for sharing ideas and asking questions as children talk about something that interests them,
- having children supply questions of the week and rewarding them for improvements in their question asking,
- helping children write lists (or record lists for nonreaders) of questions they have about something they have studied. These questions can be excellent means for

FIGURE 6.7   How Should You Respond to Children's Questions?

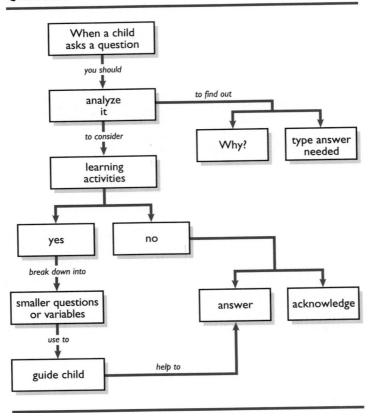

review, for showing further interest, and for providing an informal evaluation of how clearly you have taught a topic.

Question Asking and Evaluation. Have children form questions as another way of evaluating their learning. This factor can stimulate habits of question asking and is different than if you, as teacher, ask questions children must answer. Include a picture or description of a situation in a test occasionally, and call for children to write productive questions about it. In another approach, the children list questions they believe are important for a more complete understanding of the material they have just studied. Lists of children's questions can be evaluated for the number and the quality of the questions; quality should refer to the relevance of the question to the topic as well as the thought required to answer it.

How Can You Use Children's Questions Productively?

When children ask, focus your listening on the ideas represented by their questions. You will need to help them clarify their questions until they learn to ask better ones by themselves. Sheila Jelly[50] offers a strategy you can use to turn children's questions into productive learning opportunities. Figure 6.7 is based on Jelly's recommendations.

CHAPTER SUMMARY

If there is a universal teaching tool, the question is it. Questions provide unique opportunties for teachers and students to become involved in productive dialogue; questions invite both teachers and children to think and respond in many different ways.

We know that the potential of questioning is underused and that many teacher questions are closed and stimulate low-level thinking. Questions may be misused if the wrong types of questions are used before children are capable or ready to respond at the level demanded. Appropriate questions stimulate productive thinking and curiosity. Effective questions contribute to children's improved attitudes, expanded capability for thinking, and increased achievement.

As teachers, we need to afford all children equal opportunities to learn through our questioning techniques. Old habits may have to be changed. We must strive to give children adequate time to think by expanding wait-time; screen textbooks,

tests, and other print materials for evidence of good questions; and help children develop the habit of reflecting by encouraging them to ask their own questions.

All questions are not equal; they come in such different types as Bloom's taxonomy, open/closed, science processes, memory, and evaluation. Questions should be selected or composed for specific purposes.

You can question well by using the keys for good questioning described in this chapter. Periodically analyze how you use questions and form a plan for self-improvement. Check your skills against your plan and revise as necessary.

Children's questions provide benefits for teachers, children, and the science program. Teachers can encourage children's questions if they use materials and activities that simulate questions, model good questioning skills, provide a supportive classroom atmosphere, and include children's question asking in evaluation techniques.

DISCUSSION QUESTIONS AND PROJECTS

1. Based upon your school experiences, what differences have you noticed about how your teachers used questions? How do your elementary, secondary, and college teachers compare on using questions?

2. What types of questions do your teachers usually ask? How well do the questions match with the teachers' intentions? Justify your answer.

3. How do the elementary teachers you have observed use questions to begin a lesson? to focus children's observations? to lead children toward conclusions? to bring closure to a lesson?

4. What priority do you believe teachers should give to children's questions? What strategy should they use?

5. How important is it for teachers to monitor their own uses of questions?

6. How well do you use questions? What evidence do you have to support your answer? What do you think you can do to improve your questioning skills? Audio- or videotape yourself using questions when you practice teaching. Use the recommendations of this chapter to focus an evaluation of your questioning skills, and begin by comparing the numbers of closed and open questions you use.

7. Using any of the methods for classifying questions described in this chapter, write and label samples of two questions for each level. Work within class groups to evaluate the quality of the questions. How well do you avoid yes-no questions, require more than rote memory, and avoid unproductive questions?

8. Use several of the questions you have written to speculate about pupil replies and appropriate teacher responses. List the questions and the replies for the pupil and teacher.

9. Observe a science lesson. Record the number and types of questions asked by the teacher and try to measure the average wait-time. How do your observations correspond to the average uses of questions and wait-time described in this chapter?

10. Tape record a class session in which children ask questions. Transcribe these questions and describe how you could respond to them if you were the teacher. How does your response method compare with Sheila Jelly's suggestion?

NOTES

1. L. B. Gambrell, "The Occurrence of Think-Time During Reading Comprehension," *Journal of Educational Research*, 75 (1983), pp. 144–148.

2. T. Levin and R. Long, *Effective Instruction* (Washington, DC: Association for Supervision and Curriculum Development, 1981).

3. Ralph Martin, George Wood, and Edward Stevens, *An Introduction to Teaching: A Question of Commitment* (Boston: Allyn and Bacon, 1988).

4. Ibid., p. 357.

5. Mary Budd Rowe, *Teaching Science as Continuous Inquiry* (New York: McGraw-Hill, 1973), pp. 337–338.

6. William Wilen, *Questioning Skills for Teachers* (Washington, DC: National Education Association, 1986), p. 22.

7. Ibid., p. 21.

8. Hilda Taba, S. Levine, and F. F. Elsey, *Thinking in Elementary School Children*, U.S. Office of Education Cooperative Research Project No. 1574 (San Francisco: San Francisco State College, 1964).

9. D. S. Arnold, R. K. Atwood, and U. M. Rogers, "An Investigation of the Relationships Among Question Level, Response Level, and Lapse Time," *School Science and Mathematics*, 73 (October 1973), pp. 591–595.

10. J. J. Gallagher and M. J. Aschner, *A Preliminary Report on Analyses of Classroom Interaction*, pp. 183–195.

11. Francis P. Hunkins, "Analysis and Evaluation Questions: Their Effects Upon Critical Thinking," *Educational Leadership*, 27 (1970), pp. 697–705.

12. Dorothy Alfke, "Asking Operational Questions," *Science and Children* (April 1974), pp. 18–19.

13. Barry J. Zimmerman and Early O. Pike, "Effects of Modeling and Reinforcement on the Acquisition and Generalization of Question-Asking Behavior," *Child Development*, 43 (1972), pp. 892–907.

14. Iva D. Brown, "Topic 4: Teacher Questioning Techniques," *Staff Development Project—Science Grades K–6* (Jackson, MS: Mississippi Association for Teacher Education, 1986, ERIC Document no. ED 285726), p. 152.

15. Kenneth G. Tobin and William Capie, "Wait-Time and Learning in Science," *AETS Outstanding Paper for 1981* (ERIC Document no. 221353, 1982), p. 3.

16. Ted Bredderman, "Activity Science—The Evidence Shows It Matters," *Science and Children* (September 1982), pp. 39–41.

17. E. Z. Rothkopf, "Variable Adjunct Question Schedules, Interperson Interaction, and Incidental Learning from Written Material," *Journal of Educational Psychology* 63 (April 1972), pp. 87–92; and O.D. Hargie, "The Importance of Teacher Questions in the Classroom," *Educational Research* 20 (February 1978), pp. 99–102.

18. Barak Rosenshine, "Classroom Instruction," in W.L. Gage (ed.), *The Psychology of Teaching Methods* (Chicago: University of Chicago Press, 1976).

19. Barak Rosenshine, "Content, Time, and Direct Instruction," in Penelope L. Peterson and Herbert L. Walberg (eds.), *Research on Teaching: Concepts, Findings, and Implications* (Berkeley, CA: McCutcheon, 1979).

20. Kenneth Tobin, "Effects of Extended Wait-Time on Discourse Characteristics and Achievement in Middle School Grades," *Journal of Research in Science Teaching*, 21, 8 (1984), pp. 779–791.

21. Joseph P. Riley II, "The Effects of Teachers' Wait-Time and Knowledge Comprehension Questioning on Science Achievement," *Journal of Research in Science Teaching*, 23, 4 (1986), pp. 335–342.

22. Ted Bredderman, "The Influence of Activity-Based Elementary Science Programs on Classroom Practices: A Quantitative Synthesis," *Journal of Research in Science Teaching* 21, 3 (1984), pp. 289–303.

23. N. E. Kroot, "An Analysis of the Responses of Four, Six, and Eight Year Old Children to Four Kinds of Questions" (Doctoral dissertation, Indiana University, 1976); J.J. Koran and J.L. Koran, "Validating a Teacher Behavior by Student Performance" (Tallahassee, FL: Florida State Department of Education Report no. FSDE–730–063, 1973).

24. Carol P. Barnes, "Questioning Strategies to Develop Critical Thinking Skills" (ERIC Document no. 169486, 1978).

25. Los Angeles Unified School District, title IV-D, "Effects of Teacher Expectation on Student Learning Project," *The Reflector* (Los Angeles, CA: Unified School District Office of Instruction, December, 1977), 7.

26. Mary Budd Rowe, "Wait-Time and Rewards as Instructional Variables, Their Influence on Language, Logic and Fate Control: Part One—Wait-Time," *Journal of Research in Science Teaching* (vol. 11, 1974), pp. 263–279.

27. Riley, p. 335.

28. Tobin, p. 779.

29. Riley, p. 335.

30. Tobin and Capie, p. 3.

31. Mary Budd Rowe, "Wait-Time and Rewards as Instructional Variables: Influence on Inquiry and Sense of Fate Control," *New Science in the Inner City* (New York: Teachers College, Columbia University, September, 1970).

32. William J. Bennett, *What Works* (Washington, DC: U.S. Department of Education, 1986), p. 38.

33. J. E. Habecker, *An Analysis of Reading Questions in Basal Reading Series Based on Bloom's Taxonomy* (Doctoral dissertation, University of Pennsylvania, 1976).

34. Gregory P. Risner, "Cognitive Levels of Questioning Demonstrated by Test Items that Accompany Selected Fifth-Grade Science Textbooks" (ERIC Document no. 291752, 1987).

35. Mary Jo Puckett Cliatt and Jean M. Shaw, "Open Questions, Open Answers," *Science and Children* (November/December, 1985), pp. 14–16.

36. Jos Elstgeest, "The Right Question at the Right Time," in Wynne Harlen (ed.), *Primary Science: Taking the Plunge* (London: Heinemann Educational Books, 1985), p. 37.

37. Ibid., pp. 36–37.

38. J. J. Gallagher and M. J. Aschner, "A Preliminary Report on Analyses of Classroom Interaction," *Merrill-Palmer Quarterly* 9 (1963), pp. 183–195.

39. Carol L. Schlichter, "The Answer Is in the Question," *Science and Children* (February 1983), p. 10.

40. Ibid.

41. This section is based on the work of Iva D. Brown, "Topic 4: Teacher Questioning Techniques," *Staff Development Project—Science Grades K–6* (Jackson, MS: Mississippi Association for Teacher Education, 1986, ERIC Document no. ED 285726), pp. 156–158; and William W. Wilen and Ambrose A. Clegg, Jr., "Effective Questions and Questioning: A Research Review," *Theory and Research in Social Education* (vol. XIV, no. 2, Spring 1986), pp. 153–161.

42. Sheila Jelly, "Helping Children Raise Questions—And Answering Them," in Wynne Harlen (ed.), *Primary Science: Taking the Plunge* (London: Heinemann Educational Books, 1985), p. 54.

43. Susan Pearlman and Kathleen Pericak-Spector, "Expect the Unexpected Question," *Science and Children* (October 1992), pp. 36–37.

44. Fred Biddulph, David Symington, and Roger Osborn, "The Place of Children's Questions in Primary Science Education," *Research in Science and Technological Education* 4 (1986, 1), pp. 77–78.

45. John Holt, *How Children Learn* (London: Penguin Press, 1971), p. 152.

46. Biddulph et al., p. 78.

47. Jelly, p. 51. Ideas are paraphrased from this source.

48. Catherine Valentino, *Question of the Week* (Palo Alto, CA: Dale Seymore Publications, 1985), Question 5.

49. J. Richard Suchman, "Motivation Inherent in the Pursuit of Meaning: Or the Desire to Inquire," in H. I. Day, D. E. Berlyne, and D. E. Hunt (eds.), *Intrinsic Motivation: A New Direction in Education* (Toronto: Holt, Rinehart & Winston, 1971).

50. Jelly, p. 55.

ADDITIONAL READINGS

If you are interested in learning more about some of the topics raised in this chapter consider the following sources.

J. T. Dillon, *Questioning and Teaching: A Manual of Practice* (New York: Teachers College Press, 1988).

Dillon's manual focuses on skill development. Chapters are devoted to student questions and teacher questions, with particular emphasis given to questions used with recitation and discussion. A lengthy appendix provides classroom transcripts, which are useful for seeing concrete relationships between the pedagogy and effects of questioning.

William W. Wilen (ed.), *Questions, Questioning Techniques, and Effective Teaching* (Washington, DC: National Education Association, 1987). This source provides some of the most extensive coverage on questioning we have seen in one book. This collection provides a rationale for using questions, a review of the years of research on questioning, and information on the multiple uses of questions. Question classification, wait-time, effective question uses, and students as question askers are covered. A chapter is also devoted to improving teacher's questions.

Arthur Carin and Robert B. Sund, *Creative Questioning and Sensitive Listening Techniques—A Self-Concept Approach* (Columbus, OH: Merrill Publishing, 1978). This is an authoritative text for increasing your questioning skills in a unique way. The end product of effect questioning, according to the authors, is improving children's self-concepts. Many practical examples are given.

Patricia Blosser, *How to Ask the Right Questions* (Washington, DC: National Science Teachers Association, 1991). This booklet includes questions for science, discusses the value of science, describes important factors relevant to questioning, and provides descriptions of techniques you can use to analyze your questioning style.

Susan Pearlman and Kathleen Pericak-Spector, "Expect the Unexpected Question," *Science and Children*, October 1992. This article provides a brief list of children's amazing questions. Sources they recommend for finding the answers include B. Ardley, *The Random House Book of 1001 Questions and Answers* (New York: Random House, 1989); D. McCaulay, *The Way Things Work* (New York: Houghton Mifflin, 1988); J. Makower, *The Air and Space Catalog* (New York: Tilden, 1987); S. Parker, *McGraw-Hill Encyclopedia of Science and Technology* (vols. 1–20), (New York: McGraw-Hill, 1987); and R. H. Wynne, *Lizards in Captivity* (Neptune, NJ: T. F. H. Publications, 1981).

ANSWERS TO EXERCISE 6.1

1. Observing
2. Hypothesizing/experimenting
3. Generalizing/predicting
4. Observing
5. Communicating
6. Measuring
7. Hypothesizing/experimenting
8. Comparing/contrasting
9. Generalizing/predicting
10. Measuring

Questions come from the following sources:

1. Seymour Simon, *Exploring Fields and Lots: Easy Science Projects* (Champaign, IL: Garrard Publishing, 1978).

2. Jeanne Bendick, *How to Make a Cloud* (New York: Parents' Magazine Press, 1971).

3. Seymour Simon, *Science in a Vacant Lot* (New York: Viking Press, 1970).

4. Bernie Zubrowski, *Bubbles: A Children's Museum Activity Book* (Boston: Little, Brown, 1979).

5. Seymour Simon, *Exploring Fields and Lots: Easy Science Projects* (Champaign, IL: Garrard Publishing, 1978).

6. Al G. Renner, *Experimental Fun with the Yo-Yo and Other Scientific Projects* (New York: Dodd, Mead, 1979).

7. Harry Milgrom, *Adventures with a Straw: First Experiments* (New York: E. P. Dutton, 1976).

8. Millicent E. Selsam, *Play with Seeds* (New York: William Morrow, 1957).

9. Seymour Simon, *Discovering What Frogs Do* (New York: McGraw-Hill, 1969).

10. Bernie Zubrowski, *Messing Around with Baking Chemistry: A Children's Museum Activity Book* (Boston: Little, Brown, 1981).

ANSWERS TO EXERCISE 6.2

1. Divergent, because *how* many different kinds of food make *your* mouth water?
2. Convergent, saliva.
3. Convergent, gullet.
4. Convergent, small and large intestines.
5. Divergent, because this question asks for a prediction that depends on several factors that stimulate many different answers.
6. Convergent, because you are asked to select an answer from those given.
7. Convergent, because a specific concept is used to answer the question.
8. Divergent, because who knows the answer to this one? Only your imagination limits the possibilities.
9. Convergent, because descriptions about electron flow rely on a specific concept.
10. Divergent. Think about it: How many *different* ways do you use or depend on electricity?

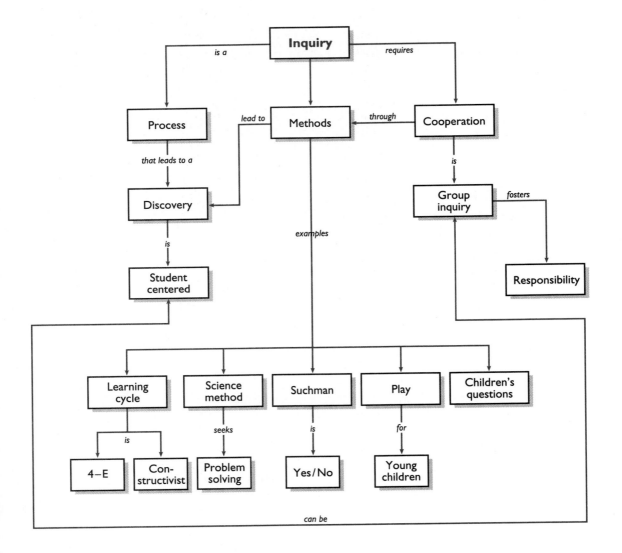

7

How Can You Use Cooperative Inquiry Science Teaching Methods?

Mrs. McDonald has loved science since she was very young.[1] She communicates this love to her students through her enthusiasm for teaching science. Her third-grade classroom is an active place to learn. A visitor walking into her room sees no nice, neat rows of student desks; rather, the desks face each other in groups of four. The walls are covered with brightly colored posters of the Young Astronauts Program. The aquariums are located along the back wall, and a gerbil's cage sits near the window.

Today the students are actively involved in making observations. It takes a moment to determine what it is that they are observing, since their heads are pressed closely together in a tight group.

"One, two, three, four, five. There are five crickets."

"No. I counted six. There's one hiding behind the stick."

"Six," says Johnny as he records the number on his worksheet.

"For the past few days we've been observing our terrarium," Mrs. McDonald says. "Can anyone tell me what the plants and animals in our terrarium need to grow?"

"Light."

"Water."

"Air."

"Very good," replies Mrs. McDonald. "Then we added some crickets to the terrariums. You have had a chance to watch the crickets for a couple of days. Today I have something new to add to your terrariums." The children murmured excitedly as Mrs. McDonald reaches into a paper bag and removes a clear plastic bag containing a chameleon.

"What's that?"

"It looks like a lizard."

"We have those in our backyard."

"Does anyone know what I have in this bag?" asks Mrs. McDonald. Several hands are raised. "Brenda."

"It's a chameleon."

"That's right. What do you know about chameleons?"

"They can change colors."

"They eat insects."

"Those are good ideas. I want each group to add a chameleon to your terrarium and observe the chameleon carefully." Mrs. McDonald moves to each group to distribute a plastic bag containing a chameleon.

"How do we get it out?" Mary asks her group.

"Just reach in and grab it."

"Don't squeeze too hard. You'll hurt it!"

After some hesitancy, Peter puts a chameleon into his group's terrarium. At first the chameleon stands still, moving its head from side to side to survey the area. Slowly it begins to move about the terrarium as the children watch, spellbound. Suddenly the chameleon lurches forward and grabs one of the crickets in its jaws.

"Mrs. McDonald! Mrs. McDonald! The chameleon ate one of the crickets."

"Oh, yech!"

"Now there are only five crickets," says Johnny, erasing his previous answer and recording the new number.

After giving the students time to observe the chameleons and the crickets, Mrs. McDonald tells them to return the terrariums to the shelf and requests their attention.

"I would like to teach you two new words," she says, writing the words *predator* and *prey* on the chalkboard. "This word is *predator*. Can you all say that with me?"

"Predator," the class echoes.

"And this word is *prey*. Can you all say that with me?"

"Prey," they respond.

"A predator is an animal that eats another animal. Can you think of any examples of predators?

"The chameleon."

"A lion."

"A hawk."

"Yes, those are all good examples. Prey is an animal that is eaten by a predator. Can you think of any examples of prey?"

"A cricket."

"A mouse."

"A small fish."

"Yes, those are all good examples of prey. Today at recess, we are going to play a game where some of you will be field mice and some of you will be hawks. It's called the Predator-Prey Game."

INTRODUCTION

Mrs. McDonald's method of teaching differs considerably from the norm in elementary science. She shares control, responsibility, and decision making in her classroom, and she uses the science text as a guide. Students learn by inquiring and by making discoveries; they read the text after they have acquired direct experiences with the science topics. Mrs. McDonald's approach involves the students in doing science; her classroom encourages cooperation.

What is the best way to teach science in the elementary school? As is often the case, the answer is not so simple as selecting a single method for all occasions. Yet, effective teachers do have a repertoire of different methods they can draw upon for maximum effect and to fit their preferred teaching styles and student learning styles. To help you expand your repertoire, the purposes of this chapter are to

1. Encourage you to explore teaching methods that use inquiry to promote student discovery and concept constructions,
2. Describe and provide examples of teaching methods that promote student cooperation,
3. Recommend effective inquiry techniques.

WHAT ARE INQUIRY AND DISCOVERY?

An understanding of inquiry and discovery is essential to promoting student discovery and concept construction.

Inquiry

Those who *inquire* exert "an effort to discover something new to the inquirer— though not necessarily new to the world."[2] Children are able to inquire when they are given hands-on learning opportunities, appropriate materials to manipulate,

Inquiry is a means to an end—the discovery.

puzzling circumstances or problems for motivation, enough structure to help them focus or maintain a productive direction, and enough freedom to compare ideas and to make personal learning discoveries. Other definitions may include:

- the process of investigating a problem,
- a search for truth or knowledge that requires thinking critically,
- making observations, asking questions, performing experiments, and stating conclusions,
- thinking creatively and using intuition.[3]

Discovery

Thinking to obtain new knowledge or to solve a problem is the single element that unites the different inquiry methods. If a child is able to "acquire a new fact, concept, principle, or solution through the inquiry, the student is making a discovery."[4] Therefore, the cognitive, affective, and psychomotor processes the child uses become the inquiry. The end result of those processes becomes the *discovery*—the substance of what is learned—what the learner constructs in the mind.

What procedures or approaches can teachers use to help children follow an inquiry learning process and construct meaning? Effective inquiry methods include the science learning cycle, Suchman's inquiry, a scientific inquiry method, playful discovery, and inquiry with children's questions. All of these methods recognize the importance of direct experience and promote it for children.

The Importance of Experience

Traditional textbook-based science programs use an inform-verify-practice approach to learning. The teacher informs or tells the students what they are to learn, the students verify that what they have been told is true, and then they practice what they have been given. This teaching and learning approach is called *teacher-centered exposition*. Experimental studies have shown that this type of learning approach in science is usually less effective than experiential learning methods, in which the instruction is more student centered and oriented toward making discoveries. Inquiry as a learning process promotes higher levels of science achievement, process skills, and attitudes.[5] Inquiry science teaching methods pay useful dividends. For example, the methods have been found to help Spanish-speaking children learn English and develop oral communication skills.[6] They also help children who have learning disabilities that affect their reading to learn to become better readers.[7]

INQUIRY SCIENCE TEACHING METHODS

Inquiry science teaching methods include the science learning cycle, the scientific method, Suchman's Inquiry, and playful science.

The Science Learning Cycle

A learning cycle is a method for planning lessons, teaching, learning, and developing curriculum. This teaching method was originally designed for the SCIS curriculum and has produced the largest achievement gains of the experimental elementary science programs of the 1960s (see Chapter 5). These increases are largely a result of the learning cycle as an inquiry teaching and learning method.

In science, a learning cycle is a way of thinking and acting that is consistent with how pupils learn. It provides an excellent approach for planning effective science instruction. The science learning cycle originally consisted of three phases: exploration, concept invention, and application. With today's goals emphasizing new dimensions of science and accountability, we recommend a 4–E learning cycle: exploration, explanation, expansion, and evaluation. Each phase, when followed in sequence (see Figure 7.1), has sound theoretical support from the cognitive development theory of Jean Piaget,[8] and applies constructivist learning procedures.

FIGURE 7.1   The 4-E Science Learning Cycle

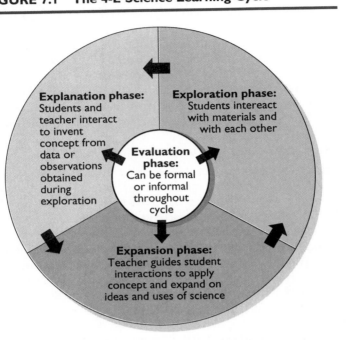

Source: Adapted from a figure by Charles Barman, ''The Learning Cycle: Making It Work,'' *Science Scope*, February 1989, pp. 28–31.

Phase One: Exploration.   The exploration phase is student centered, stimulates learner mental disequilibrium, and fosters mental assimilation. (You might review the section in Chapter 2 devoted to Jean Piaget if these ideas are unclear.) The teacher is responsible for giving students sufficient directions and materials that interact in ways that are related to the concept. The teacher's directions *must not tell* students what they should learn and *must not explain* the concept. The teacher's role is to:

- answer students' questions,
- ask questions to guide student observations and to cause students to engage in science processes or thinking skills (see Figure 7.2),
- give hints and cues to keep the exploration going.

Students are responsible for exploring the materials and for gathering and/or recording their own information. Teachers rely on questioning skills such as those shown in Figure 7.2 to guide learning.

Children must have concrete materials and experiences too if they are to construct science concepts for themselves. Use these guiding questions to help you begin your planning process:

- What is the precise concept the students will explore?
- What activities must the children do to become familiar with the concept?
- What kinds of observations or records should the children keep?
- What kinds of instructions will the children need? How can I give the instructions without telling the concept?

This last question directly transforms into verbal or written instructions you will give the children. Instructions need to direct the children's activities, suggest what kinds of records they should keep, and *not tell or explain the concept*. Instructions may be stated succinctly, perhaps in the form of an objective. What questions will you ask to encourage student exploration?

Phase Two: Explanation.   The explanation phase is less student centered and provides for learner mental accommodation. The purpose of this phase is for teachers to guide student thinking so the concept of the lesson is invented cooperatively, not merely given by the teacher. To accomplish this, the teacher selects and sets the desired class environment. The teacher asks students to give the information they have collected and helps students to process and mentally organize the information. Once the information is organized, the teacher introduces the specific language needed for the concept, much as Mrs. McDonald did *after* the children had observed and explored what happened when a new organism was introduced into their terrariums.

This phase helps to lead to mental accommodation, as described by Piaget's theory. Here students must focus on their primary findings from their firsthand explorations. The teacher must introduce language or concept labels to assist mental accommodation. These questions can help teachers guide students so they form their own explanations of the concept:

- What kinds of information or findings should the students talk about?

FIGURE 7.2   Using Questions During a Learning Cycle

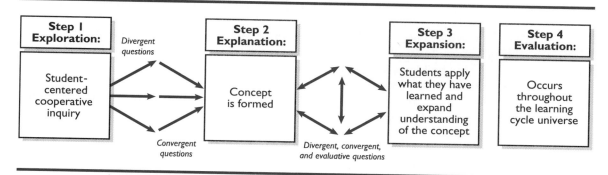

- How can I help students summarize their findings?
- How can I guide the students and refrain from telling them what they should have found, even if their understanding is incomplete? How can I help them use their information to form the concept correctly?
- What concept labels or descriptions should the students discover?
- What reasons can I give the students if they ask me why the concept is important? This question automatically leads to the next phase, expansion.

Phase Three: Expansion.   The expansion phase should be student centered as much as possible and organized to encourage group cooperation. The purpose of this phase is to help learners mentally organize the experiences they have acquired by finding connections to similar previous experiences and to discover new applications for what they have learned. Invented concepts must be linked to other related ideas or experiences. The purpose is to take the students' thinking beyond where it presently is. The teacher must require children to use the language or labels of the new concept so that they add depth to their understanding. This is a proper place to help students apply what they learned by expanding examples or by providing additional exploratory experiences for students' personal development, investigation of science-technology-society interrelationships, academic growth, and career awareness. (See goals in Chapters 3 and 4.) The expansion phase can automatically lead to the exploration phase of the next lesson; hence a continuing cycle for teaching and learning is established. Exhibit 7.1 shows how to do this in a sample lesson plan.

Teachers help students organize their thinking by relating what they have learned to other ideas or experiences that relate to the constructed concept. It is very important to use the language of the concept during this phase to add depth to the concept's meaning and to expand the range of the children's vocabulary. Consider these questions:

- What previous experiences have the children had that relate to the concept? How can I connect the concept to those experiences?
- What are some examples of how the concept encourages the students to see science's benefits? to help them realize the relationships among science, technology, and society? to help them grow academically? to help them be informed about the different careers dependent on science?
- What questions can I ask to encourage students to discover the concept's importance? to apply the concept? to appreciate the problems it solves? to understand the problems it causes? to identify the careers influenced by it?
- What new experiences are needed to apply or expand the concept?
- What is the next concept related to the present one? How can I encourage exploration of the next concept?

Phase Four: Evaluation.   The purpose of this phase is to overcome the limits of standard types of testing. Learning often occurs in small increments before larger mental leaps of insight are possible. Therefore, evaluation should be continuous, not a typical end of chapter or unit approach. Several types of measures are necessary to form a wholistic evaluation of the students' learning and to encourage mental construction of concepts and process skills. Evaluation can be included in each phase of the learning cycle, not just held for the end. Ask yourself:

- What appropriate learning outcomes should I expect?
- What types of hands-on evaluation techniques can the students do to demonstrate the basic skills of observation, classification, communication, measurement, prediction and inference?
- What techniques are appropriate for students to demonstrate the integrated science process skills of identifying and controlling variables, defining operationally, forming hypotheses, experimenting, interpreting data, and forming models?
- How can I use pictures to help students demonstrate how well they can think through problems that require understanding fundamental concepts and the integration of ideas?
- What types of questions can I ask students to help them reflect and to indicate how well they recall and understand what has been learned?

Planning and Teaching Science Learning Cycle Lessons. The four phases of the learning cycle provide most of the structure for planning an effective science lesson. Once the concept that is to be learned has been identified, the learning activity can be structured to take advantage of the learning cycle. Descriptions of ways to evaluate what the children learn also can be added. Part IV of this book contains sixty plans developed in the learning cycle that you may wish to consult as models. Also, the following questions should help you prepare for each phase of the learning cycle as you write your own lesson plans. For your convenience, a sample science learning cycle lesson plan is shown in Exhibit 7.1.

How Can a Scientific Method Become a Teaching Method?

Scientific method is defined as the systematic pursuit of knowledge involving the recognition and formulation of a problem, the collection of data through observation and experimentation (the experiential element), the formulation of a hypothesis, and the testing and confirmation (or rejection) of that hypothesis.[9]

What went through your mind as you read the definition? When and if a scientific method was taught to you it was probably taught in a high school science class separately from actually doing science. Some scientists and educators object to the notion of a scientific method and, justifiably, cite that all scientists do not think or investigate in such a linear way. Often a method is memorized as a series of steps like these:

Step 1: Define the problem.

Step 2: Find out what is already known about the problem.

Step 3: Form a hypothesis or educated guess.

Step 4: Conduct an experiment to test the hypothesis.

Step 5: Use the results to reach a conclusion.

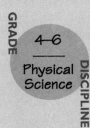

GRADE
4–6
Physical
Science

DISCIPLINE

Make a Sinker Float: Clay Boats

Concept/statement

Buoyancy: If the upward force of the liquid is greater than the downward force of the object, the object will float because it is buoyed (lifted up or supported) by the water. This concept is called *buoyancy*, and it explains why some heavy objects, such as steel ships, will float in water.

Secondary concepts that are important to expansion

Displacement, flotation, Archimedes's principle, specific gravity

Materials Needed

Small tubs or buckets to hold water, small objects that will sink or float in water, modeling clay (plasticene), small uniform objects to use as cargo (weights, such as ceramic tiles or marbles) in the clay boats, a container modified like the illustration shown in phase 3 (expansion), a small container to catch the water that spills from the modified container, and a scale or balance to measure the weight of the spilled water.

⟳ **Safety precautions:** Have children notify you in case of spills. Use a room with a nonslip floor surface if possible.

1. EXPLORATION

Instructions: Have the students examine the variety of objects given to them and predict whether each object will sink or float in the water. Have the students write their predictions on an organized data sheet that you provide. Use as one of the objects a lump of clay about the size of a tennis ball. Provide time for the students to test their predictions and then gather the students together to explore what their predictions reveal.

2. EXPLANATION

Concept: Buoyancy. If objects of different sizes and weights are used in the exploration phase, students will discover that heaviness is not the factor that determines whether an object will sink or float. For example, a large piece of 2-by-4-inch wood will be heavier than a glass marble or a metal washer, but it will float while the marble and washer will sink. Explain that Archimedes, a

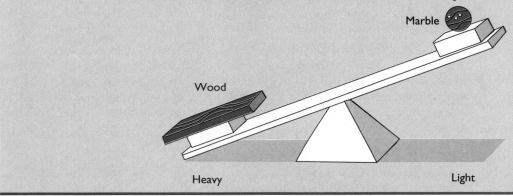

Marble

Wood

Heavy   Light

EXHIBIT 7.1   A Sample Lesson Plan Based on the Science Learning Cycle

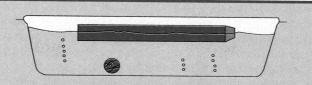

Greek philosopher, is credited with discovering that an object immersed in a liquid (water) will appear to lose some of its weight. Ask students to speculate why this seems to be. A suitable explanation may be: "If the upward force of the liquid is greater than the downward force of the object, it will float because the object is buoyed (lifted up or supported) by the water." This factor is called *buoyancy,* and it explains why some heavy objects, such as steel ships, will float in water when it can be easily illustrated that steel sinks. Steel has been given a special shape (the ship) that gives it a greater volume, which helps to spread its weight across a larger amount (volume) of the water, making it possible for the buoyant upward force of the water to be greater than the downward force of the ship's weight. How might buoyancy be affected by the amount of cargo a ship carries? Why is it important to keep a ship from taking on water?

3. EXPANSION

Weigh the lump of dry clay and the smaller container to be used to catch the water spill; record the measures. Take the lump of clay and use the device as illustrated. Carefully lower the clay into the container of water and measure its weight while it is submerged. Catch the water that spills out of the container and weigh the container again; subtract the dry container weight to determine the weight of the water displaced by the sinking clay. The weight of the submerged clay should be less than the dry weight because of the upward (buoyant) force of the water. Challenge the students to find a way to change the shape of the clay so that it will float in water. Challenge them to see who can make the clay boat that will carry the largest amount of cargo before it sinks. Have students draw pictures of their boats' shapes and/or measure the size of the boats' bottoms. Capable students could calculate the surface area of the boats' bottoms and graph the amount of cargo

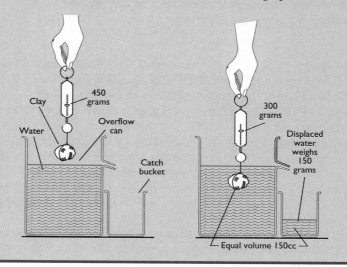

carried (before sinking) as a function of area. Ask them to observe carefully what happens to make their clay boats sink and to describe later what they observe.

Why is the idea important for personal development?
Ask the children why the Coast Guard requires flotation devices on boats and why these devices make it possible for a person who otherwise might sink to float. Why does the Coast Guard set passenger limits on pleasure craft? (Outcome 1.1)

Why is the idea important for science-technology-society?
Ask the children to search for other uses of flotation devices and applications of the buoyancy principle. Ask the children how these uses have had an impact on people. (Outcomes 2.1, 2.4) Examples might include floats connected to switches or valves that control pumps or appliances, seat cushions on airliners that are removable and can be used as flotation devices, channel buoys for navigation or to mark danger zones.

Why is the idea important for academic growth?
Ask the students to identify other examples of buoyancy in liquids and to describe differences. As examples, ask the students to redo their sink-or-float tests in denatured or isopropyl alcohol, or a mixture of alcohol and water, or water with different amounts of salt added. (This can lead to another concept and another lesson: specific gravity.) (Outcome 3.1)

Ask the students to explain why a submarine can sink and float, and how it is possible for a submarine or a SCUBA diver to remain at a particular depth. (Outcome 3.1)

Construct a Cartesian diver using a two-liter soft drink container filled with water. Place a glass medicine dropper in the container and put the cap on tightly. Squeeze the sides of the container, release, and watch what happens to the dropper. Why does the dropper sink and rise? What is necessary to keep the submarine dropper at a constant depth in the container? (Outcomes 3.1, 3.4)

Ask students to explain why it is easier to swim and float in salt water than in fresh water. (Outcomes 3.1, 3.4)

Why is the idea important to career awareness?
As an expansion assignment, have the students search for pictures and examples of careers that require some knowledge of the buoyancy concept. Examples may include ship builders, navy and marine personnel, fishermen, marine salvage crews, plumbers, SCUBA divers. (Outcomes 4.1, 4.3)

Read Pamela Allen's *Archimedes' Bath* (1980) to the class and discuss what the author needed to know about science to write this children's book. (Outcomes 4.1, 4.3)

4. EVALUATION

- Using the ball of clay and/or Cartesian diver, the students will demonstrate and explain the concept of buoyancy.
- The students will draw a picture of what happens when their clay ball is placed in water and when its shape is changed. They will write a paragraph in their own words that explains why and how the clay floats.
- The students will demonstrate proper use of the balance when weighing the clay dry and submerged.
- The advanced students will measure and calculate the area of the clay boats and graph the maximum cargo carried as a function of the surface area of the boats.

EXHIBIT 7.1 (Cont'd)   A Sample Lesson Plan Based on the Science Learning Cycle

Several developmental psychologists state that many preadolescents do not even have the thinking skills to understand the procedures of the scientific method.[10] Then why are we bringing it up in an elementary methods text? It can provide a way to form cooperative problem-solving groups, particularly when the method is used flexibly to help learners decide on an inquiry procedure they can follow. Intermediate and middle school children can learn to think according to the scientific method if it is used as a cooperative method for conducting a group inquiry. Begin simply, perhaps by saying that science deals with answering questions, or in other words: "Science invents stories and then sees if they're true."[11] Use thoughtful questions to guide classroom discussions, pursue answers to those questions, and soon you will find children asking their own questions. These questions usually serve to define the problem and point out what needs to be known and how to discover the answers.

The Scientific Method as a Teaching Strategy. The teaching strategy can have five steps that parallel those listed above. Steven Fields's fine article in *Science and Children*[12] provides many practical examples of how the steps you have memorized can be turned into a motivating, interactive, and effective teaching method. We paraphrase his ideas below.

Step 1. Have students conclude that experimenting will provide the best answer to the science question.

If a child shows interest in a topic by asking a question, or if children become curious about a topic after you ask a question, look for a way to discover the answer by acting on it. For example, how can you discover the answer to a question like "If rudders (and flaps) steer an airplane in flight, which rudders steer it in which direction?" (See Figure 7.3.) Problem questions such as this can make good challenges for cooperative group investigations in which each learner has a specific duty to fulfill.

Step 2: Focus the science question to seek a specific answer.

Try a brainstorming session. Be careful to accept all ideas related to the question, then limit the question to the kernel of the problem it poses. Identify a hypothesis from the ideas offered. Help the student groups find out all they can about the problem; then encourage them to make and test predictions. Continuing with Steve Fields's airplane example, some predictions could include:

- wing rudders control up-and-down movement,
- tail rudders control movement to the left and right,
- when rudders are set in any given way the plane will fly up and down or side to side.

Step 3: Guess the answer to the science question and use references to try to find out if the answer is already known.

Individual students and groups can brainstorm and decide the best way to find out the answer. Guiding questions can steer their thinking. Examples include:

... About the Science Learning Cycle

Jean Piaget's research on cognitive development helped to establish the first two phases of the learning cycle: exploration and explanation (concept invention). Mental activities in these phases promote what Piaget called *assimilation* and *accommodation*. Imagine the mind as a file cabinet: faced with information, the mind seeks a place to put it. Placing new information in an existing file with similar information would be an example of assimilation, as the mind adds to what already exists. However, when it does not find a file with information similar to that to be stored away, the mind must create a new file.

Robert Karplus, director of the Science Curriculum Improvement Study (SCIS), is credited with adding a third phase to the learning cycle. Karplus named this phase *discovery*, and then later changed the name to concept *implementation*. Some science educators prefer to call this the *application phase*. John Renner and Edmund Marek have made improvements and call the third phase *expansion of the idea*. There is considerable research to support uses of the learning cycle for improving children's science achievement and process skill development.

Renner and Marek note that the SCIS program relies on the learning cycle to organize its materials and to guide its teaching methods. Consequently, they have used the SCIS materials to conduct their own research, and they report conclusions that build on the effects of SCIS reported in Chapter 5.

Renner and Marek have used Piagetian mental conservation tasks to design experimental studies that indicate what effect the learning cycle may have on the intellectual development of young children. They found that when the learning cycle was used, children in an experimental group significantly outperformed other children who learned within a traditional textbook control group. Number, weight, liquid amount, solid amount, length, and area were the measures of conservation. The researchers believe "the data support the conclusion that the rate of attainment of conservation reasoning is significantly enhanced by the experiences made possible by [the first graders who learned through a learning cycle]." They also claim that the learning cycle enhances the intellectual development of young learners.

The learning cycle has also been used to test the

- "Can you find the answer in a book?" If "yes," what kind of book?
- "Whom do you know who might already know the answer?" (Other children, teachers, outside resources, experts, and so on)
- If these questions do not help, try: "How can you (we) design a test to find out the answer?" For older children, this a good place to discuss variables that can affect the outcome and reliability of an experiment.

Step 4: Follow the procedures suggested by the guiding questions in Step 3 to find the answer to the science question raised in Step 2.

Help children during this stage by limiting their temptation to overgeneralize. For example, if the wing rudders are set up and the plane flies up, guide the students to the conclusion that these settings *probably* affect all planes the same way. One could not know for certain that larger planes are affected the same way unless they also are tested.

ability of children to use science processes. In a study that investigated fifth graders who were controlled (via a matched-pairs design) for intellectual development, chronological age, gender, and socioeconomic level, Renner and Marek found that all differences in the performance of science process skills favored the group that used the learning cycle. They concluded that the learning cycle helped children learn to use the processes of science much better than did a traditional program using a conventional science textbook.

In still another study, Renner and Marek investigated the influence of the learning cycle in a science program on student achievement in mathematics, reading, and social studies. They discovered that children learned *just as much and just as well* from the learning cycle as those who learned from a traditional program on understanding mathematics concepts, learning mathematics skills, learning social studies content, and understanding word meaning. However, they conclude that *the learning cycle was superior for* helping children apply mathematics; master social studies skills that involve interpreting graphs, tables, and posters and assimilation of data for problem solving; and deter-

mine paragraph meaning. In yet another study, Renner and Marek discovered that the learning cycle used in the SCIS first-grade program helped children outperform other children in a reading program on reading readiness skills.

The researchers maintain that the learning cycle is a natural way to learn and that it fulfills the major purpose of education: helping children learn how to think. Furthermore, Renner and Marek state that their research provides a rebuttal to school people who say, "We just don't have time or cannot afford to invest in the resources to teach science." They conclude: "The truth of the matter is that any school that teaches science using the learning cycle model is teaching much more than good science; it is also teaching reading, mathematics, and social science. In fact, schools cannot afford *not* to teach science using [the learning cycle model]."

Source: Adapted and quoted from John W. Renner and Edmund Marek, *The Learning Cycle and Elementary Science Teaching* (Portsmouth, NH: Heinemann, 1988) pp. 185–199.

Step 5: After experimenting, interpreting, and concluding, have the students use what they have learned.

Focus on everyday experiences and have the children apply the main ideas they have learned—the concepts—to things they can understand. The rudder example applies to paper airplanes as well as kites, model rockets and planes, spoilers on racing cars, and rudder steering on conventional boats and swamp or airboats.

Limitations and Benefits.   Like most inquiry approaches, the scientific teaching method requires more time and planning to cover concepts. Equipment is needed, although often simple and inexpensive materials will do. Certain concepts lend themselves to experimentation more easily than others. The emphasis on concepts, however, is precisely what makes student comprehension greater and retention last longer. The cooperative group problem investigation approach helps to leverage the students' ideas by stimulating new approaches to the problem.

FIGURE 7.3   Paper Airplane Illustration   On this paper airplane, the wing rudders and vertical stablizer rudder are located as shown. Of course, creating various models of airplanes is a scientific endeavor in its own right. Let students experiment with making planes and rudders themselves.

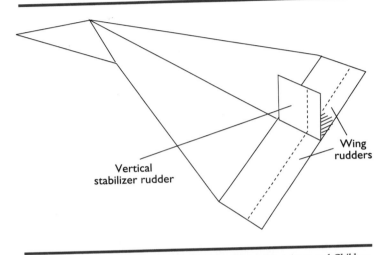

Source: Steve Fields, "The Scientific *Teaching* Method," *Science and Children,* April 1989, p. 15. Reprinted with permission from NSTA publications, 1742 Connecticut Avenue, NW, Washington, DC 20009.

Suchman's Inquiry: How Can You Get Students to Think and Question?

Science Magic?   Dressed in cape and top hat, Mr. Martinez was ready to deliver his promised special treat to the fourth-grade class. With the theatrical flair of a amateur magician he proposed to take his very sharp magic wand (the straight steel shank cut out of a coat hanger and filed to a pin-sharp point on one end) and pass it through a balloon without bursting it. Mr. Martinez played the crowd. He blew up a balloon, tied it off, and enlisted the aid of the audience by having them chant "I believe! I believe!" and then on his signal say the magic words. As the magic wand of a super-sharp pin was about to touch the stretched side of the balloon, several children furrowed their brows and covered their ears. And with good reason: Pop!

The giggles were meant to tell Mr. Martinez "I told you so," but he persisted with jabs about not all of them believing or not selecting the right magic words. "Let's try again," he said as he began working the crowd again. Martinez blew up another balloon, tied it, and then remembered that he should add a drop of elixir from an oil can to his magic wand. Through the routine they all went, again, and this time to the amazement of the children the wand pierced one end of the balloon and slowly came out the other—a perfect axis through the top of the balloon and at the bottom near the knot. The children clapped and immediately wanted to know how he did it.

Mr. Martinez explained that he was not aware of any magic that really worked and that part was only an act. He emphasized that there are usually scientific explanations for the discrepancies we observe. But he assured the children that the balloon trick was no illusion. To convince them, he passed the balloon around for the children to inspect and then said: "You usually expect for me to ask *you*

FIGURE 7.4 Balloon Discrepant Event

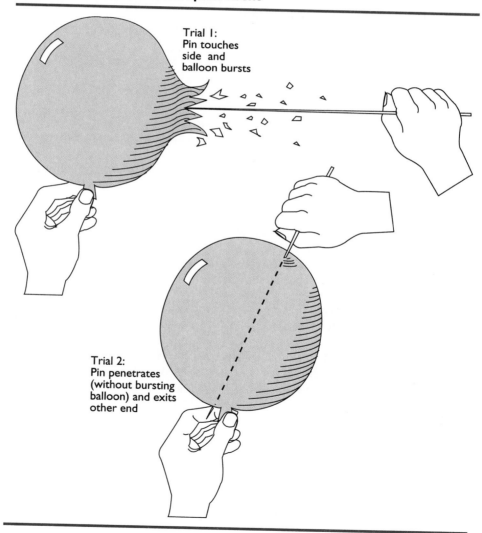

Trial 1:
Pin touches
side and
balloon bursts

Trial 2:
Pin penetrates
(without bursting
balloon) and exits
other end

questions, but today is a special opportunity for *you* to ask the questions. Let's pretend you are super sleuths who are going to find out the explanation for this balloon trick. You can ask me all the questions you want, but there are some special rules you must follow. First, you can only ask me questions I can answer with a 'Yes' or 'No.' Second, begin by asking questions to establish the facts of what you have just seen. Don't take anything for granted: Verify that it was done as you *think* you saw it. Finally, after you think you have all the facts you need, tell me the reason you think this trick was possible. Let's begin. Lucinda?"

"Did you do anything special to the second balloon, like make it stronger?"

"No."

Then other children asked:

"Were they the same kind of balloons?"

"Yes."

"Were they the same size? I mean when you blew them up?"

"Yes—I *tried* to have them the same."

"Did you let a little air out of each one?"

"Yes."

"Does the oil make it work?"

"That sounds like an explanation type of question to me. Let's hold that one a while until after we uncover some more facts," said Mr. Martinez. Then the lesson continued until eventually the children discovered the *real* answer, and it wasn't because of the oil. The answer was related to the thickness of the balloon.

Discrepant Events.   This inquiry technique was developed by J. Richard Suchman[13] and relies on the use of discrepant events. Discrepancies are differences from what we normally expect, like the sharp pin penetrating the balloon without bursting it. Theory has it that the human mind is intolerant of discrepancies and needs to maintain consistency.[14] The theory refers to an inconsistency between two cognitions—cognitive dissonance—between what one observes and what one believes. The balloon is a good example: Everyone knows sharp objects cause them to pop, but that one didn't!

The Method.   Your students' needs for cerebral consistency can motivate even those who are less alert and attentive. Why not use it to your advantage and teach science concepts with it? Suchman's method uses inquiry to help children construct theories (best explanations) for the discrepancies they observe. The approach is student centered and requires children to ask the questions—possibly a difficult task, because it requires considerable thought to ask useful questions and to build the answers into some order that will explain the discrepancy. The approach can be cooperative if the class is divided into detective teams to organize questions, conduct research, and form scientific explanations. The questions to use are convergent and must be answered with either a *yes* or a *no*. See Figure 7.5 for a visual map of how the inquiry is structured. These are the phases of Suchman's method:

1. Present the discrepant event.
2. Students ask yes-no questions to verify the events and collect information.
3. Students discuss ideas and do library research or further investigations to gather additional information to help them form explanations or theories.
4. The teacher reconvenes the class and leads a discussion to help students give and test their explanations or theories.

Suchman's approach is successful with intermediate and middle school children, but younger children need more teacher guidance. With K–2 children we

FIGURE 7.5 Discrepant Event Map

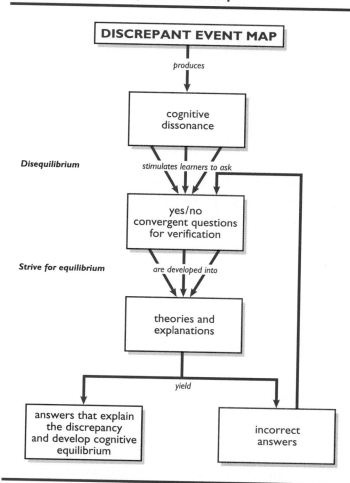

have successfully used versions of the game Twenty Questions to accomplish the same outcome. The Additional Readings section at the end of this chapter provides sources for discrepant teaching events you can try.

The need to know is the powerful force of motivation with this type of method. However, this power can lead to student frustration and unproductive activity. Robert Shrigley suggests bringing closure or resolution to the discrepant event at least by the end of the class period; otherwise, the discrepancy can lead to an overload of frustration.

> At an inservice meeting . . . teachers had sat through a lengthy inference demonstration using a mystery box with objects sealed inside. Announcing that they should learn to live with the unknown, the science educator refused to open the box for inspection or tell the participants what its contents were. During the break, one teacher, who until that point had been poised and cooperative, bolted to the table on which the box had been left, and ripped off the lid to see what was inside.[15]

Can Children Learn Science Through Play?

Playful discovery is a method based on the innate curiosity of very young children, in which play becomes the method for learning science. The method uses some of the elements of inquiry, but it is much more open ended. Children are natural investigators. Combine a child's interest with some adult encouragement and opportunities to play around with interesting materials, and playful discovery becomes a method that is useful for helping very young children begin to form fundamental science concepts they can build on for the rest of their lives.[16] The method also encourages cooperation among very young learners.

Playful discovery is based on the theories of John Dewey and Jean Piaget, who stated that young children learn best through active involvement with interesting and meaningful materials. Dewey and Piaget, however, reminded us that we as teachers must go beyond simply passing out interesting materials and letting children play with them. Both theorists believed that teachers should direct the hands-on learning through encouragement and guiding questions. Dewey was most concerned about the quality of this hands-on experience, about which he wrote:

> Everything depends upon the quality of the experience which is had. The quality of the experience has two aspects. There is an immediate aspect of agreeableness or disagreeableness, and there is an influence upon later experiences.[17]

Versions of playful discovery strive to provide young children with a variety of rich and immediately agreeable experiences. The method is used in child care centers and preschools with three- to five-year-old children and in progressive kindergarten classrooms. Playful discovery is stimulated initially by teacher-planned experiments that are based on phenomena, substances, and/or materials that are interesting and familiar to the children. For science, the learning activities can promote positive attitudes, lay the foundation for learning simple science concepts, and stimulate development of such process skills as observation, comparison, classification, prediction, and interpretation. The following scenario helps to illustrate the method. Figure 7.6 briefly describes its six stages.

Christopher: A Blossoming Scientist.[18] Mrs. Kousaleos invited her group of four- and five-year-olds to gather by her and experiment with ice cubes in hot and cold water. Five small bodies were arched over the two containers of water observing and comparing the effects. Christopher suddenly announced with obvious excitement, "Look! The ones in hot water are really getting small." At Mrs. K's suggestion to check the water with their fingers, the children were surprised to discover how very cold the formerly hot water had become.

A week later, after repeating the ice activity, Mrs. K suggested another experiment to find out how to most quickly melt an ice cube. Eager children generated ideas, then tested them by several methods. Putting ice cubes into mouths and breaking ice cubes into smaller pieces were by far the most popular methods. Midway through the experiment, however, Christopher, eyes wide open and a "Eureka" tone in his voice, proclaimed, "Let's try hot water!"

After duplicating the ice experiments with slight variations (such as exploring effects of amounts of water, numbers of ice cubes, and sizes of containers), the children began to ask permission to conduct their own experiments, Christopher in particular. These requests usually meant making ice in some uniquely shaped container, mixing various ingredients together, or adding a variety of materials to water.

During one of Christopher's self-initiated experiments, he noted that pouring salt into a container of water made the water "lift out." Since Christopher seemed intrigued with this phenomenon, Mrs. K planned some activities on displacement.

Later, when Christopher took a vacation, his parents sent a postcard that said, "Christopher is spending much time on the beach experimenting with water, observing changes as he adds shells and sand." Christopher had become fascinated by how the water "came out" when he and his dad jumped into their vacation swimming pool.

When Christopher returned, his class did a displacement experiment using different sizes of containers and different amounts of water with marbles, to assess and extend some of his vacation learning. After exploring the effect of adding marbles to water in narrow and wide containers, Christopher observed, "When the water's up high, the marbles lift the water out." He later concluded in response to a question about the difference between the narrow and wide containers that "in a fat one the water spreads out. In a thin one it goes up to the top."

The Playful Science Classroom. Christopher's is an example of what can happen when sensitive teacher guidance and well-planned experiences are combined to set the stage for the high-quality "later experiences" John Dewey wrote about. Numerous and different ongoing experiments will be evident in the playful discovery classroom. Many experiences will be based on common activities that use ordinary materials such as sand, water, and blocks.

FIGURE 7.6   Six Stages of Playful Discovery

Stage 1: Self-selected teacher-proposed experiment.
Encourage children to discover if ice cubes melt at the same rate in hot and cold water.

Stage 2: Repeat experiment with slight variation.
Encourage children to

• Vary amount of water used.
• Vary size of containers used.
• Determine if stirring the water makes a difference.
• Vary number of ice cubes placed in water.

Stage 3: Elaborate further on completed experiment.
Encourage children to discover how many ways you
can break up ice cubes (with hands, feet, teeth,
hammer, and so on).

Stage 4: Provide opportunities for and actively
encourage children's self-initiated experiments.
Make a variety of materials accessible, read books,
use teacher questioning. For example:

• Child makes ice cubes in a variety of containers (egg carton, muffin tin, plastic
  bottle, small bucket.)
• Child also explores ways to remove ice from container and uses knowledge from
  Stage 1 to solve problems.
• Child discovers whether or not magic markers melt in hot water.

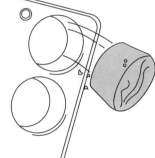

Stage 5: Communicate with parents and inform them of
child's interest.

• Parent encourages child to experiment at home and
  while on vacation (exploring ice cubes in bath water, mixing
  sand and water, discovering effect of jumping in water).
• Parent provides materials as child expresses interest.

Stage 6: Conduct a new experiment.
Encourage

• Children to explore the effect of pressure or force on water.
• Children to explore the effects of adding sand to container of
  water (e.g., displacement).

Source: Dwight L. Rogers, Ralph E. Martin, Jr., and Sharon Kousaleous, "Encouraging Science Through Playful Discovery," *Day Care and Early Education,* vol. 16, no. 1, Fall 1988, p. 23. Reprinted with permission.

Playful discovery gives young children opportunities to explore freely and to begin to understand the nature of materials *before* more structured lessons try to teach them concepts. Figure 7.6 outlines the stages Mrs. K followed to guide the children and improve the quality of their experiences. First she stimulated interest by proposing class experiments; later she stimulated sustained learning and experiential elaboration by permitting children to self-select experiments. Children will function at different stages at different times. For example,

> Some children may not go beyond Stage 1 because of lack of interest or understanding, and the teacher must proceed to Stage 6 for them. Others may spend a great deal of time on Stages 1 and 2, but not be able to make the leap to Stages 3 and 4. In this case it may help to skip these stages and go to Stage 5, so as to promote elaboration and self-initiation [by] suggesting that parents provide experiences in "science experiments" at home.[19]

Is this approach worth the effort? How long do the experiences endure? Perhaps you will find the answer here in the words of Sharon Kousaleos:

> Even months after the [first ice] experiment, a mother of one of the children [said] that when she was trying to figure out how to get ice cubes in a small-necked thermos, her four-year-old daughter suggested she could melt them a little in hot water first so they would fit.[20]

Playful discovery works best when the experiments chosen deal with phenomena and substances that the children encounter every day. The everyday environment adds a very practical aspect to science by showing its usefulness, and it helps the children to construct a better understanding of their own world.

How Can You Turn Children's Questions into an Inquiry Teaching Method?

Fred Biddulph and Roger Osborne[21] provide an inquiry approach to teaching that involves children in science investigations that are based on *their* own questions. They believe children's questions ought to be central to the process of inquiry because they show the extent of the present ideas children have about a science topic, and they can be used to generate interest. Basing inquiry on children's questions

- helps children gain understanding,
- provides children a powerful incentive to improve their own information-processing skills,
- helps children learn to interact with ideas and construct meanings for themselves from an interesting situation or topic,
- gives children occasional opportunities to learn from their own mistakes.

The teacher's role in this approach is to

- encourage children to ask questions about their encounters,
- encourage children to seek more information and rely less on teachers and others,

TEACHERS ON SCIENCE TEACHING

What Is a Question Box?

By Mary Ann Sloan
Grade 1 Teacher, Paumanok Elementary School, Dix Hills, New York

My first-grade classroom can best be described as a whole science classroom, where cooperative learning takes place throughout the day. I have found that cooperative learning is a powerful tool. In my classroom, science provides the platform for an interdisciplinary approach. The children raise questions; make predictions; devise plans; obtain, organize, and analyze data; and make many decisions while they gain experiences in using science inquiry skills. All of this is the result of the introduction of a very simple device—a question box!

The question box has helped me to begin the process of transforming the class into groups of cooperative learners. This strategy takes full advantage of the children's natural curiosity and allows them to become active participants in the learning process.

To make the question box, cover a cardboard box about the size of a mailbox with dazzling foil paper. Then cut out five-inch question marks from bright construction paper. Be sure to have one for each child and one for you, too. To introduce the question box to your class and to provide a model for the first questions, select an exciting book to read to the whole class. One of the books that I have used with great success is *Papa Please Get the Moon for Me*,

by Eric Carle. After reading the story, I ask the children what questions they would ask Monica, the main character, if she could come to our classroom and visit them. I record the questions they ask. Now I take out the question box. I explain that the question box is the place where they can put any questions they would like to have answered, that they can write their questions on their own or have someone help them, and that I will set aside time each day to work with the question box. I invite each child whose questions I recorded to put his or her question into the box. While we decorate our paper question marks, I move from table to table, modeling the kind of on-task behavior I expect. As I decorate my question mark, I think aloud of questions I might put into the question box and ask them about the questions they may be considering.

After a few days of working with the box—reading the questions aloud and adding more of their questions to it—I randomly select a question to be answered. Our first question was: Are elephants afraid of mice? The children made a list of what they already knew about elephants. When we reread the list, they decided that they needed to know more. They wanted to know: How big are elephants and

- help children find ways to test their ideas,
- help children construct well-reasoned explanations for their questions.[22]

Table 7.1 provides a quick visual outline of the method. We paraphrase Biddulph and Osborne's work in the following steps.

Step 1. Elicit and record the children's questions.

Time required is perhaps one lesson. It is easier for children to ask questions if they already know something about the topic from prior experience. If experience is lacking, provide a demonstration, perhaps a discrepant event; show a film, poster,

their trunks? Why does an elephant have a trunk? Had anyone ever seen a mouse attack an elephant? We made predictions and developed a plan of action. The children began to meet in their cooperative learning groups. Each group worked to answer one of the questions. Now science became what we do to find answers, and the children loved it!

One product that developed from their explorations was a full-size painting of an African and an Indian elephant, with attention to the length and width of the trunk, which demanded measuring with many different devices. Three charts showing objects bigger, smaller, and the same size as an elephant were completed, requiring lots of comparisons. Two world maps showing where elephants and mice are found were drawn using the overhead projector. A diorama, using clay and construction paper, was created to depict an elephant habitat. Marker drawings of the kinds of foods elephants eat were labeled. Clocks were made to show when elephants sleep, eat, and travel. One group found that elephants don't breathe through their trunks and that it takes lots of food to keep an elephant healthy. This news helped the group that was working to determine how elephants actually use their trunks. They made paper bag elephant costumes and

put on a play. The last group wrote letters to the Big Apple Circus, the Bronx Zoo, the Washington Zoo, and the San Diego Zoo. None of the zoo personnel had ever seen a mouse attack an elephant. In fact, they wrote to say that in their experiences mice seemed to be afraid of elephants. We made elephant T-shirts that the letter-writing group designed. This group was also responsible for keeping a record of money collected. They enlisted a mom to help them buy the shirts. She also helped with the stenciling.

This was just the beginning of the question center. Throughout the year, many questions are answered, and the children have many opportunities to classify, create models, generalize, form hypotheses, identify variables, infer, interpret data, make decisions, manipulate materials, measure, observe, predict, record data, replicate, and use number and language skills. You will know when your class is a community of cooperative learners. I promise this center will never be empty. The children will not want to leave for recess or lunch, and three o'clock will come too soon. They will miss school on weekends and won't be able to wait until Monday mornings, when they can put more questions into or take another question out of the question box.

photograph, or slides; give descriptions of situations, encounters, or examples of the topic; read them a relevant story; or give them time for free exploration with materials.

These opportunities may spark a wide range of questions; it may be necessary to help the children focus the points of their questions. Children may be reluctant or uncertain about how to form good questions if they have not had practice. Teacher modeling of proper question-asking behavior can help; so can using divergent questions to stimulate thoughtfulness and multiple possibilities. After a while, eliciting questions is not a great matter of concern; however, deciding *when* to stop is.

TABLE 7.1   Children's Questions as an Inquiry Approach

Step 1: Provision of inititating activities.   Provide your children with experiences that will enable them to ask questions. Record their questions.

Step 2 Decision about questions.   Decide which questions are to be investigated.

Step 3: Guidance with planning.   Assist the children to plan their investigations.

Step 4: Assistance with investigations.   Provide assistance to the children during their investigations.

Step 5: Help with findings.   Assist the children to record, interpret, and report their findings.

Source: Fred Biddulph and Roger Osborne, "Children's Questions and Science Teaching: An Alternative Approach," *Learning in Science Project* (Primary), working paper no. 117 (Hamilton, New Zealand: Waikato University, February 1984, ERIC Reproduction Document no. ED 252400), p. 4.

Step 2. Decide which questions to investigate.

Time required is up to one lesson. Once you have obtained genuine questions to which students do not know the answers, selection must occur. These are some possible ways to proceed:

- Have individual children select questions for independent projects or have groups choose a question of interest and work on it collectively.
- When separate questions may be related, let the children group them in ways that make sense to them.
- Refine the selection process by classifying the questions according to which may be investigated by practical activities or by consultation with books or people. Eliminate or defer questions that are outside the range of the science topic or that may be too difficult conceptually for the children.

Step 3. Help children plan their investigations.

Time required is one or more class periods. Encourage practical hands-on investigations as well as consultations with resources. Guide the children so that they learn to

- identify and use appropriate materials,
- carry out fair and accurate tests of their ideas,
- select and consult suitable print, media, and human resources,
- collect useful information,
- have realistic expectations for how long the children will need to test their ideas,
- show concern for the environment and treatment of people.

Intermediate and middle grade children may benefit from a written framework to help organize their investigation, such as the one in Table 7.2.

Step 4. Monitor the children's investigations and provide assistance.

Several class periods will be needed for this. Young or inexperienced older children will need considerable help as they concurrently develop research and thinking skills while they pursue science learning. You can encourage children by showing empathy for their frustrations and providing sympathetic challenges to strength-

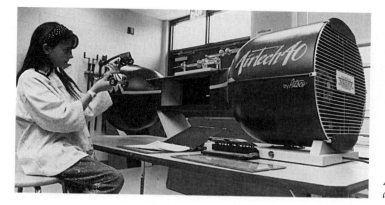

A child's question can become the source of an important experiment.

en their ideas. You can support children's inquiry by directing their attention to factors they may have overlooked or by suggesting alternatives.

Step 5. Help the children record and report their findings.

Several class periods may be necessary. Consider that children probably will need help with:

- knowing what to record and learning that several tests (repeated measures) will provide more accuracy than a single measure;
- organizing information to record it in chart, table, graph, or narrative form (this is a good place to integrate mathematics and language arts skills);
- knowing what meaning is or is not possible to take from certain information; meaning can be enhanced if children are encouraged to use analogies;
- reporting the results in an organized format such as posters, charts, models, film, video, and so on.

Will You Survive?

Inquiry teaching methods have risks and potential difficulties. The children or group may pursue several different questions and work on various projects at the

---

TABLE 7.2   Organization Framework

1. Name
2. Science topic
3. My question
4. My investigation
    a. What do I want to ask someone?
    b. Whom can I ask?
    c. What should I read about?
    d. What could I *do* to find out?

same time. This presents management and organization difficulties for most teachers. Sufficient resources may also be in short supply. Postponing or even canceling lessons are options if the initial difficulties become too much to risk. With encouragement and time to develop the needed skills, children can grow into the role of posing questions and need less help researching their answers. With practice you too will become more skilled at managing the busy class activity and know better what questions and needs to anticipate. You will also learn many fascinating things about science that you probably never had a chance to investigate. One procedure that can help you manage the inquiry from children's questions is associated with learning teams or cooperative groups.

Children learn responsibility by sharing tasks in cooperative groups.

Cooperative Inquiry Groups.   Three to five is a functional number for inquiry groups or cooperative learning groups. When each group member has a special job, the group inquiry process can be both effective and functional. The research on this management approach shows that "students who work in groups learn concepts just as well as those who work individually, with the added bonus that students who work together can develop both interpersonal skills and a sense of group responsibility."[23]

Form groups, assign roles, and give each child a job description. Roles may include principal investigator, materials manager, recorder, reporter, and maintenance director. Job descriptions may be labeled as creatively as these:[24]

The *principal investigator* (PI) is in charge of managing the group. Duties are to check the assignment and ask the teacher any clarifying questions, then lead the group by conducting the activity for the rest of the group or by assigning duties to the other group members. The PI is also in charge of safety.

The *materials manager* is in charge of picking up and passing out all equipment and materials that are necessary. Inside the classroom, the materials manager is usually the only student who has a reason to be moving around.

The *recorder* is in charge of collecting the necessary information and recording it in the proper form: graph, table, tape recorder, and so on. The recorder works with the principal investigator and the materials manager to verify the accuracy of the data.

The *reporter* is in charge of reporting the results, orally or in writing, back to the teacher or the entire class.

The *maintenance director* is in charge of cleanup and has the power to involve others in this group responsibility. Equipment must be returned and consumables must be cleaned up.

Recorder and reporter can be combined, as can materials manager and maintenance director for groups as small as three. Badges, sashes, headbands, photo IDs, or other role-identifying management devices can be used to limit confusion. Rotate the roles and form different groups often to promote fairness and group responsibility. This group technique can be used with any inquiry method in which groups are used. Robert Jones provides further tricks of the trade in Table 7.3.

RECOMMENDATIONS FOR SUCCESSFUL COOPERATIVE INQUIRY TEACHING

All of the inquiry methods we have presented are student centered to various degrees. They engage children in active thinking and learning and differ only in approach, but despite these procedural differences, each method guides children toward making discoveries. What elements unite these different procedures, which lead to a common outcome?[25]

TABLE 7.3   Tricks of the Trade for Cooperative Group Inquiry Activities

- Let each group choose a name for itself. It is a good social activity, and the names will help you identify the different groups.
- Change group members from time to time. Try out introvert-extrovert or boy-girl teams; experiment with cultural and racial mixes; form academically heterogeneous groups.
- Talk only to the principal investigators about the activity. This will set up a chain of command and prevent a repetition of questions. The students should discuss questions and problems among themselves so that it will only be necessary for you to clarify points with the principal investigator.
- Employ both indoor and outdoor activities. The badges work well indoors; armbands and headbands are more visible on school grounds. Hand-held walkie-talkies (inexpensive children's type) are also useful and (if they are available) should be used by the principal investigators.
- Use groups of three when working outdoors or on a field trip. This size group is better for safety.
- To ensure clear communication, post class rules, group names, job descriptions, and any other important information on a bulletin board in the classroom.
- Develop a system for rotating roles.
- Use job descriptions for classroom management and discipline. Most of the time you will simply need to ask which person has which role to resolve problems.
- Develop a worksheet, data recording sheet, or some other instrument for each activity.
- Make yourself a badge and join in the fun.

Source: Robert M. Jones, "Teaming Up," *Science and Children,* May 1985, p. 23.

1. **Successful inquiry teachers model scientific attitudes.** The scientific attitudes we most wish to develop in children must be evident in the people who teach them. Successful inquiry teachers must be curious, open minded, tolerant of different viewpoints, skeptical at times, willing to admit it when they do not know answers to all questions, and able to view those occasions as opportunities to expand their learning.

2. **Successful inquiry teachers are creative.** Effective teachers find ways to make deficient materials effective. They are masters at adapting others' ideas, and they become comfortable taking risks with the unknown. Successful inquiry teachers encourage creativity in children by being creative themselves.

3. **Successful inquiry teachers are flexible.** Inquiry takes time. Children need time to explore, think, and ask questions. Successful inquiry teachers are patient and use time flexibly to afford children the time they need for effective inquiry learning.

4. **Successful inquiry teachers use effective questioning strategies.** Types of questions used, wait-time, and proper uses of praise, reinforcement, and encouragement are the fodder of inquiry learning.

5. **Successful inquiry teachers focus their efforts on preparing children to think as they discover science content.** The inquiry teacher most wants children to develop an ability to solve problems. Successful problem solving depends on numerous thinking skills that arise from the processes of science that guide all phases of inquiry. The end result of the inquiry process is the discovery of science content. The end justifies the means, but exclusive focus only on the end product does not provide the means for future problem solving.

Take the first step by beginning small. Trying to adapt all lessons into a student-centered approach is an overwhelming task and can be frustrating. If yours is a conventional textbook science program, focus on only one or two chapters at first by mapping the concepts. Then develop the material into good inquiry activities or find other supplementing resources. Each year add more, and soon you will develop an effective collection of material. Combine your efforts with those of other teachers (particularly those who teach the same grade level), pool your materials, improve them, and help your program become more effective. Read such journals as *Science and Children* for elementary teachers and *Science Scope* for middle and junior high teachers. These journals are available from the National Science Teachers Association. They always contain activities reported by experienced teachers and describe new materials available through government-sponsored programs and commercial publishers.

CHAPTER SUMMARY

Cooperative inquiry teaching methods are interactive: Children and teachers investigate together and share many responsibilities that are carried only by the teacher in conventional classrooms. Inquiry is a family of science teaching methods that promote student-centered learning in a hands-on, minds-on way. Inquiry is a process, a way of pursuing learning. The outcome of its methods are children's discoveries. All inquiry methods are based on a belief about the power of experience. The methods rely on effective questioning to promote concept development.

Five inquiry-based science teaching methods are described in this chapter. The science learning cycle is appropriate for concept development in all grades and is particularly well suited for implementing the new goals in science education described in Chapters 3 and 4. A sample plan is included in this chapter and is representative of the resource plans located in Part IV of this text.

A scientific teaching method is an approach for turning what is usually a memory exercise into a powerful teaching and learning method. This approach is most suitable for the intermediate through middle school grades and lends itself to cooperative inquiry groups.

Suchman's inquiry makes use of puzzling phenomena—discrepant events—that permit teachers to build on intrinsic motivation and turn children into questioners and pursuers of explanations. Playful discovery is a little-known inquiry method that was developed for very young children. Preschool and kindergarten children benefit from its playful atmosphere, accumulating agreeable and valuable experiences that help them build concept structures for later study. Inquiry with children's questions is another approach for turning children's questions into a teaching and learning method. With so many possible different questions children may wish to pursue, classroom management can become nightmarish; therefore, we offer practical recommendations for using inquiry groups.

Effective teachers who use inquiry methods demonstrate several common attributes: They model science attitudes; they are creative in their approaches to science material and flexible in classroom management; and they tend to focus more on developing children's abilities to think than on mere acquisition of subject matter. Research verifies the superior effects of student-centered inquiry approaches over traditional text-based teaching methods for science achievement, attitudes, and process skills.

DISCUSSION QUESTIONS AND PROJECTS

1. What arguments support using cooperative teaching methods, inquiry in particular? What barriers seem to limit inquiry's acceptance and use in elementary classrooms? Will you use inquiry? Why?

2. What are the similarities and differences in the approaches described in this chapter? Under what circumstances would you favor any one approach over the others?

3. Why is it that as children get older and presumably more capable of thinking independently, they appear to rely more on an authority figure for information than on their own experiences for discovering it?

4. Cooperative inquiry methods tend to promote greater independence among learners. Name several things you can do to help children become more independent learners.

5. Inquiry teaching strives to accommodate individual student differences. Individual differences do, however, tend to complicate teaching. What are some things you could do to manage the diversity of individuality without losing your cooperative focus?

6. How do inquiry methods help slow and fast learners?

7. Select an inquiry method and prepare a lesson for it. Teach the lesson and evaluate the effects of the method. How could you modify the method to make it more effective?

8. Try teaching lessons the conventional way and then with a suitable inquiry approach. Determine the extent to which children obtain and retain the points of the lesson. What does your analysis reveal?

9. Investigate the ways you use questioning during inquiry lessons. Report the frequency and your use of different types of questions, the frequency and different types of children's questions, and uses of wait-time. What skills can you use to make the inquiry more effective?

10. Develop original lessons for each of the methods described in this chapter. How do these lessons vary? What aspects of planning are emphasized more and less as the instruction becomes more cooperative?

NOTES

1. This scenario is excerpted with permission from Steven J. Rakow, *Teaching Science as Inquiry* (Bloomington, IN: Phi Delta Kappa, Fastback #246, 1986), pp. 8–11.

2. Howard H. Birnie and Alan Ryan, "Inquiry/Discovery Revisited," *Science and Children* (April 1984), p. 31.

3. Ibid., p. 31.

4. Ibid.

5. See the studies reported by James A. Shymansky, William C. Kyle, Jr., and Jennifer M. Alport, "How Effective Were the Hands-On Science Programs of Yesterday?" *Science and Children* (November/December 1982), pp. 14–15; and Ted Bredderman, "Activity Science—The Evidence Shows It Matters," *Science and Children* (September 1982), pp. 39–41. The effects of these studies were described in Chapter 3.

6. Imelda Rodriguez and Lowell J. Bethel, "An Inquiry Approach to Science and Language Teaching," *Journal of Research in Science Teaching*, vol. 20, no. 4, (1983), pp. 291–296.

7. Mary P. Windram, "Getting at Reading Through Science Inquiries," *Roeper Review* (March 1988), pp. 150–152.

8. For a comprehensive description of the learning cycle and the theory upon which it is based, see John W. Renner and Edmund A. Marek, *The Learning Cycle and Elementary School Science Teaching* (Portsmouth, NH: Heinemann, 1988).

9. Steve Fields, "The Scientific *Teaching* Method," *Science and Children* (April 1989), p. 15.

10. Ronald G. Good, *How Children Learn Science* (New York: Macmillan, 1977).

11. M. Reecer in Fields, p. 15.

12. Fields, p. 17.

13. J. Richard Suchman, *The Elementary School Training Program in Scientific Inquiry*, Report to the U. S. Office of Education, Project Title VII (Urbana: University of Illinois, 1962).

14. R. E. Petty and J. T. Cacioppa, *Attitudes and Persuasion: Classic and Contemporary Approaches* (Dubuque, IA: William C. Brown, 1981).

15. Robert L. Shrigley, "Discrepant Events: Why They Fascinate Students," *Science and Children* (May 1987), p. 25.

16. Margaret McIntyre, *Early Childhood and Science* (Washington, DC: National Science Teachers Association, 1984).

17. John Dewey, *Experience and Education* (New York: Collier Books, 1937), p. 27.

18. Dwight L. Rogers, Ralph E. Martin, Jr., and Sharon Kousaleos," Encouraging Science Through Playful Discovery," *Day Care and Early Education*, vol. 16, no. 1 (Fall 1988), p. 21.

19. Ibid., p. 23.

20. Ibid.

21. Fred Biddulph and Roger Osborne, "Children's Questions and Science Teaching: An Alternative Approach," *Learning in Science Project* (Primary), working paper no. 117 (Hamilton, New Zealand: Waikato University, February 1984, ERIC Reproduction Document no. ED 252400).

22. Ibid., p. 2.

23. Robert M. Jones, "Teaming Up," *Science and Children* (May 1985), p. 21.

24. Ibid., pp. 21–23.

25. Rakow, pp. 16–18, 30–31.

ADDITIONAL READINGS

If you are interested in learning more about some of the topics raised in this chapter consider the following sources.

Wayne W. Welch, "Inquiry in School Science," in Norris C. Harms and Robert E. Yager (eds.), *What Research Says to the Science Teacher,* vol. 3 (Washington, DC: National Science Teachers Association, 1981), pp. 53–74. Welch reviews the desired and actual state of teaching science as inquiry. Discrepancies between these two states are further explored as dilemmas; alternatives are provided.

Emmett L. Wright, "Fifteen Simple Discrepant Events that Teach Science Principles and Concepts," *School Science and Mathematics,* November 1981, pp. 575–580. Wright describes fifteen different discrepant events, many of them in disciplines other than physical science. Materials, procedures, and explanations are given.

Tik L. Liem, *Invitations to Science Inquiry* (Lexington, MA: Ginn Press, 1987). This is the largest collection of discrepant events we have seen assembled. Liem's 411 activities span seventeen chapters representing science areas such as the environment, energy, forces and motion on earth and in space, and living things. Detailed drawings by the author and explanations for the phenomena make this an easy-to-use book.

Maeve Zamarchi Foley, "What? Me Teach?" *Science and Children,* January 1988, pp. 10–13. Foley describes another approach to using student groups. Her technique motivates students to become teachers of fellow sixth-grade science students.

Steve Fields, "Introducing Science Research to Elementary School Children," *Science and Children,* September 1987, pp. 18–20. Fields's practical approach gives more insight into using a form of the scientific method as an approach for science teaching. He focuses on helping children become classroom researchers.

Thomas R. Lord, "Right-Handed and Left-Footed? How Andrea Learned to Question the Facts," *Science and Children,* October 1986, pp. 22–25. Using the left-brain, right-brain dominance theory as a backdrop, this scientist describes how he worked with his daughter to pursue her questions and discover that the teacher's textbook was *wrong!* This article is a good example of how children's questions can be used for inquiry and science discoveries.

James T. Scarnati and Craig J. Tice, "Lighting that One Little Candle," *Science and Children,* March 1988, pp. 31–33. Fifth graders become patient and observant enough to list fifty things they discover by observing a candle. This article is a good one for reminding us about how often we overlook that which is under our very noses—and how much we can learn if we follow the suggestions of inquiry.

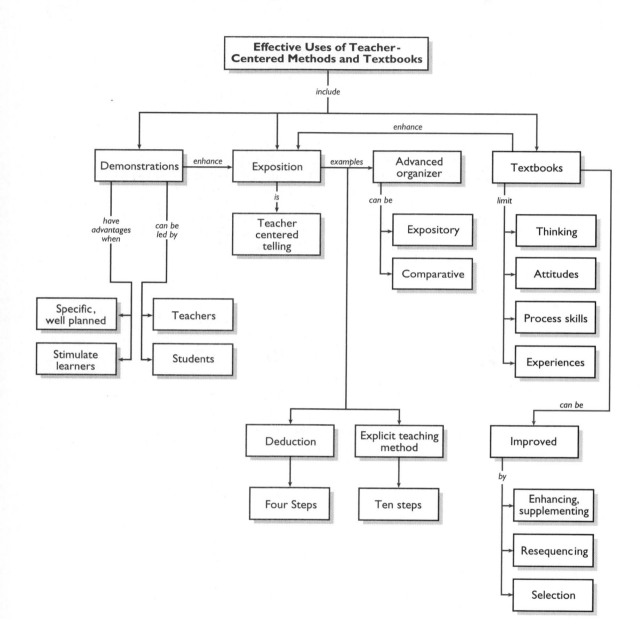

What Is the Best Way to Use Teacher-Centered Methods and Science Textbooks?

D oris Smith's classroom is next door to Mrs. McDonald's (of the Chapter 7 scenario).[1] Mrs. Smith is also conducting a lesson on predator-prey relationships in animals. Her approach to the lesson differs dramatically from Mrs. McDonald's. Mrs. Smith's style reflects, in part, her lack of confidence in teaching science. She does enjoy teaching, however, especially teaching reading.

Her classroom is arranged much more conventionally—five rows across and six seats deep. There are posters on the walls featuring Newbery Award books and travel posters of interesting places to visit. In front of the classroom is a student duty chart: class monitor, pledge leader, and so on.

"In our science reading today, we will learn two new words," begins Mrs. Smith as she writes the words *predator* and *prey* on the chalkboard. "This word is *predator*. A predator is an animal that eats other animals. A hawk is a predator because it hunts field mice. The other word is *prey*. Prey is an animal that is eaten by other animals. The field mouse is an example of prey. Please open your science text to page 48. Who would like to begin reading? Adam."

"Many animals live together in the forest. Some of these animals hunt other animals for food. These hunters are called pred . . . , pred . . ."

"Pred-a-tors," says Mrs. Smith, pronouncing each syllable.

"Predators."

"Who would like to continue? Rebecca."

"The animals that are eaten for food are called prey. Predators and prey are part of the life cycle of all living things."

The children continue reading until they have finished the section on predators and prey. "Please take out a pencil," says Mrs. Smith. "I would now like you to complete this worksheet on predators and prey."

INTRODUCTION

Avoiding Authoritarianism and the Exclusive Use of Textbooks

Mrs. Smith's approach is typical of about 90 percent of today's traditional science teachers. They use a textbook about 95 percent of the time[2] and rely on teacher-centered methods consisting of lectures, reading, and questions and answers. Their approaches are often limited to the information provided by the adopted textbook and assume that

> students should mainly pay attention to teacher presentations, read textbook passages, participate in teacher-led discussions, answer questions from the textbook and teaching plans, complete worksheets, and carry out hands-on activities as directed. Both the student textbooks and teacher lesson plans give students a mainly passive role as receivers and memorizers of information rather than as active seekers of answers to important scientific questions, although some [textbook science programs do] offer follow-up suggestions for keeping records of observation, writing reports, taking field trips, and caring for living things.[3]

Texts are *not* all bad. They do cover science content and help to promote the goal of academic preparation. Complete reliance upon textbooks, however, usually means students will be deprived of other worthy science education goals relevant to personal development, societal and technological issues, and career education.

Reliance on the science textbook can promote an authoritarian approach to teaching and learning. The text or the teacher becomes *the* authority, with the text becoming the principal determiner of what is taught. The science topic usually is selected because it is "in the book."[4] Furthermore, textbooks by themselves, without teacher modification usually do not promote or encourage the development of scientific thinking or attitudes; nor do they engage students in applying the cognitive processes that are basic to understanding the content covered. If teachers use these programs to teach science without drawing on supplementary resources, students will understand science mainly as a collection of conclusions to be memorized: They will not be brought to an adequate understanding of the nature and methods of science nor will they be afforded sufficient opportunities to explore the relationship of science to technology and to the problems of living in the modern world.[5]

Recognizing the Importance of the Interactive Classroom

An authoritative method, such as the lecture, is not recommended for extensive use in elementary science teaching. What is recommended are *interactive* teaching approaches. Mary Iatridis tells us that the young child's "capacity to think and reason is limited by extreme dependence on experience."[6] Mary Willert and Constance Kamii also remind us that authoritative teacher-centered forms of direct instruction are "based on the erroneous assumption that children are like empty glasses who learn by having bits of knowledge poured into them, and that the sooner we start to fill the glasses, the sooner this process will be completed."[7]

Interactive classrooms are places where teachers and students exchange ideas and observations. Classrooms of this type produce children who are intrinsically motivated and who will go much further than those who wait to be told what to learn.[8] The purpose of this chapter is to help you to

1. Explore ways of making a teacher-centered classroom more interactive.
2. Develop skills in giving effective teacher demonstrations.
3. Learn how to teach more effectively for those lessons when you may choose to use exposition as a method.
4. Become informed about how to select and use science textbooks more effectively.

HOW CAN YOU USE TEACHER DEMONSTRATIONS EFFECTIVELY?

With most demonstrations, a central figure stands before a class and shows something and then tells what happened. The central authority figure, often a teacher, usually is the only individual actually involved with the demonstration. Children's reactions to demonstrations may range from wide-eyed excitement to sleepy apathy.[9] How can you conduct a demonstration that stimulates curiosity and motivates the children so they actually *want* to hear an explanation? Clara Guerra[10] succeeds nicely, combining a bit of showmanship with the magic of science. She describes an exciting demonstration that can be done safely with sufficient planning and safety protection. We recommend that the demonstrator wear approved safety goggles, have a fire blanket on hand, and seat the front row of students at least ten feet from the demonstration table; the observers should wear goggles as required by state law. Let's watch her approach and learn about her techniques.

Creative demonstrations help to increase interaction with pupils.

A Bit of Science—A Bit of Magic

"A Bit of Science—A Bit of Magic" is a presentation I do for the elementary schools. It is nothing more than simple science dressed up as magic. I am the magician and the children are my dutifully amazed audience. I explode cans based on the rapid oxidation principle, I turn liquids blue with chemical reactions, and I pull the tablecloth out from under dishes, thanks to Newton's law of inertia. While many in the audience may remember only the razzle-dazzle, the pops and bangs of the show, every so often one of their parents will tell me later that their son or daughter wants to be a scientist. That's when I know that a spark has been ignited. Someone has taken the first step toward discovering the real magic of science.

"Ladies and gentlemen, boys and girls, I am a scientist!" I begin, standing in front of the students in a sorcerer's hat. "I am someone who sees things a little differently." As I talk, the house lights go out and black lights come on. My hat, decorated with stars and crayoned with fluorescent colors, catches the light and seems to stand alone on the stage. Without a drum roll or a more formal fanfare, the show begins.

Nothing quite catches the attention of a young audience like a big bang does. And a big bang is what they get with the exploding dust can trick.

To perform this, I use a candle and candle holder, lycopodium powder (flour will also work) and a small metal doll's cup, a paint can with the cup inside, and an air hose leading into the cup.

First, I fill the cup half full of the lycopodium powder and place it in the paint can. Then, I place a lit candle in its holder inside the paint can and put the lid back on. The air hose has been inserted through a hole in the side of the paint can and sits in the cup. I take a deep breath, blow deeply into the air hose, and stand back quickly. (See Figure 8.1.)

Within seconds, the top explodes off the can. Then I explain. When I blew into the can, I made the dust spread throughout it. The candle then ignited the mixture, causing the gases in the air to expand. When the gases expanded, they needed more space than the inside of the can had. There was only one place for the gases to go—out of that can. I tell the children this sometimes happens in grain dust elevators or flour mills or even in the family woodworking shop.

After the explosion, I set the lit candle on the table. I sprinkle a small amount of lycopodium dust onto the lid of the paint can. Holding the lid, I sprinkle some of the dust directly into the candle's flame. This shows the children what happened inside the can. A word of caution, if you try this: Move away from the candle quickly, and don't wear flowing sleeves.

FIGURE 8.1   The Exploding Can Demonstration

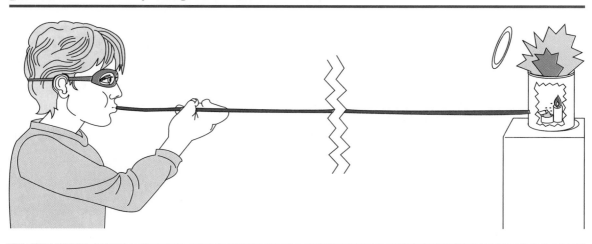

Tips for Effective Demonstrations

Ms. Guerra's technique provides a vivid illustration of several effective tips for planning and delivering classroom demonstrations. We do *not* suggest the science teacher must be an entertainer. However, a little panache does enliven the class. Demonstrations can be effective teaching tools if you follow these suggestions:

1. *The demonstration should have a specific purpose, and this purpose must be clear to all learners.* Focus on the point to be learned and make it evident in the demonstration. Also discuss how it relates to past or future lessons. If it is intended only to entertain and not teach a concept, the demonstration has little value.

2. *Plan carefully.* Collect all the necessary materials and practice the demonstration in advance. Follow the instructions and inspect them for inaccuracies. Modify the demonstration, if necessary, for *safety.* Remember, we recommend that you use goggles, distance, and fire protection if you try the demonstration. Sometimes a substitution may be useful; a safer but still exciting alternative to explosion is implosion. For example, try a clean, empty metal can with a top (like a rinsed ditto fluid can). Add about a quarter cup of water and heat it to a boil on a hotplate (without the cap). Wearing oven mitts, remove the can from the heat, replace the cap, cool it under a faucet or in a bucket of cold water, and watch what happens. (The can is crushed by a greater air pressure outside the can than inside.)

3. *Involve the children when possible.* Let the children participate in the demonstrations, or permit them to conduct the demonstration. Interactive teaching techniques such as questions and guess-making stimulate thinking, enthusiasm, and participation.

4. *Stimulate thinking and discussion.* "What do you think will happen if. . . ?" questions help stimulate original thinking and bring forth children's ideas for productive discussion. This technique also releases you from giving away too much information before the demonstration and running the risk of destroying interest.

5. *Repeat the demonstration.* A rapid flash, a loud bang, or an imploding can is sure to get attention and will demand a repeat performance. During the repeat, children will pay closer attention and powers of observation will be keener. Also, they will be given chances to acquire ideas or form mental connections that seem simple for us, but are difficult for them because of their limited experiences.

6. *Use simple materials.* Unfamiliar equipment may distract the children's attention. Familiar objects and equipment will help children focus on the cause of the action or the purpose of the demonstration rather than on the gadgets being used. Children may also choose to try the demonstrations for themselves. Importation of high school equipment for elementary classroom use should be selective and always screened for safety (see Chapter 11).

7. *Keep the demonstration easily visible.* A cluttered demonstration table will distract children from seeing what you intend. Likewise, objects that are too small to be seen by those sitting beyond the first row will frustrate viewers and cause them to lose interest. Use a tall table or counter, gather the children around when feasible (and when safe), or consider using such projection devices as the overhead projector or microcomputer.

8. *Connect with the children's environment.* Connect the point of the demonstration with the children's personal development, community, or career opportunities to expand the benefits of the demonstration and the scientific concepts or principles. Ms. Guerra did this when referring to the grain elevator, flour mill, or family wood shop.

9. *Rely on quality, not quantity.* Avoid a large number of demonstrations hoping the children learn *something*. A single well-designed, timely demonstration can communicate powerful ideas more effectively than an overwhelming number of entertaining shows. Focus on a central concept.

When Should You Use a Demonstration?

"To keep the room neat" and "to prevent the kids from tearing things up" are *not* good reasons for doing demonstrations. These reasons only prevent children from gaining necessary experience with the materials and also prevent them from learning how to interact appropriately with learning aids. However, reasons for teachers to do demonstrations *do* include:

- to avoid putting children in danger by using a demonstration as a safer alternative;
- to help children learn such skills as the proper ways to use equipment or the proper way to handle and care for plants and animals,
- to stop the class action so it can be focused on an important event for concept development,
- to overcome equipment shortages when there is not enough equipment for all children to benefit firsthand from the exercise,
- to arouse student interest, raise important questions, or pose learning problems that require critical and creative thinking,
- to help solve academic problems,
- to apply what has been studied to new situations by expanding experiences,
- to encourage slow learners and challenge rapid learners.

When Should the Children Do a Demonstration?

Student demonstrations may also be helpful. Proper times for children to demonstrate for their peers include:

- when the child has designed an original activity and should receive recognition for the effort,
- when a child's demonstration and explanation will help other students understand better,
- when a child cannot otherwise tell in words what has been done,
- to help children build self-confidence by speaking before others, to help build verbal communication skills, to help the rapid learner gain new insights.

Demonstrations inevitably open the door for questions. Along with questions come children who are intrinsically motivated and who want more information.

HOW CAN YOU USE EXPOSITION EFFECTIVELY?

Exposition, or lecture, is an efficient way to convey information. While it may be time efficient, exposition is not necessarily effective unless certain steps are taken. Exposition consists of verbal teaching by an authority such as a teacher, textbook, speaker, film, or video. Information is presented without planned interaction between the authority and the student. Teacher lecture and textbook reading are the most common forms of exposition. The way to use exposition most effectively is rather simple: Plan for interaction to occur often between the authority and the student.

Problems and Uses

Exposition carries several problems when used in elementary classrooms. Young children need concrete experiences during most of the elementary grades: verbal presentations of information are difficult for them to follow and their attention span is limited. The logic of the adult mind may not match well with that of the younger mind, and textbook-ordered information has this same problem. Two other problems also are related to exposition: Under the best circumstances the most capable learners only retain about one half or less of what they hear, and what is said is not always what is heard.

Expository teaching does have several appropriate uses: to provide necessary background information before the lesson, to provide important instructions for an activity, and to summarize or bring a lesson to a close.

What can you do before the lesson to help the children understand the concept?

Before the Lesson.   The Advance Organizer is an effective verbal device to use *before* an expository method (Chapter 2). According to David Ausubel,[11] its purpose is to provide a mental structure or framework for thinking before the lesson begins, before the actual material is taught. Advance organizers "are broadly defined as bridges from the [learner's] previous knowledge to whatever is to be learned; they are supposed to be more abstract and inclusive than the more specific material to be learned, and to provide a means of organizing the new material."[12] The lesson then may progress with a teacher presentation, reading, film, or video program; the students already know which important points they should attend to. Use of the advance organizer promotes more active mental participation during the presentation and has contributed to significantly greater pupil learning and retention because presentations are made more meaningful to learners.[13]

There are two types of advance organizers. *Expository* organizers are used with unfamiliar material, often at the beginning of a unit or lesson. For example, a teacher may begin a lesson by saying: "Today we are going to begin a study of animal habitats with an activity. At the end of the activity you should be able to define 'habitat' by describing its parts and how they are related. A habitat consists of five main parts: food, water, shelter, space, and arrangement. Look for examples of these as we do the activity and then read about habitats in our textbooks."

Comparative organizers work well when the children are going to learn new material, but already are familiar with the topic in other ways. Comparative organizers help to link new information with what is already known. A lesson with a comparative organizer may begin this way: "Doors and gates open and close. A switch is like a door or a gate. It opens and closes a circuit. When the switch is open the circuit is open and will *not* permit the electrical device to operate. When the switch is closed, the electricity can pass through the circuit and the devices connected to it *will* work. Today we are going to make switches and construct different types of circuits to see how they operate."

To Provide Instructions or Give Directions.   Exposition is always used when a teacher gives instructions to the class. Effective steps for giving directions include: read, review, and question. It is incorrect to assume that the children will read and follow the directions by themselves if given printed instructions. Instead, read the directions to them or invite a student to read to the class or for a cooperative group, and then ask the children what should be done first, second, and so on. Next, answer their questions. If the children have no questions, offer some of your own that they may think of later, and be prepared to review the answers again. All of this should be done *before* the children receive the materials to ensure safe, orderly completion of the learning activity.

For Summary or Closure.   Exposition can be a useful tool for review at the end of the lesson or the activity if modified from a teacher-centered approach into one that is more student centered. The teacher can review for the children the important points by linking them with specific experiences and by redefining or reexplaining. Ask review questions to encourage the children to construct the summary for themselves. These techniques can help the important concepts to be developed in the same order of the lesson and to be linked with what the children have experienced.

These three uses of expository teaching complement parts of a deductive teaching method. They may be used within a larger framework of deductive teaching and thinking for effective exposition.

Using Deduction

Exposition often follows a deductive approach and is organized from the general idea of the lesson to the specific participation of the learners. Figure 8.2 shows a general deductive model, with four steps proceeding from the broad, general base to the specific learner experiences provided by the lesson. Simple enhancements can be added to make the teaching more interactive. In the case of our chapter scenario, Mrs. Smith's lesson could have proceeded along the following steps if she had chosen to use deduction.

Step 1: Give the Generalization.

"Predators and prey are part of the life cycle of all living things. Our lesson today is about predators and prey."

FIGURE 8.2   Deductive Science Teaching   In deductive teaching, the lesson progresses from the general (a rule, concept, or formula) to the specific student experience (a learning activity, seat work, problem solving).

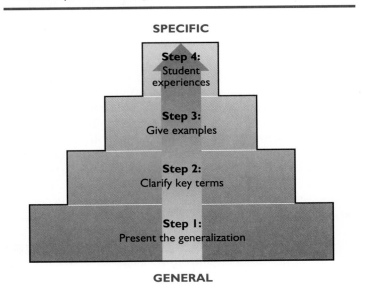

Step 2: Clarify Key Terms.

"Pred-a-tor [written on the chalkboard and carefully pronounced for the class, and then with class participation in its spelling and pronunciation] refers to animals that hunt other animals for food. Prey [written, spelled, and pronounced] is the name given to the animals that are hunted and eaten by other animals."

Step 3: Give Examples.

"Some examples include hawks that catch and eat mice, spiders that catch other insects in their webs, foxes that prey on a farmer's young chickens, and big fish, like a largemouth bass, that eat smaller fish." Textbook reading can also help to give examples.

Step 4: Students Gain Experiences by Working With and/or by Giving Specific Examples.

"Here is a list of animal names. I'd like you to look at it and tell which are the predators and which are the prey: lion, skunk, insect, frog, human, cow, pig, deer, rabbit, fish, bear." After a while the children classify the animals into a predator and prey list, but with difficulty since some animals may be both predator and prey. The children also learn that a single predator may prey upon more than one type of animal and that humans are predators too, an idea that many students had not recognized but now think about as they eat and help parents shop.

"Now please add to our list of predators and prey." Ideas are obtained from the children until two long lists are constructed with a wide variety of animals represented. The teacher then groups the children, has them draw pictures of the animals, and adds them to a mural of an outdoor scene constructed during a previous lesson on habitat. Children then take string or yarn and use tape or thumbtacks to connect the predators with their prey, noting the multiple connections between several and the web of life that is a part of the life cycle of all living things. A discussion about what happens to predators when their preferred prey is not available could close the lesson.

For expansion or for pupil evaluation, the children could write stories to describe or perform skits to demonstrate the relationship between predator and prey, including stalking and hiding habits. Children can also research what happens when predators hunt *not* to eat, such as poachers who prey on the rhino for its horn or on elephants for their ivory tusks. Student research can lead to position statements on ethics and any responsibility governments may have for regulation of commerce, export, or import. Research is also useful for comprehending the difference between preservation and conservation and possessing a better understanding of wildlife protection careers.

Teaching Explicit Material

Science textbooks introduce more new words or phrases than are introduced in foreign language textbooks![14] This type of treatment assumes explicit material must be learned and that it is the teacher's job to present it so learners can master it. Exclusively treating science material in this fashion does a disservice to the learners

Explicit teaching requires teacher guidance.

and misrepresents science. However, there are occasions when a body of information or well-defined skills must be taught. Science facts, some concepts, selected laboratory skills, and science vocabulary may be taught effectively with explicit teaching methods. Barak Rosenshine identifies the actions of effective teachers when they teach facts, concepts, or skills explicitly.[15]

1. Begin a lesson with a brief statement of goals.
2. Begin teaching with a brief review of the previous lesson.
3. Present new material in small steps with practice after each step.
4. Give clear and detailed instructions and explanations.
5. Provide active practice for all children.
6. Ask many questions to check for learner understanding; obtain responses from all children.
7. Guide children when they first start to practice.
8. Provide systematic feedback for all children, and correct their mistakes.
9. Provide explicit instruction and practice for seatwork and monitor learner progress.
10. Continue practice until all children are independent and confident.

Rosenshine clusters the major parts of this method into several small steps, as shown in Table 8.1. He concedes that this approach does not apply to all students or for all teaching situations.

The method is based on information processing research that recognizes the limits of human memory, the importance of practice, and the elements of task mastery. Children can only attend to and process effectively small amounts of information. Abstract learners can only process seven unrelated items at a time without confusion; learners whose cognitive development has not reached that level (which includes most elementary children) can process even fewer than seven. Material must be processed before it can be remembered and used. Active mental processing such as reviewing, summarizing, and rehearsing moves material into long-term memory. Teacher questions, student summaries, and active supervision assist this processing. Finally, if learning is to appear automatic through effortless recall, extensive practice and frequent review are necessary.

TABLE 8.1   Explicit Teaching Functions

1. Teaching for review
    * review homework
    * review previous learning important to the present lesson
    * review prerequisite skills and information needed for the present lesson
2. Presenting the lesson
    * state the lesson goals and/or outline the lesson
    * teach in small steps
    * model the skills and procedures children are to follow
    * provide concrete positive and negative examples to assist comprehension
    * use clear language
    * check for student understanding
    * avoid digressions or tangents
3. Guide the practice
    * use many questions to help guide practice
    * ensure that all students respond and receive feedback about their learning
    * strive for a high success rate; optimal is 75–80 percent correct answers during guided practice
    * continue guided practice until all students are competent
4. Make corrections and give feedback
    * give process feedback when children are correct but hesitant
    * when children are incorrect, give them clues or encouragement
    * reteach when necessary
5. Provide for independent practice
    * actively supervise to give children help
    * continue practice until students can respond automatically (when this applies)
    * use routines to help slower pupils; this may include peers helping peers
6. Use weekly and monthly reviews to strengthen learning
    * select a special day to review the previous week's concepts
    * use a TV show format
    * involve children in constructing questions
    * develop a special monthly format and promote it like the coming big event on television

Source: Adapted from Barak V. Rosenshine, "Synthesis of Research on Explicit Teaching," *Educational Leadership* (April 1986), p. 65.

Interaction is a concept that can unite the methods presented in this chapter. Interaction can be used to make teacher-centered methods less authoritarian, less reliant on a textbook, and more effective by

- stimulating students' interests
- more actively involving children in the lesson
- promoting more thinking and information processing
- providing relevant learning experiences

Teacher-centered methods work well with science textbooks. Aside from you the teacher, the single most dominant factor in most elementary science programs is the textbook. Selection of an appropriate text and effective use of it can improve your students' achievement, skills, and attitudes.

HOW CAN YOU USE SCIENCE TEXTBOOKS EFFECTIVELY?

Reams of research reports support the superiority of activity-based science programs and teaching methods.[16] Unfortunately, "what was intended to be joyful discovery for students too often turned out to be a lost sojourn into the abstract and difficult"[17] because teachers returned to textbooks even though textbooks continue to be criticized for their shortcomings.

Be Aware of Shortcomings and Differences

Elementary science texts vary considerably on such factors as readability, reading and study aids, treatment of gender, and emphasis given to vocabulary versus concepts. Readability studies show greater levels of difference mostly for the upper elementary and the middle grades. Students' science achievements decline when they use texts written above their reading ability levels. Reading and study aids, such as chapter headings, help pupils comprehend and recall, particularly when children are taught to use these features. Gender bias has been reduced in texts recently, with more balance now seen toward male and female representation. However, children and professionals who are handicapped and/or nonwhite often do not receive substantial recognition in textbooks. Science vocabulary is emphasized much more than science concepts, although researchers report that textbooks that emphasize concepts rather than vocabulary do *increase* science achievement.[18] In contrast to this finding, Paul D. Hurd has found science texts often introduce "as many as 2,500 technical terms and unfamiliar words."[19] He notes that a beginning course in foreign language only attempts to cover half as many new words.

A comparison of eleven elementary science textbook series that represent over 90 percent of the national science textbook market shows some improvements, but there are still tremendous shortcomings in the quality of science texts. For example, Elliott and Nagel's analysis claims that elementary textbook series "do not promote or encourage the development of scientific thinking or attitudes, nor do they engage students in applying the cognitive processes that are basic to understanding the content covered."[20] In addition, Staver and Bay's[21] analysis reports:

- Most text prose focuses on academic science.
- Most remaining text prose focuses on personal goals.
- The career and societal goals receive only minor attention.
- Text illustrations exhibit a pattern similar to text prose.
- Text activities and experiments are academic in orientation, almost to the exclusion of other goals.
- End-of-chapter sentences are largely academic.
- Inquiry is absent or present only in limited forms in text activities and experiments.
- Texts allocate only a minor portion of space to activities and experiments.

Staver and Bay also found some decreases in the amount of academic emphasis with accompanying increases in the remaining science goals—a positive feature. Figure 8.3 shows four graphs that represent the portions of process skills, concept development, application, and science-based societal is-sues recommended by the National Science Teachers Association for grades K–12.[22] Staver and Bay's research reveals that some texts come close to meeting two recommendations (application and science-based social issues), while science process skills consistently receive only minor treatment in all elementary science texts.[23]

Who decides what material science textbooks will include and how they will be organized? Recommendations from credible sources such as the National Science Teachers Association or the American Association for the Advancement of Science do not always drive the development or revision of printed materials like school textbooks. Authors, teachers, editors, marketing staffs in publishing houses, boards of education, and textbook censors have less influence than you may imagine. A single large state, such as Texas, that adopts one or two elementary science textbook series for use by all schools, carries a tremendous influence because of its large market. What one large state wants in a text, it usually receives, and therefore it influences what the books contain for the rest of the country. Approaches and material that appear radical or unconventional stand little chance despite their academic merits, origin, or proven effects.

If it seems unlikely that textbooks will be dramatically improved, what options do you have? You *do* have a choice of programs. The choice you make will influence the amount of teacher direction you use to guide your students and the extent of the positive impact upon their interactive learning experience. You can

- enhance the text in use,
- change the sequence of topics to better reflect the concepts to be learned,
- select the text that most closely represents the needs of your students and fulfills the recommendations for effective science teaching and learning.

Enhancing the Text

Each teacher can enhance the text to include more effective learning activities and interesting information, rather than wait for authors and publishers to do it. You can

FIGURE 8.3   Recommended Percentage of Instructional Time by Grade Level   The percentage of instructional time that should be devoted to process skills, concept development, application, and science-based societal issues, as recommended by the National Science Teachers Association.

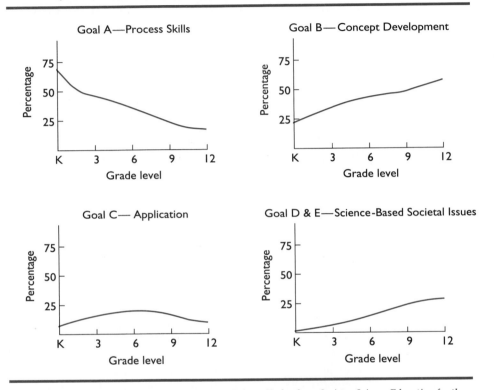

Source: National Science Teachers Association, *Science-Technology-Society: Science Education for the 1980s,* Position Statement (Washington, DC: NSTA, 1982).

add enhancements that are timely and that match learner interests and abilities. Some ways you can enhance textbooks include:

1. *Combine the best elements from published programs.* Use old editions or the most interesting materials from unadopted examination copies of textbooks. Cut out pictures, information, and activities to make mini-books or a resource file by topic.

2. *Select relevant supplements from laboratory programs.* Experimental programs like ESS, SCIS, and SAPA may have been used and then discarded by your school. Remnants can often be found stored away. Conduct an inventory of equipment and teaching materials from the past and select useful materials that enhance the concepts you are teaching.

How are Scientists Portrayed in Children's Literature?

Allen Evans, assistant professor and fifth-grade teacher at the Ackerman Lab School at Eastern Oregon State College in La Grande, investigated popular children's literature to uncover the ways scientists are portrayed to children. His research was stimulated by his students' stereotypical images of scientists. Children's literature is rapidly replacing a single text in classrooms where whole language approaches are favored. Therefore, it is important to expand our concerns about textbooks to the collection of literature used with children. We use many of Evans's words to report what he found.

> Elementary classroom teachers have long been aware that books influence children's perceptions of the world. Characters found in children's books provide inspiration, consolation, and motivation. They entertain, inform, and encourage, and they can provide positive examples for overcoming adversity.
>
> Sadly, however, not all characters in children's books present accurate depictions of their real-life counterparts, and teachers must be vigilant in looking out for stereotypes in order to make informed and appropriate choices of instructional materials.
>
> With recent trends of "reading-across-the-curriculum," classroom teachers, and science teachers in particular, need to know how scientists are portrayed in children's books. Is the image of the scientist an accurate one? Or, do children's books reinforce the absentminded, bubbling-pot, blow-up-the-laboratory stereotype? Furthermore, as teachers encourage their students to consider careers in science, knowledge of the scientists in children's books becomes more important. If children's books do in fact depict scientists in stereotypical ways, children may be less likely to view science as a desirable career choice. To answer these questions, I decided to investigate the portrayal of scientists and science-oriented characters in seventeen selected children's fiction books.

The selection criteria resulted in books that had either a science-oriented plot or at least one science-oriented character, were written for upper elementary or middle school children, had been published within the last twenty years (the majority were published during the last ten), were realistic fiction or science fiction books, and had been cited and reviewed in at least one major professional journal devoted to children's literature.

Twenty-five science-oriented characters were found, and 88 percent were male. Eleven of the seventeen books were written by females. Sixty percent of the science-oriented characters were adults, 20 percent were teenagers, and 20 percent were children. Science teachers, professors, and laboratory researchers represented 52 percent of the characters; 20 percent had a personal interest in science, perhaps as a hobby; 4 percent were involved in school science activities; the rest had an unclear orientation toward science. Evans's report sums up the portrait of a scientist in children's literature this way:

> Scientists are adult males whose orientation is due to a professional relationship. They are generally ordinary in their actions and mannerisms, as well as ordinary in their physical appearance, and are of above-average intelligence. For concerned science teachers, the news is good—the image of the scientists appearing in these books is one that is reasonably free of the typical stereotypes.
>
> There does, however, appear to be room for improvement. While it is true that the sciences are currently a white-male-dominated field, more and more women and minorities are pursuing science as a viable career option. Therefore, the inclusion of female and minority science-oriented characters in children's books must be encouraged.
>
> Science teachers in particular should benefit from an increased awareness of how scientists and science-oriented characters are portrayed in children's books. With that understanding, teachers can work more closely with other nonscience professionals, such as reading teachers and librarians, in identifying and selecting children's books depicting scientists in positive, nonstereotypical roles.

Source: Allen Evans, "A Look at the Scientists as Portrayed in Children's Literature," *Science and Children,* March 1992, pp. 35–37.

3. *Identify local resources.* School and community professionals, local businesses, parks and recreation facilities, libraries, and museums all provide rich enhancement sources for classroom speakers and field trips. These enhancement resources also help to demonstrate the relationship of science and everyday life as well as update or fill in gaps not covered by dated textbooks. (See Chapter 12 for more ideas.)

4. *Check with your state's department of education.* Some states compare commercial materials and keep on file survey-style coverage of important science findings and laboratory programs that make fine enhancements for standard textbook programs. An example is the California *Science Addendum.*

5. *Screen supplementary materials for the appropriate reading level.* Deemphasize use of a text written on a reading level too high by substituting suitable materials. Use accelerated material if the text is too simple.

6. *Select evaluation devices that reflect the objectives.* If your objective is development of a particular process skill, select performance-based evaluation tasks that

Student activities can enhance the use of a textbook.

require the children to demonstrate the skill. Carefully screen all text questions and written exercises and select those that match the intended level of thinking and skills. Adapt project ideas and improve the types of questions used in the text or teacher's guide.

7. *Work to organize building- or district-level committees in which teachers form supplement teams.* More hands make lighter work, and more heads generate a greater number of effective ideas. Teams of teachers can work together to enhance the text by sharing the research and swapping ideas.

8. *Attend professional conferences.* States have affiliates of the National Science Teachers Association, and large cities have their own science education organizations. Attend their annual conferences and listen to other teachers to get ideas for your own classroom. Adapt these ideas to enhance your science program. Remember, your ideas are just as important as those of others: Why not make your own presentation at a conference or provide a workshop for other teachers?

9. *Relearn the concepts and processes of science.* Take workshops or courses to learn about the most recent ideas in science and its teaching. This continues your education and professional development; both can help you enhance the science text. Request a staff development program for yourself and for helping the other school staff members relearn and elevate their own levels of scientific literacy. Other teachers will be more likely to enhance the text if they feel more confident and informed.

Change the Sequence

The text's chapter order and the organization of the information within chapters may not be what is best for your students. Perhaps some simple resequencing will bring improvements in science achievement, attitudes, and interest.

Cognitive scientists emphasize the importance of anchoring ideas to the learner's mental structure. New information becomes more meaningful when it can be attached to concepts already in the children's minds. Science material is better understood when it interrelates "in such a way as to make sense to the learner."[24] Resequencing text material so ideas relate in ways that make more sense to the children adds meaning. In a study of sixth graders,

> the findings revealed that students for whom content structure was clarified through resequencing general science chapters exhibited significantly higher science achievement, significantly more positive attitudes toward science, and significantly greater interest in science than students for whom general science content was not resequenced.[25]

Concept mapping is a method of sequencing the ideas of a lesson, and a version of it can be used to sequence the text effectively. A concept map shows ideas graphically according to their relationships. (See Chapter 4 for more information.) The relationships communicate important connections that show an intended mental structure to be formed about the map's topic. Consider the following when resequencing:

FIGURE 8.4   A Sample Hierarchical Structure of Science Content

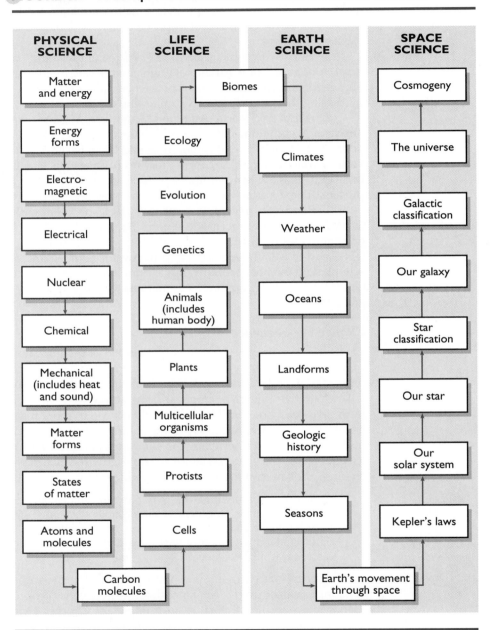

Source: Linda Hamrick and Harold Harty, "Influence of Resequencing General Science Content on the Science Achievement, Attitudes Toward Science, and Interest in Science of Sixth Grade Students," *Journal of Research in Science Teaching,* vol. 24, no. 1 (1987), p. 19. Reprinted by permission of John Wiley & Sons, Inc.

1. *Proceed from the smallest to the largest ideas, or from the simple to the complex, when resequencing a text.* Researchers recommend that rearrangments first be made into an interrelated pattern based on the size of the ideas.[26] A hierarchy of ideas is formed; perhaps physical science leads to life science topics, which progress to earth and space science concepts. See Figure 8.4 for an example of the hierarchy of ideas and Table 8.2 for an example of a typical textbook sequence of topics with a revised sequence. You can determine the children's hierarchical views of the material by doing a webbing exercise in which they refer to the table of contents or chapter titles of the text and connect them in a web that makes sense to them. Begin at the chalkboard with a single word such as *science* and have the children refer to the ideas in the chapter titles and sections within chapters to add the ideas of science to the chalkboard. Engage the children in a discussion of how they see these ideas of science connected; ask for their reasons. Your prompts can help them to order material from the simple to the more complex in a way that is more understandable. At the same time, you will be reinforcing higher levels of thinking.

2. *Convey the interrelated structure to the students.* An overview of the restructured material can be made on a student handout, placed in a notebook, and used for clarification, reinforcement, and review throughout the year. Children can check off the major concepts as they are studied. This serves as a structure of information for learners, gives you an opportunity to teach for concepts, and provides a ready guide for reinforcement. Figure 8.5 shows an example of a student handout with text overview.

TABLE 8.2   A Sample Comparison of Unrevised and Revised Textbook Content Sequence

Textbook Sequence	Revised Content Sequence
Animals with backbones	Matter (elements and compounds)
Classifying animals without backbones	Sources of energy
Plants	Light
Life cycles	Electricity and magnetism
Matter (elements and compounds)	Communications
Electricity and magnetism	Energy outcomes and the future
Sources of energy	Energy for living things
Light	Life cycles
Communications	Plants
Climates of the world	Classifying animals without backbones
Energy for living things	Animals with backbones
Energy outcomes and the future	Climates of the world

Source: Linda Hamrick and Harold Harty, "Influence of Resequencing General Science Content on the Science Achievement, Attitudes Toward Science, and Interest in Science of Sixth Grade Students," *Journal of Research in Science Teaching*, vol. 24, no. 1 (1987), p. 20. Reprinted by permission of John Wiley & Sons, Inc.

3. *Clarify the content structure for the children.* Learners will not absorb all the ideas of the resequencing overview at once. Take advantage of any opportunity to discuss the structure of the material you have chosen for your class by painting the big picture and showing how the smaller ideas fit into a pattern with the larger ideas.

FIGURE 8.5   A Sample Student Overview of Resequenced Material with Chapter Numbers

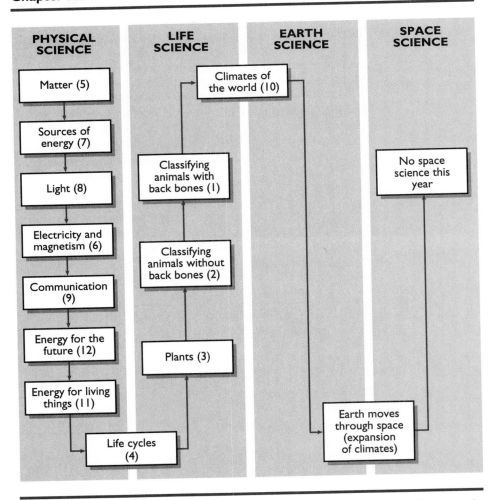

Source: Linda Hamrick and Harold Harty, ''Influence of Resequencing General Science Content on the Science Achievement, Attitudes Toward Science, and Interest in Science of Sixth Grade Students,'' *Journal of Research in Science Teaching,* vol. 24, no. 1 (1987), p. 21. Reprinted by permission of John Wiley & Sons, Inc.

*The best science textbook will challenge
children to improve their thinking.*

Selecting the Best Textbook

Not one of the recent best-selling textbooks was in the top thirteen in 1979.[27]
Teachers are becoming more selective, and it may be that their efforts to identify the
best are having effects on textbook changes.

Textbooks are often selected because they offer many activities, worksheets,
tests, and programmed teacher's guides. They appear busy or glitzy and may
require little more than reading and writing exercises. Such textbooks fall short of
meeting recommendations for effective science instruction.

Selecting a best text consists of more than determining its readability level. Of
course, we want to have texts written on an appropriate level, but there are more
than thirty different readability formulas,[28] and they do not all measure the same
thing, making it impossible to compare one formula's measure with another's. It is
a better approach to ask "What thinking is required?" rather than "What is the
reading level?" Many science activities have obvious answers. Students simply read
them and know the answer or find the exact wording required in a predictable place.
Also, doing the activities may not be required, and little thought may be elicited by
the prose or chapter questions.

TEACHERS ON SCIENCE TEACHING

How Can Toys Enhance Your Teaching?

By Michael E. Cawthra
5th Grade Teacher, Kyffin Elementary School, Golden, Colorado

There are literally dozens of books out on the market to help teachers bring science demonstrations into the classroom. I know, I'm on the mailing list for all of them. But it is worth it to have an assortment of ideas at your fingertips. Don't let anyone tell you that you must teach the textbook and never vary from it. Textbooks are nice, but you have to be yourself. Go for it!

When you start to do classroom demos, make sure you have practiced and are prepared. Nothing can kill the demo faster than the teacher leaning over the file cabinet or searching through the closet muttering, "Just a second kids, I'll have what I need. Just sit still." Yeah, right. Before you can turn around, Johnny is all over the room and into everything you had out for the demo. Likewise, nothing can get and hold their attention like all the equipment laid out on the table.

Speaking of equipment, it would be great to have thousands of dollars' worth of glassware, burners, chemicals, and such. But you can also use mason jars and propane torches and check out the chemicals that are sold over the grocery store counter. Ping pong balls—I keep at least a dozen on hand for all sorts of demonstrations: atomic structure (color them

and give kids colored marshmallows for their set so they can eat them at the end), planets, physics—well, you get the idea. A globe and a ball, the diameter of which is the same as the distance from San Francisco to Cleveland on your globe, will be the perfect model for the earth and the moon. Also include a string that has been wrapped around the globe ten times; that's the distance from the earth to the moon. And never underestimate the toy department. Oh boy, my wife won't let me go in unescorted. Slinkies, cars, marbles, magnets, and models—models of space shuttles, human bodies, eyes, just about anything.

Yes, I must admit, my room looks like a toy store. But the bottom line is this: Are the kids learning? You bet your atom they are. Because I also don't just sit. When kids with ping pong balls are walking around the room imitating electrons moving about the nucleus, and another kid is trying to hit a ball with a marshmallow, they understand the reason electrons pass through matter without hitting anything, that atoms are mostly empty space. Yeah, they learn. And that is the whole point, the "Ah-hah" moment we all live for, when Suzy says, "I get it, Mr. C!"

The research of Gregory Risner, Dorothy Skeel, and Janice Nicholson[29] reveals a surprising reverse trend in the most popular science textbooks since emphasis has been placed on school reform. On the matter of end-of-chapter questions and test bank questions in the teacher's manuals, the newer editions have gotten worse instead of better. Risner, Skeel, and Nicholson used textbook adoption information from the state departments of education in Alabama, California, Tennessee, and Texas to obtain a rank ordering of the fifth-grade science textbooks used most frequently. Earlier editions ("old," 1983–1984) were compared to more recent editions ("new," 1989). The percentages of knowledge-level and above-knowledge-level questions were determined and are shown in Figures 8.6 and 8.7. These questions were reasonably well distributed earlier in the decade, but were less so in later editions. The questions were found to be less productive and unchallenging.

FIGURE 8.6   Old Science Textbook Editions (1983–1984)

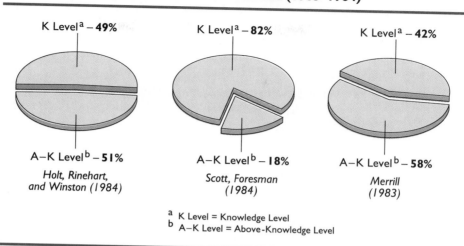

K Level[a] – **49%**

K Level[a] – **82%**

K Level[a] – **42%**

A–K Level[b] – **51%**

A–K Level[b] – **18%**

A–K Level[b] – **58%**

Holt, Rinehart,
and Winston (1984)

Scott, Foresman
(1984)

Merrill
(1983)

[a] K Level = Knowledge Level
[b] A–K Level = Above-Knowledge Level

Reprinted by permission, National Science Teachers Association, 1742 Connecticut Avenue, NW, Washington, DC 20009.

FIGURE 8.7   New Science Textbook Editions (1989)

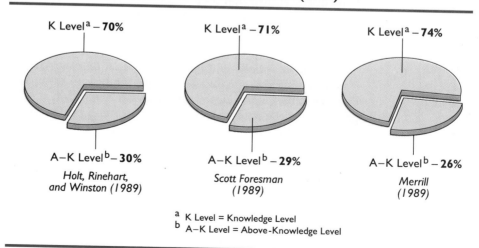

K Level[a] – **70%**

K Level[a] – **71%**

K Level[a] – **74%**

A–K Level[b] – **30%**

A–K Level[b] – **29%**

A–K Level[b] – **26%**

Holt, Rinehart,
and Winston (1989)

Scott Foresman
(1989)

Merrill
(1989)

[a] K Level = Knowledge Level
[b] A–K Level = Above-Knowledge Level

Reprinted by permission, National Science Teachers Association, 1742 Connecticut Avenue, NW, Washington, DC 20009.

It seems the expectations for students slipped. Little attention was given to application, analysis, synthesis, and evaluation; this lack reveals a gap between the stated goals of elementary science and the classroom practice promoted by texts. What can you do to select a better text or to use the text you have in ways that improve the experience for students? As a starting point for screening texts, ask yourself

- What does the text expect my students to do?
- What should they be able to do after they study the text that they could not do before?
- For every student activity, project, or question, ask "What kind of thinking is required?"
- Examine the texts for inclusion of the science goals (Chapter 3) and ask "To what extent is each dimension emphasized?" and "How is it included in the text?"
- Consider the goals of Project 2061 or the National Standards (Chapter 3), especial-ly conceptual emphasis, and ask "How well do the text's concepts represent those recommended?"
- Summarize your initial screening by asking "Will this text really help my students reach the goals I have set for them—or is it going to waste their time?"

Look again at those texts that pass your initial screening. Now is the time to be more critical. An effective text should involve children in the processes of science by guiding them toward making discoveries. The activities should not be cookbook recipes that encourage learners to mindlessly follow the steps. Focus upon the student activities, sample several from each text, and ask these questions:

- Are students required to make careful observations?
- Are students encouraged to make inferences?
- Is classification a skill used in the experiments?
- How often are students asked to make a prediction based on observation or data?
- How often are students encouraged to display data in a systematic way that will enhance their ability to communicate?[30]

These questions will help you select a text that delivers a strong blend of expository information and productive interaction through sound activity-based learning. Table 8.3 provides a list of factors to beware when selecting a text. Table 8.4 provides a brief instrument for screening texts and printed curriculum materials. All the information in this section of the chapter can be developed into your own customized form for rating and selecting textbooks or other printed curriculum materials.

We cannot force students to learn. We can help them discover for themselves, and our guidance is an important factor. Go slowly and guide with purpose. Perhaps cover less information by striving for quality rather than quantity. Remember the maxim: Less is more. Listen to students more and talk less. Try to emphasize student cooperation instead of competition. Blend learning activities to include discovery opportunities, group work, and learning that requires different types of information processing—thinking. Try to concentrate on students doing right

TABLE 8.3 Things to Beware when Choosing a Textbook

At least two issues must be considered when choosing a textbook: the pedagogical (teaching method) points, and the content (subject matter) points.

Pedagogical Points

1. Beware a text that claims to cover all students need to know about a subject. Consider instead a text that is selective and attempts to cover the important ideas of a subject area, not one that looks like an encyclopedia and expects students to memorize a great deal of information.
2. Beware a text that emphasizes large amounts of science vocabulary and expects students to memorize it. Page after page of bold vocabulary words distract readers from the important ideas. Specialized vocabulary should not be overrepresented, but selected useful vocabulary can serve to broaden understanding.
3. Beware the text that does not read well. Avoid texts that use short, choppy sentences to focus on detail and offer many conclusions. The ideal text will maintain the narrative of inquiry and will not provide a passive reading experience.
4. Beware the dogmatic text. The information of science changes as new discoveries are made and new ideas replace the old. Avoid texts that show science as absolute and unchanging. Also avoid the other extreme. Texts that appear to show science as a body of untested hypotheses and guesses do not represent science properly.
5. Beware the text as the sole source of information. A good text should be adequately supplemented with learning activities, project ideas, and lists of resources that can be used to expand children's thinking and their experiences.

Content Points

1. Beware the text that does not represent the nature of science. One chapter or a paragraph about the scientific method is inadequate and a waste of time. Scientists do have methods, but they do not follow them in the single artificial step-by-step fashion portrayed. The processes of science should permeate the text and give children opportunities to investigate interesting topics and outcomes that are unknown to them, just as scientists do.
2. Beware the text that does not clearly show the role of controlled experiments, development of hypotheses, and uses of theory. These are the real tools of scientists, which are not easily mastered and certainly not turned into skills by reading about them. They must be practiced.
3. Beware the text that emphasizes only one aspect of a science discipline. No single text can cover all viewpoints about a subject, but each should include acceptable alternatives. As an example, biology topics often include only morphology and systems, but they should include topics like ecology, genetics, growth and development, evolution, and behavior. If these areas are included, a student's personal development and academic growth will be enhanced. Science texts should never be written in isolation from society and technology; career opportunities should be liberally represented.
4. Beware the bland textbook. Texts written to avoid controversy will not accurately portray science, nor will they expose children to its value. Unresolved problems of science should be discussed. Children should be presented with accurate information and be given opportunities to process the information, make up their own minds, and defend their positions.
5. Beware the classical textbook. Science portrayed retrospectively will not deal with current areas of research and problems. This approach will not contribute to the preparation of children to face and function in the future.

Source: Adapted from William V. Mayer and James P. Barufaldi, *The Textbook Chooser's Guide* (Berkeley, CA: National Center for Science Education, 1985).

thinking rather than getting right answers. If you must use a text and teacher-centered approaches, incorporate several of the suggestions offered in this chapter to make your classroom more interactive. Chances for effective teaching will be greater through your efforts, and your reward will be improved student achievement, positive attitudes toward science, and greater interest in school.

TABLE 8.4   Screening Texts and Other Printed Curriculum Materials

You can learn about the science program by examining the textbooks and other written curriculum materials available. The following simple screening device is excerpted from Kenneth R. Mechling and Donna L. Oliver's *Characteristics of a Good Elementary Science Program*.[31]

	Yes	No	Unsure
Science Content			
1. Is there a balanced emphasis among the life sciences, earth sciences, and physical sciences?	___	___	___
2. Do the materials include study of problems that are important to us now and in the future? Examples: acid rain, air and water pollution, effects of spraying, energy production and availability, medical research, world hunger, population, deforestation, ozone depletion	___	___	___
3. Do the materials require students to apply major science concepts to everyday life situations?	___	___	___
4. Other	___	___	___
Science Processes			
1. Do the materials include liberal amounts of hands-on investigations and activities the children can do?	___	___	___
2. Are uses of scientific processes an important part of the materials the children will read? Examples: observing, measuring, predicting, inferring, classifying, recording and analyzing data, and so on	___	___	___
3. Do the materials encourage children to explore, discover, and find answers for themselves rather than tell them how things should turn out?	___	___	___
4. Do the materials require children to apply science processes to problem-solving situations?	___	___	___
5. Other	___	___	___
Other Considerations			
1. Are the materials consistent with the science goals of your school (or in the absence of such goals, those of the National Standards or your state framework of science goals)?	___	___	___
2. Are the materials clearly written, accurate, up to date?	___	___	___
3. Do the materials proceed from the simple to the complex, and are they designed for the children's developmental levels?	___	___	___
4. Is the information written at the proper grade level?	___	___	___
5. Do the materials for children appear interesting and relevant?	___	___	___
6. Are there opportunities for children to learn about science-related careers?	___	___	___
7. Are valid evaluation materials used or included? Examples: tests, record sheets, performance demonstrations, reports	___	___	___
8. Is a teacher's guide included, and is it helpful for using the materials?	___	___	___
9. Do the materials include enough application of science content and processes to make science meaningful to students?	___	___	___
10. Other	___	___	___

CHAPTER SUMMARY

About 90 percent of science classrooms use a single text the majority of the time for instruction. The teaching methods used are often teacher centered and authoritarian, even though considerable evidence reveals the limits of these approaches and more effective methods are available. Teacher-centered methods can be made more effective by using interactive techniques that enhance the children's learning experiences and help meet the goals of an effective science education.

The interactive techniques described in this chapter include demonstrations, exposition, deductive teaching, explicit teaching, and uses of textbooks. Exposition includes use of advance organizers, giving directions, and summary techniques for lessons. Deductive teaching organizes lessons from science generalizations to specific learner experiences. Explicit teaching is a technique of interactive lecture, student recitation, feedback, and practice. It is based on the effective teaching research.

The quality and features of textbooks vary considerably. The last section of this chapter acquaints readers with the shortcomings and differences of textbooks. Positive actions teachers can take to use textbooks more effectively include enhancing the text, changing the instructional sequence of textbook topics, mapping the chapter concepts, and exercising discretion when selecting a textbook.

DISCUSSION QUESTIONS AND PROJECTS

1. Why do most teachers revert to teacher-centered methods and authoritarian treatment of science through extensive use of the textbook even though they may know about more effective alternatives?

2. What can be done to motivate teachers to use more interactive teaching methods with young children?

3. How does the planning teachers must do to use the methods recommended in this chapter compare with the planning required by the cooperative inquiry methods described in Chapter 7?

4. What do you think are the characteristics of the ideal science textbook?

5. Why do you think something as simple as resequencing the topics of a textbook is related to increased student science achievement?

6. What signs indicate that a text should be considered or avoided?

7. How can teachers evaluate process skills and higher thinking? To what extent are these promoted by teacher-centered methods and textbooks?

8. How can reading enhancements (such as bold print for special words) found in textbooks interfere with the goals of science education? Do you believe the goals for scientific literacy run counter to the goals of general literacy? Why?

9. Plan a lesson (or a unit) using an advance organizer, demonstration, and techniques of deductive and/or explicit teaching with a textbook. Teach the lesson and have it recorded (video preferred). Compare your skills with the ideal requirements for each method described in this chapter. How do your skills compare? What can you do to become more effective? Which methods made it possible for you to be more interactive with the children?

10. Examine a school's science program for inclusion of the methods of effective teacher-centered teaching. To what extent is each method encouraged? Write a summary and offer recommendations for improving the program.

11. Analyze several science textbooks written for the same grade level. What are their advantages and shortcomings? Which text do you prefer? Why? What is needed to overcome the shortcomings of your preferred text?

12. Analyze your preferred science text (or texts from different publishers) across grade levels. Use the criteria for selecting the best textbook given in this chapter. Which text series do you prefer and why? Which series comes closest to fulfilling the recommendations of the science goals given in Chapter 3, or those of Project 2061 or the National Standards?

13. Examine a school district's course of study and compare it with the actual science program or text used. Which was done first, the writing of the course of study or the selection of the science program? To what extent does the course of study reflect the organization of the program or text? Compare your findings with those of your classmates. What do you conclude about the extent to which a program relates to a course of study?

14. Use the ideas provided in this chapter to develop your own form for science textbook and curriculum materials analysis. What are the main categories you feel must be included to yield a useful form?

Try your form and ask others to try it. What revisions may be necessary and why?

15. Write to your state's department of education and ask what information it provides to help teachers and school districts improve science programs. Does your state have recommended programs or textbooks? If yes, determine how they were selected for recommendation. If no, determine why your state takes no position and what services it does provide to teachers and schools who want assistance.

16. Select a text, read one of its chapters, and record the science words emphasized in the titles, headings, and bold or italicized print. Develop a strategy for mapping the concepts of these words and for helping students understand the connections between and among the concepts.

NOTES

1. This scenario is excerpted from Steven J. Rakow, *Teaching Science as Inquiry* (Bloomington, IN: Phi Delta Kappa, Fastback #246, 1986), pp. 8–11. Reprinted with permission.

2. David Holdzkom and Pamela B. Lutz (eds.), *Research Within Reach: Science Education* (Charleston, WV: Research and Development Interpretation Service, 1984).

3. David L. Elliott and Kathleen Carter, "'Scientific Illiteracy' in Elementary Science Textbook Programs," a paper presented at the Annual Meeting of the American Educational Research Association, San Francisco, CA, April 1986 (ERIC Document no. 269257), p. 11.

4. John R. Staver and Mary Bay, "Analysis of the Project Synthesis Goal Cluster Orientation and Inquiry Emphasis of Elementary Science Textbooks," *Journal of Research in Science Teaching*, vol. 23, no. 7 (1987), pp. 629–643.

5. Elliott and Nagel, p. 11.

6. Mary Iatridis, "Teaching Science to Preschoolers," *Science and Children* (October 1981), p. 26.

7. Mary K. Willert and Constance Kamii, "Reading in Kindergarten: Direct vs. Indirect Teaching," *Young Children* (May 1985), p. 3.

8. Ibid., p. 8.

9. Donna M. Wolfinger, *Teaching Science in the Elementary School* (Boston: Little, Brown, 1984), p. 223.

10. Clara J. Guerra, "Pulling Science Out of a Hat," *Science and Children*, (March 1988), pp. 23–24. Guerra's article also provides several other effective demonstrations with illustrations and scientific explanations.

11. David P. Ausubel, *Psychology of Meaningful Verbal Learning* (New York: Greene and Stratton, 1963).

12. Carol Leth Stone, "A Meta-Analysis of Advance-Organizer Studies," a paper presented at the Annual Meeting of the American Educational Research Association, New York, 1982 (ERIC Document no. 220476), p. 1.

13. Ibid., pp. 6–7.

14. Robert E. Yager, "The Importance of Terminology in Teaching K–12 Science," *Journal of Research in Science Teaching*, vol. 20, no. 6 (1983), pp. 577–588.

15. Barak V. Rosenshine, "Synthesis of Research on Explicit Teaching," *Educational Leadership* (April 1986), pp. 60–69.

16. Linda A. Meyer, Eunice A. Greer, and Lorraine Crummey, *Elementary Science Textbooks: Their Contents, Text Characteristics, and Comprehensibility*, Technical Report no. 386 (Champaign, IL: University of Illinois, ERIC Document no. 278947, 1986), p. 4.

17. Kenneth R. Mechling and Donna L. Oliver, "Activities, Not Textbooks: What Research Says About Science Programs," *Principal* (1983), p. 43.

18. Meyer, p. 5.

19. Paul DeHart Hurd, "Middle School/Junior High Science: Changing Perspectives," *The Middle/Junior High Science Bulletin*, vol. 5, (May 1982), p. 12.

20. Elliott and Carter, p. 1.

21. Staver and Bay, p. 629.

22. National Science Teachers Association, *Science-Technology-Society: Science Education for the 1980s*, Position Statement (Washington, DC: NSTA, 1982).

23. Staver and Bay, pp. 640–641.

24. Linda Hamrick and Harold Harty, "Influence of Resequencing General Science Content on the Science Achievement, Attitudes Toward Science, and Interest in Science of Sixth Grade Students," *Journal of Research in Science Teaching*, vol. 24, no. 1 (1987), p. 16.

25. Ibid., p. 15.
26. Ibid., p. 18.
27. Meyer, pp. 6–7.
28. George Wheeler and Thomas F. Sherman, "Readability Formulas Revisited," *Science and Children*, vol. 20, no. 7 (April 1983), pp. 38–40.
29. Gregory P. Risner, Dorothy J. Skeel, and Janice I. Nicholson, "A Closer Look at Textbooks," *Science and Children* (September 1992), pp. 42–45, 73.

30. R. J. McLeod, "Selecting a Textbook for Good Science Teaching," *Science and Children* (October 1979), pp. 14–15.
31. Kenneth R. Mechling and Donna L. Oliver, *Characteristics of a Good Elementary Science Program*, Handbook III (Washington, DC: National Science Teachers Association, 1983), pp. 6–8. Reprinted with permission.

ADDITIONAL READINGS

If you are interested in learning more about some of the topics raised in this chapter, consider the following sources.

Paul Eggen and Donald Kauchak, *Strategies for Teachers: Teaching Content and Thinking Skills* (Englewood Cliffs, NJ: Prentice Hall, 1988). Teacher-centered models of teaching are described, with an emphasis on developing skills. Each chapter includes brief concept maps and is easily organized for study about the methods; each method is described in terms of teaching phases to be accomplished. Most strategies promote teacher-pupil interaction.

Kenneth Hoover, *The Professional Teacher's Handbook* (Boston: Allyn and Bacon, 1982). This book is designed for middle and secondary school teachers. It is conveniently divided into several units: preinstructional activities, individual and small-group methods focus, large-group methods focus, methods for effective learning, assessment techniques, and working with special students.

David Jacobsen, Paul Eggen, and Donald Kauchak, *Methods for Teaching* (Columbus, OH: Merrill, 1989). Units Two and Three most apply to the topics of this chapter. Unit Two covers questioning skills, expository and discovery teaching, and classroom management approaches. Unit Three is devoted to measurement and pupil evaluation.

Peter Geaga, "Convert Your Text Series into a District Science Program," *Science and Children*, (November/December 1982), pp. 28–30. This article provides practical examples for supplementing or supplanting the typical science text. Geaga offers a case against the packaged program and urges teachers to draw on many printed resources; he gives examples of practical approaches that any teacher can try.

James Scarnati and Cyril Weller, "The Write Stuff," *Science and Children*, (January 1992), pp. 28–29. The authors describe ways to use science inquiry skills to help students think positively about writing assignments.

Candy Carlile, "Bag It for Science!" *Science and Children* (March 1992), pp. 15–16. This article describes a book-bag approach in which interesting trade books, teaching materials, instructions, and student enthusiasm combine for hands-on learning in an easy-to-manage fashion.

How do reading ability and listening ability affect science test scores? To find out, review articles with similar titles in the September 1991 and October 1991 issues of Science and Children.

Thomas Gee and Marly Olson, "Let's Talk Trade Books," *Science and Children* (March 1992), pp. 13–14. Suggestions for using science trade books for children effectively are offered in this article.

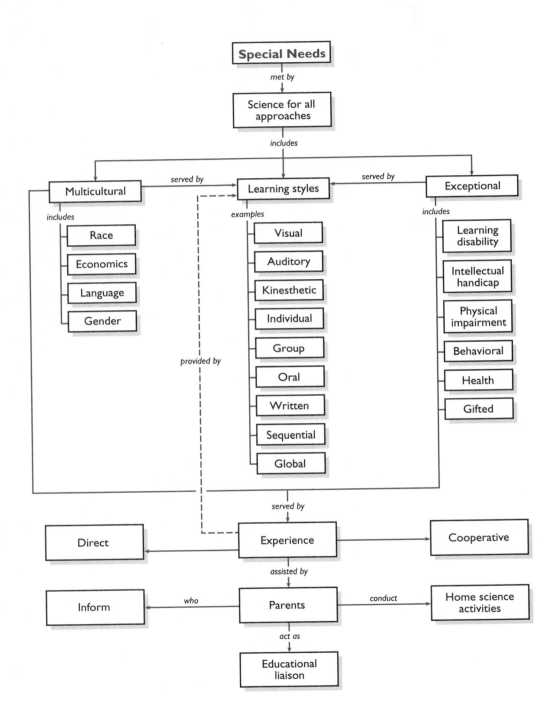

How Can You Teach All Children?

Jeannie Rae Rice[1] is an Indianapolis teacher of students with learning disabilities. She describes how her class began its trek toward a science fair: a project familiar to many children but unfamiliar to her students. While they worked on their projects, the students with learning disabilities learned more than anyone imagined they possibly could. They taught many other teachers and students an important lesson about the low expectations and unfair attitudes people often hold toward those with special needs.

It had been at least seven years since my school had a science fair. Late in the fall I asked my principal if I could organize and sponsor a school science fair for my class and the other students in grades four through six. My main concern would be to get as many students as possible to follow a project through to completion so they could experience the reward of displaying their work. She immediately gave her permission and support.

My sixteen boys and one girl, aged 11 to 13, have reading abilities ranging from beginning first grade to high third grade. Their math skills are somewhat higher, while handwriting and spelling skills vary but are generally low.

According to intelligence test scores, these students have at least average potential, but they have not achieved at the same rate as most of their peers. They have been placed in my class in order to receive special and individualized instruction.

The behavior and attitudes of children with learning disabilities have been described as impulsive, distractible, frustrated, stubborn, disruptive, defiant, obstinate, and extremely disorganized. One word I would never use to characterize my students, though, is "unmotivated." Of course their motivation varies according to the activity at hand, but when their interest has been roused, they really get into gear. Fortunately, my explanation of a science fair induced every member of the class to decide to enter a project.

During the three months our school was involved in the science fair, I noticed some important changes in my own students and in other students and the faculty.

Learning-disabled children have difficulty getting along with one another in group situations. They are easily frustrated and tend to argue and become angry. Much to my surprise, however, this did not occur when my students worked on their science fair projects. I must stress the significance of this change in behavior. Naturally it improved the quality of their work for the science fair, but it also demonstrated to me—and to them—that they could control themselves and cooperate to solve difficult problems.

While my students' perceptions of what they could do were changing, the attitudes of other students towards my class were also shifting. At the beginning, most of the other students in the school had little information about learning-disabled children. They only knew that my students were somehow different, and they usually called ours the "dummy class." I, of course, was the "dummies' teacher." But during preparations for the science fair, the perceptions of some of these other students began to change. They found it difficult to understand how a "dummy teacher" could run a science fair and why she'd want to. The fact that I seemed to be doing a good job created a halo effect that was important: As my image began to improve among students throughout the school, so did the image of my students. For the first time, members of my class began to develop friendships with other students.

Many teachers were as uninformed as their students about the limitations and the capabilities of learning-disabled children. These colleagues often viewed students in my class simply as behavior problems. This misapprehension is not necessarily the fault of the teachers, since many of them finished college before courses in special education and learning disabilities had become part of the curriculum.

I initiated our science fair with one goal—to have my students complete and display science projects. However, as preparations for the fair progressed, it became clear that my students were learning more than I had originally imagined possible. I was curious about their perceptions of what they were accomplishing, so I asked them.

My students had no doubt that they'd learned some valuable lessons by participating in the science fair and neither had I. In fact, it seems to me that several important academic and personal goals can be accomplished by involving learning-disabled children in a science fair.

For me and my students, the school science fair was an extremely satisfying experience. Of the nine winners chosen by outside judges, four were from my learning-disabled class. And while getting prizes was exciting, equally important for my students were the intangible rewards of embarking on a joint enterprise with others, and discovering within themselves capabilities of which they had not been aware.

INTRODUCTION

Have you ever heard someone reason like this: "If you can't walk, talk, or hear, or if you look or sound different, you must be intellectually and socially inferior." Most physical differences have no connection to one's intellect or mental capability. The biases of our hypothetical conversationalist are based upon two important factors: stereotypes and a lack of information. Stereotypes caused the learners without disabilities in Ms. Rice's school to refer to her students as "dummies." The uninformed teacher can insufficiently stimulate the intellect by holding low expectations for children with learning disabilities. Without realizing just how unfairly their expectations may treat the children, teachers may actually reinforce the wider perception that learners who have disabilities or are different in some other way are dummies, and this type of teacher behavior may tend to reinforce the prejudices held by others.

Children with learning disabilities are only one example of students who have special needs. Each child is a special case and deserves special attention and encouragement. You will be in a better position to teach, to strike down unfair stereotypes, and to serve the needs of *all* learners if you become informed about the special needs many of our school children have. This will be a great service for all of your students and will especially benefit those who need special assistance.

This chapter is about teaching science to serve *all* children's needs. Technically speaking, all students are culturally different; each family is unique and has its own identity. The multicultural focus of this chapter explores the special needs of culturally diverse populations (groups of students with home environments very different from society's mainstream in terms of economics, ethnicity, religion, race, and/or language) and learners who have distinct exceptionalities (children with differences in vision, hearing, speech, emotions, giftedness, and so on). In both instances, the authors believe that the science teaching techniques recommended to help the few students in your class who may have special needs, will actually better serve the needs of all learners.

The chapter begins with an investigation of several general factors that impede science learning and provides teaching recommendations beneficial for all children. After reading the first part of this chapter, you should be able to:

1. Describe the special needs of children who are members of minority groups, culturally different, and/or multilingual.
2. Practice techniques that help meet their special needs.
3. Promote gender equality in your classroom.
4. Identify the different learning styles.
5. Discuss management and teaching practices that encourage all learners.

The second part of this chapter should help you to:

1. Identify characteristics of the exceptional students who will enrich your classes,
2. Practice classroom techniques that help meet these special needs.

The third part of this chapter explores the ways we can include parents in science teaching.

SCIENCE FOR ALL

In previous chapters we have described the many benefits science offers children. Most of these benefits appear to be oriented toward academic growth through expanded powers of thinking and problem solving and positive attitudes toward functioning in a school environment. But not all children come to school able to function effectively within a school's culture. Some children lack the skills necessary to cope with the routines or rigors of schooling. These children often feel hostile toward school and toward any authority figure, especially a teacher.

Being different carries liabilities. The price of being different may be exclusion from social groups at school and prejudiced treatment from those who appear not to be different. Cultural differences can contribute to the difficulties and problems of school children. The principles of multicultural education can help us meet the special needs of all children.

Multicultural Education

All children are culturally different. Multicultural education strives to promote the often-overlooked contributions made by less dominant cultures. Children who are culturally different may include those of minority races or children with special needs, as well as children who come from home environments out of the mainstream of society. Cultural differences include those of race, religion, economic level, ethnic background, the primary language used by the child, and in some instances gender. Different backgrounds often offer rich heritages beneficial to all. Cultural pluralism brings the perspectives of many cultures to our schools. The history of our nation is strong as a result of the contributions of this heritage.

The importance of cultural pluralism is recognized and supported in the 1991 Position Statement on Multicultural Science Education from the National Science Teachers Association. This statement encourages teachers to seek resources to ensure effective science learning for culturally diverse populations. The position statement urges that teachers

- provide access to high-quality science education experiences so that culturally diverse populations can become successful participants in our democratic society,
- select and use curriculum materials and teaching strategies that reflect and incorporate diversity,
- become aware of children's learning styles and instructional preference,
- expose culturally diverse children to career opportunities in science, engineering, and technology.[2]

Multicultural education advocates effective and appropriate schooling for all children, with subsequent acceptance by those who are part of the majority culture

All children benefit from learning science.

of the community. Multicultural education helps to enlighten the children of the majority about the value of the culture from which the minority or special-needs child comes, and it helps to enhance the self-esteem of all children. It is easier for children to understand and accept cultural differences among people if they are exposed to and taught to accept differences of all sorts at an early age.

The many fields of science offer an enormous variety of topics for children to explore. Science teaches children to think more logically and reason about why things are as they are. It helps children learn to analyze and evaluate myths and stereotypes and to overcome prejudice. Science also provides important opportunities for children to study the contributions of scientists from culturally diverse backgrounds. If we are to promote multicultural education effectively, we must:

1. Stop believing in assimilation, in which the minority group loses all its distinctive characteristics and is ultimately absorbed by the majority group.
2. Help minority and majority children maintain their distinct ethnic identities within the culture of the school's values, such as equal treatment, equal opportunity to participate fully in school, equal protection by law, and equal freedom of cultural and religious expression.[3]

Who Makes up Culturally Diverse Populations?   Often the African-American child who lives in poverty is envisioned as a typical example of one who is culturally different. This is an inaccurate stereotype of African Americans. While the example does apply, culturally different children are as likely to come from the hills and mountains of Appalachia, Spanish-speaking communities of the Southwest, French settlements of the northernmost regions of Maine, or Asia. Let us not overlook the Native Americans who once were the majority on this land. They, too, are now culturally different from a changed mainstream society. In fact, each of us can become culturally different when we enter a community or region where we are not among the majority of the residents.

How Can You Use Cultural Differences to Promote Greater Science Understanding?   Your science classes can reflect greater cultural diversity if your instruction reflects contributions made by people all over the world. Often our print materials and media leave the impression that science is a recent white European construct. In fact this impression is very wrong. Consider that

> Over 5000 years ago in Egypt and Mesopotamia copper was being extracted from its ores, glass was made, and fabrics were dyed with natural colours. . . . Iron swords are known to have been produced over 3000 years ago. . . distillation was used in Mesopotamia as far back as 1200 BC. for the production of perfumes. . . . Many of the techniques and much of the terminology of modern chemistry derives from ancient times; for example, *alkali* from the Arabic *al qality*—the roasted ashes; *soda* from Arabic *studa*—a splitting headache.[4]

You can promote multicultural education in your science class by:

Developing science themes that are related to conservation and pollution, disease, food and health, and population growth and teaching with consideration for humankind as a whole. Develop an understanding among your students about the interdependence of people and unequal distribution of natural resources.

Selecting classroom teaching examples that address the contributions and participation of people from a range of backgrounds, cultures, and genders.

Considering carefully any issues of race, gender, and human origins by exploring the myths that surround them.[5]

Challenging inaccurate statements students make about ethnic minority communities and people. Statements may refer to different physical features, countries of origin, religion, language, and customs.[6] For example, we have all heard myths about the strengths and weaknesses of blacks, Asians, women, and so on. As educated adults, we understand that these alleged qualities cannot be applied to all members of a group, and that beliefs like these arise from ignorance. We know that human beings are much more alike than they are different. Use science teaching as an opportunity to refute these myths when children repeat them.

A multicultural approach to education rejects the merely color-blind view that strives to treat all children the same. Advocates of multicultural education believe that the needs of all children differ and that these differences should be taken into account. Because all children *are* different, they should be treated differently, where appropriate. Special provisions can sometimes help children with language differences, minority status, and low-income backgrounds to develop positive self-images.

What Are the Characteristics of Children from Different Cultures?   Although they come from different backgrounds and ways of life, culturally different children seem to share some characteristics. Here are some tips for meeting their needs:

Children with different experiences: What most of us take for granted may be completely lacking from the childhoods of children who are culturally different, minority, low income, or disabled. For example, herds of domestic animals, menageries of pets, and/or wild animals that roam at will may be as foreign to a city dweller as the piles of wind-tossed convenience packaging, crowds of densely packed people, and clouds of smog are to the rancher. Classroom activities, videos, and field trips with planned comparative discussions help to build awareness about and tolerance for differences by adding new experiences. Yet real experiences are a better choice. Activity-based science learning helps the student who is culturally different reach higher levels of science achievement, develop better process skills, and develop more logical thought processes.[7]

A desire for action rather than words: Few children who are multilingual or multicultural will be patient enough to listen to long instructions or descriptions. Get to the point. Provide simple, direct demonstrations and concrete experiences. Indeed, all children will benefit from the clarity and directness of this approach.

Children who need a better vocabulary: The rough, blunt street talk or backwoods language of some children can cause quite a culture shock. In the same way, the child with limited English proficiency who speaks haltingly may have difficulty following a normal conversation. Children need a vocabulary suited to the mainstream if they are to become competitive in the workplace. Science offers abundant opportunities for developing vocabulary and effective communication skills.

Disorganized children: Children can become frustrated and misunderstand the purpose of an activity if there are too many choices or if your instructions are too flexible. Some children may live in cultures in which they are not encouraged to make many of their own decisions. Be definite and clear with your instructions.

Children need genuine (rather than patronizing) relationships: Be empathetic rather than sympathetic. Looking down on the students' different social or economic standings is demeaning despite your best intentions.

Children cannot easily learn to control their own destinies: Poverty tends to produce feelings of hopelessness and desperation. Children who are culturally different, minority, low income, or disabled may feel that they have little or no control over their lives and may look for immediate gratification. *Fate control* is defined as the belief that you can control what happens to you. Many children from culturally different backgrounds believe that what happens to them happens by chance or that their future lies in the hands of others who are more powerful and beyond influence. Science experiments help children to learn that variables can be manipulated to produce different outcomes. This understanding about variables can be applied to themselves and can be used eventually to help shift the locus of fate control to a point where they perceive the power to control their own lives.[8]

How Can You Help Non–English-Speaking Students?

Lack of familiarity with the dominant spoken language can also cause students to believe their fate is beyond their control. Bruce Reichert,[9] a science teacher with the American Cooperative School in Tunis, has taught students who speak several different languages. He offers the following tips for assisting the non-English speakers in your classes.

Helping Students Help Themselves.   Ideally, students should learn to help themselves learn. Try these approaches:

Distribute a vocabulary list and/or copy of the curriculum guide at the beginning of each unit. This material helps students know exactly what will be expected of them and will give them additional time to master the difficult terms.

Ask students who are readers of their native language to carry pocket dictionaries (English-to-native language and vice versa). At times simple words create communication barriers. These pocket dictionaries can solve the problem and help create the self-sufficient habit of looking up unfamiliar words. English-speaking students can be encouraged to do the same as a way of learning words in another language.

Invite the students who are uncomfortable with English to ask questions. This personal invitation, in a nonthreatening environment, will help students to overcome fear of using the new language. The joy of being successful at expressing opinions or asking questions becomes a positive reinforcer.

Be patient. Wait-time is particularly important for multilingual speakers, to allow them to form their questions or answers.

Encourage the children to write their own translations of words in their notes. As you examine lab notebooks and see translations, you will be aware that the student has looked up the words and probably understands them better.

Encourage students to read science articles and books in their own languages. Additional supplemental readings such as those available from *Scholastic* provide brief, popular articles and photographs that encourage additional practice with the language.

I Hear and I Forget. For those times when you feel you must lecture, try the following to help students remember:

Speak slowly and enunciate clearly. All students benefit from this because the technical words of science at times seem like a foreign language.

On the chalkboard or overhead projector, display an outline or definitions, descriptions, or figures to add meaning to your spoken words.

Add emphasis to the main ideas. Underline concepts or highlight the important meanings. Non-English speakers will remember to look them up later, while other students will treat the emphasis as a study cue.

I See and I Remember. A picture really is worth a thousand words: It provides another mode for learning, and it is helpful for memory retention. Try these suggestions:

Use visual aids as often as possible. The problem in science education is deciding what to teach and what materials to use, not the availability of interesting, useful materials. Check the school district's resource center or curriculum library or the education resource co-op that serves your school. There is a wealth of films, videos, film strips, bulletin board ideas, computer programs, models, posters, and charts. Old, discarded science textbooks or magazines can be salvaged for useful visual aids.

Nurture animals and plants. They add excitement and can also make superior visual aids.

Use artwork. Add your own artwork and invite talented student artists to contribute to your notes, transparencies, learning activity illustrations, and lab activities. Stick figures with details are fine, too.

I Do and I Understand. All three learning approaches—hearing, seeing, and doing—are important, especially when all five senses are stimulated. Combined approaches provide better opportunities for understanding than a single approach.

The power of activity learning stimulates improved communication as well as greater levels of science achievement, process skill development, scientific attitudes, and logical thinking than traditional teaching, in which teacher talk and student reading dominate.[10] Keep these suggestions in mind while working with non-English speakers:

Have students do hands-on, lab-type learning activities often. The minds-on experiences that accompany hands-on learning can enhance language and reading development. Some non-English-speaking students may not understand a lecture, discussion, or teacher demonstration, but once they have done it themselves, the experience is easier for them to link with the language.

Coordinate your teaching with the English as a Second Language (ESL) teacher. Blend the grammar and vocabulary used in both classes so the students have a double exposure to the science vocabulary.

Link science concepts with the students' background experiences. Learn what you can about the children's countries of origin and refer to geographical locations, climate conditions, fauna and flora, and so on to link the new science concepts with what the students already know. Why is it always necessary to mention the Rocky Mountains or the Mississippi? The rest of the class will benefit from the geography enrichment.

Use guest speakers and field trips. These are good ways to help multilingual students become more accepted and feel at home in their new environment and with science. Be aware of the linguistic and cultural differences and include all children in the full range of activities. Invite speakers from the students' countries of origin to help classmates become familiar with people from other cultures.

Try to Reduce Test Anxiety.   Children from other countries often attach more importance to testing and achievement than native-born American children might. The mere mention of a test can evoke much more anxiety because of its importance in determining children's academic futures in other countries, and a test in the English language can pump anxiety to counterproductive levels. The following suggestions offer some ideas for reducing test anxiety:

Try puzzles. Crossword puzzles assist spelling and provide additional cues for correct answers. Students seem to do better when they know how many letters to expect in an answer. A list of words helps, too, for crosswords and fill-in-the-blank questions.

Encourage children to draw. Invite children to draw answers rather than write. This is a good way to communicate ideas as the child gets around the temporary language barriers.

Encourage students to check their work. At the end of each test, consider allotting three to five minutes for students to check answers. Permit them to use books, notes, and class handouts.

Try bonus points for extra credit. Offer bonus points for student creations. Science-oriented jokes, riddles, poems, and songs that use the concepts and vocabulary being studied can be a great way to encourage review and creativity. Permitted as homework, this can also be a good way to promote language study between the child and parents.

Is Gender Equality a Special Need?

Females do not have equal access to or receive equal encouragement for careers in science. This appears to be a cultural problem linked to how females are socialized in the mainstream of society; it is not a women's problem. Both males and females, by age 11, have developed strong sex-stereotyped attitudes concerning socially appropriate behavior and gender roles in society.[11] Although improvements have been made, many people still attribute cultural differences to gender. Cultural gender differences play an important role in career selection.

Females deserve equal encouragement and access to science.

How Does Culture Affect Females in Science?   There are cultural disincentives for women to pursue careers in science, technology, and mathematics. Proportionally fewer women and minorities have sufficient background for scientific careers, and they are underrepresented in these careers. While our country's population is 51 percent female, and 43.2 percent of our workforce is composed of women, women represent only 3 percent of our nation's engineers[12] and about 6 percent of our scientists.[13] In addition, the U.S. Senate Report on the Education for Economic Security Act of 1984 reports that many young women score lower on standardized achievement tests in mathematics and science than their male classmates. The report from the 1990 National Assessment of Education Progress illustrates this fact: In fourth grade, the average science proficiency for males and females was approximately the same; a small, but significant, performance gap was evident by eighth grade; the gap widened to ten scale points by twelfth grade. At age 17, roughly 50 percent of the males demonstrated the ability to analyze scientific procedures and data, but only 33 percent of the females could do the same.[14]

Some of the achievement differences can be traced to low enrollment of women in advanced science courses. Generally there are equal numbers of males and females enrolled in high school general or physical science, biology, and chemistry courses, but only 5.6 percent of physics students are female.[15] But encouraging females to take more science courses is not always the way to reduce the achievement deficit. The large difference in science achievement performance by gender cannot be explained entirely by the number of courses taken. In some cases, the proficiency gap between high-school-aged males and females actually increases as more science courses are taken.[16] It appears that in some cases, taking more science courses could actually do more harm to females than good, particularly if the extra courses give them negative experiences.[17]

Other aspects of the gender inequality problem can include the following factors:

Parents, teachers, school counselors, and peers discourage females to pursue scientific careers.[18]

Most elementary teachers are women and lack strong background in science; their lack of confidence can reinforce children's beliefs that women are not supposed to like science.[19]

A shortage of appropriate female science and engineering role models reinforces the belief that science is a male domain.[20]

Young males report more positive attitudes toward science and young females less positive attitudes; females report less confidence and more fear of success in careers like engineering; females report that physics courses are too difficult.[21]

Females may not be socialized at home or at school to develop and demonstrate scientific skills and may not be encouraged to develop practical ability, independence, and self-confidence. Several studies reveal that skills and characteristics associated with scientists are those often attributed to masculine characters: high intellectual ability, persistence at work, extreme independence, and apartness from others. Females may be hesitant to pursue science because they fear that they

FIGURE 9.1 **Distribution of Students and Average Academic Proficiency by Gender**

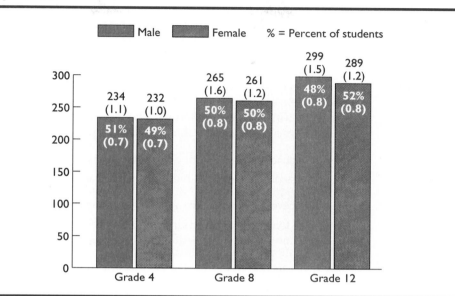

Source: Lee R. Jones, Ina V. S. Mullins, Senta A. Raizen, Iris R. Weiss, and Elizabeth A. Weston, *The 1990 Science Report Card, NAEP's Assessment of Fourth, Eighth, and Twelfth Graders* (Washington, DC: U. S. Department of Education, 1992), p. 11.

will be considered unfeminine.[22] Even the toys typically given to boys require more assembly and manipulation than the toys given to girls.

When women have problems, they tend to blame themselves for the problems or the inability to solve them, whereas when men have difficulties they tend to place the blame outside themselves. These differences can tend to develop female feelings of learned helplessness and may cause females to believe that they are not intellectually capable.[23]

Teachers reflect the values and expectations thrust upon them by the dominant society and can unintentionally perpetuate sex stereotypes in science. In addition, sex bias can be observed in the practices of teachers and the assignments of science teachers. Female science teachers usually are assigned to introductory science classes and biology, whereas males more often are high school department chairmen and are assigned to teach such advanced science classes as chemistry and physics.[24]

How Do Teachers Contribute to Gender Problems in Science? While the role of teachers perpetuating sex-role stereotypes has not been fully explored, the literature indicates that teachers are not consciously and intentionally sex stereotyping students. Many teachers do try to treat males and females fairly and equally. Often teachers tell us that they want all children to develop to their full potential. But some effects are larger than life. We were all raised in a society where gender differences are prevalent. Parents, school counselors, other teachers, social workers, books, and television have taught teachers (even you!) that certain behaviors are appropriate for females and others are appropriate for males.[25] Bias by gender will only begin to change when you are able to recognize the subtle messages that steer males and females toward particular behaviors and career choices.

Considerable evidence indicates that what teachers expect from their students affects the students' performance. Cooper's model[26] (Figure 9.2) is based on this evidence and explains how sex differences in achievement may be due to differences in teacher expectations. The model can be useful for overcoming gender stereotypes and consists of the following steps:

Step 1. Teachers form different expectations for students.

Regardless of gender, hold high but realistic expectations for all students.

Step 2. Believe that females are as capable in science as males.

Do not be tempted to assign class roles or jobs based on flawed beliefs that females are better note takers and writers and males are better handlers of equipment.

Step 3. Encourage females to take the lead in activities, to make lab decisions, to take measurements and handle equipment.

Do the same for males, but without leading them to believe they are better at it than females.

Step 4. Strive for equal amounts and types of nurturant contact with females and males.

Several studies in preschool and elementary classrooms indicate that males often receive more attention from teachers and more feedback about their performance.[27] Added attention can bolster student beliefs about the importance of their effort and encourage them to work harder.

Step 5. Provide opportunities for success.

As children master classroom tasks, they become more motivated to strive for even higher quality. Females will undertake and excel at physical science study instead of achieving dramatically less than males do by the seventh grade.

What Can You Do to Overcome Gender Inequality in Science? Realize that gender bias begins at an early age. The younger the child when you begin to address the issue, the better your chances of having an impact. From early childhood, males are expected to be more independent, creative, and manipulative. These early experiences may affect their development of spatial and verbal abilities.[28] Males have many more opportunities to experience science-oriented activities than females, although females have the interest to become more involved in science, if given the opportunity.[29] Some things you can do to help promote gender equality in your science class include the following:

Strengthen your science preparation. Particularly if you are a female, strive to strengthen your experience with science and project the importance of science to your students. You do not want to suggest that science is not for women. Your attitude toward the subject will have a powerful effect on all the children.

Strive to become aware of your own subtle biases and different expectations for students. Examine how you assign classroom tasks and the daily life examples you use of science at work for evidence of subtle gender bias.

Experiment with single-sex class groups. Until you develop more skills at creating and maintaining a nonsexist learning environment, females may receive less biased treatment if they are not paired with males for small-group activities. Females in mixed groups have been found to spend more time than males watching and listening, whereas in same-sex groups females spend the same amount of time as males in same-sex groups on hands-on science processes and experimental tasks.[30]

Expect the same from females as from males. Examine your reinforcement for equality, fairness in discipline, and encouraging nonverbal behavior toward females, especially during science class. Ensure that females participate fully in all science activities.

Be aware of the difficulties some females experience when using equipment unfamiliar to them. Differences in social expectations often lead parents to give

FIGURE 9.2   Overcoming Gender Stereotypes

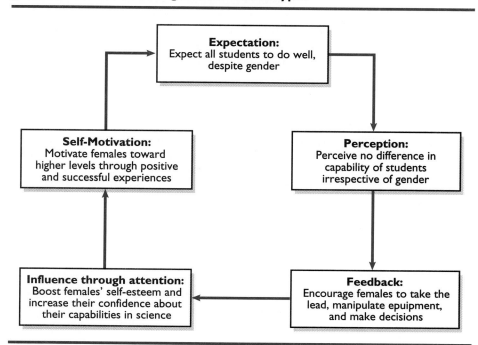

different types of toys to boys and girls and encourage different types of social interactions through games and sports. Young males are often encouraged to manipulate objects that are very similar to the tools and equipment of science. Young females may not have the same opportunities and, therefore, could have some initial difficulty with science equipment. A little extra time and encouragement early on will help females build their confidence so they can cope easily.

Hands-on learning is a great equalizer. Science process-oriented learning tasks help females to acquire manipulative experiences that put them on par with males, making access to science learning more equal.[31]

Treat science as gender free. Do not always refer to scientists as males.

Screen teaching materials. Examine all print materials and media for gender bias. Posters, textbooks, filmstrips, and other media should have equal representations of males and females.

Invite female science role models. Males will be well served too, because they will see new opportunities for females.

Help female students develop personal characteristics that are associated with success in science. Encourage them to break away from any submissive behavior patterns and encourage them to become more independent and self-reliant. Also encourage females to explore new topics and materials and to test out their new ideas and interests.[32]

Similarities in Learning

Children from other cultures or who are not English speakers benefit from specific management and teaching techniques. The recommendations we have offered reveal some similarities. Indeed, most children can benefit from the suggestions recommended for special groups of learners. Children benefit when they are taught beginning with the learning styles they prefer.

Learning Styles.   The concept of learning styles arises from the general acceptance that we all learn in a variety of ways, that those ways can be identified, and that teachers can teach in ways that capitalize on student preferences. If they begin from a position of strength (preferred learning style), learners can be exposed to other ways of learning and expand their repertoires as they overcome weaknesses.

Teaching to accommodate different learning styles helps teachers reach each individual. Students who need special assistance receive instruction through their preferred learning style during the intervention process. Children learn about how they learn and are encouraged to use their strengths. All benefit from the variety of approaches. Teachers also plan instruction carefully to make certain that all children have an opportunity to learn through their own preferred styles.

Types of Styles.   Learning styles are often classified by function. As learners, we have different modes of perception, we prefer various environments, we are motivated by different things, we express ourselves uniquely, we think differently, and we prefer various levels of mobility as we learn. True individualization is

Children perceive in different ways and prefer various learning environments.

a challenge. At least nine learning styles can be identified by function for those children who are

- visual and prefer to perceive by seeing words, numbers, charts, models, objects, and so on;
- auditory and prefer to perceive meaning by hearing;
- bodily kinesthetic and prefer to be self-involved, hands on;
- individual learners and prefer to work alone; this type of student may be more confident in his or her own opinion than in the ideas of others;
- group learners and prefer to learn with at least one other child;
- oral expressive and can easily tell or explain their ideas and opinions; they may know more than they can reveal on a test;
- written expressive and who write fluent essays or good answers on tests; their thoughts are organized better on paper than they are presented orally;
- sequential learners and have the ability to arrange thoughts and ideas in a linear, organized fashion;
- global learners and have the ability to be spontaneous, flexible thinkers; these learners may be quiet and intuitive and order their thoughts randomly, preferring to do things their own way.[33]

All learners do not fit exclusively into one style. Many may share strong preferences among several styles. All students can be served better when learning opportunities are provided in multisensory, multiexpressive, and multi-environmental modes. The following suggestions can help a wide variety of learners, particularly those who have special needs.

Establish classroom and study routines. Many children are unable to organize unaided, and traditional school learning cannot occur until organization is established. You can provide a helpful model for children if you are well organized and consistent in your classroom. Children will then know what to do and how to do it.

Limit choices. Democratic learning and cooperative learning encourage choices, but this approach may not help children who get confused easily. Asking "Would you like to . . ." implies choice. As an example, if your intention is to have a child put science equipment back on the storage shelf or follow a specific instruction, it is better for the child if your instructions are explicit and/or provide limited choices.

Make certain the children are attending to what is going on. Asking students to repeat instructions or information, requesting a response to a specific question, requiring that a child complete a specific motor task, and maintaining eye contact are some ways to determine the extent to which a child may be attending to what is going on around him or her. Focus on each child often.

Give clues to help remembering. Use mnemonic devices, rhymes, auditory associations, linking associations, and visual clues to help the child remember. Help the children construct personal memory devices.

Sequence instruction carefully. Concept mapping and task analysis can help you to find the most logical sequence of any task. The four Ws help to begin a task analysis: *what* to teach, *where* to begin, *when* the objective has been met, and *what* to teach next. Figure 9.3 provides a more detailed model for analyzing and determining the sequence for science concepts.

Separate teaching and testing. Worksheet assignments may seem to the students more like a test than the type of reinforcement activity you may intend. Provide instructional assistance to encourage learning and to help lower the failure rate. An example at the top of a worksheet or a list of guiding questions can transform the assignment from a test into a learning task. Also provide models, cues, verbal and written prompts, and correct answers as feedback.

Be specific with criticism and praise. Tell the child exactly why the response is correct or wrong. Telling the child to try number two again will cause him or her to change an answer, but he or she will not know what to change. When part of the answer is correct, tell the child; also identify what is not correct.

Provide time clues. Some children may have difficulty remembering time sequences, estimating time intervals, and determining the amount of time needed to complete tasks. By routinely displaying schedules in prominent places and referring to time in the classroom, you can help students learn to structure their school work.

Confer with special education teachers, second language teachers, and gifted and talented coordinators. Continuity of content and consistency of management and routines help many children. Coordinate your classroom activities with those of other classes the child attends.

FIGURE 9.3   Concept Analysis Model for Teaching Children with Special Needs

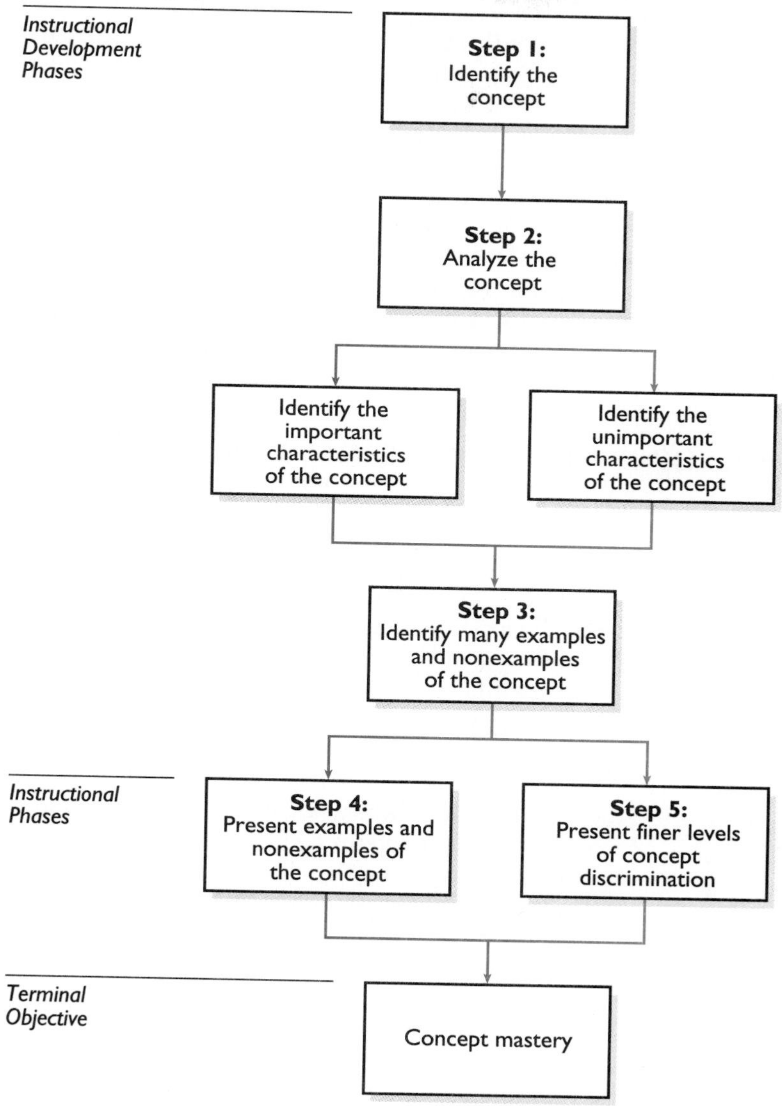

Instructional Development Phases

Step 1:
Identify the concept

Step 2:
Analyze the concept

Identify the important characteristics of the concept

Identify the unimportant characteristics of the concept

Step 3:
Identify many examples and nonexamples of the concept

Instructional Phases

Step 4:
Present examples and nonexamples of the concept

Step 5:
Present finer levels of concept discrimination

Terminal Objective

Concept mastery

Source: A modified version of "Concept Analysis: A Model for Teaching Basic Science Concepts to Intellectually Handicapped Students" by Jack T. Cole, Margie K. Kitano, and Lewis M. Brown in Marshall E. Corrick, Jr. (ed.) *Teaching Handicapped Students*, NEA, 1981, p. 52. Reprinted with permission.

Show empathy, encouragement, sensitivity, and understanding for each child's attempts to learn, to remember, and to conform to your routines. Point out the child's abilities and respect the child as a human being.

Provide kinesthetic experiences, practical hands-on learning activities with concrete, relevant materials. Children who are experience deficient will benefit, as will children who prefer this type of learning. Hands-on experiences stimulate minds-on learning.

Identify desired behaviors, set clear expectations, and reduce distractions.

Simplify. Break each task down into its simplest steps; assist the students with step-by-step instructions.

Give frequent feedback. Small improvements deserve praise, and precise direction helps children continue to improve.

Use the preferred learning mode. If the child has a dominant mode of learning (visual, tactile, auditory), use it. Regard the preference as a strength and try to build success on it. Then use this preference to help build self-esteem on successes before tackling learning weaknesses.

SCIENCE FOR EXCEPTIONAL CHILDREN

Public Law 94–142 of 1975 (the Education for All Handicapped Children Act) is part of a federal law (Individuals with Disabilities Education Act, IDEA) that helps ensure a place for handicapped students in American public schools. The law requires that every handicapped student must be provided an appropriate education in the least restrictive environment possible. The law includes nine specific categories of handicap: deafness, hearing impairment, mental retardation, orthopedic impairment, other health impairment, serious emotional disturbance, specific learning disability, speech impairment, and visual impairment.

The "least restrictive environment" provision requires that whenever possible students with disabilities be educated with their nonhandicapped peers. Students with handicaps who are included in regular classrooms are placed there because it has been determined to be the most appropriate environment for them. These decisions are based on extensive assessment, parental consent, and decision making among school personnel that must follow due process of law.

The presence of students with disabilities in regular classrooms does not mean that the curriculum must be the same for all children. Federal law states that the schooling of children with disabilities must be differentiated according to their special needs and provided with necessary support. This may require a degree of individualized education not usually found in typical classrooms. The Individualized Education Program (IEP) prescribes goals for the school year based on present performance levels, specific educational services the school must provide, the extent to which the student participates in the regular classroom, and schedules and procedures for evaluation. Indeed, many educators believe the intent of the IEP benefits all children. Table 9.1 provides a brief description of adaptations that help students who have special needs.

Teaching Children Who Have Learning Disabilities

A child with a learning disability has the intellectual potential to succeed in school. But for some reason, the child's academic achievements are significantly below the expected level of performance in a specific subject such as reading or mathematics.

What Is a Learning Disability? A child can be identified as having a learning disability if a school evaluation team finds a severe discrepancy between the child's achievement and intellectual ability in one or more of seven areas: oral expression, listening comprehension, written expression, basic reading skill, reading comprehension, mathematics calculation, and mathematics reasoning.[34] The child may perform at or above the expected level in some school subjects but poorly in others. When this happens it is especially frustrating for the child and makes identification of the disability difficult. The child may develop failure-avoidance techniques that surface as behavior problems to draw attention away from areas of academic failure.

Nearly 5 percent of school-age children have learning disabilities. Perhaps five to ten million children today may have some type of learning disability. The

Exceptional children learn science with the proper type of support and encouragement.

TABLE 9.1   Teaching Children Who Have Special Needs

Special Need	Environmental Adaptation	Materials Adaptation	Teaching Adaptation	Assessment Adaptation
Cultural	Carefully select visuals and non-print materials for cultural inclusion. Represent plural culture. Maintain clear classroom organization. Establish empathic relationships.	Use culturally representative materials. Avoid cultural stereotypes. Use broad themes to include all cultures.	Set explicit expectations, give explicit instructions. Use divergent questions to encourage pluralism and inclusion. Challenge inaccurate statements. Include careful consideration of issues. Use experience-rich methods.	Provide and accept diverse contexts for assessment activities.
Non-English Speaking	Be patient. Use visual aids to help communicate. Provide direct experience. Encourage high levels of activity.	Maintain a conceptual focus. Enrich vocabulary development. Use supplemental, high-interest readings.	Be verbally clear. Maintain written clarity; use outlines. Emphasize concepts. Link concepts to experiences. Use guest speakers and field trips. Reduce text anxiety.	Encourage the use of pocket translators and dictionaries. Use pictorial assessment devices, puzzles, and performance tasks.
Gender	Nurture independence and self-confidence. Use hands-on learning activities. Use female role models in the sciences.	Identify and eliminate gender bias in materials. Use a wide variety of manipulatives.	Experiment with heterogeneous and single-sex grouping. Use cooperative learning techniques. Maintain high but realistic expectations for all. Provide frequent progress feedback.	None
Learning Style Preferences	Include all styles.	Select a balance of visual, auditory, kinesthetic, oral, and written materials.	Provide activities to match preference for individual, group, sequential, visual, verbal, auditory, and global learners.	Assess concepts through verbal, written, kinesthetic, individual, and group opportunities.

Special Need	Environmental Adaptation	Materials Adaptation	Teaching Adaptation	Assessment Adaptation
Learning Disability	Show empathy. Focus attention. Seat away from distractions.	Use concrete manipulatives. Screen out irrelevant materials and distractions.	Show clear expectations. Simplify; give cues and specific praise. Use dominant learning mode and multisensory activities. Use concept analysis.	Provide specific criticism and praise. Try oral tests. Modify reading and writing exercises if needed.
Intellectual	Limit visual and verbal distractions.	Select appropriate reading level. Use concrete, relevant manipulatives.	Use concept analysis. Simplify. Praise. Use repetition. Maintain eye contact. Engage in physical activity. Give feedback, use cues, cooperative learning. Use examples and nonexamples. Use brief periods of direct instruction.	Verbal tests. Provide assistance with written tests. Provide small-step progress checks.
Visual	Provide clear, predictable traffic pathways. Maintain organized, predictable locations for materials and storage. Provide good lighting. Seat student near activity. Sighted student tutor can assist.	Use voice and audio tapes. Print materials should be large, clear, and uncluttered with numerous colors and geometric designs. Adapt materials to special equipment student may have to use.	Emphasize uses of other senses. Taped instructions or science information can be provided. Pair with sighted students.	More verbal assessment. Assist with written assessment. Assist with physical manipulation of objects during performance assessment.
Hearing	Seat so vision is not obstructed. Seat away from distracting background noises.	Modify for making observations through other senses. Use captioned films and videos. Use printed text to accompany audio tapes. Model or illustrate spoken instructions.	Face the child when speaking. Speak distinctly; do not shout. Use written outlines. Pair with nonhearing-impaired student.	Avoid spoken forms of assessment.

TABLE 9.1 (cont'd)   Teaching Children Who Have Special Needs

Special Need	Environmental Adaptation	Materials Adaptation	Teaching Adaptation	Assessment Adaptation
Orthopedic	Identify and remove physical barriers. Provide adequate space for movement. Seat near exits for safety. Check tables and desks for proper height.	Identify devices that assist handling of objects, such as spring-loaded tongs, accountant's pencil grips, test tube racks.	Encourage physical manipulation of objects. Pair with nonimpaired student peer. Provide student training time with equipment prior to use.	Provide assistance with writing and manipulation of materials.
Behavior	Seat away from distractions. Provide well-lighted quiet space for study.	Train in use prior to providing special equipment.	Use brief activities. Give praise and cues. Reinforce desired behaviors. Obtain attention and establish eye contact prior to discussion or giving instructions.	None
Gifted	None	Advanced reading materials. Greater application of technology.	Emphasize problem solving. Accelerate pace. Arrange mentorships. Emphasize processes, mathematics, and uses of technology.	Increase expectations for analysis, application, and hypotheses. Use open-ended assessment devices.

numbers have increased over time, in part because of greater sensitivity in assessment and diagnosis and teacher alertness for possible learning disabilities. Nationwide, nearly 30 percent of the students who receive special education services attend regular classrooms.[35]

Learning disabilities are not diseases. There is no single learning disability. Disabilities include dysgraphia, disorders in written language; dyscalculia, disorders in arithmetic; dyslexia, disorders in receptive and expressive language and reading; and difficulties in perception of spatial relations and organization.[36] Some famous people who have had learning disabilities include Thomas Edison, Albert Einstein, Winston Churchill, Cher, and Tom Cruise.

How Can You Help a Child with Learning Disabilities? Structure is the most important concept when teaching children with learning disabilities. These children have perceptual and cognitive difficulties. Such difficulties may make it impossible for children to mask out unnecessary stimuli such as sights and sounds in the background of the classroom. Ways to promote structure include class and study routines, limited choices, focused attention, memory clues, sequenced instruction, clear distinctions between instruction and testing, specific criticism and praise, time clues, conferences with special education teachers, and empathy and encouragement.[37]

Teaching Children with Intellectual Handicaps

Some children in your classes will have intellectual handicaps, also referred to as *mental retardation.*

Who Are Children with Intellectual Handicaps? There are different categories of mental retardation, and each has a range of different functions the child is expected to achieve. Mental retardation characterizes approximately 25 percent of the total population of students with handicaps, and of that portion nearly one third may be successful in regular classrooms.[38]

Children with a mild degree of mental retardation may be mainstreamed into your classroom. Their IQs can range from 52–67 on the Stanford-Binet test. *Educable mentally retarded* (EMR) is the term used to describe this level of intelligence. The American Association of Mental Deficiency describes children who have mental retardation as having subaverage intelligence and being deficient in behavior and responsibility for their age-related cultural group. These limitations affect academic and motor skills. Children with intellectual handicaps are capable of learning some academics, acquiring social skills, and developing occupational skills.

How Can You Teach Children Who Have Intellectual Handicaps? Peer acceptance is very important for the child with an intellectual handicap. By acquiring as much information as you can about the child, you can prepare to emphasize strengths while teaching to overcome weaknesses. School support services and special education personnel can make situation-specific suggestions to assist any particular child. However, the recommendations in Table 9.1 can help you enhance the child's academic skills.

Concept analysis is a strategy that has great potential for teaching science to children who have intellectual handicaps or learning disabilities as well as children who are not disabled. Figure 9.3 is a visual guide to the five distinct steps of concept analysis.[39]

Step 1. Identify the concept.

Select the main idea to be taught.

Step 2. Analyze the concept.

Identify the concept's critical attributes (characteristics that make the concept different from others) and its noncritical attributes.

Step 3. Identify several examples and nonexamples of the concept.

Examples illustrate the critical attributes, and nonexamples do not contain the attributes.

Step 4. Present the examples and nonexamples of the concept.

Use a variety of media and hands-on experiences to present the examples of the concept and to expose the children to nonexamples as well. The examples should be used to help children identify other examples that you have not identified for them. Comparisons with the nonexamples help to identify the attributes and nonattributes and help children transfer their learning to other situations.

Step 5. Present finer levels of discrimination.

A funnel approach can be used to move the children from making simple discriminations to more difficult comparisons.

Teaching Children Who Have Physical Disabilities

Physical disabilities include visual, hearing, and orthopedic impairments. Conservative estimates suggest that one percent of school children may have visual impairments, and hearing and orthopedic impairments may affect 6 and 5 percent respectively.[40]

What Barriers Do Children with Physical Disabilities Face?   Although few in number, children with physical disabilities carry huge burdens that limit their access to science education. Most of these burdens arise from the barriers the children encounter, such as[41]

- parents and school advisors who limit the children through stereotypes and low expectations,
- classroom structures that limit accessibility and reduce exposure to tactile manipulative experiences that are critical to basic learning in science,
- science programs that have not been modified or adapted to meet the needs of children who have physical impairments,
- teachers who may harbor fearful or negative attitudes or who may treat the children in an overly protective or cautious manner.

Why Is Science Important for Children Who Are Physically Disabled?   Science instruction should begin at an early age and continue throughout schooling for physically disabled children. The National Science Board Commission on Precollege Education in Mathematics, Science, and Technology offers three reasons for this early and sustained education in science:[42]

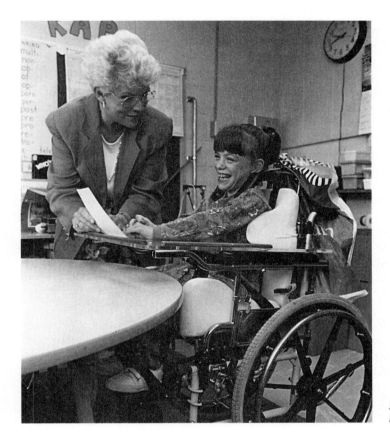

Help children to overcome barriers to learning science.

1. Science emphasizes hands-on experience and exploration of the environment. It can help to fill some experiential gaps that may have evolved because of extensive hospital stays and/or overprotectiveness of schools or parents. Science can help to develop the individual's independence and overall positive self-image.

2. Recent scientific and technological advances have provided tools such as computers, talking calculators, control systems, versabraille hook-ups to computers, and special telephone systems. These advances can help to mitigate the limitations imposed by a physical disability and can enable the individuals to become independent contributing members of society. Science instruction that emphasizes making observations, collecting and organizing information, and making conclusions can help develop the individual's mental and manipulative readiness for using new technology.

3. Job opportunities in the future will require greater knowledge and understanding of technological devices. Computers will continue to be an important part of many jobs. Advances in technology have helped children with physical disabilities learn and provide new employment opportunities for them. Children with physical disabilities will need the background, training, and self-confidence to seek these opportunities.

Visual Impairments.   Children who are *educationally blind* and *partially sighted* are increasingly benefiting from regular education experiences. The educationally blind cannot read printed materials and must learn from voice, audio tapes, braille reading, and other forms of nonprinted materials. They may have residual vision and should be encouraged to use it as widely as possible. Children who are partially sighted can read printed materials, but that material must be larger than standard school print. Magnifying devices can also be used to enlarge standard print.

Children with severe vision problems are identified at an early age. However, less severe problems often go undetected for years. Regular classroom teachers may be the first to notice sight problems. Some behaviors that may indicate vision loss include squinting at the chalkboard, holding a book closer or farther away than most children, blinking or otherwise distorting the eyes, holding the head at an odd angle, and unusual sensitivity to light.[43] Refer all children who demonstrate any of these behaviors to the school official who can arrange a vision screening. Parents and children appreciate early notification.

Teaching Children with Visual Impairments.   An audio-tactile teaching approach helps children who have visual impairments. Verbal lessons can be audiotaped for later playback, written assignments and tests can be tape-recorded, and a personal recorder with headphones can be used by children who are educationally blind without disturbing the rest of the class. (Be certain to provide verbal or tape-recorded feedback about answers too.) Magnified print materials and visual aids with high contrast can help children who are partially sighted.

Science process skills (Chapter 1) can provide helpful tactile experiences for the student with a visual impairment. Tactile experiences that require more than passive participation include:[44]

- modeling various birds and habitats with clay,
- illustrating the carbon cycle of a forest with papier mache,
- constructing leaf print books from old newspapers,
- designing constellations by constructing paper stars,
- illustrating a food chain by using natural objects,
- designing cloud formations from cotton balls,
- building bridges and other structures using drinking straws,
- building a replica of a coral reef,
- illustrating an electromagnetic wave by using iron filings and magnets,
- constructing replicas of prehistoric tools.

Instruction that stimulates the greatest range of senses (multimodal instruction) is vital for children with physical impairments. Commercial materials exist and may be modified to assist the student who is visually impaired. Programs such as the Elementary Science Study and Science: A Process Approach II have been used with over 3 million students. Teacher supplements are available with suggestions for modifications for students with disabilities. Adapting Science Materials for the Blind (ASMB) was developed from two Science Curriculum Improvement Study units for use with visually impaired children in mainstreamed classrooms. Science Activities for the Visually Impaired (SAVI) have been designed especially for middle-level children.

Pair children with visual disabilities with sighted children. Several researchers have found that this approach enables the child with a visual impairment to achieve on par with their nondisabled peers. The sighted member of a team can translate the class experiences to the child with a visual disability who can obtain an understanding through other senses. Together both can report the results of an experiment or activity. The team pairing approach has shown outstanding promise.[45]

Hearing Impairments. *Deaf* and *hard of hearing* are two types of hearing impairments. Regular classroom teachers occasionally work with children who have profound hearing losses, but more often have students with some lesser degree of hearing loss. Common types of hearing impairments concern volume and pitch. Another type is intelligibility—the volume of a sound may be adequate, but it is garbled. Hearing aids, lipreading, expressions, and gestures help the child with a hearing disability succeed in the regular classroom.

Deafness is often identified early in childhood, but mild hearing losses frequently go undetected. The following behaviors may signal a hearing impairment that should be referred to school personnel for screening: odd positioning of the head while listening, inattention during discussions, often asking the speaker to repeat, and asking classmates for instructions.[46]

Teaching Children Who Have Hearing Impairments. Language development is one of the major problems for the hearing impaired. Researchers have concluded that direct experience with objects is essential if children are to develop language sufficiently and that objects from a child's environment enhance learning of scientific concepts.[47] When we provide rich experiences, children who have hearing impairments can improve

> language performance, observing and listening skills, vocabulary, the learning of science concepts and development of cognitive skills through direct experiential experiences in science. In order for this learning to occur, students must have the opportunity of "doing science" by hands-on, inquiry, real-life experiences through direct physical manipulation of objects that focus attention on patterns of interaction in physical and biological systems. The pairing or coupling of handicapped and nonhandicapped children also seems to be an effective means for students to learn science.[48]

Observations students must make can be adapted. For example, auditory observations may be changed to visual observations, as in the case of the sounds made by different sizes of tuning forks. Have the child transfer the sound wave to water or sand and compare what happens as an alternative to hearing. Other techniques teachers can use are similar to those used for multilingual children, including seating the child near the front of the room so vision is not obstructed, looking directly at the child and obtaining his or her attention before speaking, shaving beards or mustaches so lips are visible for the student's lipreading, speak-

TEACHERS ON SCIENCE TEACHING

What Is Science Integration Through Inclusion?

By Najwa Abdul-Tawwab
Grade 2 Teacher, Oliver Wendell Holmes School, Dorchester, MA

The integration model of the newly opened Oliver Wendell Holmes School in Boston promises an exciting, creative inclusive model to teaching science and integrating special-needs children who have mild to moderate learning and behavior difficulties. These twenty children attend full-day classes. Fourteen of the children receive regular education, and six have special needs. Each child has strengths and weaknesses that must be addressed in this classroom setting for optimal learning to occur.

Oliver Wendell Holmes is a science-based school. For me, science on the primary level of instruction is not a complicated process. Imagination, enthusiasm, excitement, and clear and logical thinking are crucial. I look at science instruction as basic as reading, writing, and mathematics. For my special education students it is one of the few ways in which their varied disabilities now become a strength. Science-based instruction allows all of our students to consider themselves observers, experimenters, investigators, and questioners. Most of all they become risk takers.

The process of scientific thinking mandates that one must ask questions and develop hypotheses through repeated practice or experiments or by just looking at something over time. When we made rock crystals, we expected the solution to harden in three weeks. We clearly learned the value of patience and perseverance as it took our solutions three months to solidify. Those of us who shook the solution or stuck our fingers in it

quickly found out how variables affect the scientific process.

My focus is not one specific area of science. It is my job to prepare my students to love and be curious about all branches of science as they move up the ladder of education. In time, answers come, and they come from everyone, not just the teacher. Through this process I have found that the weak links in my special education students now have become their strengths. An observer of these twenty children would find it hard to determine who is or is not special education. My children have begun to develop consistency, patience, and perseverance. Most importantly, I see the light of self-confidence, which was ever so dim, now growing brighter and stronger. They are prepared to believe in their own ability to grasp and understand new concepts. They are also discovering techniques that help them see their own problems, claim ownership of them, and move on to solve them. Could there be a better approach to problem solving?

A Team Approach to Developing Units

Our philosophy is based upon inclusion in the broadest sense. Once I have determined my theme, I call a team meeting. I invite parents, the eduactional team leader, an occupational therapist, an adaptive physical education specialist, a speech therapist, and art and music teachers. I also approach faculty from colleges that have partnerships with our school. All of these people are invaluable assets to the developing loudly and distinctly without shouting, pairing students, and using a written outline for activities that require several steps.

Orthopedic Impairments.   Orthopedic impairments are disabilities caused by diseases and deformities of the muscles, joints, and skeletal system. Examples

ment and execution of a project. We explore discussions, activities, and materials that will allow all students to discover the connections between what they already know and the various science topics to be studied. We plan how I can integrate science with other areas of the curriculum.

Each participant recommends resources, approaches, and projects that will address objectives outlined in the individualized education programs. All team participants spend time in the class observing and taking ethnographic notes that will be discussed later during planning periods. The service providers bring their skills into the classroom. They work in small groups as well as with the entire class. This integration model does not support pull-out programs. Inclusion is the number-one priority. These team members are all part of my class in spirit, content, and approach. Our school motto is "It takes an entire community to educate our children."

Are the Connections Being Made?

I believe this is a question that remains with all educators. We don't need to have lectures, readings, or workshops on what to teach; rather, we need to look at process, assessment, learning styles, and inclusion. These are areas that I have attempted to address. Any strong school of education's science department can give you content. How do you as an educator know that you are reaching and serving the diverse children in front of you?

My science themes are based on the seasons.

That leaves a lot of territory to be covered. The children sitting in front of me have an abundance of academic, social, and behavioral needs. My neediest child requires the services of all the itinerant people assigned to the school. His short attention span, weak muscle tone, poor social skills, and limited writing ability force me to provide lessons that are intellectually challenging, require minimum writing, coloring, or sitting, and allow lots of movement about the room. For those children who have cultural, ethnic, and geographical ties around the world, our approach to the seasons transcends typical gender and race stereotypes. Our school librarian helps by reading and providing books that meet our needs. Our public librarian will make visits to share cultural and seasonal activities. Science is all about learning, questioning, discovering and sharing. It's also about brainstorming and taking these ideas, experiments, and observations and writing and publishing our own chapter in the biggest science book in the world: the creation and nature.

Last but not least, for those children who have volcanic, eruptive behaviors periodically because they don't feel they are equal to their peers, a science discovery assisted by a caring parent, an inquisitive college professor, or the calmest child in the class often proves to be a remedy. Science points out to them that there are many beautiful, positive ways for them to be discovered or noticed. It gives them a chance to say, "Look at me—notice and discover the wonders in me, too."

include cerebral palsy, spina bifida, amputations, birth defects, arthritis, and muscular dystrophy. Temporary injuries are not addressed by Public Law 94–142 because they can be corrected. A child with an orthopedic impairment may require an appliance such as a wheel chair, walker, crutches, or skeletal braces.

Teaching Children with Orthopedic Disabilities.   Generally, the way an orthopedically handicapped child learns is not affected. Adjustments are more physical than educational. Be aware of and attempt to remove physical and psychological barriers in your classroom. Examine the curriculum materials and activities and modify them to include the child with a disability without sacrificing their purpose or science content. Do not underestimate the capabilities of the child. Become familiar with the function and maintenance of any appliance the child uses.[49]

Teaching Learners Who Are Gifted and Talented

Children who are gifted or talented are not protected by Public Law 94–142. However, gifted or talented children do have special needs that are not usually served well by the instruction given to most children. Gifted and talented children are included in this chapter because most teachers already have children of this type in their classrooms, and authorities have questioned the wisdom of pulling gifted children out of the regular classroom for special instruction. Like children with disabilities or cultural differences, gifted and talented children

> require a balanced view of humanity, and they must prepare to work and live in the greater society. This preparation can best be accomplished within the regular classroom. This does not imply that curriculum, materials, and instruction for the gifted should be the same as for the nongifted. What it does imply is that the gifted, like everyone else, should be considered individuals, with unique needs and abilities. Their education should attend specifically to those needs and abilities.[50]

Who Are Gifted and Talented Learners?   Children who are gifted and/or talented show promise of making superior progress in school. These children may demonstrate advanced progress in academic achievement in a school subject or exceptional ability and creativity in the arts. Their special talents are observed and may be verified by achievement and IQ tests or superior performance in a subject or artistic area. In addition, gifted children may demonstrate other traits such as sensitivity to the needs of other children, a need for independence, a predisposition for expression, a capacity for social leadership, broad interests in different school areas, apparent natural talents in the arts, and such noticeable behaviors as intensity, persistence, self-assured introversion, or detachment from what they believe are mundane topics.[51]

Children who are gifted and talented have a wide range of possible characteristics. This range makes it difficult to generalize about all gifted children. Gifted and talented children can represent a tremendous challenge to the elementary science teacher.

Academically gifted children may appear to become easily bored with instruction offered to the rest of the class. If you have not majored in science, you may have some anxiety about having a scientifically gifted child in your class. Fear not. Feeling unprepared in science should not stop you from teaching gifted children. Perhaps your anxiety will be eased if you can keep the issue in perspective. Remember that you are an adult who teaches children, and the experiences of adulthood provide advantages when working with the student who is gifted. Despite all the knowledge a young gifted learner may have, he or she is still an elementary or middle school student, and the student's social, emotional, physical, psychological, and cognitive development is not complete. As an adult, you still have much to offer. All learners enjoy seeing their teacher get excited about their students' work. Having a gifted child in your science class is reason to rejoice and will give you a wonderful opportunity to become a real facilitator and guide, rather than a messenger.

How Can You Teach Learners Who Are Gifted in Science? Children who are gifted in science often are capable of accelerated and more detailed learning. You can enrich their experiences by encouraging them to pursue the subject to a greater depth. You may also accelerate their instruction by drawing on topics from advanced grades or by arranging for the child to work with a mentor (perhaps an older student, another teacher, or a science career professional) on special science topics. It is not uncommon for gifted students to perform two or three years above grade level in the subject or area where they show talent.[52] Therefore, more flexibility in written assignments and higher expectations for verbal communication are necessary. Try having gifted learners engage in more speculation about scientific events, hypothesize, and develop arguments and counterarguments that pertain to scientific/social issues. Have gifted learners demonstrate the application of science as well as the relationships between science and material learned in other subjects. The following teaching strategies are often appropriate for gifted learners.

Open-ended learning activities. Whereas children who have learning and intellectual disabilities benefit from narrowly focused, sequential activities, children who are gifted should be challenged to develop their intellectual reasoning through open-ended activities that have many possible outcomes. These activities avoid step-by-step recipe procedures and do not have predetermined results. Several of the cooperative inquiry teaching methods of Chapter 7 and the tools of questioning in Chapter 6 are useful when working with gifted learners.

Use the gifted students as classroom leaders. These children may become reliable informal teachers of their peers who can greatly enhance the classroom atmosphere. Children who are gifted can also be used as resource persons, researchers, science assistants, and community ambassadors for exciting school programs.

Use technology, science processes, and mathematics. Scientific observation can be enhanced through mathematics. Encourage gifted children to use higher forms of mathematics and statistics as often as possible. Engage them in more precise measures and more extensive uses of science process skills. Technology will

Teaching Exceptional Students

Who has the wisdom and ability to predict which of our students will succeed and which will not? People with disabilities are often erroneously thought to be mentally deficient, but the prevailing social attitude is slowly changing. Thanks to federal laws, inclusion, and local school efforts to service better the special needs of children are greater than at any time in the history of schooling. All children are given more encouragement and are provided with more opprotunities to achieve their full potential.

After decades of turning away students with handicaps, universities are now accepting them for scientific career training. A three-year survey by the American Association for the Advancement of Science reported a resource group of more than 700 scientists with disabilities. People with handicaps *can* do science. But our schools still must do more. Robert Menchel, a senior physicist for the Xerox Corporation who has been deaf since the age of seven, has visited many schools. He says:

> The lack of development of a basic science curriculum from kindergarten to the twelfth grade is a national disgrace and one that puts the deaf child at

a disadvantage in comparison to the nonhandicapped child. Furthermore, these students are still being pushed into stereotyped job roles and dead-end jobs. For the female students it is even worse.

Robert Hoffman, a researcher who has cerebral palsy, speaks about the effects of isolation due to a disability:

> When one is born with a disability severe enough so society shoves him into a special program (which nonhandicapped people develop), one becomes separated from "normal" persons. All through his school years, he learns from other disabled students, and the teachers design studies to fit the limitations of his physical handicap.

John Gavin, a research scientist with a physical impairment, cautions those who have no apparent disability:

> One of the least desirable traits of the human condition is our propensity to avoid those among us who are afflicted with overt physical disabilities. While this may be an inherent psychological carryover from those days of survival of the fittest, it is more likely we do not wish to have a reminder

challenge gifted students to expand research capabilities as well as quantify and communicate their scientific findings.

Reinforce and reward superior efforts. Some school gifted and talented programs use pull-out approaches. The learners are placed in special programs or given accelerated instruction. Mainstreaming can also benefit children who are gifted. Adaptations of science content and changes in instruction with more options for the gifted learners can provide suitable instruction in the regular classroom. Science content adaptations could include emphasizing higher levels of thinking, abstraction, and independent thinking. The challenge is fundamentally the same as with any child: Help the child learn how to learn. Reinforcement and rewards for effort and work well done are usually all that is necessary to help gifted children keep their high level of motivation for learning. Some suggestions for reinforcing and rewarding superior effort include public recog-

that we are potentially and continually eligible to join them.

Teachers become the key. A caring teacher with a positive can-do attitude is consistently ranked highly by children with handicaps. Teachers who care seem to expect that their students can learn at a high level. These teachers try to see that all children fulfill the high expectations held for them.

Language development is one of the major problems of children with hearing impairments. Researchers report that direct experience with objects is essential and that utilization of objects from a child's environment enhances his or her learning of concepts.

The most significant changes needed for teaching children who have visual impairments are related to the adaptation of educational materials and equipment to take advantage of each child's residual vision.

Children who are orthopedically handicapped are a heterogeneous group, and it is difficult to prescribe general methods and adaptations that will serve *each* child well. However, pairing a child with an orthopedic impairment with a nonhandicapped child helps both. The child who is impaired still needs direct physical experience with the science phenomena to the greatest extent possible. For example,

a magnet can be taped to the arm or leg. Another student can bring objects in contact with the magnets. The child should be able to feel and see which objects interact with the magnet and which do not. In this way, the child [with a handicap] is involved in the decision making and discovery that is the major emphasis of [the] lesson.

Dean Brown's research shows that children with physical handicaps can learn to understand science concepts and that they can develop higher levels of reasoning skills if given the opportunity. Children with handicaps need direct, experiential, sensory experiences in science. Many researchers repeatedly express the need for doing science through hands-on, inquiry-based, real-life experiences.

Source: Adapted from the literature review by Dean R. Brown, "Helping Handicapped Youngsters Learn by 'Doing'," in Mary Budd Rowe (ed.), *What Research Says to the Science Teacher*, vol. 2 (Washington, DC: National Science Teachers Association, 1979), pp. 80–100.

nition for effort, extra credit or waiver of standard assignments, positive teacher comments, extra leadership opportunities and/or classroom responsibilities, and encouraging students to do real research projects.

Provide extra- or cocurricular learning opportunities. Your classroom will have limited teaching resources, and your time will also have limits. Out-of-class or out-of-school learning options may also help the gifted student continue to learn science. Use community library resources or make arrangements for the child to do special work at a community college or nearby university. Develop and utilize community resource personnel: Construct a network of science-related resource people and arrange mentor-intern relationships. Start a science club for students with special interests. Begin an after-school science lab—encourage the learners to design and pursue experiments. Student teachers or field experience interns from a nearby university may be able to assist with the science lab instruction and programming.

HOW CAN PARENTS HELP MEET CHILDREN'S SPECIAL NEEDS?

More parents are realizing the importance of science. Reinforce its importance often with those parents who are already aware of it. For those parents who are unaware, share these ideas through school or class newsletters and during conferences with parents.

Science Is Important to Their Children's Future

Children will have a much better chance of finding a job if they have a good background in mathematics, science, and computers. The College Board of New York, for example, estimates the unemployment rate of African-American scientists and engineers at 2.5 percent. This compares with an overall unemployment rate of 14.5 percent for African-American adults. Unemployment for Hispanic adults is 11.5 percent, but for Hispanics who are scientists and engineers it is only 2.1 percent. Unemployment statistics are inexact for Native Americans, but they show the same trends for those with a background in science.[53]

Skills in mathematics and science will help children earn more money when

Science is found in all aspects of life and is important to children's successful futures.

they enter careers. A scientist or engineer from a minority background earns well over twice the annual salary of the average person from the same background.[54]

Science can help break the cycle of unemployment, underemployment, and poverty in culturally different and special-needs populations. Scientific careers command higher levels of pay, and demands for personnel are increasing.

Science skills develop over time, and development builds upon older skills. "If you don't use it, you'll lose it" applies here. The science foundation begun during childhood will increase each individual's potential for later success. Also, science depends on mathematics. Students should be encouraged to study mathematics every school year.

All students learn science through hands-on, minds-on experiences. Children should be encouraged to handle physical objects, make measurements and direct comparisons, and ask frequent questions about what they observe and experience.

How Can Parents Help Their Children Study and Prepare for Science?

Parents are invaluable when it comes to educating children. They are closest to the special needs their children may have and are naturally protective of their children's best interests. Parents can help their children succeed in science by following these suggestions:

Stimulate interest in and foster feelings for science. Parents can help their children realize that science can be fun and help them experience success, with its feelings of excitement, discovery, and mastery.

Include science in the child's everyday experiences. Children can be asked to count and form sets of utensils at dinner time and can help to measure ingredients. Include them also in repairing broken appliances or building a model airplane.

Establish a regular study time and provide a designated space for study away from distractions. Work with the teachers to develop effective ways to communicate with children who have vision and hearing disabilities. Equipment modifications can be developed for children who have physical disabilities, and these can be shared with the school.

Parents should check with their children every day to make sure homework and special projects are completed. They should ask to see completed homework and any tests or projects that have been graded or returned.

Parents should offer to read assignment questions. Even if the parents do not know the answers, a stronger academic bond will be formed between parent and child. The child will benefit from an interested adult role model, forming the impression that school, homework, and effort are important.

Parents should ask if their children have any difficulties with science or mathematics. Suggest that parents talk with their children at least once per week about this and then follow up by communicating with you if there appear to be problems.

Teachers can offer to set up a homework hotline. This may be school based or supported only by yourself for your classes during designated hours.

What Are Some Extra Science Activities Parents Can Do to Help Their Children?

Some teachers, even entire schools, arrange home-based science activities to supplement school instruction. Parents become enthusiastic and develop a stronger bond with the school. They often say, "Let's have parent involvement programs more often." "It helps me keep in touch with my child." "The activities didn't take too much time, so it was simple to include them into our busy evening schedule." "I think it's great to get the parents involved. Each activity we did benefited our older child and the younger child who is not even in school!"[55]

The rich variety of science teaching resources makes it easy to suggest home study extensions. Giving parents options to choose from helps them overcome limits of time and materials. When selecting options and making suggestions to parents, keep these criteria in mind:[56]

The activities should be at grade level and developmentally appropriate for the child. Select options with the special needs of the children in mind.

Activities should require materials that are available at home. No parent will welcome traveling to gather together materials, and many cannot afford the expense.

The activities should supplement what is taught in school, not duplicate what you teach. Do not expect parental teaching to be a substitute for your own responsibility.

The activities should require only a brief amount of time. There are many simple, inexpensive activities that require only ten or twenty minutes. (See Table 9.2.)

Provide complete and accurate instructions. Try the activities yourself before sending them home. Do they work? Are the instructions clear? Are they safe? Can a child do the activity with minimal adult guidance? Revise the instructions as necessary for the children you teach, again being mindful of the special needs of the children.

Select activities that emphasize simple and accurate concepts. Cross-check the concepts of the activity with those of your text or science program. Are they consistent? Or are there differences in terminology and accuracy of information? If they are different, modify them or select another activity. Choose activities that emphasize a main science idea, and encourage the parents to continue emphasizing this main idea.

The activities should be fun. Parents and children will enjoy a special time together when the activity is fun. No one, not even an adult, will do something that is not enjoyable if it can be avoided. Encourage parents to share the joys and mysteries of science with their children. Scientific attitudes and positive values parents give to science at home also will benefit school science.

Table 9.2 provides a brief list of science resources useful for home learning activities. Ideas similar to the following may be selected from sources such as those shown in the table.[57]

TABLE 9.2   Science Resources for Home Activities

J. Abruscato and J. Hassard, *The Whole Cosmos Catalog of Science Activities* (Glenview, IL: Scott Foresman, 1977).

J. Barber, *Bubbleology* (Berkeley, CA: Great Exploration in Math and Science, Lawrence Hall of Science, 1986).

V. Cobb, *Bet You Can* and *Bet You Can't* (New York: Avon Books, 1980).

J. DeBruin, *Creative, Hands-On Science Experiences* (Carthage, IL: Good Apple, 1986).

J. Echols, *Buzzing a Hive* (Berkeley, CA: Great Explorations in Math and Science, Lawrence Hall of Science, 1986).

D. Herbert, *Mr. Wizard's Supermarket Science* (New York: Random House, 1980).

D. Herbert and H. Ruchlis, *Mr. Wizard's 400 Experiments in Science* (North Bergen, NJ: Book Lab, 1983).

C. Shaffer and E. Fielder, *City Safaris* (San Francisco: Sierra Club Books, 1987).

Smithsonian Family Learning Project, *Science Activities Calendar* (New York: GMG Publishing, annually).

Develop the concepts of sink or float and density by floating common objects such as straws and plastic buttons in plain water and in salt water. Because the density of salt water is greater, objects that sink in plain water often float in salt water. Try adding different amounts of salt to water to explore the effects of salt concentration on density and floating.

Explore primary and secondary colors. Following the directions on food coloring packages, prepare different colors and arrange them in glass jars. Dye macaroni or paper to represent the colors of a rainbow. Combine the three primary colors to produce every color.

Demonstrate magnetism by having children compare the effects of magnets on different objects in the kitchen. Let the children predict which objects will and will not be attracted to the magnets.

Use building blocks to develop the concepts of set and order. Lay a foundation of three blocks; then place two blocks on the next layer and one on the top layer. Ask the children to count the blocks and to estimate how many blocks would be necessary to build towers six and ten blocks high.

CHAPTER SUMMARY

A single science teaching method by itself is insufficient. Each hands-on science lesson must be accompanied by adaptations to suit the needs of each special student. Nothing is so unequal as equal treatment without exception.

There is no single method or science program that can be used to teach all children fairly and equally all the time. However, one single factor does benefit *all* children: hands-on science. This approach has the potential to become the great equalizer. Children who are culturally different may acquire missing experiences through hands-on science. Non-English-speaking children can use science to learn and develop language skills. Young females can overcome skill deficits, gender stereotypes, and career limitations through hands-on, minds-on science. Exceptional children are given new opportunities because of hands-on science and its ability to include all children in minds-on experiences. Gifted and talented children also benefit as they are introduced to new experiences and are motivated to process those experiences at an advanced intellectual level.

Parents play a vital role with students who have special needs. Teachers should inform parents about the importance of science and offer activities to strengthen the school-home learning connection.

DISCUSSION QUESTIONS AND PROJECTS

1. Cultural differences can have a positive impact on the social climate of a classroom. What are some ways you can encourage the expression of differences and make a positive impact on all children?

2. Take the picture of a scientist you drew in Chapter 1, and draw another one now. How do the pictures compare? What features are similar? How many of these features do you observe: male, middle aged, bald, glasses, facial hair, lab coat with pocket protector, test tubes? How can these features reflect bias, attitudes, stereotypes, and values? Where did the impressions portrayed in the pictures come from? What types of multicultural education concepts are reflected in the picture? How can social context and media influence impressions? How are the impressions you have of science and scientists likely to influence young children?

3. Blindfold yourself or attend a class while wearing earplugs. How is your ability to function impaired? What long-term cumulative effects could result from your temporary disability if it were to become permanent? How could those effects influence your ability to function in a regular classroom?

4. Brainstorm ideas suitable for teaching science to gifted students. What differences are found on your list according to grade level? How would you work with a youngster who is gifted and who also has a cultural or language difference and/or a disability?

5. Brainstorm ideas related to classroom organization. How can a typical self-contained room be converted to better suit the needs of special students? Look especially for barriers that might limit the inclusion of children who have physical disabilities. What complications might a teacher encounter? What are some ways to overcome these complications?

6. Interview a teacher whose students are culturally different from him- or herself. Inquire about how the science program or instruction has been modified to recognize and use cultural differences in a positive way. What effects have the teacher's efforts had on all of the children?

7. Peruse several elementary science textbooks from different publishers. Report observations about possible gender bias, omitted discussion of cultural differences, and potential for adaptation for non-English-speaking, disabled, and/or gifted children. What suggestions are provided in the teacher's guide?

8. Choose any lesson from an elementary science text or hands-on program. Demonstrate how you would adapt it to provide special instruction for female students or children with learning disabilities, intellectual handicaps, impaired vision, hearing loss, or orthopedic impairment.

9. Sketch the floor plan of an elementary classroom. Examine the floor plan carefully and make changes to show adaptations that would assist children with orthopedic impairments.

10. Use the concept analysis model presented in this chapter (Figure 9.3) to make changes in a science lesson plan. How would you use the model to instruct children who are learning disabled or intellectually handicapped? How could the model be used with all children? What are the possible benefits and limits?

NOTES

1. Jeannie Rae Rice, "A Special Science Fair: LD Children Learn What They Can Do," *Science and Children* (January 1983), pp. 15–16. Reprinted with permission from NSTA publications.

2. "An NSTA Position Statement: Multicultural Science Education," *NSTA Reports!* (October/November 1991), p. 7.

3. George Antonouris, "Multicultural Science," *The School Science Review*, vol. 70, no. 252 (March 1989), pp. 97–100.

4. I. W. Williams, "Chemistry," in Alma Craft and Geoff Bardell, *Curriculum Opportunities in a Multicultural Society* (New York: Harper & Row, 1984), pp. 133–146.

5. Antonouris, p. 98.

6. Ibid., pp. 99–100.

7. Ted Bredderman, "Activity Science—The Evidence Shows It Matters," *Science and Children* (September 1982), pp. 39–40.

8. Mary Budd Rowe, "Wait-Time and Rewards as Instructional Variables, Their Influence on Language, Logic, and Fate Control: Part I—Wait Time," *Journal of Research in Science Teaching*, vol. 13, no. 2 (1974), pp. 81–94; and "Part II—Rewards," *Journal of Research in Science Teaching*, vol. 13, no. 4 (1974), pp. 291–308.

9. Bruce Reichert, "What Did He Say? Science in the Multilingual Classroom," *Science Scope* (November/December 1989), pp. 10–11.

10. James A. Shymansky, William C. Kyle, Jr., and Jennifer M. Alport, "How Effective Was the Hands-On Science of Yesterday?" *Science and Children* (November/December 1982), pp. 14–15.

11. Geoff Chivers, "Intervention Strategies to Increase the Proportion of Girls and Women Studying and Pursuing Careers in Technological Fields: A West European Overview," *European Journal of Engineering Education*, vol. 11, no. 3 (1986), p. 248.

12. Lynn Edward Elfner (ed.), *Exemplars: Women in Science, Engineering, and Mathematics* (Columbus, OH: Ohio Academy of Science, 1988), p. 3.

13. M. Gail Jones and Jack Wheatley, "Factors Influencing the Entry of Women into Science and Related Fields," *Science Education*, vol. 72, no. 2 (1988), pp. 127–142.

14. Lee R. Jones, Ina V. S. Mullins, Senta A. Raizen, Iris R. Weiss and Elizabeth A. Weston, *The 1990 Science Report Card, NAEP's Assessment of Fourth, Eighth, and Twelfth Graders* (Washington, DC: U. S. Department of Education, 1992), p. 11.

15. Jones and Wheatley, p. 128.

16. Ina V. Mullis and Lynn B. Jenkins, *The Science Report Card: Elements of Risk and Recovery* (Princeton, NJ: Educational Testing Service, 1988), p. 7.

17. Ibid., p. 90.

18. Elfner, p. 3.

19. Chivers, p. 249.

20. Jones and Wheatley, p. 130.

21. Ibid., p. 129.

22. Ibid., pp. 129, 130.

23. Ibid., p. 130.

24. Ibid., p. 131–132.

25. David Sadker, Myra Sadker, and D. Thomas, "Sex Equity and Special Education," *The Pointer*, vol. 26, no. 1 (1981), p. 33.

26. H. M. Cooper, "Pygmalion Grows Up: A Model for Teacher Expectation, Communication, and Performance Influence," *Review of Education Research*, vol. 49 (1979), pp. 389–410.

27. Jones and Wheatley, pp. 133–134.

28. D. U. Levine and A. C. Ornstein, "Sex Differences in Ability and Achievement," *Journal of Research and Development in Education*, vol. 16, no. 2 (1983), pp. 62–66.

29. J. B. Kahle and M. K. Lakes, "The Myth of Equality in Science Classrooms," *Journal of Research in Science Teaching*, vol. 20, no. 2 (1983), pp. 131–140.

30. Leonie Rennie and Lesley Parker, "A Comparison of Mixed-Sex and Single-Sex Grouping in Year 5 Science Lessons," a paper presented at the Annual Meeting of the American Educational Research Association (San Francisco: Educational Resource Information Center Document no. 273 441, 1986), p. 10.

31. Eve Humrich, "Sex Differences in the Second IEA Science Study—U.S. Results in an International Context," paper presented at the Annual Meeting of the National Association for Research in Science Teaching (Lake of the Ozarks, MO: Education Resource Information Center Document no. 292 649, 1988), p. 5.

32. Jones and Wheatley, p. 137.

33. Rita Dunn and Kenneth Dunn, "Finding the Best Fit—Learning Styles, Teaching Styles," *NASSP Bulletin* 59 (October 1975), pp. 37–49.

34. U. S. Office of Education, "Education of Handicapped Children: Assistance to the States: Procedures for Evaluating Specific Learning Disabilities," *Federal Register, Part III* (Washington, DC: U.S. Department of Health, Education, and Welfare, December 29, 1977).

35. Deborah Deutsch Smith and Ruth Luckasson, *Introduction to Special Education* (Boston: Allyn and Bacon, 1992), pp. 18, 77.

36. Mary MacCracken, *Turnabout Children* (Boston: Little, Brown and Company, 1986).

37. Charles R. Coble, Betty Levey, and Floyd Mattheis, "Science for Learning Disabled Students" (Educational Resource Information Center Document no. 258 803, 1985), pp. 7–10.

38. C. M. Charles and Ida M. Malian, *The Special Student* (St. Louis, MO: C. V. Mosby, 1980), p. 155.

39. These examples are adapted from Jack T. Cole, Margie K. Kitano, and Lewis M. Brown, "Concept Analysis: A Model for Teaching Basic Science Concepts to Intellectually Handicapped Students," in Marshall E. Corrick, Jr. (ed.), *Teaching Handicapped Students Science: A Resource Book for K–12 Teachers* (National Education Association, 1981), pp. 51–53.

40. Charles and Malian, p. 19.

41. Greg P. Stefanich et al., "Addressing Orthopedic Handicaps in the Science Classroom" (Educational Resource Information Center Document no. 258 802, 1985), pp. 8–9.

42. National Science Board Commission on Precollege Education in Mathematics, Science, and Technology, "A Revised and Intensified Science and Technology Curriculum for Grades K–12 Is Urgently Needed for Our Future" (Washington, DC: National Science Foundation, 1983), Educational Resource Information Center Document no. 239 847, 1983, p. 27.

43. Charles and Malian, pp. 28–29.

44. Randall Harris, "An Audio-Tactile Approach to Science Education for Visually Impaired Students," in Marshall E. Corrick, Jr. (ed.), *Teaching Handicapped Students Science* (Washington, DC: National Education Association, 1981), p. 40.

45. Dean R. Brown, "Helping Handicapped Youngsters Learn Science by Doing," in Mary Budd Rowe (ed.), *What Research Says to the Science Teacher*, vol. 2 (Washington, DC: National Science Teachers Association, 1979), p. 85.

46. Charles and Malian, p. 21.

47. Rodger Bybee and P. W. Hendricks, "Teaching Science Concepts to Preschool Deaf Children to Aid Language Development," *Science Education*, vol. 56, no. 3 (1972), pp. 303–310.

48. Brown, p. 89.

49. Stefanich, pp. 9–15.

50. Charles and Malian, p. 181.

51. Ibid., pp. 181–182.

52. Michael Piburn and Morris Enyeart, "A Comparison of the Reasoning Ability of Gifted and Mainstreamed Science Students," a paper presented at the Annual Meeting of the National Association for Research in Science Teaching (Educational Resource Information Center Document no. 255 379, April 1985).

53. College Board, "Get into the Equation: Math and Science, Parents and Children," (College Board, NY: 1987), Educational Resource Information Center Document no. 295 785, pp. 6–7.

54. Ibid.

55. Comments are representative of those found in Mary Williams-Norton, Marycarol Reisdorf, and Sallie Spees, "Home Is Where the Science Is," *Science and Children* (March 1990), pp. 13–15.

56. Ibid., p. 14.

57. College Board, pp. 20–21.

ADDITIONAL READINGS

If you are interested in learning more about some of the topics raised in this chapter consider the following sources:

Deborah Deutsch Smith and Ruth Luckasson, *Introduction to Special Education* (Boston: Allyn and Bacon, 1992). This text provides interesting descriptions of students who are members of minority groups, non-English speaking, and who also have mental, learning, or physical impairments.

William L. Heward and Michael D. Orlansky, *Exceptional Children*, 3d ed. (Columbus, OH: Merrill, 1988). This is one of many fine texts that delve deeper into the characteristics of special children. Included is extensive coverage of federal law, the philosophy of special education, and specific detailed descriptions of exceptionalities. Teaching and educational service alternatives are offered.

Michael E. Corrick, Jr., (ed.), *Teaching Handicapped Students Science* (National Education Association, 1981). This book is a concise collection of essays that address goals, approaches, materials, barriers, and evaluation practices. This is a worthy personal reference for any science teacher.

Francis X. Sutman, Virginia French Allen, and Francis Shoemaker, *Learning English Through Science* (Washington, DC: NSTA, 1986). A guide to collaboration for science teachers, English teachers, and teachers of English as a second language, this book offers practical suggestions for setting up classrooms and science programs as models for cultural pluralism through multilingual efforts.

Patricia B. Campbell has written a series of brochures (published by the U. S. Department of Education, 1991) about females in mathematics and science. The brochures cover such topics as appropriate ways to evaluate programs for girls in math, science, and engineering; designing effective programs; working in and out of school to encourage young females; and the kinds of things parents can do.

William D. Romey and Mary L. Hibert, *Teaching the Gifted and Talented in the Science Classroom* (Washington, DC: National Education Association, 1988). This guide offers practical suggestions for creating a learning environment that nurtures giftedness. It includes several science activity ideas.

Some sources of information for science for students with special needs are:

Center for Multisensory Learning
Lawrence Hall of Science
University of California
Berkeley, California 94720

Exceptional Children Science Education Project (ECSEP)
Science for the Learning Disabled
Charlotte-Mecklenberg Schools
PO Box 140
Charlotte, NC 28230

The Project on the Handicapped in Science
American Association for the Advancement of Science
1776 Massachusetts Avenue, NW
Washington, DC 20036

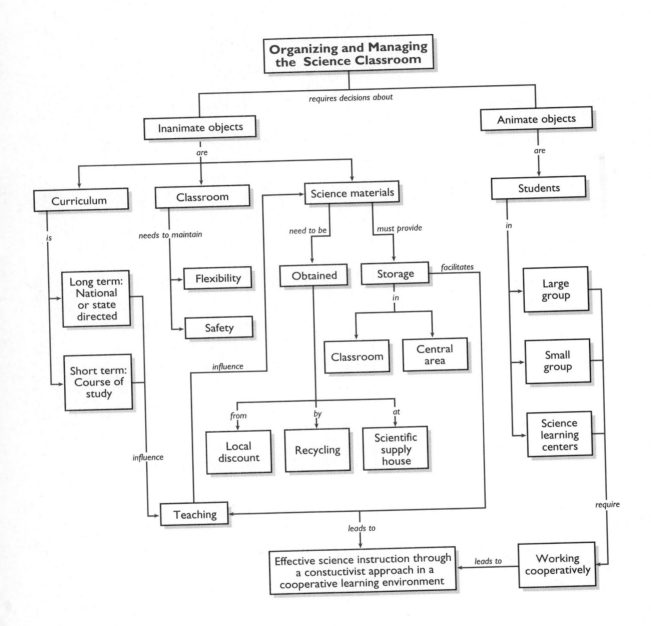

How Can You Create an Efficient, Activity-Based Science Classroom?

CHAPTER 10

N ine-year-old Celeste sat reading her current issue of *3–2–1 Contact Magazine*. She was intrigued by an article about volcanoes. At the end of the article was an activity on making a volcano. She read over the list of materials she needed. "Let's see," she said half out loud, "the water I can get from the sink; in the bottom cupboard I can find the large baking pan; in the upper cabinet there's the white vinegar, red food coloring, baking soda, and dishwashing liquid; in the first drawer on the right I should find the glue, masking tape, and scissors; and in the drawer on the left I can find the tin foil and teaspoons." Celeste collected the materials from their storage areas. She found the clay flower pot and the potting soil stored with the garden supplies. Celeste checked over the materials list once again. "I think I have just about everything I need to make my own volcano," she announced to Sarah, who was passing by. Ten-year-old Sarah looked over Celeste's shoulder at the magazine; then she took a quick inventory of the materials Celeste had collected. "You forgot an empty tuna can," Sarah proclaimed. Celeste looked pensive for a moment and then shouted, "I know, I can go to the recycling bin—I'll probably find just what I need in there!"

In a few moments Celeste was back with an empty tuna can. The two girls arranged the materials according to the directions in the magazine. They dumped the baking soda down the vent of their newly formed volcano. They mixed the vinegar, dishwashing liquid, water, and food coloring together. They were just about to pour the vinegar mixture into the vent when they were startled by a frantic cry from an adult yelling, "STOP! What do you think will happen to you if you continue to look down that vent as you pour in the liquid? How are you going to protect your eyes and your clothing? Do you think it's a good idea to do that on the carpet?"

A surprised look came over their faces. "Oh, I'm sorry! I forgot about that," said Celeste. "I guess I was so excited after reading this article, I really wanted to try it out as quickly as possible. Come on Sarah, let's move this off the carpet and then go get our goggles and put some old sweatshirts on before we make our volcano erupt."

INTRODUCTION

An activity-based science classroom does not mean a chaotic classroom. In fact, the teacher who is committed to an activity-based science program will find that the key to success is organization. Whether you choose to set up learning centers or work with all the students at once, the most effective teaching will come about when materials are stored in an organized fashion, allowing for easy access.

The scenario above could have taken place in any activity-based science class where the teacher gives the students time to engage in different kinds of inquiry at a science learning center. The girls were able to create the volcano to immediately satisfy their natural curiosity because they knew where the materials were stored and could easily obtain them. The person who stopped them to remind them of some simple safety rules, however, was not their teacher. It was their mother! The sisters know where everything is kept in their home. When they want materials for a project, such as building a volcano, they know where to get them. This same familiarity with storage of materials that children feel in their homes, down to knowing what things they are allowed to touch and those materials they are to keep away from, should go on in the classroom.

This chapter examines the tasks necessary to create an efficient, activity-based science classroom:

1. Deciding what should be taught in the long and short term.
2. Storing equipment and materials.

3. Distributing, taking care of, and inventorying those materials.
4. Establishing the physical surroundings and the rules that will maximize the learning experience for all the children involved.

ORGANIZING THE SCIENCE CLASSROOM

By the time the students join the teacher in an activity-based science classroom, most of the teacher's work is done. The most important and time-consuming tasks are completed before the teacher ever deals with the students. The first task is for the teacher to decide what will be taught. This is more than just a matter of opening up the elementary science textbook and following the table of contents. You may be involved in the long-term planning for science—creating the science curriculum for your state, school district, or individual school; or for the short term, simply deciding, once the science curriculum is in place, which concepts you can effectively cover within a given time frame.

Long-Term Planning

Some states already have a recommended science curriculum that individual school districts have agreed to incorporate as their own. Others may be just starting the process of science curriculum reform. You may even know of veteran teachers who have been involved in planning the state curriculum.

The individual school districts may be required to accept the state curriculum, or this may come from the state in the form of a recommendation. It is then up to individual districts to decide their courses of action. If your school decides to work with the state document, you as a science teacher are expected to plan your lessons around the concepts or themes recommended for your grade level. Although this may seem rather restrictive, many excellent state science curricula still allow for individual teacher preferences and leave room for a creative teacher to introduce other science concepts to his or her students.[1]

School districts in states where no mandated science curricula exist are usually left with two choices: creating a district-wide science curriculum or allowing the individual schools to determine what science concepts will be taught at each grade level. You may become a part of this planning team. There are probably as many ways to go about creating an effective science curriculum as there are grains of sand in the Sahara. The important things to keep in mind during this type of long-term planning for science teaching are the overall goals and objectives of your science program. What is your mission? What do you think is important for elementary school children to know in the sciences by the time they get to the secondary school? Will your district or school advocate any particular teaching method as the best way to go about achieving its goals?

There are many problems and questions to be answered as one looks at the long-term planning necessary to create an effective activity-based science program. These problems are not insurmountable. Teachers with a strong commitment to science education, a clear understanding of science concepts, and the willingness to listen to the ideas of peers can work to create an effective activity-based science program.

Short-Term Planning

As a new teacher, you may simply be handed the school science course of study and told to follow it for your grade level. If this is the case, the greatest planning task has already been done for you. Your next step is to ask yourself, "Knowing that these are the concepts I'm expected to teach my students, what is the best way I can go about doing that?"

While the elementary textbook may serve as a source of information to your students, as a teacher you should not limit yourself to the text as you plan your lessons. The textbook may provide useful background information about a science concept for your students, but it is often limited. It is usually necessary for you to consult trade books to gain further understanding of the concept. As you broaden your knowledge base, you should become more comfortable seeking out other sources for science activities, aside from those presented in the text. It will be your responsibility to determine not only if your students can understand the concept presented through the activity, but also if they have the psychomotor skills necessary to carry it out.[2]

If you decide to set up science learning centers within the classroom, activity in this area may not be related to the specific structured activities you presented to the entire class. You will need to brainstorm a list of all of the possible activities a child can engage in to satisfy his or her scientific curiosity. Once you have determined the appropriate activities to meet the course of study or activities that the children may decide to do at a learning center, the next step is to determine what materials are necessary to perform the activities.

Necessary Materials

The concepts have been determined, the textbooks have been perused, the activity supplements have been scoured. Now you need to ask yourself, "What materials will I need to enhance my science teaching or to create the most stimulating activities for my students?" After going through equipment lists from your chosen activities and considering additional materials for a learning center, your first step is to find out what your classroom or school already has at your disposal. The large equipment needs or the more costly items like microscopes or balances may already exist in some other teacher's classroom in your school. Find out if these items are intended solely for one teacher's use, or if they were meant to be shared. Don't be surprised if the amount of material available to you begins to grow once you begin asking questions!

Once a classroom or school inventory has been taken, the next step is to determine what materials are left to purchase. A good suggestion is to divide the remaining items into categories:

- items to be purchased through a scientific supplier,
- items that can be purchased locally through a discount or hardware store,

• items that can be made for little or no cost from recycled materials.

Using a sheet like the "Science Activity Planner" in Figure 10.1 for each activity presented will facilitate ordering. This sheet should be filled out at least six weeks before you teach the lesson. Time must be allotted for vendor shipping and/or the steps your order must go through for approval of purchase and appropriation of funds in your school district. Figure 10.2 provides an example of how this form can be used.

Items Purchased Through a Scientific Supplier. Items such as microscopes, slides, cover slips, thermometers, magnets, electrical bulbs, and so on are the typical kinds of materials supplied by many reputable science equipment vendors. Science teachers in your school may already have suppliers they regularly deal with. Talk with fellow teachers about companies they have used in the past. If you are uncertain, the best thing to do is to ask each of the companies for their supply catalogues. Imagine that you are spending your own money. Don't be quick to order from the first catalogue you look through. Be a wise shopper: Compare prices and quality. Ask questions of others who may have ordered materials from a particular vendor before. "How good is their service? Are they willing to meet my needs quickly or are they slow in processing orders? What type of return policy do they have? Are they willing to take a purchase order or do they need to be paid up front?" A complete listing of science vendors is available from the National Science Teachers Association. This comprehensive list is updated yearly.

FIGURE 10.1   Science Activity Planner

Concept to be taught: _____
_____
Material needs: _____
_____
Items available through school inventory: _____
_____
Items available at no cost/recycle: _____
_____
Scientific supplier: (Indicate vendor name, catalogue number, description, number needed, cost per unit, total cost.)

Local store: (Indicate store name and exact cost.)

FIGURE 10.2   Science Activity Planner Example

Concept to be taught: The circular path electrons follow is called a *circuit.*

Material needs: *For Each Student:* Battery, flashlight bulb, insulated copper wire, switch, bulb socket, cardboard tube (toilet paper tube), paper clip, two brass fasteners, plastic cap from a gallon milk container or a 35mm film can.

Items available through:

School inventory	Bulbs, switches, wire
No cost/recycle	Cardboard tubes, milk caps, film canister caps
Scientific supplier	Delta Supply, Nashua, New Hampshire
	57–020–9769, Bucket of Batteries, 30, $29.95, $29.95
	57–020–5644, Bulb Sockets, 30, $4.85/pkg. of 6, $24.25
Local store	John's Dime Store on Main Street
	1 box of paper clips, 79¢
	2 boxes of brass fasteners, $1.45

Does your current textbook publisher supply prepackaged kits that go along with their activities? If so, will it be necessary to replenish materials in those kits? Is there a specific supplier you should order those kits from? If your answer to these questions is "Yes," then determine which items need to be replaced and if it is possible to simply replace the used items or if it is necessary to order a new kit. You may often come across prepackaged general science kits, such as one that supplies all the materials you will need to do a unit on electricity. Under both circumstances you must determine your needs. Will you use all of the materials provided in the kit? Will it be less expensive to order the items individually?

It is helpful to carefully look through the supply catalogues. Often you will spot an item that could enhance a lesson, an item you didn't even think of in your original materials list. Perhaps you found the item in two different catalogues, each at a different price. As you gain experience in ordering, you will find that some of the companies have different prices on many equivalent items. If you are making a big order with one company, it is usually more economical to purchase the higher-priced item from them along with the rest of your order. The money you would save on the price of the item with a different vendor could be spent on shipping charges, if you are ordering only one item. A list of supply items available from commercial vendors is found in Table 10.1.

The task of ordering supplies with school money may appear overwhelming. But if you follow a few easy steps, the work is painless. First of all, plan ahead! Avoid waiting until the last minute to order supplies. Often district paperwork or supply availability may delay shipment. Live plant or animal specimens can be

TABLE 10.1 Commonly Used Supply Items Available from Commercial Vendors

Item	Description
Beakers	Available in glass or plastic. Plastic may not be heated over an open flame. Commonly used sizes are 250-, 500-, and 1000-milliliters.
Bulbs	Small flashlight bulbs available with various resistances, commonly used for basic electricity units.
Dry Cells	Order according to their voltage ratings. They come in multiples of 1.5 volts. The commonly used D batteries found in flashlights are 1.5 volts. Another commonly used size is the 9-volt transistor battery.
Flasks	Two types are available: the triangular-shaped Erlenmeyer flask and the rounded Florence flask. Erlenmeyer is less likely to get knocked over in an elementary class. They should be made of heat-resistant glass. Sizes most often used are equivalent to the English units of a cup, a pint, and a quart, that is, 250- 600-, and 1000-milliliters.
Funnels	Available in glass or plastic. At the elementary level, long-tube plastic funnels may be purchased in a variety of sizes.
Goggles	Protective eyewear is available in adult and child sizes. Goggles designed to seal comfortably on the face provide the best protection.
Magnets	Horseshoe, bar, or ring magnets are most commonly used in elementary science activities. Purchasing a remagnetizer to realign magnetic fields of frequently dropped magnets will eliminate the need to buy new magnets.
Magnifiers/Microscopes	Plastic hand lens magnify objects from 2x to 8x. Hand-held microscopes capable of 30x magnification are available. Light microscopes can be purchased with magnification up to 750x. Fiber-optic scopes designed for durability are also available. The type to purchase will depend on budget and need.
Stoppers	Buy to fit test tubes and flasks; solid, one-hole, and two-hole are available.
Test Tubes	Available in a variety of sizes, typically glass; some sizes in plastic available. Test tube racks help store filled tubes.
Thermometers	V-back metal with dual Fahrenheit/Celsius readings.
Wire	Available both covered and bare. Gauge depends on use.

ordered several months in advance with an indication of when you want them shipped. Once you have determined what items will be needed and from which suppliers, you probably will have to obtain a purchase order. It is best to check with your principal or school district treasurer about the proper procedure. Most often this involves filling out the purchase order completely. *Completely* means not only names of items, but catalogue numbers, quantities, prices, shipping charges, complete name, address, phone and/or fax number of vendor. Remember, one purchase order per vendor! Once it is completed, you will need to obtain the authorized signatures before you can mail it. If the purchase order form has duplicates, mail the original to the vendor. If it is a single copy, make a copy for the administration and one for yourself.

If you decide to phone in the order, be sure to provide the vendor with all the information included on the purchase order, especially the purchase order number. After the initial order is placed, it is customary to write on the purchase order the date and time the order was phoned in. You may be required to send the vendor a copy of that purchase order. If so, make sure to write on the purchase order "This is a copy of a phone order."

Items Purchased Locally.   Consumable items such as paper cups, bags, and straws are some of the common items purchased through local vendors. If you teach in a community that is very supportive of its local schools, with a little effort you may be able to get donations of consumable items. Local restaurants, grocery stores, or discount stores are often willing to donate such items. You might surprise yourself once you begin calling around to local stores. Even the local lumber yard may be willing to supply a class with yard/meter sticks or scrap lumber.

William E. Mills

Local restaurants, grocery stores, or discount stores are usually willing to donate items such as paper cups, containers, or straws to meet your science activity needs.

Discount stores that specialize in overruns are one of the best sources for science supplies. Often you can simply peruse the aisles, scanning shelves with this in mind: "What science concept can I teach with that item?" You may be surprised at what you come up with. Simple toys like yo-yos, ball and jacks, paddle balls, or rubber balls can be used to teach a variety of scientific concepts. Paper clips, masking tape, batteries, or wire can start you on the way to a terrific electricity unit. Inexpensive bubble gums or chocolate chip cookies can lead to exciting lessons that focus on the scientific method! Never underestimate the science in a discount store!

Local stores may already have agreements with your school district, such as charge accounts or cash credit accounts. Check with the school district treasurer. You may be able to charge the items at those stores. Other stores may take purchase orders. Occasionally you may have to provide your own money up front. If this is the case, find out what the procedure for reimbursement is in your school. Does the principal have a fund from which you can immediately be reimbursed upon turning in your receipt? Is a receipt necessary? Do you need a petty cash voucher from the school before you make a purchase? What kind of information does the vendor need to supply on that voucher? Do you need to supply the vendor with a tax-exempt number from the school so that you are not charged sales tax? All of these questions should be asked before you go out and spend your own money. You don't want to find out after the fact that since you didn't complete the proper paper trail, you will not be reimbursed!

Items Made from Recycled Materials.   Once again you were caught rummaging through the bin at the local recycling center. Embarrassed? There's no need to be when it's done in the name of science! What was it this time? Looking for cans to paint black for a unit on heat? Was it a plastic pop bottle to make another Cartesian diver? Did you need various size jars for a sound unit? Whatever the science topic, usually one or two items can be found in a recycling bin. Of course you can avoid those embarrassing moments by encouraging your students to bring in materials they would ordinarily throw away. Setting up a recycle area in your classroom will not only provide a quick source for those necessary items, but will also teach the students the importance of recycling.

In the opening scenario, Celeste needed a tuna can. Her home had an area where recyclables were stored; thus she did not have to hold off creating the volcano for lack of a tuna can. Cans are not the only useful recyclable item. Styrofoam plates from prepackaged meats are useful in many activities. They make great place mats for messy activities that involve liquids. Styrofoam egg cartons can be turned into charcoal crystal gardens in no time, or they can be used to stack small items like rock collections. Toilet paper or paper towel tubes can be used to make flashlights, while aluminum pie plates are useful for heating water. Plastic containers with lids, often seen storing frosting in the grocery store, can be used to store paints, playdough, or silly putty in the classroom. Your imagination is your only limit when it comes to deciding what to do with recycled materials.

Central or Classroom Storage Access

The biggest task is over, or so you think. The materials have been ordered and are beginning to arrive. So where do they go? Many variables should be considered. Does your school have an existing central storage area for science materials? Are the materials you ordered solely for your classroom use or will you be sharing them with other teachers? Who will be allowed access to the materials? Do you have the space to store materials in your classroom? Before you begin stocking your classroom shelves you should find the answers to these questions.

Central Storage Area.   Some schools have designated one room or area as the space where all science materials will be kept. If this is the case at your school, find out who is responsible for maintaining that area.[3] Careful inventory should be maintained of the items stored there. It is best if one person is responsible for keeping the inventory current. Teachers who borrow materials should be held responsible for their return. One person should have the authority to request the return of borrowed materials after a reasonable time period. Sign-out sheets like the one in Figure 10.3 should be completed by any staff member who uses materials from the central storage.

The teachers should determine who will have access to the central storage area. Will only science teachers be allowed to use it? Will an art teacher who needs an item used by science teachers have access to the storage area? Will students be

FIGURE 10.3   Science Equipment Checkout Form

Science Equipment Checkout Form

Name: _____

Grade and/or subject area: _____

Room number: _____

Date of checkout: Expected date of return:

_____   _____

Items borrowed:

_____

_____

_____

Signature: _____

allowed to borrow items from central storage? Who will be responsible for disseminating the materials? Will it be done on an honor system? While these questions may appear trivial, once you count on items for a particular activity only to find that someone has borrowed them without formally signing them out, you will not be too happy. Oftentimes it becomes a wild goose chase, hunting down this teacher or that one to find out who used the materials last. If the search comes up short, you may end up omitting a valuable lesson for lack of supplies. Some ground rules set down by the faculty in advance can avoid any unnecessary searches or hard feelings.

Classroom Storage.   While waiting for ordered materials to arrive in your classroom, you must plan where the materials will be stored. The first thing you should decide is who will have access to those materials. Will the students be allowed access to everything? Will safety reasons prohibit total access? Where can you store materials that you consider dangerous to the students?

A very real issue concerns the storage of live specimens. If plants are brought into the classroom, is an area available near windows to facilitate plant growth? Is shelf space available near a window, or will you have to place a table or bookshelf near a window for plant use? Can artificial lights be used on the plant? If window space is minimal, where will this designated artificial light be? Should the students have access to these plants? Do they present any potential harm to the students if ingested?

What about live animals? Are adequate cages or containers available for the animals' safety? What about your students' safety near the animals? Is a water source available for the animals? What are their food requirements? How and where will their food be stored? Care should be taken to insure that improper storage of animal food will not draw pests to your classroom. If a decision has been made to keep a live animal in the classroom, you should be aware of your responsibilities to the animal and most importantly your responsibility for the students' health and safety. Learn the school's policy on live animals in the classroom. Find out if any of your students have allergies to certain animals. Learn what kind of insurance coverage you need should a student become injured while handling the animal. Make sure that any animal kept around children is not a carrier of infectious diseases.

If you know that the students will need access to certain materials, try to arrange it so that these materials are on shelves or in cabinets they can reach easily. If there are certain materials, such as chemicals or cleaners, that need to be out of the students' reach, a locked cabinet or cupboard is a necessity. Plans should be made to make shelves or cabinets if these do not exist in your classroom. Rather than looking at your classroom negatively and simply deciding that there's no place to put anything, try to find some positive aspects of your classroom. Could an unused corner make an ideal storage area? Could you get a local office to donate some unused book shelves or storage cabinets? Will it be necessary to ask the school's maintenance personnel to make some shorter shelf units for student access? Try to have these problems solved before the materials arrive.

Certain items may never be stored away. For instance, if you have a learning center that constantly requires the use of a balance, then leave it out. Other activity areas may be set up where materials are always left out. The students should know that they are free to move items from one center to another. For example, going back to the opening scenario, if Celeste and Sarah were working on their volcano at school in the science activity center and realized that they needed red food coloring, which was always out at the food center, they could easily go over and get the food coloring without having to ask for permission to move it from one center to the next.

Freedom to move materials creates a learning environment that is adaptable to the students' needs. Of course this may create an inventory nightmare for the teacher. Some simple task assignments can alleviate this problem. Most children like to be useful and help the teacher. In the primary grades the teacher can create a poster for each center with a picture of the necessary items. Older students can have a written supply list for each center. Students can be assigned to the different centers on a rotating basis. The students are responsible for making sure that at the end of the school day the items for their assigned center are in place. When consumable items are needed, the students should write them on a master list for the teacher, indicating the item needed and at which learning center. The teacher can then use this list to obtain the needed materials. The teacher should give the needed items to the student responsible for that center to put in their proper place. Gentle reminders to the students about returning items to the place where they found them will facilitate the task of taking inventory.

Material Storage

No matter where materials are stored, you will need to decide how to store them. Will they be arranged according to units, such as electricity, weather, and simple machines, or will the items be stored separately? Once you make this decision, you must choose from among many ways to arrange the items, from shelves to shoe boxes to plastic storage bins.

Units versus Individual Storage.   Articles in science magazines often suggest handy ways to store materials for individual lessons. However, we question the value of storing in separate containers all the items necessary for each activity. In the short term, it does make a quick and convenient way of planning a lesson. If you know you have all the materials organized in shoe boxes for seven groups of students to make circuits and ultimately flashlights, then you can present that lesson at any time without expecting the students to rummage through the shelves for the necessary materials. In the long run, what usually happens is that you need the batteries for a different activity before you get to the prepackaged activity. The boxes will be robbed before your planned unit is presented. Then another time the wire is needed for something else, and soon your perfectly organized lesson is missing half its materials. If you happen to be at a school where materials are abundant, then organizing materials into prepackaged units will not be a problem. In fact it will be an asset. However, if you are at a school where resources are scarce, or if you have to store materials in a central area where other teachers have access to them, it is a waste of energy to prepackage activities. Materials stored individually will be easier to collect, no matter what the lesson.

Labeling Shelves.   Advantages: Whether you're stocking shelves in a central storage area or in your own classroom, a quick and easy way to arrange materials is to label certain areas of the shelves for each letter of the alphabet. Items can be placed on the shelf according to the letters of the alphabet they begin with. When you are filling an equipment request, it's a simple matter of looking for the items alphabetically.

Disadvantages: This method works well for storing chemicals, but for items like magnets or marbles, or any items that are small or in multiple quantities, too much space is wasted, and materials may be scattered all over. Oftentimes it's impossible to determine where one letter ends and the next begins. Soon, especially with multiple users, the items are misplaced. You will frequently need to rearrange the shelves.

Proper materials storage makes preparation and replacement easier.

Plastic Bags.   Advantages: Sealable plastic storage bags are ideal for small items. The outside can be labeled with permanent markers. The bags can be obtained in a variety of sizes to accommodate various sized materials.[4]

Disadvantages: They eventually begin to tear, especially with frequent use. If the seal is not made, items may fall out and get lost. After extended use, labeling done even with a permanent marker begins to wear off.

Shoe Boxes and Cardboard Boxes.   Advantages: A very inexpensive way to store multiple items like thermometers, marbles, or bar magnets is by using a cardboard box of some sort. Shoe boxes seem to be the ideal size for storing things on shelves. They can be easily labeled. For prolonged use they may be covered with an adhesive plastic.

Disadvantages: Even if they are covered, these too will eventually wear out. Also, because the boxes are opaque, it is often necessary to open them up to determine the contents unless they are properly labeled.

Plastic Storage Bins.   Advantages: Plastic storage bins come in a variety of shapes and sizes. Many are clear so that items stored inside are visible. They can be labeled with permanent markers. They last much longer than shoe boxes, and many are guaranteed to last at least for five years of normal use.

Disadvantages: The better-made containers can be costly. The lids will crack on the less expensive ones if heavy things are stacked on top.

Color Coding.   Usually your budget will determine which storage method you choose. Whether it's simply labeling the shelves or buying expensive plastic storage containers, one thing that will facilitate access to the materials is color coding items.

Dangerous chemicals or equipment that can cause a safety problem should always be labeled in a noticeable color. If you do not have hot orange safety stickers or a bright orange marker, some other hot color will work. Whatever the color, you need to make sure that you only use that color label for dangerous items. Dangerous items should also be locked up. The cabinet where they are kept can be marked with the same color label.

Items that are quickly consumed carry a different color label. For instance, paper cups, straws, paper towels, and the like are items taken from shelves and rare-ly returned. If the staff knows that a particular color identifies those materials, a simple glance looking for that particular color will tell the observer whether these items need to be replaced or not. Labeling the cabinet where the consumable items are stored with that color will make it easier for someone looking for paper towels, for example, to know where to go to find them. If you're getting items from a central storage area, keeping inventory will be easier if all the consumables are kept in one cabinet.

Whatever you decide to color code, remember it will only be efficient if everyone who has access to the materials understands the code. Posting a color code key will make it easier to locate the materials.

Dispensing Materials

Whether items are kept in a central storage area (see Figure 10.4) or in the classroom, you still need to think about how the students will collect them for a particular activity. When items are stored in a central location, a teacher may want to collect the materials at least a day ahead of time to make sure the items necessary for a given activity are still available. Decide how many of what item you will need. Once the items are in the classroom, you can appoint students to arrange the materials for the various working groups.

FIGURE 10.4 Central Storage Area Design

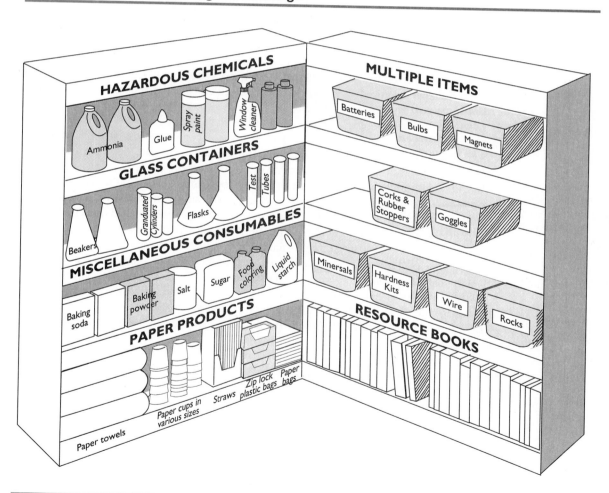

In an efficient, activity-based science classroom, the teacher does not have to do all the advance work for a particular science activity. The teacher can appoint responsible students to collect the science materials. A simple way to disseminate the materials is to have a materials list posted for the given activity, assign particular students to gather materials, and provide those students with buckets or plastic bins to put the collected materials in for that activity. Each materials manager for the day should be responsible for collecting the correct number of items for his or her group to do the activity. That materials manager will also be responsible for counting the materials at the end of the lesson, collecting them in the bucket, and returning them to their proper place at the end of the activity.

The teacher could appoint one or two students to count the items in the buckets, making sure everything is returned after use. The teacher can put the used materials back in their proper storage areas in the classroom or assign students to help with that task. If the materials go back to a central storage area, the teacher should make sure they are returned to their proper place as soon as possible. Remember, other teachers may be counting on the use of those materials also!

Issues raised in Chapter 11 on safety need to be kept in mind when returning used materials. Were hazardous materials used during the activity? Any material labeled toxic, ignitable, corrosive, or reactive should be considered hazardous.[5] Many common household items used at the elementary level in science activities could fall into these categories. Items such as bleach or ammonia, carpet shampoos, window cleaner, paints, and glues commonly fall under the heading *hazardous*. Does your school have an appropriate system to handle disposal of these wastes? Which materials could be recycled? What procedures should be followed to dispose of used materials? Remember, hazardous waste improperly handled can pollute drinking supplies, poison humans, or contaminate soil and air. The teacher should be responsible for disposing of used hazardous materials. If you are uncertain about disposing of a particular item, check with the local fire marshal or local office of the Environmental Protection Agency. These agencies will be able to instruct you on proper disposal. Many local fire departments are equipped to handle low-level toxic waste. A local high school should already have a plan in place for handling waste from the chemistry classes. Check to see if your district has one. If not, work with local agencies to develop a safe and reliable disposal system.

Room Arrangement

Carefully planned lessons and ample supplies are not enough to carry off a successful inquiry-based science activity. The physical arrangement of the classroom is an important consideration. Barriers such as classroom size, traffic patterns, blind spots, poles, and walls will require a teacher to be creative about utilizing the space available.

Before you begin moving furniture around, it may help you to draw to scale a floor plan of your classroom (see Figure 10.5). Ask yourself the following questions when deciding how to arrange the classroom:

- What is the best way to utilize the space I have available?
- What kinds of activities will my students be involved in?
- What kinds of materials will be used?
- What type of furniture do I have in my classroom?
- Will I need any additional furniture, or should I eliminate some of the furniture that is already there?
- What kind of flooring does the classroom have? Is it appropriate for the activities my students will be engaged in?
- Where are the entrances and exits in this classroom?
- Where are the electrical outlets?
- What kind of traffic patterns do I wish to develop?
- What are the potential hazards with the arrangement I have in mind?

The suggestions that follow are designed to help you arrange your classroom to maximize your students' science experiences while allowing you to maintain flexibility to accommodate the teaching of other subject areas.

FIGURE 10.5   Classroom Floor Plan

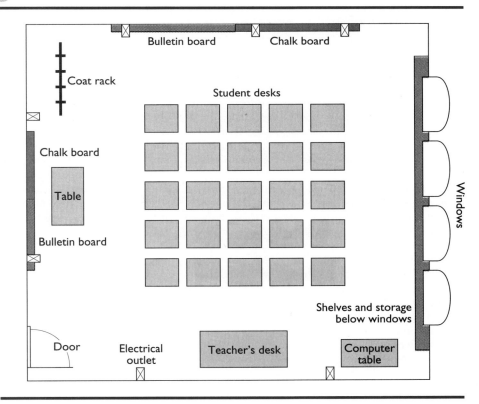

Large-Group Science Activities.   Flat surfaces offer the best means of engaging in science activities when working with an entire class. If you are in a classroom with tilted desk tops, then you will need to be more creative. Child-sized tables are one alternative. Another is to designate space on the floor for children to participate in science activities. Divide the class into small working groups. Cooperative groups of three or four function well in a small area. Current recommendations are that elementary school classrooms should provide at least 30 square feet of space for each student, and have no more than twenty-four students for labs and activities (see Chapter 11). Although elementary science classes are not laboratory based, to provide all students with sufficient feedback and guidance in science projects twenty-four students is a manageable number. While the physical constraints of your classroom may not allow you this much area, or your class size puts you beyond the twenty-four student limit, whenever possible optimum space should be allocated and ideal class size should be maintained.

Whether the students are working at small tables, several flat-topped desks pushed together to make a larger working area, or on the floor, consider the type of flooring found within the classroom. While a nonslip tile floor works best, it is not

WHAT RESEARCH SAYS

About Class Size and Science Achievement

First, small classes are supported in primary grades. Kindergarten, first, second, and third grade classes should be as small as economically feasible. If cost were not an issue, the limiting factor to reducing class size . . . seems to be the social value of cooperation among very young children.

Second, . . . it seems evident that these changes should be accompanied by research-based changes in teaching methods that take advantage of these changes. One prominent study concludes that reducing class size and proportionally increasing educational expenses by as much as 50 percent might be necessary to increase the students' achievement by a mere 10 percentile points. It may be that reducing class size in itself is not an efficient use of public funds.

Third, the research on teaching and learning (rather than the research on achievement) supports the idea that very large class sizes cannot provide students with reasonable instructional and motivational systems. Safety problems also increase with class size.

Small groups make it easier for teachers to monitor problem solving, attempt to improve understanding, and create an atmosphere of scientific inquiry. . . .

Fourth, teachers must couple their arguments for smaller classes with requests for other improvements that would help their students achieve. . . . Most science classrooms. . . lack adequate supplies and equipment. . . . Such tools, along with reasonable inservice, might make science truly exciting and academically productive.

. . . Teachers need small classes [to] conduct hands-on laboratory activities and intense follow-up discussions. In large classes, it is unlikely they can prepare and inspire students for tomorrow's world of science.

Source: Excerpted from William G. Holliday, "Should We Reduce Class Size?" *The Science Teacher* (January 1992) pp.14–17.

a necessity. Carefully taping down an inexpensive vinyl floor remnant in the designated science area will save a carpet from messy spills and facilitate cleanup.

Create an area where you can collect materials for science activities before the class uses them. This place should also function as an area where science demonstrations occur. Preferably, this area should be close to the science storage area if supplies are stored within the classroom. Storage space for student projects should also be planned near this area. If possible, choose an area near the sink if there is one.

The physical arrangement of the desks and/or tables should be dictated by the type of activity going on in the classroom on any particular day. If space and furniture availability permit, a permanent science area can be maintained within the classroom. However, if space is a problem, desks and/or tables that can be moved into configurations like those shown in Figure 10.6 will facilitate learning in an activity-based science classroom. Whenever possible, this area should be near

FIGURE 10.6   Arranging an Activity-Based Classroom

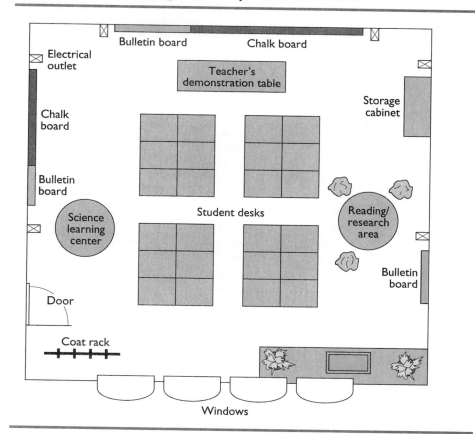

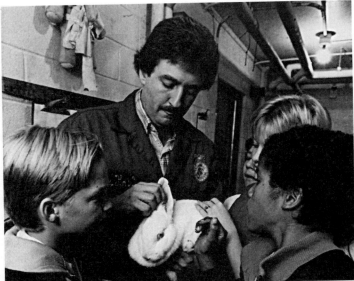

Animals brought into the classroom should be used to enhance the students' understanding of and respect for the animal.

William E. Mills

windows to allow the use of natural light. Space should be arranged to eliminate traffic congestion and to provide a clear path to all classroom exits.

Science Learning Centers.   A teacher committed to learning cycle/constructivist approaches, when working with the entire class for science lessons, will find that science learning centers satisfactorily accommodate additional expansion activities for each lesson. The teacher can design the learning center so that it focuses on a particular concept brought out in a class lesson and provides additional experiences for the students, who will then come to a greater understanding of the concept. The center should not simply be a place where the brighter students or those who finished their assignments first get to go. All students should be encouraged to use the learning center at their convenience, to engage in activities that provide additional experiences with a particular science concept.[6] Once all the students have had sufficient time to utilize that expansion activity, change the activity at the center to address whatever new concept you are teaching.

Another approach to science learning centers is to design them so that students gain greater experience with the *processes of science*. When you present science lessons to a large group of students, the chance that each student will have adequate time to make observations, predictions, measurements, and so on are slim, if a more-skilled peer blurts out the answer first. The learning center can be designed so each child has a chance to work in the area, gain experience in solving problems, measuring, predicting, using scientific instruments, and so on. The teacher can change the learning center weekly, with different process skills as the focus (see Figure 10.7).

FIGURE 10.7   Process-Oriented Science Learning Center Lesson

1. Obtain light bulb record books

Process Skill: Recording data

Each student will receive a light bulb record book. The outer covers are made from yellow cardboard. Several sheets of white paper for students to record their data are stapled between the covers.

4. Record book, battery, bulb, wire

Process Skill: Manipulating materials

Card numbered 4 near a battery, bulb, and wire, asks the students to do the following:

> *Label the next blank page of your record book MANIPULATING MATERIALS. Take the battery, bulb, and wire from the table. Using only those three pieces of material, get the bulb to light. Record in the record book drawings of ways you manipulated the materials—whether the bulb lit or not.*

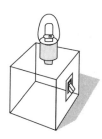

2.   Page 1 of record book

Process Skill: Observing

On the table is a box with a bulb sticking out of the top. A switch protrudes from one side. A card near the box states:

> *Make as many observations as possible. Write the word OBSERVA-TIONS on the top of page 1 in the light bulb record book. Record your observation on that page.*

5. Record book, battery, bulb, wire, bulb holder, switch

Process Skill: Manipulating materials

At the next station the above materials will by laying near card number 5. The students will be asked to do the following:

Label the next blank page of your record book MANIPULAT-ING MATERIALS. Take the battery, bulb, wire, bulb holder, and switch from the table. Get the bulb to light as you did at station 4, this time wire it so that the switch will turn the bulb on and off. Record in the record book drawings of ways you manipulated the materials, whether the bulb lit or not.

3. Record book

Process Skill: Predicting

A card that is numbered with a 3 and has a drawing of the box with the bulb will be at the center with the following directions:

> *Label the next blank page in your record book PREDICTIONS. Predict what is inside the box causing the bulb to light. List and/or draw your prediction(s) on that page.*

6. Record book, box, battery, bulb, bulb holder, wire, switch

Process Skill: Interpreting data, inferring, formulating models

The above materials will be found at station 6. The students will be asked to do the following:

Label the next blank page of your record book INTERPRETING DATA, INFERRING, FORMULATING MODELS. Using the materials given and your results from activities 4 and 5, try to create a box like the one you observed at station 2 and 3. When finished go back to your prediction page in the record book. Was your prediction correct?

A science learning center can also be designed as a discovery area—a place where children create inventions from a variety of provided materials. They can be challenge areas, where the teacher creates a problem for the week, and using the materials provided, the students work to solve the problem. Science learning centers can also be areas where students can play science games prepared by the teacher or commercially prepared.

Whatever you decide the focus of your science learning center should be, a few simple rules must be upheld to insure its success. The guidelines for a science learning center are found in Table 10.2.

Figures 10.8 and 10.9 show examples of science learning centers. Centers should be found in an area of the classroom where they are least likely to interfere with normal classroom operations. A review of the information provided in the chapter on classroom safety will facilitate the placement of the science learning center.

A pegboard or felt board can be designed so that it will stand on its own atop a table or desk, and when necessary can easily be stored. Pockets made from cloth or heavy cardboard serve as areas to hold activity cards, instructions, or small materials needed for the activity. Any material sturdy enough to withstand student wear, without being so heavy that it topples over, will serve as the backdrop for your science learning center.[7] Pictures or diagrams that enhance the lesson should be displayed on this board. If the activity requires a more formal means of record keeping, then appropriate record sheets or assessment sheets can be kept in a pocket on the board. Figure 10.10 provides an example of a typical science learning center backdrop.

Bulletin Boards and Displays. The physical arrangement of an activity-based science classroom should include a science bulletin board and a science display area. Lettering used for the bulletin board should be no smaller than four inches high. Don't use too many words. Plan the topic to be addressed, and focus on one concept.

TABLE 10.2   Science Learning Center Guidelines

1. The purpose and objectives for the activity are made clear; the students understand what they are supposed to do at each center. The activity is designed so that it enhances the students' understanding of a concept, rather than serving to frustrate and confuse.
2. *All* students have an opportunity to work at the center before the activity is changed.
3. Activities at the center do not interfere with other lessons going on in the classroom. Activities that require darkness, loud noises, or excessive amounts of physical activity are not appropriate for a learning center. The center is in an area where the teacher can readily observe the children in action.
4. At least one two-feet-by-four-feet table or work area of equivalent size is dedicated to this center. If the activity requires additional space, adequate floor space will be allocated. If audiovisual materials are to be used, electrical outlets are close by.
5. Consumable materials at the centers are replenished frequently.
6. When water is required for an activity, the center is located close to a water source. If this is not possible, care is taken so that children running to sinks or water fountains are not interfering with students engaged in other classroom tasks.

FIGURE 10.8 Science Learning Center

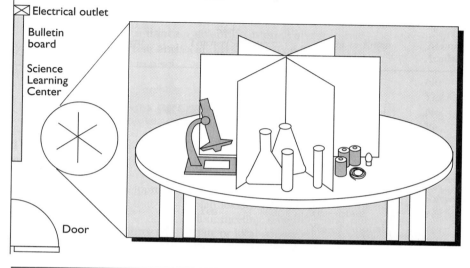

- Outlets should be available when needed
- Bulletin board contains pertinent science information
- Center is located near door to gain access to water from fountain in hall since no water is available in this classroom

⊠ Electrical outlet

Bulletin board

Science Learning Center

Door

Try to find visuals that will enhance students' understanding of the concept, but avoid using too much material. Frequently changing colors, sizes, and shapes create a bulletin board that is too busy and distracts from the intended message.[8]

Science displays should be designed to enhance the students' natural curiosity. They can be theme oriented and designed by the teacher or a collection of unrelated items provided by the students. A theme, for example, could be mammals. The display table could contain pelts of various mammals for the students to touch and to compare. It could contain antlers or horns for the students to determine the animal it came from and its age. There may be footprints of various mammals with a challenge to the students to determine which animal left the print. Books or picture of various mammals would be left at the table.

In a hodge-podge approach, the display area may be simply a catch-all for the various science-related items children come across that they would like to share with their peers. Items on the display table should be ones the children are allowed to touch. These can be household items, like an old radio or clock that the children are allowed to take apart to examine the inner works. Unusual rocks or plant parts may serve to pique a student's curiosity. If a student brings in an item that requires

FIGURE 10.9   Science Learning Center

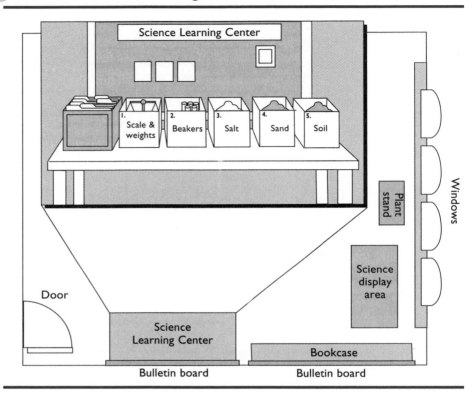

special care, like a geode or a parent's rock collection, then this may be better suited for teacher-supervised display.

Animals brought into the classroom should be used to enhance the students' understanding and respect for the animal. Of course common sense should prevail. Children cannot be permitted to bring in stray squirrels, raccoons, and similar animals. However, an occasional lady bug or cricket can teach valuable lessons. When live animals are brought into the classroom, follow the twenty-four hour rule recommended by the American Humane Society.[9] The students should be allowed to study the animal during the course of the day. Encourage the children to use resource books to determine the animal's food, shelter, and space needs and to make as many observations about the animal's behavior as possible. After a day in the classroom, return the animal to the place where it was found or a similar habitat.

Large-group instruction or small science learning centers? No matter the mode of instruction, science learning will be facilitated when you give careful thought to

FIGURE 10.10 Science Learning Center Backdrop

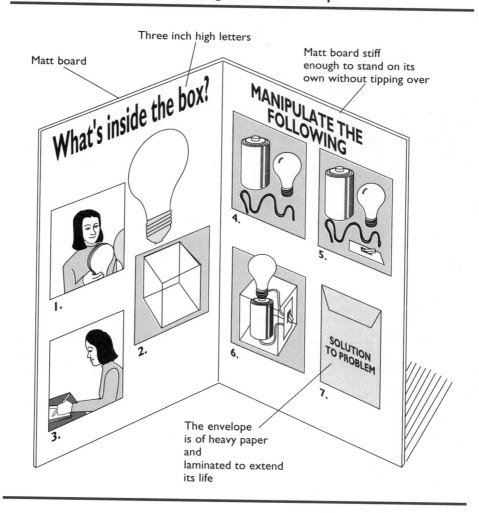

the physical arrangement of the classroom. Allowing the students to freely travel to learning centers implies that certain behavior is expected of the students. Just what these expectations are and who decides them will be discussed next.

MANAGING THE SCIENCE CLASSROOM

A teacher committed to having students *do* science rather than talk or read about it understands that children learn best when they are actively engaged in the processes of science, constructing science knowledge out of their own experiences.

TEACHERS ON SCIENCE TEACHING

What Does an Effective Science Classroom Look Like?

By Johanna Ramsey
Grade 6 Science Teacher, Marion Elementary School, Palmyra, New York

Teaching sixth-grade science by using the hands-on method has many challenges. I found this to be true when I began teaching science seven years ago. One of the challenges is to arrange the classroom to promote student activity and student learning. The classroom should be laid out in such a way that the students can move freely around the room. At times the students need to work in the lab, get equipment, get into small discussion groups, and/or meet for large-class discussion and directions. Since there is movement in class, there should be a good flow pattern to the room.

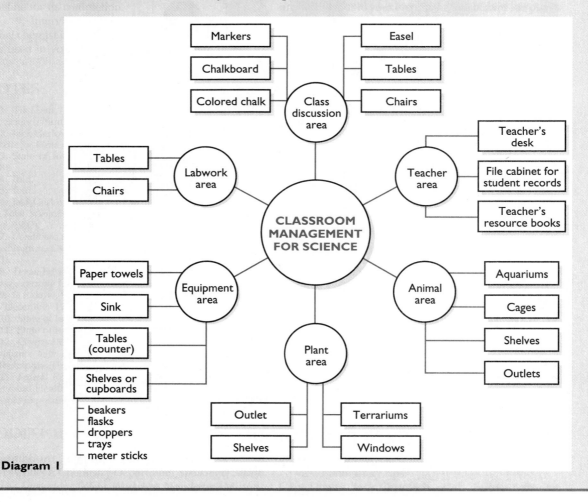

Diagram 1

The plant and animal areas are in the room for the students to enjoy throughout the year. Much on-the-spot learning takes place about plant and animal life this way; sometimes more so than a prepared lesson. They learn things such as the parts of a plant, the changes a flowering plant goes through, animal behavior, animal reproduction, and plant and animal care.

Besides having a set display of plants and animals, the students have the opportunity to bring in other small animals and insects (you need to make sure that they are not harmful before allowing them in the classroom). Students are very curious about their surroundings, so why not tap into their interests? This makes learning fun, and the students don't realize they're learning when they're having fun!

When I began teaching science I brainstormed on areas I wanted in my classroom. See Diagram 1 for the ideas I planned out. Diagram 2 helps visualize what my classroom looks like today. The students come into my room and meet in the class discussion area for directions and/or questions. From here they are dismissed to go to their lab work areas. They move to the equipment area as they need pieces of equipment for their experiment. All materials are clearly labeled so the students know exactly what they need, and each work area is clearly posted so there is no confusion as to where in the room the students belong. During lab work time the students conduct their experiments and discuss their procedures and results in small lab groups of four. Once experiments are complete, the class gets back together in the class discussion area to discuss the results they found in their small groups. Much learning takes place through this cooperative sharing of ideas and results.

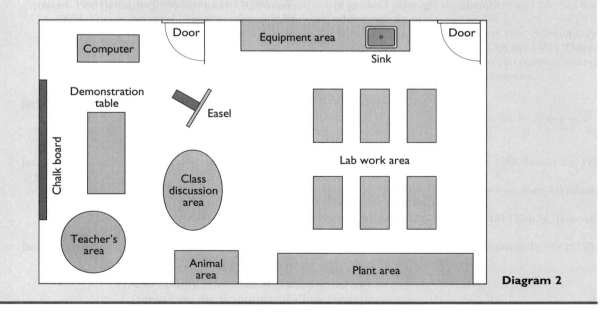

Diagram 2

A constructivist approach allows children to engage in their own experiments to build explanations and theories about the world and the way it works. The teacher helps learners build theories by providing materials and experiences to help them become active participants.

If all teachers were responsible for only one student at a time, this constructivist approach to science education would be greatly simplified. Problems arise when two or more children are actively trying to construct their knowledge of a particular science concept without concern for the needs and wants of the other students. Cooperative strategies should be employed so that all students can engage in science processes at the same time. Arranging the students into small heterogeneous groups to work on science activities will help to create a cooperative environment. Assigning each child in a group a specific task and holding him or her accountable will also eliminate any confusion or disruptive behavior. In any well-designed teacher-facilitated science activity, there will be a need for a principal investigator, a recorder, a maintenance director, a materials manager, and a reporter. These roles are defined in Chapter 7. If you find that some cooperative groups finish before others, you can add the role of student facilitator, in which teams who complete activities first help teams having difficulty. While serving in this capacity, the student facilitators must be sure they simply facilitate and do not take over a flailing group.

Successful, problem-free science lessons can occur if each member of the group understands the importance of his or her role. In a cooperative learning environment, the groups are purposely comprised of boys and girls of different ability levels. Each student realizes that on any given day, he or she could serve in any capacity as a member of the cooperative group. Therefore, each member is responsible for learning the material. The grade earned by participating in the lesson is a reflection of the group effort, not an individual. The group is interdependent; they will sink or swim together. The students within a group need to communicate to one another problems, observations, and successes before they go to the teacher with them. Courtesy, respect, and encouragement are interpersonal skills needed by each member of the cooperative group.

One useful cooperative method is known as a *jigsaw approach*.[10] Use it, for example, when you are teaching third-grade students about the state tree, flower, and bird. Within each cooperative group, a different member will be assigned one of the following tasks:

- to determine the criteria for becoming the official state tree,
- to determine the criteria for becoming the official state flower,
- to determine the criteria for becoming the official state bird,
- to find out who suggested the state tree, bird, or flower, and where these are found in the state,
- to learn what the state tree, bird, and flower are in one bordering state.

The students in the cooperative groups should decide which student will take on each of the five tasks. Once these students are determined, then all of the students in the class assigned to task one should get together to find answers to that task, those assigned to task two should do the same, and so on. After a sufficient amount of time has passed (for this topic with third graders, two or three 35 to 40 minute class periods should be enough time) the students should have found answers for their task. They must now return to their original cooperative groups to share their information. The success of the cooperative group will depend on how well the expert gets his or her information across to the members of the group. After two class periods of sharing information from the five tasks, it is time for the quiz. This can be done by student experts for task one, moving to different cooperative groups. Those experts will then quiz each member of a different cooperative group individually on task-one information. After task-one experts quiz the students and record their results, then task-two experts will do the same, and so on. The success of each student will be reflected by how well his or her cooperative group expert prepared the group for the quiz.

CHAPTER SUMMARY

Organizing and managing a science classroom requires decisions about inanimate objects—the curriculum and science materials—and animate objects—the students in the class. Long-term curriculum planning may be nationally or state dictated. Short-term planning allows the teacher to decide how the concepts will be taught. This short-term planning determines which science materials will be necessary and how they will be acquired. Once they are obtained, storage of these materials will depend on school building space restrictions.

The physical arrangement of the classroom directly affects the success of an activity-oriented science lesson. When physical barriers impede the completion of an activity, the students become frustrated and disillusioned. If materials are not readily available to bring a child from a state of disequilibrium to equilibrium, then those teachable moments may be lost. A flexible learning environment, carefully planned, and designed to promote student exploration will greatly facilitate science learning.

Decisions on the inanimate objects within a classroom generally reflect the decisions made about the animate objects, the students. Is whole-group instruction necessary, or can students work in smaller groups? While classroom size limitations may affect the choice made here, often it is the short-term planning, deciding how to teach a particular concept, that will determine what is done with the students. A constructivist approach to science teaching is enhanced by dividing the students into cooperative learning groups. Discipline problems are minimized when students work together to solve problems or to engage in scientific explorations. When students learn to rely on one another, when they realize that the success of an individual is directly dependent upon the success of the group, order is created out of chaos. Cooperative learning encourages students to become active learners, to engage in explorations to construct theories, and to become better at articulating the science concepts they have learned.

DISCUSSION QUESTIONS AND PROJECTS

1. Interview an elementary science teacher responsible for ordering science equipment. Find answers to the following questions:

- What vendors does he or she use to purchase science equipment and why?

- How good is the service provided by that vendor?
- How quick is the vendor to process orders?
- What type of return policy does the vendor have?

- Does the vendor take purchase orders, or is payment required up front?
- What procedures does the school follow when placing and paying for orders?
- If you had to set up an ordering system, would you recommend the one used by the teacher you interviewed? If not, how would you design it differently?

2. Choose a science lesson from the activities section of this book. What materials do you think you could purchase locally to do this activity? Make recommendations about the most economical route to follow when preparing materials for this lesson. What will be your total cost to prepare materials for this lesson?

3. Visit an elementary school that has a central storage area for science materials. Does this area appear to be well maintained? Is someone responsible for checking materials in and out? Who keeps inventory of supplies? How well managed do you think their storage area is? What recommendations would you make for this storage area?

4. Using the floor plan and furniture below, redesign this classroom so that an efficient activity-based science class could take place in here. Bring in any additional furniture you think you may need.

5. Design a science learning center for sixth-grade students with outer space as the theme, or select your own theme. What kinds of items, activities, and experiments would you place there? Draw a diagram of what this will look like. How would you change this design if it were for a second-grade class? Explain and provide another diagram.

6. During a unit on insect behavior, several children bring into school both live and dead insects. What should be done with the dead insects? What will you do with the live ones? Should the students be encouraged to bring insects into the classroom? Why or why not? What do you believe your responsibility is to the insects and for the students' attitudes toward insects?

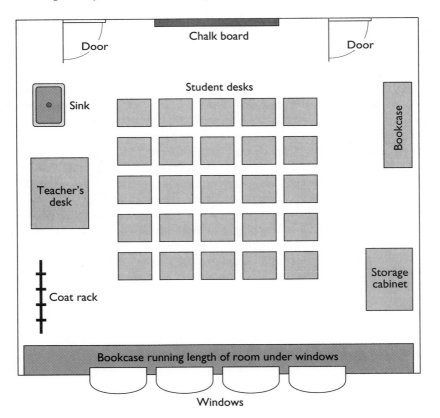

NOTES

1. John E. Penick and Robert E. Yager, "Trends in Science Education: Some Observations of Exemplary Programmes in the United States," *European Journal of Science Education*, vol. 8, no. 1 (1986), p. 3.

2. Bruce Watson and Richard Konicek, "Teaching for Conceptual Change: Confronting Children's Experience," *Phi Delta Kappan* (May 1990), pp. 680–685.

3. Penick and Yager, p. 2.

4. Nancy R. Romance and Michael R. Vitale, "Sealable Science for Busy Teachers," *Science and Children* (February 1991), pp. 24–26.

5. Linda L. Cronin-Jones, "Is Your School a Dumping Ground?" *The Science Teacher* (October 1992), pp. 27, 28.

6. Pat Piech, "Science Learning Centers: Seatwork Alternatives," *The Reading Teacher*, vol. 44, no. 6 (February 1991), pp. 446–447.

7. Ibid.

8. Cindy Mason, "Bulletin Board Idea," *Science Scope* (October 1991), p. 40.

9. David C. Kramer, Animals in the Classroom (Menlo Park, CA.: Addison-Wesley, 1989).

10. Scott B. Watson, "Cooperative Methods," *Science and Children* (February 1992), pp. 30–31.

ADDITIONAL READINGS

If you are interested in learning more about the topics raised in this chapter consider reading the following:

David C. Kramer, *Animals in the Classroom* (Menlo Park, CA: Addison-Wesley, 1989). This book serves as a reminder of teacher responsibilities when animals are brought into the classroom. Whether it's an invertebrate or a vertebrate, this book tells how to care for those visitors. Resource books for children and adults are listed, as well as addresses for state wildlife agencies.

Victor M. Showalter, *Conditions for Good Science Teaching* (Washington, DC: National Science Teachers Association, 1984). This easily read booklet provides the reader with information on classroom organization recommended by the National Science Teachers Association (NSTA). In addition to resources, current NSTA recommendations for science instruction and professional growth are provided.

Christine Chaille and Lory Britain, *The Young Child as Scientist: A Constructivist Approach to Early Childhood Science Education* (New York: HarperCollins, 1991). This short book details the constructivist learning theory and provides models for classrooms where this approach is utilized. An entire section is devoted to constructivist science, with examples of science activities in physics, chemistry, biology, and ecology.

Shlomo Sharan (ed.), *Cooperative Learning; Theory and Research* (New York: Praeger, 1990). Many essays and articles have been written on the theory behind cooperative learning and examples of its implementation. This book collects much of that work into one volume.

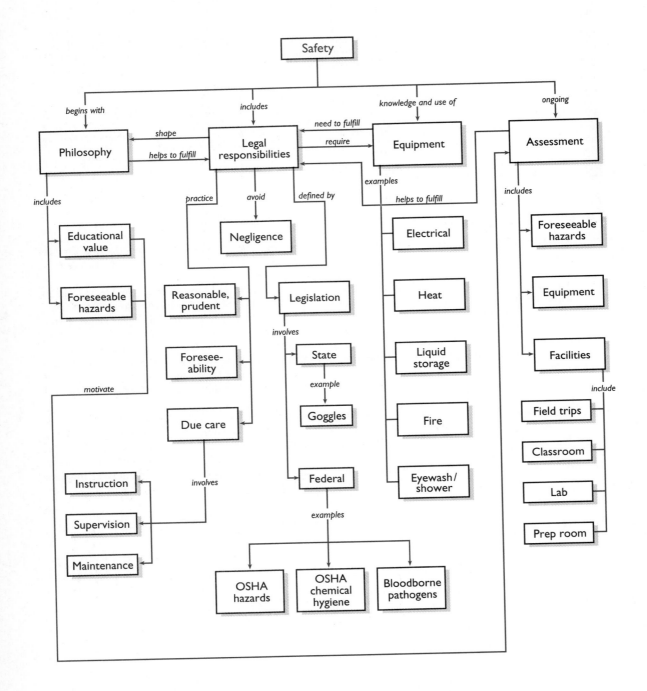

How Can You
Teach Science Safely?

T he scenarios that follow are based on factual situations, although some components have been disguised. The purpose of this section is to provide a platform for the presentation of safety concerns and help prevent similar events from occurring with other teachers.

Scenario 1. Miss M.'s science classroom was a beehive of activity when the students entered the room. Students were discussing the water-reactive metals project as if it were a Disney World event. The noise level was now disturbing, especially near the brightly colored translucent containers on Miss M.'s demonstration table; these containers held the golf-ball-size pieces of sodium and potassium.

Finally, Miss M. calmed the class and asked them to take their seats for a final briefing before proceeding outside. The excitement was infectious. "Please remember to walk quietly through the halls to the central courtyard. We do not want to disturb the other classes. Take your science notebooks with you. Recorders need not approach the plastic swimming pool until we are ready add our chemicals to the water. Please recall that although I have performed this activity before, it has always been on a very small scale using chips of these chemicals watch glasses with a tablespoon of water. I do not know for sure how this reaction will take place. That is part of science, I guess."

"Do we need our safety goggles or fire equipment?" a Billy B., the class safety officer.

"Of course not," quipped Miss M. "We're not testing the

Each of the thirty students picked up his or her chemical tic bomb." out of the room. As they entered the school's central courtyarer and filed composure and simply rushed to the wading pool.   lost their

Sally looked about the courtyard and noticed the faces of many peering at them through their class windows. Sally thought, "I bet the friends were out here doing this science activity."   they

"Okay," reminded Miss M., "get your heads over the pool so you reaction of these materials with the water. On the count of three, everyone chemicals into the water."

The explosion that occurred when all the chemicals hit the water s neously was blinding and caused serious burns on the heads and faces of sev the students standing near the pool.

How could this scenario have been avoided? Did Miss M. commit any er of judgment?

Scenario 2.   The Roosevelt sixth-grade class finally arrived at its destination, the old Wilson farm. As the bus rolled to a stop, Mr. J. arose and addressed the class. "Please remember our purpose here today. We are visitors to these animals' homes, so do not disturb them or the plants. In science we observe, measure, and record, we don't destroy or disrupt. Let's review our lesson plans for today's environmental science."

Following a five-minute clarification of the outcomes and precautions for the activity, Mr. J. answered student questions. "Now for our safety guidelines," stated Mr. J. "Are there any questions concerning the safety items on your activity page, such as equipment operation, accident procedures, and the buddy system? Remember to stay with your buddy and never allow yourself to be separated from myself, Mr. P., Mrs. M., or Ms. O. by more than fifty feet in this pasture area. If you need help in an emergency, please use your whistles. We adults were here earlier this morning checking out the area and can assure you that there are no hazards to worry about during this mapping exercise. Please be careful, just in case."

Mark and Alicia filed off the bus, confident of their purpose. "Let's see," said Alicia, "we need to proceed fifty meters to the northeast to pick up our first marker, then sixty meters to the east for our second one. Do you have the map, compass, and whistle ready, Mark?"

"Yes, I do," replied Mark. "Put on your helmet."

As the students proceeded about twenty meters into the trees, they noticed that the terrain became more rugged and difficult to negotiate. "See these little lines, Alicia?" asked Mark. "They're the little hills we're walking over now. Another thirty meters and we should spot the first marker."

Just as they came over the next hillock, they both spotted a large green disk, partially hidden in the leaves. "What's that?" asked Mark.

"I don't know. Let's check it out," replied Alicia. As they cautiously lifted the disk, it broke into several pieces. Revealed before them was a deep hole about a meter in diameter. It did not appear to have a bottom. However, there was water down about two meters.

"Let's explore it," suggested Alicia.

"No way! Let's get help!" Mark answered.

"Don't be silly," she said. "We can check it out, finish our assignment, and return before anyone knows. It could be our secret."

"What if that water is over your head?" asked Mark. "How long could you stay afloat? I say we get help before some animal or another person falls into it."

"I guess you're right," agreed Alicia. "Use that whistle!"

What was the difference between the safety emphasis in this scenario and that in the first scenario? Could you credit the judgment simply to the older age of the students?

Scenario 3.   Twanna returned from the supply table of the second-grade classroom with her hands full of materials. "Did you get the paper, iron filings, hand lens, and magnets?" asked José.

"Yes, I did," responded Twanna. "Let's get going."

"First, we need to be sure we have plenty of room," stated José, the manager and recorder for the science activity. "Are you sure you have all the materials now, Twanna?" Twanna was the materials manager for the activity.

"I forgot the shoe box," stated Twanna. "I'll be right back." In a few minutes she returned from the supply table with a shoe box with one end cut out of it.

"Now," said José, "the directions say to lay the shoe box flat on the table and put the white paper over it. While I'm doing that, Twanna, you need to pour some iron filings onto the second sheet of paper and look at them with your hand lens." José went about his work while Twanna poured the filings from the glass jar onto the paper.

"Wow!!" squealed Twanna, "Look at these things, they look like baby fish hooks and spears. Why are they so jagged?"

"Maybe they were made using a file on an old piece of pipe," said José. "My father makes them all the time when he puts new pipes in people's houses."

"Okay," said Twanna. "Are you ready for the filings now?"

"Sì," replied José. "Put them on the paper covering the shoe box now." Twanna poured half of her filings onto the paper and leaned forward to watch José. José picked up the large bar magnet and reached under the paper with it. "Watch to see what happens to the iron filings as I move the magnet around under the paper."

Both students were leaning very close to the shoe box now. Just as José touched the lower right edge of the paper with the magnet, Twanna sneezed. The iron filings sprayed into José's face, and a few of them flew into his right eye. "OOWWW!" shrieked José as he twirled from his chair, eyes buried in his hands. "Help me, please!!!"

How could this accident have been prevented? Did you notice any oversights?

INTRODUCTION

With this chapter we intend to help you avoid the situations in the first and third scenarios and to help you teach your students how to act safely, as the children in the second scenario did. To accomplish this mission, we

1. encourage you to develop a philosophy of safe science teaching,
2. help you understand your legal responsibilities,
3. help you understand when and how to use safety equipment,
4. encourage you to perform safety assessments of your classroom, lab, field site, or working space.

A SAFETY PHILOSOPHY

Children are natural scientists because they are curious about everything in their natural world. Given the opportunity, they will investigate events and objects from all avenues. They see beauty and intrigue in events that adults accept as mundane. Being children, however, it is sometimes difficult for them to separate danger from fascination. It is the teacher's responsibility to balance these two factors, with input from publishers, science experts, peers, and their own teaching environment (student abilities and maturities, equipment available) in order to ensure that science learning is effective, yet safe.

Tik Liem has said that students are best motivated to learn science when they become intrigued by a *discrepant event*.[1] Discrepant events are produced when students observe something that is inconsistent with what logic or their senses suggest. Filling a wine glass with colored water, placing a light piece of plastic covering over the opening, and then inverting the glass creates a situation in which students expect the water to spill. When it does not, students become curious about the discrepant event. They are now receptive to learning the science of the event.

Capitalizing on natural events as learning situations for science is very effective with elementary students. Ice storms, tornadoes, thunderstorms, floods, the first snowfall, a gentle rain, and the changes of the seasons are all natural phenomena elementary students are curious about. When such events impact on the local community, students become more curious about their cause, and they become receptive to learning the science that caused the events.

In order to keep students safe while attempting to resolve discrepant events and/or exploring the scientific principles of natural phenomena through hands-on science activities, the teacher must have a simple, yet effective *safety philosophy*.

What follows leads to a safety philosophy that we provide to help teachers develop their own attitudes and self-imposed instructional safety limitations. These questions have been effective at helping teachers recognize hazards and avoid potential or real hazards to their own students. This philosophy is based upon two important questions.

What is the Educational Value of the Activity?

First, teachers should assess the activity students are about to participate in for its real educational value. Does the activity really have a logical, essential place in the scheme of learning within this class, or is it taught based simply on tradition or for entertainment? Ask yourself if a respected peer would use this activity to teach the concept. Would he or she use the same materials you have selected? Would he or she have made any other adjustments due to the general makeup of this group of students (emotional, social, academic handicaps)?

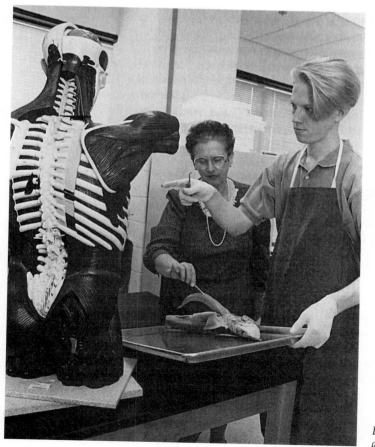

Determine the educational value of an activity before doing it.

What Are the Foreseeable Hazards Associated with the Activity?

Next, review the activity carefully for foreseeable hazards. Be sensitive to such things as chemical problems about which you have insufficient knowledge, fire hazards, potential eye injuries from sharp objects or flying projectiles, and over-crowding. If the foreseeable hazards exceed the educational value of the knowledge or experience students could gain from their direct participation in the activity, the teacher has some choices to make. Consider the following:

1. Provide additional safety precautions, such as safety goggles, fire blankets, eyewashes, and additional supervision.
2. Limit the activity to a teacher demonstration, in which the teacher is the only one who manipulates the equipment. Students become active observers. In many instances this is the most logical and educationally responsible choice.
3. Eliminate the activity entirely from the curriculum. Unless you have recently performed a detailed assessment of the entire science curriculum across grades, you might be surprised at how many duplicate activities without real value exist in science classes. They are being taught based primarily on tradition.[2]

Additional information concerning how to assess your room and activities for safety will be provided in the section entitled Performing Safety Assessments.

WHAT ARE YOUR LEGAL RESPONSIBILITIES?

Although this section will focus on tort law as it relates to science teaching, the principles and philosophy apply to all areas of education.

Tort

A *tort* is a wrong or injury that someone has committed against someone else. The injured party generally wants restitution for the injury or damages. The resolution of such conflicts between litigants (plaintiffs being those who bring the claim, and defendants being those whom the claim has been filed against) generally occurs in a court, involving lawyers, judges, jurors, and witnesses, and is referred to as a *lawsuit*.

Reasonable and Prudent Judgment

It is important to remember that the legal system of this country does not require educators to be superhuman in the performance of their duties. It is only expected that educators be reasonable and prudent in their judgment when performing their duties with students. Educators need only do what reasonable persons with parallel training would do in similar situations. They must ask themselves if their peers would endorse the activities being performed with students. Only if these questions can be answered affirmatively should teachers proceed with confidence. If not, teachers should add more safety features, limit the activity to a demonstration, or eliminate it entirely. Educators must attempt to anticipate hazards, eliminate them, or be confidently prepared to address them.

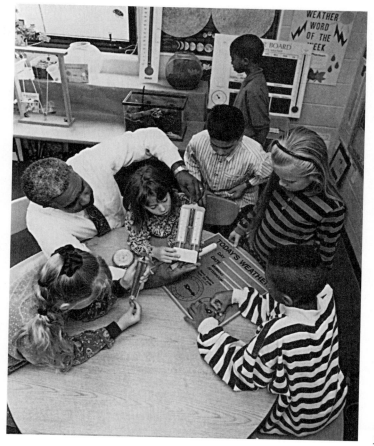

Prudent judgment and proper supervision fulfills most legal responsibilities.

Foreseeability

If a teacher discovers something amiss in his or her teaching environment, he or she should initiate corrections, preferably in writing, as soon as possible. Essential items such as fire extinguishers, fire blankets, eyewashes, or safety goggles need to be addressed immediately, while less important items, like nonskid floor wax, could be discussed with administrators for future correction. All such known hazards and appropriate emergency reactions should be explained to students as well.

The foreseeable hazards of all activities, as well as appropriate emergency reactions, should be completely explained to students *prior* to an activity. Field trip sites should be reviewed very carefully by the teacher before students are ever involved there. Communications between the teacher and the owner or proprietor of the field site should include any known hazards or potential hazards to this age group of students. Any sensitivities to foods the class might be working with should be ascertained before the activity begins. Any phobias should be known before

TEACHERS ON SCIENCE TEACHING

How Can Chemicals Be Used Safely in Schools?

The following is a transcript of an interview with Donald Murphy, teacher at Hoover High School, Des Moines, Iowa, who has taught chemistry, physics, physical science, and biology for twenty-nine years.

Question: Don, a great many elementary educators have a significant fear of chemistry. In many instances they feel that the subject is simply too dangerous to teach at the elementary level. Do you agree with this perception?

Answer: Personally, no. I do not think chemistry is too dangerous for elementary teachers to address as long as they follow some very basic guidelines of safety and they use chemicals that are appropriate for their knowledge level and that of their students. I would personally recommend that they limit chemical use to common household items about which they are knowledgeable. To say that chemistry is too dangerous is a dramatic oversimplification of the question. The subject can and should be addressed at the elementary level, but not to exceed the comfort level or knowledge level of the teacher.

Question: Are there chemicals which you feel are too dangerous to use at the elementary level?

Answer: Yes, there definitely are! I feel that Ammonium dichromate used to create a colorful and dramatic volcano effect for elementary students, and similar strong and rapid-reacting chemicals are definitely too dangerous for all concerned. Baking soda and vinegar can provide the same effect with a lot less potential hazard to teacher and students. Strong acids and alkalis should also be avoided due to their rapid and potentially violent reactions with other chemicals and human tissue. It is best to limit chemicals to dilute forms, and household items, at the elementary level.

Question: How should elementary teachers prepare for the safe use of chemicals?

Answer: Teachers should be certain that they are comfortable and knowledgeable of any chemicals with which they work. I also think that it would be a great idea to have high school students come to the elementary class to help the teacher with the chemicals. Teachers should also emphasize that random mixing of chemicals is

students are placed in potentially frightening situations. The teacher *must* know as soon as possible about any medical problems that students may have. These might include medication schedules, allergies, fears, and anxieties. This list, although incomplete, should provide the teacher with a sample of the kinds of things he or she needs to know and ask about before ever involving students in activities. Simply ask yourself, "What could go wrong with this activity, and am I prepared to address the problem?" If you can answer the questions affirmatively, proceed with confidence.

Negligence

Before a person can be held accountable for personal injury accidents, it must be proven that he or she was negligent. Negligence has been defined as "conduct that falls below a standard established by law or profession to protect others from harm."[3] It is sometimes described as failure to exercise due care.

inappropriate. Chemists always approach the analysis of chemical problems with a logical plan in mind.

Question: What safety equipment do you consider essential to the safe use of chemicals?

Answer: I think that there are a couple of items that should be available to all elementary teachers who address chemistry. Kitty litter is a porous, dry clay and is very effective in cleaning up liquid spills. The litter is sprinkled on the spill, allowed to sit until the liquid is absorbed. It is then swept up and disposed of in the trash. For the types of chemicals to be used in elementary programs, kitty litter is a very effective cleanup tool.

If open flames are to be used, the teacher should have available a fire extinguisher and fire blanket. They *must* know how to use these items and have them close at hand also.

Safety goggles are essential any time chemicals are to be used that could cause eye irritation if splashed in them.

Rubber gloves may also be helpful when working with slippery glassware.

Question: Do you have any summarizing recommendations to elementary teachers who wish to address chemistry in their classrooms?

Answer: As a high school chemistry teacher, I would like very much to see chemistry addressed at the elementary level. The concern for safety must accompany this interest, however. Elementary teachers should not hesitate to ask their high school chemistry teacher for materials, student help, and advice on the subject. We as chemistry teachers are proud of our subject and generally want very much to share our excitement with others. The incorporation of the subject into elementary science also provides an excellent opportunity for articulation across the grades as well as communication among professional educators.

Chemistry is an exciting, and appropriate endeavor for elementary study as long as teachers are knowledgeable of the items with which they are working, they have the safety equipment items necessary, and they ask questions when they feel the need.

Due Care

Due care can be defined as the educators' duty to protect the students in their charge.[4] For younger or handicapped students, the degree of care provided must be increased. Teachers must remember that they are the authority in the classroom. They or an equally qualified adult substitute must be present at all times, especially when the potential for student injury exists. During science activities, when materials and/or chemicals are being manipulated, a teacher's presence is essential. If the teacher needs to leave the room during such activities, he or she must make certain that an equally qualified person assumes this responsibility. Due care is often summarized in three teacher duties: instruction, supervision, and maintenance.[5]

Instruction. Educators must ensure that the instruction being offered is appropriate for the physical and mental development levels of their students. Since textbooks form the basis of many science programs, teachers would be wise to be sure that safety is an integral and conspicuous component. Teachers need to be certain that textbooks selected are parallel in teaching philosophy to their own. Remember the philosophy we presented earlier.

> All activities students are involved in are weighed for their educational value versus the hazards involved in having students perform them. If the foreseeable dangers outweigh the educational value of the activity, it must be limited to teacher demonstration, have more safety features added, or be eliminated from the science experience.[6]

In many instances, instructional guidelines for science settings and activities have been developed and disseminated through science teaching professional journals and monographs. Educators should become active members of their state and national science teaching association so that they can receive these materials. At the national level, educators should think seriously about joining the National Science Teachers Association (NSTA) and receiving their science teachers' journals. For information, contact:

Science and Children (for elementary teachers)
Science Scope (for middle school teachers)
National Science Teachers Association
1742 Connecticut Avenue NW
Washington, DC 20009
(202) 328-5800

Educators should also become aware of newsletters supplied by safety-conscious scientific supply companies. Many equipment-supplier newsletters include safety columns and hints as well as effective safety equipment ideas for young students.

Rules.   Rules should be clearly written and explained to students. Copies of the most important rules should be posted conspicuously throughout the room. Serious consideration should be given to developing and implementing a *student safety contract* for students in the upper grades (4–6) that identifies all foreseeable hazards and appropriate actions to be taken, describes the location and proper use of safety equipment items, and explains essential rules. At this level, students should sign such contracts indicating their understanding of the provisions. It is best to explain and have students initial only a couple of items each day. Teachers should collect these forms between each event and retain them for dissemination at the next safety discussion session. In some instances, teachers may wish to administer safety tests to determine the degree of student understanding.

Discipline during science activities should be fair, consistent, and strictly enforced. If safety is that important, no one should be exempt! The only exceptions should be based on a student's obvious physical or mental limitations. Students will support teachers in their activities a great deal more if they feel that everyone is treated fairly. Teachers may also wish to involve students in establishing some disciplinary policies.

Role Models.   Teachers should become role models for students to emulate in all safety procedures. Students cannot be expected to take safety seriously if their teacher does not observe all guidelines. Teachers should be especially careful to wear safety equipment items (goggles) and to observe all safety rules themselves. Teachers should also be careful to explain all safety considerations and have all safety equipment items available and explained to students before beginning any activities. Safety should be something that students expect their teacher to enforce with them.

Supervision.   The duty of supervision, as part of due care, can be a significant challenge. Teachers should always be in the classroom when scientific equipment or chemicals are accessible to students. The only exceptions to this rule would be during extreme emergencies or when the supervision has been delegated to another equally qualified person.

Overcrowding.   There is increasing evidence that overcrowding is the root cause of accidents in science settings. It is recommended that supervision should increase with the perceived dangers involved in the activity being undertaken, with increased percentages of handicapped students in the class, and with the degree to which the learning environment differs from the conventional classroom setting. Teachers must be aware of overcrowding and initiate corrections as soon as possible. The NSTA and numerous other professional science teaching organizations recommend that the teacher:student ratio never exceed 1:24 during science labs and activities.[7] The Texas Education Agency recommends at least thirty square feet of floor space for each student (including storage and teacher preparation area) in elementary school science classes.

Class Size.   The classroom teaching environment has a significant influence on the safety that can be provided to students. In their 1989 safety guide,[8] the Texas Education Agency recommended two types of floor plans for teaching elementary school science that may provide a model for the nation. Emphasis was placed on safety equipment, a maximum of twenty-four students during science activities, and extensive open space leading to at least two exits. There is adequate room for students to move about without bumping into each other or equipment. Students can also be readily supervised by the teacher from any point in the room—there are no blind spots.

Field Trips.   For field trips, teachers should ensure that parent/guardian release forms or waivers have been obtained and that the administration is apprised of the event. The activity should be an integral part of the course. Teachers should use only school-sanctioned and insured vehicles. Supervision should generally be increased to one teacher or other qualified adult to ten students. It is imperative that teachers

What must a teacher do to assure safe field trips?

and other assisting adults preview the field site carefully for hazards *before* students are involved. Students should be apprised of any known hazards and appropriate reactions in an emergency. Be careful to consider poisonous plants and plants with thorns or other irritating parts, and check for poisonous or biting animals. On the school grounds, it can often be vital that the teacher check for broken glass, holes, drug paraphernalia, and other unexpected items.

Implement the buddy system[9] on field trips. Each student is paired with and responsible for another student. Should something go awry, buddies can apprise adults of the problem. Of course, very young students (grades K–3) should not be separated from adult supervision at any time. The teacher should arrange for regular meeting times and locations for upper elementary students, and they should be adhered to explicitly.

Maintenance.   Maintaining the educational environment is the third teacher duty. It is imperative that educators attempt to foresee hazards and expedite their correction. Again, it is not expected that educators be supernatural in their identification and correction of hazards; however, a logical, regular review of the teaching environment is a reasonable expectation. The information available in the safety equipment and safety assessment sections of this chapter can help with maintenance.

Federal and State Legislation

A vital state law or statute about which you should instruct students relates to eye protective equipment (safety goggles).[10] Teachers must insist that whenever the potential for eye injury exists, appropriate American National Standards Institute

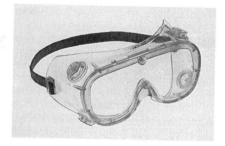

(ANSI)[11] approved eyewear is provided to all students. These federal equipment criteria were established to ensure minimum quality standards. Educators must insist that such eyewear meets ANSI standards and that they are worn!

Compliance with these federal equipment standards is ensured when you see *Z87* printed on the goggle itself. The faceplate will not shatter, splinter, or fall backward into the face of the wearer if impacted by a one-inch ball bearing dropped from fifty inches or by quarter-inch ball bearings traveling at 150 feet per second. In addition, the frame will not burn. It is the teacher's responsibility to insist that the purchasing agent orders only goggles that conform to these standards.

Insist that students wear the goggles whenever there is the slightest chance that someone could sustain an eye injury in your classroom. Remember that injuries can happen when students are walking about the room where others are performing science activities. Think also about injuries that could happen with even such simple chemicals as salt or vinegar, or with flying objects like rubber bands or balloons. Attempt to foresee such problems and act accordingly. Goggles that do not meet ANSI Z87 standards, that do not fit the students, or that have scratched faceplates, missing vent plugs, or damaged rubber moldings or headbands should not be used.

Most state statutes also require that goggles be cleaned before students wear them. Such equipment should also be stored in a relatively dust-free environment, such as a box or a cabinet. Educators should secure a copy of their state Eye Protective Equipment Legislation from their state department of education or school administration, and check for specific details. Remember, in many states this is the law!

Teachers need to understand and comply with applicable federal and state legislation as another way of ensuring proper and safe instruction. Contact the science consultant at your state department of education to secure copies of relevant science education legislation. Examples of such legislation include goggle laws, chemical right-to-know laws, bloodborne pathogen legislation, and other applicable Occupational Safety and Health Administration (OSHA) regulations.

The Occupational Safety and Health Administration (OSHA) Hazard Communication Standard

Also called the *right to know* (RTK), this OSHA legislation pertains to hazardous chemicals in the workplace.[12] All privately financed educational institutions are covered by the federal standard. Publicly funded schools must comply with their respective state government statutes. All RTK legislation is designed to help employees recognize and eliminate the dangers associated with hazardous materials in their workplaces.

Such legislation requires that chemicals be labeled and stored properly. Teachers must know the properties, hazards, and appropriate actions to take in the event of an emergency involving chemicals. They should instruct students *before* they ever use potentially dangerous chemicals. There are several resources outlined in the reference section of this book that would be helpful to educators in this regard. Teachers should also know what safety equipment items should be used whenever certain chemicals are present. These might include safety goggles, water in the event that chemicals are splashed in students' eyes, fire extinguisher, fire blanket, and most importantly a material safety data sheet (MSDS) citing the hazards and safe handling for the specific chemical.

The legislation requires that a *written program* be developed and that all affected employees know its contents. The details of such legislation will vary from state to state, so check with your department of education, federal or state OSHA office (Table 11.1), or department of labor. (For chemical emergency procedures and right to know questions, call 1-800-424-9346.) The plan need not be lengthy, but it must include these components:

1. Written hazard assessment procedures, including designation of responsible individuals or agency, consideration of scientific evidence for health hazards, evaluation of physical hazards, consideration of regulated chemicals, and assessment of chemicals prepared on site.
2. Material safety data sheets (MSDSs), including designated person responsible for maintaining the sheets, procedures for apprising employees and allowing employees access to them, procedures to follow when MSDSs are not received, procedures for updating the sheets, and descriptions of alternatives to actual sheets in the work area.
3. Labels and warnings, including the designated person responsible for ensuring proper labeling of chemicals, description of the labeling system, and procedure for updating the labeling information. Most states are using the National Fire Protection Association (NFPA) hazard diagram shown at the beginning of this chapter. The four-part square provides hazard information concerning fire, reaction with other chemicals, human health hazard, and other special information. Items are rated from zero, no hazard, to four, extreme hazard.
4. Employee training, including designation of the person responsible for conducting training, format of the program, documentation of training, and procedures for training new employees. The ultimate purpose is to assure a safe workplace.[13]

Occupational Safety and Health Administration (OSHA) Chemical Hygiene Plan

The OSHA chemical hygiene plan is a standard that applies to all employers engaged in the laboratory use of chemicals. *Laboratory* is defined below and may or may not include upper elementary science activities, depending on the types of chemicals and program involved. A laboratory is a place where

chemicals are manipulated on a laboratory scale; where the chemicals are handled in containers designed to be safely and easily manipulated by one person; multiple chemical procedures are used; procedures are not of a production process; protective laboratory equipment and practices are in common use to minimize employee exposure.[14]

The legislation became effective in 1991. It requires that employers, including schools, develop a comprehensive plan for identifying and dealing with chemical hazards. The plan must include all employees who could be exposed to these chemicals, and it must be updated annually.

Bloodborne Pathogen Legislation

In 1992, OSHA released the Bloodborne Pathogens "Standard Summary Applicable to Schools."[15]

The intent of this standard summary is to offer schools an overview of theOSHA standard to eliminate or minimize occupational exposure to Hepatitis B virus (HBV), which causes hepatitis B, a serious liver disease; Human Immunodeficiency Virus (HIV), which causes Acquired Immunodeficiency Syndrome (AIDS), and other bloodborne pathogens. Based on a review of the information in the rulemaking record, OSHA has made a determination that employees face a

TABLE 11.1 OSHA Offices by Region

Region I (CT, MA, ME, NH, RI, VT) 6-18 North St. 1 Dock Square Bldg. 4th Floor Boston, MA 02109 (617) 565-1145	Region II (NY, NJ, PR, VI) 201 Varick St. Room 670 New York, NY 10014 (212) 337-2325	Region III (DC, DE, MD, PA, VA, WV) Gateway Bldg. Suite 2100 3535 Market St. Philadelphia, PA 19104 (215) 596-1201
Region IV (AL, FL, GA, KY, MS, NC, SC) 1375 Peachtree St., NE Suite 587 Atlanta, GA 30367 (404) 347-3573	Region V (IL, IN, MI, MN, OH, WI) 230 S. Dearborn St. 32d Floor, Room 3244 Chicago, IL 60604 (312) 353-2220	Region VI (AR, LA, NM, OK, TX) 525 Griffin Square Bldg. Room 602 Dallas, TX 75202 (214) 767-4731

Region VII (IA, KS, MO, NE) 911 Walnut St. Room 406 Kansas City, MO 64106 (816) 426-5861	Region VIII (CO, MT, ND, SD, UT, WY) Federal Bldg., Room 1576 1961 Stout St. Denver, CO 80294 (303) 844-3061	Region IX (AZ, CA, HI, NV, 3 Terr.) 71 Stevenson St. Room 415 San Francisco, CA 94105 (415) 995-5672	Region X (AK, ID, OR, WA) Federal Bldg. Room 6003 909 First Ave. Seattle, WA 98174 (206) 442-5930

significant health risk as the result of occupational exposure to blood and other potentially infectious materials because they may contain pathogens. OSHA further concludes that this exposure can be minimized or eliminated using a combination of engineering and work practice controls, personal protective clothing and equipment, training, and medical surveillance.

Educators should simulate foreseeable emergencies and proper responses. After instruction, students might be evaluated based on their proper and expeditious performance during such simulations. *Be careful to protect students from any hazards during the simulations.* Examples of such simulations might be a student receiving a chemical splash to his or her clothing, face, or eyes; a classroom or clothing fire; securing other adult emergency assistance; or emergencies requiring the rapid evacuation of the room.

Should an accident occur, it is imperative that educators collect as much information as possible from witnesses (student and staff) in the form of an accident or incident report. Should legal repercussions arise from the incident, these accounts are powerful firsthand evidence of what actions were taken and the teacher's commitment to safety. When the statute of limitations for legal actions passes for the incident, dispose of the reports. These reports can also be very effective learning tools when used with other classes.

SAFETY EQUIPMENT

Certain safety equipment items are essential when teaching science activities. Teachers should be confident that such items are immediately accessible when needed, that teachers and students can operate them, and that they are appropriate for the student audience being served. Students should also be taught the location and proper operation of all safety equipment items they might need to use. These should include fire extinguishers, fire blankets, eyewashes, safety goggles, and a telephone or intercom, if available. This might necessitate having duplicate safety items in more than one location in the room. Every student should have a set of goggles during science activities.

Electrical Equipment

It is recommended that whenever possible hot plates with on/off indicator lights replace open flames. This simple change could eliminate many fire situations from science rooms. You should not have to use extension cords for hot plates, since the room should have sufficient electrical outlets. Extension cords on the floor create tripping hazards unless they are in cord protectors. Do not allow cords to be draped across desks or other work areas in order to prevent students from inadvertently upsetting apparatus. Electrical outlet caps should be in place when the outlets are not in use. In primary grades, they should be covered at all times; this will help prevent students from putting metal items in the plug holes, which could cause electrocution or burns.

Heating Equipment

If open flames are periodically necessary, be certain that emergency fire equipment is functioning properly and is immediately available. If alcohol lamps, sterno cans, or candles are to be used, place them in pie pans filled with damp sand. Should a spill accidentally occur, the pie pan would prevent the liquid from spreading onto clothing, tables, and so on. Since alcohol looks like water, it is essential to keep it off items where it might be treated like water. If you put alcohol in lamps, add a small amount of table salt so that the flame burns a bright orange color. Large quantities (one-half liter or more) of alcohol or other flammable liquids should never be brought into the room, and students should never have access to quantities of these liquids.

Flammable Liquid Storage

If teachers are storing flammable liquids such as alcohol, they should do so only in small quantities in the manufacturer's original container or in an approved safety can. A safety can is made of heavy-gauge steel or polyethylene. It has a spring-loaded lid to prevent spilling and to vent during vapor expansion caused by a heat source. It also has a flame arrestor or heat sump in the throat of the spout to help prevent explosions.

Hair and Loose Clothing

Loose clothing and long hair should be restricted when students are working with open flames. This seems obvious; however, it still commonly causes accidents among students. Be careful to pull long hair back so that it does not hang down over the flame. Loose clothing, especially sweaters, can be hazardous near open flames.

Fire Blanket

Fire blankets should be of the proper type and size and in the proper location. They should not be so large that students could not easily use them in an emergency. Check to be certain that they are placed in conspicuous locations and easily retrievable by both handicapped and nonhandicapped students and staff. Unless otherwise recommended by your fire marshal, these blankets should be made of

wool Fire blanket display and storage containers should be carefully checked for proper function. Be sure to eliminate containers with rusted hinges and latches, blankets still stored in plastic wrappers, and blankets made with asbestos fiber. Six-foot vertical standing fire blanket tubes should be avoided since they can result in facial burns. Do not attempt to extinguish torso fires by having a student stand and be wrapped in the fire blanket: This results in a chimney effect, which pushes heat across the student's face and causes unnecessary facial burns. The stop-drop-and-roll procedure endorsed by fire departments appears to be most effective at extinguishing body fires and presents the fewest drawbacks.

Fire Extinguishers

ABC triclass fire extinguishers are usually preferred by fire departments due to their ability to extinguish most foreseeable fires from products likely to be found in elementary science settings (such as paper products, electrical items, grease). In settings where microcomputers are used regularly, it might be wise to investigate

halon extinguishers. These have been used in aviation for years because their fire-extinguishing chemicals do not foul the contacts in delicate electronic navigation and communications equipment and microcomputers as dry chemical types will. Halon has also been preferred over carbon dioxide for extinguishing fires within electronic equipment, such as computers, because it does not cause a cold thermal shock to sensitive electronic microcircuits. Teachers should confirm such suggestions with their local or state fire marshal. The major disadvantage to halon is its harmful effect on the earth's ozone layer. Since halon contains such small quantities of this ingredient, and such emergency tools are used so infrequently, we feel that the benefits outweigh the drawbacks.

It is a good idea to have fire department personnel come into your room and demonstrate for students appropriate fire procedures and equipment. Teachers should be confident and comfortable in using their fire equipment items. Teachers should also be in the habit of checking the pressure valves on fire extinguishers in or near their rooms to ensure that they are still adequately pressurized. It would also be wise for students to heft extinguishers, unfold and use a fire blanket, and rehearse foreseeable emergencies involving fire.

Eyewash and Shower

It is recommended that fifteen minutes (2.5 gallons per minute) of aerated, tempered (60–90° Fahrenheit) running water be deliverable from an eyewash to flush the eyes of a person who has suffered a chemical splash. At the elementary level, eye irritants could include salt, vinegar, sand, alcohol, and other chemicals. Teachers should explore the installation of the fountain fixture type of eyewash station.[16] It is very inexpensive ($60–$70) and easy to install: Screw it into an existing gooseneck faucet. The fixture allows the plumbing to be used as both an eyewash and a faucet, simply

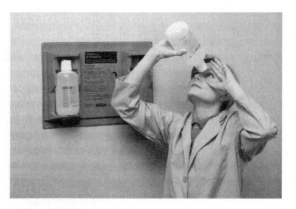

by pushing a diverter valve. Should traffic patterns or room designs change, such fountain fixtures can easily be moved to other faucets. Check the equipment and chemicals reference section of this book for sources. On a temporary basis, educators can stretch a piece of surgical tubing over a gooseneck faucet in order to deliver aerated running water to the eyes of a chemical splash victim. Again, it is critical that such equipment be easily accessible to all staff and students. Be certain that the hot water faucet handle has been removed from any sink eyewash to prevent accidental burns caused by hot water.

Bottled water stations are not recommended for use during science activities because they can be contaminated, and they cannot deliver fifteen minutes of aerated running water. They should only be used when there is no alternative, such as in field settings, and where the teacher maintains very strict control of them.

Critical safety equipment such as fire blankets, fire extinguishers, eyewashes, and drench showers should be located within thirty steps or fifteen seconds of any location in the science room. These vital equipment items should be checked for proper operation every three to six months.

When working with chemicals, it is imperative that teachers understand the properties, hazards, and appropriate emergency procedures to follow in the event of an accident. Material safety data sheets (MSDS)[17] and the Merck Index[18] provide this comprehensive information from chemical manufacturers. They identify the material, listing hazardous ingredients, physical and chemical characteristics, fire and explosion hazards, reactivity with other substances, health hazards, precau-

Most states have a goggle law.

tions for safe handling and use, and control measures. Teachers can secure MSDSs from the U.S. Government Printing Office or directly from the manufacturers or suppliers from which the schools purchase their chemicals.

It is also recommended that educators secure a copy of *School Science Laboratories: A Guide to Some Hazardous Chemicals*[19] or *The Total Science Safety System.*[20] Both of these documents encompass chemical management systems; check the references section of this chapter for addresses.

In some states, requirements regarding the handling, storage, and emergency response to chemical accidents are included in right-to-know legislation. In addition to understanding the properties and effects of chemicals, educators must ensure that chemicals are properly labeled. All chemicals should be stored in lockable cabinets or storerooms when not in use. Check with your state-level environmental protection agency, department of natural resources, or department of education to be certain that you know the requirements in your state.

Table 11.2, a 1991 survey of the fifty state departments of education, indicates the following:

- Forty states observe the goggle legislation requirement;
- In legislation, nine states observed the NSTA requirement for one teacher to

TABLE 11.2   What Requirements Are Observed by the States?

State	Goggle Legislation	NSTA Teacher/Student Ratio	State Teacher/Student Ratio	Right-to-Know Legislation	Safety Manual Available
AL	Yes	No		Yes—National	Yes
AK	Yes	No		Yes—National	No
AR	Yes	No	Yes 1:30	No	No
AZ	Yes	No		Yes—National	No
CA	Yes	No		Yes—State	Yes
CO	No	No		No	
CN	Yes	Yes	No	Yes—National	Yes
DE	Yes	No		Yes—State	Yes
FL	Yes	No	Building capacity	Yes—State	No
GA	Yes	No	Yes 1:28	No	
HI				Yes—National	
ID	No	No		No	
IL	Yes	No		Yes—State	No
IN	Yes	No	Yes 1:30	Yes—National	No
IA	Yes	No		Yes—National	No
KS	Yes	No		Yes—State	No
KY	Yes	No	Yes 1:28	Yes—National	No
LA	Yes	Yes	No	Yes—State	No
MA				Yes—State	
ME	Yes	No	K–8=1:25 9–12=1:30	Yes—State	Yes
MD	Yes	No	Yes	Yes—National	Yes
MS	Yes	No	Yes 1:33	Yes—State	No
MI				Yes—National	
MN	Yes	No	Yes	Yes—National	Yes
MO	Yes	No	Yes 1:28	Yes—State	Yes
MT	No	No		Yes—State	Yes
NE	Yes	No		No	In progress
NV	No	No		No	

twenty-four students, while seventeen states had their own individual requirements;
- Thirty-nine states currently recognize either federal or state versions of the right-to-know (RTK) legislation;
- Eighteen states had their own science safety manuals for teachers.

State	Goggle Legislation	NSTA Teacher/Student Ratio	State Teacher/Student Ratio	Right-to-Know Legislation	Safety Manual Available
NH	No	Yes	No	Yes—State	No
NJ	Yes	No	Yes	Yes—State	Yes
NM	Yes	No		Yes—State	No
NY	Yes	No		Yes—National	Yes
				Yes—National/State	
NC	Yes	Yes	No	Yes—National	Yes
ND	No	No		Yes—State	No
OH	Yes	No		No	Yes Software
OK	Yes	No	Yes	Yes—State	Yes
OR	No	No		Yes—National	Yes Software
PA	Yes	No		Yes—State	Yes
RI	Yes		Yes State Monitors	Yes—State	No
SC	Yes	No	Yes 1:30	Yes—National	Yes
SD	Yes	No		No	
TN	Yes	No	Yes 1:35	Yes—National	No
TX	Yes	Yes	No	Yes—State	Yes
UT	Yes	No		Yes—National	No
VT	Yes	Yes	No	Yes—National	No
VA	Yes	No		Yes—National	Yes
WA	Yes	No		Yes—National	No
WV				Yes—State	
WI	Yes	No	Yes 35 ft^2 per student	Yes—State	No
WY	No	No		No	Yes
DC	Yes	Yes		No	Yes
Am. Samoa	No	No		No	
PR	Yes	No		No	Yes Chemistry

Source: Jack Gerlovich, "Science Safety Survey of State Departments of Education," Electronic Survey of State Science Consultants via the Council of State Science Supervisor (CSSS), People Sharing Information Network (PSInet), August, 1991.

This information should be useful to teachers when assessing their needs and the state services available to them.

PERFORMING SAFETY ASSESSMENTS

Teachers of elementary school science must be prepared to assess the safety situation within their teaching environments (classrooms or field trips) regularly and accurately. The best way to accomplish this task is to develop and use safety software checklists regularly. The Total Science Safety System—Elementary[21] is available in Macintosh, Apple, and IBM formats and is cited in the reference section

---

FIGURE 11.1   Science Safety Checklist

This listing is only representative of teachers' safety duties. Check off those items you are well informed about or prepared for and ask your instructor for more information about the remaining items.

Item	Well Prepared or Informed	Item	Well Prepared or Informed
Teachers understand their teaching duties of		Teachers ensure that all safety equipment is functioning and available	___
Instruction	___	Teachers ensure that all science equipment is of the right size and is appropriate for their students	
Supervision	___		
Maintenance of the environment, equipment	___		___
Teachers attempt to foresee hazards and correct them	___	Teachers ensure that students know how to use safety and other science equipment items	___
Teachers' activities are consistent with those recommended by their textbooks, professional organizations, state agencies, federal standards	___	Teachers ensure that the following fire safety equipment is available whenever they are using open flames:	
		Fire blanket	___
		Fire extinguisher	___
Teachers use student safety contracts with upper elementary students	___	Fire alarm	___
Teachers use only ANSI Z87 approved safety goggles	___	Teachers ensure that loose clothing and long hair are confined when students are using open flames	___
Teachers insist that students wear safety goggles whenever the potential for an eye injury exists	___	Teachers ensure that an eyewash is available and functioning whenever the potential for an eye injury exists	___
Teachers ensure that classes are not overcrowded (fewer than twenty-four students per teacher)	___	Teachers use only chemicals for which they have MSDS sheets that they have reviewed for hazards	___
Teachers ensure that field trips are not overcrowded (fewer than ten students per adult)	___	Teachers ensure that extension cords are used only when absolutely necessary, and then only grounded types	___
Teachers review the field trip site before taking students	___	Teachers ensure that all electrical outlets are capped when not in use	___
Teachers use the buddy system on field trips	___		

Source: Jack Gerlovich and Kenneth Hartman, *The Total Science Safety System—Elementary* (Waukee, IA: Jakel).

of this chapter. There is also a reply card included in new copies of this book that teachers can return to JaKel, Inc., to receive the software at a significant discount. Teachers are encouraged to use an interactive program so that they can conveniently customize their assessment systems to their academic and facilities needs. Teachers can also create complete and easily accessible records that can be updated regularly and printed as needed. These records could also provide a defense in the case of an unforeseeable accident or injury lawsuit.

Elementary and middle school science safety checklists should include but not be limited to the components outlined in Figure 11.1. The assessments should be performed every semester in order to ensure that safety problems are identified and corrected expeditiously.

Any safety problems should be corrected as soon as practical. This is best accomplished by informing the administration of the problem in writing. State the problem matter-of-factly, without explanation. Request an answer within ten days.

The Total Science Safety System[22] provides checklists concerning life, earth, and physical science activities and procedures, a student safety contract, an accident/incident report, and request for correction forms.

CHAPTER SUMMARY

In order to prevent injuries, teachers must attempt to foresee problems and address them immediately. They need to teach appropriately for the emotional, physical, and intellectual levels of their students. Teachers must also provide adequate supervision applicable for the environment and the degree of hazards anticipated, in addition to ensuring that the environment and equipment items are properly maintained. If teachers can be sure that they have addressed all of these concerns, they should proceed with confidence. If they cannot, adjustments should be made, including the addition of more safety features, limitation of the activity to a teacher demonstration only, or elimination of the activity.

DISCUSSION QUESTIONS AND PROJECTS

1. You are planning a field trip to the local prairie ecosystem (or other special local ecosystem) to study plants with your first-grade class. All parent/guardian release forms have been returned with the exception of one. Would you allow the student to attend the activity anyway? Give three reasons for your answer.

2. There has been a significant increase in the number of accidents in science classroom and lab settings in recent years. What are three possible reasons for this change?

3. A student in your third-grade class comes to you one day and asks if he can bring his pet northern banded water snake to class to show during your rep-

tile unit. What would be your response? What information would you want to support your decision? Where would you secure such information?

4. As part of your animal study unit for fourth grade, you are planning the dissection of a cow's eye. What safety considerations should you plan for? How would you respond to a parent who says the activity is not safe?

5. You are planning a unit on the study of molds with your fifth-grade students. You will have the students growing mold on bread. What safety considerations should you plan for? Where would you secure information on molds and their potential hazards to students?

6. You are preparing to do a simple chemistry experiment with your sixth-grade class. A student comes to you and says that she has new safety glasses provided by her optometrist and that she would rather wear them than your safety goggles. What would be your response? Why?

7. Develop a complete plan for an elementary science field trip to a natural forested area in your region. Be sure to include all preplanning, transportation, and student groupings in your plan.

8. Develop a written plan for conducting a safety assessment of a school science classroom in your area. Include all necessary forms and checklists as well as a timeline for its completion.

9. Interview a chemistry teacher or other professional chemist in your district. With a list of the chemicals used in your science program, ask him or her to help you rate the items as to their hazards to your students. Consider the following ratings: safe, requires special attention, and unsafe.

10. Ask the local fire department to visit your classroom and demonstrate the proper procedure for dealing with a personal-clothing fire and the proper use of fire extinguishers. If possible, ask that the fire personnel set small demonstration fires outside in containers and show how the various extinguisher types put out paper, electrical, and grease fires.

11. Select an elementary school in your area and develop a written checklist for performing a safety assessment of its grounds. Be sure to address items that are indigenous to your area, including hazardous plants and animals, automobile traffic, difficult-to-supervise areas, natural hazards (streams, lakes, and so on), and human problems (construction areas, glass).

NOTES

1. Tik Liem, *Invitations to Science Inquiry,* 2d ed. (El Cajon, CA: Science Inquiry Enterprises, 1989).

2. Jack Gerlovich and Kenneth Hartman, *Science Safety: A Diskette for Elementary Educators* (Waukee, IA: JaKel, 1990).

3. State of Iowa, *School Code of Iowa,* (Des Moines, IA, 1988).

4. Ibid.

5. Ibid.

6. Jack Gerlovich, Kenneth Hartman, and Timothy Gerard, *The Total Science Safety System for Grades 7–14* (Waukee, IA: JaKel, 1992).

7. *Conditions for Good Science Teaching in Secondary Schools* (Washington, DC: National Science Teachers Association, 1983).

8. Texas Education Agency, *Planning a Safe and Effective Science Learning Environment* (Austin, TX, 1989).

9. S. Rakow, "Safety Supplement," *Science Scope* (November/December 1989).

10. State of Iowa.

11. State of Iowa.

12. *Compact School and College Administrator's Guide for Compliance with Federal and State Right-to-Know Regulations* (Philadelphia: The Forum for Scientific Excellence, 1989).

13. *Federal Register,* Department of Labor, Occupational Safety and Health Administration, 29, CFR, Part 1910, Occupational Exposures to Hazardous Chemicals in Laboratories, Final Rule, Wednesday, January 31, 1990, U.S. Supt. of Documents, Government Printing Office, Washington, DC.

14. *Federal Register,* Department of Labor, Occupational Safety and Health Administration, Rules and Regulations (FR Doc. 91-288886), vol. 56, no. 235, December 6, 1991.

15. *Federal Register,* Department of Labor, Occupational Safety and Health Administration, 29, CFR, Part 1030, Subpart Z, the Department of Labor, Occupational Safety and Health Administration, 1992, U.S. Supt. of Documents, Government Printing Office, Washington, DC.

16. Sargent-Welch Scientific Co., *Equipment Catalogue* (Skokie, IL: Sargent-Welch Scientific).

17. *CHRIS: Hazardous Chemical Data,* U.S. Department of Transportation, Superintendent of Documents, U.S. Government Printing Office, Washington, DC.

18. S. Budavari et al., *The Merck Index: An Encyclopedia of Chemicals, Drugs, and Biologicals,* 11th ed. (Rahway, NJ: Merck & Co., 1989).

19. Consumer Products Safety Commission, *School Science Laboratories: A Guide to Some Hazardous Substances* (Washington, DC, 1984).

20. Gerlovich and Hartman.

21. Jack Gerlovich and Kenneth Hartman, *The Total Science Safety System—Elementary* (Waukee, IA: JaKel).

22. Ibid.

ADDITIONAL READINGS

Information

Curry College, Chemistry Department, *Speaking of Safety: The Laboratory Safety Workshop Newsletter* (Milton, MA 02186). Excellent reference for case study reviews and safety tips.

Gary Downs, Jack Gerlovich, et al., *Science Safety for*

Elementary Teachers (Ames, IA: Iowa State University Press, 1984). This book provides educators with accident statistics, liability information, and safety considerations for physical science, life science, and chemicals. In addition, first aid and outdoor activities are addressed.

Flinn Scientific Co., *Flinn Chemical Catalogue Reference Manual* (Batavia, IL: Flinn Scientific, 1992). This annual publication provides science educators with a listing of chemicals sold by Flinn Scientific, as well as quick reference items regarding their storage, handling, and disposal.

Florida Department of Education, *Science Safety: No Game of Chance!* (Division of Public Schools, Bureau of Elementary and Secondary Education, Tallahassee, FL 32399). This guide assists school personnel in developing a personal safety plan for their districts or schools.

Forum for Scientific Excellence, Inc., *Handbook of Chemical and Environmental Safety in Schools and Colleges,* The Forum for Scientific Excellence, J.B. Lippincott Co., Philadelphia, PA, 1990. This brief monograph provides practical suggestions to schools and colleges relative to chemical use.

Jack Gerlovich and Kenneth Hartman, *The Total Science Safety System: Elementary,* 2d ed. 1990. Secondary, 6th ed. 1993 (JaKel, Inc., 585 Southfork Dr., Waukee, IA 1993). This is the most complete science safety system for teachers of science available. The set encompasses K–12 and includes laws, codes, and standards; case studies; forms and checklists for safety assessments; and chemical management information.

Jack Gerlovich, Gary Downs, et al., *School Science Safety: Elementary* (Batavia, IL: Flinn Scientific, 1984). This paperback provides a rich reference for elementary teachers of science.

Jack Gerlovich and Timothy Gerard, "Don't Let Your Hands-On Science Program Blow up in Your Face," *American School Board Journal* (May 1984), pp. 40–41. This article, written by a science safety consultant and an attorney, emphasizes the team approach to safety in school science settings.

Jack Gerlovich, "Safety First in the Elimination of Hazardous Chemicals from School Science Settings," in

D. A. Pipitone, *Safe Storage of Laboratory Chemicals,* 2d ed. (Somerset, NJ: John Wiley & Sons, 1991), pp. 249–261. This chapter provides educators with a safe and cost-effective means for eliminating unwanted chemicals from schools on a statewide basis.

Lab Safety Supply Co., *Safety and Compliance Directory 1992* (Janesville, WI 53547-1368). This is an excellent handbook for information from safety hotlines, government agencies, professional societies, and private agencies.

National Science Teachers Association, *Science Scope: A Journal for Middle/Junior High School Science Teachers—Safety Supplement,* vol. 13, no. 3 (November/December 1989). This excellent safety monograph addresses chemicals, overcrowding, living materials in the program, and more.

New York State Department of Education, "Elementary Science Program Evaluation Test (ESPET)" (Washington Ave., Albany, NY 12234). This test, which was shown on PSInet (People Sharing Information Network) on October 16, 1989, assesses student mastery of science process skills.

Lloyd Phillips and Jack Gerlovich, *Fifty Safe Physical Science Activities for Teachers,* (Skokie, IL: Sargent Welch Scientific Co., 1988), 1-800-SARGENT. This booklet contains eighty-five activities for students in grades 7 through 10. Chemistry and physics are addressed.

Donald Phillips, "Chemistry for the Elementary School," *Science and Children,* (October 1981). This is an excellent overview of chemicals commonly used in elementary school science programs.

Equipment and Chemicals
These organizations could be useful to teachers when securing necessary safety equipment items.

Lab Safety Supply Co., P.O. Box 1368, Janesville, WI 53547-1368. 1-(800) 356-0783

Nasco Scientific Co., 901 Janesville Ave., Fort Atkinson, WI 53538. (414) 563-2446

Flinn Scientific Co., P.O. Box 219, 131 Flinn St., Batavia, IL 60510. (708) 879-6900

Science Kit, Inc., 777 E. Park Dr., Tonawanda, NY 14150-6781. (718) 874-6020

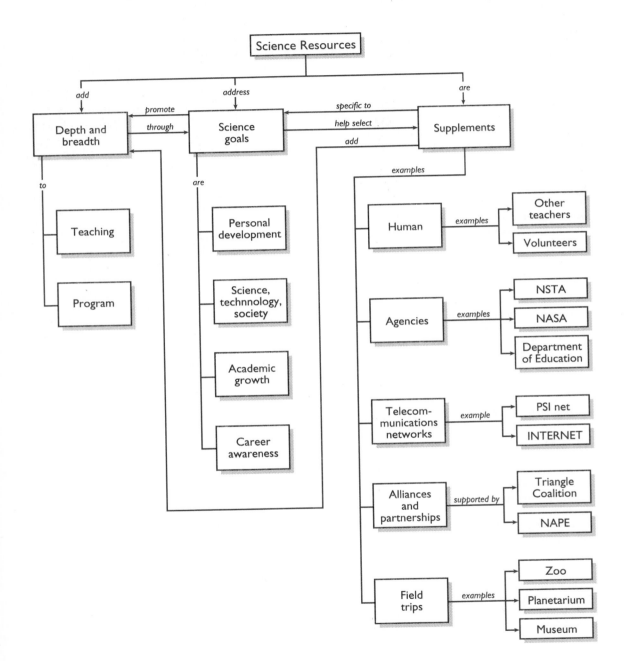

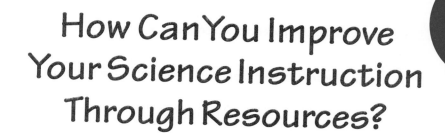

How Can You Improve Your Science Instruction Through Resources?

12

"I wish I knew more about environmental education. I don't remember covering much content during my undergraduate work," said Rosita Martinez, a third-grade teacher, while she was eating lunch with fellow teachers.

Another third-grade teacher, Kara Larson, said, "I don't either. I know it's important for students to be concerned about the land and its resources, and an appreciation of conservation is something they have to learn. It's scary to think what our land will be like in thirty years. Resource management and education are both critical, and education is our job."

Overhearing the discussion, Cade Beaver, a fifth-grade teacher, said that he had attended a good session on environmental education presented by a state naturalist at the last state inservice meeting.

359

He said, "I think I can find her name for you." He also suggested putting a message on the state telecommunication network for science teachers. He added, "I often get help with activities from other teachers and staff at state and national agencies."

Kara suggested, "You might want to look at the school resource file in the principal's office for information on volunteers and field trips within the community. This information can be very helpful."

Later that afternoon, Cade used the school computer to connect to a science education network and requested information or assistance for Rosita. After the school day, he found his program from the state meeting and identified the naturalist, copied her name and agency, and left them in Rosita's school mailbox. When Rosita found the note from Cade, it reminded her to stop at the principal's office to review the school resource file that Kara had mentioned. Instead of one file, she found a complete file drawer filled with information on many community resource persons, volunteers, and field trip locations.

Within two days, the network had provided several suggestions from teachers across the state. Many cited examples of activities, lesson plans, and resources. Three messages from teachers suggested that Rosita obtain two supplementary curriculum programs, Project WILD and Project WILD—Aquatic.[1] One teacher even provided the name and phone number of the state director of these programs.

Rosita called the state director only to find that she was also the science education consultant. The director described Project WILD and Project Learning Tree as teacher-tested supplemental activities designed to provide information to help students evaluate choices and make decisions about the environment. She also described the inservice workshops funded through the state's Dwight D. Eisenhower Mathematics and Science Education Program inservice funds. Rosita promptly enrolled in an upcoming Project WILD workshop.

The two-day Project WILD workshop provided Rosita with a book of hands-on elementary activities that closely matched the goals and objectives of the unit she would be teaching. During the workshop she also met the naturalist who had made the presentation at the state conference. Rosita asked the naturalist to visit her class, to bring some animals, and to arrange for the class to visit the park where she worked.

Rosita's class received enriched educational experiences because she used resources to enhance her teaching. Her students became bears searching for food during "Carrying Capacity," and artists in "Adaptation Artistry," both Project WILD activities. Rosita's students became active participants in their own learning experiences by direct, active contact with the naturalist and the animals.

INTRODUCTION

Can you look into your past and recall a school experience that led you to further learning or that excited you about a topic? The learning experiences and opportunities people most often recall are those that included active participation. "I remember when we held the snake, . . . when we went to the zoo, . . . when I stood inside the six-foot tall eye at the science museum." Students learn best when they are actively involved with their learning and when the topics are of interest to them. Today's students have grown up exposed to active hands-on enterprises as they sit for hours in front of TV screens both as inactive and active participants in videos, video games, and cartoons. They interact constantly with software that offers instant motion and movement, and they often become involved to excess. These experiences require active and innovative classroom instruction.

Think comprehensively about the educational experiences you offer your students. Consider their interests, learning styles, and educational needs. The learning experiences and opportunities you provide to your students should be varied and multifaceted. You can use the read-write-review-test approach to textbook material. Or you can actively engage your students in activities that will help them develop the skills required to be scientifically literate citizens or even scientists; to explore their surroundings; and to make connections between themselves and their world, rather than to accept the secondhand experiences provided in textbooks.

Rosita's program is just one example of extending the classroom beyond its walls. Let us examine the resources she utilized:

- colleagues,
- state professional organization,
- state telecommunications network,
- state science consultant,
- supplementary curriculum materials
- volunteer,
- inservice provided through a federally funded program,
- school-level resource file.

Each resource provided an additional facet to the instruction her students received.

Resources that you bring to the classroom are the key to enhancing the instruction and providing the stimulus to excite and engage your students in learning. If science is a way of doing and learning from doing, then it is mandatory that you provide the resources for the experiences that enable students to do the work of science. Using outside resources is an effective way to provide educational experiences that address the goals of a balanced, comprehensive science education program.

To assist you in incorporating resources into your program, this chapter will

1. examine why outside resources are necessary,
2. describe types and examples of available resources,
3. describe procedures for the varied and safe use of resources.

WHY USE OUTSIDE RESOURCES?

A teacher who uses the textbook as the entire teaching guide limits the variety and quality of instruction. Adding community resources enhances learning opportunities, allows experiences that address the goals of a comprehensive science education program, provides the link between the students' present and future experiences,

Community resources stimulate children's interests in science and its practical value.

and makes the teaching process personal for both the students and the teacher. Including additional resources requires time and planning, but teachers discover through experience that the addition of information and hands-on activities goes beyond the walls of the classroom and the world of academia and often creates the most memorable learning experiences of all.

For example, the Thomas Jefferson Magnet School in Euclid, Ohio, involves animals in its curriculum. Each room has permanent animal residents: chinchillas, hamsters, a pot-belly pig, iguanas, finches, a turtle, a python snake, a parakeet, a parrot and a rabbit all live at the school. An English springer spaniel resides in the office and greets all arriving guests. This novel use of resources within the class-room provides an exciting learning experience.

The Voyage of the Mimi (see Appendix A), a resource often used in middle schools, excites students and raises questions about their interaction with the environment. Could this knowledge be intensified if adapted to the students' own surroundings? A trip to a nearby stream, river, lake, bay, or ocean allows a student to learn and apply skills. Such an investigation leads to students' enthusiasm, engagement, and interest in their own surroundings and may provide the spark needed to develop a future oceanographer. It can also help students who feel like outsiders to become part of a team. You will only need to view the faces and hear the enthusiasm of students as they bring their first specimens in from bay water to appreciate the value resources add through the use of hands-on activities.

You may never fully know the effect any learning activity has on your students, but many class reunions are spent discussing the memorable events of the school years. You should hope that the experiences you provide your students will be remembered and valued. The classroom is the location of learning, but the walls need to be extended to the community where students will spend their lives. Resources from academia and the outside community need to be entwined with the curriculum to provide meaningful learning experiences.

The link between the community and the classroom is not a new concept. John Dewey made the following statement in his *Democracy and Education* in 1916:

> The development within the young of the attitudes and dispositions necessary to the continuous and progressive life of society cannot take place by direct conveyance of beliefs, emotions, and knowledge. It takes place through the intermediary of the environment; the environment consists of the sum total of conditions which are concerned with the execution of the activity characteristic of the living being. The social environment consists of all activities of fellow beings that are bound up in carrying on the activities of any of its members. It is truly educative in its effect, in its efforts, in the degree in which an individual appropriates the purpose which actuates it, becomes familiar with its methods and subject matters, acquires needed skills, and is saturated with its emotional spirit.[2]

The need for relevance in education is paramount now as the country finds its educational system questioned in light of a new technological and global society. Society's ability to respond to profound and rapid changes is dependent upon an adequate and educated human resource base. Society must educate highly competent scientists, professionals, and managers to meet the challenges of the future. It must also prepare an educated and scientifically literate citizenry capable of responding to technological advances. Demographic studies predict that fewer students will be prepared for and interested in pursuing science in the 1990s. The characteristics of the future workforce likely will mirror changing demographics, with more minorities and women. Programs within our schools must respond to these changes, promote a comprehensive understanding of the role of science in human affairs, and stress the importance of a scientifically literate workforce.

Areas of emphasis within the classroom should include

- encouraging student interest in science by broadening K–12 initiatives that emphasize the interrelatedness of science and society,
- strengthening curricula to better address societal and ethical concerns, internationalize course content, and focus on communication and analytical skills,
- utilizing an innovative instructional delivery system to reach wider audiences more economically with more effective learning experiences,
- promoting education that relates to emerging technologies and careers, includ-

ing the development and dissemination of career information, networking with science professionals, and stressing scientific literacy in grades K–12.

The overall goals of education lead to the conclusion that society and the community have a significant impact on each child as a student and as a member of society. This impact cannot be ignored in science education. Lawrence Cremin summarized the rationale for community involvement:

> In sum, to think comprehensively about education we must consider policies with respect to a wide variety of institutions that educate, not only schools and colleges, but libraries, museums, daycare centers, radio and television stations, offices, factories, and farms. To be concerned solely with school, given the education world we are living in today, is to have a kind of fortress mentality contending with a very fluid and dynamic situation.[3]

Gladys Dillion, inservice director of Flint Community Schools, Flint, Michigan, contends that the use of community resources

- gives learning in school closer relations with actual life situations, needs, and problems,
- develops the kinds of interest in schoolwork that impel (rather than compel) children to come to school,
- clarifies teaching and learning by making use of concrete, firsthand illustrations and demonstrations,
- provides experience in planning, problem solving, and critical thinking,
- develops skills of observing, asking questions, searching for information, and seeing relationships,
- places knowledge and skill in the context of functional learning: learning to use by doing,
- brings related content areas and skills together and uses them to meet problems and situations,
- provides common learning and common adjustment to problems and differences in needs, abilities, and interests,
- emphasizes achieving good human relations and practicing them,
- increases opportunities for understanding and practicing the responsibilities of community citizenship.[4]

The community can become a laboratory and a supplement to assist the teacher with effective and relevant teaching, but the use of the community resources can also help the teacher get parents involved. Daniel Safran gives examples that directly relate to teachers. Community involvement

- enables teachers to draw upon supplemental and often unique adult resources,
- provides teachers with additional information about the children they teach,
- encourages teachers to recognize other perceptions of what they do,
- permits teachers to understand more about the community their school serves,
- makes possible political alliances between teachers-as-workers and parents-as-consumers to contend with school bureaucracies.[5]

WHAT RESOURCES ARE AVAILABLE?

Before we delve into the use of resources, a definition is in order. *Resources* are "something that can be turned to for support or help."[6] Let us also look to the word *resourceful*. Its definition, "readily able to act effectively"[7] adds additional meaning to our discussion. A teacher uses resources to be effective in the classroom, to provide the most appropriate and meaningful learning experiences to the students. To teach science well and avoid the read-recite-test cycle often present in science instruction, you need to use appropriate and accessible resources.

Now that we are challenged to acquire and use resources, two questions need to be asked: What resources are available? Where can they be located? This chapter will attempt to answer both of these questions. It will be, however, only a partial answer, as you as a teacher must continually attempt to provide the best combination of curriculum, resources, and instructional alternatives as possible. You will add to your resources list as you teach.

Human Resources

A readily available and often ignored resource is your colleagues. As a teacher you may often feel isolated in the classroom. This is not necessary. Using colleagues as resource persons for instructional guidance and assistance enables you to broaden

Volunteers can enrich your science teaching and help children learn to appreciate the community.

educational activities and expand the cooperative nature of the educational enterprise.

Your colleagues—other classroom teachers, the principal, the school nurse, the resource teacher, and the librarian—are all sources of assistance. The experienced teacher who is willing to share activities, materials, and support is a natural aide. Do not overlook a teacher in another school or grade level, as he or she might be able to suggest teaching activities and supply equipment and materials. Upper grade level students are also sources of help to you, as they are often available to provide a demonstration or serve as a teaching assistant or tutor.

Another source of assistance is community volunteers. They can provide a varied and rich composite of expertise. Most communities contain engineers, professors, sewage treatment personnel, medical professionals, computer specialists, and mechanics who are interested in education. In addition, look to parents for suggestions. Corporations and institutions may have an educational officer who can assist by providing names of employees who are willing to volunteer their time and talent to assist within the schools. You should also consider contacting retirement groups, as these individuals are experienced and may have time to volunteer. Contact chambers of commerce, local women's clubs, local, state, or national agencies, or even the yellow pages.

A volunteer can allow the teacher to devote more time to planning, diagnosing the individual needs of students, and prescribing learning activities to meet these needs. Volunteers can offer other benefits, including the following.

- Volunteers increase the number of people available to help the teacher. Educators for years have called student:teacher ratios too high.
- Volunteers often bring skills that professional educators do not have. The educational process maximizes opportunities for all students.
- Perhaps more important than all the other reasons, however, is the positive effects volunteering can have on the volunteers themselves. And the public relations value is certainly important.[8]

Table 12.1, Science Classroom Volunteers, provides a listing of vocations your volunteers might have. Look to individuals such as these to serve as volunteers for your school program.

Not all volunteers, however, want to come into a classroom and make a presentation on their particular areas of expertise; they may prefer instead to be involved in one or more of the following ways:

- demonstrating scientific concepts,
- serving as a mentor,
- tutoring,
- providing science fair project assistance,
- providing career choice assistance,
- reviewing school safety equipment,
- assisting in science competition instruction,

TABLE 12.1 Science Classroom Volunteers

Animals

Zoologist, entomologist, microbiologist, zookeeper, veterinarian, beekeeper, marine biologist, paleontologist, cytologist, animal trainer, physician, forest ranger, physiologist, chemist, ecologist, neurobiologist, wildlife manager, farmer, rancher, geneticist, anatomist, mammalogist, limnologist, nurse, dietitian, X-ray technician, pharmacologist, forensic specialist, pharmacist

Plants

Botanist, paleobotanist, agronomist, horticulturist, farmer, forest manager, chemist, ecologist, geneticist, paleontologist, nutritionist, landscape architect, soil pathologist, soil scientist, conservation officer, park ranger, agricultural extension agent

Weather

Meteorologist, ecologist, agronomist, TV weather forecaster, airport flight controller, geologist, oceanographer, climatologist, fisherman, boat captain, farmer, pilot, environmentalist, soil and water conservation agent

Physical and chemical properties

Chemist, biochemist, pharmacologist, architect, inventor, mechanic, carpenter, molecular biologist, physicist, ecologist, musical instrument maker, musician, toxicologist, metallurgist, geologist, photographer, builder, police lab forensic criminologist, materials scientist, technician, water company technician, chemical engineer, textile engineer, industrial engineer, cosmetics developer, gemologist, acoustical engineer, optical engineer, mechanical engineer, civil engineer, building inspector, potter, nuclear engineer, agricultural engineer, ceramic engineer

Electricity

Physicist, geologist, computer hardware/software designer, electrician, radar technician, amateur radio operator, designer, industrial engineer, electrical engineer, telephone system technician, thermal engineer, mechanical engineer, electronic engineer, electrical inspector, inventor, radio/TV engineer

Earth and space science

Astronomer, geologist, paleontologist, pilot, astronaut, geographer, cartographer, ecologist, physicist, biologist, chemist, surveyor, geotechnical tester, aerial photographer, volcanologist, seismologist, oceanographer, soil scientist, aeronautical engineer, aviation engineer, construction engineer, civil engineer

Behavioral and social science

Animal psychologist, clinical psychologist, marketing professional, business manager, psychiatrist, sociologist, anthropologist, city planner, applied economist, school psychologist, historian, archaeologist, geographer, pollster, market research analyst, demographer, statistician

Source: North Carolina Museum of Life and Science, *Science in the Classroom,* as cited in Triangle Coalition for Science and Technology Education, *A Guide for Planning a Volunteer Program for Science, Mathematics, and Technology Education* (College Park, MD: Triangle Coalition, 1992), p. 59.

- demonstrating societal and technological applications of content,
- furnishing specialized equipment,
- assisting in speakers' bureaus,
- spearheading public awareness campaigns,
- encouraging projects for girls and minorities,
- arranging field trips,
- maintaining equipment,
- assisting with special demonstrations.

Help volunteers feel comfortable in their roles. They may not always be aware of the relevance of their knowledge and skills to elementary students; tell the volunteer about the benefits the students will receive from his or her assistance. The following advice was adapted from a list of suggestions for volunteers prepared by the Lane County Juvenile Department of Eugene, Oregon.

- Invite volunteers to serve as partners.
- Clearly define the differences in the tasks and roles of employees and volunteers.
- Screen volunteers and accept only those who can contribute; check references and interview each candidate as you would a prospective employee.

Give volunteers tips that will help them be successful with your students.

TABLE 12.2 Tips for Teachers Working with Volunteers

Volunteers will come from a wide variety of backgrounds. You as a teacher will want to help the volunteer understand your teaching standards and performance. Your responsibilities to the volunteer include the following:

1. Take time to talk with the volunteer outside the classroom, explaining class procedures, schedules, expectations, and objectives.
2. Prepare the volunteer with specifics about the assignment, where materials can be found, and what the learning objectives are.
3. Make the volunteer comfortable by explaining the obvious support facilities: where to place personal items, find a rest room, and get a cup of coffee.
4. Keep channels of communication open with the volunteer; exchange home telephone numbers if appropriate and convenient. Plan and follow the schedule developed for the volunteer. Inform the volunteer of any schedule change as soon as possible. Keep in mind that volunteers have other responsibilities and cannot be expected to wait for an assignment or materials preparation and that their responsibilities may prevent them from fulfilling their commitment. You will need to be understanding if this occurs.
5. Keep a special folder for regular volunteers with current assignments.
6. Inform volunteers about the students' level of ability and special problems.
7. Encourage your volunteers to sign in and to wear name tags. Other faculty members and administrators will want to acknowledge volunteers in the building.
8. Let every volunteer know how much you and the class appreciate the help. A thank-you note goes a long way toward making the experience a rewarding one for a volunteer.
9. Evaluate the volunteer encounter. Consider the specific request, the background of the volunteer, and the constraints of the situation.

Source: Project Technology Engineering Applications of Mathematics and Science, Yakima Valley/ Tri-Cities MESA, *Tips for Teachers Working with Volunteers,* as cited in Triangle Coalition, p. 54.

- Require a specific commitment of time and resources from volunteers.
- Provide an orientation program to acquaint volunteers with the their functions.
- Provide supervision.
- Make assignments based upon the volunteers' skills, knowledge, interests, capacity to learn, time available, and resources.[9]

For additional information on using volunteers in the classroom, contact the Triangle Coalition for Science and Technology Education (Appendix C). This organization published *A Guide for Planning a Volunteer Program for Science, Mathematics, and Technology Education.*[10] It includes tips for volunteers, volunteer applications, a community organizational needs assessment, tips for volunteers on making presentations, and other related topics. Another source of information on orientation, recruitment, recruitment techniques, volunteer recognition, and volunteer evaluation is *Community Involvement for Classroom Teachers,* by Donna L. Hager-Schoeny et al.[11]

TEACHERS ON SCIENCE TEACHING

How Can You Supplement Science Instruction?

By Barbara J. Smith,
K–1 Science Teacher, Wainwright Elementary School, Houston, TX

There is no better opportunity to show students the relevance of scientific studies than utilizing outside resources from the real world. Students are allowed to see the application of skills, the need for maintaining bases of information, and maybe most importantly, the satisfaction professionals derive from their studies in various branches of science.

One of the easiest sources of information to access is the public museums of natural history. Before taking our children to a museum, someone goes to the exhibits and plans a route and schedule for various groups, taking into account interest levels and curriculum requirements. He or she studies exhibits and writes a study guide with questions covering the main points of the subject. These study guides require our students to apply some thought to their museum time and not just wander from case to case. After the museum trip, we discuss what we have seen, and make the connections between the classroom work and the exhibits.

At Wainwright Elementary, we have an office that serves the magnet math and science program within our school. We have organized a resource file accessible to any staff member on campus. It is there that we collect specialty books, curriculum guides, industry/education guides, handouts from workshops, and teacher-made modules. These modules contain outlines, resource lists, activities, and student work examples from special-interest units that teachers have developed. We also maintain a display area to showcase some of the completed projects.

In addition to talent right here on campus, we frequently look to supplement instruction with the experiences of others. At the beginning of the school year, I have each student fill out an information card that includes a question about what the student's parents do for a living and for hobbies. I usually find several parents with connections to oil, petrochemical, or botanical industry who can help discover resources available through their employers. These parents are more tenacious in finding help with samples, speakers, pamphlets, or other freebies than might be someone who answers my initial phone calls. Additionally, my school district maintains and publishes a speakers' bureau listing.

Organizational and Agency Support

Professional organizations can provide a richly varied form of support. The leading national organization in K–college science education is the National Science Teachers Association (NSTA). It provides services to nearly 50,000 members in the United States and Canada; its activities include professional conventions, publications and journals, and science education position statements.

NSTA holds three regional conventions each fall and an annual national convention in early spring. Attendance at NSTA's national conferences has reached as high as 18,000 science educators. The organization also produces journals appropriate for different grade levels: *Science and Children* for elementary schools; *Science Scope* for middle schools; and *The Science Teacher* for secondary schools. NSTA has developed policy papers on a wide range of topics including technology, the environment, science safety, ethics, drug abuse, and so on. Membership ap-

Alliances with businesses frequently yield a variety of resources and offers. One of my students' favorite field trips is to compete in our business partner's Paper Airplane Contest with some of their engineers. After a module with me, studying the four forces of flight and making many different models, the students start working on their own designs. On the day of the contest, we meet the engineers on the top floor of their parking garage. Categories are set up for time aloft, distance, design aesthetics, and speed. Students and adults compare designs and results, and establish a strong connection between theory and practice.

Single print resources are never enough to support my instruction in science. I begin with the basic parameters established by my state and school district, then comb the book for interesting activities and reading selections. After I align chapters with my plan of attack, the field is wide open to me. I look for activities, names, and ideas in trade journals, newspaper articles, and television programs. Many of the experiment books for children are also help-

ful. I stumble across some of these every time I attend a children's book fair. I prefer to make collections of interesting activities and then figure out how to make them align with curriculum objectives.

I often submit wish lists to our school librarian even when there are no funds available. My recommendations come to mind when funds do become available, and nearly guarantee the usefulness of the new books in our program.

When all else fails, I start asking around. If I have difficulty finding resources for some particular lesson or unit, I mention it to colleagues and friends. Through that route, I have collected non-Newtonian fluid recipes, hosted a visit from a gentleman with a reptile collection, and shown actual core samples from a drilling rig.

Resources are a means to raise interest levels in science and help eliminate some of the learned helplessness that seems so prevalent in science. An added benefit is that it keeps me on my toes and interested in what I am presenting to my students!

plications, samples of their publications, copies of the policy position statements, and an annual catalog of resources and materials can be obtained from the NSTA national headquarters at 1742 Connecticut Avenue NW, Washington, DC 20009-1171. The phone number is (202) 328-5800.

NSTA also has chapters and affiliated groups in most states. The activities of the state organizations vary, but they are an excellent resource for you as a teacher. Their membership fees are usually very low, and they provide a mechanism for you to build your professional contacts and learn from other colleagues. There are also other organizations that provide services to the elementary teacher; see Appendix D for a listing of many of these organizations.

In addition to professional organizations, look for state and federal agencies that provide educational services. The agricultural extension service in each county in the country is a great source of information on soils, insects, and other related material. They are directly connected with a university and will help you to locate additional information. The U.S. Department of Agriculture has many initiatives directed at improving the science education in K–12, through both nontraditional areas such as 4-H and traditional resource curriculum offerings. Another source is the land management or natural resources department within your state government. These offices or departments usually have education directors who provide assistance and training to teachers and who are pleased to recommend such classroom volunteers as geologists, conservationists, and agronomists. To contact agency personnel, use the telephone book for your county seat or state capital.

The National Aeronautics and Space Administration (NASA) has an extensive education infrastructure throughout the country. Regional centers offer educational resources that include lesson plans and extensive slide, photo, and video libraries. Teacher workshops are also arranged through the agency. NASA provides a mobile display bus for hands-on activities for both students and teachers. A listing of the centers can be found in Appendix E.

Your state's department of education is also a source of information and resources. States organize their agencies differently, but most have at least one science consultant. Many states are organized around regional centers that provide inservice training, equipment, and assistance to the classroom teacher. Write to your state science consultant for specific information. Addresses for all state and territorial education agencies can be found in Appendix B.

Telecommunication Networks

A source of a vast amount of assistance is a telecommunications network. The electronic age offers an end to teacher isolation. Beverly Hunter contends that the challenges in scientific research require collaboration among geographically disparate institutions, disciplines, and individuals and also that the challenges of education require new kinds of collaborations across institutional boundaries among individuals whose work was previously isolated.[12] A network increases professionalism as a teacher collaborates with other educators concerning such issues as educational reform or systemic change. By eliminating barriers of time and place, networks provide teachers with greater access to information, knowledge, and points of view. Networkers discuss issues with increased comfort in the absence of traditional hierarchical barriers. They have access to varied resources, including other teachers and resource agencies. A network provides the opportunity to practice deliberation, collegial consensus building, and development of ideas and concepts related to the teaching profession.

Educational researchers are teaming with classroom practitioners to form action collaboratives; parents and teachers are cooperating with school board members and state and national reform organizations; engineers from industry are serving as mentors for teachers and students; experts at supercomputer centers are corresponding with and assisting high school teachers; and professors are working with inner-city science teachers. In science education, closer links between the science practitioners, the community, teachers, and students enable all to participate in the methods, tools, and content of current and relevant scientific investigations.

Networks help you and your students to have greater access to ideas.

Computer communication networks can help these diverse individuals and groups form new kinds of collaboratives that facilitate both classroom instructional practices and the educational reform and restructuring processes. These networks can contribute to the development of a support system for the classroom teacher in the following ways:

- Networks create linkages with other teachers, experts in various disciplines, curriculum developers, state education agencies, professional societies, colleges and universities, business and industry practitioners, federal- and state-supported education projects, and scientific research centers and students.
- Networks increase the access to resources. As national standards are developed and implemented, learning goals and classroom practices will change. Educators need timely access to instructional materials, research, software, and data bases.
- Networks contribute to new paradigms for learning and teaching as collaborative efforts contribute to the accumulating research in education.[13]

Experience with networks has provided lessons of interest to teachers. A partial list of benefits of networks of classroom teachers follows.

- Networks provide support for rapid diffusion of innovative techniques and procedures among teachers. Examples: cooperative learning, field trip sites, national standards.
- Elementary students can actively participate in inquiry-based education in collaboration with other students and scientific resource individuals. Example: comparative water studies between geographically dispersed students (fresh water versus sea water).

- Telecommunications provide a mechanism by which business and industry, the science research communities, and practitioners can make substantive contributions of expertise directly to students and teachers in the schools. Example: scientists at a research facility who answer students' questions without leaving their place of work.

Network technology changes quickly as new software builds bridges between incompatible systems and as hardware changes. Currently, a cost-effective network is PSInet (People Sharing Information Network) software.[14] This telecommunication network software uses a batch-processing system and does not depend on real-time phone connections. All reading and composing of communications is done without connection to a phone line, while data file maintenance is done in short periods of on-line time. The system can be accessed at the user's convenience and provides messaging, conferencing, and data management. The conference structure evolves as users develop topics for discussion. The PSInet software has provided a cost-effective and useful tool for the science educator.

The National Science Foundation (NSF), through a grant to the Council of State Science Supervisors (CSSS), has provided a state server to all states and territories. In addition, some states have developed extensive intrastate networks using PSInet software, and parallel networks have been produced for state and national mathematics leadership and for the members of the Triangle Coalition for Science and Technology Education.

Other networks also exist. The activities on these networks include professional collaborations among teachers, student collaboratives, access to scientific expertise, access to information (libraries, databases), access to computing resources (machines, software), electronic delivery of instructional materials, teacher education enhancement, and electronic publications. Contact your state science consultant (Appendix B) for information on how to access a network.

Alliances and Partnerships

School reform is complex. The late 1980s brought recognition by all facets of society that science and mathematics education is an issue we all must face. Many challenges face the educational system, including converting from an industrial to a technology-driven information age and changing social, cultural, moral, and political forces. Education must become a partnership effort involving educators and parents, business and industry, professional organizations and community-based organizations and alliances. Collaboratives or partnerships, referred to as alliances, can be a key ingredient in educational reform. Business, industry, and labor organizations, in addition to professional associations, are interested and are rapidly getting involved in educational reform. An alliance provides business and education a mechanism for addressing the goal of a better-educated American public.

Alliances can provide

- volunteer scientists/engineers,
- inservice workshops,
- scholarships, fellowships, awards,

TABLE 12.3   An Alliance

- Counters isolation by opening dialogue between teachers and other professionals
- Creates links between communities and schools
- Provides a forum for a systemic approach to solving education problems
- Identifies the elements needed to bring about educational change and develops projects that focus on these elements
- Connects school science with real-world experience
- Provides a broader information base from which teachers can help students make decisions about educational goals and future employment opportunities
- Speaks in a collective voice about education needs, potentials, and strategies
- Aspires to inform the general public and bring about consensus on education problems, needs, and progress
- Empowers all its partners and promotes collaboration
- Provides a mechanism for talented people from various sectors of society to volunteer their expertise for the welfare of America's youth
- Forges creative programs designed to improve precollege science, mathematics, and technology education to help meet the special needs of disparate school districts
- Ties economic development to education by identifying the competencies that will be needed by future workforces, acknowledging that human resources are an important infrastructure for economic development

Source: Adapted from the Triangle Coalition for Science and Technology Education, *A Guide for Building an Alliance for Science, Mathematics, and Technology Education* (College Park, MD: Triangle Coalition for Science and Technology Education, 1991), p. 3.

- clearinghouse/resource databases,
- resource directories,
- satellite or distance learning systems,
- gifted and talented programs,
- traveling science programs,
- speakers' bureaus,
- computer-based instruction,
- internships,
- mentors,
- sabbaticals,
- mini-grants,
- support of educational reform,
- tutors,
- support for statewide systemic change,
- support for legislative action.

There are many associations and agencies that provide technical assistance to alliances. Two groups that provide extensive information and assistance are the National Association of Partnerships in Education (NAPE) and the Triangle Coalition for Science and Technology Education (see Appendix C). If your school is not currently part of an alliance, you may find yourself the initiator of this effort. Contact one of the aforementioned groups for assistance.

FIGURE 12.1   Typical Alliance Interactions

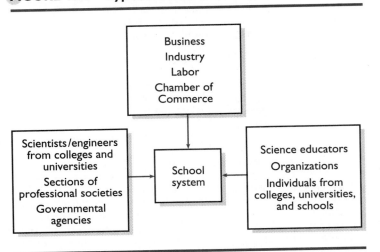

Source: Triangle Coalition for Science and Technology Education, *A Guide for Planning a Volunteer Program for Science, Mathematics, and Technology Education.* (College Park, MD: Triangle Coalition for Science and Technology Education, 1991), p. 4.

Field Trips

A Scenario.   Robert Keddell, Sheryl Barr, Lee Ann Matheu, and Liz Bartley team teach science, mathematics, and social studies at the Patuxent Valley Middle School in Maryland. They provide a comprehensive program of integrated learning that includes hands-on activities within the school and in the nearby Chesapeake Bay area. Field trips, excursions, and environmental hands-on activities abound for their sixth-grade students. Keddell, Barr, Matheu, and Bartley have said:

> The annual excursion to Camp Letts for all sixth graders is an experience we all look forward to. The seventh and eighth graders fill the ears of our current sixth-grade students with tales of the aches and pains, the cold showers, the terrible food, and the reality of living without hair dryers; nevertheless, all students are enthusiastic about the trip.
>
> Our classroom activities prepare our students for a three-day, two-night field trip at a YMCA camp at the mouth of a river that ends in the Bay. It provides us with various types of water specimens and a close, beautiful, and safe environmental field trip. It also allows the parents who serve as chaperons to enjoy the time with their own children and about twenty friends.
>
> Participation is almost 100 percent, as costs are kept at a minimum and the PTA provides scholarships for those in need. Arrangements for these scholarships are made through the school guidance counselors, who contact all parents of students who receive free or reduced-price lunches. None of our students miss the trip due to cost.

*Successful field trips require thoughtful
planning and a philosophy of safety.*

We prepare extensively for safety and keep the parents informed. We have a 24-hour camp nurse who staffs the camp medical central. He is a certified paramedic and provides both emergency care and pampering; he contacts the parents if problems arise. He is also responsible for administering all medications per parents' instructions. Our most serious accidents have all been to parents, several of whom have gone home on crutches following events like the parents' volleyball game.

We require all students to have a series of permission slips signed by their parents or guardians, who are also invited to a parents' information meeting prior to the permission slip deadline. Parents as well as students study the camp map, the class schedule, and of course, the cabin assignments.

We begin to prepare for the trip at the beginning of the school year through outdoor activities and lessons that relate to the classes held during the field trip. Our preparatory activities include investigative studies in salinity, turbidity, food chains, and water studies. Our students use Project WILD and Project WILD Aquatic activities, and we rely heavily on Living in Water, which is provided by the National Aquarium in Baltimore. These activities help students understand the fascinating world of aquatic habitats. Procedures for outdoor excursions, including teaming, movement, and social interactions and responsibilities are also modeled. One of the trip's purposes is to help our students develop an awareness of the ecological balance on earth, as well as the knowledge, skills, and commitment that will enable them to make responsible and informed decisions concerning their environment.

All of the classes scheduled for the trip are taught by teachers from our school. Many sixth-grade teachers accompany the group on the trip and continue assignments from their own classroom instruction. Poetry readings and discussions of societal issues related to the environment and the field trip activities are included in the classroom instruction before the trip. Activities and lessons are integrated across the curriculum and across different subject areas. Some of the field trip staff are also seventh- and eighth-grade teachers with special talents and knowledge.

Our students attend the following classes on a rotating basis during the three days: beach studies, canoeing, seining, swimming, orienteering, nature hiking, the confidence course, insect studies, crabbing, and water testing. All classes contain hands-on, minds-on, full-participation activities. Data collected during the field trip are then interpreted in classroom lessons upon our return. Having completed four trips, we are now able to study trends and periodic variations in the data related to turbidity, water samples, and specimen types.

Although the time and effort of organizing this extended field trip are extensive and involve many participants, we have found it to be one of the most rewarding events of the school year for our students, the parents who volunteer, other colleagues, and ourselves. Using the entire year to prepare lightens our task and builds the enthusiasm and motivation for the students. This trip allows nature to creep into the students' minds, causing a new way of thinking that stimulates wonder, excitement, and interest in their environment that they have not experienced before. The time and effort required to organize and facilitate this adventure seem small in comparison to the benefits to our students.

Planning a Field Trip or Other Excursion.   A trip away from school to a zoo, planetarium, nature park, or science-technology center is an exciting and memorable event for the elementary school student, and it can also be a very educational experience. For urban children, the visit may be their first encounter with animals and plants, telescopes or a computer. The educational potential of an off-site visit is high, but the trip must be organized to provide the educational outcomes expected.

The Worst Scenario.   Angelica Sebik and Ed Hart fall into the school bus seats after loading their third grade students, lunches, notebooks, and cameras for a trip to the local science museum. The trip was planned quickly, as the PTA discovered that there was a small amount of money in the field trip account at the end of the school year.

Ed sighed, "It's good that we're allowed to take this trip, but I feel totally unprepared. Being new to the area, I've never visited the center. Where will the bus

Andrew Mackenzie and Richard White studied the effects of field trips on retention of geography concepts. They used a control group who received only classroom instruction, which included viewing slides of geographic features. The remaining group was split in half. One group took a field trip, listening to further descriptions and checking items off in a manual. The other group participated in activities that required them to observe, record, draw, and make comparisons. All three groups were tested immediately after the trip. Results of this test indicated that the experimental (third) group scored 33.1 compared to the traditional (second) group's 29.2 on the 35 objectives. The control group scored 26.3. A follow-up test a few months later showed a more pronounced difference. The experimental group outscored the traditional group by 29.7 to 17.2. The control group retained the fewest facts, scoring only 13.2. The results are clear: The students who were actively engaged in the learning process learned more and retained more. Active field trips promote higher achievement and more extensive retention.

Source: A. A. Mackenzie and R. White, "Field Work Geography and Long-Term Memory Structures," *American Educational Research Journal*, vol. 19 (1982), pp. 623–632.

park? What displays will be appropriate for our students? How will we ever get them back to the bus?"

Angelica was a little calmer as she responded, "I was there some time ago, and they were remodeling. At that time, there was a live animal area, some interactive computer displays, and a traveling exhibit on dinosaurs. However, I have no idea what displays are currently there or what the remodeling did to the structure. I guess we'll see soon enough."

When they got off the bus, the students spread throughout the building. Several bolted up the stairs to the history avenue, others to see the airplane hanging from the ceiling, while others sat in the boat that floats on a waterbed. Joseph and Marty shot each other with water pistols at a water demonstration in the preschool area.

Some time into the morning, the paging system in the museum called for Angelica or Ed to report to the office. Jennifer had fallen as she ran down the stairs and had a painful ankle. The consensus of the staff was that she needed medical care, but it was soon discovered that the parental permission slips had been left at school and there was no student medical information readily available. Angelica would spend the next two hours trying to contact Jennifer's parents.

Too soon for the students, but not nearly soon enough for Angelica and Ed, it was time to load the bus to return to the school. Students piled on the bus with the usual negotiating about who sits with whom, and the trip home began.

The principal was awaiting the bus and greeted Angelica with an unhappy face. Her look was quickly explained as she stated, "The museum called to tell us that Karen is still there. I have called her stepfather and he is at this moment driving to the city to pick her up. It appears they have one scared little girl!"

Following further discussions and the principal's retreat to her office, Angelica and Ed said simultaneously, "Never again!"

The idea of leaving the classroom and taking students outdoors or to another location can be unnerving for some teachers and students, but field trips and out-of-classroom experiences are important and can be educationally beneficial. Concrete experiences

- help students understand and retain concepts and terms they have read about and discussed in class,
- provide students unique access to resources not available in the classroom,
- help them acquire and retain basic science skills,
- assist students in learning how to observe, record, and interpret data in a meaningful way.

The field trip can be one of the hardest instructional events to control. Unlike the classroom, where students and teachers rely on predictable routines and surroundings, the outside excursion does not contain much that is familiar. Students and teachers may become anxious, resulting in unacceptable behavior by the students and rigid expectations by the teacher. In new situations and surroundings, children need an opportunity to adjust to the location. Angelica and Ed's students were unprepared to focus on any specific activities or demonstrations at the museum. The experience became a social and entertaining event rather than an educational opportunity. If students had been prepared for the educational opportunities provided by the trip, their in-class learning would have been enhanced.

For this reason, field trips should not be a once-a-year occurrence, the last week of school. Excursions of short length with a single goal should start at the beginning of the year, followed by many more extensive and well-planned field trips.

If students are to learn from these out-of-classroom field trips and excursions, they must be planned with a deliberate purpose, and they must use proper teaching methods. Children do learn from fun activities, but to get maximum benefit from an activity it must relate to a topic already studied within classroom or develop skills necessary for this study. This relationship can only be developed through extensive planning prior to the experience. The teacher must determine what concepts are best related to outside-the-classroom experiences and then develop lesson plans that will meet the lesson objectives. The full value of a field trip can only be realized with careful planning, execution, and follow-up.

Preparations before the trip are extremely important. One first grader was very fearful of attending a circus because he thought the animals would not be caged and would be a threat. An explanation during the preparation phase of the field trip assured him that there was no danger. The students must understand why they are going and what they must watch for while they are there. Other preparatory activities include using pictures and books, learning vocabulary words, and having preliminary discussions.

In addition to instructional planning, the teacher must be attentive to the policies and procedures. Such matters as permission slips, insurance, provisions for eating, transportation, and safety precautions are examples of programmatic plan-

FIGURE 12.2   Parental Permission for Out-of-Classroom Activity

Date: _____

School: _____

     Your child's class is planning a school trip on (date) _____ to

_____

as part of their class studies. The group will leave the school at _____ and will

return at approximately _____. Your child will be under the same supervision as is

maintained during time spent in the school.

     This excursion will enhance in-class studies on the topic of _____.

Attendance at the field trip will enable your child to participate in educational activities that

meet the planned objectives of classroom learning.

     If you have any questions relating to the trip or its educational value, feel free to

contact _____ (teacher) at _____ (telephone number).

     Please express your approval of participation by signing the slip below and returning

it to the teacher.

_____

    Teacher

_____

    Principal

- -

     I give permission for my child, _____ to attend the

trip scheduled on _____ (date) to _____ knowing

that every precaution will be taken for his or her safety.

_____

   Date   Parent or guardian

Source: Adapted from Donna L. Hager-Schoeny and Diane Galbreath, *Utilizing Community Resources in the Classroom: An In-Service Reference Collection* (Charlottesville, VA: University of Virginia, Mid-Atlantic Center for Community Education, 1982), p. 39.

ning. Your supervisor should be involved in planning for a field trip, in addition to students and parents.

    Permission slips are customary and required by most school administrators. An example of such a permission slip is shown in Figure 12.2; note that a parent or guardian's signature is required only after all information concerning the trip is provided. This signed slip is not a waiver of responsibility to the teacher or school system by the signer. It is merely evidence that the signer knew and approved of the activity. Adherence to the recommendations of Table 12.4, Safety Considerations for Field Trips, will alleviate many potential problems.

Field trips need not be long. Many educationally sound trips are possible within the school grounds or the community very near the school. Such trips are inexpensive and provide the advantage of allowing follow-up through return visits to the site for extended observations. Look for opportunities within the school grounds: Take a walk, looking for animals, shadows, trees, houses, or insects. Allow students to explore the dirt in the playground for soil studies or rock samples; then enhance these studies by inviting a local geologist or agronomist to visit. A problem-solving activity for a future archaeologist can be developed in a vacant lot. Students can study insects, smells, and weeds and other plants through a visit to a small patch of grass. Worms, ants, beetles, and slugs can be found within a foot of soil. Recycling, erosion, and raindrop effects are other examples of opportunities for science study within your own schoolyard. Use your imagination and creativity to design valuable field trips that utilize local facilities.[15]

Other traditional field trip facilities are accustomed to guests and are very helpful with trips. Many museums and zoos offer a packet for teachers to use in the classroom prior to the visit. Through these materials students learn concepts like *rare animals, captivity,* or *ecosystems.* The educational value of a field trip can be related to the science goals discussed in Chapter 3. A sense of custodianship (collective responsibility for the environment over a period of time) is one example of a program goal that is enhanced by a field trip. Look to traditional locations for some not-so-traditional trips. For example, a visit to the library can provide an exceptional opportunity to study the chemistry of paper preservation.

Also look to nontraditional locations like a hospital to study technology developments. The local dairy, beach, mountain, quarry, military base, fish farm, sewage and water treatment plants, or a neighbor's home are other sites to visit. Such nontraditional sites as a motorcycle shop can demonstrate a complex machine; a visit to a photography studio can demonstrate chemical reactions in film development.

Teachers can assist each other by developing a school resource file that lists human resources, governmental agencies, and local community resources arranged in categories. Including the name of a contact person and appropriate lesson plans would also be helpful. It is most useful if one or two individuals are responsible for organizing the information provided by the entire staff. The files should be kept current and updated as necessary.

The best source currently available for resource lists is published by the National Science Resources Center of the Smithsonian Institution. This book, entitled *Science for Children: Resources for Teachers,*[16] is an outstanding source of information. It includes curriculum materials, supplementary resources, and sources of information and assistance.

Field Trip Procedure Review.   Table 12.5 provides an outline of the advantages, objectives, preparation, follow-up, and selection criteria for field trips.

TABLE 12.4 Safety Considerations for Field Trips

1. The teacher has visited the field trip site prior to involving students there.	____
2. The activity is a well-planned part of the science course.	____
3. The activity is appropriate for the mental and physical age of the students taking the trip.	____
4. Transportation is via school or school-sanctioned vehicles only.	____
5. Clear, appropriate rules of behavior are established, and the students understand them.	____
6. All field trip dangers are pointed out to students in advance and again when students arrive at the site.	____
7. Students are dressed according to the demands of the environment and weather.	____
8. Supervision is increased according to the novelty and danger inherent in the field trip environment.	____
9. Equipment is in a proper state of repair.	____
10. Equipment is designed for the mental and physical ages of the students using it.	____
11. Students know how to use the equipment properly.	____
12. If students are to be separated from the teacher at any time, prearranged meetings are planned.	____
13. The buddy system of pairing students in teams is used to help ensure safety and mutual responsibility.	____
14. The teacher is aware of any student medical needs (allergies, medication schedules, phobias).	____
15. Signed parent or guardian permission forms have been received and processed.	____
16. For extended-length field trips, appropriate medical and liability insurance policies have been obtained.	____
17. First-aid kits appropriate for the environment are available.	____
18. All safety procedures have been demonstrated and are understood by students.	____
19. The teacher has talked with the landowner or proprietor concerning hazards and special points of interest before involving students at the site.	____

Source: Jack Gerlovich, *Safe Science Teaching: A Diskette for Elementary Educators,* computer program (Waukee, IA: JaKel, 1990).

CHAPTER SUMMARY

Sometime in the future, you and your students may pick up a newspaper and read a headline like "Genetic Engineering Unravels the Aging Process" or "Ozone Hole Increases." The stories following these headlines will be important to both you and your students. They will affect your lives, and as citizens you may need to form an opinion or make a decision concerning your future related to this information. Being able to understand the consequences of your choices is very important to you and to your students.

As a teacher, you will need to ask yourself if you have done your best to provide your students with the skills they need to make these decisions. The scientific and technological knowledge in our world is changing so rapidly that it is difficult to prepare students for any decision. Textbooks cannot keep pace with the new discoveries in science,

TABLE 12.5   Field Trips

A field trip

- blends school life with the outside world, putting children in direct touch with things, people, environments, occupations, and trends under learning situations
- involves the consideration and solution of problems arising from individual and group participation in natural social situations
- affords opportunities to develop keenness and accuracy of observation
- helps children to organize new information in relation to their experiences
- develops initiative and self-motivation, making pupils active agents rather than passive participants
- arouses ambitions, raises aspirations, and determines aims
- provides valuable correlation of subjects
- affords opportunities for practicing cooperative learning by giving students the chance to take part in group discussions, distinguish facts from opinions, listen to what other individuals have to say, and discuss important problems
- provides a means of sharing ideas

Objectives of a field trip are to

- provide first-hand observation and new information
- stimulate interest in a topic
- broaden students' backgrounds and provide new vistas
- provide common experiences in planning
- enable the teacher to observe behavior in new situations
- build group morale
- provide experiences for learning social skills
- study concepts acquired in class
- arouse the interest and curiosity of students
- utilize magazines, newspapers, picture books, textbooks, and other mass media productions
- elicit main areas of interest

Student and teacher preparation should include

- learning which resource location would be most valuable to study
- planning activities for the trip
- post-trip interpretation of data
- field trip protocol

Preparation steps include

- clearance with parents and administrators
- insurance for long trips
- advance visit by teacher to site
- simple rules of conduct and dress
- safety precautions
- clearance with other teachers
- means of safe transportation
- provisions for meals

Follow-up activities may include

- diaries, photo collections, bulletin boards, articles in school and/or town newspaper, thank-you notes
- in-class interpretation and analysis of data, if appropriate

Criteria for selecting a field trip are that it

- relates to a topic under discussion, is a follow-up on a topic, or will spur study of a new topic
- provides opportunities for learning that can be better facilitated by direct experience than through textbooks, films, or other methods
- gives students experiences that they cannot easily have alone, in small groups, or with parents
- leads to a variety of classroom activities, such as oral and written reports, dramatizations, expression through art and music, reading and research, graphic displays, bulletin board exhibits, interpretation of data, and prediction skills
- is not be too long for the time available, is inexpensive, and can be offered to all students
- has the approval of parents and school administration

Source: Adapted from Donna Hager-Schoeny and Diane Galbreath, *Utilizing Community Resources in the Classroom: An In-Service Reference Collection.* (Charlottesville: University of Virginia, Mid-Atlantic Center for Community Education, 1982), pp. 37–43.

but you as a classroom teacher can supplement your text and your program with other experiences and opportunities.

You can stimulate learning by serving as the bridge between the resources that are relevant and available to you and the students in your classroom. The effective use of a volunteer or a field trip may bring the real world outside of the classroom inside to your students. An alliance with a business may provide the expertise and equipment needed for laboratory studies in a sci-

ence learning center, while a telecommunications network may provide you with current and timely education reform information. Safe field trips allow your students to learn science in relevant and cutting-edge locations.

Your use of resources is only limited by your imagination and energy. They can provide learning opportunities that stimulate your students to scientific interest and inquiry. Science can be fun, and resources can be the toys.

DISCUSSION QUESTIONS AND PROJECTS

1. Brainstorm resources not mentioned in this chapter that are useful in elementary science instruction. How can you enhance your instructional methods by including resources in your teaching plans?

2. Brainstorm ideas related to the development of a school resource file and ways to ensure that it is useful and current.

3. Compose a list of supplemental resource curricula that you would like to include in your lesson plans on three different topics. Compare your list with that of two or more other classmates; combine the lists to keep for future reference.

4. Locate three hands-on resources not mentioned in this chapter that have the potential to be used within an elementary classroom for science instruction. Define the planned use and identify specific goals that would be met by the use of these resources.

5. Identify one resource that will enhance lessons in environmental education, electricity, digestion, and plate tectonics and indicate the correlation with your stated goals and objectives.

6. Identify an activity from one resource curriculum that will enhance a lesson by providing experiences that will increase your students' skills in observing, questioning, classifying, measuring, and using numbers.

7. Identify three resources useful in the instruction of students with special needs.

8. Research the purposes, fee structure, and services of the National Science Teachers Association and identify publications that will be useful to you as you plan lessons in science. Locate membership information, meeting schedules, and publications from your state or local science education organization.

9. Identify three locations in your geographic area that are appropriate for a field trip for elementary students. For each location, identify the goals and objectives of the current instruction that will be enhanced by the field trip, how the field trip will engage the abilities and interests of the children, the planning needed prior to the field trip, and a list of classroom activities to be included in instruction because of the trip.

10. Identify resources that will assist in making your classroom instruction non-gender biased.

11. Visit a science museum or other facility in your local area. Compile a list of exhibits that would be appropriate for elementary students. Indicate the topics and student skills that would be enhanced by a field trip.

12. Compare and contrast the two field trip scenarios in this chapter. Develop a list of procedures that Angelica and Ed should have followed prior to their trip.

NOTES

1. Western Regional Environmental Education Council, Project WILD and Project WILD—Aquatic (Golden, CO, 1987).

2. John Dewey, *Democracy and Education* (New York: Macmillan, 1916), as cited in Larry E. Decker, *Foundation of*

Community Education (Charlottesville, VA: Mid-Atlantic Center for Community Education, 1981), p. 39.

3. Lawrence A. Cremin, *Public Education* (New York: Basic Books, 1976), pp. 22–23.

4. Gladys Dillion, mimeograph cited in Donna L. Hager-Schoeny et al., *Community Involvement for Classroom Teachers*, 2d ed. (Charlottesville, VA: Community Collaborators, 1977), p. 27.

5. Daniel Safran, *Preparing Teachers for Parent Involvement* (Menlo Park, CA: Center for the Study of Parent Involvement, 1974), p. 1.

6. Funk & Wagnalls, *Standard Dictionary* (New York: Reader's Digest, 1968), p. 1073.

7. Ibid.

8. Donna L. Hager-Schoeny and Diane Galbreath, *Utilizing Community Resources in the Classroom: An In-Service Reference Collection* (Charlottesville: University of Virginia, Mid-Atlantic Center for Community Education, 1982), pp. 47–52.

9. Hager-Schoeny, p. 20.

10. Triangle Coalition for Science and Technology Education, *A Guide for Planning a Volunteer Program for Science, Mathematics, and Technology Education* (College Park, MD: Triangle Coalition for Science and Technology Education, 1992).

11. Hager-Schoeny.

12. Beverly Hunter, "Linking for Learning: Computer-and-Communications Network Support for Nationwide Innovation in Education," *Journal of Science Education and Technology*, vol. 1, no. 1, 1992, pp. 23–34.

13. Ibid.

14. International Business Machines, *People Sharing Information Network, PSInet 1.01*, computer program (Palo Alto, CA: IBM Palo Alto Scientific Center).

15. Jacalyn K. Wood, "Take a Field Trip Close to Home," *Science and Children* (October 1986), pp. 26–27.

16. National Science Resources Center, *Science for Children: Resources for Teachers* (Washington, DC: National Academy Press, 1988).

17. Hager-Schoeny, pp. 37–43.

ADDITIONAL READINGS

If you are interested in learning more about the use or source of resources raised in this chapter consider the following sources.

Barbara S. Spector, *Community Resources for Meaningful Learning* (Dubuque, IA: Kendall Hunt Publishing, 1988). This is one of many fine books available that delves into the use of community resources to enhance classroom practices. It provides both traditional and nontraditional community resources.

Ellen Doris, *Doing What Scientists Do: Children Learn to Investigate Their World* (Portsmouth, NH: Heinemann, 1991). This easy-to-read and informative book provides insights into creating an environment for science in the classroom and discusses interpreting children's work.

Marvin N. Tolman and James O. Morton, *Earth Science Activities for Grades 2–8*, *Life Science Activities for Grades 2–8*, and *Physical Science Activities for Grades 2–8* (West Nyack, NY: Parker Publishing, 1986). This series is a collection of hundreds of stimulating hands-on experiences to develop students' thinking and reasoning skills along with important science concepts and facts.

T. K. Leim, *Invitation to Science Inquiry* (Lexington, MA: Science Inquiry Enterprises, 1987). This text provides hands-on activities for use in the classroom.

David L. Drotar, *Learn and Discover: Fun Science* (New York: Creative Child Press, 1988). This inexpensive coloring-book-like publication serves as an excellent source of easy, inexpensive demonstrations for teachers to use in the classroom.

Sara Stein, *The Science Book* (New York: Workman Publishing, 1980). This book provides knowledge in the areas of Outsides (animals in the home); Insides (observations on the inside of plants and animals); and Invisibles (things too small to see).

Science and Children, published by the National Science Teachers Association, Washington, DC. This periodical provides information on content, teaching practices, educational research, and professional activities of elementary school science.

Science for Children: Resources for Teachers, published by the National Science Resources Center of the Smithsonian Institution and the National Academy of Science (Washington, DC: National Academy Press, 1988). This document contains a comprehensive listing of curriculum materials, supplementary resources, and sources of information and assistance.

Science Scope is published by the National Science Teachers Association, Washington, DC. This periodical provides information on content, teaching practices, educational research, and professional activities related to middle school science.

PART FOUR

Learning Activities and Teaching Materials to Meet the Goals of Elementary and Middle School Science

The next three sections contain examples of commercial and public domain supplementary materials as they are *modified* to meet the goals for elementary science. Section I is devoted to life science lessons, Section II includes physical science lessons and Section III contains earth science lessons. Our intention is to show the techniques for modification, planning, and methods of teaching emphasized in earlier chapters. Part IV is a resource for ideas and an exemplar of modification techniques.

The following section contains over 150 activities for life, physical, and earth science. These activities are found within sixty lessons designed to fit the 4–E science learning cycle format suggested in the text. A teacher making use of this format is most concerned with the science to be taught in the lesson—the concept. A clearly written concept statement can be found at the beginning of each lesson. Any secondary concepts that may be important to the lesson are also identified in the beginning of the lesson.

The student outcomes or behavioral objectives are included in the evaluation phase of each lesson. This phase identifies what is expected of the student by the time he or she completes all the activities in the lesson. Those of you who expect to see objectives or learner outcome listed first in an activity are encouraged to carefully look at the evaluation phase of each lesson before starting the exploration phase.

The grade levels suggested in the beginning of each lesson are simply that—suggestions. Each teacher knows best his or her students' limitations. If, upon reading the lesson, you find the activities too difficult or too easy for your students, then by all means find a lesson more suitable for your students' ability levels.

You will not find a time limit on the lessons.

Lessons using a science learning cycle format may take one forty-minute class period or may take several class meetings. One lesson may represent a unit or just one piece of that unit. The length of time for each lesson will depend on the ability level of your students and the amount of detail for each activity. Generally, the lessons are set up so that the exploration phase will take one or two class meetings, the explanation phase one class meeting, and the expansion phase one or two class meetings. Questions that cover the goals of personal growth, science-technology-society, academic growth, and career awareness may be asked at any time during the lesson. Just because they are listed after the expansion phase does not mean they have to wait until after expansion to be asked. The evaluation phase may also be given in parts, during or after the exploration phase, as part of the explanation phase, and during or after the expansion phase.

These lessons are designed to give your students a chance to thoroughly explore a science concept. Your students will enjoy the lessons when they are given a chance to engage in the science thinking skills to create the concepts for themselves. The teacher's work comes before the students set foot in the classroom. Collect all the necessary materials for each activity. Assign members of a cooperative group to gather these materials for their group. Make sure that each student is aware of any safety precautions before engaging in the science activity. If certain skills are required before the students can engage in an activity, then spend the time teaching those skills before starting the new activity. The advance work done by the teacher will insure the success of a lesson presented in a science learning cycle.

SECTION I

Life Science Activities

Lesson Name	Grade Level	Activities
Plant Parts and Needs	K–2	Plant Dig • Eggshell Planters • Food Storage
Chlorophyll Production: Changing Leaf Color	K–2	Leaf Collection, Press, and Mobile • Life of a Tree Drama
Osmosis and Capillary Action	2–5	Colored Carnations • Three-Way Split
Plant Photosynthesis	5–8	Radish Growth: Light versus Dark • In a Bag • In Soil
Starch Exploration	6–8	Microscopic Starch • Beans and Starch Grains
Colors of Wildlife	K–2	Animal Similarities and Differences • Create a Rainbow Animal
Shelter	K–2	Shelter Drawing • Animal Homes
Wildlife and Domesticated Animals	K–3	Animal Needs • Domestic versus Wild Charades
Habitat	3–6	Basic Needs Lap Sit • Animal Habitat Research, Collage, and/or Diorama
Crickets: Basic Needs of an Organism	5–8	Cricket Needs • Cricket Behavior
Animal Adaptations	6–8	Mitten and Tweezer Beaks • Fish Adaptations
Owl Pellets	6–8	Owl Pellet Dissection • Owl Research or Field Trip
Humans and Trash	K–2	Trash and Animals • Classroom Landfill and Recycling
Useful Waste	4–6	Rating Garbage • Litter-Eating Critter • Making Paper
Litter in Our Waterways	3–6	Sink-or-Float Litter • Plastic Food
Slogans and the Environment	6–8	Slogan Categorization • Environmental Slogans
Sense of Taste	K–2	Tongue Mapping • Chocolate Chip Tongue Maps and Peanut Tongue Maps
Skeleton	1–3	Bones Assembly Line • Newsprint Bone Bodies • Hokey-Pokey Skeleton
Temperature Receptors on Skin	3–5	Soaking Hands • Hot/Cold Receptor Mapping
Building Microscope Skills	4–6	Microscope Use and Crystal Comparisons • Charcoal Crystals

GRADE K–2

Life Science

DISCIPLINE

Plant Parts and Needs

Concept to be invented
Main idea—The basic parts of a plant are roots, stems, and leaves.

Secondary concepts that are important to expansion
Soil or some nutrient containing medium, air, water, and light are necessary for plant growth.

Materials needed
For exploration:

large paper or large plastic
 bags
spoons for digging, or a spade or
 shovel
white paper

resource books on plants
poster paint
art paper
crayons
markers

For expansion:

eggshells (halves or larger)
potting soil
mung beans

water
sunlight or artificial light
colored markers

⊃ **Safety precautions:** Always have proper adult:student ratio when taking the students away from the school campus. Make sure that the students are buddied up and that they are able to cross streets safely and know enough not to talk to strangers while walking to the dig site or while on the site.

Make sure all students can identify any poisonous plants at the dig site, such as poison ivy or poison oak. If large amounts of poisonous plants are in the area it may be better to simply choose a different site.

Demonstrate to the students a safe method for digging up the plants and make sure they practice what was demonstrated. Remind the students never to put anything in their mouths unless the teacher gives prior approval. Do not eat the plants!

1. EXPLORATION: Which process skills will be used?

Observing, identifying, comparing

What will the children do?

Plant, dig

Take the students on a walking field trip to an area near the school where plants can be dug up without harming the environment. Identify the plants the students may dig up and then allow them time to dig, making sure they get most of the root systems. Instruct the students to put their plants in bags and bring them back to school. Once back in class, ask the students to choose one of their plants and spread it out on a piece of white paper. Ask them to use the materials provided to draw pictures of their plants.

2. EXPLANATION/CONCEPT INVENTION: What is the main idea? How will the main idea be identified?

Concept: The basic parts of a plant are roots, stems, and leaves.

Once the students have drawn their pictures, provide them with resource books that identify other plants. Ask the students the following questions: How are these plants different from the plant in front of you? How are they the same? What do all of our plants have in common? Continue with this line of questioning until the students understand that the basic parts of a plant are roots, stems, and leaves. Ask the students to return to the drawings they created of their plants. Ask them to label the roots, stems, and leaves in their drawings. At this time the teacher may provide the students with the common names for their plants, or ask the students if they already know what they dug up, or ask them to look through the resource books to identify their plants.

3. EXPANSION OF THE IDEA: Which process skills will be used?

Observing, gathering data, recording data, interpreting data, manipulating materials.

How will the idea be expanded?

Eggshell planters

Help the students collect eggshells (halves or larger). Ask the students to draw two eyes and a nose on their eggshells with colored markers. Provide potting soil so that the students can fill the shells with soil and sprinkle mung beans on top. Have them put a little more soil on top of the seeds. Sprinkle a small amount of water on the soil. Place the filled shells near the window. Challenge the students to observe the shells each day. When they discover bean sprouts appearing, have them draw a smile on the shell to complete the face.

Once the beans are well grown, ask the students to pull one of the sprouts out. Can you identify its root, stem, and leaves? Ask the students to describe what they did to help the plant grow from the bean seed to the sprout. What things were necessary for plant growth? Make a list on the board. Review with them why the items they identified are necessary for plant growth. Discuss the fact that leaves are necessary to plants because they are the place in the plant where food is created. The water and minerals are taken from the soil through the roots and brought up to the leaves. Gases from the air enter the plant through the leaf, and with the help of sunlight the leaves make food for the plant.

Additional ideas for expansion

Food storage

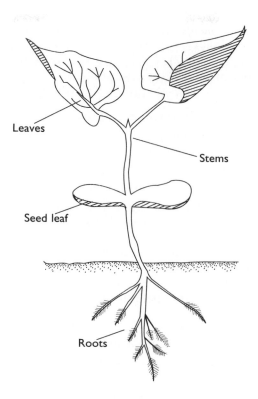

The teacher can share with the students ways in which plants store food and what humans do with this knowledge. For instance, when food is stored, such as in nuts and seeds, the leaves drop off because they are no longer needed. Also, food is stored in various parts of plants. Provide the students with actual fruits, vegetables, and seeds (or pictures of them) to classify. Make a bulletin board of drawings done by students of roots, stems, leaves, flowers, fruits, and seeds eaten by man. Hang the pictures near the appropriate term. Some possibilities are roots (beets, carrots, radishes, sweet potatoes), stems (asparagus, celery, green onions), underground stems (onions, potatoes), leaves (lettuce, spinach, cabbage), flowers (artichokes, broccoli, cauliflower), fruits (apples, pears, tomatoes, peaches, plums, apricots), seeds (nuts, peas, beans).

Why is the idea important for personal development?

- What would your life be like without plants? Why do you need to take care of plants?
- Do you think taking care of plants develops responsibility?
- Ask the students if any of their parents or grandparents have a garden or grow plants indoors. Discuss the special care these plants need. Discuss how large fields of plants can be watered.

Why is the idea important for science-technology-society?
- Why is research done on growing plants?
- Why do plants sometimes need to be fertilized?
- Do all plants have to be in soil in order to grow? Hydroponic farming does not use soil. Can you think of what it uses instead of soil to grow plants?

Why is the idea important for academic growth?
- Why do you need to know what plants need to grow?
- What must we do to keep the plants healthy?
- During what part of a plant's life cycle can it grow without sunlight? Why?

Why is the idea important for career awareness?
- Discuss with the students jobs or professions that involve caring for plants, such as gardening, working as a forest ranger, selling vegetables in a grocery store, or working in a nursery or flower shop.
- Growing and caring for plants takes a lot of work; some of the people who do this are agronomists, horticulturists, florists, botanists, and nutritionists.
- Ask your parents to help you discover what Luther Burbank and Gregor Mendel did to help us understand plant growth better.

4. EVALUATION: How will the students show what they have learned?

Upon completing the activities the students will be able to
- identify the root, stem, and leaf on a complete plant;
- name the four things most plants need to live;
- when given potting soil, sunflower seeds, water, and a cup, demonstrate the steps necessary to grow and care for a plant;
- when given a beet, spinach, and a piece of asparagus, identify which is a root, which a stem, and which a leaf.

Chlorophyll Production—Changing Leaf Color

GRADE
K–2
Life
Science
DISCIPLINE

Concept to be invented
Main idea—Living green plants produce chlorophyll for food.

Secondary concepts that are important to expansion
Trees can be classified into two groups—those that lose their leaves and those that do not.

Materials needed
For the entire class: Sharon Gordon, *Now I Know Trees* (Mahwah, NJ: Troll Associates, 1983), or an equivalent; collection bags (one per student, paper lunch bag size), wax paper, electric iron, hole punch, yarn, scissors, towel.

⊃ **Safety precautions:** Pair up the students with buddies before taking them outdoors. Go over safety rules when outside the school building: Stay with your buddy. Respect the other students who are still indoors by staying quiet. Do not talk to strangers who may come on the school grounds. Stay within eyesight of the teacher. Do not eat anything you find outside. Wash your hands after collecting the leaves. Do not poke each other with the scissors; use them only while seated. Stay away from the hot iron.

1. EXPLORATION: Which process skills will be used?

Observing, questioning, classifying, using time relationships, making assumptions, inferring, hypothesizing, drawing conclusions, communicating

What will the children do?

Leaf collection

Begin the lesson by reading *Now I Know Trees* or any book that introduces students to the idea of trees losing leaves and the production of chlorophyll. Use the story to initiate a discussion about leaves on trees.

Give each student a collection bag. Take the students outside. Let them explore the area and use the bag to collect different kinds of leaves. Ask the students to look for signs that fall has arrived. Gather the students together to discuss their findings. Ask them to describe their observations in terms of colors, shapes, and sizes. Return to the classroom.

2. EXPLANATION/CONCEPT INVENTION: What is the main idea? How will the main idea be identified?

Concept: Living green plants produce chlorophyll for food.

Ask the students the following questions to help invent the concept: How many different colors did you find? What do you think causes the leaves to change color? What do plants use as food?

All plants, including trees, make their food, called chlorophyll, using sunshine and water. The chlorophyll makes the leaves turn green. Why are the leaves green? Green is the color of the chlorophyll. What do you think would happen if the trees didn't get any water? Any sunlight? When fall comes the amount of sunlight decreases. As the ground hardens due to colder weather, it becomes more difficult for the tree to get water out of the ground and up to its leaves. As a result, the trees cannot produce as much food. Since food is scarce, the tree shuts off the food supply to the leaves in order to have enough for itself. Without the chlorophyll, the leaves are no longer green.

What color are the leaves on the ground? Why are they no longer green?

Did all the trees you observed lose their leaves? Why or why not? Some trees stay green all year long. Does anyone know what these trees are called? There are two kinds of trees. The ones that lose their leaves are called *deciduous.* The second kind are called conifers. Most conifers remain *evergreen,* but some, like the larches, lose their leaves.

3. EXPANSION OF THE IDEA: Which process skills will be used?

Formulating models, experimenting, communicating

How will the idea be expanded?

Life of a tree drama, leaf press, and mobile

Have the students find their own space in the classroom with plenty of room to move. The students will dramatize the life of a tree. The teacher will narrate, talking through the seasons and the loss of the leaves. Free expression should be encouraged. Suggest using the arms for branches and hands for leaves.

Help the students to create leaf mobiles. The teacher will press the students' collected leaves between layers of waxed paper. The students can cut around the shape of the leaves, punch holes, and hang with yarn.

Why is the idea important for personal development?

- How does the approach of fall affect your life? How does the change of any season affect you?
- What do you think you would need if you could make your own food like a tree?

Why is the idea important for science-technology-society?

- Do you think we can trick a tree into never losing its leaves? What would we need to do in order for that to happen? How would this benefit society?

Why is the idea important for academic growth?

- How and why do leaves change colors?
- What is chlorophyll?
- Do all trees loose their leaves in the fall?
- Are the needles on a pine tree leaves?

Why is the idea important for career awareness?

- Who might we ask to find out more about leaves and the change of the seasons?
- Would a Christmas tree farm owner have a job if Christmas trees were deciduous?

4. EVALUATION: How will the students show what they have learned?

Upon completing the activities the students will be able to

- explain what chlorophyll does for plants,
- name the two groups of trees,
- dramatize how and why a tree loses its leaves.

2–5

Life
Science

Osmosis and Capillary Action

Concepts to be invented

Main idea—Fluid is drawn up the stem of a plant by osmosis and capillary action.

Secondary concepts that are important to expansion

Fiber membranes run throughout a flower from the roots to the petals.

Materials needed

For exploration (per student group):

two to three white, long-stem
  carnations
food coloring

two clear cups or glass beakers
water
knife or sharp blade

⊃ **Safety precautions:** Take care not to drop glass or beakers thus increasing the likelihood of cuts. Use caution if using the knife or sharp blade.

1. EXPLORATION: Which process skills will be used?

Observing, predicting, reasoning, inferring, recording data

What will the children do?

Colored carnations

Separate the class into groups of four to six students. Give each group two carnations and two beakers or clear cups. Fill the cups or beakers with water. Dissolve one color of food coloring in one cup and a different color in the other. Dark colors like red or blue work well. Take one of the carnations and cut a fresh end on the stem (this may be done by the teacher with students in each group assisting). After this cut, split the stem in half, starting a cut with the knife and further splitting it along the fibers without breaking them. Place each half of the stem in each beaker and observe the white flower. Record your observations over three-minute time periods for a total of 30 minutes.

2. EXPLANATION/CONCEPT INVENTION: What is the main idea? How will the main idea be identified?

Concept: Fluid is drawn up the stem of a plant by osmosis and capillary action.

Ask the students questions such as the following to help invent this concept: What did you observe during the first three minutes of this experiment? How long did it take before you observed any changes in your flower? What were these changes? Why do you think they happened?

The stems of green plants support the plants and hold up the leaves and flowers. Some plants, like this carnation, have thin, green stems. Other plants,

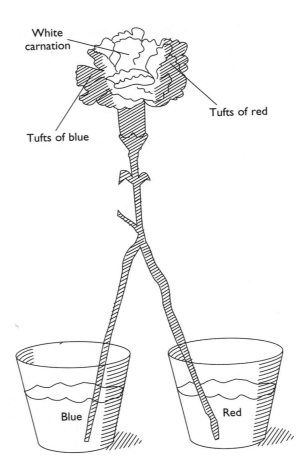

White carnation

Tufts of red

Tufts of blue

Blue

Red

such as trees, have thick wooden stems. The trunk of an oak tree is its stem. It holds heavy branches and thousands of leaves. Water and food move up and down the plant through the stem. Water moves through special tubes in the stem. The water goes from the roots to the leaves and other parts of the plant. Other tubes carry food from the leaves to the roots and other plant parts. The colored water in our experiment is drawn up the stem of the carnation by osmosis and capillary action. The water molecules diffuse through the fiber membranes from a less to a larger concentration of plant sap (osmosis). The fibers are so tiny that the adhesive force of the water molecules to the fiber walls becomes very great. This capillary force in combination with the osmotic pressure sucks the water up the flower.

3. EXPANSION OF THE IDEA: Which process skills will be used?

Communicating, problem solving, experimenting, recording data

How will the idea be expanded?

Three-way split

When the stem is split three ways, it is very likely that the flower will be three colored. Ask the students to design an experiment to demonstrate this. This will show that the fibers must somehow run all the way from the stem to the petals of the flower. Encourage the students to experiment with how many ways they can get the stem to split to create as multicolored a flower as possible.

Ask the students to think about the following: What would happen if the stem were cut irregularly, such as diagonally? What if a cut was made that was jagged and cut across the fibers? How many other types of plants can be used to demonstrate this same phenomenon? Demonstrate this.

Why is the idea important for personal development?

- If you wanted to give someone a bouquet of carnations to celebrate the Fourth of July and could only find white ones, what can you do to those to get red and blue ones too? Do you think the same thing is done by florists?
- If you were to receive a bouquet of flowers and you wanted them to stay fresh for a long time what should you do for them, and why?

Why is the idea important for science-technology-society?

- How has knowledge of capillary action been used to create more efficient car engines?
- Artificial hearts and other organs are continuously being developed. How will osmosis and capillary action of blood affect the function of these artificial organs?

Why is the idea important for academic growth?

- What force is pulling the colored solution up the stem of the carnation in this activity?
- What if the flower were placed in *clear* water? Would the liquid still be drawn up the stem? How could you tell?
- Could a plant live without a stem? Why or why not?

Why is the idea important for career awareness?

- Can you name some people who work with plants?
- Why do you think it might be important for a farmer to understand plant growth? A florist? A grocer?
- Would you like to work in any of these occupations? Why or why not?

4. EVALUATION: How will the students show what they have learned?

Upon completing the activities the students will be able to

- explain the purpose of splitting the stem in two during this lesson;
- demonstrate their knowledge of capillary action by explaining the process using a piece of celery, food coloring, a beaker, and water;
- observe several plants in various stages of watering (underwatered, overwatered, just right) and explain why the plant looks as it does.

GRADE

5–8

Life
Science

DISCIPLINE

Plant Photosynthesis

Concept to be invented

Main idea—Plants are capable of making their own food by a process called *photosynthesis.*

Secondary concepts that are important to expansion

Seeds, moisture, chlorophyll, designing investigations.

Materials needed

For each student group:

Radish seeds
two ziploc bags (larger storage size)
two paper towels

one piece of aluminum foil
paper towels
metric ruler

⊃ **Safety precautions:** Do not put anything in your mouth. Avoid eating leaves or seeds of plants. Do not play with plastic bags; keep them away from your face.

1. EXPLORATION: Which process skills will be used?

Predicting, observing, inferring, controlling variables, experimenting, reducing experimental error, analyzing

What will the children do?

Radish growth: light versus dark

Provide each group of students with some radish seeds, two ziploc bags, two paper towels, and one piece of aluminum foil. Challenge the students to design a way in which they could use these materials to compare the growth of radish seeds. Explain to them that the variable to be manipulated in this experiment is light. All other factors must remain constant. The students must write up the method they plan to use; do not be concerned if the students change too many variables. This will be a valuable lesson to them, as they will soon discover by their experimental results. Once they have designed and written up their experimental methods, including predictions of potential outcomes, then give them time to act on their design. Check their uncovered bags each day. When leaves begin to grow in the uncovered bag, uncover the covered bag and compare the two environments.

2. EXPLANATION/CONCEPT INVENTION: What is the main idea? How will the main idea be identified?

Concept: Photosynthesis, a process in which chlorophyll-bearing plant cells, using light energy, produce carbohydrates and oxygen from carbon dioxide and water. Simply put, it is a way in which green plants use the sun's energy to make their own food.

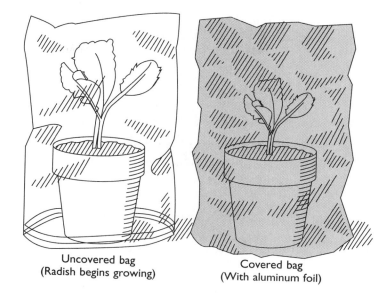

Uncovered bag
(Radish begins growing)

Covered bag
(With aluminum foil)

Have the students share the data they collected. Where did you place your bags in the room? Were they both put in the same place? Why is it important to make sure the bags were in the same area? What about the number of seeds you used? Was that kept constant? Is it important to keep the number of seeds the same? Why or why not? What happened inside both of your bags? Was it as you predicted? If so, can you explain why? If not, why not? Did the seeds sprout leaves in both the covered and uncovered environments? What color were they? Which environment appears more successful? Where did the green leaves come from? What gives your skin color? (Pigment.) Do plants have pigment? Does anyone know the name of the pigment that gives plants their green color? (Chlorophyll.) Do you think, based on your experimental results, you can determine what the chlorophyll does for the plant? (It makes food for the plant.) What do we call the process whereby the chlorophyll makes use of light energy to make food for the plant? (Photosynthesis.)

3. EXPANSION OF THE IDEA: Which process skills will be used?

Experimenting, hypothesizing, predicting, observing, analyzing, controlling variables, inferring, recording data

How will the idea be expanded?

Radish growth: light versus dark in soil

Challenge the students to design another experiment, this time planting the seeds in soil instead of bags. Once again make light the manipulated variable. Predict the outcome, plan and record the methods, and act on your design. Once the seeds in the light begin to sprout, compare these results to the bag experiment. Were your predictions accurate? Why do you think you obtained the results you did? Did photosynthesis occur in the covered pot? The uncovered pot? Why? Continue to grow the plants and measure and record the results for one month.

Why is the idea important for personal development?
- How do plants help man survive on this planet?
- What would your life be like without plants?

Why is the idea important for science-technology-society?
- Because they need land to live and grow things on, some people in Brazil are cutting down the tropical rain forests. Should this concern you?
- Of what advantage has hydroponic farming been to the people of the world?

Why is the idea important for academic growth?
New concepts to be identified for invention in new lessons include growth rates, leaf shapes, deciduous versus coniferous, and so on.
- Can photosynthesis occur if a plant does not contain chlorophyll?
- Does photosynthesis take place in plants that grow on the ocean floor?

Why is the idea important for career awareness?
- What impact has the farming industry had on our daily lives? On the lives of people throughout the world?
- Who was Gregor Mendel (1822–1884)? How did his knowledge of photosynthesis open up an entirely new field of genetics?
- Can just anyone become a landscape architect? What kind of background knowledge does a person in this field need?

4. EVALUATION: How will the students show what they have learned?

Upon completing the activities the students will be able to
- when provided with two of the same plant, one grown in a shady environment and the other in a sunny one, identify which was grown where;
- observe plants growing around the classroom. They will be able to accurately predict what will happen to the leaves if a small piece of paper is clipped over part of a leaf for one week;
- read a problem about a science exploration and accurately determine which variable should be manipulated and which should be controlled.

GRADE

6–8

Life Science

DISCIPLINE

Starch Exploration

Concept to be invented

Main idea—Starches have a structure that is unique for each type of vegetable.

Secondary concepts that are important to expansion

Starch grain, hilum, slide preparation, microscope use.

Materials needed

For each student group:

microscope	rice that was soaked in water for at least four hours
five slides	kidney beans
one scalpel	corn kernels
coverslips	potatoes
tapioca	

⊃ **Safety precautions:** Although the starches are edible, the students should be discouraged from tasting them. Caution should be used around electrical outlets for the electric microscopes. The bulb for the microscope will get hot. Students should be reminded of safety techniques when using the scalpel.

1. EXPLORATION: Which process skills will be used?

Observing, predicting, comparing, manipulating materials, recording data

What will the children do?

Microscopic starch

The students will prepare slides of each of the given vegetables by using the scalpel to gently scrape a newly cut surface of the vegetable. A very small speck of each should be placed on each slide with a drop of water. A cover slip should be applied. The students should make predictions before observing the different starch grains. Will all of them look alike, since they are all starches? What do you think? Record this prediction. The students should observe each prepared slide under the microscope and draw their observations of the starch from each vegetable.

2. EXPLANATION/CONCEPT INVENTION: What is the main idea? How will the main idea be identified?

Concept: Starches have a structure that is unique for each type of vegetable.

Key questions to ask the students to help them come to these conclusions are: What did you observe as you looked at the potato grains? How were they different from the corn or rice? What did the bean and tapioca starch look like? Ask the students to compare their drawings to actual pictures of the various grains. Were you able to observe the detail these pictures show? Can you differentiate between parts of the grain?

Additional information to help develop the concept

The students should find countless oval, ellipsoidal, or even triangular shaped, almost transparent bodies that look like miniature oyster shells when they observe the potato starch grains. Since they are not flat, it may help if the students slowly rotate the fine adjustment back and forth to get all the parts in focus. Usually on the narrower end the students will find a tiny dark spot that is not in the center of the grain. This is called the *hilum,* the oldest part of the starch grain, around which the remainder of the shell has grown layer by layer until fully formed. If you focus up and down at this point, you will find concentric lines or rings called *striations,* which indicate the layers where the grain has grown larger and larger.

Corn starch is different from potato. The grains may have an irregular globular shape or a very distinct polygonal shape. The shape will vary depending on the part of the kernel the students take their samples from, the horny or the floury portion. Corn starch has a central hilum that is usually a point, but sometimes shows two, three, or four radiating clefts.

Rice starch grains are very small and many sided. They may be square, triangular, or pentagonal in shape. The hilum is not distinct, but in some grains a central portion appears brighter. This difference may be due to the drying of the grain. Ovoid or spherical shapes are usually due to a number of grains being compacted together.

Bean starch grains are usually ellipsoidal or kidney shaped. They have an irregular branching cleft running out from the center that appears black because of enclosed air.

Tapioca grains are usually circular or loaf shaped, depending on whether they sit on their flat surfaces or on their sides. The hilum is centrally located, usually coming to a point or small cleft. When students view the flattened surface, the hilum may appear triangular.

3. EXPANSION OF THE IDEA: Which process skills will be used?

Observing, predicting, comparing, manipulating materials, recording data, hypothesizing

How will the idea be expanded?

Beans and starch grains

- The students may brainstorm a list of other starch-containing foods. Obtain these foods, prepare slides, and check their predictions by looking for evidence of starch grains. Are they similar to any of the grains previously identified? Are they different? What kind of starch do you think this food contains?
- The students may obtain several different kinds of beans. Pose a question:

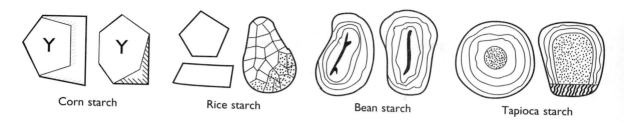

Corn starch   Rice starch   Bean starch   Tapioca starch

Will all beans contain the same kind of starch grains, no matter the type of bean? Allow the students to design an experiment to answer that question.

Why is the idea important for personal development?

- Do you think the differences in the starch grain will affect your ability to digest that starch? Why or why not?
- Are there any other kinds of plants that contain starch grains that humans do not eat? What are these? Why do you think we do not eat them?
- Why are starches important in a person's diet?

Why is the idea important for science-technology-society?

- Why does the United States send starchy foods to underdeveloped countries? What kinds of conditions are necessary to grow starch-containing foods? Is our society doing anything to help these underdeveloped nations to grow starches on their own?
- What kinds of products have modern industries created that make use of starches? How have these helped modern society? How have these hindered modern society?

Why is the idea important for academic growth?

- Are all starch grains, no matter the plant they come from, the same? Will starch grains from many different varieties of potatoes look the same? Why or why not?
- What is the name of the oldest part of the starch grain? Does finding this structure under the microscope help in identifying the type of plant the starch grain came from?
- The process skills the students had to engage in to do these activities (predicting, manipulating materials, forming hypotheses, solving problems, recording data, making careful observations) enhance their overall academic growth.

Why is the idea important for career awareness?

- Why do you think a person responsible for creating frozen dinners should understand that different vegetables have different starch structures?
- What kinds of jobs entail making careful observations and accurately recording what was observed?
- Do you think an insurance adjuster could benefit by learning the skills you utilized while participating in this lesson?

4. EVALUATION: How will the students show what they have learned?

Upon completing these activities the students will be able to

- prepare a slide of starch grains,
- accurately draw starch grains observed under a microscope,
- identify with 80% accuracy the various starch grains and their sources,
- explain in writing or verbally why certain starches can be digested by humans while other starches cannot.

Colors of Wildlife

Concept to be invented

Main idea—Wildlife occurs in a wide variety of colors.

Secondary concepts that are important to expansion

Camouflage allows an organism to blend in or hide in its environment.

Materials needed

For the entire class:

Magazines that have a wide variety of animal pictures, such as *National Geographic, Ranger Rick, National and International Wildlife, Audubon.* Try to have magazines that can be cut up.

Construction paper, crayons or markers, scissors, glue, felt, cotton balls, natural materials from outdoors (acorns, leaves, grass); an appropriate story book with a wide variety of different colored animals in it will also help introduce the topic. A book such as Richard Buckley and Eric Carle's *The Greedy Python* (New York: Scholastic Books, 1992) is a good selection.

⊃ **Safety precautions:** Do not poke each other with the scissors; use them only while seated.

1. EXPLORATION: Which process skills will be used?

Observing, comparing, generalizing

What will the children do?

Animal similarities and differences

Introduce the lesson by reading the students a book like *The Greedy Python.* Encourage the students to make note of the color of the python and of all the other animals it comes across. You will return to the ideas provided by the story later.

After the story and brief discussion about it, provide each student group with several wildlife magazines to look at. Ask the students to find pictures of animals, make observations about the animals, and compare the animals to one another. Create two lists on the board. Title one list *similarities*, the other *differences*. Ask the students to share their observations about the animals they found by providing information about the similarities and differences of the animals. Ask the students to each cut out three different animals.

2. EXPLANATION/CONCEPT INVENTION: What is the main idea? How will the main idea be identified?

Concept: Wildlife occurs in a wide variety of colors.

Refer back to the story you read. For instance if *The Greedy Python* was used, you might ask the following questions to help invent the concept: What animals did you see in the book? What colors were they? Why do you think the python was so successful in eating all the animals? Could a green python hide easily in a jungle?

Hold up a variety of different-colored pieces of construction paper. Ask the students to identify the colors. Then ask the students to raise their hands if they cut out animals that match the color of the paper you are holding. Assist them in concluding that animals appear in a variety of colors.

Let the students help in gluing the animals on to the construction paper that matches the animal's color. Hang these animal pages around the room. Ask the student furthest from each picture if it is difficult to identify the animal on the page, that is, a red animal on a red piece of paper. Ask why they think it is difficult. How would this coloration help it survive in the wild? Draw the students to the conclusion that camouflage allows an organism to blend in or hide in its environment.

3. EXPANSION OF THE IDEA: Which process skills will be used?

Observing, manipulating materials, generalizing, comparing, communicating

How will the idea be expanded?

Create a rainbow animal

Use the materials from the material list to have the students create their own animal. The animals may be real, or they can make them up. Encourage the generalization that wild animals appear in a wide variety of colors and that the animals' colors and markings help them survive. Encourage the students to look for rainbow animals—those that have three or more distinct colors on their bodies. Ask the students to share their creations with one another. Get them to communicate to one another how their animal can hide in its environment.

Why is the idea important for personal development?

- Where would you find _____? (Insert an animal name.)
- Do you think it is as important for a pet to blend in with its surroundings as it is for wild animals? Why or why not?

Why is the idea important for science-technology-society?
• Do we need to protect the environment where some animals live? Why?
• What are some things society can do to protect animal environments?

Why is the idea important for academic growth?
• Where could you learn more about a particular animal?
• What are some ways that color helps animals survive?
• Besides color, what other kinds of things can animals use for camouflage?

Why is the idea important for career awareness?
• Can you think of any jobs in which people work or study animals?
• Can you think of any job in which people work with aquatic animals?
• Can you think of any animals that work? (Police dogs, seeing-eye dogs, sled dogs, horses, pigeons, animals that help on a farm.)

4. EVALUATION: How will the students show what they have learned?

Upon completing the activities the students will be able to

• construct an animal using a variety of colors when given materials,
• explain how a cartoon animal relates to a real animal,
• make a graph of animals that have one, two, or more colors.

GRADE **K–2** **Life Science** **DISCIPLINE**

Shelter

Concept to be invented
Main idea—Shelter is a necessary condition for the survival of many animals.

Secondary concepts that are important to expansion
Food, water, and space are other conditions necessary for the survival of an animal.

Materials needed
For each student:

Construction paper and crayons or markers.

⊃ **Safety precautions:** Remind the students to use crayons and markers properly. Do not place them in your mouth.

1. EXPLORATION: Which process skills will be used?

Inferring, predicting, analyzing, comparing, generalizing, communicating, manipulating materials, recording data

What will the children do?
Shelter drawing

Ask the students to draw a picture of the place they live in. Upon completion, allow each child to hang his or her picture in the classroom. Be sure all the drawings can be easily viewed by the students. Ask the students to determine what each has in common. Possible answers include roofs, ceilings, walls, floors, doors, windows. Ask the students to determine how each is different. Suggestions may include apartment, trailer, house, size, color, materials dwelling is made of.

Ask the students to draw another picture of items found inside their home. To simplify, ask them to focus upon their favorite room in the house. Once again, display the pictures. Ask the students to view the pictures and decide what items a home may have more than one of, such as refrigerators, beds, lamps, pictures in frames. Ask the students to identify the things the children must have, such as food, water, space, clothing. Ask the students to identify the items that make living in the home more fun or easier, such as television, radio, chairs.

2. EXPLANATION/CONCEPT INVENTION: What is the main idea? How will the main idea be identified?

Concept: Shelter is a necessary condition for the survival of many animals.

Carry on a discussion with the students centered around this question: What would happen if we didn't have a place to live? Be sure to mention that we would be affected by the weather, we could get sick, be harmed by animals, get dirty, and so on.

Focus again on the first pictures drawn. Be sure the following idea comes out during discussion: All homes may not be the same, but they serve the same purpose—for protection.

Ask the children if they think anything beside humans need homes. Lead the discussion toward animals. Why do animals need a shelter? Is it for the same reason as humans? Help the students to conclude that shelter is necessary for the survival of many animals, humans included.

3. EXPANSION OF THE IDEA: Which process skills will be used?

Observing, communicating, problem solving, formulating models, classifying, questioning, hypothesizing

How will the idea be expanded?

Animal homes

Ask each child to choose an animal and draw a home for that animal. Display these drawings. Discuss how the animals' homes are the same and how they are different. Compare the animals' homes with the drawings of the children's homes. Discuss with the students the answers to the following questions: Do animals live in bigger or smaller homes than humans? Why don't animals live inside a building like humans? Where do animals get their food? Where do humans get their food? Do animals have furniture in their homes? How many people live in your home? How many animals live in their homes?

Be sure the students understand that although animals do not live in houses, trailers, or apartments, they do live in homes in nature where they are protected from the weather and other animals, where they sleep, eat, and care for their young. Food, water, and space in a suitable arrangement are basic needs that every animal has. This arrangement is different for different animals; for example, humans live in neighborhoods that may meet all of their basic needs.

Why is the idea important for personal development?
- If you had to choose only three items from your home to keep, which items would you choose? Why did you choose these items? Do you need these things to stay alive?
- If you found a bird's nest, would you pick it up or leave it alone? Why?

Why is the idea important for science-technology-society?
- How can humans make homes for animals? What kinds of things must humans use to make animal homes?
- What do you think happens to animals when humans tear down forests (where many animals live) to build human homes or office buildings? Do you think this kind of action is responsible human behavior?

Why is the idea important for academic growth?
- What kinds of things do humans and animals need in their homes to survive?
- Where can animals' homes be found?
- Can animals live in human homes?
- What kinds of animals live with people?

Why is the idea important for career awareness?
- What kinds of supplies do construction workers use to build homes for people? How are these supplies like those that animals use?
- If you were a community developer and you were offered a large space of land to build an amusement park if you cut down a forest, would you cut down the forest to build the park? Why or why not? What if you could build homes for people on that same land; would you do it?

4. EVALUATION: How will the students show what they have learned?

Upon completing the activities the students will be able to

- choose from various items found in a home those that are necessary for living;
- classify homes according to human or animal homes when given several pictures of various human and animal homes,
- explain similarities and differences between human and animal homes and explain why humans and animals need shelter,
- list the four items necessary for life: food, water, shelter, and space.

Wildlife and Domesticated Animals

GRADE

K–3

Life
Science

DISCIPLINE

Concept to be invented
Main idea—Wildlife includes animals that are not tamed or domesticated.

Secondary concepts that are important to expansion
Endangered animals, extinct, threatened, safe.

Materials needed
For exploration:

Pictures of both wild and domesticated animals, attribute blocks.

⊃ **Safety precautions:** Do not throw attribute blocks; use care when acting out animals in expansion activity so as to not hit any other student.

1. EXPLORATION: Which process skills will be used?

Observing, hypothesizing, inferring, categorizing, recording data

What will the children do?

Animal needs

Using attribute blocks, ask the students to place these blocks into two different groups. This activity will ensure that the students understand the concept of grouping. Next, ask the students to look around the room at the pictures hanging up. What do you observe in the pictures? (Animals.) Divide the class into groups of four to six. Provide them with pictures of both wild and domesticated animals (at least as many pictures as there are students in a group). Each student in the group will pick up an animal and record characteristics that make that animal different from any other. Some prompting questions could be: Where do they live? How do they get their food? Are they dependent upon humans for their survival? Once each child in the group has listed the characteristics of the animal he or she chose, ask the students to decide how they could put their animals into two different groups. Once they make that decision, then divide the animals.

2. EXPLANATION/CONCEPT INVENTION: What is the main idea? How will the main idea be identified?

> *Concept:* Wildlife includes animals that are not tamed or domesticated.
>
> Ask the students questions such as the following to help invent this concept: How did your group decide to divide your animals? What characteristics of your animals led you to this decision? How do the animals in one of your groups get their food? How do the animals in your other group get their food? Do either of your groupings separate the animals into whether or not they rely on humans for their survival?
>
> Animals that do not rely on humans for survival and that are neither tame or owned are called wild. Domesticated animals rely on humans for their survival.

3. EXPANSION OF THE IDEA: Which process skills will be used?

> Observing, classifying, analyzing, inferring, communicating

How will the idea be expanded?

Domestic versus wild charades

Ask the students to choose an animal, and without telling anyone else in the class, write down the name of that animal. The students may choose one from a picture in the room or think of one on their own. Divide the class in half, and collect their listed animals in two groups. Explain to the students how the game of charades is played. Have students from one half of the class pick from a pile of animals that came from the other half of the room and vice versa. Ask the students to look at the name of the animal on the card, and without saying what is written on the card, act out the behaviors of that animal for the students on your side of the room to guess. Write the words *domestic* and *wild* on the board. Once the students guess which animal was acted out, ask the student who just acted out the animal to decide whether that animal should be listed as domestic or wild. Make sure all of the students agree on the listing before acting out the next animal.

Wild	Domestic

Why is the idea important for personal development?

- Name some of the domesticated animals that we could find around your neighborhood. What would the neighborhood be like if these animals were wild?

- What do you think life would be like if any of the wild animals we acted out no longer existed, that is, they became extinct?
- What do you think would happen if you tried to tame a wild animal?

Why is the idea important for science-technology-society?
- Why is a wildlife preserve important to our society?
- Can the study of wildlife give us any ideas about how man behaves?

Why is the idea important for academic growth?
- What important facts must we remember when dealing with wildlife?
- What things are important to remember when taking care of pets?
- What is the difference between a wild and a domesticated animal?

Why is the idea important for career awareness?
- What type of job requires knowledge of wildlife or requires someone to work with wild animals?
- Interview a zookeeper. What special skills does someone in this line of work need?
- What kind of jobs would have to be created if wildlife started taking over our community?

4. EVALUATION: How will the students show what they have learned?

Upon completing the activities the students will be able to

- give two examples of a wild animal,
- give two examples of a domestic animal,
- list the characteristics of a wild and domestic animal,
- draw a picture of an animal and identify it as wild or domestic by drawing an appropriate habitat for it.

GRADE

3–6

Life Science

DISCIPLINE

Habitat

Concept to be invented

Main idea—An animal's *habitat* is an environment in which there is a suitable arrangement of its basic needs—food, water, shelter, and space.

Secondary concepts that are important to expansion

Niche.

Materials needed

For each student:

one large sheet of newsprint
scissors, glue
markers, crayons
old magazines to cut up

construction paper of various colors
resource books that provide information
    on different animals' habitats and
    their niches in those habitats

⊃ **Safety precautions:** Remind students about the safe use of scissors.

1. EXPLORATION: Which process skills will be used?

Predicting, hypothesizing, inferring

What will the children do?

Basic needs lap sit

Begin the session by asking the students to think about the last meal they ate. Could they have gotten by without it? How long could they have gone without eating? Why is food necessary? Could you survive without it? After a discussion on food move on to a similar line of questioning, getting at the necessity of water and shelter. After there is consensus through effective questioning techniques on the necessity of food, water, and shelter, ask all the students to get out of their seats and direct them to some small space or corner of the room. Encourage all of them to crowd into a small space. Keep encouraging them to get as close to one another as possible. After they have spent a few moments crowded into a small space, if there is not too much protest, begin your line of questioning about how they feel right now. If they really begin to complain, allow them to return to their seats; then continue a discussion about the importance of suitable space. How necessary is it?

Once the students have reached agreement on the importance of food, water, shelter, and space in their lives, move the class to a room or outdoor setting where they will have plenty of space to stand up and form a circle. The teacher should stand at the center of the circle and lead a discussion about the importance of food, water, shelter, and space, not just for humans, but for all living organisms. Assign each student in the circle one of the four necessities—food, water, shelter, or space. When assigning the students, make sure that you try to assign at least three students in a row the same necessity. Take for example these ten students, who were standing in the circle in the following order: John, water; Kevin, food; Mary, shelter; Carol, space; Colette, food; Charlie, food; Pat, food; Trudy, water; Joshua, shelter; Calvin, space; José, water; Yolanda, shelter. This assignment of necessities will be used later to help invent part of the concept.

As the students are facing you in the center of the circle, ask them to turn to their right and place their hands on the shoulders of the person in front of them. Encourage them to get as close to one another as possible while still maintaining a circle formation. They may have to take one or two steps toward the middle of the circle to close their ranks. Once *they* believe their circle is tight enough, ask the students at the count of three to slowly sit down on the knees of the person behind them. (Note: Some shuffling and rearranging of bodies may occur to tighten the circle some more once the students hear this direction. If this does not happen, if the circle has a lot of empty space between bodies, do not tell them to tighten up the circle. The students will soon realize this on their own after one try at the lap sit. They may even decide that their sizes will affect the

success of the lap sit and try to arrange themselves before the sit so that the tallest student is not expected to sit on the lap of the shortest student.) If the lap sit falls apart, encourage the students to get up and try it again. Once it is successful, the students are ready to help invent the concept.

2. EXPLANATION/CONCEPT INVENTION: What is the main idea? How will the main idea be identified?

Concept: An animal's *habitat* is an environment in which there is a suitable arrangement of its basic needs—food, water, shelter, and space.

As the students are sitting in a successful lap sit, remind them that each student represented a basic necessity—food, water, shelter, or space. Tell them that some terrible natural disaster came along, like a flood, that wiped out most of their food source. Ask three fourths of the students who represented food to leave the lap sit. What happened to the lap sit once those students left? Could the lap sit survive? In a circle where several students next to one another represented the same necessity it is virtually impossible to maintain the lap sit. It quickly falls apart. The teacher should lead a discussion by asking the students why they think the lap sit fell apart. What could have kept the lap sit together? Could they have arranged themselves differently in the lap sit so that it would not fall apart if a few people from one type of necessity were asked to leave? Could animals survive if only one of the areas where they get food (or water, shelter, space) from was wiped out? Can they survive if all of their food (or water, shelter, space) is in one place and it gets wiped out? Help the students conclude that food, water, shelter, and space are all needed in a *suitable arrangement* to help insure the animal's survival. This area where there is a suitable arrangement of the animal's basic needs is called its *habitat*.

3. EXPANSION OF THE IDEA: Which process skills will be used?

Observing, gathering data, recording data, interpreting data, manipulating materials

How will the idea be expanded?

Animal habitat research

Ask each student to choose an animal in which he or she has a particular interest. Encourage the students to be creative, to suggest a variety of animals, not just dogs and cats for everyone. If necessary, assign animals. Provide the students with the materials listed above. Ask the students to do some research on the animal they chose using the resource books provided or books they find through a library research time. During their research they should find out as much as possible about that animal's habitat. What are its needs for food, water, shelter, and space? What role does it play or *niche* does it occupy in its environment? Encourage them to find one other interesting fact about their animal.

Once they have completed their research, ask them to use the materials to create a pictorial representation of the animal's habitat. This can be done as a diorama, collage, drawing, or other medium. On the back of their creation they should provide in writing a brief description of the animal's habitat indicating how its basic needs are met.

Why is the idea important for personal development?
- How are your basic needs similar to those of the animal you studied? How are they different?
- In what ways has man been able to alter his habitat?
- Do you think there will come a time when even humans will not have their basic needs met? Do you think some humans are already at that point? Why or why not?

Why is the idea important for science-technology-society?
- What is the Biosphere II Project in Arizona all about? What can be learned by creating artificial habitats?
- Of what importance is our understanding of the concept of habitat to the success of a space station?
- Should logging be allowed in a national forest that is the only known habitat for a particular species of owl?

Why is the idea important for academic growth?
- What are the basic needs for a human?
- Can an organism survive in a habitat where one of its basic needs is low or missing?

- Can two different animals with basically the same habitat survive in an area if the role they play in the environment (their niche) is different?

Why is the idea important for career awareness?
- What do you think a wildlife officer does?
- Does an animal behaviorist discipline animals? If not, what kind of a job does this person have?
- Can a social worker apply the idea of a *suitable arrangement of basic needs* to his or her job? Why might he or she want to, and how would it be done?

4. EVALUATION: How will the students show what they have learned?

Upon completing the activities the students will be able to

- describe the *basic needs* for a human,
- draw a picture of an ideal habitat for an organism of their choice,
- engage in a healthy discussion of where in society they think humans have applied their understanding of habitat to cure a social problem,
- explain the difference between a habitat and a niche.

GRADE

5–8

Life Science

DISCIPLINE

LIFE SCIENCE

Crickets—Basic Needs of an Organism

Concept to be invented
Main idea—All organisms, no matter the size, have a basic need for food, water, shelter, and space in a suitable arrangement.

Secondary concepts that are important to expansion
Living organisms respond to stimuli from their environment. Animals in captivity must be able to adapt to their environment in order to survive.

Materials needed
For each group of students:

one terrarium
one plastic pint container with
  screen top
one hand lens

one piece of black construction paper
seeds (six each of clover, grass, wheat,
  radish, and bean)

For the entire class:
Eric Carle's *The Very Quiet Cricket* (New York: Philomel Books, 1990); four plastic bags, each containing eighteen crickets; felt pen, paper clips, tape or staples, chart paper.

⊃ **Safety precautions:** Remind the students to wash their hands after handling the crickets. Do not eat the seeds or put them in your mouth. Do not poke each other with the staples or paper clips.

1. EXPLORATION: Which process skills will be used?

Observing, recording data, experimenting, drawing conclusions

What will the children do?

Cricket needs

Begin the lesson by doing something that students of this age level would never expect. Read very animatedly *The Very Quiet Cricket,* by Eric Carle. Although not age appropriate, the story is very effective in getting students to think about the task to come. Divide the class into research groups of four. Allow library time for the students to find answers to the following questions: What is necessary for the survival of a cricket? Are their needs similar to human needs? What requirements do they have for food, water, and shelter? Can many crickets live in a small space? How many can live comfortably together?

2. EXPLANATION/CONCEPT INVENTION: What is the main idea? How will the main idea be identified?

Concept: All organisms, no matter the size, have a basic need for food, water, shelter, and space in a suitable arrangement.

Ask the various student groups to report on the results of their inquiries. Through their reporting continue to question them to clarify the results of their research efforts. Help the students to draw the conclusion that all organisms, no matter the size, have a basic need for food, water, shelter, and space in a suitable arrangement.

3. EXPANSION OF THE IDEA: Which process skills will be used?

Observing, communicating, problem solving, formulating models, classifying, questioning, hypothesizing

How will the idea be expanded?

Cricket behavior

Set up a terrarium with a few crickets living in it. Encourage the students to make observations about the crickets in the terrarium as they are collecting their data. Assign each of the different research groups from the exploration phase of this lesson one of the following tasks so that they will understand the behavior of a cricket:

• Take a cricket from the terrarium. Place it on a smooth surface and then on a rough surface. Watch the cricket for three to five minutes on each surface. Record your observations. Which surface causes the greatest obstacle to movement? Why do you think this is so? Try manipulating the environment in other ways: hot versus cold surface or light versus dark conditions. Return the cricket to the terrarium.

- Obtain a shoe box. Cut a hole on one side about the size of a small flashlight. Cut a hole on the other side just big enough for your eye to peep inside. Take a cricket from the terrarium. Place the cricket in the dark end of the shoe box (opposite end from the flashlight hole) and put on the lid. Cover the flashlight hole with your hand in an effort to make the box as dark as possible inside. Watch the cricket's behavior for five minutes. Record your observations. Now place a small flashlight in the hole and turn it on. Observe the cricket for another five minutes. Record your observations. Were there any differences in the cricket's behavior when the lights were on versus when they were off? If so, why do you think this occurred? Return the cricket to the terrarium.

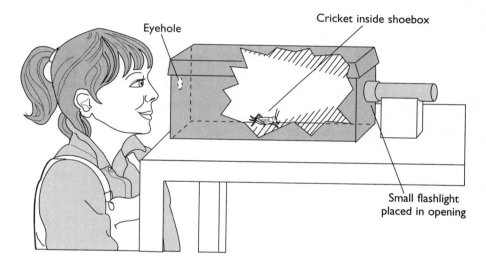

Eyehole

Cricket inside shoebox

Small flashlight placed in opening

- Take a cricket from the terrarium and place it in a shoe box. As a group, decide on three different kinds of food you think a cricket might like to eat. Place the three types in front of the cricket. Make sure you keep accurate records about the amount of food placed in the box. It may be important to weigh each food choice. Put the lid back on the box. Place the box in a dark, quiet place in the classroom. Ask the group members to make predictions about which food type they think the cricket will choose. Make and record observations every thirty minutes for one school day. Did the cricket choose the food you predicted? Why or why not? Do you think more than one cricket should be used in this experiment? Why or why not? Return the cricket to the terrarium.

Ask each of the different research groups to report on their findings. Encourage all the students to communicate to one another exactly what they did, why they did it, and what they discovered as a result. Help them in their discussion to come to the following conclusions: Living organisms respond to stimuli from their environment. Animals in captivity must be able to adapt to their environment in order to survive.

Why is the idea important for personal development?

- What could you do for an animal if it has lost its mother? How could you help it survive without removing it from its environment?
- Why would it be important for you to know how to care for an animal in a situation like that?

Why is the idea important for science-technology-society?

- What legends exist about crickets? How and why have these been handed down through generations?
- Do you think fluctuations in cricket populations could tell us something about what people are doing to their environment?
- Do you think it is important that humans understand something about other animals no matter what their size? Why or why not?

Why is the idea important for academic growth?

- Why does a terrarium need to have soil in it?
- Can a cricket drink water out of a bowl? Why does a cricket rub its wings?
- What are the basic needs of a cricket?

Why is the idea important for career awareness?

- What kinds of occupations deal with a variety of animal species? (Game wardens, zookeepers, wildlife officers.)
- What would it be like if there was no one who understood the basic needs of certain animals?
- What does an entomologist do?

4. EVALUATION: How will the students show what they have learned?

Upon completing the activities the students will be able to

- design and build their own terrarium for a cricket, making sure that it is designed to meet all of the cricket's basic needs;
- pick one animal and determine what are its basic needs for food, shelter, water, and space;
- pick a domesticated animal such as a chicken, dog, or hamster and describe the adaptations necessary for that animal to survive in the wild;
- participate in a discussion of how man would have to adapt in order to survive in the wild.

Animal Adaptations

Concepts to be invented

Main idea—The shape of a bird's beak determines the type of food it will eat. This is one form of an adaptation.

Secondary concepts that are important to expansion

Many animals have developed specialized adaptations in order to survive in their environments. Fish utilize adaptive coloration, body shape, and mouth placement to help them survive in different aquatic environments.

Materials needed

For exploration:

Enough tweezers and mittens so that each student in the class has one or the other of these. Numerous pipe cleaners, paper wads, and strips of construction paper to serve as "food" for the birds. Place pictures of various kinds of birds with different feeding habits all around the classroom.

For expansion:

Pictures of various kinds of fish placed around the room. The fish should demonstrate such differences in coloration as light-colored belly, dark upper side, mottled, vertical stripes, or horizontal stripes. Differences in body shape could be flat bellied, torpedo shaped, horizontal disc, vertical disc, or hump-backed. The mouth shapes may be an elongated upper jaw, duckbill jaws, an elongated lower jaw, an extremely large jaw, or a sucker-shaped jaw. A fish tank with fish that live at different levels of the tank would also serve to emphasize the secondary concept. Art materials like crayons, markers, scissors, scrap material, construction paper, chalk, old buttons, yarn, pieces of felt, and so on are also needed.

⊃ **Safety precautions:** Remind the students to walk, not run, while participating in the bird-feeding activity. Use caution with scissors in the expansion activity.

1. EXPLORATION: Which process skills will be used?

Observing, inferring, experimenting, analyzing

What will the children do?

Mitten and tweezer beaks

Distribute the pipe cleaners, paper wads, and paper strips throughout the room. Place some on the floor and some of them in harder-to-get-to places. Each student will choose the type of "beak" (mitten or tweezers) that he or she wants to use. The students will explore a bird's eating habit by trying to pick up the different types of food using the beak they chose.

2. EXPLANATION/CONCEPT INVENTION: What is the main idea? How will the main idea be identified?

> *Concept:* The shape of a bird's beak determines the type of food it will eat. This is one form of adaptation.
>
> Ask the students questions such as the following to help invent this concept: Why was it easier for _____ (student's name) to pick up the paper strips than _____ (a different student's name)? Do you see any pictures of birds in this room with a beak that would work like the tweezers? Can you think of any others? What do you think they use these beaks for? What types of food can a bird with a beak like a pair of mittens eat? Birds have a variety of adaptations that help them survive in their environment. Their beaks are one such adaptation.

3. EXPANSION OF THE IDEA: Which process skills will be used?

> Hypothesizing, observing, questioning, classifying, analyzing, inferring, manipulating materials, communicating
>
> How will the idea be expanded?
>
> Fish adaptations
>
> The students will look at pictures of different types of fish and try to categorize them in three different ways: coloration, mouth shape, and body shape. A

discussion should ensue on how these three classifications are important adaptations to insure the fish's survival in its environment. After the discussion, the teacher should assign each student or group of students a par-ticular combination of adaptations from each of the three groups, such as mottled coloration, torpedo body shape, and sucker-shaped jaw. Ask the students to use the art materials provided to create fish with those three types of adaptations. Ask them to create environments in which fish with those adaptations could survive. Have the students share their creations.

Why is the idea important for personal development?

- What are some ways in which man has adapted to his environment?
- What are some ways in which we share our environment with the birds? The fish?

Why is the idea important for science-technology-society?

- What has society done to improve the lives of animals in their habitat?
- What are some disadvantages of taking an animal out of its natural habitat? Could an animal adapt quickly enough to survive in a new environment? Why or why not?

Why is the idea important for academic growth?

- Can an animal's inability to adapt to rapid changes in its environment lead to its extinction? What other events may lead to the extinction of an animal?
- Is there any one species of bird that has a beak that allows it to winter in an area with a relatively cold climate? What advantage does this beak shape have over any other?
- If you were to buy a fish from a pet store and wanted one that would clean the food off the gravel in the bottom of your fish tank, what kind of a mouth shape would you choose?

Why is the idea important for career awareness?

- If you were to make a hummingbird feeder, would it be useful to know the type of beak this bird has, and why?
- How important is it for a zookeeper to understand the special feeding adaptations many animals have developed? Why?
- If you were working at a nature center and were responsible for creating an aquarium that made use of fish found at a local lake, what kinds of things would you need to know about the local fish to make your display enjoyable for center visitors?

4. EVALUATION: How will the students show what they have learned?

Upon completing the activities the students will be able to

- identify bird beak adaptations and explain how these contribute to the survival of the bird;

- design an ideal habitat for an animal of their choice, emphasizing that animal's special adaptations for survival in its environment;
- explain why several species of fish can live together in one lake without competing with one another for food.

Owl Pellets

Concept to be invented
Main idea—Owl pellets contain undigested parts of animals eaten by the owl, such as hair and bones.

Secondary concepts that are important to expansion
Digestion, eating habits.

Materials needed
For each student group:

One owl pellet, which may be obtained through a local department of natural resources wildlife division for the state. Sterilized pellets can be ordered through a supplier. One dissecting kit, glue, handouts of the skeleton of a vole, mouse, or rat.

⊃ **Safety precautions:** Remind the students to use caution when handling the sharp dissecting tools.

1. EXPLORATION: Which process skills will be used?

Observing, predicting, inferring, hypothesizing

What will the children do?

Owl pellet dissection

Provide each pair of students with an owl pellet and a dissecting kit. Ask the students what they think this is. How was it created? What do you think you will find in here as you carefully pick the matted hair away from the owl pellets? After student predictions are shared, instruct the students to keep everything they find as they pick away carefully at the pellets. Try to reconstruct a skeleton of a rodent, using the picture as a guide.

2. EXPLANATION/CONCEPT INVENTION: What is the main idea? How will the main idea be identified?

Concept: Owl pellets contain the undigested parts of animals eaten by the owl, such as hair and bones.

Ask the students questions such as the following to help invent this concept: What kind of rodent do you think your owl ate? Did you find the remains of

Vole Skelton

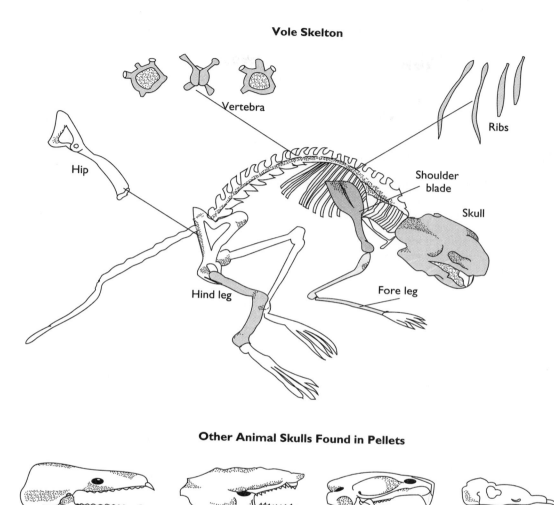

Other Animal Skulls Found in Pellets

Shrew Mole Rat Sparrow

more than one kind of rodent? What do these findings tell you about the type of food an owl eats? What is an owl capable of digesting?

3. EXPANSION OF THE IDEA: Which process skills will be used?

Observing, communicating, problem solving, formulating models, recording data

How will the idea be expanded?

Owl research or field trip

- Take the students on a field trip to an area where owls are known to nest. Look carefully on the ground around the area. What do you expect to find to indicate to you that owls may be in the area? How are pellets different from owl scats?
- Invite a wildlife specialist to bring an owl to visit your classroom to discuss its characteristics and habitat. Ask your class to prepare in advance sound questions to ask the visitor about the owl.
- Assign each student team to write a report about a different species of owl. This report should include such things as where it is found and its life span, habitat, and food preferences.

Why is the idea important for personal development?
- What might happen to owls if humans disrupt their habitats?
- What are some ways that owls are adapted to their environment?
- How are we adapted to our environment?

Why is the idea important for science-technology-society?
- What has technology done to improve the lives of animals in their habitats? What could society do?
- What are some disadvantages of taking an animal out of its natural habitat and placing it in another environment?

Why is the idea important for academic growth?
- What special needs does an owl have in order to survive in any habitat?
- Why were the bones and hair of the rodents not digested by the owls?

Why is the idea important for career awareness?
- What kinds of professions are dedicated to ensuring animal safety? What kinds of careers endanger animals?
- In this activity you found the bones of a rodent and reconstructed them to determine which rodent it was. Do any other careers expect you to take evidence and reconstruct it to find answers? Which ones?

4. EVALUATION: How will the students show what they have learned?

Upon completing the activities the students will be able to:
- construct a food chain, placing the owl at the highest level,
- dissect an owl pellet and use the bones found to reconstruct the skeleton of a rodent,
- speculate on how information provided through owl pellet dissection can assist man in enhancing the survival rate of many owl species.

GRADE

K–2
——
Life
Science

DISCIPLINE

Humans and Trash

Concept to be invented

Main idea—Man-made trash affects all living matter.

Secondary concepts that are important to expansion

Recycling can decrease the amount of waste created by man.

Materials needed

For exploration:

Selected (clean) trash, drawing paper, crayons, glue, stapler. Enough of these materials should be collected so that each child in the class can actively participate in the lesson. One large box filled with a piece of trash for each child, five or six medium-sized boxes that can be labeled for glass, paper, plastic, aluminum, tin, and so on.

⊃ **Safety precautions:** Remind the students to use caution when handling the trash. Do not put fingers in mouth. Wash hands thoroughly after handling the trash.

1. EXPLORATION: Which process skills will be used?

Questioning, inferring, predicting, hypothesizing, communicating, manipulating materials.

What will the children do?

Trash and animals

Before doing this lesson with the class, collect enough trash so that each child in the class may have several pieces to choose from. Be sure that any trash chosen is free of rough edges, broken glass, or sharp points so that the children will not be harmed during the lesson. Wash out any plastic bags and cans used as trash.

Ask each student to think of an animal and draw a picture of it.

Supply the students with a large selection of trash. Ask the students to choose one piece that particularly intrigues them. Ask the students to draw a picture of how that piece of trash would hurt their animal if the animal came across that piece of trash while outside. Ask the students to attach the piece of litter to their picture. Each student should be allowed to share the picture with the class, explaining how their animal was harmed by the piece of trash they chose. Encourage the students to act out how the animal moved both before and after the trash affected them.

2. EXPLANATION/CONCEPT INVENTION: What is the main idea? How will the main idea be identified?

Concept: Man-made trash affects all living matter.

Ask the students questions such as the following to help invent this concept: What's wrong with leaving our garbage just anywhere? How do you think trash can hurt animals besides the ways each of you just shared? The teacher can give such examples as: How many of you have been fishing? What happens when your line gets stuck? Just as it tangles up in the weeds, if you simply cut the line and leave it in the water, it can get tangled on ducks' necks, legs and beaks. It can keep them from walking, flying, and swimming. Sometimes it may become wrapped around their beak and they starve to death.

Hold up a ring from a six-pack of cans. Could this hurt an animal? How? Explain how fish or birds can get tangled up in it. Check the local wildlife office for pictures of tragedies like these. Show the students how to break up the plastic rings before they place them in the garbage. Explain to them that even though they put them in the garbage, eventually that garbage bag will break down and that plastic ring will be left to cause possible harm to some animal. If they cut it up before placing it in the trash, there is less of a chance of it harming an animal.

In what ways do people get rid of their trash? Do you think the way in which we get rid of our trash harms animals? What do you think we can do to get rid of litter? (Pick up litter alongside the road, reduce our use of materials in excessive packaging, recycle, and so on.)

3. EXPANSION OF THE IDEA: Which process skills will be used?

Observing, communicating, problem solving, formulating models, classifying, questioning, hypothesizing

How will the idea be expanded?

Classroom landfill and recycling

Refer back to the explanation phase of this lesson. Remind the students of the conversation they had in which you asked about the ways people get rid of their trash. Perhaps some students mentioned that their garbage is hauled away by a service. Ask them to think about where that trash goes after hauling. Introduce the term *landfill* (the place where trash gets hauled to be buried in the ground) if they are not already familiar with it. Ask them to suggest alternatives to taking trash to a landfill. As they make suggestions list them on the board.

After the students have created a list, show them a large box in the front of the room labeled *landfill*. (Note: The teacher should have filled this box with a piece of trash for every child in the class.) Have each child pick out one item. Ask them if they think it can be recycled. If so they should place it in the appropriately labeled medium-sized box. Sum up this activity by getting the children to surmise that recycling can decrease the amount of waste created by man.

Why is the idea important for personal development?

- What can you do to help eliminate excessive trash?
- Do you know what to do with recyclable materials where you live? If not, why not ask your parents to help you work on recycling some of your trash?

- Do you think twice about buying a toy that is not only boxed but then wrapped in paper and then in plastic? Do you think the practice of excessive packaging affects our environment?

Why is the idea important for science-technology-society?
- What are some ways businesses can cut down on their trash?
- How can companies that make different products help the environment?
- Do you think businesses have a responsibility to other people to reduce the amount of trash they create?

Why is the idea important for academic growth?
- What kinds of household items can be recycled?
- How does trash harm animals?
- How does trash harm plants?
- It has sometimes been said that "one man's trash is another man's treasure." After doing these activities, how true do you think that statement is?

Why is the idea important for career awareness?
- Who is responsible for making sure that animals are not harmed by human trash?
- Who is responsible for making sure that plants are not harmed by human trash?
- Do you think you could make a career out of collecting recycled trash? Can people make money from recycling?

4. EVALUATION: How will the students show what they have learned?

Upon completing the activities the students will be able to

- separate recyclables into appropriate groups,
- state three ways in which trash harms animals,
- draw pictures of our environment before trash was recycled and after it was recycled. The students will be able to explain the difference between the two drawings.

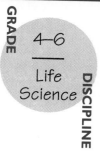

GRADE 4–6 · Life Science · DISCIPLINE

Useful Waste

Concept to be invented

Main idea—A great majority of man-made waste can be recycled or reused.

Secondary concepts that are important to expansion

Recycle, reuse, water, litter, useful and nonreusable waste, landfill, hazardous waste.

Materials needed

For exploration:

aluminum can
glass bottle
newspaper
plastic pop bottle
tin can
cigarette butt
rope

bug spray can
orange peel
art supplies (crayons,
    markers, scissors,
    construction paper,
    glue, scrap paper)

bottle cap
blender
water
old piece of screen
rolling pin

⊃ **Safety precautions:** Be careful of the sharp edges and glass. Exercise care when carrying and using the scissors and blender.

1. EXPLORATION: Which process skills will be used?

Observing, questioning, hypothesizing, predicting, reasoning, recording data

What will the children do?

Rating garbage

Separate the class into groups of four to six students. Give each group the materials listed above (except for the art supplies) concealed in a brown grocery bag. Ask the students to remove the items from the bag, make observations, and rate or arrange the items in order from the most usable to the least usable. The students' reasoning behind their rating scheme should be recorded.

2. EXPLANATION/CONCEPT INVENTION: What is the main idea? How will the main idea be identified?

Concept: A great majority of man-made waste can be recycled or reused.

Ask the students questions such as the following to help invent this concept: What did you find in your bags? How did you rank these items from most usable to least usable? Why did you put _____ (name item) as the most usable? Why did you put _____ (name item) as the least usable? Man-made refuse is often regarded as useless waste and ends up in landfills and pollutes our environment. Although not all man-made materials can be recycled, they can be reused in a number of ways not originally intended. Why is it important for us to recycle and reuse? What is the difference between recycling and reusing? What can you do to see that materials such as those found in your bags are recycled or, if possible, reused?

3. EXPANSION OF THE IDEA: Which process skills will be used?

Communicating, problem solving, interpreting data, classifying, making assumptions, drawing conclusions, manipulating materials

How will the idea be expanded?

Litter-eating critter; making paper

- Ask the groups of students to decide what kind of litter-eating creature they could create using the materials found in their grocery bags and the art supplies you make available. After they create plans for their creatures, allow them sufficient time to make and explain to the class just how their litter-eating creatures function.
- Hold up the bug spray can in order to introduce hazardous wastes that are found in the home. Ask the students if they can think of any household items that cannot be disposed of in a regular fashion. Some examples of items that are dangerous and need to be disposed of properly are paint thinners, paints, and motor oils. Ask the students if they are aware why these items cannot be dumped in regular landfills. Explain in detail their impact on the environment.
- Encourage the students to learn how to recycle paper by doing the following activity with them: Collect different types of paper scraps, and using a blender, cut the paper into very small pieces. Mix the fine paper to a pulp mixture with water. Pour out of the blender and roll flat. This can be done on an old piece of screen using a rolling pin. Place an old towel over the pulp as you roll it flat to help squeeze out some of the excess water. Allow the new piece of paper to dry before use.

Why is the idea important for personal development?

- What things can you do to reduce litter in your home? What plans do you have for reducing, reusing, and recycling waste materials you generate?
- Do you think you have a responsibility to future generations to reduce the amount of waste you create? Why or why not? Do you think your parents and

grandparents thought about the amount of waste they generated in the past and how it affects the quality of your life?

Why is the idea important for science-technology-society?

- How can reducing, reusing, and recycling our resources insure that future generations will have a lifestyle comparable to or better than our present one?
- How does a landfill function? Who is responsible for selecting a site for the landfill? How long can we continue dumping our waste into the same landfill?
- What technological advances have decreased the amount of waste we put into our landfills? What technological advances have added to the problem of overflowing landfills?

Why is the idea important for academic growth?

- How can a product be recycled or reused?
- Can all waste products be recycled? If not, is there anything else that can be done with that waste product first before you throw it away?
- Should cost factors prohibit you from recycling waste products? Why or why not?

Why is the idea important for career awareness?

- How many different jobs are involved in the recycling of any product?
- Aside from using natural resources, what other sources can manufacturers go to in order to obtain materials to create their products?

4. EVALUATION: How will the students show what they have learned?

Upon completing the activities the students will be able to

- differentiate between litter and waste in terms of definitions and usefulness,
- rank a pile of materials according to which are the most to least recyclable and which are the most to least reusable,
- identify and collect from home one clean waste item, one clean recyclable item, and one clean reusable item,
- start a recycling project for the entire school.

Litter in our Waterways

GRADE **3–6**

Life Science

DISCIPLINE

Concepts to be invented

Main idea—Irresponsible actions by man are causing the earth's waterways to become littered. This upsets the ecological balance of the water.

Secondary concepts that are important to expansion

Beaches, floating, lakes, litter, oceans, recycling, rivers.

Materials needed

For exploration:

aquarium   water to fill aquarium three-fourths full
plastic six-pack holder   empty aluminum pop can

empty tin can

empty glass pop bottle

empty plastic 2-liter pop bottle

metal can opener

metal bottle cap

⊃ **Safety precautions:** Be careful of the sharp edges and glass. Keep hands away from the aquarium.

1. EXPLORATION: Which process skills will be used?

Observing, questioning, hypothesizing, predicting, experimenting, recording data

What will the children do?

Sink or float litter

- Display the seven litter items listed above next to the aquarium. Ask the students to predict which items will sink when placed in the water. Record their predictions. Allow student volunteers to place each item in the water (one at a time) and observe what happens. Record the results and compare with the initial predictions made by the students.
- Ask the students if they think any of the items that floated could sink eventually. After soliciting several answers, point out that some empty containers may fill with water and sink. The time they take to sink may vary based on certain conditions, such as rough water or human manipulation.
- Ask the students to generate a list of litter they think may be underwater in lakes and rivers. Ask the students how they think it got there.

2. EXPLANATION/CONCEPT INVENTION: What is the main idea? How will the main idea be identified?

Concept: Irresponsible actions by man are causing the earth's waterways to become littered. This upsets the ecological balance of the water.

Ask the students questions such as the following to help invent this concept: What types of litter sank to the bottom of the aquarium? What types of litter floated on top? Do you think that those that floated may eventually sink? How do you think litter such as this could end up in a lake or river? What do you think happens to the litter after it sinks? How do you think this affects water life, such as aquatic plants and animals? What do you think will happen to an aquatic animal if it eats a piece of litter such as a plastic bag?

Litter that floats is easily mistaken for food by many aquatic animals. It is not uncommon for sea turtles to mistake plastic bags for jellyfish and eat them. When this happens the sea turtle thinks it is full because the plastic bag is stuck in its stomach. It eventually starves to death. Ducks and some fish get their beaks or bodies tangled in six-pack rings. This prevents them from eating, and they starve to death. Litter that sinks is not always considered a nuisance. Some sunken ships become places for coral reefs to grow upon.

3. EXPANSION OF THE IDEA: Which process skills will be used?

Communicating, problem solving, interpreting data, classifying, making assumptions, drawing conclusions

How will the idea be expanded?

Plastic food

Ask the students to collect and save every piece of plastic waste used in their homes for one week, clean the waste, and bring it to school. Divide the class into groups of four to six. Ask them to pool their plastic collection. Ask the students to classify the waste according to how an aquatic animal might look at that plastic as a source of food. The categories might be definitely, somewhat likely, unlikely. List some animals that would go for the food in each of the categories. Share these divisions with the class. Once they have discussed their divisions, ask the students to divide the plastic waste according to whether or not an animal could get tangled up in it. Again, discuss the classification scheme the students developed and why. Ask the students as a summary activity to state one positive thing they could do to prevent further pollution of a waterway.

Why is the idea important for personal development?

- Does litter affect your everyday life? If so, how?
- What could you do to cut down on litter?
- Why should someone who lives far from a major waterway be concerned with litter in our waters?
- Do you and your family recycle? If so, what and how?

Why is the idea important for science-technology-society?

- Who in our community should be responsible for cleaning up our waters?
- What are some projects in your neighborhood that deal with litter control?
- What are some different litter control agencies operating in your community?

Why is the idea important for academic growth?

- Are pollutants that float in a waterway just as dangerous as pollutants that sink? Why or why not?
- Are people in danger if they play on beaches near polluted water? Why or why not?
- Can a sunken ship ever be beneficial to aquatic organisms?

Why is the idea important for career awareness?

- Are there any special precautions one must take if his or her job is to clean up a waterway?
- How could an oceanographer use his or her knowledge of ocean currents to help the Coast Guard to identify businesses or cruise ship lines that pollute the waterways?
- Do health care workers have a responsibility to the rest of us to know exactly where their garbage will be disposed? How can they prevent it from ending up in the nation's waterways?

4. EVALUATION: How will the students show what they have learned?

Upon completing the activities the students will be able to

- explain how plastic bags could cause the death of a sea turtle,
- give an example of a piece of plastic litter that can be harmful to aquatic life and propose a solution about how this product could be eliminated from the environment without harming wildlife,
- write a letter of concern to a product manufacturer that they believe uses excessive amounts of plastic packaging on their products.

GRADE **6–8**

Life Science

DISCIPLINE

Slogans and the Environment

Concept to be invented

Main idea—Slogans are used to get a message across.

Secondary concepts that are important to expansion

Campaign slogans, public service slogans, advertising slogans, media, target audience.

Materials needed

For exploration:

Slips of paper with slogans written on them, an overhead transparency with the definition of a slogan on it and examples of slogans, scrap paper for all students, and slogan planning sheets such as the following:

Name: _____   Date:_____

Important Issue:

_____

_____

_____

Form of Advertising:

_____

_____

Selected Audience:

_____

How will your audience get the message?

_____

_____

Rough Draft for Advertisement:

⊃ **Safety precautions:** None needed.

1. EXPLORATION: Which process skills will be used?

Observing, inferring, categorizing, experimenting, recording data

What will the children do?

Slogan categorization

Give each table several slips of paper with one message printed on each. Choose messages with advertising your students are familiar with. As a group, arrange the messages into two or more categories. One suggestion is to read all of the messages and then to decide the criteria they will use to separate them. This will make it easier to put them into categories. Ask the students to record their categorizations.

2. EXPLANATION/CONCEPT INVENTION: What is the main idea? How will the main idea be identified?

Concept: Slogans are used to get a message across.

Ask the students questions such as the following to help invent this concept: What are some ways in which slogans are advertised? Can you think of any slogans for which you are the target audience? For one of the slogans that your group discussed, what is the slogan's purpose? How did you classify the slogans? What important things do all of these slogans include?

Slogans are short phrases used by businesses, public parties, or the like to advertise their purposes. They are meant to influence a certain group of people (target audience) in some way. The following information can be placed on a transparency:

Slogans:

Short phrases used over and over again in advertisements.

Good slogans are easy to remember and tend to stick in people's minds.

Examples:

Product slogan: *Can't beat the real thing* (Coca-Cola)
Restaurant slogan: *Have it your way* (Burger King)
Company slogan: *I love what you do for me* (Toyota)
Political slogan: *Make peace not war* (Peace)
Environmental slogan: *Reduce, reuse, recycle* (Recycling)
Public service slogan: *Just say No!* (Drugs)

3. EXPANSION OF THE IDEA: Which process skills will be used?

Hypothesizing, observing, questioning, classifying, analyzing, inferring, manipulating materials, communicating

How will the idea be expanded?

Environmental slogans

Encourage the students to create a list of important environmental issues that effect their area. Ask the students to work in small groups to do the following: (1) choose an issue from the list generated by the class; (2) create a slogan pertaining to this issue using the slogan planning sheet. Is your slogan one that people could easily remember? Is the purpose clearly stated?

Why is the idea important for personal development?

- Do you think you can be affected by slogans without even realizing it? Can you give any examples of this happening? (Subliminal messages.)
- Do you think the use of subliminal messages is ethical?
- Are slogans always truthful? How do you know when to trust the message of a slogan?

Why is the idea important for science-technology-society?

- Do you think the number of billboards on highways should be limited? Do they serve a purpose? If so what is it? Can this purpose be served in a different manner, without the use of a billboard?
- What are some effective environmental slogans that have been used to improve the world we live in?

Why is the idea important for academic growth?

- What is the purpose of a slogan? What is it intended to do?
- Can the slogan your group created be used to influence the other students in your school about their actions toward the environment? Design a way in which your message could reach a large proportion of the student population in this school.

Why is the idea important for career awareness?

- Which occupations rely on one's ability to quickly create slogans that send powerful messages?
- How do the following occupations utilize slogans to sell their product: Media executive, political advisor, restaurateur, beautician, vitamin manufacturer, construction company executive, soft drink bottlers?

4. EVALUATION: How will the students show what they have learned?

Upon completing the activities the students will be able to

- cooperatively create a slogan on an important local issue,
- choose a medium to advertise the slogan,
- suggest a target audience for the slogan,
- choose a different environmental issue, create a slogan, and design a T-shirt with the slogan on it.

GRADE

K–2

Life
Science

DISCIPLINE

Sense of Taste

Concept to be invented
Main idea—The tongue can detect four different tastes: sweet, sour, bitter, and salty.

Secondary concepts that are important to expansion
Taste buds in different areas of the tongue detect different tastes. Information from the taste buds is interpreted by the brain.

Materials needed
For each pair of students:

four paper cups	cocoa powder
eight cotton-tipped swabs	water
brown sugar	food coloring
lemon juice	a variety of different foods—salty, sweet,
salt	sour, and bitter

Preparation
For each pair of students, fill three paper cups with water. Dissolve salt, cocoa,

and brown sugar (corn syrup may also be used instead of brown sugar) in the individual cups. Add the lemon juice to the fourth cup. Label the cups A, B, C, and D. Create an outline of the tongue on a sheet of paper and duplicate it for each pair of students.

⊃ **Safety precautions:** Before distributing the cotton-tipped swabs, remind the students that they are to be used carefully and cautiously to avoid eye injury. Also, to avoid contamination of the unknowns and to inhibit the spread of germs, students should be reminded not to put used cotton-tipped swabs back into the cups after they place them on their tongues.

1. EXPLORATION: Which process skills will be used?

Observing, predicting, experimenting, evaluating, generalizing, inferring, recording data

What will the children do?

Tongue mapping

Ask the students to choose a partner. Each set of partners should be provided with four paper cups labeled A, B, C, and D, each filled with a different liquid. One student will dip a clean cotton swab into the paper cup labeled A, then touch the cotton swab to the tip of his or her partner's tongue. He or she will then touch the back and the sides of the tongue. Remember that a clean swab should be used for each cup and by each student.

Record how your partner thought liquid A tasted—sweet, sour, salty, or bitter? On what part of the tongue did your partner taste the liquid? Using the drawing of the tongue provided, label where liquid A was tasted. Label whether liquid A was sweet, sour, salty, or bitter. Repeat this procedure using liquids B, C, and D. Be sure to record the observations.

2. EXPLANATION/CONCEPT INVENTION: What is the main idea? How will the main idea be identified?

Concept: The tongue can detect four different tastes: sweet, sour, bitter, and salty.

Ask the students questions such as the following to help invent this concept: How did your partner think each liquid tasted? On what part of the tongue did your classmate taste each liquid?

The students should find that the sugar water could be detected on the tip of the tongue. The salt water could be detected on the sides of the tongue near the tip, the lemon juice on the sides near the back, and the cocoa on the back of the tongue. Also note that salt may be detected on several parts of the tongue.

Your tongue is the organ that gives you your sense of taste. The parts of your tongue that can sense taste are called the taste buds. Thousands of tiny taste buds cover the surface of your tongue. They are in the little bumps that make your tongue look rough. The bumps are called *papillae.* Each one contains about 200 taste buds. You also have taste buds in your throat and on the roof of your mouth. You have about 9000 taste buds in all. Your taste buds contain nerve cells that can sense the substances in food that make each food taste the way it does.

In order to really taste your food, you must chew it. Chewing grinds up your food. It also wets the food by mixing it with saliva. Saliva is a liquid made by small organs in your mouth. When your food is well mixed with saliva, your taste buds can pick up messages about its flavor. Nerves take these messages to taste centers in each side of your brain. Your brain then decides what you are tasting.

The tongue maps should look close to the following:

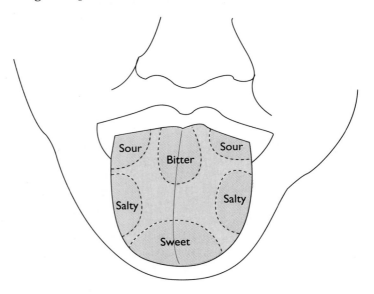

Your taste buds can sense four basic tastes: bitter, salty, sweet, and sour. Foods can still taste different because the four basic flavors combine in many ways. Your brain can tell the mixtures apart. Each mixture is like a different flavor.

Your sense of taste and smell work closely together. The taste of many foods is really a mixture of taste and smell. Food often seems to have no taste when you have a cold. The cold stops up your nose and dulls your sense of smell. When you cannot smell the food, a part of its taste seems to be missing.

3. EXPANSION OF THE IDEA: Which process skills will be used?

Communicating, problem solving, experimenting, recording data

How will the idea be expanded?

Chocolate chip and peanut tongue maps

To reinforce this concept, the students should be given the opportunity to taste real foods such as chocolate chip cookies or peanuts to determine what parts of their tongues can taste the flavors. Create chocolate chip cookie tongue maps and peanut tongue maps.

Why is the idea important for personal development?

- On what parts of the tongue did your partner taste the sweet liquid and the sour, salty, and bitter? Was it the same place as you?
- Are any flavors tasted on more than one part of the tongue? Which?
- Why can many adults tolerate flavorings like hot pepper sauce that if given to a baby would surely make him or her sick?

Why is the idea important for science-technology-society?

- Ask the students to generate a list of spices used in cooking. Assign each student a spice. From which country does it originate? How does it grow? How is it harvested? How important is that spice to the society of the country in which it grows?
- Do you think that people from countries other than your own have different amounts of taste buds on their tongue? How do you explain that many cultures tolerate food much spicier than typical American fare? Does the number of taste buds have anything to do with it?

Why is the idea important for academic growth?

- Why do you think the taste buds are located in different areas of the tongue?
- What do you think might happen if the different kinds of taste buds were located all in the same area on the tongue?

Why is the idea important for career awareness?

- In which careers would people find information on taste buds useful? How would they use this information?
- Do you think someone with permanent damage to his or her nose resulting in the loss of the sense of smell would have a promising career as a professional chef? Why or why not?

4. EVALUATION: How will the students show what they have learned?

Upon completing the activities the students will be able to

- list the four kinds of taste buds found on the tongue,
- locate the positions of the different kinds of taste buds on the tongue,
- eat a piece of chocolate candy and draw a tongue map identifying the various tastes sensed while eating the candy.

Skeleton

Concepts to be invented

Main idea—The internal support system for muscles in most mammals is the bones. All the bones arranged together make up the skeleton.

Secondary concepts that are important to expansion

Joints help skeletons move.

Materials needed

For each student:

One large sheet of newsprint, markers, crayons, several brass paper fasteners, a packet of paper bones that when put together will create a replica of a human skeleton.

⊃ **Safety precautions:** Explain to the students how to use the brass fasteners. Remind them that they could hurt themselves if they poked themselves or others with the pointed edge.

1. EXPLORATION: Which process skills will be used?

Observing, questioning, manipulating materials, analyzing

What will the children do?

Bones assembly line

Introduce the lesson by reading two poems from *A Light in the Attic,* by Shel Silverstein. The poems are "Day After Halloween" and "It's Hot!" Begin a discussion with the students about the ideas behind the poems. Ask questions such as: What would it be like if we didn't have a skeleton? Why do we need bones in our bodies?

Give each child several brass fasteners and a packet containing paper bones cut into the different major bones of the body. Ask the students to empty the packets and to manipulate the materials in any way they wish in an effort to determine what they can create with all the bones. Encourage them to use the brass fasteners to assemble the bones. Walk around the room asking questions like: What do you think all of these different parts make up? Do you think you know where all the parts go? What could the brass fasteners represent in a real body that helps us to move? How do the bones in our body connect for real?

2. EXPLANATION/CONCEPT INVENTION: What is the main idea? How will the main idea be identified?

Concept: The internal support system for muscles in most mammals is the bones. All the bones arranged together make up the skeleton.

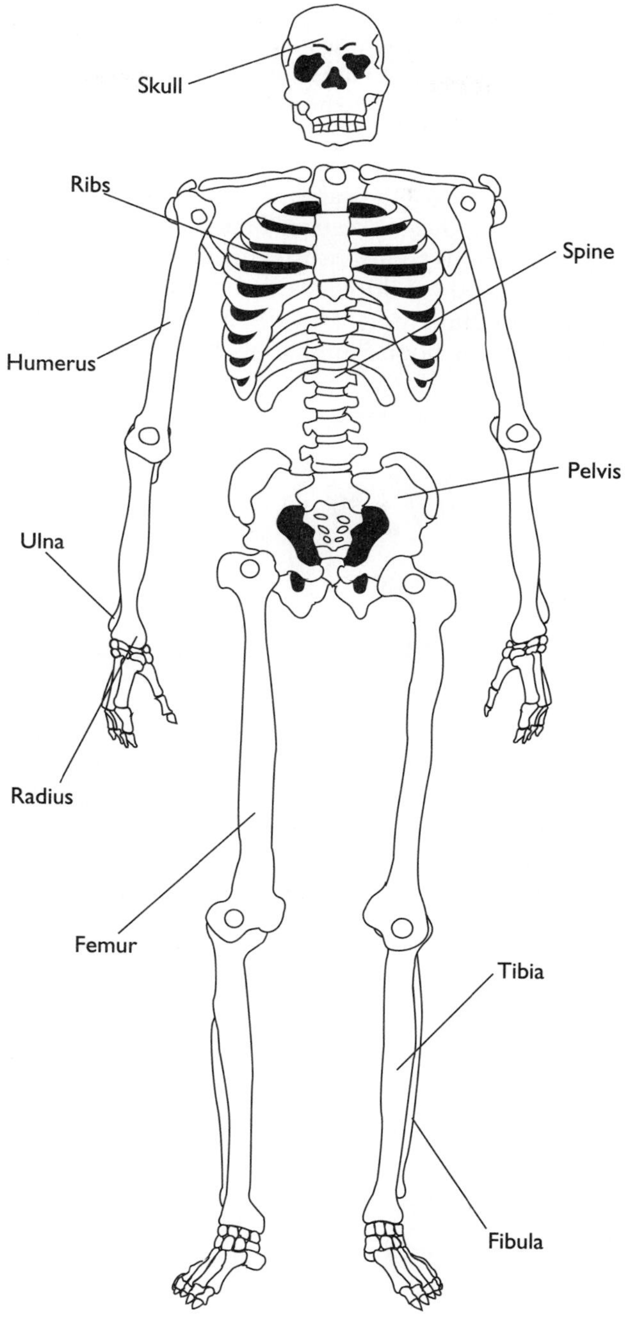

Skull

Ribs

Spine

Humerus

Pelvis

Ulna

Radius

Femur

Tibia

Fibula

Using a picture of a skeleton and a life-size skeleton, ask the children if they know the nonscientific names of the bones. Write these on the board. If students offer the scientific names, list those as well; compare them to the common name. Show a picture of the muscle system of the human body. Explain to the students how the bones help give the muscles support.

Walk around the classroom very stiffly. Encourage some or all of the students to do the same. Really play it up: Tell them they cannot bend their elbows or knees. You used brass fasteners to connect the bones in your skeleton. Do you think those are used in our bodies? Of course not; what do we use? Joints.

Ask the children to demonstrate what would happen to them right now (as they are standing) if they did not have bones in their body. The students should drop to the floor. Summarize that the skeleton supports our muscles.

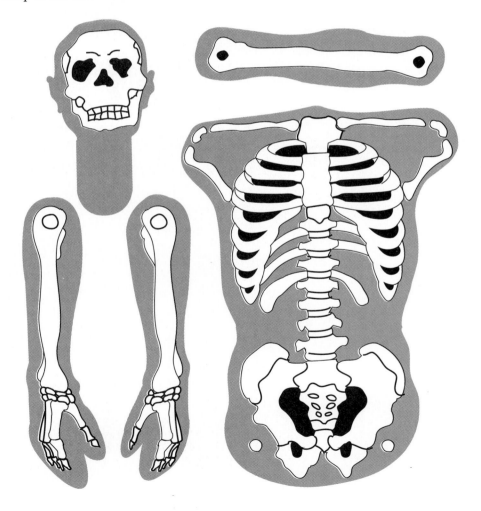

3. EXPANSION OF THE IDEA: Which process skills will be used?

Observing, classifying, recording, manipulating materials

How will the idea be expanded?

Newsprint bone bodies

Pair up the students and provide each child with a large sheet of newsprint and a pencil. Ask the students to spread the paper out on the floor. The paired children should take turns. One child should lie flat on the paper with his or her face down. The other child should outline the body. Let each child switch roles. After they have created their outlines, have each child fill in the outline with the bones of the body.

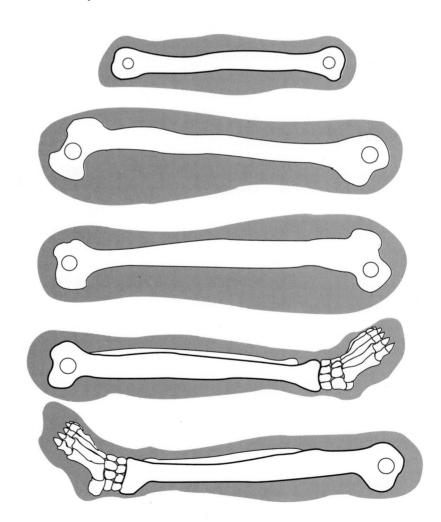

Why is the idea important for personal development?

- Do you think it is good to know what is inside our body? Why?
- How do joints help us move?
- Could you do the same activities you do on a daily basis if you didn't have a skeleton?

Why is the idea important for science-technology-society?

- What do you think scientists do with bones found in nature?
- Do you think bones found by scientists tell them anything about the organism and the environment it lived in?
- How do you think we see our bones inside of our body? What is that picture called?

Why is the idea important for academic growth?

- How do bones connect together?
- Why do you think it is good to understand how our bodies move?
- Why do you think we have two bones in our forearms and lower legs?

Why is the idea important for career awareness?

- What is the name of the person who shows you pictures of your bones inside you?
- If you had some back problems and you wanted your spine readjusted, what type of professional would you go to?
- What would you call a person who went to different locations to dig up buried bones and artifacts?
- What would happen if you went to a doctor and he or she didn't know what parts of your skeleton were hurting you? Would you trust that doctor?
- What does a doctor do if you have a broken bone?

4. EVALUATION: How will the students show what they have learned?

Upon completing the activities the students will be able to

- assemble a paper skeleton,
- identify at least five bones in the body with common names,
- understand why we need joints in our bodies and explain what they do,
- play Hokey-Pokey Skeleton, using the common names of bones to stick in and out.

Temperature Receptors on Skin

Concept to be invented
Main idea—Our bodies have separate spots, called receptors, for feeling temperatures that are hotter or colder than body temperatures.

Secondary concepts that are important to expansion
Water can feel hot and cold to our bodies at the same time.

Materials needed
For each student group:

a source of hot and cold water
three bowls
six nails

two fine-tipped pens, each a different
  color
paper towels

⊃ **Safety precautions:** Do not poke each other with the nails. Use care around the water: If it is knocked over, be sure to clean it up immediately. Make sure hot water is not so hot that it will scald.

1. EXPLORATION: Which process skills will be used?

Observing, questioning, designing an experiment, recording data, predicting, generalizing

What will the children do?

Soaking hands

Divide the students into cooperative working groups of four. Ask the materials manager to obtain three small bowls. Fill one with hot water, one with cold water, and the third with warm water. The groups' mission is to find out how hands feel when placed in water of different temperatures. Encourage the groups to design an experiment to solve this problem. Ask them to record their data. Their experimental designs may look something like this: Each student in the group will take turns placing one hand in hot water and the other in cold. Hands should be left for several minutes in the water. Remove hands from those bowls and immediately immerse them in the warm water. They should be able to describe what happened next. There may be some variations to this plan. Teachers may find that some groups first put both hands in cold and then in hot. They all should be able to help invent the concept no matter the experimental design.

2. EXPLANATION/CONCEPT INVENTION: What is the main idea? How will the main idea be identified?

Concept: Our bodies have separate spots, called *receptors*, for feeling temperatures that are hotter or colder than body temperatures.

To help invent this concept, ask each of the student groups to report on the experiment they designed. What did you do? What results did you get? Did the water feel hot and cold at the same time? How can that be? Does it have to do with the temperature of the water your hand was in first or just the temperature of your hand? The students should be able to conclude that it has to do with the temperature of the water their hand was in first. On their skin are receptors that sense temperatures different than normal body temperature.

3. EXPANSION OF THE IDEA: Which process skills will be used?

Observing, classifying, recording, predicting

How will the idea be expanded?

Hot/cold receptor mapping

Ask each student to use one of the pens provided to the groups to draw a square on the back of his or her hand. Place one nail in the bowl of cold water and another in the bowl of hot water. Ask the group members to pair up. Ask one student from each pair to take the nail from the cold water and touch the tip of the nail to any spot in the square of his or her partner's hand. If it feels cold, mark that spot with the pen (marking all the cold ones in the same color). Now switch so that each partner has cold receptors marked. Other student pairs in each cooperative group can be doing the same thing with the hot water and a nail. Be sure to use a different color pen for hot spots. Now exchange bowls and make marks for the opposite water type. Are you surprised at where you find the hot and cold receptors?

Why is the idea important for personal development?

- People say that to test bath water you should use your elbow or to test a baby's bottle you should use your wrist. Why do you think they chose those particular body parts?
- Which would you test your bath water with, your hand or your toes? Why?

Why is the idea important for science-technology-society?

- On a hot summer day it is nice to enter an air-conditioned building. After you've been in the building for an hour you begin to think the air conditioning

has been shut off. Why do you think you feel this way?
- How has technology allowed us to exist comfortably in the winter and the summer?

Why is the idea important for academic growth?
- Could you find a way to pick up a snowball and not feel the cold?
- Which part of your hand is most sensitive to hot things?
- What is a receptor?

Why is the idea important for career awareness?
- Why do people who work in meat lockers wear gloves?
- Do you think it is important for someone involved in child care to make sure that his or her heat receptors are not damaged? Why or why not?

4. EVALUATION: How will the students show what they have learned?

Upon completing the activities the students will be able to
- identify the different hot and cold receptors on each hand,
- explain how water can feel hot and cold at the same time,
- identify the child with the cold hands when looking at a picture of children involved in building a snow fort (the one without gloves),
- view a picture of working firefighters with and without fire coats and identify which ones will feel hot. Why is this not the same as pictures of children in the winter with and without coats?

GRADE **4–6**

Life Science

DISCIPLINE

Building Microscope Skills

Concept to be invented

Main idea—A microscope is used to identify objects not visible to the naked eye.

Secondary concepts that are important to expansion

Identifying a compound by its characteristic crystal shape, slide preparation.

Materials needed

For exploration:

noniodized salt	water	microscope
iodized salt	eye droppers	scale
sugar	cups	graduated cylinder
alum	slides	pictures of crystals
borax	slide covers	

For expansion:

water	laundry bluing
noniodized salt	household ammonia

⊃ **Safety precautions:** Avoid placing hands near eyes or mouth while working with materials to prepare slides. When using an electric microscope, be sure to use proper safety measures near electrical outlets. The microscope lamp may be hot to touch. Apply the usual safety standards when working with such chemicals as bluing and ammonia.

1. EXPLORATION: Which process skills will be used?

Observing, classifying, recording data, diagramming, and comparing, manipulating instruments

What will the children do?

Microscope use and crystal comparisons

Measure out 5 grams of each solid. Dissolve each in a separate cup containing 25 ml of water. Be sure to label the cup with the name of the material dissolved in the water. As the solution is forming, label a slide for each solute. Place a drop of each solution on its assigned slide. Allow the water to evaporate. Carefully place the cover slip over the remaining crystals on the slide. Focus each slide under the microscope and record your observations for each at low power. Focus under a higher power and again record observations.

2. EXPLANATION/CONCEPT INVENTION: What is the main idea? How will the main idea be identified?

Concept: A microscope is used to identify objects not visible to the naked eye.

Key questions to ask students to help them come to this conclusion are: What shapes did you observe on the slide? How does it compare to a drawing of the crystal shape? Can you share a diagram of those shapes with the class? How are these shapes similar? How are they different? How did the microscope help you to observe the crystal?

3. EXPANSION OF THE IDEA: Which process skills will be used?

Graphing, classifying, experimenting

How will the idea be expanded?

Charcoal crystals

- Use the results of the previous crystal comparison activity to graph the crystal shapes versus the number of substances that have that particular shape.
- The students should be encouraged to brainstorm a list of other possible substances that contain crystals. Observe these under the microscope.
- The students will grow a crystal garden in a Styrofoam egg carton by first placing pieces of charcoal into the egg sockets. In a separate container mix the following substances:

6 tablespoons of water	6 tablespoons of laundry bluing
6 tablespoons of noniodized salt	2 teaspoons of household ammonia

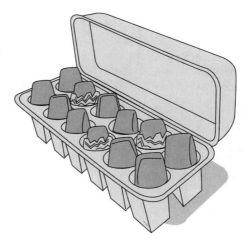

Once this solution is prepared the students should carefully pour it over the pieces of charcoal in the egg container. The students can then place these in an area in the classroom where they will not be hit or bumped. The crystals will grow for several days. If the students want colored crystals, they may place a few drops of food coloring on the charcoal after the solution is poured on them. The students may wish to make each egg socket a different color. Once the crystals have grown, the students may safely carry them home in their egg cartons. If the crystals do get bumped in transit, sometimes they can be revived by putting a little water on them.

Why is the idea important for personal development?

- While rummaging through your kitchen for a salt shaker, you come across a container you think will work. After placing the salt into the container, you find that no salt comes out of the holes when you shake the container. Why do you think this happened? Will the size of the salt crystals determine the size of the holes that should be on top of a shaker?
- Do you think there are any other areas of your life where the skills you learned in this lesson can be applied? If so, where?
- How do you think your increased knowledge of crystal shapes will help you become a better consumer? Would you buy ice cream that contained frost crystals? Why or why not?

Why is the idea important for science-technology-society?

- Knowing that salt or sugar can be placed in solution allowed past generations to preserve foods more easily, thus insuring their survival. How have our present-day technologies expanded on these early ideas?
- Think about the frozen food industry. How do they make use of their knowledge of crystal formation?

Why is the idea important for academic growth?
- What scientific concepts did you discover while participating in these activities?
- What problem-solving techniques did you employ?
- What procedures were used with the microscope?

Why is the idea important for career awareness?
- How important is it for a gemologist to understand the differences between crystal shapes? Why?
- In addition to knowledge about crystals, what other kinds of skills would a geologist need? A gemologist? A hospital laboratory technician?
- Are there any other careers you can think of that would require the skills you obtained while participating in these activities?

4. EVALUATION: How will the students show what they have learned?

Upon completing these activities the students will be able to

- demonstrate proper slide preparation techniques,
- prepare a slide of a crystal and focus it under a microscope,
- identify on a diagram the basic crystal shapes,
- state why different compounds may have different crystal shapes.

SECTION II

Physical Science Activities

Lesson Name	Grade Level	Activities
Sound versus Noise	2–3	School Sound Search • Magazine Sound Search • Music or Noise Search
Sounds Are Different	2–4	Megaphones and Vibrating Straws • Bell Ringers
Vibrations Causing Sound	2–4	Sound Makers • Waxed Paper Kazoo
Loudness and Pitch	2–4	Pop Bottle Orchestra • Cigar Box Strings • Fish Line Harps
Sound Movement as Waves	2–4	Vibrating Fork • Clapping Blocks • Tapping Tank • Paper Cup Telephone
Sound Waves	2–4	Soup Can Reflectors • Slinky Waves • Sound Waves and the Ear
Sound Production	5–7	Noise/Sound ID • Sound Movement • Sound Game
Characteristics of Matter	2–6	Plastic Bag Chemistry • Marble Matter • Chemical Nomenclature and/or Balancing Equations
Physical Properties of Matter	K–6	Egg-citing Observations • Chocolate Chip Exploration • Paper Towel Testing
Changing Matter	3–6	Physical and Chemical Paper Change • Polymer—Rubber Balls
Identification of an Unknown	5–8	Physical Properties of an Unknown • Chemical Properties of an Unknown
Using the Scientific Method to Solve Problems	3–6	Exploring with Efferdent Tablets • Exploring with Corn Starch
Heat Energy	1–3	Liquid Birthday • Liquids to Solids
Structure Strength	1–3	Straw Construction
Mirrors and Reflection	1–3	Mirrors and Reflectors • What's a Mirror? • Mirror Writing
Paper Chromatography	3–6	Moving Black Ink Dots • Moving Colored Ink Dots and Snowflakes
Toys in Space	3–6	Toy Behavior in Zero Gravity • Toys and Newton • Toy Design
Simple Machines—The Lever	4–8	Lever Creations • Spoons and Nuts • Lever Scavenger Hunt

PHYSICAL SCIENCE

GRADE 2–3

Physical Science

DISCIPLINE

Sound versus Noise

Concept to be invented
Main idea—Sound can be considered useful or simply noise.

Secondary concepts that are important to expansion
Sound can be pleasant or unpleasant.

Materials needed
Whistle   tape recorder (if possible, one per group)
magazines for cutting up   one blank audio tape per group

⊃ **Safety precautions:** The students should be reminded of the importance of walking, not running, as they move through the school to find a place to listen to different sounds. They should use care when carrying pencils or pens to record their observations. Exercise caution when using the scissors in the expansion activity.

Discrepant event
While the children are working quietly at their desks, make sure no students are looking, and then take out a whistle and blow it loudly. Ask the children what they first thought when they heard the whistle. Record some of their thoughts on the board.

1. EXPLORATION: Which process skills will be used?

Observing, classifying, predicting, describing, recording data, communicating

What will the children do?

School sound search

Divide the class into four groups. Send each group to different parts of the school building, such as the janitors' work room, the playground, the gym or music room, their own classroom. Ask them to go to these areas quietly. Have them sit quietly in their areas for three minutes. Create a list of all of the sounds they hear in those areas. Return to the classroom. Instruct the students to work with the people in their group to decide if there is any way they could group the sounds. When all of the groups have analyzed their lists, share the categories of sounds with the rest of the class. Ask the students if any of the groups came up with categories your group never thought of?

2. EXPLANATION/CONCEPT INVENTION: What is the main idea? How will the main idea be identified?

Concept: Sound can be considered useful or simply noise.

Place on the board in separate columns the terms *useful, noise, pleasant,* and *unpleasant.* Ask the students if any of these terms fit the feelings they had when

I blew the whistle unexpectedly? Do any of these terms fit the categories you placed your sounds under? If so, which of your sounds would go under the different headings? Encourage members of the group to write their sounds under the appropriate headings. Do all sounds fall *only* into one classification? Fire alarms, whistles—where do they fall? Sounds can be useful or noise depending on circumstances. Sound can be harmful. We need ear protection from some sounds.

3. EXPANSION OF THE IDEA: Which process skills will be used?

Observing, classifying, communicating, inferring, manipulating materials, interpreting data

How will the idea be expanded?

Magazine sound search

The children will work in groups, looking through magazines, cutting out possible sources of sound. Each group will create an audiotape, mimicking the sounds that the different items they collected make. Each group will place their pictures on a poster. They will then play their tape to the other groups. The members of the other groups will guess which item the sound goes with, and then determine if it is useful or noise, pleasant or unpleasant, or any combination of these. They must be able to explain why they would classify the item that way.

Why is the idea important for personal development?

- When listening to a radio with headphones on, is it wise to have the volume so loud that those around you can hear it?
- If you were asked to create a sound that would serve as a warning for some devastating disaster like a tornado, what would this sound be like? How would you categorize it? How unique would it have to be?

Why is the idea important for science-technology-society?

- Why was it necessary for the Occupational Safety and Health Administration (OSHA) to set standards for an acceptable noise level in work areas?
- Personal computers have changed our lives in many ways. While they have been a help, they have also created problems. How have they contributed to the problem of noise pollution, and what has the computer industry done to eliminate some of this noise?
- Many airports near major cities were built in areas long considered migratory routes for some animals, mating habitats for others. The constant roar of jet engines affects the behavior of these animals. What has man done to eliminate some noise hazards brought upon these creatures? What must we continue to do?

Why is the idea important for academic growth?

- How would you classify the sound best suited for quiet study time?
- Can sounds be classified into more than one category?

PHYSICAL SCIENCE

Why is the idea important for career awareness?

- Which type of work do you think would be most affected by noise pollution? Least affected? Which type of work would you choose? Why?
- Do you think it is important for a music critic to distinguish between a useful sound or noise, a pleasant or unpleasant sound?

4. EVALUATION: How will the students show what they have learned?

Upon completing the activities the students will be able to

- listen to an audiotape of various sounds and classify them according to useful/noise and pleasant/unpleasant,
- take one of the assigned categories—useful/pleasant; useful/unpleasant; noise/pleasant; noise/unpleasant—and given a week, will be able to find some music that they think fits into their assigned category and explain why they believe it does. They are encouraged to get their families involved in their search. If they cannot find some music that fits their category, they can create their own sound.

Sounds Are Different

GRADE 2–4

Physical Science

DISCIPLINE

PHYSICAL SCIENCE

Concept to be invented
Main idea—Sounds vary in loudness and pitch.

Secondary concepts that are important to expansion
Loudness is determined by the strength of the vibration. Pitch is determined by the length of the vibrating object. Magnification of sound is achieved by megaphones and speakers.

Materials needed
several large and small bells
pieces of at least 8-in x 8-in
   square paper

tape
paper straws
scissors

⊃ **Safety precautions:** Be careful when using the scissors. Remember basic scissors safety. Be careful when placing the straws into your mouth. During the expansion activity, do not ring a bell in anyone's ear.

Discrepant event
Find a time when the students are working quietly in their seats. Take a large and a small bell and ring them at the same time. Ask the students: "Did I get your attention? Did you hear just one noise or two? Did one sound softer than the other? Higher than the other?"

1. EXPLORATION: Which process skills will be used?

Observing, communicating, inferring, predicting

What will the children do?

Megaphones and vibrating straws

Ask half the students to shout "hello" to you from their seats. Now ask them to cup their hands around their mouths and shout "hello" again. Ask those who did not yell if they noticed a difference in the sound produced. Now let the other half try it. Give the children pieces of paper and have them roll them into cones. Tape the sides together to maintain the cone shapes. Use the scissors to cut away about one inch of the pointed end of each cone. Once again have half the class shout "hello," and then shout again, holding the cut ends of the cones by their mouths. Once again ask the listeners if they noticed a difference in the sound produced each time. Allow the other half to test their cones too.

Give the students one straw each. Ask them to cut a little piece off both sides of one end so that what remains looks like an inverted V. Ask them to predict what will happen when they blow into the cut end of the straw. What do they need to do to get the cut V-shaped pieces to vibrate? As they hold the straws in their mouths, they should continue to blow into the straws and start cutting off pieces at the ends of the straws. What is happening to the sound as the straw gets shorter?

2. EXPLANATION/CONCEPT INVENTION: What is the main idea? How will the main idea be identified?

Concept: Sounds vary in loudness and pitch.

When did the "hellos" sound the loudest? When you used nothing, your hand, or your school-made megaphone? What does a megaphone do? It magnifies sound. It increases the strength of the vibration, thus making the sound louder.

What happened to the sound produced by the straw as you cut it? Was the loudness of the sound the same? What property of sound changed? The pitch got higher. *Pitch* is determined by the length of the vibrating object.

3. EXPANSION OF THE IDEA: Which process skills will be used?

Predicting, designing an experiment, communicating, controlling variables, experimenting, observing, recording data, hypothesizing, inferring

How will the idea be expanded?

Bell ringers

Divide the students into groups. Provide for each group at least four different-sized bells. Before ringing each bell, ask the students to create a prediction sheet identifying the loudness and pitch of the bell. Have each group design a way that will most fairly and accurately ring the bells. Emphasize the importance of keeping all other variables constant when comparing the four bells, such as having the same person ring the bells for each trial, or having each person in the group ring each bell to see if the person doing the ringing affects the loudness or pitch. After filling out their prediction sheet and designing a way to ring the bells without letting their predictions prejudice them, they should ring the bells. Record your results. Did your results match your predictions? Is there any way you can alter the bell to magnify the sound coming from it?

Why is the idea important for personal development?

- What harm can the earphones on headsets have on your eardrums? What does the magnification of sound do to your eardrums?
- Would the magnification of sound be useful at a baseball or football game? Why or why not? Would everyone at these games appreciate sound being magnified?

Why is the idea important for science-technology-society?

- How has knowledge of loudness, pitch, and magnification led to the creation of devices that are important for crowd control? For large group communication? For the production of music?
- Why do you think a baseball stadium needs to be designed differently than a concert hall? In which would you want the sound to be louder? To be magnified?

Why is the idea important for academic growth?

- How could you control the loudness of the sound created by a piano?
- How could you change the pitch of a guitar?

Why is the idea important for career awareness?

- In what careers would you need to understand that loud sounds could set objects vibrating, which could cause structures to collapse? (Safety engineers, contractors, civil engineers, hotel/motel managers, high-rise office building workers.)
- How can a cheerleader save his or her voice by knowing about sound, loudness, pitch, and magnification?

4. EVALUATION: How will the students show what they have learned?

Upon completing the activities the students will be able to

- infer, when given a set of pictures (large bell, small bell, siren, whistle) which would create a loud or soft sound;
- infer, when given another set of pictures (long and short guitar strings, large bell, small bell, man's voice, child's voice), which would create a high or low sound;
- give at least three ways in which one could magnify one's voice.

Vibrations Causing Sound

Concepts to be invented

Main idea—Vibrations are caused by the movement of air molecules due to a disturbance.

Secondary concepts that are important to expansion

There are many ways to produce sounds. You may not be able to see all vibrations.

Materials needed

For exploration:

Prerecorded tape of classroom sounds, tape player, string, wire, meter stick, drum and beans, tuning forks and rubber mallet, pans of water, kitchen fork.

For expansion:

Combs and waxed paper squares.

⊃ **Safety precautions:** Remind students of the importance of using the rubber bands as instructed. Any other use may result in injury to eyes or faces. Exercise caution when carrying the kitchen forks during the exploration activity.

Discrepant event

Ask the students to listen carefully as you play the tape recording of classroom sounds. Try to guess what these familiar sounds are. Can you give me any descriptive terms to remember them by?

1. EXPLORATION: Which process skills will be used?

Observing, communicating, recording data, experimenting, predicting, inferring

What will the children do?

Sound makers

- Have the children place their hands on their throats and make sounds. Record what it feels like.
- In groups, ask the children to stretch and pluck rubber bands and strings. Record their observations.
- Have the students place the handle end of a kitchen fork between their teeth. Quickly flick the other end of the fork. What do your teeth feel like?
- In groups, ask the students to tap pans of water and observe.
- In groups, have the students tap tuning forks with rubber mallets and observe. Ask them to predict what will happen if they strike a tuning fork and quickly thrust it into a pan of water. Have them check their predictions.

2. EXPLANATION/CONCEPT INVENTION: What is the main idea? How will the main idea be identified?

Concept: Vibrations are caused by the movement of air molecules due to a disturbance.

What did it feel like when you placed your hands on your throat and made sounds? Did your hands begin to tingle? What happened to the rubber bands when you stretched them out and plucked them? How did your teeth feel when you flicked the kitchen fork? What path did the water create when the pan was gently tapped? Did the tuning fork tickle your hand when you struck it with the rubber mallet? What happened when you thrust the tuning fork into the water? Was it as you predicted? Elicit the idea that sound is produced by movement. If no one says "vibrate" introduce this term now.

3. EXPANSION OF THE IDEA: Which process skills will be used?

Inferring, experimenting, hypothesizing, communicating

How will the idea be expanded?

Waxed paper kazoo

Have each child make a comb-and-waxed-paper kazoo by folding a piece of waxed paper over the teeth of a comb. Instruct to the children to place their lips

on the wax paper and to hum a tune. How is the sound being produced? What is vibrating?

Why is the idea important for personal development?

- How is sound made? Can you avoid sound?
- Do sounds affect the way you feel and act?
- Would you want to attend a concert or go to a movie where the sound kept echoing off the walls? Why or why not?

Why is the idea important for science-technology-society?

- The quality of speakers and sound systems relies heavily on sound vibrations; how has modern technology eliminated a lot of excess vibrations?
- How important a role does the design of a room play in carrying sound vibrations?
- How did an understanding of sound vibrations help in the creation of the microphone, the phonograph, the telephone, underwater depth sounding, and ultrasound? How have these inventions changed the world?

Why is the idea important for academic growth?

- Knowing that sound is produced by a vibrating object, do you think you can make a bell ring under water? Try it.
- Some birds, like loons, can dive under water for their food and stay down for an extended period of time. Do you think they call to one another while they are under the water? Can they hear each other? What could you do to determine whether or not your answer is correct?

Why is the idea important for career awareness?

- Who was John William Strutt, also known as Baron Rayleigh? What role did he play in helping us understand how sound behaves? [For second grade, the teacher could give a brief biography of Baron Rayleigh. He was born in England in 1842. While many people before him expressed opinions about the nature of sound (Pythagoras, Galileo, Mersenne, Chladni—"the founder of modern acoustics,"—Colladon and Sturm, and von Helmholtz), Baron Rayleigh was the first to put it all together in a book titled *Theory of Sound,* which he published in 1877. A second edition was published in 1894. In 1904 Rayleigh won the Nobel Prize for physics, mainly for his work that lead to the discovery of argon and other inert gases. Baron Rayleigh died in 1919.]
- Sound production is important in entertainment—develop a list of entertainment careers that utilize sound.

4. EVALUATION: How will the students show what they have learned?

Upon completing the activities the students will be able to

- predict from a given set of objects which will vibrate and produce sound (nerf ball, drum, taut rubber band, loose rubber band, ruler, feather).
- spend one week in which they will be expected to test various wall surfaces to

determine which one allow for maximum and for minimum sound vibrations. They will share their findings with the class and, based on these findings, accurately predict which type of wall surface would be best for a movie theater or a concert hall.

Loudness and Pitch

Concept to be invented
Main idea—Sounds vary in loudness and pitch.

Secondary concepts that are important to expansion
Size and strength of vibration will affect loudness and pitch.

Materials needed

drinking glasses	wooden board with hooks and fish line
large nail	oatmeal boxes
empty pop bottles	wood blocks
water	pan lids
cigar box	guitar or piano
rubber bands	

⊃ **Safety precautions:** Care should be taken when handling any of the glass containers used in many of the activities. Protect eyes against flying rubber bands—wear goggles!

Discrepant event
Ask the students to predict what will happen to the sound as you tap an empty glass with a nail and gradually add water as you tap. Once all predictions are given, begin to tap the bottle and fill it as you do so. Did the sound behave as you predicted? What happened to the sound as more water filled the glass? Do you have any ideas why this happened?

1. EXPLORATION: *Which process skills will be used?*

Observing, manipulating materials, predicting, communicating, recording data, inferring, hypothesizing

What will the children do?

Pop bottle orchestra, cigar box strings, fishline harps

Divide the class into four groups. Have each group rotate through the following activities:

• Pop bottles, glasses, water, nails: Set up a center with glasses and bottles filled with water at varying levels. Have children explore sound variation with

Soda bottles filled with water at varying levels

Glasses filled with varying levels of water

water levels in both glasses and bottles. Ask them to record their observations, taking special note of the relationship between the sound produced and the amount of water in the different containers.

• Rubber bands of varying widths and lengths, open cigar box: Stretch the different-sized rubber bands over the open cigar box. Pluck the rubber bands. What kinds of sounds do they make? Record the sounds made by the different-sized rubber bands.

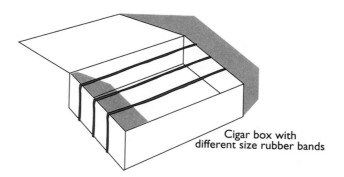

Cigar box with
different size rubber bands

• Make a fish line harp by cutting at least eight different lengths of fish line. String each line through two eye hooks that are screwed into a foot-long piece of board (a 1 x 8 will do) the same distance apart as the string length. (The teacher can make this harp ahead of time.) Pluck the strings. What do you observe about the relationship between the string length and the sound produced? Is there a relationship between the sound produced and the tightness of the string?

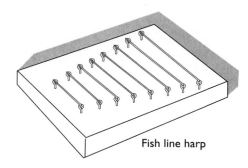

Fish line harp

• Strum a guitar, or play a piano in which the guts are exposed. If you are using a guitar, what relationship do you observe between the size of the guitar string and the sound it produces? For the piano, what relationship do you observe between the size of the piano string and the sound it produces?

2. EXPLANATION/CONCEPT INVENTION: What is the main idea? How will the main idea be identified?

Concept: Sounds vary in loudness and pitch.

What did you observe when you tapped the various glasses and bottles? What happened to the sound if you used a lot of force to strike the nail to the container? In which containers were the sounds higher?

How were you able to make the rubber band sound loud when plucked? What type of sounds were produced with very skinny, tightly stretched rubber bands? Very fat, loosely stretched ones?

When you played the harp, which length string gave you the highest sound? The lowest? Did you try loosening the strings? What happened to the sounds when the strings were loose?

When you played the guitar or piano, what did you do to create a very loud sound? How were you able to get a very high sound? A low sound?

Summarize all the answers by reinforcing the following: Loudness is determined by the strength of vibration. Pitch is determined by the length of the vibrating object.

3. EXPANSION OF THE IDEA: Which process skills will be used?

Predicting, communicating, experimenting, interpreting data

How will the idea be expanded?

Homemade music

Based on your conclusions from the previous activities, choose a song familiar to everyone in your group and try to play that simple melody on the glasses, the bottles, or any of the other instruments. Each group will take a turn performing for the other groups.

Why is the idea important for personal development?

- The ability to produce music enriches the lives of children and can lead to a lifetime skill. The ability to control sound enhances self-concept.
- How could you use sound to help you determine how much pop you have left in a can? Or how much milk is left in a carton? Or how much laundry detergent is left in its container? Or if a new bottle of perfume or aftershave is totally full?

Why is the idea important for science-technology-society?

- Many video games use sound to heighten the suspense and action of the play. Do you think these games would be as popular if all sound were eliminated?
- What effect does the loudness and pitch of music have on moviegoers? Would scary movies be as effective without the sound effects?
- How has the computer industry made use of the loudness and pitch of sounds in personal computers?

Why is the idea important for academic growth?

- What properties affect the pitch of a sound? The loudness of a sound?
- Can you create an instrument with high pitch and soft sound? With low pitch and loud sound?

Why is the idea important for career awareness?

- Children enjoy music for listening and movement and may look to a future as an entertainer.
- Where do you think someone with a background in music production, sound engineering, or the creation of musical instruments could use his or her talents?

4. EVALUATION: How will the students show what they have learned?

Upon completing these activities the students will be able to

- predict whether a high or low pitch will be produced by looking at pictures of various-sized strings or columns of water,
- predict loudness and softness of sound when given pictures of thick or thin strings of the same length,
- create a high-pitched sound when given a straw,
- create a low pitch with a pop bottle.

PHYSICAL SCIENCE

GRADE **2–4** *Physical Science* **DISCIPLINE**

Sound Movement as Waves

Concepts to be invented

Main idea—Sounds move in the form of waves through air, water, wood, and other solids.

Secondary concepts that are important to expansion

Sound waves must strike your eardrum for you to hear sound, sound waves weaken with distance.

Materials needed

Set up the following as activity centers:

(1) fork and string chime, (2) metal rod, (3) meter stick, wood blocks, (4) pieces of cloth, cotton balls, feathers, cork, nerf ball, (5) ten-gallon fish tank filled with water.

Per student pair:

Two paper cups and two paper clips per student; string for telephone; tin can and fishline telephone for comparison with paper cup telephone.

⊃ **Safety precautions:** Care should be taken when handling the kitchen fork and tuning forks; keep them away from your own eyes and those of your friends. Be careful where you place your fingers as you bang the two wood blocks together; avoid crushing them between the blocks.

Discrepant event

Ask the students to listen as they tap the sides of their desks. Now ask them to lay their ears on their desk tops while tapping the sides of the desks with the same force as before. Have them describe the sounds they hear. Are there any differences? Why?

1. EXPLORATION: Which process skills will be used?

Observing, recording data, predicting, inferring, describing, communicating, measuring, defining operationally

What will the children do?

Divide the class into five groups. Have each group record their observations as they rotate throughout the following activity centers.

• Tie about a 12-inch length of string to the handle end of a fork. Allow it to bang on the side of a desk or a wall as you set it in swinging motion. Write a description of the sound it creates. Can you manipulate the string or fork in any way to change the pitch or loudness of the sound? Can you feel the vibrating fork through the string?

• Hold the metal rod and strike it against a wall, a book, a desk, a variety of surfaces. Is sound produced? Which striking surface will make the rod sound the loudest? The softest? Why do you think this is so?

• Take turns with members of your group clapping the two wood blocks together. Use the meter stick to measure at what distance the clapping blocks sound the loudest. How far can you move away from the clapping blocks and still hear them?

• Using the cloth, cotton, feathers, cork, and nerf ball, try to produce a sound. Is it possible to create a sound if you simply drop the items on your desk? What if you strike them with your hand? Are these items capable of producing sound? Why or why not?

• Place your ear to one end of the filled fish tank. Have another student gently tap the glass on the other side of the tank. Can you hear this sound? Did the sound travel through the glass or through the water? This time place your ear so that it is directly above the tank. Have a friend gently drop a quarter into the fish tank when you are not looking. Could you hear when the quarter hit the bottom of the tank?

2. EXPLANATION/CONCEPT INVENTION: What is the main idea? How will the main idea be identified?

Concept: Sounds move in the form of waves through air, water, wood, and other solids.

Were you able to make the fork sing? How did you do this? Did the hand that was holding the string feel anything as the fork sang? What about the metal rod? How did you get it to sound the loudest? Could you see the rod moving as it made sound? What about the wood blocks; were they very loud? How did your hands feel as you banged the blocks together? What about the cloth, cotton, feathers, cork, and nerf ball? Were you able to get them to make a sound when they were dropped? Why or why not? Do these items behave like the fork, metal rod, or wood blocks? What can those items do that the cloth items cannot? (Get students to realize that objects that vibrate will set the air in motion to create a sound.) Could you hear sound through the water? When was it the easiest to detect? Why is it important that your ear is facing the source of the sound? Sound waves must strike your eardrum for you to hear sound.

Based on your observations from these five activities and when we put our ears to our desks and tapped, can you tell me through which media sound waves will travel? Sounds move in waves through air, water, wood, and other solids.

3. EXPANSION OF THE IDEA: Which process skills will be used?

Communicating, experimenting, interpreting data, reducing experimental error

How will the idea be expanded?

Provide each student with two paper cups and any length of string (minimum two feet). Instruct the students to poke a small hole in the end of their paper cups

and thread the string through them. Tie the end of the string to a paper clip to prevent the string from slipping out of the cup. Ask the students to work in pairs trying out their paper cup telephones. Experiment with loose string versus tight string, long versus short string. Compare results. Touch the string as they talk to dampen the sound. Ask each pair to try using the tin can-fishline telephone. Is there any difference between this phone and the one you made? Which telephone sets up more vibrations? What can you say about how sound travels?

Why is the idea important for personal development?

- Where in your house would be the best place to set your stereo speakers, on a metal table or a cloth-covered bench? Or would neither of these be good? Can you suggest a good place?
- Why do you think most homes have doorbells? How are these better than just yelling for our friends?

Why is the idea important for science-technology-society?

- Do you think it is fair for a fisherman to use a fish echo-locator to determine where the fish are before he or she begins fishing?
- Do you think it is ethical for someone to use knowledge of sound to eavesdrop on other people for such purposes as collecting military intelligence, listening in on criminals, or listening to others talk about himself or herself?

Why is the idea important for academic growth?

- A knowledge of the conductivity of sound helps develop further concepts of controlling sound loudness, quality, and usefulness.
- What materials would you use and how would you go about building a soundproof room? Can you create a plan that would be easy to follow that takes all variables into account in building this room? Work with your parents to create a working model of your design.

Why is the idea important for career awareness?

- How have marine biologists used their knowledge of sound to study the humpbacked whale? Why should we be concerned with the singing behavior of the humpbacked whale?
- Why would a pilot be concerned with how sound travels? If you were the pilot

of the Concorde, would you have a problem trying to get permission to land your plane in Columbus, Ohio? Why?

4. EVALUATION: How will the students show what they have learned?

Upon completing the activities the students will be able to

- rank-order a given set of materials from good to poor conductors of sound: air, wood, metal rod, cotton string, wire, water, cotton balls;
- take an object that is capable of creating sound when struck and alter it so that when it is struck, the loudness of the sound is decreased.

GRADE 2–4

Physical Science

DISCIPLINE

Sound Waves

Concepts to be invented

Main idea—Sound travels in waves. Waves consist of areas of compression and rarefaction. Waves move through the air.

Secondary concepts that are important to expansion

Sound waves cause vibrations as they hit the eardrum, causing us to hear sounds.

Materials needed

For each group of students:

soup can open at both ends
balloon
rubber band
small rectangular piece of mirror
flashlight

slinkies
a model of the ear (one for the
    whole class)
a labeled diagram of the ear

Discrepant event

Stretch a piece of the balloon over one end of the soup can. Secure it tightly with the rubber band. Glue a small piece of mirror on the balloon membrane, slightly off center. Shine a flashlight onto the mirror so that its reflection shows up on the chalkboard. Ask the students to observe the mirror's reflection on the board. Ask one student to come up and speak into the open end of the can. What happens to the mirror's reflection on the chalkboard when someone speaks into the can?

1. EXPLORATION: Which process skills will be used?

Observing, experimenting, predicting, hypothesizing, inferring

What will the children do?

Soup can reflectors

Divide the students into groups depending on class size. Have one soup can reflector for each group. Provide each group with a flashlight. Ask the students to predict and then record what happens to the soup can reflectors as they vary the loudness of the sound. What do you think is causing the mirror's reflection to move? Think of this as you begin to play with a slinky. Stretch and shake the slinky, and record what the slinky looks like as you do this. A diagram may be useful at this point. Try to label where the slinky looks mashed together and where it looks thin on your diagram.

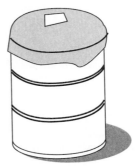

2. EXPLANATION/CONCEPT INVENTION: What is the main idea? How will the main idea be identified?

Concept: Sound travels in waves. Waves consist of areas of compression and rarefaction. Waves move through the air.

What do you think caused the mirror to move? Can you actually see the balloon moving as someone speaks into the open end of the can? Speaking into the can set the balloon membrane vibrating. Can you feel the vibration of the balloon if you lightly touch it as someone speaks into the open end? What type of pattern does the moving mirror make on the board? How is this pattern similar to the movement of the slinky?

What would be a good name to describe the path sound travels in? (Waves.) Ask for volunteer to share his or her drawing of slinky movement with the class. Reproduce this drawing for all to see. As you moved the slinky, were you able to detect areas where the slinky was mashed together? Were you able to detect areas where it was more spread out? These slinky movements are similar to sound waves. Areas where sound waves are mashed together are called compression; areas that are spread out are called rarefaction.

3. EXPANSION OF THE IDEA: Which process skills will be used?

Observing, manipulating materials, inferring, predicting, communicating

How will the idea be expanded?

Slinky waves, sound waves and the ear

Ask the students to take turns laying their heads on their desks while another student stretches the slinky out on top of the desk and releases it rapidly, or have another student hold a ruler over the edge of the desk and strike it quickly. Ask the student with his or her head on the desk what this felt like. What did your ear detect?

Provide the students with diagrams of the inner ear. Ask them to label what they believe is the path that sound takes as it reaches our ears. Use the ear model to trace this path for the students. Allow them to check their labeled predictions with the model you are tracing. Remind them that sound waves vary in strength. As the sound waves hit the eardrum, they cause it to vibrate in rhythm with them, causing sound messages to the brain. The human ear can interpret sound waves with frequencies ranging between 16 and nearly 20,000 vibrations per second. Those vibrations above 20,000 are termed *ultrasonic*.

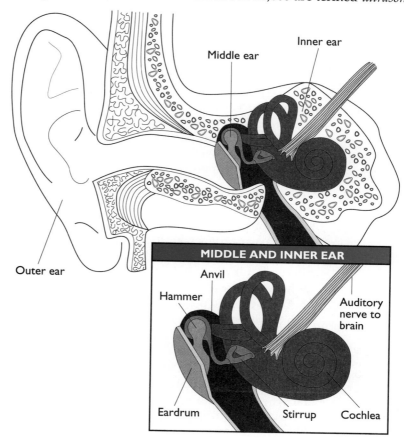

Why is the idea important for personal development?

- Why is it important that you never put anything in your ear smaller than your elbow? What kind of ear-cleaning products do you think are the safest to use?
- Have you ever tried to talk to your friends while you are under water

swimming? Is it easy to understand someone talking under water? Why or why not?

- Is it a good idea to wear headphones while riding your bicycle? Why or why not?

Why is the idea important for science-technology-society?

- How effective are ear plugs in preventing potentially damaging sounds from reaching your eardrum?
- Interview people in different lines of work who use ear plugs, such as factory workers, road construction crews, or building contractors. What types of ear plugs do they use? How well do they think their ear plugs work?
- Write to the manufacturers of the various ear plugs. What materials do they use to make their ear plugs? Is any one material better than another? What is the most widely used brand of ear plugs? (A teacher can assign this question as homework, or as another expansion activity for the class to investigate.)

Why is the idea important for academic growth?

- At a track meet, why do you think you see the spark and smoke from the starter's gun before you hear the sound made by the gun? Can you explain this phenomenon in terms of sound waves?
- If someone in the room was speaking to you and you could only detect faint, muffled sounds, what might be the probable cause for your loss of hearing? How is sound supposed to travel from your ear canal to your brain?

Why is the idea important for career awareness?

- What do you think would happen to you if you had a job working at an airport loading cargo onto planes and you did not wear protective headphones?
- Would a piano tuner need to be aware of compression and rarefaction of sound waves? How could he or she apply this knowledge in his or her work?
- Interview a local audiologist. What does his or her job entail? What kind of knowledge is needed to perform the job? Ask if he or she could share with you any cases where a person's job affected his or her hearing. Share the interview with the class.

4. EVALUATION: How will the students show what they have learned?

Upon completing the activities the students will be able to

- identify areas of rarefaction and compression on a diagram of sound waves,
- trace the path of the sound waves from its source through the ear when given a worksheet with a diagram of the ear. The students should be able to label the ear canal, eardrum, bones of the middle ear, and nerve to the brain.

Sound Production

Concept to be invented

Main idea—Sounds are produced by vibrations.

Secondary concepts that are important to expansion

A vibrating object has an energy source. Moving energy is referred to as *kinetic*. Vibrations that cause sound can be produced by hitting, plucking, stroking, or blowing an object.

Materials needed

For each student group:

pencil	one balloon
paper	small pieces of mirror
percussion instruments	one flashlight
one soup can with both ends cut out	chalkboard

⊃ **Safety precautions:** Remind the students to exercise caution when making sounds with the instruments. They should be reminded not to hold them up to a friend's or their own ear when the sound is loud or piercing. During the expansion activity they must use care when handling the mirrors, and watch for sharp edges.

1. EXPLORATION: Which process skills will be used?

Observing, recording data, predicting, hypothesizing, experimenting

What will the children do?

Noise and sound identification

Activity 1. Ask the students to close their eyes, sit perfectly still, and not speak. Tell them to listen carefully to all the noises they can hear, even the slightest sounds that they normally ignore. After a few minutes ask them to open their eyes and write descriptions of every noise they heard and if possible, identify what they believe is the source of those sounds. Students should describe noises in terms ordinarily used for sounds, such as high, low, loud, soft, hissing, rumbling, piercing, musical.

Activity 2. Tell the students that they are going to play a listening game. Ask the students to close their eyes while the teacher makes a sound and then try to guess what the sound was. The first one to guess what the sound was will make the next sound. Make sure everyone gets a turn.

Activity 3. Present various percussion instruments to the class, such as drums of various sizes, cymbals, pots, pot lids, and xylophones (toy ones will work as well). Ask the students to guess how you can get each one to produce a sound. Ask the students to predict what causes each one to make a sound. Allow the students to experiment with the various instruments, asking them to take note of how sound is produced on each instrument. Ask the students to describe what it feels like. After students have done this, have them strike the instrument again and then hold it tightly. Ask them if the sound stopped. Why did it stop?

2. EXPLANATION/CONCEPT INVENTION: What is the main idea? How will the main idea be identified?

Concept: Sounds are produced by vibrations.

Activity 1. Ask the students to go back to the first list they made. Make two columns on the board, one labeled *descriptive words* and the other *sound sources*. Ask the students to help fill in the chart from the lists they created. The class will be referring back to this list after they discuss the other two activities.

Activity 2. Ask each student: What type of sound did you make for everyone to guess? How was the sound made? What energy source did you use to make it? Add these sounds to the list on the board already; include a third column, *how made,* to the chart.

Activity 3. When you hit your instrument, what did you set up? How did you get the sound to stop on your percussion instrument? Go over the list on the board and stress that sound is a type of energy. To make sound, one form of energy is changed to another form of energy. Energy causes movement. Sounds can be produced by hitting, plucking, stroking, and blowing. All of these actions use energy to create vibrations. Vibrations are the source of sound.

3. EXPANSION OF THE IDEA: Which process skills will be used?

Experimenting, predicting, inferring

How will the idea be expanded?

Sound movement

Divide the class into groups. Have each group stretch a piece cut from a balloon over one end of a soup can, using a rubber band to hold it tightly in place. Glue a small piece of mirror slightly off center. Darken the classroom, and hold the can at an angle to the blackboard. Using a flashlight, shine the beam so that it strikes the mirror and reflects upon the board. Ask the group to predict what will happen to the mirror's reflection on the board as someone speaks into the open end of the can. Ask someone in the group to talk into the open end of the can. Ask the other members of the group to take note of what happens to the mirror's reflection as the person speaks into the can. Do your observations match your predictions? What do you think causes the changes in the reflection? What source of energy causes the balloon to vibrate?

Home assignments
Sound game, "What Is Sound?" This assignment may be done alone or with other family members.

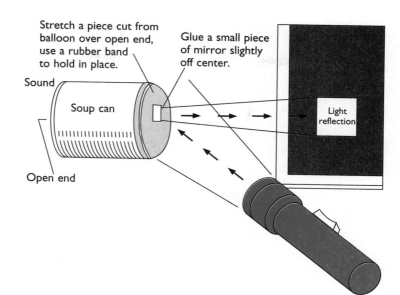

1. Go home and sit down in your bedroom or the room of your choice, close your eyes, and be very quiet for three minutes. Listen carefully. Do you hear anything? Write down the sounds you hear and describe them.
2. If you have heard new sounds, what are they and why do you think you haven't heard them before?
3. How did the quiet make you feel? (To show how the quiet made you feel, you may write a descriptive paragraph, write a poem or draw a picture.)

"How Well Can You Match Sounds?"

Students will construct a game for younger students. After the students have made the game they will take it to a primary class and supervise the younger students playing it.

Materials needed

At least twelve six-ounce unmarked metal cans, small objects (materials used in cans to make noises could include dried rice, beans, peas, marbles, BBs, gravel, sand, bits of Styrofoam, puffed rice, or any other small objects found around the house), tape.

Preparation:

Place small objects in a pair of cans and then seal the cans with tape. Be sure children cannot see in the cans and that the cans are prepared in pairs with approximately the same amount of material in each set of cans.

Procedure:

1. Shake the cans and listen to the noise they make.

2. Can you hear the different sounds they make?
3. Do any of the cans make the same sound?
4. If you find cans that sound alike, put them next to each other.
5. Have a friend listen to the cans and see if he or she agrees.
6. You may want to make more cans with different sounds to see how well your friends can tell the difference.

Why is the idea important for personal development?

- What would your life be like without sound?
- What are some sounds that you hear around you and how are they made?
- When you wake up in the middle of the night and hear creaking bed springs or creaking stairs, knowing what you now know about sound, how could you explain away any fears that you might have?

Why is the idea important for science-technology-society?

- How has man made use of his knowledge that a vibrating body will produce a sound? What types of signals have we created because of this? (Fire alarms, smoke detectors, burglar alarms, fog horns.)
- How do vibrating strings allow us to create a violin, a guitar, or a bass fiddle? Why is it that some of the sounds created by these instruments sound soothing to some, while others may think of them as simply obnoxious noise?
- How do we record and transmit the sounds we make or the sounds that are made around us?

Why is the idea important for academic growth?

- Explain how it is possible to create a percussion instrument. Make one and describe how it works. Use terms like *vibration* and *energy* in your explanation.
- Why do you think you enjoy certain types of music?

Why is the idea important for career awareness?

- Why do you think it is important that a car mechanic is able to distinguish one sound from another? How does his or her job depend on recognizing engine sounds?
- Do you think Beethoven was able to continue his musical career after he became deaf? Do you think it is possible for any deaf people to "feel" sounds?
- What other occupations can you think of in which reliance on sound is essential?

4. EVALUATION: How will the students show what they have learned?

Upon completing these activities the students will be able to

- describe sources of sound, explaining how a vibration is set up and the energy source for that vibration;
- report on their home assignment "What Is Sound?" and share with the class their poems, paragraphs, or drawings about the sounds they observed;

- work successfully with the younger students when they play the "What Is Sound?" game they made, helping the younger students invent the concept of vibration.

Characteristics of Matter

Concept to be invented

Main idea—Anything that occupies space and has mass is called *matter*. *Matter* can be found in a solid, liquid, or gaseous state.

Secondary concepts that are important to expansion

Physical versus chemical change, solutions versus mixtures, chemical symbols, chemical formulas, matter can be neither created nor destroyed.

Materials needed

For exploration (per student group):

Two zip-lock plastic bags (label one A and the other B), one teaspoon sodium bicarbonate (place in bag A and seal closed), one teaspoon calcium chloride, sold as ice melter during winter months (place in bag B and seal closed), magnifying glass, small medicine cups with 10 ml of water in each, 5–10 drops of bromothymol blue (number of drops may vary due to the alkalinity of local water supplies; when it is placed in the water, make sure the water stays blue), wood splint, matches.

For expansion:

Three clear cups or plastic beakers, marbles, sand, water, and weighing scale.

⊃ **Safety precautions:** Remind students that safety goggles must be worn at all times. Since this is a guided discovery lesson, they are to listen to the teacher at all times before they begin to manipulate the materials—this is for their safety! During the expansion activity, everyone must wear safety goggles and protective gloves when pouring the sulfuric acid. This activity should be done under a fume hood, right next to an open window, or preferably outside.

Advanced organizer used to set the stage for this guided discovery activity: Which process skills will be used?

Observing, analyzing, inferring, hypothesizing

What will the teacher and students do?

The teacher should enter the classroom with a lit candle. Ask the class the following: Why does it burn? What helps it burn? How can I make it go out? Act on student suggestions. Why does the candle go out when I place it under a glass? What is it lacking? Could I try to grow plants under glass? Could animals, like a hamster, live under this glass? Why or why not? Through questioning, the teacher should bring out the idea that a way to test for the presence of oxygen in a gas would be to see if a flame stays lit in the gas. If the flame goes out, that would tell us that a gas like carbon dioxide may be present. (If the students are not already aware of fire safety skills please review them at this time.)

1. EXPLORATION: Which process skills will be used?

Manipulating materials, collecting and recording data, communicating, observing, hypothesizing, predicting, inferring

What will the children do?

Plastic bag chemistry

Make and record their observations of two unknown white powders found in bags A and B. Use the magnifying glass to make careful observations of the two unknowns. Draw pictures of unknown white powders. (Stress importance of keeping bags sealed, and not tasting the unknown substances. Encourage the students to make observations about the shape of the unknown white powders).

Make observations of the unknown liquid placed before them; record these (work on getting students to realize that the liquid takes the shape of the container).

Introduce the mystery solution and ask students to predict what will happen when the solution is placed in the unknown liquid before them. Have them record the amount of mystery solution that was placed in the unknown liquid and the results of the mixing. (The "mystery solution" is bromothymol blue. Conceal its name on the container and move from group to group asking the students for their predictions of what it is. Then place the 5–10 drops of mystery solution in the students' cups.)

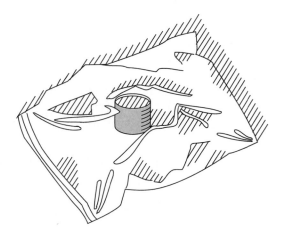

Ask the students to open bag A, taking care not to touch it or eat it, and pour it into bag B. Seal the bag, and record their observations once the two unknown powders are combined together. After they record their observations, ask the students to place the bag on its side and open it. Without mixing the unknown liquids with the unknown powders, place the container with the unknown liquids into the bag and seal it.

Ask the students to design a way in which they can mix the powders with the liquids without actually picking up the bag and shaking it. They should discuss this with the students closest to them. While they design their plan, remind them that they have been provided with a wood splint and some matches (the students should already be aware of appropriate fire safety skills). Ask the students to recall the previous candle demonstration. Do you think a gas will be given off when you mix the unknown powders with the liquids? How will you know? What can you do to determine which gas it is? Encourage the students to incorporate these suggestions into their experimental design.

After sufficient time has been allowed for the students to design their experiment, have them act on their plans. Record their observations. Encourage them to observe the bags with the magnifying glasses, make some careful observations (not only looking at the bag but also holding it to feel for any changes in temperature and using the burning wood splint to check for evolution of a gas—remember we observe with all of our senses), perhaps even drawing what they see.

2. EXPLANATION/CONCEPT INVENTION: What is the main idea? How will the main idea be identified?

Concept: Anything that occupies space and has mass is called *matter.*

By working with the unknown white powders, students can make observations in which they realize that the unknown substances are in a *solid* state of matter. By observing the unknown *liquid* and the mystery solution, also in a *liquid* state, they can see they are using another state of matter. Upon mixing the *solid* with a *liquid,* they can see the bag expanding, thus observing the third state of matter, a *gas.* Careful use of questions will also get the students to realize that *solids* always retain their shape, no matter the container. *Liquids* take up the shape of the container, and a *gas* will take up as much space as you give it.

Ask the students the following questions to help get to the ideas stated above: You drew pictures of the unknown white powders in bag A and in bag B. When you mixed them together, did they change their shape? (Work on the children's understanding of the concept of a solid, which does not change in shape. Physical change can be observed if they crush the solids; what was created is a heterogeneous mixture, a combination of two or more substances each distinct from one another.) If so, how or why? What shape was the liquid in when it was inside the cup? What about when you poured it out? Why? What happened to the liquid when the mystery solution was added? Could you tell where one liquid began and the other ended? (Work on the concept of liquids taking the shape of their container and only within the limit of the volume that the sample occupies. Also work on developing the concept of a solution). What happened when you mixed the solids with the liquids? What did you observe? (Listing all of their observations will allow you to expand on specific secondary concepts you want the students to understand, such as physical versus chemical change, heat of reaction, acid formation.) Why did your bag get bigger? How did you find out what gas evolved? If you used a bigger plastic bag, would it be blown all the way up, too? Why? (Work on the concept of a gas taking the shape of its container.)

If you are interested, use this activity to introduce the students to chemical nomenclature. Provide students with the chemical formulas for the unknowns involved in the activity (older students may help derive these formulas and help balance the equation).

$$CaCl_2 + NaHCO_3 + H_2O + \text{bromothymol blue} \rightarrow NaCl(aq) + HCl(aq)$$
$$+ CaCO_3 + H_2O$$
$$CaCO_3 + H_2O \rightarrow H_2CO_3 + CaO$$
$$H_2CO3 \rightarrow H^+ + HCO_3^- \rightarrow CO_2\ (g) + H_2O$$

3. EXPANSION OF THE IDEA: Which process skills will be used?

Measuring, predicting, hypothesizing, observing, recording data

How will the idea be expanded?

Marble matter

Provide each student group with three clear cups or plastic beakers, marbles, sand, and some water. Ask the students to weigh a cup, then ask them to fill the cup with marbles. Record their weights and number of marbles. Ask them questions such as the following: How many marbles did you put in the cup? Do you think you can put in any more marbles? Did the marbles take the shape of the cup? (Work here to make sure they understand that the marbles did not change their shape.) What was the weight of the cup? What state of matter are the marbles?

Ask the students to fill the other cup with sand. Weigh the cup, then weigh the cup filled with sand. Have them place a mark on the cup indicating the top of the sand. Use same line of questioning as for the marbles.

Now ask the students if they think both cups are full. Ask the students if they think they can pour any of the sand into the cup filled with marbles. Solicit responses. React to responses—I thought you told me the cup with the marbles in it was full; how can you possibly put anything else into this cup?

Have the students pour some sand into the cup of marbles. Mark the new level of sand on the sand cup. What happens? Were you able to add sand into an already-filled cup of marbles? Why? What is the weight of your new mixture? What is the weight of the sand remaining in the cup? Subtract this remaining weight of sand from the original weight of sand. How much sand did you lose? Subtract the original weight of the marbles from the new weight of the marble and sand mixture. Is this amount gained equal to the amount lost from the sand cup? (Reinforce the concept of matter—anything that occupies space and has mass; concept of states of matter—two different solids. Secondary concept— physical change, matter was not created or destroyed, it still has the same weight; nothing was lost, just placed in different containers.)

Fill a third cup with water. Weigh this. Ask the students if they think it is possible to put water into an already-filled cup of sand and marbles. Why? Why not? What state of matter is the water? What do you know about liquids? (For older students, instead of weighing the water in a cup, introduce them to a graduated cylinder; have them measure out so many milliliters of water and record the volume of water in milliliters that they pour into the marble-sand cup.)

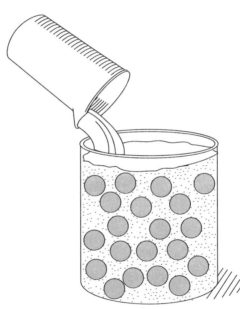

Was your prediction true? What happened when you tried to add water to the marble-sand cup? Why could the container that was already filled with marbles still hold more sand and water?

Do you think we could have started with the water, then the sand and marbles? Why? What does this tell you about the sizes of molecules of different materials or substances? (The concept of solids versus liquids leads into a discussion of the size of particles. Smaller-size particles can slip between the larger ones. Make an analogy of molecules. Introduction of this new term may lead into a new unit on atoms and molecules.)

Why is the idea important for personal development?
- Which would you rather take a bath in, water mixed with sand or water mixed with bath bubble beads? Why?
- What would happen if you burned a dollar bill? Could you tape it back together and still have a dollar?

Why is the idea important for science-technology-society?
- How has knowledge of chemical changes allowed the food industry to create cake mixes that can be made in a microwave rather than a regular oven?
- Getting matter to change its shape has allowed us to create many large buildings, like the Sears Tower in Chicago. How is this so?

Why is the idea important for academic growth?
- The students engage in manipulative skills during the activities.
- For understanding the concept of physical versus chemical change, ask the students to explain why they can heat snow and get water, or why they can mix flour, water, baking soda, and sugar together, heat the mixture, and taste not these separate ingredients but a cake.
- Why can't you put a round peg in a square hole?

Why is the idea important to career awareness?
- Using a list of all of the concepts discovered in the activities, ask the students to survey their parents and other adults to see if they make use of any of these concepts in their work. Where do they see them utilized? Are these people in typical scientific careers? Can anyone use these science concepts?

4. EVALUATION: How will the students show what they have learned?

Upon completing the activities the students will be able to
- demonstrate a physical change and then a chemical change when given a piece of paper;
- provide examples of solid matter, liquid matter, and gas;
- demonstrate how he or she could capture a gas;
- name five chemical elements;
- name and write the chemical symbols for five elements (intermediate grades). Primary grades should be able to state simple chemical symbols such as hydrogen and oxygen.
- name three chemical compounds or mixtures and provide their chemical formulas (intermediate grades). Primary grades should be able to give the formula for water.
- write, when given the chemical formula for sugar and sulfuric acid, an equation that shows what happens when the two are mixed together (once again this objective depends on student grade level).

PHYSICAL SCIENCE

K–6

Physical Science

Physical Properties of Matter

Concept to be invented

Main idea—Physical properties of matter help distinguish one kind of matter from another.

Secondary concepts

A cooked egg will spin freely, whereas a raw egg will be difficult to spin. It will have a slight wobble as it spins. The term *best* is arbitrary—members of a group must decide criteria for judging an object the best.

Materials needed

For exploration:

Cook enough white eggs for half the class. Place randomly in a bowl the cooked eggs and an equal number of raw eggs. Allow each student to pick an egg out of the bowl.

one can of broth or any canned liquid

one can of dog food paper towels

For expansion:

Three or four different brands of chocolate chip cookies, paper towels.

For each student group:

one ruler five to ten toothpicks

paper for recording data

⊃ **Safety precautions:** Remind students that although you encourage them to make as many observations as possible, they should never taste anything without your permission. Discourage the students from licking the eggshells. Remind them to wash their hands after the exploration activity, especially before they begin the expansion activity.

1. EXPLORATION: Which process skills will be used?

Observing, manipulating materials, collecting and recording data, communicating

What will the children do?

Egg-citing observations

Enter the classroom carrying the bowl of eggs and acting as if you are greatly troubled. Explain to the students that you boiled some eggs last night for a dinner party and placed them in the refrigerator. When you went into the refrigerator this morning you found that someone took the cooked eggs and combined them with the raw eggs in this bowl. Now you have to determine which are cooked and which are raw without breaking any of them. Ask the students if they can help you solve your problem.

Ask each student to choose an egg from the bowl. Ask them to make as many observations about their egg as possible. Remind them not to break the egg! Allow sufficient time for the students to collect their data. Encourage them to record their observations. For very young students, ask them to draw their observations. Once they have made their observations, move to the concept invention phase of this lesson.

2. EXPLANATION/CONCEPT INVENTION: What is the main idea? How will the main idea be identified?

Concept: Physical properties of matter help distinguish one kind of matter from another.

As the students are making their observations, move among them, encouraging those students who appear to be stumped to think of ways in which observations can be made. Ask questions like: When I make an observation am I only using my eyes? What other things can I use to make an observation? Encourage the students to think about ways they can manipulate the egg without dropping or breaking it. Remind the students to record the information they are discovering.

Once the students have made their observations, solicit them from the class. Make a list on the board. Once you have received an observation from each of the students, go back to your original question and ask the students: Now, which of these observations will help me solve my problem? Ask a student to restate the problem (which eggs are raw and which are cooked).

Through the process of elimination, the students will find that some physical properties are more distinguishing than others. For instance, simply observing that the egg is white is not going to help solve the problem, since all of the students have white eggs. However, an observation that it sounds like something is moving inside when I shake it, or my egg will spin or stand on end are observations that will help solve the problem. Ask the students: Is one distinguishing characteristic enough to decide if an egg is cooked or raw? If some students think so, then ask them to make their prediction about whether their egg is cooked or raw based on that one distinguishing characteristic. Let one student crack an egg only to find that the prediction was incorrect. (Make sure that the student chosen to bring out the idea that one characteristic is not enough has in fact made a wrong decision.)

As you progress through the list of student observations, keep referring back to the original problem. As you narrow down their observations to those that help solve the problem, you may find that the students eventually come to an observation that stumps them. Some eggs spin easily and other sort of wobble but don't spin well. The students aren't sure if it is the raw or cooked eggs that spin easily. At this point the teacher should bring out the cans of broth and dog food. (Two cans of each may be helpful.) Open the can of broth and pour it into a clear container. Ask the students what state of matter the broth is in. Now ask for a student volunteer to try to spin the unopened can of broth. Ask the student if it is easy or hard to get the can to spin.

Now open a can of dog food. Empty that into a clear container. Ask the students what state of matter the dog food is in. Now ask for a student volunteer to try to spin the unopened can of dog food. Ask the student if it is easy or hard to get the can to spin.

Ask the class to determine if the broth is similar to a raw or cooked egg, what about the dog food? Once they have decided that the raw egg and the broth are similar, and the cooked egg is similar to the dog food, ask them to tell you how you can determine if an egg is cooked or raw. Encourage them to list all the criteria that helped them come to their conclusions. The students should conclude that the cooked eggs will spin freely and the raw eggs will wobble like the broth can when spun. Through careful observation you can sense movement in raw eggs when you shake them.

3. EXPANSION OF THE IDEA: Which process skills will be used?

Designing an experiment, observing, measuring, predicting, hypothesizing, recording data

How will the idea be expanded?

Chocolate chip exploration

This expansion activity is more appropriate for students in grades 3–6. For K–2 students, you may want to lead a guided discovery activity using the following ideas:

Remind the students about the concept learned from the exploration activity: Physical properties of matter help distinguish one kind of matter from another. Explain to the students that you would like them to first design an experiment using just physical properties to determine which brand of chocolate chip cookies is the best. Allow sufficient class time for groups of students to brainstorm ways in which they could use only physical properties to determine the best brand of chocolate chip cookies. Ask the students to submit a copy of their planned experiment and a materials list to you so that they can perform their experiment in the next class meeting. Suggested materials are included in the materials list at the beginning of the lesson. Be sure to read over the designed experiments to be sure that they are only using physical properties and also that appropriate safety standards are maintained.

On the second day, allow the students to act on appropriately planned lessons. On the third day, ask the different student groups to share the methods they used for determining the *best* cookie and the results of their experiment. Once all of the groups have had a chance to share their results, and especially if the results were different, ask the students if it is necessary to set some criteria for determining which cookie is *best*. The students should conclude that the term *best* is arbitrary—the members of the group must decide criteria for judging an object the *best*.

As a final discussion question, ask the students why you asked them to design their experiment around physical properties. Why could they not taste the cookie to determine the best?

Why is the idea important for personal development?

- If you had to describe your best friend to another student, how would you do that? Would a description such as "He or she is really nice and cute" be enough? Why or why not?
- If you were talking with a group of people about the best movie you ever saw, do you think everyone in the group would agree with you? Why or why not?

Why is the idea important for science-technology-society?

- How does the mineral industry determine which mineral is which?
- Why has the auto industry gone from metal bumpers to plastic bumpers? What do properties of matter have to do with this decision?

Why is the idea important for academic growth?

- Students engage in manipulative skills during the activities.
- How can you accurately describe an object?
- How can you tell the difference between a raw and cooked egg without cracking the egg open?

Why is the idea important to career awareness?

- Pretend you want a new sidewalk in front of your house. You need to hire a cement contractor to do the work. One contractor you interviewed said it didn't matter what kind of material he or she used to pour your sidewalk. Does this person know much about distinguishing physical properties of matter? Would you be willing to hire that contractor? Why or why not?

- Who do you think should be aware of the many different physical properties of matter for their work?

4. EVALUATION: How will the students show what they have learned?

Upon completing the activities the students will be able

- to determine, when given an egg, whether it is cooked or raw,
- to design an experiment to determine the best brand of paper towels,
- to list the physical properties of three or four different things (the teacher can choose any number of items to set before the student: a rock, flower, penny, button, or anything else will work).

GRADE **3–6**

Physical Science

DISCIPLINE

PHYSICAL SCIENCE

Changing Matter

Concepts to be invented

Main idea—An alteration of the composition or the properties of matter is called a *chemical change*. An alteration of the shape of matter without a change in its chemical composition is called a *physical change*.

Secondary concepts that are important to expansion

Small, single units of matter are called *monomers*. A substance that will speed up a chemical reaction without being affected itself is called a *catalyst*. A bond linking the chains of atoms in a polymer is a *cross linker*. A compound formed by adding many small molecules together in the presence of a catalyst or by the condensation of many smaller molecules through the elimination of water or alcohol is a *polymer*.

Materials needed

Per student:

one piece of scrap paper
one clear cup
matches

one stirring rod or popsicle stick
one lunch-size zip-lock bag

For entire class:

one aluminum pie pan
three large containers of glue (enough to give each student 30 ml)
food coloring
liquid starch

borate solution (50 g borax with 100 ml of water)
beaker or graduated cylinder for measurements
paper towels for clean-up

The following items are used to introduce the problem:

Teflon pan   football helmet
compact disc   pair of nylons
plastic baby bottle

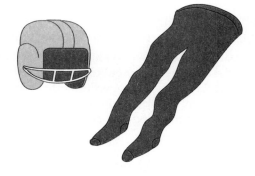

⟃ **Safety precautions and/or procedures:** During the exploration phase, when the paper is burned, the teacher should make sure there is adequate ventilation in the classroom. The teacher should also be sure the matches are kept away from the students and use care when an open flame is present: sleeves must be pushed up, hair pulled back, and eyes protected. During the expansion phase, the students should be discouraged from putting their hands in their mouths. Be sure they wash their hands as soon as they are finished with the activity.

1. EXPLORATION: Which process skills will be used?

Observing, predicting, inferring

What will the children do?

Physical and chemical paper change

Introduction: The teacher will allow the children to examine the following things: compact discs, baby bottles, Teflon pan, nylons, and a football helmet. As the children view the items, tell the children that you would like them to think about each item, and that by the time they finish the activities, they should be able to tell you what they have in common.

Student Activity: Give each child a piece of paper. Ask each of them to make it look different in some way. Then ask each to share what they did to make it look different.

2. EXPLANATION/CONCEPT INVENTION: What is the main idea? How will the main idea be identified?

Concept: An alteration of the composition or the properties of matter is called a *chemical change.* An alteration of the shape of matter without changing its chemical composition is called a *physical change.*

Ask such questions as: What did you do to make the paper look different? If they tore it up, ask, "If I taped it back together, would I still have a piece of paper? By changing its shape, did I do anything to change the molecules that came together to make that piece of paper?" Be sure to allow the children to share their comments with one another. Explain that a change in shape with no loss of molecules is called a *physical change*.

If children suggest burning the paper, ask if they think they will still be able to use the paper once you change it by burning it? Then burn it over the aluminum pie pan. Is the paper still in a usable form? Why not? Explain that the paper underwent a *chemical change*. When it burned, carbon atoms were lost.

3. EXPANSION OF THE IDEA: Which process skills will be used?

Observing, measuring, recording data, predicting, inferring

How will the idea be expanded?

Polymer-rubber balls

Do all chemical changes result in the creation of useless matter? Think about that question while you try the following activity. Ask the students to use the graduated cylinders to measure out 30 ml of glue. Pour it into the clear cup. Choose a color from the food coloring and mix it with your glue (use popsicle sticks for stirring). Do you still have glue in front of you? What kind of change did the glue undergo?

What do you think will happen if you mix the colored glue with the liquid you have in front of you? (The teacher should place in front of half of the class the liquid starch; in front of the other half a borate solution). Please make some predictions, and share them with one another on each side of the room. What do you think will happen when you mix the glue with the unknown liquid in front of you? Make your predictions and record them.

Ask the students to measure out 30 ml of either the starch or the borate solution. Encourage the students to make predictions about how much of the solution they will need to bring about a change in the glue. Since they do not know for certain how much starch or borate solution they will need, encourage the students to slowly add one of these, stirring all the time, until they see a change. Record how much starch or borate solution was necessary to bring about a change in the glue. Record any new observations you may have made about the colored glue.

Did you create anything new, or can you still tell the glue from the starch or borate solution? Can you pick up this new piece of matter? (Encourage the students to do so—the more they manipulate it in their hands, the more the water will come out, and eventually they will have created their own rubber ball.) What do you think you can do with it? What kind of change do you think you created by combining the glue with the starch or the borate solution? Why do you say this?

Go back to the original question: Do all chemical changes result in the creation of useless matter? How many of you think you created a new form of matter that is useful? What did you do differently than your classmates? What do you think you can do with your newly created piece of matter? How useful is it? As a teacher, you may encourage the students from the different sides of the room to compare their newly created rubber balls. Do they bounce the same? Roll the same? Feel the same? Here, two different catalysts were used to create this special kind of chemical change called a *polymerization reaction.* After they finish, the students may place their balls in a zip-lock bag, where they will stay fresh for a few weeks.

Do you think that other inventions could have been discovered just by people mixing things together in the lab and making careful observations about how much and of what materials they mixed together?

Teflon, used to coat pans, is one of these accidental chemical combinations that was discovered in a lab when scientists weren't looking for it. Chemists realized that it was possible to get small pieces of matter to link up chemically when a catalyst was used to force the reaction to occur. Sometimes these smaller pieces of matter, called *monomers,* add together in one long chain to create *polymers.* Saran wrap, Lucite, Plexiglas, and Teflon are polymers formed by this additive process. Polymers can also be formed by bringing monomers together, removing water or alcohol through a condensation reaction, and forcing the monomers to link together. This is what happened to form nylon, and this is what happened here to create a new form of matter—rubber balls! In addition to these manmade polymers, silk, cellulose, and rubber are naturally occurring polymers.

Go back to some of the first items shown to the students: the football helmet, the baby bottle, the CD, the nylons, and the Teflon pan. Encourage the students to think about the activities they just participated in as they try to answer the very first question you asked: What do all of these things have in common?

They were all created by a chemical change in which small pieces of matter, called monomers, were linked together to form polymers. These polymer reactions created new kinds of matter that have proven to be very useful.

Why is the idea important for personal development?
- You're tired of the color of your bedroom, and you want to change the color of your walls. Will your room undergo a physical or chemical change?
- Can you name any products created because of a polymerization reaction that have directly affected your life?

Why is the idea important for science-technology-society?
- There is much controversy over the use of Teflon bullets. Police unions bitterly oppose its use. Why do you think this product, formed from a polymerization reaction, is of serious concern to our society?
- Knowledge of chemical changes has led to the invention of many products

that have greatly changed society. Can you think of any products that were created as the result of a chemical change?

Why is the idea important for academic growth?

- Can you demonstrate the difference between a physical and a chemical change?
- Explain how a polymer can be created. How is this a unique type of chemical change?
- Can you name some monomers or polymers that are found in nature? How about some manmade ones?

Why is the idea important for career awareness?

- Do you think a cement finisher or a beautician needs to understand how a chemical change can occur? Why or why not?
- Are physical or chemical changes common in the type of work your parents do?

4. EVALUATION: How will the students show what they have learned?

Upon completion of the activities the students will be able to

- appreciate the need to think about a problem first, and then use clear, concise language to communicate the action taken on the problem;
- demonstrate the differences between physical and chemical changes;
- make predictions based on previous experiences;
- utilize the scientific method to solve a newly designed problem;
- explain how certain chemical reactions, such as polymer formation, can result in the creation of useful materials;
- explain what a football helmet, a compact disc, a Teflon pan, a baby bottle, and a pair of nylons have in common.

PHYSICAL SCIENCE

GRADE 5–8

Physical Science

DISCIPLINE

Identification of an Unknown

Concept to be invented

Main idea—Physical properties alone are not always sufficient characteristics to identify an unknown.

Secondary concepts

Indicators are used to bring about a physical or chemical change in an unknown. Common indicators are iodine, vinegar, and heat.

Materials needed

For exploration (for class of 24):

The following items make up the secret powders: four pounds of granulated sugar, two boxes of table salt, four pounds of baking soda, four pounds of corn-starch, four pounds of plaster of Paris.

The following items are necessary for all parts of the lesson: twenty plastic spoons, one box of toothpicks, ten eyedroppers, twenty small cups or containers.

Some optional materials are newspapers, paper towels, broom and dust pan, black construction paper, hand lenses or microscopes.

For expansion (for class of 24):

To perform indicator tests the following items are necessary: one quart of vinegar, one roll of aluminum foil, one ounce of tincture of iodine, one bucket of water or a water source in room, birthday candles (one per student group), small lumps of clay (one per student group), wooden clothespins (one per student group).

⊃ **Safety precautions:** Never taste any of the unknown substances unless given teacher permission. Goggles must be worn at all times! Wash hands between testing different unknowns and immediately after the lab is completed. Remove all combustible material from the area of the flame during the heat tests during expansion. Roll up sleeves and tie back hair when using an open flame.

1. EXPLORATION: Which process skills will be used?

Observing, manipulating materials, inferring, collecting and recording data, communicating

What will the children do?

Physical properties of an unknown

The teacher should start off the lesson by asking the students the following: Have you ever thought about some of the common substances we use in our homes? For instance, how many of you can name some common white powder substances we may use in our homes? (List these on the board. If the ones used as secret powders are not suggested, make suggestions that will help the students think about those possibilities.) What are they used for? How do we know that what it says on the container is really what is inside? The following activity will provide you with skills to help identify unknown substances.

Provide each student group five small cups numbered 1–5 and containing five different secret powders. The students will also receive five toothpicks to use as stirring sticks, some black construction paper to dump their powders on, and a hand lens. Ask the students to try to determine what the unknowns are, based on their observations of physical characteristics. The following questions should serve as a guide to encourage the students to focus on physical properties: How are the powders alike? How are they different? Do they feel the same? Does any powder have an odor? Are they the same shade of white? Can you list three properties of each powder? Can you list more than three? Using the hand lens, can you discover anything new about the powders? Are all the powders really powders? Can you describe the particles that make up each powder? Do you think a powder can be identified by the shape of its particles? Describe which properties of the powders seem to be the same and which seem to be different. Which properties are helpful in describing a particular powder?

2. EXPLANATION/CONCEPT INVENTION: What is the main idea? How will the main idea be identified?

Concept: Physical properties alone are not always sufficient characteristics to identify an unknown.

Ask the students to share answers to questions asked during the exploration phase. Refer back to the original list of common white powders from home. Ask the students to match up the unknowns to knowns based on physical characteristics they observed. Salt and sugar are made of cube-shaped particles, but salt is much more uniform and less broken. Cornstarch, baking soda, and plaster of Paris are similar in appearance, and it is hard to distinguish one from another simply on physical characteristics.

3. EXPANSION OF THE IDEA: Which process skills will be used?

Designing an experiment, observing, measuring, predicting, hypothesizing, recording data, evaluating, controlling variables, interpreting data, reducing experimental error

How will the idea be expanded?

Discussion before the activity: Ask students if they know why canaries were used in coal mines years ago, or what good is knowing the pH of pool water, or why a gas gauge in a car is useful. Once you obtain answers to these questions, ask what these three questions have in common. Work at getting to the idea that all of these are indicators of some sort: Canaries indicate the quality of the air, pH indicates the acidity or alkalinity of water, and a gas gauge indicates the amount of gas in the car.

Indicators can be used to conduct tests on the secret powders to assist in a more accurate determination of the unknown. These indicators may bring about a physical or chemical change in the secret powder. (Be sure the students already know the difference between a physical change—one in which a change of shape can occur, but the chemical composition of the original material is not altered, such as freezing of water or shredding paper, and a chemical change—a change in the composition of the original material in which molecules are lost and cannot be put back into the material to return it to its original composition, such as burning sugar or mixing vinegar and baking soda.)

During a discussion of the indicators, ask the students the following, to see if they can determine how the indicators can be used in determining the identity of the secret powders: What do you think might happen when water (or iodine, vinegar, or heat added) is mixed with the secret powder? How might you go about doing this without contaminating your secret powder sample? Why is it important to avoid contamination?

Action: Observe the reactions of the five secret powders when acted upon by the water, iodine, vinegar, and heat. Reaffirm the notion of contamination at this point. Have the students use separate eye droppers for the water, iodine, and vinegar. Be sure they use different toothpicks and clean containers to mix the unknown with the indicator. The students should record their results.

Water: What happens to each powder when you put a few drops of water on it? Did each powder mix with the water? Did any of the powders disappear? Did you put the same amount of powder in each cup? Is this important? What will happen if you add twenty drops of water? Fifty? Eighty? Does additional water affect the powders? Did any powders disappear? Where did they go? Did the powder leave the cup?

As students work with the water, they will discover that sugar, baking soda, and salt are soluble in water. By comparing the number of drops needed to dissolve these powders, some students may conclude that sugar is more soluble in water than baking soda and that salt is the least soluble of the three. Both cornstarch and plaster of Paris are insoluble in water. Plaster of Paris will harden if permitted to stand for a short period of time. After hardening, plaster of Paris cannot be changed back into its original state. The concepts of solubility and evaporation, as well as the differences between solution, suspension, and mixture, can be highlighted through this portion of the activity if necessary.

Iodine: Place small amounts of secret powders in five separate cups. Add a few drops of iodine. Do all the powders react to iodine in the same way? How can iodine be used to distinguish one powder from another? Take a cracker and a piece of potato; how do these react with the iodine? Was this reaction similar to any of the secret powders' reactions? What do the cracker and potato have in common?

The cup containing corn starch will show a striking blue-black color when iodine is added. A deep blue or blue-black color on contact with iodine is the standard test for the presence of starch. The starchier the food, the more obvious and deep the blue color will be.

Vinegar: Place small amounts of secret powders in five separate cups. Add a few drops of vinegar. What happens when you put a few drops of vinegar on each powder? Did any powder react more than others? Do you think that powders that dissolved in water will also dissolve in vinegar? Which powder do you think will take the least amount of vinegar to dissolve? The most? How can you find out? How can vinegar be used to distinguish baking soda from the other powders? If you place vinegar on an unknown substance and it bubbles, can you be sure that the substance is baking soda? Could it be another substance?

Baking powder fizzes actively when vinegar is added, while other powders fizz only slightly or not at all. Other powders can be tested with vinegar. A solution of powdered milk is curdled by vinegar.

Heat: Support a small candle in a lump of clay. This will supply sufficient heat to test the effects of heat on the powders. Fashion the aluminum foil into a small dish to be used to heat the secret powders. Use the clothespin as a handle for your aluminum dish when holding the dish over the flame. Be sure to make a separate dish for each powder.

Remove combustible litter from the area where the candle will be used. Roll up loose sleeves and tie back long hair while working with the burning candle. It is extremely important to use dry powder when performing this activity, to prevent spattering. Never use powders that have been mixed with any liquid. Place a small amount of powder in the dish and heat it.

Did any of the powders change when heated? Was an odor given off during heating? Do all the powders look the same after cooling? Compare them with samples of powders that were not heated. Were any new substances formed by heating?

When heated, baking soda and plaster of Paris seem to remain unchanged, while salt snaps and crackles. Starch turns brown and smells like burnt toast. Sugar melts, bubbles, smokes, smells like caramel, turns brown, turns black, and finally hardens. The heat test, then, is a good way to detect sugar, since sugar is the only one of the secret powders to melt and turn shiny black when heated. The same reaction occurs to sugar even when it is mixed with any of the other powders.

After using the indicators, ask the students to share their results to help determine the identity of the unknown powders. Which powder turned black when iodine was added? Can you name the powder or powders that are soluble in water? Which liquid added to which powder caused bubbles? How can a hand lens help you to identify a powder? Is a hand lens helpful in identifying all substances?

Why is the idea important for personal development?

- Why is it important for you to wash your hands before you eat any food?
- Has this activity changed your mind on decisions you make about whether or not you like a certain food? What about decisions on whether you want a certain person as your friend; do you base that choice on looks alone?

Why is the idea important for science-technology-society?

- Do you think an automobile manufacturer could be competitive if it based a car's performance ability on results from one test? Why or why not?

PHYSICAL SCIENCE

Encourage interested students to research the performance tests that cars undergo.

- Which properties of coal or oil make it a useful form of energy for our power plants?

Why is the idea important for academic growth?

- Students engage in manipulative skills during the activities.
- You are given one of five powders. When tested with vinegar, it bubbles. Can you identify the powder? Can you be sure of its identity?
- You are given one of the five powders. It dissolves in water. Can you identify the powder? Are additional tests needed? Can you eliminate any powders?

Why is the idea important to career awareness?

- Can you think of any jobs in which avoiding contamination of materials is important?
- What care should be taken when mixing unknown substances with known substances? What good is knowing possible reactions? In what careers might this knowledge be necessary?

  Cornstarch: The corn starch can be used to demonstrate how dust explosions occur in coal mines or grain elevators. Cornstarch can also be used to explain how bread becomes toast.

  Baking soda: The reaction of baking soda and vinegar results in the release of carbon dioxide gas. This gas can be used as a fire extinguisher. Most dry-powder extinguishers utilize baking soda; it can also be used to smother fires.

  Plaster of Paris: This is nothing more than hydrated calcium sulfate. When mixed into a paste with water, it sets quickly and expands. It is because of this property that it is used as a fine casting material.

  Salt: Salt can be used to lower the freezing point of water; examples are road salts and salt used in ice cream makers.

  Sugar: Its numerous uses in foods are obvious, but also our knowledge of the chemical composition of sugar and the food calories it provides have led man to discover sweeteners that work like sugar but with fewer calories.

4. EVALUATION: How will the students show what they have learned?

Upon completing the activities the students will be able to

- demonstrate when given five unknown powders, the steps necessary to identify them by using physical properties;
- demonstrate how water, iodine, vinegar, and heat can be used to identify an unknown powder;
- explain the advantages of an indicator test over reliance upon merely physical properties to identify an unknown.

GRADE

3–6

Physical
Science

DISCIPLINE

Using the Scientific Method to Solve Problems

Concepts to be invented
Main idea—Problems should be thought out before action is taken to solve them. The *scientific method* is a useful tool in problem solving.

Secondary concepts that are important to expansion
Matter can be combined in many ways. It can become a mixture, a solution, a suspension, or a colloid.

Materials needed
one-liter 7-Up soft drink
one liter water
400 ml alcohol (90 percent or
    higher concentration)
one gallon vinegar
one pound flour

two pounds cornstarch
Efferdent tablets or Alka-Seltzer
    tablets
plastic bins or buckets
paper towels for clean-up
balloons

The teacher may also want to obtain any other clear liquids or unknown white powders the students decide to use in the experiments they design.

⊃ **Safety precautions:** Goggles should be worn by teacher and students during all activities.

Teacher preparation
For clear liquid: Pour about 400 ml of alcohol as close to 100 percent pure as possible into a container. Typical rubbing alcohol is 70 percent; the water content will cause the Efferdent to slowly dissolve. Therefore, 98 percent rubbing alcohol, also available over the counter, will be more effective.

For white powder: Add one cup of cornstarch to a large container or plastic bin (old dishwashing containers work well). Slowly add water until a gooey consistency is reached. This material will pour or drip slowly but will not splatter when struck with a quick blow. This is a non-Newtonian fluid. Rather than a solution or mixture, it is called a colloid. The starch is suspended in the water.

1. EXPLORATION: Which process skills will be used?

Problem solving, communicating, inferring, designing an experiment, recording data, measuring, observing, defining operationally, synthesizing and analyzing information

What will the children do?

Exploring with Efferdent tablets

Ask the students to imagine traveling through space. All of a sudden the spaceship crash-lands. Tell them, "You have no idea where you landed. You do find several objects on the planet. Your hope is that manipulating these objects will give you some clues about the place where you have landed." Show them a container with a clear liquid in it. This is one of the things found at the landing site. Other items found were several packages of Efferdent tablets, used on earth to clean dentures. Ask them what they think will happen if you drop two tablets into the clear liquid. Encourage a variety of predictions. Now drop the tablets into the liquid. Did you predict accurately? What do you think this liquid could be? In a few moments you will be given a chance to experiment to determine what it is and if there is a way to get the Efferdent to dissolve in it.

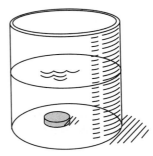

Explain to the students that in addition to the clear liquid and Efferdent tablets they found some white powder and mixed it with water from their spaceship. Show them the mixture you created. Tell them, "You were trying to figure out what the powder was, especially because it didn't get all gooey like the paste you use at school. Some of you will need to design an experiment to determine what this white powder is."

Now assign the students on one side of the room to solve for one of the unknowns (what the clear liquid is) and the students on the other side to solve for the other unknown (what the white powder is). Encourage use of the scientific method to solve for the unknowns. Use the following guide questions to help plan student experiments: What do you think the problem is? How will you go about solving the problem? What materials do you think you will need? What will you do with those materials to help solve your problem? Do you think it will be important to keep accurate records of the information you collect while doing the experiment you designed?

2. EXPLANATION/CONCEPT INVENTION: What is the main idea? How will the main idea be identified?

Concept: Problems should be thought out before action is taken to solve them. The *scientific method* is a useful tool in problem solving.

Ask the students to share with you the methods they used to go about solving their problem. Key questions to get them to share are: Do you think it is important to plan before you act? Why? What steps did you use in designing your experiment?

This methodical method of problem solving is called the scientific method. The steps to be followed are:

1. State the problem.
2. Generate predictions or hypotheses to help solve the problem.
3. Design an experiment to help solve the problem.
4. Create a list of materials needed to solve the problem.
5. Gather the materials and act on the experimental design.
6. Collect and record the data.
7. Draw conclusions and share them with peers.

3. EXPANSION OF THE IDEA: Which process skills will be used?

Problem solving, communicating, inferring, designing an experiment, recording data, measuring, observing, defining operationally, synthesizing and analyzing information

How will the idea be expanded?

Exploring with cornstarch

Ask the students from the different sides of the room to communicate the results of their experiment to one another. The students on each side will need to clearly communicate to the students on the other side exactly what they did so that the students on the other side can replicate their experiment. Allow the students time to replicate experiments. Now ask them where they think they landed. The students should reason that since they found objects on earth that behaved in ways they weren't familiar with, that perhaps they could still be on earth.

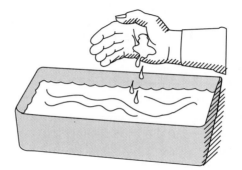

Once the students from each side of the room have discovered what the unknowns were, the students may want to play with the ooze formed with the cornstarch and water. Demonstrate to the students the balloon method for carrying their ooze in space. Obtain a plastic 1- or 2-liter pop bottle. Remove the cap and cut off the top of the bottle about two to three inches from the neck. Invert this, place a balloon over the bottle opening, pour the ooze into the funnel and milk it into the attached balloon. Knot the balloon. Stretch the balloon into various shapes. What happens? Why can you do this?

Why is the idea important for personal development?

- Do you think you can use the scientific method to help you solve personal problems you have?
- How would you go about explaining an important event that happened in your life to a friend? Will the story have the same impact if you leave out important details?
- Do you think it is as important to be able to accurately communicate your feelings about some issue as it is important to be able to give directions for performing a particular task?

Why is the idea important for science-technology-society?

- How important do you think it is to have motor oil that is the right weight in your car's engine? Can these differences in the oil's weight be affected if dirt particles were dissolved in the oil? Will dirt particles dissolve in the oil, or will they create a colloid?
- Can solutions be created when the materials involved are at temperatures close to freezing? Do you think knowledge of this will be important as we try to create space stations hundreds of miles from earth?

Why is the idea important for academic growth?

- What are the differences among solutions, mixtures, suspensions, and colloids?
- What steps are involved in the scientific method?

Why is the idea important for career awareness?

- If you were an auto mechanic, would knowledge of solutions be beneficial? What kinds of solutions does an auto mechanic work with?
- What other careers rely on knowledge of the differences among solutions, suspensions, colloids, and mixtures? Name three and state why.

4. EVALUATION: How will the students show what they have learned?

Upon completing the activities the students will be able to

- successfully take a given problem and design an experiment to solve it, using the steps in the scientific method;
- demonstrate examples of mixtures, solutions, suspensions, and colloids;
- upon looking at a diagram of a mixture, solution, suspension, or colloid, identify each combination of matter.

GRADE

1–3
—
Physical
Science

DISCIPLINE

Heat Energy

Concept to be invented
Main idea—Adding heat energy to solids causes them to liquefy.

Secondary concepts that are important to expansion
Removing heat energy from liquids causes them to solidify.

Materials needed
hot plate	saucepan	tablespoon
ten birthday candles	aluminum foil	

↪ **Safety precautions:** Do not move too close to the hot plate. Do not touch the hot melted wax.

1. EXPLORATION: Which process skills will be used?

Classifying, observing, inferring, generalizing, communicating

What will the children do?

Liquid birthday

Allow the students to handle the birthday candles. Ask them to determine whether they are a liquid or a solid. Collect their responses. Once there is consensus as to their solid state, ask for suggestions on how the solid candle could be turned into a liquid. During this discussion, if no student suggests it, the teacher should make the suggestion of using the hot plate to melt the candles. Place the candles in the saucepan over the hot plate and melt them. Ask the students to make observations as heat energy is added to the candles.

2. EXPLANATION/CONCEPT INVENTION: What is the main idea? How will the main idea be identified?

Concept: Adding energy to solids causes them to liquefy.

To help the students create this concept ask the following questions: If you place your hand close to the pan (do not touch it!) does it sense that the pan is hot? What happens to the candles as the heat energy moves from the hot plate to the pan? Can you explain why this is happening? What is a common way in which birthday candles are melted? What other types of things in your home release heat energy? As the hot plate releases heat energy to the saucepan, it is transferred to the candles, causing them to melt. What can you do to change the candles back into solids?

3. EXPANSION OF THE IDEA: Which process skills will be used?

Inferring, questioning, observing, communicating

How will the idea be expanded?

Liquids to solids

Ask the students to make predictions about what will happen to the candles once the pan is taken off of the hot plate. Give each child a piece of aluminum foil and a drop of the liquid wax. Ask the students to make observations of their wax. Divide the class in half. Ask one half to determine ways in which they can turn the liquid wax back to a solid in the shortest time possible. Ask the other half to determine ways to keep their drops in the liquid state. In which case do you need to add heat energy? Where is heat energy removed?

Why is the idea important for personal development?

- Imagine you are riding in a car on a long trip through Florida in July. During the long ride you spend time coloring and drawing pictures. You leave your crayons on the car seat when you stop to eat lunch. What do you think you will find when you return to the car after lunch? Why?
- Where in your home would be a good place to store candles? Why?

Why is the idea important for science-technology-society?

- Why do you think it is important to understand why heat energy can melt a solid?
- The oil used in a car engine is in a liquid state, yet when cool it is very thick. What do you think will happen to it as the car engine continues to run? Will this affect the design of an engine?

Why is the idea important for academic growth?

- What does it take to change a solid object into a liquid state?
- Can objects change their state of matter without gaining or losing heat energy?

Why is the idea important for career awareness?

- Aside from automobile engineers, are there other careers in which people must understand that the addition or subtraction of heat energy will change an object's state of matter?
- How do you think a hairdresser utilizes the concept identified in these

activities? If you were having your hair done by a hairdresser, would you feel more comfortable if this person understood something about heat energy?

4. EVALUATION: How will the students show what they have learned?

Upon completing the activities the students will be able to

- demonstrate how heat energy can be added to a rubber band without using fire or a hot plate,
- demonstrate how heat energy can be removed from an ice cube, draw a picture of it, and write three sentences describing how this is done.

GRADE 1–3

Physical Science

DISCIPLINE

Structure Strength

Concept to be invented

Main idea—The strength of a structure depends upon the arrangement of the materials used in construction.

Secondary concepts that are important to expansion

A variety of materials can be used to create a structure. A triangular arrangement of materials provides a more stable structure than a square.

Materials needed

straws	pins	toilet paper tubes
clay	toothpicks	paper towel tubes
washers	popsicle sticks	

⊃ **Safety precautions:** Use care in handling the pins to attach straws together. Do not stand on chairs when building tall structures; ask the teacher for help. Do not throw any of the building materials.

1. EXPLORATION: Which process skills will be used?

Observing, predicting, manipulating materials, hypothesizing, inferring

What will the children do?

Ask the students to make observations about the materials provided. Ask them to make predictions about how the materials could be used. Encourage the students to think beyond the usual uses for the materials. Allow them to manipulate the materials and to put them together in as many ways as possible. Ask the students to draw pictures of the different creations. Ask them to identify which of their creations remained standing the longest.

2. EXPLANATION/CONCEPT INVENTION: What is the main idea? How will the main idea be identified?

Concept: The strength of a structure depends on the arrangement of the materials used in construction. A variety of materials can be used to create a structure.

Key questions to ask to help identify these concepts are:

- What kinds of things did you create with these materials?
- Did anyone create a structure that remained standing?
- What did that structure look like?
- What kinds of materials did you use?
- How long did your structure remain standing?
- Why do you think one structure stood longer than another?
- Do you think you could use the same materials yet make your structure stronger? How do you think you could do that?

3. EXPANSION OF THE IDEA: Which process skills will be used?

Observing, predicting, manipulating materials, hypothesizing, inferring

How will the idea be expanded?

Allow those students who originally created some sort of building to work on making it stronger using the same materials. Encourage students who did not originally create a building to do so, trying to create as strong a structure as possible. Encourage all of the students to share with one another the structures they created. Take the time to point out which structures were sturdier than others and why. Assist the students in realizing that structures in which materials like the straws, toothpicks, popsicle sticks, or paper tubes are arranged in a triangular shape are stronger than those left as squares.

Why is the idea important for personal development?

- Take a field trip with an adult family member to the attic or basement of your house or that of a friend. What kinds of support systems are found in the house? What materials were used? In what arrangements are those support systems placed?
- Think of some common objects found around your house that you typically use once and throw away. Do you think you could use them to create a structure? How long do you think a structure would last if it was built out of the material you have in mind?

Why is the idea important for science-technology-society?

- Can you name three famous buildings that are known for the uniqueness of their structure?
- Why do you think that certain areas in the United States have strict laws about the types of structures that can be built there?

Why is the idea important for academic growth?

- Can you make a house out of a deck of cards? How is it possible? Why is it possible?
- Do you think you can support a 2-pound weight in a structure made out of old newspapers? How will you manipulate the newspapers to make this possible? Try it.

Why is the idea important for career awareness?

- Choose one of the following occupations and explain how important knowledge of structural arrangement and strength is to that occupation: mechanical engineer, civil engineer, architect, contractor.
- Do you think a paper carrier or someone working in a fast-food restaurant would use the ideas you discovered through these activities in his or her work? How?

4. EVALUATION: How will the students show what they have learned?

Upon completing the activities the students will be able to

- work in cooperative groups of four and use drinking straws and clay to build a bridge that spans across the classroom. The strength of the structure built will be tested using metal washers.
- view two toothpick structures and determine which of the two has the greatest strength and be able to explain why (Create them according to the accompanying picture).
- draw a picture of a structure that could survive in an area where strong winds occur often. Write a narrative explaining what the structure is and why it was designed as it was.

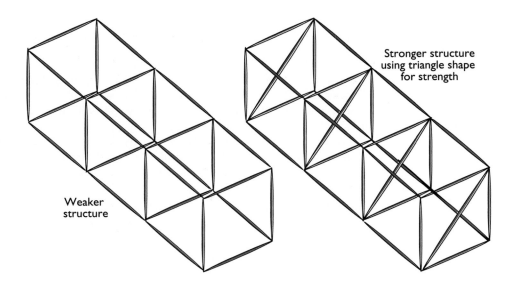

Stronger structure
using triangle shape
for strength

Weaker
structure

GRADE

1–3
—
Physical
Science

DISCIPLINE

Mirrors and Reflection

Concepts to be invented
Main idea—An object must be shiny, smooth, and reflect light to be called a *mirror*. Light bouncing off a shiny surface is called *reflection*.

Secondary concepts that are important to expansion
Mirrors with a bowl-shaped surface are called *concave;* those that are rounded outward are called *convex*.

Materials needed
For each student group:

at least one 2-inch square mirror	black paper
one metal spoon	scrap paper
aluminum foil	pencils
clear plastic	mylar paper

↪ **Safety precautions:** Be sure that rough edges on mirrors are filed or taped. Demonstrate to the students the proper handling of mirrors and mylar paper: hold them by the edges to avoid fingerprints. Stress the importance of sharing.

1. EXPLORATION: Which process skills will be used?

Observing, predicting, making assumptions, brainstorming, recording data

What will the children do?

Mirrors and reflectors

Allow the students to observe various materials and predict if they can see themselves. Ask the students to brainstorm ideas of when and where they have seen mirrorlike materials such as the ones they are working with. Manipulate the materials to see if they can see images of objects in them. Ask the students to describe their observations. Encourage the students to think about the position of that object in the mirrorlike materials versus what it looks like when they look at it directly. Ask the students to predict what their name will look like after they write it on the paper, and look at it in each of the materials. Instruct the students to write their name and view it in the mirror and each of the other materials. Can you see it in all of the objects? Does it look the same as it is written? Why or why not? Can you write it so that you can read it correctly when you look in the mirror?

2. EXPLANATION/CONCEPT INVENTION: What is the main idea? How will the main idea be identified?

Concept: An object must be shiny, smooth, and reflect light to be called a *mirror*. Light bouncing off a shiny surface is called *reflection*.

Assist the students in creating these concepts by doing the following: Refer back to the list brainstormed during the exploration phase. If terms like smooth, reflect, light, and shiny are not listed, add them to the list. Ask the students to help explain the meaning of those terms. Can an object be considered a mirror without light? Does the surface of the object need to be shiny? Can surfaces that are rough or bumpy give images as clear as shiny, smooth surfaces?

3. EXPANSION OF THE IDEA: Which process skills will be used?

Observing, predicting, manipulating materials, classifying, inferring

How will the idea be expanded?

What's a mirror?

Using the same materials from the exploration activity, ask the students to classify them into groups of things that are shiny, things that are smooth, and things that reflect light. Were you able to classify all of the materials? Could some of the materials fall into more than one group? Which materials were shiny and smooth and reflected light? Can you call these objects mirrors?

Can the spoons be considered mirrors? Describe the images seen inside the spoon. Where have you seen mirrors like these before? Have you ever been to a grocery store and seen these kinds of mirrors? What purpose do these mirrors serve? Mirrors with a bowl-shaped surface are called *concave;* those that are rounded outward are called *convex*.

Why is the idea important for personal development?

- Mirrors are used quite a bit in our everyday lives. When and where have you seen mirrors? What is their purpose?
- How often do you use a mirror? Describe the mirrors that you use.

Why is the idea important for science-technology-society?

- How do different people use mirrors? What can be learned by looking in a mirror?
- How do scientists use mirrors? Have you ever used a microscope that uses mirrors? Did you ever see a telescope that makes use of mirrors?
- Can you list at least three machines that make use of mirrors?

Why is the idea important for academic growth?

- Why is a light source needed in order for an object to be considered a mirror?
- Which type of mirror would you use if you wanted objects to appear larger than they actually are: concave or convex?
- Why do words appear to be written backwards when viewed in a mirror?

Why is the idea important for career awareness?

- What careers are linked to the use of mirrors? Do your parents use mirrors in their work?
- What career do you think you would like to have? Do you think you will use mirrors in any way?
- Would some careers be more difficult without mirrors? Think of your school bus driver.

4. EVALUATION: How will the students show what they have learned?

Upon completing the activities the students will be able to

- write their names upside down and backward on a piece of paper to illustrate their knowledge of what a mirror can do,
- describe the three properties of a mirror or mirrorlike object and use them in sentences,
- classify materials into *shiny*, *smooth*, and *reflects light* categories.

Paper Chromatography

Concept to be invented

Main idea—Paper chromatography is the separation of a mixture into its different parts through preferential absorption by a strip of filter paper.

Secondary concepts that are important to expansion

Black ink is made up of many colors.

Materials needed

Per student group:

One rectangular basin at least the size of a shoe box, enough water to fill the container to about half an inch, paper towels for spills, several sheets of filter paper (inexpensive coffee filters or white paper towels work just as well), three rubber bands, paper clips, one set of colored felt-tip pens, five or more different brands of black water-soluble felt-tip pens (each labeled with the name of a different person), scissors to make multicolored coffee filter snow flakes during expansion phase.

⊃ **Safety precautions:** Encourage the students to use caution when carrying the water-filled basins. Clean up all spills immediately. Do not poke one another with markers. Keep markers away from eyes.

1. EXPLORATION: Which process skills will be used?

Observing, predicting, questioning, making assumptions, brainstorming, recording data

What will the children do?

Moving black ink dots

Set the stage for this lesson by explaining that for different holidays you like to decorate the outside of your house. You had a decoration in front of your house and one Monday morning you woke to find it had been taken. Taped to your front door was this message. "I have your decorations. If you want them back you must bake me some cookies by Friday or else!" Ask the students to help you find out which friend took your decorations. Tell them that you don't have time to make cookies for all of your friends. You want to narrow it down so you only have to make cookies for that one friend.

Pick a number based on the number of different felt-tip black pens you were able to collect. Explain that you went to that number of friends' homes and innocently asked them if you could borrow their pen with the promise of returning it by Friday. Show the students the ransom letter and the pens. Ask them to help brainstorm ideas on how they could figure out who wrote the letter, using their pens and the ransom letter. Record these suggestions. After as many suggestions as possible are offered, review the suggestions. Help the students decide which suggestions will really work. Show them the basin with water and the filter paper. Ask them if they think they can use these to help solve your problem. If they can't figure it out, demonstrate to them by cutting a word off the ransom letter and placing it in the water. Ask the students to observe what happens to the ink as the paper becomes wet. Allow the paper to dry. Let the students examine the various colors that bled from the letters. While that word is drying, encourage the students to think about how they could use the black pens to see the colors in the ink.

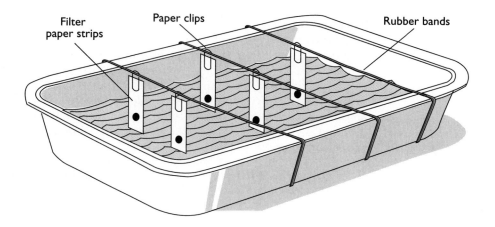

Show the students one efficient set-up to separate the ink: Stretch three rubber bands across the rectangular basin. Use the filter paper to make strips about 1–2 inches wide. Place a dot about the size of a dime about a quarter-inch from one end of the strip. Hang the strips over the rubber bands so that about an eighth-inch of the paper end closest to the dot is sitting in the water. Use the paper clips to clip the top of the strip to the rubber band. Let these strips sit until the dot slowly moves up the strip. An illustration may help in set-up.

2. EXPLANATION/CONCEPT INVENTION: What is the main idea? How will the main idea be identified?

Concept: Paper chromatography is the separation of a mixture into its different parts through preferential absorption by a strip of filter paper. Black ink is made up of many colors.

Ask the students to share their observations about the word from the ransom note when it was placed in the water. What happened to the black ink? When you placed the paper strips with the dots from each of the pens in the water, what happened to the dots? Did they appear to crawl up the paper? Did they all remain the same color? What colors did you observe? Why do you think that happened?

PHYSICAL SCIENCE

Assist the students in understanding that as the water moves up the filter paper, it takes some of the ink with it. Black ink is made up of many colors. The different colors separate out of the spot of ink. The heavy colors stay near the dot; the light ones move up the strip. Different pen manufacturers use different formulas for their black inks. This will cause a difference in the chromatogram (the colored strip of separated black ink) that is formed. When we compare the different colors in the strips to the different colors from the ransom word, we can determine whose pen wrote the note. According to your data, which friend took your decoration?

3. EXPANSION OF THE IDEA: Which process skills will be used?

Observing, predicting, manipulating materials, recording data, inferring

How will the idea be expanded?

Moving colored ink dots and snowflakes

Start this phase by reminding the students about their discoveries from the exploration phase. Ask them if they think colored markers will behave the same way as black felt tipped pens. Allow the students to make and record their predictions. Provide the students with one piece of filter paper. Ask them to make several strips and place a dot from a different colored pen on each. Hang these in the basin. Do the colors separate out? Do all of the colored pens create a chromatogram? Why or why not?

As an extra activity, give each child another piece or two of filter paper. Ask the students to use the colored and black pens to create a design in the middle of the circular filter paper (inexpensive coffee filters are great for this activity). Fold the filter paper so that the center is at the pointed end of a triangle. Ask them to make predictions about what will happen to that design after you dip the pointed tip into the basin of water. Record those predictions; then dip. Open the paper and allow it to dry. After it has dried and the various colors have bled throughout, encourage the students to refold the paper and cut out various designs. When they open it up they will have created a snowflake.

Why is the idea important for personal development?

- Do you think you could trick your friends using paper chromatography? How?
- In what ways have you ever mixed different colors together to get a different one? When you did that, did you ever wish you could separate them again? Do you think you could separate them in all cases? Why or why not?

Why is the idea important for science-technology-society?

- In industry, paper chromatography is not used as much as solid chromatography, in which solids are used to separate mixtures into their parts. In what industries do you think this type of chromatography is used?
- Do you think the paint industry has benefited from knowledge of chromatography? Why or why not?

PHYSICAL SCIENCE

Why is the idea important for academic growth?

- Can all black inks be separated into their component parts?
- What do you call separating a mixture into its parts by using a solid or paper to pull out those parts?
- How would you design an experiment to determine who wrote you an anonymous letter?

Why is the idea important for career awareness?

- Do you think the FBI makes use of paper chromatography? How do you think they might use it?
- Would a cake decorator need to understand chromatography? Why or why not?
- How do you think paint stores know how many drops of each color paint to put into a can of white to get it to match the color on the paint sample strip?

4. EVALUATION: How will the students show what they have learned?

Upon completing the activities the students will be able to

- design an experiment to determine who wrote an anonymous letter,
- explain the concept of paper chromatography to a peer,
- explain why some ink colors merely bleed while others bleed and separate.

Toys in Space

Concepts to be invented
Main idea—Things that behave one way on earth will behave differently in space due to zero gravity conditions.

Secondary concepts that are important to expansion
An astronaut will experience weightlessness while traveling through space. Toys can be used to explain a variety of scientific principles.

Materials needed
Toys in Space video (available from NASA, Lewis Research Center, Cleveland, OH) and toys used in video: wheel-o, yo-yo, paddle ball, ball and jacks, self-propelling car, magnetic marbles, spinning top, Play-Skool Flip Mouse, gyroscope.

⊃ **Safety precautions:** Teacher and students should wear goggles to be sure that no eye injuries occur.

1. EXPLORATION: Which process skills will be used?

Observing, predicting, manipulating materials, hypothesizing, inferring

What will the children do?

Toy behavior in zero gravity

Provide the students with the toys from the materials list. Ask them to play with the toys and make observations about how they function. After adequate time has been spent playing with the toys, ask the students to make predictions as to how they think the toys would function in zero gravity. Encourage the students to make as many predictions as possible.

2. EXPLANATION/CONCEPT INVENTION: What is the main idea? How will the main idea be identified?

Concept: Things that behave one way on earth will behave differently in space due to zero gravity conditions.

To assist the students in developing this concept, ask them the following questions: How do the toys work in the classroom? Can you demonstrate them for me? How does gravity behave on earth? What does it do to objects on earth? If there were no gravity on earth, how do you think these toys would behave? Have you ever seen movies of astronauts as they travel in space? How do they look?

3. EXPANSION OF THE IDEA: Which process skills will be used?

Observing, predicting, manipulating materials, hypothesizing, inferring

How will the idea be expanded?

Toys and Newton

After much discussion between the students about their predictions, show the NASA videotape, *Toys in Space*. Discuss afterward the discrepancies between the students' predictions and what really happened. An astronaut will experience weightlessness while traveling through space.

Toys can be used to explain a variety of scientific principles. If the students really show an interest in the behavior of the toys under zero gravity conditions, you may want to introduce the students to some of Newton's laws, which govern the behavior of these toys on earth. If you want the students to really understand them, then take care to plan additional activities that engage the students in science processes to enhance their understanding of these laws. The laws are as follows:

1. Law of inertia: Every body continues in its state of rest or of uniform motion in a straight line, except insofar as it is compelled by forces to change that state.
2. Force equals mass times acceleration.
3. The force exerted by an object A on another object B is equal in magnitude and opposite in direction to the force exerted by object B on object A.

Why is the idea important for personal development?

- How do you decide what kinds of toys to play with? Did you ever think that you could use them to help explain science concepts?
- Can you choose one of your toys and explain how or why it works? Ask your friends to help you decide which science concept is applied to explain why your toy works.

Why is the idea important for science-technology-society?

- Toys are actually like models of particular systems. Why do you think it would be easier to make a toy model of some invention first? What advantage would that give to certain industries?
- Why do you think you or your friends choose particular toys to play with? Is it important that you play with the same things as your friends? Why or why not?

Why is the idea important for academic growth?

- Is it possible for toys on earth to behave the same way when under zero gravity conditions? Is it possible for toys in space to behave the same way when on earth?
- Describe two different scientific concepts that can be explained using a bicycle.

Why is the idea important for career awareness?

- Do you think a wheel-o could have been invented if the creator did not understand something about magnetism?
- If you were to become a toy designer, would knowledge of science concepts be useful in your career?

4. EVALUATION: How will the students show what they have learned?

Upon completing the activities the students will be able to

- describe one scientific concept that can be explained with the use of a roller skate,
- create a toy using materials of their choice that can be fun, yet explain a scientific concept,
- design a toy that can still function in the absence of gravity and write a few sentences to describe it.

GRADE 4–8

Physical Science

DISCIPLINE

Simple Machines—The Lever

Concepts to be invented

Main idea—A lever is a rigid bar that pivots around a point, which is used to move an object at a second point by a force applied at a third point. The pivot point is the *fulcrum,* the object moved is the *load,* and the place where the force was applied is the *effort.*

Secondary concepts that are important to expansion

There are three kinds of levers. A *first-class lever* is a fulcrum between effort and load; the effort moves in the opposite direction of the load, as in a seesaw or a balance. A *second-class lever* is a load between the fulcrum and the effort; effort is applied in the same direction as the load should be moved, as in a wheelbarrow or a bottle opener. A *third-class lever* is an effort between the fulcrum and the load, which magnifies the distance moved by the load but reduces its force, as in a hammer, a catapult, or a fishing rod. Additional terms that may be introduced in this lesson are *resistance, friction, work,* and *machine.*

Materials needed

Per student group, for the discrepant event:

sandpaper   cooking oil
water   marbles or beads
hand lotion   paper towels or wipes

For exploration:

Goggles, one long piece of board (18" x 1/4" works well), one fulcrum (proportional in size to the long board—for the 18" board, triangular pieces cut out of a 2 x 4 work well), any proportionally sized objects to be used as load, such as blocks of wood, small books, metal chunks, or cylinders.

For expansion:

goggles   one rubber band
two plastic spoons   peanuts

⊃ **Safety precautions:** Remind students that safety goggles must be worn at all times. Discourage students from sending the load material flying across the room. Warn them of the potential danger to themselves and other students.

Discrepant event

Which process skills will be used?

Observing, hypothesizing, inferring, drawing conclusions

What will the teacher and students do?

Do not show the students what you are giving them. Ask them to put out their hands and place a small amount of one of the following in their hands: sandpaper, nothing, water, hand lotion, cooking oil, two or three marbles or beads. Tell them to be sure not to let anyone else see what they have. Once everyone has received one of the items, then ask the class to rub their hands together (all at the same time) with the objects still in their hands. After the students have had time to do this and to comment on what just happened, then ask questions such as: What did your hands feel like? Who had the hardest time rubbing his or her hands together? The easiest? Why? Did your hands change temperature? What do you think caused your hands to get hot/cold/no change? Why was it easy for some and not for others? What do you think is prohibiting you from sliding or rolling the objects in your hands? (Resistance.) What is this resistance to movement called? (Friction.) What did you need to do to overcome friction? (Exert some energy—effort.) By using effort to move your hands over a distance, you have done work. What do we call an object that will do the work for us? (A machine.)

1. EXPLORATION: Which process skills will be used?

Manipulating materials, collecting and recording data, communicating, observing, hypothesizing, predicting, inferring

What will the children do?

Lever creations

Instructions: Use a long board and a triangular shaped block in as many combinations as you think possible to move the weighted object (blocks, books, metal pieces). Draw the methods you tried. Discuss possible solutions with your peers. Try and record the results of those as well.

2. EXPLANATION/CONCEPT INVENTION: What is the main idea? How will the main idea be identified?

Concept: A lever is a rigid bar that pivots around a point, which is used to move an object at a second point by a force applied at a third point.

Have the students draw the results of their manipulations on the board. With help from the class, identify on their drawings the pivot point, the object being moved, and the place where they had to apply a force to get the object to move. Solicit class ideas as to names for these points. Identify the pivot point as the *fulcrum,* the object moved as the *load,* and the place where force was applied as the *effort.*

Key questions to ask: Did these inventions make it easier for you to do work? What do we call objects that make our work easier? What has the machine we invented allowed us to do? What do you think we call it? Why? Once the concept *lever* has been invented, ask the students if they can see any differences in the placement of the three points on any of their diagrams. If necessary, supply diagrams that show different placements of the points. Key questions: Is there any advantage to changing the position of the three points? What happens to the direction of the effort and load in each of the diagrams? Can you see some practical uses for the different positions of the points? As you go through the different arrangements of the points, identify the three classes of levers: A *first-class lever* is a fulcrum between effort and load; the effort moves in the opposite direction of the load, as in a seesaw or a balance. A *second-class lever* is a load between the fulcrum and the effort; effort is applied in the same direction as the load should be moved, as in a wheelbarrow or a bottle opener. A *third-class lever* is an effort between the fulcrum and the load, which magnifies the distance moved by the load but reduces its force, as in a hammer, a catapult, or a fishing rod.

3. EXPANSION OF THE IDEA: Which process skills will be used?

Hypothesizing, inferring, manipulating materials, observing, communicating, collecting and recording data, making assumptions, predicting, formulating models

How will the idea be expanded?

Instructions: Given two plastic spoons, a rubber band, and some peanuts, design

PHYSICAL SCIENCE

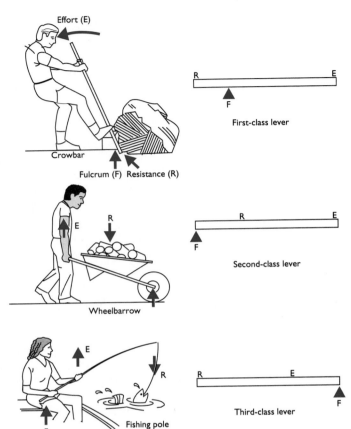

and demonstrate a first-, second-, and third-class lever. Share your inventions with the class.

Home Extension: Which process skills will be used?

Inferring, manipulating materials, making assumptions, formulating models, observing, analyzing, classifying

What will the children do?

Lever scavenger hunt: Have the students ask an adult to go with them on a lever scavenger hunt. Make a list of all of the places where levers are being used in some form or another. How many of these are combination levers? How many are compound levers of the first, second, or third class? Bring these lists back to school to share with the class.

PHYSICAL SCIENCE

Why is the idea important for personal growth?

- Where in your home did you find a lever being used? Did any of these places surprise you? Were any of these uses a case where two of the lever types were used in combination? (Nail clippers, manual typewriter, piano.) Did you find any compound levers? (Scissors, pliers, nutcracker, tweezers.)
- When you need to cut a piece of paper, why is it easier to use scissors instead of a knife? What advantage does using a pair of scissors have over using a knife for cutting?
- Which simple machine makes it possible for people to play a piano?

Why is the idea important for science-technology-society?

- Why would it be difficult for you to wear your ice skates in the house but not your roller skates? How have industries used this information to overcome friction?
- How do you think the invention of the parking meter has affected your city? How about cities like Chicago or New York?

  Example technologies include ball bearings for reducing friction, balance, wrench, seesaw, tweezers, fishing rods, manual typewriters, parking meters, pianos.

Why is the idea important for academic growth?

- Students will be able to explain the function of the fulcrum, load, and effort; various combinations of these points can create a first-, second-, or third-class lever. They will be able to explain how machines help us to do work and to overcome friction.
- This activity lays the foundation for new concepts to be identified in new lessons, such as the relationship between effort and work, mechanical advantage, other types of simple machines, and so on.

Why is the idea important for career awareness?

- Archimedes of Syracuse was perhaps the greatest of the Greek mathematicians and scientists. He lived from 287 to 212 BC. He is credited with inventing the catapult, which the Greeks used during the Second Punic War against the Roman army. It is said that Archimedes was slain during this war while he was studying mathematical figures, which he habitually drew in the dust. What do you think he meant when he said, "Give me a fulcrum on which to rest, and I will move the earth"?
- Who needs to know about levers? Which careers rely upon the use and/or knowledge of levers? (Manufacturers of playground equipment, laborers, dock workers, piano makers, typewriter manufacturers, parking meter repair persons.)

PHYSICAL SCIENCE

4. EVALUATION: How will the students show what they have learned?

Upon completing the activities the students will be able to

- classify the following items as a first-, second-, or third-class lever: hammer, nutcracker, seesaw, wheelbarrow, balance, bottle opener, fishing rod;
- identify the fulcrum, the effort, and the load on each item, when given a hammer, wheelbarrow, and nail extractor;
- predict the direction of the load when effort is applied with each of the following: fishing rod, balance, bottle opener.

SECTION III

Earth Science Activities

Lesson Name	Grade Level	Activities
The Solar System and the Universe	K–2	Rhythm Activity • Postcard Writing
The Expanding Universe	2–4	Expanding Balloon/Universe • Build a Solar System Salad
Constellations	4–7	Connect the Stars • Evening Field Trip • Create a Constellation
Earth Layers	K–2	Clay Earth Layers • Clay Continents
Fossils	1–4	Fossil Observations • Plaster Molds and Casts
Soil Formation	3–5	Soil Separation and Rock Crushing • Soil Components
Rock Types	6–8	Rock Categorization • Rock Collection Field Trip
Cooling Crystals	6–8	PDB Crystal Formation • Rock Type versus Crystal Formation
Weathering	6–8	Freezing Bottle • Weathering Field Trip • Rock Identification • Acid ID Test • Rust Exploration
Crustal Plate Movement	6–8	Moving Plates • Mapping Volcanoes and Earthquakes • Oatmeal and Crackers = Plate Tectonics
Rain Formation	K–2	Rain in a Jar • Water Drop Attraction
Dew Formation	K–2	Pop Bottle Condensation • Thermometer Reading and Dew Point
Radiant Energy	2–4	Temperature and Colored Surfaces • Temperature: Sun versus Shade • Magnifiers—Capture the Sun • Sun Tea
Weather Forecasting	4–8	Weather Log Creation • Weather Map Symbols • Weather Data Collection
Weather Predictions	5–7	Weather Map Information • Recording Weather Data and Predicting • Weather Records
Air Mass Movement	4–7	Coriolis Effect—Globe • Coriolis Effect—Top • Air Movement—Dry Ice • Oil and Water Fronts • Create a Rain Gauge • Air Masses and Parachutes
Air Pressure	5–6	Balloon Balance • Air Has Weight • Paper Blowing, Newspaper Strength • Lunch Bag Balance
Solar Heating	5–8	Temperature versus Surface Color • Optimum Thermometer Placement
Air Movement and Surface Temperature	5–7	Convection Current • Surface, Temperature • Observation Box • Paper Bag Balance
Uneven Heating of the Earth	5–7	Tower of Water • Aneroid Barometer • Air Pressure versus Water Temperature • Air Temperature versus Movement of Air • Heat Transfer on a Wire • Heat Movement Through Air • Heat Transfer Through Metal • Movement of Smoke over Hot and Cold Surfaces—Clouds

EARTH SCIENCE

GRADE

K–2

——

Earth
Science

DISCIPLINE

The Solar System and the Universe

Concept to be invented
Main idea—The earth is part of the solar system.

Secondary concepts that are important to expansion
Planets differ from one another.

Materials needed
For exploration:

Books on planets, such as Jeff Davidson, *Voyage to the Planets* (Worthington, OH: Willowisp Press,1990) and Joanna Cole, *The Magic School Bus Lost in Space* (New York: Scholastic, 1988).

For expansion:

Post card outline, poster paper, paints, and markers.

⊃ **Safety precautions:** The students should be reminded to sit and listen without poking or hitting one another. During the expansion activity they should be sure to clean up any paint spills immediately, and they should not put markers or paint brushes in their mouths.

1. EXPLORATION: Which process skills will be used?

Observing, questioning

What will the children do?

Rhythm activity

- You should read such books as *Voyage to the Planets* or *The Magic School Bus Lost in Space* to the students. Ask them recall questions as you are sharing the book with them.
- Teach the students the following chant, clapping the beat. Allow them to fill in the planet of their choice once they get the rhythm down:

  A–B–CDE, How many planets can there be?
  F–G–HIJ, There are nine we know of today.
  K–L–MNO, To which one would you like to go?
  P–Q–RST, I'd like to visit Mercury.
  U–V–WXY, I've been watching it in the sky.
  Z–Z–ZZZ, Know anyone who'll come with me?

2. EXPLANATION/CONCEPT INVENTION: What is the main idea? How will the main idea be identified?

Concept: The earth is part of the solar system.

It has been found through observations of the nighttime sky and satellite observations that the earth is just one of nine planets that move around the sun. Each of the planets has unique characteristics because of its distance from the sun. Questions students ask during the reading of the book will also assist in developing the concepts.

3. EXPANSION OF THE IDEA: Which process skills will be used?

Inferring, observing, questioning

How will the idea be expanded?

Postcard writing

Once the students know the chant and sing it with all nine planet names, ask them to choose one of the nine as a place they'd like to go on vacation. Break the students into nine planet vacation groups. Ask them to plan a drawing of their planet as close to reality as possible and then work as a cooperative group to create one drawing of that planet. Draw a sun on your mural paper. Ask the different groups to come up to the mural and place their planet in its appropriate order from the sun.

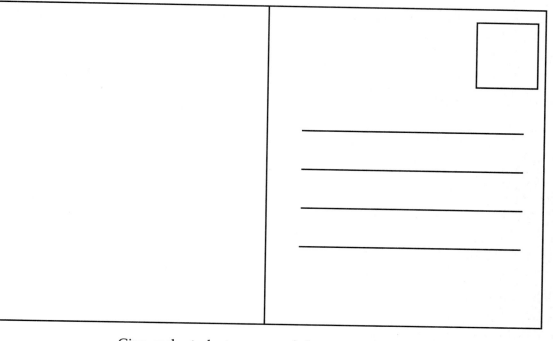

draw landscape

Give each student a copy of the postcard outline. Ask them to write postcards to family members, describing their trips to the planets they drew. Teach them how to address a postcard. Ask them to design an appropriate stamp for the planet they visited. When all of these are completed, tape the postcards near the planet of origin.

EARTH SCIENCE

Questions that help invent secondary concepts

- Is the earth all alone in space? No, there are eight other planets.
- What else is found in the earth's neighborhood? Planets, moons, dust, meteorites.
- How do we know there are other planets in our neighborhood? Has anyone ever seen them? We can see them in the sky; they look like stars. We have satellites that have gone close to them and sent back pictures to earth.
- What is unique about your planet? Answers will vary.
- How close to the sun is your planet? Answers will vary.
- Are all the planets the same size? No—go into detail about their planets.
- Do you think you could live on your vacation planet as easily as you can on earth? Why or why not?

    Students will apply knowledge they learned about their planets to answer these questions.

Why is the idea important for personal development?

- Do you think if the earth were as close to the sun as Mercury you could still live on it? Why or why not?
- If someone told you he or she could take you on a plane ride to the planet Mars, would you believe it? Why or why not?

Why is the idea important for science-technology-society?

- Do you think man can invent a way so that it will be possible to live on any of the other planets? How do you think we can do this?

Why is the idea important for academic growth?

- Students will be able to name the nine planets, list their order from the sun, and discuss one characteristic of each after completing and participating in the above activities.

Why is the idea important for career awareness?

- Do you think that a person responsible for monitoring the air quality of the planet Earth can learn anything from understanding what the atmosphere is like on the planet Jupiter?
- How important is it that space scientists know the positions of the planets before launching satellites or rockets into space? What kinds of skills do space scientists need in order to do their jobs?

4. EVALUATION: How will the students show what they have learned?

    Upon completing the activities the students will be able to

- successfully answer the questions included in the expansion phase of this lesson, as well as the new outcomes questions.
- draw lines from the picture of a planet to a group of words that briefly describe the planet. The picture question on the next page is an example of the kind of question that could be made for this assessment:

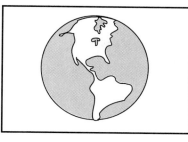

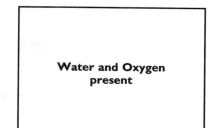

Water and Oxygen present

- create a planet mobile (this can be done as a home extension) out of the following materials: wire coat hanger, paint, tape and/or glue, papier maché or balls of different sizes, string, and cardboard, paper, or newspaper.

GRADE

2–4

Earth Science

DISCIPLINE

The Expanding Universe

Concepts to be invented
Main idea—Our universe appears to be expanding. Distances between parts of the universe are vast.

Secondary concepts that are important to expansion
Planets orbit about the sun. The planets are very small and very far away from the sun.

Materials needed
For exploration:

Round balloons (one for each student), wide-tip felt markers (black and red).

For expansion:

one fresh pea	one dried pea	one small walnut
one larger walnut	one bean	one smaller bean
one 8-inch head of cabbage	one 9-inch head of cabbage	one grapefruit
one big orange		a bicycle
the school track		

⊃ **Safety precautions:** Use extreme caution while blowing up the balloon. Do not allow children to chew on the balloon.

1. EXPLORATION: Which process skills will be used?

Observing, predicting, hypothesizing, inferring

What will the children do?

Expanding balloon/universe

Instruct each student to
- partially inflate a round balloon, pinching the neck closed with thumb and forefinger,
- make specks with a wide-tip felt marker all over the surface of the balloon, noting their positions and letting them dry,
- blow more air into the balloon and look at it, again noting the position of the specks.

2. EXPLANATION/CONCEPT INVENTION: What is the main idea? How will the main idea be identified?

Concept: Our universe appears to be expanding. Distances between parts of the universe are vast.

Help the students invent the concept by asking them such questions as:
- What has happened to the distance between the specks? *It has increased, expanded.*
- What do you think will happen to the specks if you continue to add air to the balloon? *They will continue to move away from one another.*
- Imagine that the balloon is space and one of the specks is the neighborhood the earth is found in. Put a red mark on one of the specks to represent the earth's neighborhood. Blow up the balloon some more while watching the red speck. What do you think you could say about space if you were on this red speck? *The earth is very far from other parts of the universe.*

3. EXPANSION OF THE IDEA: Which process skills will be used?

Observing, communicating, formulating models, recording data

How will the idea be expanded?

Build a solar system salad

Have students observe the fixings for a solar system salad (see materials needed). They should decide which of the items correspond to the nine planets and the

EARTH SCIENCE

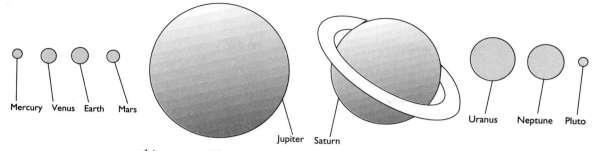

Mercury Venus Earth Mars   Jupiter Saturn   Uranus Neptune Pluto

earth's moon. The students should check with one another to come to some consensus. Then they will discuss decisions with the teacher.

After a discussion on relative sizes, take the salad items out to the school track. While bicycling around the track, drop off the planets to show their relative distance from each other. Allow all the students to participate. Some may be lap counters; others should do the riding. To make it really effective, each student should ride the bicycle. As the children grow tired, the vast distances between the planets will be apparent to them. Each lap represents 211,265 miles in space.

Mercury: 2/5 lap
Venus: 3/4 lap
Earth: 1 lap
Mars: 1-1/2 laps
Jupiter: 5-1/2 laps

Saturn: 9-1/2 laps
Uranus: 19-1/2 laps
Neptune: 30 laps
Pluto: 39-2/5 laps

Questions that help invent secondary concepts:

- Which of the salad fixings did you have a hard time assigning a planet to?
- Did you find it necessary to look in some reference books to help you decide which item represents which planet?

Mercury: Fresh pea
Venus: Walnut
Earth: Larger walnut
Moon: Dried pea
Mars: Bean

Jupiter: 9-inch cabbage
Saturn: 8-inch cabbage
Uranus: Grapefruit
Neptune: Big orange
Pluto: Small bean

- How did your legs feel after you dropped off the solar system salad fixings?
- Imagine you are out in space dropping those items off at the different planets. What would be the total distance you would have traveled? (Hint: What is the distance from the sun to Pluto?)
- If the center of the football field represents the sun, what can you say about the planets with respect to the sun? What do the planets do?

Why is the idea important for personal development?

- Do you think it will ever be possible for you to travel to the other planets? Would you like to do this? Why or why not? What do you think you would need to pack for your trip?

- Would you purchase a ticket today to spend some time in a space station? Do you think you will live long enough to use the ticket?

Why is the idea important for science-technology-society?

- Do you think space stations will solve the problems of pollution and over-population on earth?
- Do you think the vastness of space will allow us to ship our garbage out into space and never be affected by it on earth? How do you think this will be possible?

Why is the idea important for academic growth?

- The students will be able to explain the concept of the expanding universe and discuss the implications that has for life as we presently know it on earth.
- Why is it possible to view planets in the nighttime sky? Do all of the planets always maintain the same orbital paths?

Why is the idea important for career awareness?

- If it was your job to successfully create a satellite that would move through outer space, sending back to earth information about other planets, what kinds of knowledge do you think you would need to have? What would be the qualifications for your job? Pretend you need to employ someone to fill such a job. Write a job description and give it a title. Do the race or sex of the person applying matter?

4. EVALUATION: How will the students show what they have learned?

Upon completing the activities the students will be able

- to successfully complete the activities above.
- to write a few sentences after they participate in the bicycle activity about how they felt when they finished and what they think about the distances between the planets. Ask the students to share their feelings with one another. How tired they became and how much they want to share with others what they did will provide an effective measure of success.
- when provided with ten different kinds of vegetables for a solar salad, use these new items to arrange the members of the solar system. Also ask them to decide how far they would have to be from one another if one inch equals one million miles.

4–7

Earth Science

Constellations

Concept to be invented

Main idea—Constellations are groups of stars.

Secondary concepts that are important to expansion

Big Dipper, Little Dipper, Polaris or North Star, Cassiopeia, Perseus, and Pleiades found in Taurus.

Materials needed

For exploration:

Construction paper
one pen or pencil per student

overhead projector
four or five flashlights

⊃ **Safety precautions:** Remind students to be careful not to poke themselves or others with the pen or pencil.

1. EXPLORATION: Which process skills will be used?

Observing, predicting, hypothesizing, inferring

What will the children do?

Connect the stars

The students will view a dot to dot pattern presented to them and predict what the pattern will look like once the dots are connected. This pattern is made on the chalkboard by using an overhead projector and black construction paper with holes punched in it for dots as the transparency. Place several different patterns up on the overhead. Have the students take turn connecting the dots on the chalkboard.

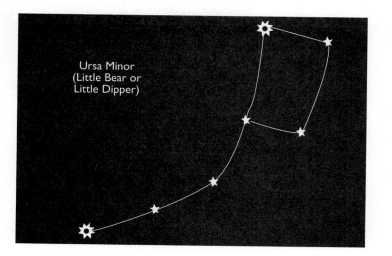

Ursa Minor
(Little Bear or
Little Dipper)

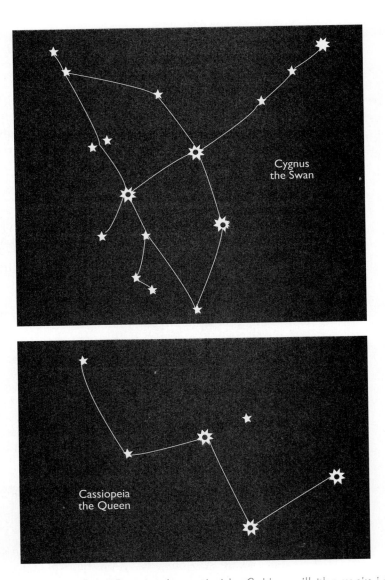

Cygnus
the Swan

Cassiopeia
the Queen

2. EXPLANATION/CONCEPT INVENTION: What is the main idea? How will the main idea be identified?

Concept: Constellations are groups of stars found in the sky.

Ask the students questions such as the following to help invent this concept: What do you think these patterns represent? Do you recall seeing these same patterns anywhere? Review each of the patterns again and ask once again if anyone recalls seeing these patterns anywhere.

Patterns represent star constellations. Star constellations are made up of a group of stars and are given a name traditionally based on the pattern they make in the sky. These constellations were named by people in the past and usually have a story or legend attached to them.

Once again, project the patterns up on the board, again connecting the dots. This time go through the names of the constellations presented, and give a brief history of how they got their names. Some easy constellations to showcase are the Big Dipper, the Little Dipper, Cassiopeia, Perseus, and Pleiades found in Taurus.

Identify the North Star—Polaris—for the students. Explain how all the other constellations in the northern hemisphere appear to revolve around this star. Thus, at different times of the year only certain constellations are visible in the nighttime sky in the northern hemisphere.

3. EXPANSION OF THE IDEA: Which process skills will be used?

Observing, communicating, formulating models, recording data

How will the idea be expanded?

Evening field trip, create a constellation

- Take the students on an evening field trip to an area where man-made lights are minimal. Be sure you pick a clear night. Ask everyone to bring a blanket and lie on the grass. Try to identify as many constellations as possible.
- Ask the students to create a constellation of their own and name it, much as the ancient Greeks and Indians did as they observed stars in the nighttime sky. Have them write reports about how their constellations got their names. Share the reports orally with the class.

Why is the idea important for personal development?

- How can star constellations help you if you get lost at night?
- How can you develop watching stars into a hobby?

Why is the idea important for science-technology-society?

- What kind of equipment can you use to improve your view of the stars?
- How has astronomy equipment been perfected since the time of Galileo's first telescope?

Why is the idea important for academic growth?

- How can we use our knowledge of constellations to find a particular star in the sky?
- Why do all stars in the northern hemisphere appear to revolve around Polaris? Is this our closest star?

Why is the idea important for career awareness?

- How are constellations used by astronomers who study other phenomena in the sky.
- Is there any difference between an astronomer and an astrologer? Do they both use their knowledge of constellations in some form? How?

4. EVALUATION: How will the students show what they have learned?

Upon completing the activities the students will be able to

- identify Polaris, the North Star,
- identify the Big and Little Dippers in the northern sky,
- explain how at least two different constellations got their names,
- identify the star closest to earth.

Earth Layers

GRADE

K–2
—
Earth
Science

DISCIPLINE

Concepts to be invented
Main idea—The planet earth is made up of three layers, the *core, mantle,* and *crust.*

Secondary concepts that are important to expansion
Large land masses found on the crust of the earth are called *continents.* Large bodies of water on the crust are called *oceans.*

Materials needed
For exploration (one per student):
2-inch diameter ball of red, yellow, and gray clay, plastic knife, white construction paper, three crayons of red, yellow, and gray.

For exploration (for entire class):
Green and blue clay, green crayon, globe of the earth, tennis ball, soccer ball. Maps of ocean floors are useful but optional.

⊃ **Safety precautions:** Remind students to be careful not to poke themselves or others with the plastic knife. Be sure to wash hands after using the clay. Remind them not to eat the clay.

EARTH SCIENCE

1. EXPLORATION: Which process skills will be used?

Observing, manipulating materials, predicting

What will the children do?

Clay earth layers

Guide the students through this portion of the lesson by first asking them to pick up the red clay and work it into a ball. Ask them to then flatten out the yellow clay and wrap it around the red ball of clay. Finally ask them to flatten out the gray clay and then wrap it around the yellow-covered ball of clay. Ask the students to carefully use their plastic knives to cut the clay ball in half. Ask them to draw on their construction paper what the sliced-open clay ball looks like.

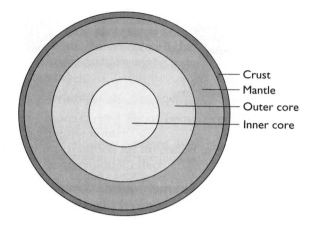

Crust
Mantle
Outer core
Inner core

2. EXPLANATION/CONCEPT INVENTION: What is the main idea? How will the main idea be identified?

Concept: The planet earth is made up of three layers—the *core, mantle*, and *crust*.

Help the students invent the concept by asking them such questions as: What do you think this ball of clay with the different colored layers represents? Accept as many suggestions as possible and provide appropriate responses all the while steering the students toward thinking about the earth. If this suggestion is never given, then tell the students you'd like them to think of the clay ball as a representation of the earth and its layers. Since the students are most familiar with things found on the surface of the earth, ask them to give you suggestions of things they find there. If possible, draw pictures of their suggestions or write the names on the board. Ask if anyone has an idea for another name to call the earth's surface. You may make an analogy to a pie that has a different material on the inside than outside. What do you call the outer covering of the pie? *Crust* —this same name is given to the outer surface of the earth. Ask the students to label the gray layer on their diagram the *crust*.

Ask the students what they think the yellow layer may be like on the earth and if they have any ideas as to its name. The yellow clay represents the mantle. This layer of the earth is in a slightly liquid form. It is under enough pressure to heat the rock and melt it. Ask the students to label the yellow layer on their diagram the *mantle*.

Continue with questions to get the children to think about what the very middle of something is usually referred to. Get the students to think about what they call the center of an apple. The *core* is represented by the red ball. Because the core is under such great pressure it is very hot, but also in a solid state. Ask the students to label the red layer on their diagram the *core*.

EARTH SCIENCE

3. EXPANSION OF THE IDEA: Which process skills will be used?

Manipulating materials, observing, hypothesizing, inferring

How will the idea be expanded?

Clay continents

Hold up the tennis ball. Ask the students how they think the tennis ball is like the earth. Encourage them to use the terms *crust, mantle,* and *core.* Hold up a soccer ball. Ask the students how the soccer ball is like the earth. Hold up the globe. Tell them that this represents what the earth would look like if they were up in the sky looking down. Ask the students to carefully observe the globe. After they look at the globe, ask the students if they think the soccer ball or the tennis ball is more like the earth's surface. Engage the students in a conversation about how the soccer ball is not one solid piece but many pieces sewn together. The crust of the earth does not look like one solid piece but like many pieces separated by water. The pieces appear to fit together. Ask the students for suggested names for the land masses and the bodies of water. If none are given, tell the students that the land masses are called *continents* and the bodies of water are called *oceans.* If maps of the ocean floor are available, share them with the students. Be sure to point out that the crust still exists below the ocean water.

Provide the students with some green and blue clay. Ask them to put their two halves of clay back together again, gently sealing the gray clay so that they have one ball of clay again. Ask the students to use the green clay to place some land masses or continents on their earth. Ask them to add blue clay between the continents to represent the oceans. Then ask them to use their green and blue crayons to draw the continents and oceans on their drawings and to label them.

Why is the idea important for personal development?

- It has been found that the movement of the semiliquid material in the mantle of the earth causes the crust to move. When the crust moves, earthquakes occur. Have earthquakes ever occurred where you live? What should be done to protect people during earthquakes?
- What continent do you live on?

Why is the idea important for science-technology-society?

- How has knowledge about continent movement changed the way we construct buildings?
- Can earthquakes be detected? How?
- Do you think if technology could come up with a way to drain the oceans that would be better for life on earth? Why or why not?

Why is the idea important for academic growth?

- Which layer of the earth is very hot, yet still in a solid state?
- The land masses on the surface of the earth appear to fit together, yet many are far apart. Do you think they were once together? If so, why?
- Is there crust under the oceans? How do we know this?

EARTH SCIENCE

Why is the idea important for career awareness?

- A seismologist would need to understand that the earth is in layers. Why do you think this is true? What do you think a seismologist does?
- Should oceanographers be concerned about the earth's layers?
- Many oil companies get their oil out of the North Sea. Do you think these companies used their knowledge of the earth's layers to find their drilling sites? Why or why not?

4. EVALUATION: How will the students show what they have learned?

Upon completing the activities the students will be able to

- draw a diagram of a cross-section of the earth and label the continents, oceans, crust, mantle, and core;
- identify from a diagram the different layers of the earth;
- explain how the earth can be compared to a soccer ball;
- point out continents and oceans on a globe.

GRADE **1–4**

Earth Science

DISCIPLINE

Fossils

Concept to be invented

Main idea—A record of an ancient animal or plant found in sedimentary rocks is called a *fossil.*

Secondary concepts that are important to expansion

Fossils provide clues to ancient environments. Evidence that man was present during primitive times is called an *artifact.* A hollow space left in sedimentary rock when a plant or animal body decays is called a *mold.* When sediments fill the hollow space and harden, the hardened sediments formed in the shape of the plant or animal are called *casts.*

Materials needed

For exploration:

A variety of fossil samples for class observations, construction paper, and crayons or markers.

For expansion:

Seashells (one or two per student)   water
one aluminum pie tin per student   one plastic spoon per student
petroleum jelly   paper towels
two paper cups per student   old newspapers
plaster of Paris

Note: The plastic samples of seashells, readily available through science equipment suppliers, may be preferred over the actual seashells. Young children will find these easier to work with.

⟳ **Safety precautions:** Students should be reminded not to eat the plaster. Take care to avoid water spills. Should they occur, wipe them up immediately.

1. EXPLORATION: Which process skills will be used?

Observing, brainstorming, predicting, hypothesizing, communicating

What will the children do?

Fossil observations

Pass the fossil samples around to the students without telling them what they are looking at. Ask the students to make careful observations about these unknown objects and to share their observations with the class. Encourage the students to think about what these things could possibly be. Is it a plant or an animal? Is it an image of a plant or an animal, or a piece of the real thing? Do you think it is still on the earth? How do you think this could have been formed? Allow the students sufficient time to brainstorm with one another ideas on their possible origins. Ask the students to draw the unknown object and to color it the way they think it would look if the actual object (plant or animal) were right in front of them. If the students are capable of writing sentences, ask them to write three or four sentences below their pictures describing how they think the image in the rock was formed.

2. EXPLANATION/CONCEPT INVENTION: What is the main idea? How will the main idea be identified?

Concept: A record of an ancient animal or plant found in sedimentary rock is called a *fossil.*

Help the students invent the concept by asking them to share with the class the drawings they created. Some questions to ask the students to help invent the concept are:

- Why did you choose those colors for your drawing?
- Depending on the unknown you observed, was it easy or difficult for you to decide what this would look like if it were right in front of you? Why?
- How do you think this was formed?
- Will you please share with us your ideas?

Through this line of questioning the process of fossilization can be brought out. When an animal or plant dies and is covered with mud, rocks, sand, and so on and pressure is applied over many years, it turns to stone, leaving an imprint of the plant or animal. The records of ancient animals and plants found in sedimentary rocks are called *fossils.* Additional source books or films on fossils may be shared with the class at this time. Also share xamples of local fossils.

3. EXPANSION OF THE IDEA: Which process skills will be used?

Observing, manipulating materials, predicting

How will the idea be expanded?

Plaster molds and casts

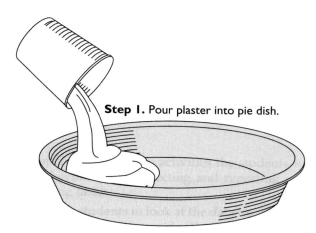

Step 1. Pour plaster into pie dish.

Step 2. Push shell into plaster; after drying an hour pop out cast and allow to dry overnight.

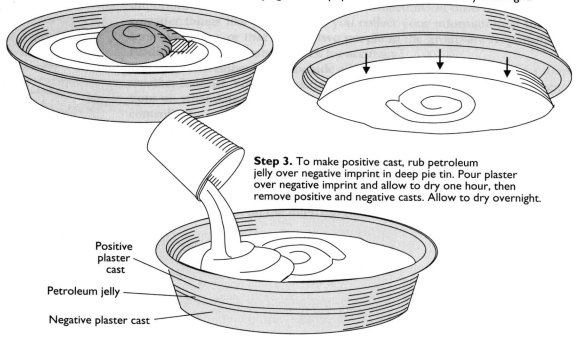

Step 3. To make positive cast, rub petroleum jelly over negative imprint in deep pie tin. Pour plaster over negative imprint and allow to dry one hour, then remove positive and negative casts. Allow to dry overnight.

Positive plaster cast

Petroleum jelly

Negative plaster cast

Ask the students to bring in seashells or leaves to use in making an image, or provide these or plastic models for them. Ask the students to use the old newspapers to cover their desk tops. Give each student a pie tin. Provide enough petroleum jelly so that the students can spread a thin to medium film over the bottom and sides of the pie tin. Remind them to be sure that the entire inside of the tin is covered with jelly. Once they have chosen the item they want to make an image of, instruct the students to cover the shell or plant with a thin layer of petroleum jelly. Place the shell or plant in the bottom of the pie tin so that the flattest side rests on the bottom of the pan.

In one of the cups for each student place enough dry plaster of Paris so that when mixed it will be enough to cover the bottom of the pie tin with about 15 mm (.5 in) of plaster. In the second cup place enough water so that each student will have created the proper consistency of plaster once he or she mixes (using the plastic spoon) the dry powder with the water. Once the students have mixed their plaster instruct them to pour it carefully over the shell or plant into the pie tin. They should allow about an hour for the plaster to harden. Remember: As the plaster dries it will become quite warm and then cool. Wait until it has cooled before removing it from the tin.

Once the plaster has hardened, turn the pie tin upside down over the paper-covered desk and tap the tin lightly to remove the plaster cast. The plaster will still be quite wet at this time, so the students need to be reminded to use care as they remove their shells or plants from the plaster. Once the shells or plants are removed, set the plaster casts in a safe place to fully cure (dry out and harden). This should take at least a day. Once the casts are cured, the students will have what is known as a *negative imprint* or *mold* of a plant or animal. If desired, a *positive imprint* or *cast* can now be created by spreading addition-al petroleum jelly over the surface of the negative imprint and placing it back into a deeper petroleum-jelly-lined pie tin. On top of the first cast pour addi-tional plaster. After it has hardened (about one hour) carefully turn the tin upside down and remove the old and new plaster casts. Since the surface of the old cast was thoroughly covered with petroleum jelly, the two casts should readily come apart with a knife blade. The new cast formed from the negative imprint is called a *positive imprint*. After this has had a chance to harden thoroughly (about one day), the students may want to paint or color with markers their newly formed fossils.

Why is the idea important for personal development?

- Why do you want to know about fossils? Has our study of fossils given you any ideas about what life was like in the past?
- Do you think you could have lived during the time when dinosaurs roamed the land? Why or why not?

Why is the idea important for science-technology-society?

- How can fossils tell us what ancient environments were like?
- Evidence left by early man is called artifacts. Some examples are arrowheads,

ancient beads, and animal skins used as clothing. Why do you think we don't call them fossils?

Why is the idea important for academic growth?

- Why can fossils only be found in sedimentary rocks?
- Can you find fossils where you live? Where do you think you would go to look for fossils?

Why is the idea important for career awareness?

- Paleontologists (fossil experts) study and learn from fossils. If you were a paleontologist, what kind of information would you share with others on the imprints you just made?
- How is an archeologist's job different from a paleontologist's? An excellent book for this topic is Gloria and Esther Goldreich, *What Can She Be? A Geologist* (New York: Lothrop, Lee and Shepard, 1976).

4. EVALUATION: How will the students show what they have learned?

Upon completing the activities the students will be able to

- demonstrate how a fossil can be formed by using sand, water, and a seashell;
- pick out the fossils when given several items to choose from, such as a seashell, a leaf, a sedimentary rock with a shell imprint or leaf imprint on it, a geode, or an igneous rock such as obsidian;
- tell or write in their own words what a fossil is and what information it can provide humans.

GRADE

3–5

Earth Science

DISCIPLINE

Soil Formation

Concept to be invented
Main idea—Soil is made from finely ground rock and organic material.

Secondary concepts that are important to expansion
The rocks and plants found in the local area will determine the kind of soil that is formed. Large amounts of weathered sandstone will create a sandy soil. Slightly smaller particles create a silty soil. Very fine particles will make a clayey soil.

Materials needed
For exploration:

Soil samples from local area
one piece of white construction
   paper per student

old newspapers
one magnifying glass per student

EARTH SCIENCE

local sedimentary rock samples
  (these are easily broken)

one pair of goggles for each
  student

For expansion:
sand
organic matter such as leaves or
  grass clippings
soil samples from local area

two small baby food jars with lids
  for each cooperative group
water

⊃ **Safety precautions:** Make sure that all students are wearing goggles while smashing rocks with hammers. Wrap the rocks in newspaper and then strike them with a hammer. This will prevent rock pieces from flying everywhere.

If you choose to take the students outside to collect soil samples, be sure proper safety procedures are followed. Pair up the students and make sure they know the boundaries for soil sample collection.

1. EXPLORATION: Which process skills will be used?

Observing, recording data, classifying

What will the children do?

Soil separation and rock crushing

Provide the class with soil samples collected from the local area, or if possible, take the students around the school grounds to collect soil samples. Ask the students to cover their desktops with old newspapers and then place the white construction paper on top of the newspaper. Arrange the students in cooperative groups of three to four to make observations of the soil samples. Use the

magnifying glasses to make detailed observations of the individual particles. Encourage students to draw or write a description of their observations.

After the students have made as many observations as possible, ask them to try to separate their soil samples into different parts. How many different ways can you separate the soil samples?

Give each cooperative group a hammer and several pieces of local sedimentary rocks like sandstone or limestone. Remind students to *put on and keep on* their goggles at all times during this section of the activity. Over the news-paper-covered desks, ask the students to wrap the rock samples in newspaper and then pound the rocks with hammers. Do the materials formed look similar to the materials you separated out from the local soil sample?

2. EXPLANATION/CONCEPT INVENTION: What is the main idea? How will the main idea be identified?

Concept: Soil is made from finely ground rocks and organic material.

Ask the students to share the results of their observations. What kinds of things did you observe? Were all parts of the soil the same size? How many different ways did you separate your soil samples? Suggestions may include by size or color and rocklike or plantlike. What did your rock look like before you crushed it with the hammer? What about afterwards? Is there any similarity between the crushed rock and your soil sample? Continue questioning students until they come to the conclusion that soil is made up of small pieces of rock and plant matter.

3. EXPANSION OF THE IDEA: Which process skills will be used?

Manipulating materials, observing, inferring, classifying, estimating, predicting

How will the idea be expanded?

Soil components

Provide each cooperative group with two small baby food jars with lids. Ask the students to label one jar *local soil* and the second *home-made soil*. Ask the students to fill the first jar up halfway with one of the local soil samples. Ask the students to place in the second jars some of the crushed rock they just smashed, some sand, and some grass clippings or leaves, so that one half of the jar is filled. Into both jars pour enough water to cover all of the solid materials. Place the lids on the jars and shake vigorously. Solicit predictions about what will happen in each jar after it has sat for one hour, for three hours, and overnight. Ask the students to record their predictions and then place the jars where they will not be disturbed for the times indicated. Ask the students the following questions to help them conclude that the rocks and plants found in the local area will determine the kind of soil formed. Weathered sandstone will create a sandy soil, more finely ground particles will create a silty soil, and very fine particles will create a clay soil. What did the two samples look like after one hour? After three hours? The next day? If you did not look at jar labels and just at samples, could you tell the difference between the *soil* in the two jars? How were they similar? Different? Look at the settled materials. Can you estimate how much of the sample is sand? Silt? Clay? How would you classify the soil? What do you think will happen to the grass or leaves if you let the jar sit for one week, one month, or three months? Solicit predictions and then set the jar in a safe place so that students can observe it over a three-month period.

Why is the idea important for personal development?

- What kind of soil is found around your home? Would it be a good soil if you wanted to grow potatoes in your garden?
- Do you think it is better to have a sandy or a silty soil in your garden? Do you put fertilizers on your soil? If so, why?

Why is the idea important for science-technology-society?

- As you have discovered, not all soils are alike. Do you think it was important to keep this fact in mind as tractor tires were developed?
- Should people be concerned about farmers using excessive amounts of fertilizers in soils? What can be done to prevent excessive use of fertilizers?
- What do you think *no-till* means, and why would farmers be urged to use this method of farming?

Why is the idea important for academic growth?

- List at least three components of soil.
- What influence does local bedrock have on the type of soil found in an area?
- Does the rate of weathering and erosion in an area effect the formation of soil?
- Where do you think the minerals found in soils come from?

Why is the idea important for career awareness?

- What are the responsibilities of a soil agronomist?
- How important is it for a land developer to understand soil formation?
- What is organic farming? How do these methods of farming differ from other methods?

4. EVALUATION: How will the students show what they have learned?

Upon completing the activities the students will be able

- to take a given soil sample and demonstrate the steps necessary to estimate the amount of sand, silt, and clay in the sample;
- to explain how the type of soil found in a local area is dependent upon the local bedrock and ground cover;
- to write a persuasive argument on why grass is necessary to cover soil, or on how soil is different from dirt.

EARTH SCIENCE

Rock Types

Concepts to be invented

Main idea—Rocks may be classified into three groups: *igneous*, *sedimentary*, and *metamorphic*.

Secondary concepts that are important to expansion

Igneous means fire formed. Cooled magma and lava create igneous rocks such as granite and obsidian. *Sedimentary* rocks are formed in water due to layers of sediments building up from weathered igneous, metamorphic, and other sedimentary rocks, or decaying organic matter; examples are limestone and sandstone. *Metamorphic* rocks are very hard rocks that may be formed from igneous or sedimentary rocks under extreme heat and pressure; marble and gneiss are examples.

Materials needed

For exploration (for each cooperative group of students):

several samples of igneous rocks, sedimentary rocks, metamorphic rocks, one jar, two sheets of construction paper, sand, mud, and pebbles.

For expansion (for each student):

Goggles, hammer and chisel, collection bag, three empty egg cartons, old newspapers, and a marker.

⊃ **Safety precautions:** Remind students to handle rock samples carefully. No throwing rocks! If you choose to take the students outside to collect rock samples, be sure proper safety procedures are followed. Pair up the students and make sure they know the boundaries for rock sample collection.

1. EXPLORATION: Which process skills will be used?

Observing, classifying, inferring

What will the children do?

Rock categorization

Divide the class into cooperative learning groups of three or four students. Provide each group with sand, numerous rock types, and pebbles. Ask the students to categorize the rocks. What's different about them? How are they alike? After the students have shared the results of their categorizing, ask them to set those samples aside in the categories they identified.

Give each cooperative group a jar and ask them to put rocks, sand, mud, and water into it. Put a lid on the jar and shake it for a few moments. Ask the students to draw a picture of what the jar looks like after the materials have settled.

2. EXPLANATION/CONCEPT INVENTION: What is the main idea? How will the main idea be identified?

Concept: Rocks may be classified into three groups—igneous, sedimentary, and metamorphic.

Ask the students to fold a sheet of construction paper into three parts. Now go back to the different piles of rocks the students first categorized. Ask them what kinds of differences they noted. Explain that rocks come in all shapes, colors, and sizes. However, they weren't all made the same way. Use the example of lava from a volcano. What happens to the lava when it dries? It becomes a hard rock called *igneous,* meaning fire formed. Cooled magma and lava create igneous rocks like granite and obsidian. In the first part of the construction paper draw or describe how igneous rock is formed. Provide the students with various samples of igneous rocks to observe.

Refer back to the shaken jar. What does it currently look like? Steer the students toward looking at the layers of materials. Did your group classify any of the rock samples based on whether or not you could see layers? What do you think rocks formed from the buildup of materials in layers are called? *Sedimentary* rocks are formed in water due to layers of sediments building up from weathered igneous, metamorphic, and other sedimentary rocks, or decaying organic matter. Limestone and sandstone are sedimentary. In the second part of the construction paper draw or describe how sedimentary rocks are formed. Provide the students with various samples of sedimentary rocks to observe.

Ask the students if they think they classified any rocks that have not yet been described. Have the students share those rocks with the rest of the class. Make sure they do not fit under igneous or sedimentary categories. Explain to the students that the igneous or sedimentary rocks can be put under extreme heat and pressure inside the earth, which changes the look of the rock. These are called metamorphic rocks; examples are marble and gneiss. Metamorphic rocks are very hard. In the third part of the construction paper draw or describe how metamorphic rocks are formed. Provide the students with various samples of metamorphic rocks to observe.

3. EXPANSION OF THE IDEA: Which process skills will be used?

Observing, classifying, collecting, comparing, communicating

How will the idea be expanded?

Rock collection field trip

This expansion activity may be done as a home extension activity or as a class field trip. Identify a site where students will be permitted to collect rock samples. Either take them as a class or provide instructions to parents to take the students to the collection site. Be sure the students are given instruction on how to use the hammer and chisel to extract rock samples from the bedrock. Encourage the students to break their samples into pieces small enough to fit into the egg carton depressions. Remind the students to think about the different colors and textures that different kinds of rocks have. Classify the collection into igneous, sedimentary, and metamorphic and designate one egg carton for each rock type. After a sufficient amount of time has passed (one or two months) ask the students to bring their collections to school to share with the class.

Why is the idea important for personal development?

- If you were going to build a home along the ocean, would you want the underlying rock to be igneous, sedimentary, or metamorphic? Why?
- Have you ever washed your hands with a pumice-based soap? Have you ever used a pumice stone to smooth away rough skin? Where do you think this comes from?

Why is the idea important for science-technology-society?

- Which type of rock is best used for building purposes?
- Would you trust a bridge made of sedimentary rocks? Do you think it would last as long as a bridge made with igneous rocks? What about a bridge made of metamorphic rock?
- Which type of rock would be a wise choice to build a dam with?

Why is the idea important for academic growth?

- Where in the world would I easily find an igneous rock? A sedimentary rock? A metamorphic rock?
- Can an igneous rock be formed from a sedimentary one? Can a sedimentary rock be formed from a metamorphic or igneous rock?
- What kind of rock is the local bedrock?

Why is the idea important for career awareness?

- Would a civil engineer responsible for placing a bridge across the Mississippi River between Illinois and Missouri need to understand the type of bedrock found in the area before plans for the bridge could be made? Why or why not?
- As a construction worker you decide to build your own home. You want to make it out of stone. Which kind of rock type would you use and why? Is it important that a construction worker or even a home owner know the differences among igneous, sedimentary, and metamorphic rocks?

4. EVALUATION: How will the students show what they have learned?

Upon completing the activities the students will be able to

- look at six different rocks and identify whether they are igneous, sedimentary, or metamorphic;
- identify different areas of the world where the three different rock types can be found;
- reflect, and then write a description of an igneous rock formed when lava cooled outside the earth.

EARTH SCIENCE

Cooling Crystals

Concept to be invented
Main idea—The rate at which a crystal cools affects the size of the crystal.

Secondary concepts that are important to expansion
Crystals can be seen in many rocks.

Materials needed
For exploration (for each group):

three glass caster cups
three small test tubes (10 ml)
test tube holder
Paradichlorobenzine (PDB) flakes
    (found in supermarkets, hardware
    stores, pharmacies)

one hand lens per student
grease pencil
crushed ice
two 500-ml beakers
one 150-ml beaker
tongs

For exploration (for entire class):

hot plates, paper towels

For expansion:

Samples of the igneous rocks rhyolite, granite, and obsidian; one hand lens per
student.

⊃ **Safety precautions:** Extreme care should be used near the hot plate and in
handling the hot water and PDB. Goggles should be worn at all times. Be sure
the room is well ventilated when melting the PDB.

1. EXPLORATION: Which process skills will be used?

Observing, predicting, manipulating materials, recording data, drawing conclusions

What will the children do?

PDB crystal formation

Ask the students to fill one of the 500-ml beakers with 300 ml of water. Place a
caster cup in the beaker. Boil the water on the hot plate. Fill the other 500-ml
beaker with crushed ice. Place the second caster cup in the beaker. Leave the
third caster cup at room temperature.

Carefully observe some PDB flakes. Record those observations. Fill each of
the three small test tubes with PDB flakes. Half-fill the 150-ml beaker with water.
Place the three test tubes in the beaker. Place the beaker with the test tubes on the
hot plate. Heat the beaker gently until the PDB melts.

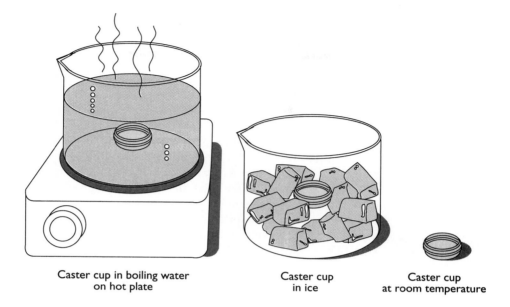

Caster cup in boiling water
on hot plate

Caster cup
in ice

Caster cup
at room temperature

Using the tongs, carefully remove the caster cup from the boiling water. Dry the cup and label it *A*. Using the test tube holder, remove one test tube and pour the PDB into this caster cup. Time how long it takes for the PDB to completely become a solid. Record the time. Record your observations of the PDB flakes for cup A.

Remove the second caster cup from the beaker with ice. Dry the cup quickly and completely. Label it *B*. Pour the second test tube of PDB into this cup. Time how long it takes for the PDB to turn completely solid. Record the time. Record your observations of the PDB flakes for cup B.

Pour the third test tube of PDB into the cup at room temperature. Label it *C*. Again, time how long it takes for this PDB to completely solidify. Record the time. Record your observations of the PDB flakes for cup C.

2. EXPLANATION/CONCEPT INVENTION: What is the main idea? How will the main idea be identified?

Concept: The rate at which a crystal cools affects the size of the crystal.

How does the rate of cooling affect the size of crystals? Record the cooling times for samples A, B, and C on the board. Look at the contents of each caster cup with the magnifying glass. Draw the contents of each caster cup on your paper. When the PDB was placed into the test tubes there was no difference between tubes. Once it was placed into cups A, B, and C, a change occurred. How are they different? What caused this difference? What conclusions can you draw? The students should conclude that the rate at which a crystal cools affects the size of the crystal formed.

EARTH SCIENCE

3. EXPANSION OF THE IDEA: Which process skills will be used?

Observing, recording data, generalizing, formulating models

How will the idea be expanded?

Rock type vs. crystal formation

Ask the students to observe the crystals in the samples of granite, rhyolite, and obsidian with a magnifying glass. Draw the crystals in each sample on your paper. Compare the crystals in the caster cups to the samples of granite, rhyolite, and obsidian. Which PDB crystals are most similar to the crystals in the rock samples? [Answer: cup A, granite; cup B, obsidian; cup C, rhyolite.]

Granite, rhyolite, and obsidian are igneous rocks essentially made of the same material. Explain why they look different. Where would igneous rocks have a chance to cool slowly? Where would igneous rock cool rapidly? If you saw a rock that contained large interlocking crystals, what would you say about the way it formed? The more slowly a crystal cools, the larger the crystals are. Granite cooled slowly and crystals were able to form. Rhyolite cooled more rapidly than granite, but more slowly than obsidian. Igneous rocks cool slowly deep in the earth. They cool rapidly on the surface. Large interlocking crystals form slowly inside the earth.

Why is the idea important for personal development?
- What kinds of crystals do you eat regularly? [Salt and sugar]
- How does the size of a crystal determine its quality? Do you think your knowledge of how crystals form will assist you in determining the quality of precious rocks and gems?

Why is the idea important for science-technology-society?
- The strength and quality of rocks are important for construction. What is the best type of rock for long-lasting buildings?
- How has the scarcity of quality gems on the market affected your life, your community, or the world?

Why is the idea important for academic growth?
- What kinds of rocks are found in the area where you live? Can you classify them according to their crystal structure?
- Can crystals be found in sedimentary rocks? Why or why not?

Why is the idea important for career awareness?
- What kinds of careers would use information on crystal formation? Some possibilities include geologist, geophysicist, volcanologist, jeweler, sculptor, and geographer.
- Choose one of the career suggestions from the question above and research the skills necessary to enter that career. Provide an oral report to the class.

4. EVALUATION: How will the students show what they have learned?

Upon completing the activities the students will be able

- to correctly identify where a crystal cooled (on the earth's surface or inside the earth) and at what rate when given drawings of crystals of different shapes and sizes;
- to examine samples of igneous rocks and explain why they have different sized crystals;
- to explain how the prices of precious jewels are affected by crystal formation.

GRADE **6–8** Earth Science **DISCIPLINE**

Weathering

Concept to be invented
Main idea—*Weathering* is the name given to the various mechanical and chemical processes that break down rock.

Secondary concepts that are important to expansion
Erosion, soil formation, rock formation—igneous, sedimentary, metamorphic.

Materials needed
For discrepant event:

Pop bottle and cap, water, freezer.

For exploration:

Field site to collect data, stereo-microscope, hammer.

For expansion:

Dilute hydrochloric acid (HCl), igneous, sedimentary, and metamorphic rock samples.

⊃ **Safety precautions:** Review with the students ahead of time the rules that should be followed for everyone's safety during the field trip. Visit the field site before the students do to guard against any possible hazards at the site.

Discrepant event—Freezing bottle
The day before you begin this lesson, take a glass pop bottle and ask a student to fill it with water all the way to the top. Cap the bottle so that no water can escape. Now ask the students what they think will happen to this bottle if you place it in the freezer for a day. Record their predictions on the board, where they will remain untouched until the next day. Twenty-four hours later remove the

bottle from the freezer. If the bottle was totally filled before freezing, it should now be cracked, as the ice expanded upon freezing. Ask the students what they observe. Did it behave according to their predictions? Why did this happen? What happens to water when it freezes? Based on your observations, do you think water could do this to other items besides glass? Think about this as we engage in today's activity.

1. EXPLORATION: Which process skills will be used?

Observing, hypothesizing, predicting, measuring, using spatial relationships, recording data

What will the children do?

Weathering field trip

The students will go on a field trip around the school grounds. An old road or empty prairie or field will be an ideal site. Before beginning the trip, the students will be reminded about appropriate care of a collection site. Remind them to take care as they travel through the site and to try not to destroy any animal homes or wildflowers or plant growth. Ask the students to look for rocks that appear to be broken apart. They are to record a description of the area in which they find them, taking care to note the soil conditions (wet, dry, sandy, clayey), an estimate of the original size of the rock, a physical description of the rock (color, shininess, hardness, porosity), and a prediction based on their findings as to what they think caused the rock to break apart. A small sample of the rock should be collected for further study in the classroom. Upon returning to the classroom, the students will make a composite chart of their field observations. Headings for this chart could include collection site, soil conditions, rock size, physical properties (color, luster, hardness, pore size), possible cause for breakage.

2. EXPLANATION/CONCEPT INVENTION: What is the main idea? How will the main idea be identified?

Concept: Weathering is the name given to the various mechanical and chemical processes that break down rock.

Draw the students' attention to the composite chart in the front of the room. In order to guide the students in inventing the concept of *weathering*, ask such questions as: In looking at this chart, are there any we can group together? Do any of them sound as if the different groups of investigators were looking at the same rocks?

Ask the students to bring up the sample rocks whose descriptions sound similar. Do you think these are the same rocks?

Once double sightings have been eliminated, then begin to focus on the chart again, this time asking, "Is there any one area where broken rocks were found more often than any other? Or is there any one soil condition where broken rocks are found more often than any other?"

If this is the case, then ask the students if they think this soil condition contributed to the presence of broken rocks. If it is a very wet area, then you can relate this back to the discrepant event—how the freezing and thawing of water will contribute to the cracking of the rocks. If this is a dry area, ask the students if they made note of any vegetation growing in the area. They may have found the broken rocks due to roots growing through the surface of the rock. It may be a very dry area where wind blows through rather rapidly causing the rocks to break up.

Ask the students if they know of a term to describe the breaking up of rock due to running water, wind, rain, or roots. Introduce the term *weathering* at this point.

What happens to the rock pieces as they are carried by the rain, wind, or running water? What term can we use to describe the carrying away of this weathered material? *Erosion.* Ask the students if they observed the soil where they found the rock. Was it similar in composition to the rock itself? Engage the students in a discussion of how the weathering of rocks assists in soil formation.

3. EXPANSION OF THE IDEA: Which process skills will be used?

Observing, classifying, experimenting, predicting, inferring, interpreting data, recording data, communicating

How will the idea be expanded?

Rock identification, acid test, rust exploration

If your students collected rock samples that fell into one type (all igneous, or all sedimentary, or all metamorphic) then in addition to their samples, provide them with rock samples from the missing rock groups. Ask the students to try to group the rock samples according to the characteristics from the composite chart from the first activity. Suggest to them that based on hardness, porosity, and composition, they should be able to group their rock samples into three different groups.

Once they have their samples in three groups the students can then perform the following experiments to determine possible sources of weathering.

Acid Rain. Take one sample from each rock group. Predict what will happen to the rock when you drop three drops of dilute HCl on it. Do you think each rock will react the same way? Which one do you think will weather the most? In nature, what type of weathering could we consider this to be? (This is known as *chemical weathering.*)

Oxidation. Do you notice any color changes in your rock? Are there what appear to be rust spots on the rock? What do you think causes this?

Water. Cover the three different rock samples with water and place them in a freezer for a day. Do the rocks crumble easily in your hands? If you strike it with a hammer lightly do they fall apart? Are the insides still wet? Which rock type was most susceptible to the freezing water? Since the water simply froze and broke the rock apart, this is known as *mechanical weathering.*

Roots. In what area did you find this rock? Are there still traces of plant matter on the rock? Did you see any roots pushing up right through the surface of the rock? Do the roots cause chemical or mechanical weathering? Overall, which rocks are most easily weathered and which are most difficult to weather? Can you guess how each of these rock groups were originally formed based on your weathering observations? Lead to a discussion on rock formations—igneous, sedimentary, and metamorphic. Detailed discussions will be provided in a separate lesson for each rock type.

Why is the idea important for personal development?

- Why does one need to use special fishing lures if a river or lake is muddy or murky due to erosion?
- What would you suspect was happening if the water in your favorite fishing stream looked clean, yet the number of fish began to dwindle? You have noticed that some of the rocks along the bank are beginning to crumble and

wash downstream. What could you do to verify your suspicions? Whom would you talk to about this problem?

Why is the idea important for science-technology-society?

- What role does strip mining of coal or clear cutting of timber play in allowing the forces of weather to affect erosion?
- How has an increased understanding of the forces of weathering and erosion caused us to change our farming practices since the Dust Bowl days of the 1930s?

Why is the idea important for academic growth?

- How does weathering differ from erosion? What factors contribute to soil formation? What processes have occurred to create the different rock types? Can you name the three different rock types?
- In which rock formation would you most likely place a building like the Sears Tower? Why? Which rock type would you be least likely to choose to build a house of? Why?

Why is the idea important for career awareness?

- What role have geologists played in the production of fuel and plastics?
- Why would a civil engineer need to understand the processes of weathering and erosion?
- Do you think a contractor or cement finisher would find knowledge of weathering, erosion, soil and rock types useful in his or her work?

4. EVALUATION: How will the students show what they have learned?

Upon completing the activities the students will be able

- to draw a diagram showing the relationships among rock types, soil types, weathering, and erosion;
- when given a weathered rock sample and a description of where the sample was found, to suggest the most probable source for its weathering;
- to list at least four agents of erosion;
- to discriminate between constructive and destructive geologic forces.

GRADE 6–8

Earth Science

DISCIPLINE

Crustal Plate Movement

Concept to be invented

Main idea—The theory of plate tectonics states that the crust of the earth is not one solid piece, but rather several separate plates that are in motion on top of molten material.

Secondary concepts that are important to expansion

Continental drift, earthquakes, volcanoes.

EARTH SCIENCE

Materials needed

For exploration (for each group of four to six students):

four wood blocks
one liter of water
a heat lamp or 150–200-watt
    bulb and socket

plastic shoe box
food coloring
stacks of books to raise box above
    lamp

For expansion:

Maps of the world showing the crustal plate boundaries, a list of places famous for volcanic eruptions, a list of sites of recent earthquakes.

⊃ **Safety precautions:** The students should be reminded to use care with the heat source. Don't place the heat source too close to the plastic box or books. Use care around water and electricity. Wipe up any water spills immediately. Do not touch heat source with wet hands.

1. EXPLORATION: Which process skills will be used?

Experimenting, observing, predicting, inferring

What will the children do?

Moving plates

Each student group should place its plastic box on two stacks of books. The box should be high enough so that a heat source (lamp) will fit beneath. Pour water into the box. Place the four small wood blocks in the box. All the blocks should touch, forming a square. Place the heat source beneath the box directly under the center of the blocks. Turn the light on and place a drop of food coloring in the water where the four blocks meet. Observe the blocks for about five to ten minutes. What happens to each of the four wood blocks? What happens to the food coloring?

2. EXPLANATION/CONCEPT INVENTION: What is the main idea? How will the main idea be identified?

Concept: The theory of plate tectonics states that the crust of the earth is not one solid piece, but rather several separate plates that are in motion on top of molten material.

Ask the students to share their observations on the movement of the four wood blocks and the food coloring. Why do you think this happened? If you were to relate this activity to the earth's crust, what do you think the blocks represent? (Early land masses that separated millions of years ago.) What would the water represent? (The molten layer of the earth called the mantle.) What happened to the temperature of the water over time? (It warmed up.) What happened to the food coloring? (It slowly moved along the surface as the water continued to warm.) Through questioning along this line, help the students to conclude that

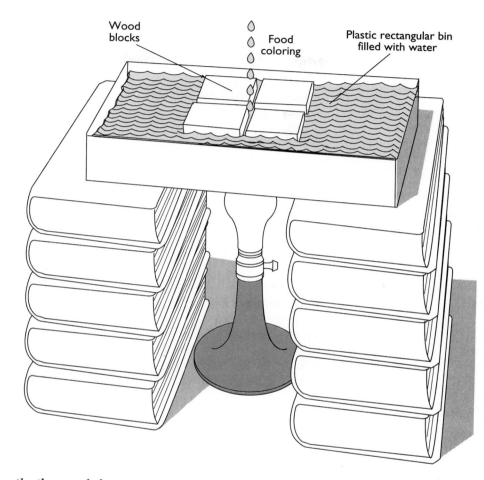

Wood blocks

Food coloring

Plastic rectangular bin filled with water

the theory of plate tectonics states that the crust of the earth is not one solid piece, but rather several separate plates that are in motion on top of molten material.

3. EXPANSION OF THE IDEA: Which process skills will be used?

Observing, predicting, making conclusions

How will the idea be expanded?

Mapping volcanoes and earthquakes

Pair up the students. Provide each pair with a world map indicating the boundaries for the crustal plates. The students should be free to mark on the maps you provide. Provide the students with a recent list of volcanic and earthquake activity. Ask them to plot on the map the places where the most recent earthquakes and volcanoes have occurred. You may give them a list of volcanic and earthquake activity for the past fifty years to plot. Ask the students

EARTH SCIENCE

to share some observations they have made about the relationship between earthquakes and volcanoes from this exercise. The students should conclude that most earthquake and volcanic activity occurs where two or more crustal plates come together.

Why is the idea important for personal development?

- Would you choose to live along a crustal plate boundary? If you did, how might it affect your life?
- Do you think the government should help pay to repair homes for people who chose to build their homes on a known crustal boundary?

Why is the idea important for science-technology-society?

- Are you aware of any other theories about formation or movement of the earth's crust? What part do you think technology has played in theory change and advanced knowledge about different phenomena?
- How do we use our knowledge about movement of the earth's crust when we construct buildings in areas where crustal plates are known to move?

Why is the idea important for academic growth?

- Is there still movement of the earth's crust? How do we know?
- A lot of volcanic activity occurs in the Hawaiian Islands. Are they on the edge of a crustal plate? If not, what is causing the volcanic activity? Research the formation of these volcanic islands.
- Explain how a solid crust can move. What does the mantle layer of the earth have to do with this movement?

Why is the idea important for career awareness?

- Who is Charles Lyell? What career changes led him to many geological discoveries?
- Would a seismologist be concerned with crustal plate movement? Why?
- Why would a civil engineer be concerned with the location of crustal plate boundaries? What does a civil engineer do?

4. EVALUATION: How will the students show what they have learned?

Oatmeal and cracker plate tectonics

Upon completing the activities the students will be able

- to demonstrate the theory of plate tectonics by using a bowl of oatmeal and some soda crackers;
- to identify the area known as the Ring of Fire on a world map and explain what it is;
- to briefly explain the theory of plate tectonics.

EARTH SCIENCE

K–2

Earth
Science

Rain Formation

Concepts to be invented
Main idea—Raindrops form as water vapor condenses and falls from the sky.

Secondary concepts that are important to expansion
Water cycle, condensation, evaporation, precipitation.

Materials needed
For exploration (for each group of four to six children):
1-quart glass jar with lid, hot-to-boiling water, ice cubes.

For expansion:
Clear plastic lid (coffee can lid), pencil, water, plastic cup, eye dropper, paper towels.

⊃ **Safety precautions:** The students should be reminded to avoid bumping the tables once the exploration activity is set up. If the hot water spills out it could hurt the children. If the glass jar breaks it could cut someone.

1. EXPLORATION: Which process skills will be used?

Observing, predicting, recording data

What will the children do?

Rain in a jar

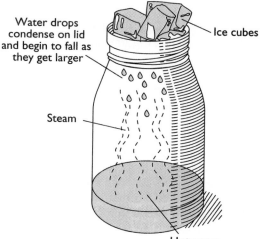

Water drops condense on lid and begin to fall as they get larger

Ice cubes

Steam

Hot water

Set groups of four to six children around a table. In the middle of the table place a 1-quart jar with enough hot-to-nearly-boiling water to cover the bottom of the jar. The teacher should ask the students to make predictions about what will happen when they cover the jar with the lid turned upside down, holding three or four ice cubes. After the students have recorded their predictions and shared them with the class, instruct someone from each group to carefully place the lid over the jar and place the ice cubes on top of the inverted lid. Ask the students to watch the jar for four or five minutes. What did you observe? Was it as you predicted? Record those observations.

2. EXPLANATION/CONCEPT INVENTION: What is the main idea? How will the main idea be identified?

Concept: Raindrops form as water vapor condenses and falls from the sky.

The students should have observed that water drops collected on the inside of the lid. As time progressed more water drops formed. As the drops became bigger it got to the point that the lid could no longer hold the drops. At that point the drops began to fall back into the jar. Ask the students the following questions to help them conclude that raindrops form as water vapor condenses and falls from the sky. What observations did you record? Where do you think the drops of water on the lid came from? (From the *condensation* of water vapor inside the jar. The hot water in the jar *evaporated* and changed into a *gas*—water vapor. When the water vapor hit the cool lid, it *condensed* and changed back to a *liquid*.) What happened to the drops of water as they collected on the lid? (They got bigger as more water vapor *condensed* and collected on the jar lid.) At what point did the water drops starts to fall from the jar lid? (As they collected on the lid they grew bigger and soon pulled together with other drops. Their weight pulled them down.) What do you call water drops that fall from the sky? (Rain.)

3. EXPANSION OF THE IDEA: Which process skills will be used?

Observing, inferring, measuring

How will the idea be expanded?

Water drop attraction

Pair up the students. Provide each pair with a plastic coffee can lid or the like, an eye dropper, a cup of water, and some paper towels. Ask the student pairs to do the following: One student should hold the plastic lid bottom side up. The other student should fill the eye dropper with water and squeeze as many separate drops of water on the lid as possible. The child holding the lid should then quickly turn the lid over. Hold the lid at least eight to ten inches over the table top, directly over some paper towels. Ask the student not holding the lid to use the point of a pencil to move the tiny drops together. What happens when you do this? Ask the students to switch roles, allowing one to hold the lid and flip it and the other to use the eye dropper and pencil. Did the same thing occur?

The water molecules appear to attract one another. As you pull them together it seems as if they readily jump to one another. As they grow bigger, they eventually are overcome by gravity and fall from the lid. Water may fall like this from the sky, not just in the form of rain. The teacher may solicit ideas from the students on other forms in which water falls from the sky (snow, sleet, hail). Explain to the students that all of these are called *precipitation*.

Why is the idea important for personal development ?

- Why do you think it rains more in certain places than in others?
- Read the poem "Little Raindrops," by Aunt Effie (Jane Euphemia Browne), to the class. After it is read ask the students if they think they are affected by emotional changes with changes in the weather.

Why is the idea important for science-technology-society?

- Why do you think meteorologists study rain patterns? Do these patterns affect where people will build cities?
- Why do scientists *seed* rain clouds in dry areas? Do you think farmers in these areas want to be able to make it rain when water is scarce? Why?

Why is the idea important for academic growth?

- What do you call it when water turns into water vapor? (Evaporation.)
- When water vapor collects on an object to form water droplets, what is it called? (Condensation.)
- What do you call water that falls from the sky? (Precipitation.)
- What do we call the process by which water evaporates, condenses, and falls from the sky? (The water cycle.)

Why is the idea important for career awareness?

- How important do you think it is for a farmer to understand the water cycle?
- If you were a botanist working in the desert, why would you be curious about how a cactus grows?
- When you watch a local weather forecast, does the meteorologist help explain where the next rainfall will come from?

4. EVALUATION: How will the students show what they have learned?

Upon completing the activities the students will be able

- to show how they can make rain when given a jar of hot water, a pie tin, and some ice cubes;
- to successfully explain where evaporation, condensation, and precipitation are occurring in the jar demonstration they set up;
- to draw a picture of something they think they would not have in their life if it did not rain. Ask them to explain the reasoning behind choosing that object.

EARTH SCIENCE

Dew Formation

Concepts to be invented
Main idea–Cold surfaces collect more water drops than warm surfaces do.

Secondary concepts that are important to expansion
Dew, frost, temperature measurement with a thermometer, dew point.

Materials needed
For exploration (for each group of four to six children):
Minute timer or clock with minutes marked off, glass pop bottle, clear container large enough for the pop bottle to fit in, ice cubes, water, paper towels.

For expansion:
Drinking glass, thermometer, ice cubes, water, paper towels

⊃ **Safety precautions:** The students should be reminded to use care when handling the bottles. Wipe up any water spills so that students do not slip on wet surfaces.

1. EXPLORATION: Which process skills will be used?

Observing, predicting, measuring, inferring, recording data

What will the children do?

Pop bottle condensation

Set groups of four to six children around a table. In the middle of the table place a container large enough to hold a pop bottle. In this jar place four or five ice cubes and enough water so that once the pop bottle is placed in the jar, it will be

covered with cold water up to its neck. Give one child in the group a glass pop bottle. Remind the other students that they each will get a turn. If enough pop bottles are available, each child may be given one at this time. Ask the children to wrap their hands around the bottle for two minutes to try to get it very warm. When the two minutes are up, ask the students to exhale inside the bottle. What did you observe? Record those observations.

Then ask the students to make predictions about what will happen after they put the bottle into the container of ice water for two minutes, take it out, quickly wipe it off, and again exhale into the bottle. After they have recorded their predictions and shared them with the class, the students should then take turns putting their bottles into the ice water container, taking them out, wiping off the excess water, and then exhaling inside them. What did you observe? Was it as you predicted? Record those observations.

2. EXPLANATION/CONCEPT INVENTION: What is the main idea? How will the main idea be identified?

Concept: Cold surfaces collect more water drops than warm surfaces.

When the students exhaled into their warmed bottles they may have observed some condensation, but very little. Their warm breath and the warmed bottle did not differ greatly in temperature. Therefore, water vapor did not condense readily. When the students exhaled into the cooled bottles, the difference in temperature between their breath and the bottles was enough to make water drops collect on the cold bottles. The students will be able to conclude that cold surfaces collect more water drops than warm surfaces when you ask them the following questions about what they did. What observations did you record when you exhaled on the warmed bottle? What observations did you record when you exhaled on the cooled bottle? Was there a difference between the two? Why do you think this happened? Do you ever walk through grass on a spring or summer morning? What happens to your shoes on those mornings? (If the students said yes, they may begin to think about getting wet shoes as they walk through the grass. If the students start to respond along these lines, then ask the next set of questions.) Why do you think your shoes got wet? Do you think the grass or the air was warmer? Which was cooler? (The cool grass allowed water vapor to come out of the warm air and condense on the grass.) Do you know what we call the water you find on grass in the morning? (Dew.) When it's a cold morning this dew appears to be frozen. What name do we give it then? (Frost.)

3. EXPANSION OF THE IDEA: Which process skills will be used?

Thermometer reading and dew point
Observing, measuring, comparing, recording data

How will the idea be expanded?

Pair up the students. Give each pair a thermometer. Practice reading the thermometer. Be sure each student knows how this is done. As the students work in pairs ask them to fill a glass with ice and add enough water to cover the ice.

Record the temperature their thermometer is currently reading. Place the thermometer in the glass. Watch the outside of the glass and record the temperature at which water begins to form on the outside of the glass. Explain to the students that for this particular day, with this particular amount of moisture in the air, the temperature they just recorded would be called the *dew point* for the day. When the air reaches that temperature then *dew* will begin to form on the grass outside.

Why is the idea important for personal development?

- Other than the noise involved, why do you think it is not a good idea to mow grass very early on a summer morning?
- Explain how your feet could get wet when you run through the grass in the spring.
- Why does frost form on car windows in the winter?

Why is the idea important for science-technology-society?

- Do you think auto manufacturers are concerned with dew formation when they build new cars? Do you think the auto manufacturers think carefully about the kind of paint they put on new cars because they know dew may form on them? What would happen to a car if dew formed on it day after day and there was no protective paint on it? Would the same thing happen to your bicycle?
- How does a rear window defogger/deicer eliminate frost on the car window?

Why is the idea important for academic growth?

- What do you call it when water turns into water vapor? (Evaporation.)
- When water vapor collects on an object to form water droplets, what is it called? (Condensation.)
- When water collects on a cold surface what may form? (Dew or frost.)
- What is a *dew point*?

Why is the idea important for career awareness?

- Why would a landscaper be concerned about dew/frost formation? Have you ever seen plants wrapped in cloth or covered in plastic bags? Why do you think landscapers or homeowners do this?
- Do you think a person in the lawn-care business should pay attention to weather forecasts that give the dew point? Do you think it could be used to help the person decide when to start work in the morning?

4. EVALUATION: How will the students show what they have learned?

Upon completing the activities the students will be able to

- use a bottle and a bowl of ice water to demonstrate how dew can form,
- demonstrate how to determine dew point using a glass, ice cubes, and a thermometer,
- explain why their shoes get wet when they run through grass on a sunny summer morning.

Radiant Energy

Concept to be invented

Main idea—The sun produces energy in the form of heat—this is referred to as *radiant energy.*

Secondary concepts that are important to expansion

The sun's heat can be used to perform work.

Materials needed

For Activity 1:

Two pie pans, sand, two coins, two black plastic bags.

For Activity 2:

Large glass jar with lid, water, thermometer, graph paper.

For Activity 3:

Magnifying glasses, sheets of paper.

For expansion activity:

Tea bags, paper cups, large jar.

⊃ **Safety precautions:** Before starting the activities go over the following safety rules:

• The students should call the teacher if the thermometer is dropped and broken. Avoid touching broken glass or the liquid inside the thermometer.
• Activity 3 should only be done by a teacher or other adult.
• Avoid playing with the magnifying glass or placing a hand between the paper and magnifying glass.
• Do not let children stare at or touch the point of light during Activity 3.

1. EXPLORATION: Which process skills will be used?

Predicting, observing, hypothesizing, measuring, recording and analyzing data, graphing

What will the children do?

Activity 1. Temperature and colored surfaces. Ask the children to fill the pie pans with sand. Put one pan of sand, one coin, and one garbage bag in direct sunlight. Put the other pan, coin, and bag in shade. Predict what the differences will be between the objects in the sun and those in the shade. After a while have the children feel and compare the objects. How did the objects that were in the sun feel? What about the ones that were in the shade? Why do the things that were in the sun feel warm? Why do they feel cool if they were in the shade?

Activity 2. Temperature, sun versus shade. On the second day, have the students fill two jars with water. Record their starting temperatures. Place one of the jars in the sun and one in the shade. Predict how much temperature change will take place in both as time progresses. Have students record the temperatures of the two jars every half hour for a total of three hours. Take a final temperature reading. Graph the results with a bar graph using different colors for the sunny and shady sites.

Activity 3. Magnifiers capture the sun (to be done on day two while waiting for the results of Activity 2). On a sunny day, hold the magnifying glass over a piece of paper until the light comes to a point. Hold it there for a few seconds. What happens to the paper? What made the hole in the paper? What does this tell you about what the sun does for us? What can the sun do to your skin and eyes?

2. EXPLANATION/CONCEPT INVENTION: What is the main idea? How will the main idea be identified?

Concept: The sun produces energy in the form of heat—this is referred to as *radiant energy.*

What does your graph tell you about a sunny environment versus a shady one? Why do you think there were such temperature differences at the two sites? What does the sun do for the earth? What do you think might happen if the earth were closer to the sun? What if the earth were farther from the sun? What would life be like in either case?

3. EXPANSION OF THE IDEA: Which process skills will be used?

Predicting, observing, inferring, hypothesizing

How will the idea be expanded?

Sun tea

Fill a large jar with water and six tea bags. Record its temperature. Predict what will happen to the water after a few hours. (Suggest to the students that they might want to think about more than just a temperature change.) Decide where you would place the jar if you wanted to make tea. Place the jar in that spot. Throughout the day check the jar and record the changes. Ask: "What do you think is happening inside the jar? How did the water change into tea? What part did the sun play in this process? What other ways can the sun's heat be harnessed to help things to work?"

Why is the idea important for personal development?

- Why is the sun important to us?
- What are some of the things we need to be aware of when we are in the sun?

Why is the idea important for science-technology-society?

- What are some ways in which people use solar energy? (Solar batteries, skylights, heating water to warm rooms, and so on.)

EARTH SCIENCE

- Are these beneficial? In what ways?
- Why might we need to explore ways to use solar energy in the future?
- Why do clothing manufacturers create lighter-colored clothing for the summer months? Would a manufacturer make more money selling black or white T-shirts in the summer?

Why is the idea important for academic growth?

- Why are people more careful about being exposed to the sun during the summer than during the winter?
- New concepts to be identified for invention in new lessons: global warming, the ozone layer, the greenhouse effect.

Why is the idea important for career awareness?

- What are some careers in which people can work with solar energy?
- Why would it be important for a botanist, a florist, or a gardener to understand how the sun heats the earth?

4. EVALUATION: How will the students show what they have learned?

Upon completing the activities the students will be able

- while blindfolded, to tell which objects were in the sun and which were in shade, and give reasons for the answers;
- to create a collage showing the many uses of solar energy;
- to draw pictures showing ways they can protect themselves from the damaging effects of the sun.

GRADE **4–8**

Earth Science

DISCIPLINE

Weather Forecasting

Concept to be invented
Main idea—Weather data can be collected and reported.

Secondary concepts that are important to expansion
Controlling variables, use of symbols, cloud types.

Materials needed
For exploration:

barometer	wind vane	anemometer
thermometer	rain gauge	clinometer
sling psychrometer	cloud charts	nephoscope

The students should have had prior experience with this equipment as they were learning about individual weather phenomena such as air pressure, humidity, temperature, air masses, fronts.

EARTH SCIENCE

For expansion and evaluation:

Weather instruments listed above, collection of weather maps from newspapers.

⊃ **Safety precautions:** Use care with weather instruments when collecting data. Outdoors, obey school rules. Avoid talking to strangers, and exercise caution if inclement weather prohibits data collection.

1. EXPLORATION: Which process skills will be used?

Brainstorming, observing, formulating models, predicting, measuring, questioning

Teacher introduction: How many of you have nicknames? When you write letters or your name in school, do you write your full name or your nickname? Which is easier for you to write?

Try to picture in your mind a McDonald's or a Kentucky Fried Chicken restaurant. Imagine you are in their parking lot, or you are riding down the road and you spot one of these places. What image comes to mind first? How many of you remembered a shape or a symbol for the restaurant first?

Can you think of any other things in your life, like toys, games, or bicycles, where you might remember the symbol for the manufacturer rather than the actual name of the company?

For which stores, restaurants, toys, or games do you find the symbol easiest to remember? How often do you use the item or frequent the store? Do you find that the more you use the item or frequent the store, the easier it is to remember the symbol?

Now imagine you're a meteorologist and you collect weather data every day for years. Just like you and your nickname or McDonald's and their golden arches, would it help the meteorologist to have symbols to record data with instead of words? Why or why not?

What will the children do?

Weather log creation

Challenge the students to prepare a weather log or a data chart that they will use to collect weather information. Encourage them to keep in mind the previous discussion. Allow the students to break into their own groups. This will help when the students eventually collect weather information on weekends.

Try to give as little input as possible. Give the students time to brainstorm all the factors that may be important to forecast weather. Have the instruments available for them to look over as they try to think of what they need to create a good weather forecast.

Encourage the students to use their designed chart for one week. At the start of the next week, ask the student groups to share the information they obtained. As a class, determine the group which was the most accurate in predicting daily weather.

2. EXPLANATION/CONCEPT INVENTION: What is the main idea? How will the main idea be identified?

> *Concept:* Weather data can be collected and reported.
>
> Controlling variables is important to making reliable weather observations. Each separate weather measurement is a variable that cannot be controlled. Ask the students the following questions to help them invent the concept:
>
> - Did the weather factors you chose to observe give you enough information to forecast the weather?
> - Could you have been more accurate had you collected other types of data?
> - Which factors could increase error in your data?
> - Did you try to control any human factors that might have made your readings faulty?
> - Can you simplify the way in which you recorded your data?

3. EXPANSION OF THE IDEA: Which process skills will be used?

> Observing, interpreting data, inferring, creating models, making conclusions
>
> How will the idea be expanded?
>
> Weather map symbols

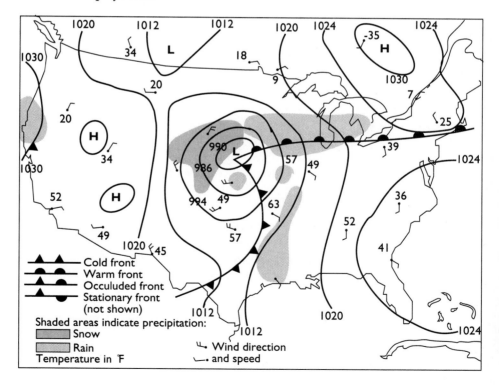

Symbols can be used to designate some weather observations. Collect a supply of weather maps from as many different newspapers as possible. Once you have a number of maps that vary in sophistication, distribute them to your students and ask if they can interpret them. Create a list on the board of all of the different symbols they observe on the maps. Encourage the students to speculate about what each symbol represents. After exploring the various symbols found on the map, break the class up into six groups. Assign each group one of the following tasks:

- Draw a station model diagram that shows wind direction and speed, type of high cloud, type of middle cloud, sea-level pressure, pressure change, type of low cloud, dew point, sky cover, present state of weather, air temperature.
- Create a chart that shows the weather map symbols for highs, lows, fronts, isobars, and air masses.
- Create a chart titled "Present State of the Weather" that shows and briefly describes the symbols for precipitation.
- Create a chart titled "Sky Cover" that shows the symbols for the different fractions of cloud coverage.
- Create a chart titled "Major Cloud Types" that shows the symbols for and names the major cloud types.
- Create a chart titled "Wind Scale" that lists the speed and shows the symbols for the wind.

Weather data collection. As the student groups report on the symbols they discovered to represent the various weather phenomena, ask them to decide how they could use some of this information to make recording weather information easier. How can you use this information to predict weather?

Why is the idea important for personal development?

- What changes have you experienced in the amount of attention you pay to weather forecasts now that you have had a chance to collect weather information yourself?
- Do you think you can create a family weather station at your house without spending a large amount of money on expensive weather equipment? What types of weather instruments could you create?

Why is the idea important for science-technology-society?

- In the summer of 1990 a sudden flood wiped out a town called Shadyside, Ohio. Could an improved weather radar system helped to save lives? Could it have prevented the sudden flood?

Why is the idea important for academic growth?

- Create graphs for each of the weather factors collected over the one-month time period. Study your graphs. Do you see any great fluctuations in any of the readings over time? If so, with which weather factor?
- Was there ever a dramatic rise or decrease in the barometric pressure?

EARTH SCIENCE

- Did you examine your graphs to see if any other factor changed dramatically when the barometer did? If you did find some changes, with what other factors?
- What kind of pressure system was over the area when the barometer changed dramatically?
- What conclusions can you draw about the relationships among different weather factors?

Why is the idea important for career awareness?

Survey local radio and television stations. Where do they get their weather forecast information from? Is there a resident meteorologist who prepares the forecast? If so, see if you can interview that person. Prepare some key questions you would like to have answered in light of the experiences you have just had collecting your own weather data.

4. EVALUATION: How will the students show what they have learned?

Upon completing these activities the students will be able to demonstrate the use of symbols for collecting and reporting weather data by completing the following tasks:

- Ask the students to look at the data they collected from the exploration phase of this lesson and consider the following questions: Is there a weather factor you did not consider collecting which you would add now? Would it be important to be consistent in your data collection? In other words, did you consider things like making sure you collect your information at the same time every day, or that at least two people in the group are responsible for reading the instruments to check for accuracy?
- Revise your weather log to include all the factors necessary to make a sound weather forecast. You may ask the teacher for sample weather logs or suggestions on what data to collect. Be sure the variables that can be controlled are controlled!
- Once you have revised your log, show it to the teacher. If it is judged complete, then collect weather data for a month.

Some teachers may have their students so proficient on the various weather instruments that it becomes second nature to them. Weather data is collected every day for the entire school year. Your class may want to give a daily weather report to the school on the intercom each day.

EARTH SCIENCE

5–7
———
Earth
Science

Weather Predictions

Concepts to be invented
Main idea—Many aspects of weather need to be considered before one can make an accurate prediction of the weather.

Secondary concepts that are important to expansion
Types of storms, seasonal weather change, and climate zones.

Materials needed
For exploration:

Numerous copies (at least two for each student) of weather maps from newspapers and/or those available from NOAA, weather map symbol key.

For expansion:

rain gauge
wind vane and anemometer or an
    aerovane that combines the two
thermometer

sling psychrometer
mercury barometer or the more
    convenient aneroid barometer
cloud charts

⊃ **Safety precautions:** Handle weather instruments with care. Avoid dropping them. Be sure you understand how they are used to prevent damage.

1. EXPLORATION: Which process skills will be used?

Hypothesizing, recording data, classifying, predicting, formulating models, analyzing, making conclusions, evaluating, communicating

What will the children do?

Weather map information

Ask the students to generate a list of variables that need to be taken into account in order to accurately predict the weather in their area. Place this list on the board, numbering each item. (This part of the activity requires them to reflect on results of previous activities in which they studied phenomena like air pressure, cloud types, temperature, relative humidity, air masses, wind speed, and so on.) After the class has had ample opportunity to add to this list, ask the students to take two or more of the weather maps and go on a scavenger hunt. They are to use the weather map key to help them in their hunt. Circle the items from the list on the board that are found on the map. Place the number from the list on the board next to the circle on the map. Do your maps contain enough data to accurately predict what the weather will be in your area? If so, predict the weather. If not, what do you think is missing? Why?

2. EXPLANATION/CONCEPT INVENTION: What is the main idea? How will the main idea be identified?

Concept: Elements of the weather can be recorded and used to forecast weather change.

- What role do air pressure, relative humidity, wind speed and direction, and cloud cover play in predicting weather?
- Without being aware of any other weather component, if your city was trapped under a low pressure system, what kind of weather would you predict you would have?
- What types of storms can form in a low pressure system?
- What types of information are better than others for making accurate forecasts?

Time should also be set aside for problems students had in making predictions.

3. EXPANSION OF THE IDEA: Which process skills will be used?

Observing, questioning, measuring, predicting, using numbers, mapping, recording data, making assumptions, formulating models, inferring, analyzing, interpreting data.

How will the idea be expanded?

Recording weather data and predicting weather records

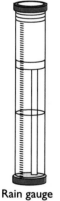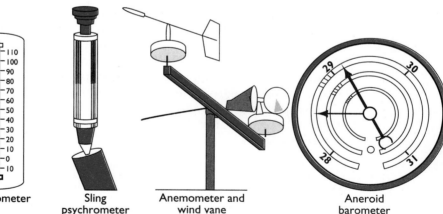

| Rain gauge | Thermometer | Sling psychrometer | Anemometer and wind vane | Aneroid barometer |

The students will generate a list of materials needed to create an amateur weather station on the school grounds. The students will work with the teacher to obtain these materials. They will work together to learn how to use these instruments. Divide the class into groups, assigning each group a week in which they will be responsible for reading and recording the weather instruments each day. From their observations, the use of weather maps, and how they chart the air movements on their own weather maps, the group is to predict the weather each day for one week. Offer a prize to the group that gives the most accurate weather forecast. After each group has had a week to predict the weather, determine the winning group and award the prize!

Why is the idea important for personal development?

- Why is it is important to know proper safety procedures during severe storms?
- Do you think you are affected by emotional changes with changes in the weather?

Why is the idea important for science-technology-society?

- How were many historic events shaped by changes in weather and climate? Examples are the potato famine in Ireland, the Dust Bowl days of the 1930s in the United States, the Shadyside floods in Ohio during the spring of 1990, and various Revolutionary War battles.
- How has the number of commuters into cities like Los Angeles or New York altered the weather conditions of these cities? How has the formation of smog in and around metropolitan areas altered the climate of the surrounding region?

Why is the idea important for academic growth?

- Charts can be useful in organizing various kinds of data. Past experience can assist one in making accurate predictions of future events.
- What factors do you need to be aware of in order to make an accurate weather prediction?

Why is the idea important for career awareness?

- Why is it important for those who work outdoors to pay attention to daily weather reports on TV, radio, or newspapers?
- In addition to meteorologists, in what other careers is the accurate prediction of weather essential? Why?
- Why do those who install or make insulation, heat pumps, and air conditioners want to neutralize weather extremes?

4. EVALUATION: How will the students show what they have learned?

Upon completing the activities the students will be able to

- make short-term forecasts or predictions of weather conditions using an available weather record with 75% accuracy,
- describe typical weather conditions for various climate zones,
- identify a weather trend on a weather map and use it to predict changes over twenty-four hours.

Air Mass Movement

Concept to be invented
Main idea—When moving air masses of different temperature and different moisture content come in contact, it results in precipitation and other identifiable weather phenomena.

Secondary concepts that are important to expansion
Fronts, cold and warm.

Materials needed
For exploration:

globe of the earth	paper	thermometer
medicine dropper	marking pen	hammer
colored water	dry ice	matches
flat-sided top	container of water	string

For expansion:

Clear bottle with screw cap   cold water
   (small juice bottles work well)   red and blue food coloring
cooking oil

⊃ **Safety precautions:** Use extreme caution when handling the dry ice. If the students are immature, the teacher or another adult may need to handle the dry ice for that part of the experiment. Heavy-duty safety gloves should be made available for anyone handling the dry ice. Care should be taken when handling any of the instruments. Exercise care with glass containers.

1. EXPLORATION: Which process skills will be used?

Observing, measuring, recording data, formulating models

What will the children do?

Station A, coriolis effect—globe. Spin the globe quickly so that it moves in a west-to-east direction. Pretending that you are on the globe at the North Pole, use the medicine dropper to start some colored water rolling in a stream south toward the equator. Carefully record your observations, being sure to include the movement of the water both north and south of the equator.

Station B, coriolis effect—top. Obtain a small flat-sided top. On a piece of paper draw a circle the size of the top. Push this down over handle of the top and center it on the top. As you spin the top in a counterclockwise direction (from west to east) with one hand, hold a marker in your other hand and try to draw a straight line on the paper attached to the top. Record what happens when you do this.

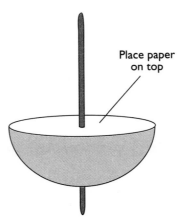

Place paper
on top

Station C, air movement—dry ice. Break a piece of dry ice with a hammer and place a few small pieces into a container of water. Be sure to use caution when working with the dry ice (gloves and goggles). Observe the air around the container over a period of time. Measure the temperature of the air mass (a) just above the container, (b) about one meter above the container, and (c) near the base of the container. Record these readings.

Light one end of a piece of string and then blow out the flame. The end should begin to smoke. Give the smoking string to the students and have them wave it around the container. Ask them to record their observations of the movement of the smoke.

2. EXPLANATION/CONCEPT INVENTION: What is the main idea? How will the main idea be identified?

Concept at Stations A and B: Air masses, low-pressure areas, and fronts move generally from west to east.

- At Station A, in what direction did the stream turn in the northern hemisphere? In the southern hemisphere?
- What effect do you think the land masses with their mountain ranges will have on the moving air?
- At Station B, what happened when you tried to draw a straight line on the paper from the center to the edge of the top?
- Because of the earth's rotation, the motion of a body as seen from earth ap-pears to deflect to the right in the northern hemisphere. This fictitious deflecting force is also called the Coriolis effect. How do you think the Coriolis effect can help explain the results you obtained when trying to draw a straight line on the paper on the spinning top?

Concept at Station C: When moving air masses of different temperature and different moisture content come in contact, it results in precipitation and other identifiable weather phenomena.

- Where was the air mass the highest?
- What happened to the air as it cooled?
- What were your temperature readings around the container? If there were differences, why do you think they occurred?
- What happened when you waved some smoking string in the air around the container? In what direction did the air flow around the container?
- What kind of precipitation do you think could occur if warm air were blown over the cold air flowing from the container?

3. EXPANSION OF THE IDEA: Which process skills will be used?

Manipulating materials, formulating models, hypothesizing, inferring

How will the idea be expanded?

Oil and water fronts

Half-fill a bottle with cooking oil. Add some red food coloring, cap the bottle, and shake well. This will represent a warm air mass. In a separate container, add blue food coloring to cold water. What do you think will happen as you pour the cold water into the bottle of oil? Slowly pour the water into the bottle.

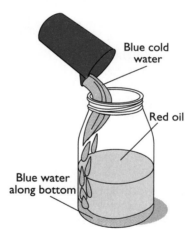

Blue cold water

Red oil

Blue water along bottom

The following concepts can be demonstrated with this arrangement of materials:

- Lines of temperature differences between two air masses are called fronts.
- A warm front is caused by a relatively warm mass of air advancing over a mass of relatively cold air.
- A cold front is caused by a mass of relatively cold air displacing relatively warm air.
- Advancing cold fronts lift warm air. Advancing warm fronts result in the warm air being lifted.
- Fronts do not all move at the same speed or in the same direction.
- The amount of moisture in the air controls the kind of weather along the front.

EARTH SCIENCE

Questions that help students invent expansion concepts:
- What happened when you poured the cold water into the oil? Did it behave as you predicted? Which liquid is more dense? How do you know?
- Place the screw cap on the bottle. Slowly turn the bottle on its side. How does the heavier liquid move, and what is its final position?
- If a cold air mass moves toward a warm air mass, would the leading edge of the cold air mass be at the ground level or above the ground? Why? (Remember that the blue water represents the cold air mass, and the red oil is the warm air mass.)
- If a warm air mass moves toward a cold air mass, would the leading edge of the warm air mass be at the ground or above the ground? Why?
- How would you describe a stationary front? What factors affect its formation?

Why is the idea important for personal development?
- If you were planning a picnic for Saturday and you heard on a Thursday weather forecast that a warm front would be moving into the region on Friday evening, would you switch the day of your picnic to Sunday? Why or why not?

Why is the idea important for science-technology-society?
- What effect do extremes in precipitation have upon area populations (not just human)?
- How do you think knowledge of such weather phenomena as air masses, fronts, and precipitation have assisted in the invention of the material Goretex, which is now used in running clothes, tents, tarpaulins, and so on? How has this invention allowed us to enjoy our environment more, no matter what the weather conditions?

Why is the idea important for academic growth?
- What kind of pressure system do you think would bring your area a large amount of precipitation? A small amount?

Use the following materials to create your own rain gauge: large straight-sided jar, long narrow jar or large test tube, meter stick, metric ruler, and masking tape. Place a ruler vertically in the large jar and pour in water until it reaches the 10-mm mark on the ruler. Pour this water into the narrow jar, to which you have attached a strip of masking tape. Mark the masking tape at the exact level of the water. This represents 10 mm in the jar. Repeat this procedure for levels of 20 mm, 30 mm, and so on.

Place the large jar outside, away from any obstruction, to collect rain. Why is that important? The top of the jar should be about 30.5 cm above the ground. To read the amount of rain, empty it into the measuring jar at the same time each day. Keep a daily record in a chart form.

Do you think you can determine how much snow you would have had if you had 50 mm of rain collected in your gauge? What about if you have 50 mm of snow—how much rain would that be? The student can do two things here: (a) Obtain a tall, straight-sided container, such as an empty juice can. Carefully fill it with loose snow, but do not pack the snow in the can. Heat the snow until it is completely melted. Use the rain gauge to measure the amount of water. If you know the length of the can you can compare amount of snow to rain. (b) The student could guesstimate the amount of rain the snow is equal to by knowing that the ratio of snow to rain is usually 10 to 1. A wet, heavy snow may have a ratio as low as 6 to 1, while in dry, fluffy, new-fallen snow the ratio may be as high as 30 to 1.

Why is the idea important for career awareness?

- How is it possible for airplanes to fly in the eye of the storm during a hurricane? What kind of information do pilots need to understand about air masses in order to do this?
- Create a list of all of the types of jobs that can be affected when air masses of different temperatures and moisture contents come in contact. Are any of those jobs in areas you would like to work?

4. EVALUATION: How will the students show what they have learned?

Air masses and parachutes: The following parachute activity, as well as the questions covering personal development, science-technology-society, academic growth, and career awareness could be used to assess the students' knowledge of the relationships among air masses, fronts, and precipitation.

Parachute Materials

12-inch square sheet of tissue paper
eight glue-backed hole reinforcers
four strings 10 inches in length

washer for weight
paper person (for decorative purposes only)

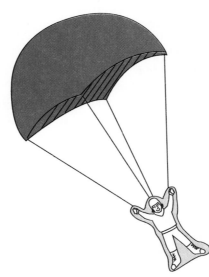

Punch a hole in each corner of the tissue with a pencil point. Place a hole reinforcer on each side of the hole. Tie the four strings to each hole. Tie the loose ends of the strings together around the washer. Be sure the strings end up being of equal length. Decorate with a paper person attached to the washer. You may find that a small hole in the very center of the tissue will help the parachute open more quickly.

Fold up your chute and throw it into the air. Have a partner time from the moment you release it until the moment it begins to descend. Time its descent separately.

- Which is faster? Why?
- How does the parachute depend on air pressure?
- What if your parachute came from several hundred meters above the earth's surface? Would it fall any differently?
- Would the parachute fall differently if a cold front were in the area? What about a warm front?
- What if a warm front were just moving into the area, replacing a cold front. Would it be safe to parachute during that time? Why or why not?

Air Pressure

GRADE 5–6

Earth Science

DISCIPLINE

Concept to be invented
Main idea—Air has weight.

Secondary concepts that are important to expansion
Air can exert pressure. Temperature and air movement are factors that influence air pressure.

Materials needed
For each student group:

modeling clay	three balloons	straw
pencil	two books	one index card
yardstick	one piece of 8.5-inch	one glass of water
string	by 11-inch paper	one sandwich bag

For teacher demonstration:

One beach ball

For academic growth questions and evaluation:

two paper lunch bags	one lamp or candle
two balloons and string for	one straw and one ping pong ball per
each student group	student

⊃ **Safety precautions:** The students should take care that when blowing during the activities they don't hyperventilate and get dizzy. Have a paper bag available for any hyperventilating student to breathe into slowly. This will balance the oxygen-carbon dioxide ratio and return the student to normal.

1. EXPLORATION: Which process skills will be used?

Observing, predicting, comparing, questioning, describing, manipulating materials, recording data

What will the children do?

Provide the students with modeling clay, pencil, yardstick, three balloons, and a string. Ask them to manipulate these materials so that they can create a balance such as in the diagram.

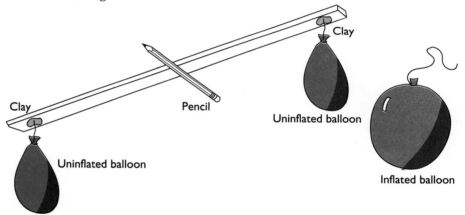

Clay

Pencil

Uninflated balloon

Clay

Uninflated balloon

Inflated balloon

Suspend and balance two uninflated balloons. Ask the students to record their observations. Then ask them to predict what would happen to this balanced system if they were to replace one of the uninflated balloons with an inflated balloon. Record their predictions. Now replace one of the uninflated balloons with an inflated balloon. Record students' observations. Do they match their predictions?

2. EXPLANATION/CONCEPT INVENTION: What is the main idea? How will the main idea be identified?

Concept: Air has weight.

What kind of data did you collect? Did you obtain results as you predicted? Hold up an uninflated beach ball. Ask the students to help you weigh it. Now ask one of the students to blow it up. Ask for their predictions as to whether or not it now weighs the same. How is this demonstration similar to the balance you just created? What happened with your balance when you replaced the uninflated balloon with an inflated balloon? Weigh it. Does it weigh the same? Why? Air has weight!

3. EXPANSION OF THE IDEA: Which process skills will be used?

Observing, predicting, comparing, manipulating materials, recording data, hypothesizing

How will the idea be expanded?

Ask the students to place two books (at least a quarter- to a half-inch thick) three inches apart on a desk top. Place a sheet of 8.5-inch by 11-inch paper across the book lengthwise. Have the students predict if they can blow the paper off the books by blowing into the space between the books. Record your predictions, then try it! Repeat the experiment, this time using a straw placed just under the edge of the paper to blow between the books.

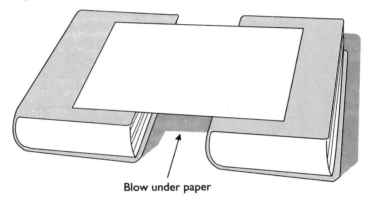

Blow under paper

What happened to the paper when you blew without the straw? With the straw? Were you able to blow the paper off the books either time? Did the paper move at all? If so, how? This activity demonstrates that air has pressure. Air moving fast, such as the air you blew out between the books and underneath the paper, creates a lower pressure than the pressure above the books. Thus you see a slight dip in the paper. When you use a straw to blow through, the straw creates a narrow high-speed path of low pressure between the books. Now the pressure underneath the paper bridge is much lower than the pressure above the paper, thus you observe a big dip in the paper bridge. This dip is caused by the higher air pressure on top of the paper. Thus, air exerts pressure!

A good teacher demonstration to emphasize this fact is to take a yardstick or some other relatively long, thin piece of wood and place it on a table top. Smooth out a large piece of newspaper over the wood. Leave about six to eight inches of wood sticking out one side. Make sure there are no air spaces between the newspaper and the table top. Ask the students if they think you can hit this stick and make the paper go flying. Once you take several predictions, hit the stick. What happened? The stick broke and the paper remained on the table top. Why? Because on every square inch of that paper air is exerting a pressure of 14.7 pounds per square inch. A full sheet of newspaper is typically

27 inches by 23 inches or 621 square inches. If there are 14.7 pounds of pressure exerted on every square inch of the newspaper, that means that there is 621 square inches times 14.7 pounds per square inch, or 9128.7 pounds of pressure being exerted by the air on that paper. You would have to hit the stick with a force equal to that amount to get the paper to move!

Why is the idea important for personal development?

- What does air pressure have to do with a smooth ride on your bike or in a car?
- What happens when your bike gets a flat tire? What does this do to the air pressure in the tire?

Why is the idea important for science-technology-society?

- In the second activity you found that faster moving air causes lower air pressure. How do you think this fact has influenced the design of airplanes?
- Ask a student to demonstrate lift by taping a narrow strip of paper to a pencil. Hold the pencil by your mouth and blow over the strip of paper. What happens to it? How do you think this movement is similar to air blowing over the wing of an airplane?

Why is the idea important for academic growth?

- Does all air have the same weight? Ask the students to replace their uninflated balloons in the balanced system with two paper lunch bags. Get the system to balance. Now place a lit lamp or candle several inches below one of the bags. What happened to that balanced system? Which weighs more, cold or hot air?
- What kind of air pressure do you think would be associated with a cold front? A warm front?

EARTH SCIENCE

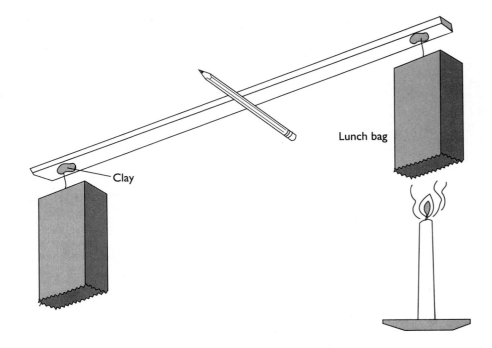

Why is the idea important for career awareness?

- Ask the students to share information with one another on Daniel Bernoulli (1700–1782). He was a Swiss doctor, mathematician, biologist, physiologist, physicist, astronomer, and oceanographer. Can you think of any people today who are as well versed in as many areas as Daniel Bernoulli was? Do you think it is more difficult to be an expert in all of these areas today? Why?
- Invite a pilot to come speak to your class. Ask him or her to explain how knowledge of air pressure helps him or her to control an airplane.

4. EVALUATION: How will the students show what they have learned?

Upon completing these activities the students will be able to

- predict and then explain why two balloons suspended on equal-length strings about three inches apart come closer together when the students blow between them. They will be able to demonstrate this phenomenon.
- look at a picture of an unbalanced system, in which one balloon is inflated and the other is uninflated, and explain why this system is unbalanced.
- demonstrate that a ping pong ball can hover over the end of a drinking straw. They will also be able to explain why this happens and be able to share and explain this phenomenon to children in a primary grade.

EARTH SCIENCE

5–8

Earth
Science

DISCIPLINE

Solar Heating

Concept to be invented
Main idea—The earth's surfaces are heated unevenly.

Secondary concepts that are important to expansion
Uneven heating creates wind and makes the water cycle occur. The sun is the source of energy that determines the weather on earth.

Materials needed
For exploration (per student group):

three paper cups	three thermometers	three metal cans
dark soil	one lamp	white enamel paint
light sand	satellite photographs	matte black paint
water	of the earth's surface	Styrofoam cups

For expansion (per student group):
One thermometer

⊃ **Safety precautions:** The students should be careful when using the lamp and around electricity.

1. EXPLORATION: Which process skills will be used?

Observing, predicting, comparing, questioning, describing, manipulating materials, recording data

What will the children do?

Temperature versus surface color

Ask the students to cut the tops off the paper cups so that they are about 4 cm deep. Fill one with dark-colored soil, one with light-colored sand, and the third with water. Instruct the students to place a thermometer into each cup, covering the bulb with about 0.5 cm of soil, sand, or water. Record the temperature of each surface. Place a lit lamp so its bulb is about 15 cm from the tops of the cups. After five minutes, record the temperature of each cup. Identify which cup gained heat the fastest and record this information. Remove the lamp from the cups. Predict which cup you think will loose heat the fastest. Record your prediction. Leave the cups untouched, and after ten minutes, record the temperature of each cup. Which lost heat the fastest? Record this data. Was it as you predicted?

2. EXPLANATION/CONCEPT INVENTION: What is the main idea? How will the main idea be identified?

Concept: The earth's surfaces are heated unevenly.

What kind of data did you collect? Did you obtain results as you predicted? How

EARTH SCIENCE

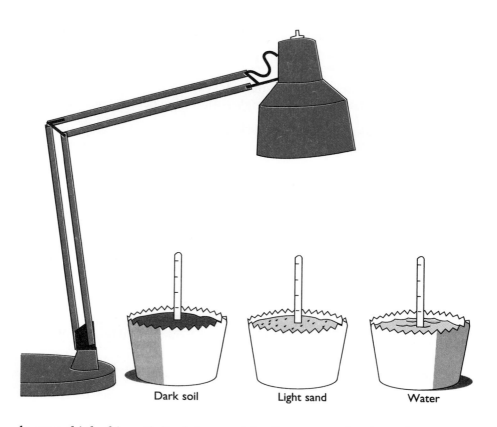

Dark soil   Light sand   Water

do you think this activity helps explain the uneven heating of the earth's surfaces?

Look at satellite pictures of the earth. Describe the different surfaces. Why do dark-colored surfaces absorb more heat energy from the sun? What do lighter-colored surfaces do that would prevent as much absorption of the sun's energy as dark surfaces? The lighter surfaces reflect more of the sun's energy, whereas dark land absorbs it. Also, dark land loses its heat faster than water.

3. EXPANSION OF THE IDEA: Which process skills will be used?

Observing, predicting, comparing, manipulating materials, recording data, hypothesizing

How will the idea be expanded?

Optimum thermometer placement

The teacher should ask the students where they think they should place a thermometer to measure the air temperature every day. Ask the students to first predict and then record air temperature taken on blacktop, grass, in the shade of a tree, a sandy area, and a gravel area. Take these readings at ground level and at one meter from the ground. Does this make a difference? Will the time of day make a difference? Have the students record the temperature at these various sites during different times of the school day. Which gives the most accurate reading for actual air temperature? Once the class decides this, then at that site and time, daily temperature readings can be taken for a weather log for the class. The students can also practice taking temperature readings as degrees Celsius and Fahrenheit.

Why is the idea important for personal development?

- What are ways of staying cool on a hot day or warm on a cold day?
- Why are swimming pools, ponds, lakes, or oceans good places to cool off?
- What kinds of clothes will help keep you cool in summer? What kinds will keep you warm in winter? How and why?

Why is the idea important for science-technology-society?

- How do we attempt to control the temperature in our homes? What kinds of heating and cooling systems do we utilize?
- What alternative sources of energy, aside from fossil fuels, should we continue to develop? How efficient do you think these are or will be?

Why is the idea important for academic growth?

- Aside from unequal heating of the different-colored surfaces of the earth, temperature is also determined by many other factors. Discuss how the following could affect air temperature: cloud cover, time of day, time of year, wind, latitude, altitude, and oceans or other large bodies of water.
- At what temperature in degrees Celsius does water freeze? Boil? At what temperature will water freeze and boil in degrees Fahrenheit?

Why is the idea important for career awareness?

- Who helps supply energy to keep our homes cool in summer and warm in winter? (Coal miner, lumberjack, oil-field worker, power plant operator, heating-ventilation-air conditioning personnel, and so on.)

4. EVALUATION: How will the students show what they have learned?

Upon completing these activities the students will be able to

- fill three identical-sized cans with tap water. Insert a thermometer through a cover made out of the bottom of a Styrofoam cup. One can should be painted dull black, one left shiny metal, and the last painted shiny white. Ask the students to predict what will happen to the temperature of the water when the cans are placed in direct sunlight or equally distanced from a 150- to 300-watt light bulb. The students should be able to record the temperature of the water in the cans at one-minute intervals. They should be able to write a short report of their observations.
- record the temperature of the cans in Celsius and Fahrenheit.
- choose an optimal location outdoors to record daily temperature observations.

EARTH SCIENCE

Air Movement and Surface Temperature

Concept to be invented
Main idea—Air moves downward over cold surfaces and upward over warm surfaces.

Secondary concepts that are important to expansion
A volume of warm air has less mass than an equal volume of cool air; particles of warm air are farther apart than particles of cool air. Cold air, being heavier than warm air, sinks, pushing warm air upward.

Materials needed

For exploration to make an observation box:

one cardboard box (about 30 cm
   x 30 cm x 50 cm)
clear plastic food wrap

plastic tape
one plastic straw

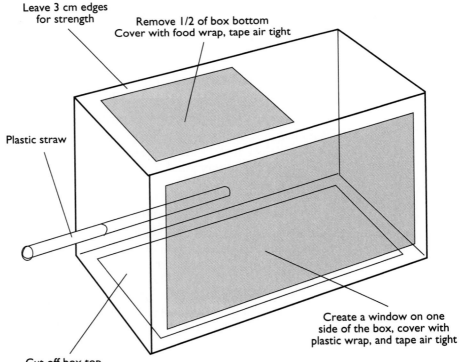

Leave 3 cm edges
for strength

Remove 1/2 of box bottom
Cover with food wrap, tape air tight

Plastic straw

Create a window on one
side of the box, cover with
plastic wrap, and tape air tight

Cut off box top,
leave 3 cm edge for strengh

Remove the top of the box. Leave a 3 cm edge for strength. Turn the box over. Cut a window in the new top, leaving half of the top intact. Cut out one side, again leaving a 3 cm edge for strength. Tape clear plastic food wrap to the side and the half window on top. In one end of the box, cut a small hole just large enough to insert a plastic straw. See figure for assistance in construction.

Additional materials for exploration:

one 35 ml syringe	scissors
one plastic straw (cut into three even pieces)	matches
	ice water
heavy cotton string (three 4 cm pieces)	aluminum pan
	metric ruler

For expansion:

one dowel rod (3 feet long x .75 inch wide) with hole drilled exactly in center
one dowel rod (1 foot long x .25 inch wide) to be placed through hole in larger rod
one paper clip used as a sliding clip to balance the rod
two small paper bags of equal size
two thumbtacks of equal size and weight
one 150-watt bulb and socket
extension cord if necessary

⊃ **Safety precautions:** Use caution around open flame.

1. EXPLORATION: Which process skills will be used?

Observing, experimenting, formulating models, questioning, communicating, inferring

What will the children do?

Take a piece of string and fold it in half. Place the folded end into one of the pieces of straw, allowing about 0.5 cm to hang out the end. Be sure it fits snugly in the end. Do this for each piece of straw.

Slip the open end of the prepared straw onto the syringe. Light the string. Collect smoke in the cylinder by slowly pulling out the plunger. Remove the straw and lay it aside where it won't burn anything. You may need more smoke later.

Place a pan of ice water inside the observation box. Be sure the straw is in place through the end of the box, but not hanging over the pan. Let the pan sit for three or four minutes. After the wait, insert the smoke-filled syringe into the straw of the observation box. Gently force the smoke through the straw into the box. Carefully observe what happens to the smoke as it moves over the pan of ice water.

Complete the procedure above using a pan of hot water instead. Once again, make careful observations of the smoke as it moves over the hot water.

2. EXPLANATION/CONCEPT INVENTION: What is the main idea? How will the main idea be identified?

Concept: Air moves downward over colder surfaces and upward over warm surfaces.

- What path did the smoke take as it moved over the cold surface? (It spread out slowly over the pan, staying close to the pan's surface.)
- What path did the smoke take as it moved over the hot surface? (It slowly spread out and upward.)
- Do you think a force is acting on the smoke as it moves above the warm or cold surfaces? (A force is something that causes a change in shape or a change in motion of a body. It is easy to see the change in shape; this also shows the change in motion.)

3. EXPANSION OF THE IDEA: Which process skills will be used?

Experimenting, making conclusions, evaluating, generalizing

How will the idea be expanded?

Set up the dowel rod balance as in the figure. Fasten the two paper bags to the balance rod using the thumbtacks. Balance the rod using the sliding paper clip.

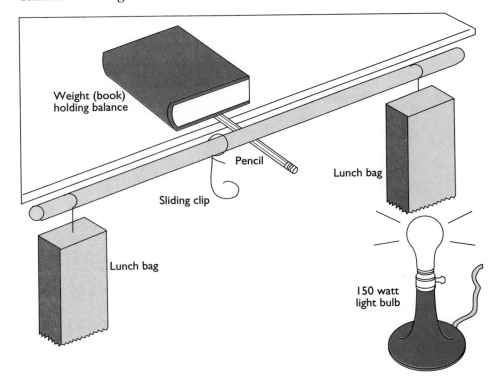

Weight (book) holding balance

Pencil

Lunch bag

Sliding clip

Lunch bag

150 watt light bulb

EARTH SCIENCE

Hold the rod stationary. Put the lighted bulb just below the open end of the bag on one side. Keep the bulb under the bag for thirty seconds. Then gently let go of the bar. Observe the bag for several minutes.

Questions that help invent secondary concepts:
- What happened to the bag on the side near the bulb?
- How do you know this?
- Was the temperature of the bag away from the bulb colder or warmer than the bag near the bulb?
- What happened when you gently released the balance?
- From your observations, which has the greater mass? Is it the bag of warm air or the bag of cool air?
- The bags in this activity have the same volume. Which do you think has more gas particles? Why?
- What do you think this activity demonstrates about what happens to a substance when heated?

Warm air has less mass than an equal amount of cool air: particles of warm air are farther apart than particles of cool air. Cold air, being heavier than warm air, sinks, pushing warm air upward.

Why is the idea important for personal development?
- How would the absence of wind affect your life? Do you think life would be changed in any way if there never was a wind?
- How does the presence of wind affect you personally? How do you think strong winds would affect you if you lived in a coastal city?

Why is the idea important for science-technology-society?
- How has wind power become a source of energy in some regions of the world? How has this harnessing of the wind changed the lives of people living there?
- How has knowledge of air mass saved lives? In what circumstances?

Why is the idea important for academic growth?
- The students will develop process skills needed to identify moving air as wind and to determine that air has mass.
- The students will be able to explain the movement of air over surfaces of varying temperatures and apply this knowledge to explain why wind occurs.

Why is the idea important for career awareness?
- How will knowledge of wind behavior assist a pilot in flight? What kind of training must a pilot undergo in order to understand how wind behaves? Can just anyone become a pilot? What skills do you think are necessary to become a successful pilot?
- Read a book on Amelia Earhart. What do you think happened to her when she vanished in her plane over the Pacific Ocean?
- Can you list any other occupations in which knowledge of wind and its behavior is necessary?

EARTH SCIENCE

4. EVALUATION: How will the students show what they have learned?

Upon completing the activities the students will be able to

- successfully answer the questions included in the explanation phase and expansion phase of this lesson as well as the questions in personal growth, science and technology interrelationships, academic growth, and career awareness;
- demonstrate the movement of smoke over cold air and warm air to a group of younger students or parents and be able to explain the concept behind the movement;
- demonstrate that cold air sinks and warm air rises when given a thermometer, a pan of ice water, and a fan.

GRADE **5–7**

Earth Science

DISCIPLINE

Uneven Heating of the Earth

Concepts to be invented
Main idea—Uneven heating of the earth affects air pressure.

Secondary concepts that are important to expansion
Uneven heating of the earth gives rise to wind patterns that move locally and around the globe.

Materials needed
For exploration:

long clear tube
two rubber stoppers to fit
    tube (clear caps)
tub of water
two baby food jars (one larger
    than the other)
balloon

six rubber bands
clear tape
one tongue depressor
one straw
scissors or knife
one marking pen

For expansion:

two clear-glass drinking cups
    of the same size
water
food coloring
index card
wire
candle

two large can lids
clay
two tacks
small lamp
oven mitt
glass beaker

⊃ **Safety precautions:** The students should take care when using any glass containers. Exercise extreme caution when using the hot water to avoid burns.

Also, when using the lamp, remember that the bulb can get hot. When using the candle, be watchful of the open flame. Be sure all sleeves are rolled up, all hair is pulled back, and no shirts are dangling into the flame.

1. EXPLORATION: Which process skills will be used?

Observing, measuring, questioning, recording data, predicting, formulating models

What will the children do?

The following two activities could be done ahead of time to introduce the concept of air pressure. Once the students understand this concept, then the third activity can be performed to teach the concept at hand.

Tower of water. Close one end of a long clear tube with a stopper or cap. Stand this in a tub of water. Fill the tube with water. Seal the top end of the tube with the stopper or cap. Remove the seal at the bottom, keeping the opening of the tube under water. What happens to the water in the tube? Why? What do you think will happen if you remove the stopper from the top of the tube? Try it! Was your prediction correct? Why does all of this happen?

Aneroid barometer. Cut the open end off a balloon. Obtain a large-size baby food jar and extend the balloon over the mouth of the jar. Make sure the balloon is stretched taut. While you hold it, have your partner fasten it in place with a rubber band. Be sure to make a tight seal. Use the second rubber band to make sure the seal is tight. Why do you think a tight seal is important? Draw a sketch of your jar. Show what the balloon seal would look like if the pressure inside the jar were greater than the pressure outside of the jar. Cut one end of the straw at an angle to make it pointed. Gently place a 3 cm strip of tape on the uncut end. Place this on the center of the balloon-covered jar. Be sure it sits securely in the center. Attach a tongue depressor to the smaller jar at the top and the bottom of the jar, using two rubber bands at each location (a total of four). Place the two jars side by side on a level support so that the pointed straw is in front of the tongue depressor. Label the point where it hits 0 to show the starting position.

Questions for student activities:

- What do you think will happen to the pointer as the air pressure outside the jar increases?
- What about when the air pressure outside decreases?
- Try increasing the air pressure within the jar by placing your hands over the balloon jar for about ten minutes. What happens to the pointer?
- Try decreasing the air pressure within the jar by placing the balloon jar in a pan of ice water. What happened to the pointer?

Uneven heating and air pressure. Make use of the barometers created in the second activity or provide the students with comercially made aneroid barometers. After the students have had a chance to observe how their barometers work, divide the class into three groups. In the very beginning of the school day, instruct one third of the students to place their barometer in the same safe place in the playground in the sun on the blacktop or gravel; one third in the same safe place in the playground in the shade on the grass near a tree; one third in the same area of the classroom. Instruct each group to place a thermometer in their area also. Ask the students to take readings from their barometers and thermometers throughout the course of the school day. Instruct the students to also note any changes that occur in the area where they placed the barometer, such as the amount of sunlight, changing shade conditions, or wind picking up or dying down. Remind them about the importance of keeping a careful record of their observations.

2. EXPLANATION/CONCEPT INVENTION: What is the main idea? How will the main idea be identified?

Concept: Uneven heating of the earth affects air pressure.

If the students have made careful observations and recorded their data accurately, you should be able to create a class chart of data collected at the three sites. Ask the students from each of the groups to examine their data as a group first. If their data for the different time readings are not all the same, ask them to average the readings for that time period. These averages could be placed on the chart.

Through careful questioning and calling attention to the group data, the children may find that the barometric readings as well as thermometer readings were different at each of the sites. Ask them if they see some sort of relationship between the temperature at the site and what was happening with the barometer. What happened to the barometric reading as your temperature increased? As it decreased? Were the barometer readings any different in the shade than in the sun or the classroom? Why or why not?

The earth is heated unevenly due to varying types and colors of surfaces found on the earth. What was the color of the site where you placed your barometer and thermometer? Which color site had the warmest temperatures? The coolest? Were the barometer readings different for these sites? What conclusions can you draw about uneven heating of the earth and air pressure?

3. EXPANSION OF THE IDEA: Which process skills will be used?

Observing, hypothesizing, predicting, communicating

How will the idea be expanded?

Concept: Uneven heating of the earth gives rise to wind patterns that move locally and around the globe.

Set up stations around the classroom so that the children can practice the following:

Air pressure versus water temperature. Fill two clear glasses with water. Place an index card on the top of one. Holding the card in place, invert the cup and place it on top of the other cup. Remove the card. Obtain some very hot water.

Put food coloring into it. Use this to fill one of the clear glasses used in your practice session above. Do the same with cold water and a different color of food coloring. Place a card over one of the cups. Be sure to wear an oven mitt to hold the hot glass. Try inverting the cold over hot and hot over cold. What happens in each set of cups? Why?

Air temperature versus movement of air. Draw a spiraling line on an index card. Cut out this snake and tape a thread to the center of it. Blow on the snake from the bottom. What happens to the snake? What do you think will happen if you suspend it above a burning candle? Try it! Why is this snake moving?

Heat transfer on a wire. Light a candle and allow the melting wax to harden at different spots on a wire. Hold one end of the wire in a candle flame. What do you think will happen to the wax drops on the wire? Does something happen to all of the drops at the same time? How is heat transferred from one end of the wire to the next?

Heat movement through air. Remove the shade from a lamp and plug it in. Place your hand carefully near the side of the bulb, keeping the light off. Turn on the lamp. Did you notice a change in the temperature of your hand? Place a cool beaker around the lit bulb. Can you feel the heat from the bulb?

Heat transfer through metal. Cover one side of a large tin can lid with candle soot. Fix a tack to the opposite side with candle wax. Fix a tack to the side of a clean tin can lid. Support each lid in a clay mound so the tacks are directly opposite the candle flame, a small but equal distance away. Which tack do you think will fall first and why? Did it occur as you predicted?

As the students rotate through the five stations, set up a sixth demonstration area so that the small groups can come and observe the teacher perform the following activity.

Make an observation box before beginning the demonstration. The following materials will be needed: one cardboard box (about 30 cm x 30 cm x 50 cm), clear plastic food wrap, plastic tape, one plastic straw.

Remove the top of the box. Leave a 3 cm edge for strength. Turn the box over. Cut a window in the new top leaving half of the top intact. Cut out one side, again leaving a 3 cm edge for strength. Tape clear plastic food wrap to the side and the half window on top. In one end of the box, cut a small hole just large enough to insert a plastic straw. See figure for assistance in construction.

Additional materials:

one 35-ml syringe	scissors
one plastic straw (cut into three even pieces)	matches
	ice water
heavy cotton string (three 4 cm pieces)	aluminum pan
	metric ruler

Teacher demonstration—movement of smoke over hot and cold surfaces to make clouds:

• Take a piece of string and fold it in half. Place the folded end into one of the

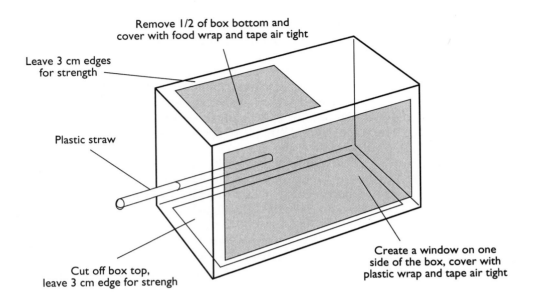

Remove 1/2 of box bottom and
cover with food wrap and tape air tight

Leave 3 cm edges
for strength

Plastic straw

Cut off box top,
leave 3 cm edge for strengh

Create a window on one
side of the box, cover with
plastic wrap and tape air tight

pieces of straw, allowing about 0.5 cm to hang out the end. Be sure it fits snugly
in the end. Do this for each piece of straw.

- Slip the open end of the prepared straw onto the syringe. Light the string.
  Collect smoke in the cylinder by slowly drawing out the plunger. Remove
  the straw and lay it aside where it won't burn anything. You may need more
  smoke later.
- Place a pan of ice water inside the observation box. Be sure the straw is in place
  through the end of the box, but not hanging over the pan. Let the pan sit for
  three or four minutes. After the wait, insert the smoke-filled syringe into the
  straw of the observation box. Gently force the smoke through the straw into
  the box. Carefully observe what happens to the smoke as it moves over the pan
  of ice water.
- Complete the procedure using a pan of hot water instead. Once again ask the
  students to make careful observations of the smoke as it moves over the hot water.

Additional activity/demonstration materials needed:

Observation/convection box	paper clips	scissors
	tape	empty soda pop bottle
drinking straws	index cards	small fan
straight pins	clay	

Activity. Remove the pan of water used in the figure above and replace it with a
candle. Cut a 10 cm hole in the observation box in the lid directly above the
candle so that the observation box now looks like the figure below. Light the
candle and place it inside the box directly under the hole. Once again inject air

through the straw to keep the wick smoking. Observe the behavior of the smoke in the box. Which direction is the smoke in the straw coming from: horizontal or vertical? Place a pan of ice cubes directly below the smoking wick and leave the burning candle in place. What happens to the smoke as it moves over the pan and on toward the candle?

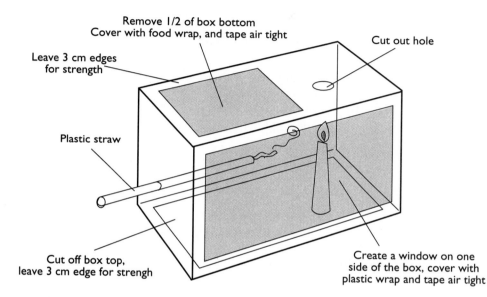

Remove 1/2 of box bottom
Cover with food wrap, and tape air tight

Cut out hole

Leave 3 cm edges for strength

Plastic straw

Cut off box top, leave 3 cm edge for strengh

Create a window on one side of the box, cover with plastic wrap and tape air tight

Concept: Uneven heating of the earth gives rise to wind patterns that move locally and around the globe. Convection is hot air rising above cold. Conduction is heat transferred through surface of objects. Radiation is heat energy that travels in waves.

Questions for student activities:

- What three types of heating did you experience in the above activities?
- When warm air rises over cold air, what type of current does this represent?
- If you had a choice of the type of heating for your home, would you choose one that made use of conduction, convection currents, or radiation? Which do you think is the most efficient? The least efficient?
- How can a toaster be used to demonstrate the three different types of heating?

Questions for teacher demonstration:

- What path did the smoke take as it moved over the cold surface? (It spreads out slowly over the pan, staying close to the pan's surface.)
- What path did the smoke take as it moved over the hot surface? (It slowly spread out and upward.)
- What path did the smoke take as it moved over the ice and on toward the candle? (It stayed close to the pan's surface and then rose up over the candle.)

EARTH SCIENCE

- Do you think a force is acting on the smoke as it moves above the warm or cold surfaces? (A force is something that causes a change in shape or a change in motion of a body. It is easy to see the change in shape; this also shows the change in motion.)
- What name could you give this change of motion? Why do you think it occurs? (Wind is caused by the uneven heating within the observation box. Teacher should elaborate on this concept of local and global winds.)

Why is the idea important for personal development?

- How would the absence of wind affect your life? Do you think life would be changed in any way if there never was a wind?
- How does the presence of wind affect you personally? How do you think strong winds would affect you if you lived in a coastal city?

Why is the idea important for science-technology-society?

- How has wind power become a source of energy in some regions of the world? How has this harnessing of the wind changed the lives of people living there?
- How has knowledge of air mass saved lives? In what circumstances?

Why is the idea important for academic growth?

- The students will develop process skills needed to identify moving air as wind.
- The students will be able to explain the movement of air over surfaces of varying temperatures and apply this knowledge to explain why wind occurs.

Why is the idea important for career awareness?

- How will knowledge of wind behavior assist a pilot in flight? What kind of training must a pilot undergo in order to understand how wind behaves? Can just anyone become a pilot? What skills do you think are necessary to become a successful pilot?
- Read a book on Amelia Earhart. What do you think happened to her when she vanished in her plane over the Pacific Ocean?
- Can you list any other occupations in which knowledge of wind and its behavior is necessary?

4. EVALUATION: How will the students show what they have learned?

Upon completing these activities the students will be able to

- compare cloud patterns of different areas when given satellite photographs,
- look at an aerial map of a coastal state and be able to predict where most of the clouds will form,
- demonstrate the ability to read a barometer,
- explain the difference in barometric readings over land and sea,
- explain why you would expect the air to be warmer in the daytime over land than sea,
- engage in a reflective discussion on the cause of wind and its importance.

Appendixes

Curriculum Projects

The National Science Foundation and other organizations and agencies supported many science curriculum projects during the sixties and seventies. Many were innovative and presented new and different approaches to science education. Some have endured, while others are no longer available in print. In addition, the educational reform movement has brought new curricula into existence. Below you will find a list of the notable projects complete with short descriptions.

Projects marked with * are currently in development. The date following the asterisk indicates the anticipated year of completion.

Activities to Integrate Mathematics and Science (AIMS)
P.O. Box 7766, Fresno, CA 93747; (209) 291-1766

Activities to Integrate Mathematics and Science publishes elementary and middle school integrated curriculum materials (K–9) that have been produced and tested by teachers. It conducts national leadership training and local workshops and seminars.

Topics include Down to Earth, Fall into Math and Science, Floaters and Sinkers, From Head to Toe, Fun with Foods, Glide into Winter with Math and Science, Hardhatting in a Geoworld, Jawbreakers and Heart Thumpers, Math + Science - A Solution, Our Wonderful World, Out of this World, Overhead and Underfoot, Pieces and Patterns, Popping with Power, Primarily Bears, Seasoning Math and Science: Spring and Summer, Seasoning Math and Science: Fall & Winter, The Sky's the Limit!, Spring into Math & Science, and Water, Precious Water.

AIMS was developed through Fresno Pacific College as an outgrowth of a National Science Foundation project.

Arkansas's Project MAST: Mathematics and Science Together (*93)
University of Arkansas, College of Education, Gifted Programs, 2801 South University, Little Rock, AR 72204; (501) 569-3410

This project uses existing materials along with materials developed for the project to introduce integrated science and mathematics instruction in grades 2–6. The program emphasizes critical thinking and utilizes instructional technology. Intensive teacher training focuses on content knowledge and familiarity with the instructional materials.

Bottle Biology
Department of Plant Physiology, University of Wisconsin–Madison, 1630 Linden Drive, Madison, WI 53706; (608) 263-5645

This booklet contains suggestions for activities that use a variety of throwaway containers, primarily plastic beverage bottles, in constructing experiments and life science exploration. Activities can be adapted to all K–12 instructional levels.

Chemical Education for Public Understanding (CEPUP)
Lawrence Hall of Science, University of California, Berkeley, CA 94720; (510) 642-8718

The Chemical Education for Public Understanding project produces modular materials stressing chemical concepts and processes associated with current societal issues and risk assessment. The hands-on orientation addresses topics such as pollution, household chemicals, toxic and municipal waste, and chemical in foods. The modules contain student materials and laboratory kits for grades 6–8.

595

Distributors include Addison-Wesley Publishing Company; Lab-Aids, Inc.; Fisher Scientific; Science Kit and Boreal Laboratories; and Sargent-Welsh Scientific Company.

Conceptually Oriented Program in Elementary Science (COPES)

No longer active: materials available on *Science Helper, K–8*

COPES is a general K–6 science program developed around five major conceptual schemes: structural units of the universe, interaction and change, conservation of energy, degradation of energy, and a statistical view of nature.

Conservation for Children

6560 Hanover Drive, San Jose, CA 95129; (408) 725-8376

Conservation for Children consists of activities designed to educate students in grades 1–6 about basic concepts of ecology and conservation through integration with mathematics, social studies, and language arts. The group publishes a curriculum guide and conducts staff development programs.

Curriculum in Human Biology for the Middle Grades (*92)

Stanford University, School of Education, Stanford, CA 94305-3096; (415) 723-4662

This two-year human biology course is designed for seventh- and eighth-grade students. The course includes human physiology, anthropology, psychology, and sociology topics that are relevant to adolescent maturation. Videotapes are being developed to provide teachers with background for the print materials. Summer institutes will be offered for teachers interested in more assistance with course content.

Denver Audubon Society's Education Project

Denver Audubon Society, 975 Grant Street, Denver, CO 80203; (303) 860-1476

The materials train volunteers to work with small groups of children from a variety of socioeconomic backgrounds. They explore, study, and participate in hands-on experiences with plants and animals that grow in surrounding neighborhoods. The handbook is designed to assist organizations developing similar programs.

Developmental Approaches in Science and Health (DASH)

University of Hawaii, Manoa, College of Education, 1776 University Avenue, Honolulu, HI 96822; (808) 956-6918

This program provides sequential, integrated curricula in science, health, and technology for students in grades K–6. It also offers alternative instructional strategies for teaching a heterogeneous population; its instructional materials require minimal preparation times and are easy to use and to organize. Concepts in biology, physical and earth science, and applications in health and technology are taught through practical and applied situations.

Eco-Inquiry

New York Botanical Garden, Institute of Ecosystem Studies, Box AB, Millbrook, NY 12545-0129; (914) 667-5976

This ecological curriculum features an emphasis on the conceptual underpinnings of ecological literacy (nutrient cycling and energy flow); commitment to demystifying the practices of scientists; and the development of students' inquiry skills and dispositions through modeling the scientific methods.

Eighteenth-Century Electricity Kit

The Bakken, 3537 Zenith Avenue South, Minneapolis, MN 55416; (612) 927-6508

These materials use depictions and recreations of eighteenth-century electricity experiments to promote

better understanding of physics. They incorporate historical information and can be easily integrated into existing curricula. They were developed for grades 7–12. The kits include laboratory kits, teacher materials, and informational videos.

Distributor: Sargent-Welch Scientific Company

Elementary School Science and Health

Biological Science Curriculum Study, 830 North Tejon, Suite 405, Colorado Springs, CO 80903; (719) 578-1136

This K–6 program divides instructional units among life, health, earth, and physical sciences. Students learn science content and process skills as well as social skills, problem solving, decision making, and use of technology.

Distributor: Kendall/Hunt Publishing Company

Elementary Science Study (ESS)

Education Development Center, Inc., Newton, MA 02160; (617) 969-7100

Several modules may be purchased from Delta Education; some activities are available on *Science Helper K–8*.

The Elementary Science Study consists of fifty-six hands-on units that can be used as a complete curriculum or as resource units in a general elementary curriculum. They were extensively revised for commercial use. Revised copies are available through Educational Resource Information Center and Delta Education.

Units include Animal Activity; Animals in the Classroom; Attribute Games and Problems; Balloons and Gases; Behavior of Mealworms; Batteries and Bulbs; Batteries and Bulbs II; Bones; Brine Shrimp; Budding Twigs; Butterflies; Changes; Clay Boats; Colored Solutions; Crayfish; Daytime Astronomy; Drops, Streams, and Containers; Earthworms; Eggs and Tadpoles; Gases and "Airs"; Geo Blocks; Growing Seeds; Heating and Cooling; Ice Cubes; Kitchen Physics; Life of Beans and Peas; Light and Shadows; Mapping; Match and Measure; Microgardening; Mirror Cards; Mobiles; Mosquitoes; Musical Instrument Recipe Book; Mystery Powders; Optics; Pattern Blocks; Peas and Particles; Pendulums; Pond Water; Primary Balancing; Printing; Rocks and Charts; Sand; Senior Balancing; Sink or Float; Small Things; Spinning Tables; Starting from Seeds; Stream Tables; Structures; Tracks; Water Flow; Where is the Moon?; and Whistles and Strings.

Explorations in Middle School Science (*93)

Jostens Learning Corporation, 6170 Cornerstone Court East 5300, San Diego, CA 92121-3710; (619) 391-9900

This computer-based program will provide ninety computer lessons in life, earth, and physical science for students in grades 6–9. The heart of each lesson will be a computer-simulated laboratory to improve student achievement, critical thinking, communications and scientific process skills, and attitudes about science. Extension activities provide hands-on learning. The lessons, designed for a networked system, will use on-line tools.

Explorations in Science

Roy Beven, Jostens Learning Corporation, 6170 Cornerstone Court East, San Diego, CA 92121; (800) 521-8538 x6372

Explorations in Science provides student lessons in physical, life, and earth science on a CD-ROM and local-area computer network (IBM, Mac, Apple IIGS) for grades 6–9. Computer-simulated laboratories and hands-on activities guide students in acquiring scientific concepts and developing critical-thinking skills. Computer laboratories allow

students to conduct experimental activities in physical, earth, and life science that are too dangerous, too difficult, or too time consuming to be done in the classroom.

Foundation and Challenges to Encourage Technology-based Science (FACETS)

American Chemical Society, 1155 16th Street NW, Washington, DC 20036; (202) 872-6179

This two-year curriculum uses a balanced treatment of science, technology, and society in a hands-on and cooperative learning approach. Topics are studied in the context of problems relevant to middle school students' lives. There is a teacher/administrator training component and a newsletter to network teachers and students using the materials.

Foundational Approaches in Science Teaching (FAST)

Curriculum Research and Development Group, University of Hawaii, 1776 University Avenue, Room UHS 2-202, Honolulu, HI 96822; (808) 948-7863

Foundational Approaches in Science Teaching uses laboratory and field activities to engage students in investigations of physical science, ecology, and relational study. Students use the knowledge gained in studying the environment to develop concepts related to technology, resource management, and conservation. Designed for use in grades 6–8.

Full Option Science System (FOSS)

Lawrence Hall of Science, University of California, Berkeley, CA 94720; (510) 642-8941

Materials include student equipment kits, student print materials, and alternative assessment materials for grades 3–6. All materials are designed to engage students in actively con-

structing scientific concepts through hands-on laboratory activities. Several types of assessment tools are included as an integral component of instruction. Sixteen modules exist in four topic areas: life science, physical science, earth science, and scientific reasoning and technology.

Current distributor: Encyclopaedia Britannica Educational Corporation

Franklin Activity Kits

Franklin Institute Science Museum, Museum To Go Science Resource Center, 20th and the Parkway, Philadelphia, PA 19103; (215) 448-1297

Two to four kits for each grade level (K–6) provide students with hands-on learning experiences in physical, earth, and life sciences. Both the kits and the eight or ten exercises per kit can be used independently, allowing teachers maximum flexibility in their use, and enabling kits to reach larger numbers of students within a school. Teacher training is provided to increase confidence in the use of science materials.

Distributor: Science Kit and Boreal Laboratories

Great Explorations in Math and Science (GEMS)

Lawrence Hall of Science, University of California, Berkeley, CA 94720; (415) 642-7771

Great Explorations in Math and Science offers twenty-four publications that integrate mathematics with the life, earth, and physical sciences. The materials consist of teacher guides, presentation materials, and exhibit guides. Designed for K–12, the lessons are written for instructors with little knowledge of mathematics and science.

Topics include Animal Defenses; Animals in Action; Bubble-ology; Buzzing a Hive; Chemical Reactions; Convection: A Current Event; Crime

Lab Chemistry; Discovering Density; Earth, Moon, and Stars; Fingerprinting; Hide a Butterfly; Hot Water and Warm Homes from Sunlight; Liquid Explorations; The "Magic" of Electricity; Mapping Animal Movements; Mapping Fish Habitats; More than Magnifiers; Oobleck: What Do Scientists Do?; Paper Towel Testing; QUIDICE; Shapes, Loops, and Images; Solids, Liquids, and Gases; Vitamin C Testing; and The Wizard's Lab.

GrowLab

National Gardening Association, 180 Flynn Avenue, Burlington, VT 05401; (802) 863-1308

These materials utilize indoor gardening as a vehicle for teaching life science and engaging students in scientific inquiry. A teacher network provides resources for connecting schools to community partners and other educators who are using the materials nationwide. Designed for K–8, the materials include teacher resource books, seed kits, planter equipment, posters, a newsletter, the teacher network, and informational videos.

Hands-on Elementary Science

Education Department, Hood College, Frederick, MD 21701; (301) 663-3131

The focus of the Hands-on Elementary Science series is on developing science process skills in grades 1–5. Materials include curriculum guides and materials kits.

Dissemination is supported through the National Diffusion Network.

Hands-on Science

Hands-on Science Outreach, Inc., 4910 Macon Road, Rockville, MD 20852; (301) 460-5922

Thematically organized materials provide recreational activities in science for use in after-school settings. The kits are organized around three themes: structure and change, patterns, and energy. Required leader training sessions facilitate effective discovery of science by participants at a wide range of ages. Consumable kits promote ownership and mastery of scientific concepts by participants, especially those from economically disadvantaged backgrounds.

Health Activities Project (HAP)

Lawrence Hall of Science, University of California, Berkeley, CA 94702; (415) 642-4193

This project provides elementary students with activities and information relevant to health and safety in their daily lives.

Topics include Action/Reaction; Balance in Movement; Breathing Fitness; Consumer Health Decisions; Environmental Health and Safety; Flexibility and Strength; Growth Trends; Heart Fitness; Nutritional/Dental Health; Personal Health Decisions; Sight and Sound; and Skin Temperature.

Horizons Plus

Houston Museum of Natural Science, 1 Hermann Circle Drive, Houston, TX 77030; (713) 639-4632

Horizons Plus consists of kits, including teacher materials and hands-on activity files for grades 1–6, to be used as a vehicle for introducing science concepts and hands-on activities in the context of students' experiences. The storybook design encourages multidisciplinary instruction and science learning in settings outside of school.

Distributor: Silver Burdett and Ginn

Improving Middle School Science: A Collaborative Approach (*93)

Education Development Center, Inc., 55 Chapel Street, Newton, MA 02160; (617) 969-7100

This multidisciplinary project for seventh- and eighth-grade students is targeted to the needs of early adolescents in urban environments. Materials integrate life, physical, and earth science within the context of science, society, and technology problems. Materials also include informal science education strategies.

Improving Urban Elementary Science: A Collaborative Approach

Education Development Center, Inc., 55 Chapel Street, Newton, MA 02160; (617) 969-7100

Materials in this K–5 project are designed to improve urban students' abilities to think critically, use language, and solve problems using the natural world as an experimental base. Life, physical, and earth science are balanced, and activities are tied to the urban setting. These activities integrate science with the rest of the elementary curriculum, particularly mathematics and language arts.

Informal Science Study (ISS)

University of Houston, Room 450 Farish Hall, Houston, TX 77004; (713) 749-1692

Through Information Science Study, students investigate physical science concepts demonstrated in such familiar contexts such as amusement park rides, sports, and playground activities. Designed for children in grades 5–12, the units consist of materials, equipment, and teacher prompts.

Dissemination is through the National Diffusion Network.

Insights: A Hands-on Elementary Science Curriculum

Education Development Center, Inc., 55 Chapel Street, Newton, MA 02160; (800) 225-4276

This elementary science program (K–6) consists of thematic modules that can be used together as a complete curriculum or as individual modules in conjunction with existing programs. They focus on a limited number of concepts and themes in depth and breadth, reflecting a balance of life, physical, and earth sciences, as well as attitudes, skills, knowledge, and values. They support cultural, racial, and linguistic diversity and are designed to be especially responsive to the needs of the urban school.

JASON Mediterranean Expedition

The JASON Foundation for Education, 395 Totten Pond Road, Waltham, MA 02154; (617) 487-9995

Instructional materials address school science and social science relevant to on-line investigations undertaken by the underwater seeing-eye robot JASON. Materials also stand alone as thematic units about the exploration of sunken vessels in the Mediterranean Sea and the Great Lakes and about life in the Galapagos Islands. The project provides teacher guides, lesson plans, and posters to prepare students and teachers for the JASON downlink to museums.

Junior High/Middle School Life Science Program

Jefferson County Public School, Science Department, 1209 Quail Street, Lakewood, CO 80215; (303) 231-2351

This year-long curriculum in life science emphasizes the understanding and care of the human body as an alternative for educators seeking materials to improve their life science curricula or a resource for educators interested in integrating health topics into their existing life science course.

K–6 Project STARLAB

Young Astronaut Council, 1211 Connecticut Avenue NW, Suite 800, Washington, DC 20036; (202) 682-1084

This project consists of science-based learning environments in two K–6 inner-city schools in Washington, DC.

The project contains science and math-based curriculum materials, teacher kits, teacher training, and supplemental activities that can be integrated into all subject areas.

Learning About Plants (LEAP)

Cornell Plantations, Cornell University, One Plantations Road, Ithaca, NY 14850; (607) 255-3020

LEAP is an activity-based life science program for grades K–6. The project integrates classroom and field experiences, emphasizing conceptual development through exploration of plants. The materials consist of four units for each grade.

Life Lab Science Program

1156 High Street, Santa Cruz, CA 95064; (408) 476-7140

Life Lab uses the garden as the basis of this program for grades K–6. Using familiar materials, it provides activities that integrate physical, life, and earth sciences; students then use the knowledge gained to analyze situations involving values and ethical issues. An earlier project was entitled *The Growing Classroom* for grades K–3, and the program contains videodisks.

Distributor: Addison-Wesley Publishing Company for *The Growing Classroom* and Video Discovery for the *Life Lab Science Program.*

Marine Science Project: FOR SEA

17771 Fjord Drive, NE, Poulsbo, WA 98370; (206) 779-5549

This project is designed to supplement existing science programs in grades 2, 4, 6, 7–8, and 9–12.

FOR SEA is disseminated through the National Diffusion Network.

Microcomputer-Based Laboratory Tools

Technical Education Research Center, 2067 Massachusetts Avenue, Boston, MA 02140; (617) 547-0430

Sensors for various physical param-

eters are interfaced to a computer so that experimental data can be easily gathered and displayed, thus providing K–12 students with a greater opportunity to actively engage in experimentation. Typical detectors include those for motion, temperature, voltage, pH, light, and sound. Instructional materials are included.

Distributor: IBM Educational Systems

Middle School Life Science

Jefferson County Public Schools, Lakewood, CO 80212; (303) 231-2351

This full-year course in life science for grades 6–8 is organized around a series of learning cycles in which students engage in hands-on laboratory activities, apply the concepts learned to other situations, and form connections between this new knowledge and other areas of inquiry. In this program, concepts are learned through active participation, rather than activities merely illustrating concepts discussed in lecture. Its goal is to effectively engage students in the discovery of scientific knowledge through connections to language arts, mathematics, and social sciences.

Distributor: Kendall/Hunt Publishing Company

Model Elementary Science Program

District of Columbia Public Schools, 415 12th Street NW, Washington, DC 20004; (202) 767-8666

This urban project for typical students is designed for teaching based on one hour of science instruction each day, research-based procedure for inquiry teaching, and experiential learning. All students are engaged in science, and interrelationships between science and technology are stressed. In this project, science is a core activity frequently integrated with other content areas, particularly mathematics and language arts.

National Geographic Kids Network

National Geographic Society, Educational Services, Dept. 5397, Washington, DC 20036; (800) 368-2728

Participating students collect scientific data in their home environments and feed it into a nationwide electronic network, facilitating the discovery of scientific concepts on a national and global scale. Students communicate with other students and practicing scientists across the country. For Apple IIGS, IBM, and Mac.

Study units include Hello, Acid Rain, and Weather.

National SERIES Project

National Series Project, 300 Lakeside Drive, Oakland, CA 94612; (510) 987-0119

High school students lead younger children (ages 9–12) in the discovery of science. Trained by adult mentors, teens guide younger students through six scientific units, addressing such concepts as chemistry and the environment, agriculture, and recycling. Each unit culminates in a community service project, giving students opportunities to apply acquired knowledge to real problems in their own communities.

National Urban League Preschool Science Collaborative

National Urban League, New York, NY 10021; (212) 310-9214

This project consists of physical science activities for preschool children and provides training for parents and teachers of this age group. Materials include a center-based science activities manual, an activities booklet for use by parents, and play areas for science explorations. A promotional videotape highlights various parts of the training and promotes use of the materials.

Operation SMART

Operation SMART, 2336 Kahn Street, Port Townsend, WA 98368; (206) 385-7585

This program of out-of-school activities emphasizes hands-on experiences in math, science, and technology for girls ages 6–18. Its activities are aimed at combating existing barriers to participation in science and mathematics by girls through the creation of positive environments for learning, special staff awareness training, and bombardment of girls with information about careers and educational opportunities not traditionally promoted among women.

Outdoor Biology Instructional Strategies (OBIS)

Lawrence Hall of Science, University of California, Berkeley, CA 94720; (415) 642-4193

OBIS consists of ninety-seven modules for students in grades 3–10. The out-of-school environment is used to increase environmental awareness through nontraditional activities such as games, crafts, and experiments. Examples: Ants, Beach Zonation, Creepers and Climbers, Fly a Leaf, Metric Capers, and Roots and Shoots.

Distributor: Delta Education

Project First Step (Science and Technology Education Program) (*93)

U.S. Space Foundation, 1551 Vapor Trail, Colorado Springs, CO 80916; (719) 550-1414

This three-year curriculum for grades 6, 7, and 8 will features hands-on inquiry learning; use of space and aviation technologies to motivate students to study life, earth, and physical sciences; concrete representations of abstract scientific concepts; and an approach that encourages gender equity and the participation of minorities and the disabled.

Project STARWALK

Lakeview Museum Planetarium, 1125 W. Lake Avenue, Peoria, IL 61614; (309) 686-6682

This National Diffusion Network-distributed program integrates field trips to a planetarium with classroom lessons about space concepts for grades 3 and 5. Materials include teacher management assistance and training materials.

Science Activities for the Visually Impaired/Science Activities for Learners with Physical Handicaps (SAVI/SELPH)

Lawrence Hall of Science, University of California, Berkeley, CA 94720; (415) 642-8941

SAVI/SELPH activities enable students with special needs to participate successfully in multisensory investigations of physical, life, and earth science. The nine modules work well in many environments and can be taught by teachers with limited science instruction experience.

Units are Communication, Environmental Energy, Environments, Kitchen Interactions, Magnetism and Electricity, Measurement, Mixtures and Solutions, Scientific Reasoning, and Structures of Life.

Science and Technology: Investigating Human Diversity (*93)

Biological Sciences Curriculum Study, 830 North Tejon, Suite 405, Colorado Springs, CO 80903; (719) 578-1136

This three-year activity-based program is available for students in grades 5–9. The program continues the K–6 materials and focuses on the specific developmental needs of the early adolescent. It also encourages the participation of female, minority, and handicapped students; emphasizes reasoning and critical thinking; illustrates careers; and introduces the science, technology, and society theme.

Science and Technology for Children (STC)

National Science Resources Center, Arts and Industries Building, Room 1201, Smithsonian Institution, Washington, DC 20560; (202) 357-2555

The National Science Resources Center provides a four-year elementary science curriculum for grades 1–6 in the areas of physical, life, and earth science. The twenty-four hands-on science teaching units focus on important age-appropriate concepts and skills. The units link science with other subjects including mathematics, language arts, social studies, and art. Each unit includes a teacher's guide, a classroom set of student activity books, a kit of equipment and materials, and an annotated list of science trade books, audiovisual materials, and computer software that can be used to supplement the unit.

Distributor: Carolina Biological Supply Company

Science—A Process Approach (SAPA/SAPA II)

American Association for the Advancement of Science, Washington, DC; 1333 H Street NW, Washington, DC 20005; (202) 326-6400

Science—A Process Approach (SAPA), produced by the National Science Foundation during the sixties, focuses heavily on the processes of science rather than on concepts. In both versions, activities form a sequential K–6 program in which mastery of specific skills is predicated upon the accumulation of experience.

Distributor: Activities are currently available on *Science Helper K–8* or as revisions from Delta Education.

Science Curriculum Improvement Study (3 versions) (SCIS/SCISII/SCIIS)

Lawrence Hall of Science, University of California, Berkeley, CA 94720; (415) 642-8718

SCIS, in all three versions, focuses on concepts and processes of science for grades K–6. Investigations in physical and life science include exploration, interpretation, and application skills.

SCIS: Beginnings; Communities; Ecosystems; Energy Sources; Environments; Interaction and Systems; Life Cycles; Material Objects; Models: Electric and Magnetic Interactions; Organisms; Populations; Relative Position and Motion; Subsystems and Variables.

SCIS II: Communities; Ecosystems; Energy Sources; Environments; Interaction and Systems; Life Cycles; Material Objects; Modeling Systems; Organisms; Populations; Measurement, Motion, and Change; Subsystems and Variables.

SCIIS/85: Beginnings; Communities; Ecosystems; Energy Sources; Environments; Interaction and Systems; Life Cycles; Material Objects; Scientific Theories; Organisms; Populations; Relative Position and Motion; Subsystems and Variables.

Distributor: Units available on *Science Helper K–8*. All three versions are available through Delta Education.

Science for Life and Living: Integrating Science, Technology, and Health

Biological Sciences Curriculum Study, 830 North Tejon, Suite 405, Colorado Springs, CO 80903; (719) 578-1136

This program is evenly divided among the life, health, earth, and physical science. Students learn science content and process skills as well as social skills, problem solving, decision making, and use of technology. Supplementary activities integrate reading, language arts, and mathematics.

Distributor: Kendall/Hunt Publishing Company.

Science Helper K–8

Room 302, Norman Hall, University of Florida, Gainesville, FL 32607; (904) 392-0761

The University of Florida has produced *Science Helper K–8*, a CD-ROM database that provides access to materials developed by the major National Science Foundation curriculum projects of the sixties and seventies. Excerpts from the actual programs are indexed by grade, subject, skill, keyword, and content. A search results in the on-screen image of a page of the document and can be printed. Curriculum projects included are COPES—Conceptually Oriented Program for Elementary Science; ESS—Elementary Science Study (partial); SAPA: Science—A Process Approach; SCIS—Science Curriculum Improvement Study; USMES—Unified Science and Mathematics for Elementary School (partial).

ScienceVision

Interactive Media Science Project, 205 Carothers Hall, Florida State University, Tallahassee, FL 32306; (904) 644-8422

These materials utilize interactive videodisks to provide students (grades 6–8) with the tools and information necessary to solve extended problems in life science, earth and space science, and physical science that are of real-world scope and significance. Videodisks allow students to visit locations, listen to experts, collect data, and reach conclusions without leaving the classroom. Materials include interactive videodisks, computer software (Apple IIGS and Mac), student log books, teacher's guides, and laboratory activities.

Distributor: Houghton-Mifflin Company

The Second Voyage of the *Mimi*

Wings for Learning, 1600 Green Hill Road, P.O. Box 660002, Scotts Valley, CA 95067-0002

A voyage into ancient Mayan civilization serves as a vehicle for teaching interdisciplinary science and mathematics. Twelve 15-minute documentary-format episodes, accompanied by student materials and hands-on activities, engage students in the discovery of mathematics and science. Software learning modules, whose themes are derived from the video series, offer flexible learning opportunities in either science or mathematics to individuals or small groups of students.

Self Help Elementary Level Science (SHELS)

Florida State University, Gainesville, FL 32611; (904) 392-0761

These are videotapes with print materials to be used as a form of staff development for teachers and administrators. The tapes include topics such as strategies for dealing with obstacles to teaching elementary science and techniques for research-based teaching.

TLTG Physical Science / TLTG Math for Science

Texas Learning Technology Group, P.O. Box 2974, Austin, TX 78768-2974; (512) 467-0222

This two-semester physical science course is delivered primarily through interactive videodisk and includes courseware, teacher resources, laboratory exercises, classroom management, testing systems, and a computer tutorial for science-related

mathematics for grades 8–10. This full-year physical science course includes units in chemistry, physics, and energy resources of the future.

Distributor: Glencoe Corporation

Terracorps

Upland Unified School District, 904 West 9th Street, P.O. Box 1239, Upland, CA 91786; (714) 981-1603

Ecological science materials have been developed for students in grades 6–8; they feature real-life applications and classroom activities. The thirty-six modules represent life, earth, and physical science topics. The units are arranged into three levels of proficiency, each with increasing skills and a higher level of measurement, concept, and knowledge. A videotape teaching training component is available.

T/S/M (Technology/Science/ Mathematics) Integration Activities

Virginia Polytechnic Institute and State University, 144 Smyth Hall, Blacksburg, VA 24061-0432; (703) 231-6480

These materials for grades 6–9 use design-under-constraint activities, in which students create their own solutions to problems given a fixed set of resources and conditions, to teach concepts in science, mathematics, and technology. Through activities such as trying to harness wind power with any apparatus constructed from provided materials, students create their own learning experiences. Because these problems do not have a single correct answer, each solution offers some opportunity for learning. While these materials require the facilities of a technology or industrial arts classroom, they are designed to be implemented through technology, science, or mathematics courses.

Unified Science and Mathematics for Elementary Schools

Education Development Center, Inc., Newton, MA 02160; (617) 969-7100

Currently inactive: materials can be obtained from ERIC. Partial inclusion has been made on *Science Helper K–8*.

This project provides a series of twenty-three guides for use in grades K–8. The units include a beginning challenge that is investigated by the students through project activity cards and background papers. Teacher instructions are limited as learning is developed through students' independent activities.

Topics include Advertising, Bicycle Transportation, Burglar Alarm Design, Classroom Design, Classroom Management, Consumer Research—Product Testing, Describing People, Designing for Human Proportions, Dice Design, Electromagnet Device Design, Growing Plants, Lunch Lines, Manufacturing, Orientation, Pedestrian Crossings, Play Area Design and Use, School Zoo, Soft Drink Design, Traffic Flow, USMES Design Lab Manual, The USMES Guide, Ways to Learn/ Teach, and Weather Predictions.

Wisconsin Fast Plants

Wisconsin Fast Plants Program, Department of Plant Pathology, University of Wisconsin–Madison, 1630 Linden Drive, Madison, WI 53706; (608) 263-2634

These rapid-cycling cabbage-related plants facilitate the study of plant biology and genetics at all levels (K–college). The manual contains suggested activities and resources for teachers using Fast Plants. Kits include seeds and instruction in addition to a teacher resource manual.

Distributor: Carolina Biological Supply Company

State Education Agencies

Each state has an agency that oversees the educational structure within the state. Below is a listing of these agencies.

Alabama
Alabama State Department of Education
Gordon Persons Building
Montgomery, Alabama 36130

Alaska
Alaska State Department of Education
P.O. Box F
Juneau, Alaska 99811

Arizona
Arizona Department of Education
1535 West Jefferson Street
Phoenix, Arizona 85007

Arkansas
Arkansas Department of Education
1535 West Jefferson Street
4 State Capitol Mall
Little Rock, Arkansas 72201

Bureau of Indian Affairs
Department of Interior, BIA
1849 C Street NW
Mail Stop 3525, Code 521
MIBWashington, DC 20240

California
State Department of Education
721 Capitol Mall, 3rd Floor
Sacramento, California 95814

Colorado
Colorado Department of Education
201 East Colfax Avenue
Denver, Colorado 80203

Connecticut
State Department of Education
P.O. Box 2219, Room 369
Hartford, Connecticut 06145

Delaware
State Department of Public Instruction
Townsend Building
P.O. Box 1402
Dover, Delaware 19903

District of Columbia
Education Program
D.C. Public Schools
415 12th Street NW, Room 1004
Washington, DC 20004

Florida
Florida Department of Education
Florida Education Center, Suite 522
Tallahassee, Florida 32399

Georgia
Georgia Department of Education
1862 Twin Towers East
Atlanta, Georgia 30334

Hawaii
Education Program
189 Lunalilo Home Road, 2nd Floor
Honolulu, Hawaii 96825

Idaho
Idaho Department of Education
Len B. Jordan Office Building
Boise, Idaho 83720

Illinois
Illinois State Board of Education
100 North First Street
Springfield, Illinois 62777-0001

Indiana
Indiana Department of Education
229 State House
Indianapolis, Indiana 46204-2798

Iowa
Iowa Department of Education
Grimes State Office Building
Des Moines, Iowa 50319-0146

Kansas
Kansas Department of Education
120 East 10th Street
Topeka, Kansas 66612-1103

Kentucky
Kentucky Department of Education
Capitol Plaza Tower, 17th Floor
Frankfort, Kentucky 40601

Louisiana
State Department of Education
P.O. Box 94064
Baton Rouge, Louisiana 70804-9064

Maine
Maine State Department of Education
State House Station #23
Augusta, Maine 04333

Maryland
Maryland State Department of Education
200 West Baltimore Street
Baltimore, Maryland 21201-2595

Massachusetts
Massachusetts Department of Education
1385 Hancock Street
Quincy, Massachusetts 02169

Michigan
Michigan Department of Education
P.O. Box 30008
Lansing, Michigan 48909

Minnesota
Minnesota Department of
Education
Capitol Square Building, Room 922
St. Paul, Minnesota 55101

Mississippi
State Department of Education
Walter Sillers Building, Suite 501
P.O. Box 771
Jackson, Mississippi 39205-0771

Missouri
Department of Education
Department of Elementary and
Secondary Education
P.O. Box 480
Jefferson, Missouri 65102

Montana
Office of Public Instruction
State Capitol Building
Helena, Montana 59620

Nebraska
Nebraska Department of Education
P.O. Box 84987
301 Centennial Mall South
Lincoln, Nebraska 68509

Nevada
Nevada Department of Education
Capitol Complex
Carson City, Nevada 89710

New Hampshire
New Hampshire Department of
Education
101 Pleasant Street
Concord, New Hampshire 03301

New Jersey
New Jersey Department of
Education
Division of General Academic
Education
CN 500
Trenton, New Jersey 08625-0500

New Mexico
State Department of Education
300 Don Gaspar Street
Santa Fe, New Mexico 87501-2786

New York
New York State Education
Department
Bureau of Professional Career
Opportunity Programs
Empire State Plaza
Cultural Education Center,
Room 5C64
Albany, New York 12230

North Carolina
Department of Public Instruction
116 West Edenton Street
Raleigh, North Carolina 27603-1712

North Dakota
Department of Public Instruction
State Capitol
Bismark, ND 58505

Ohio
Ohio Department of Education
65 South Front Street
Columbus, Ohio 43266-0308

Oklahoma
State Department of Education
2500 North Lincoln Boulevard
Oklahoma City, Oklahoma 73105

Oregon
Oregon Department of Education
700 Pringle Parkway, S.E.
Salem, Oregon 97310

Pennsylvania
Pennsylvania Department of
Education
333 Market Street, 7th Floor
Harrisburg, Pennsylvania 17126-
0333

Puerto Rico
Office of Education
Office 809
Department of Education
Hato Rey, Puerto Rico 00919

Rhode Island
Rhode Island Department of
Education
22 Hayes Street
Providence, Rhode Island 02908

South Carolina
South Carolina Department of
Education
Curriculum Section
801 Rutledge Building
Columbia, South Carolina 29201

South Dakota
Division of Education
700 Governors Drive
Pierre, South Dakota 57501-2291

Tennessee
Tennessee Department of
Education
4th Floor Northwing
Cordell Hull Building
Nashville, Tennessee 37243-0388

Texas
Texas Education Agency
1701 N. Congress
Austin, Texas 78701

Utah
Utah Department of Education
250 East 500 South
Salt Lake City, Utah 84111

Vermont
Vermont State Department of
Education
120 State Street
Montpelier, Vermont 05602

Virginia
Virginia Department of Education
P.O. Box 6Q
Richmond, Virginia 23216-2060

Washington
Washington Department of
Education
P.O. Box 47200
Old Capitol Building, FG-11
Olympia, Washington 98504

West Virginia
West Virginia Department of
Education
1900 Kanawha Blvd., East, Room
B-252
Charleston, West Virginia 25305

Wisconsin
Department of Public Instruction
125 South Webster Street
P.O. Box 7841
Madison, Wisconsin 53707-7841

Wyoming
State Department of Education
241 Hathaway Building
Cheyenne, Wyoming 82002-0050

APPENDIX C

Organizations That Support Reform in Science Education

**American Association for the
Advancement of Science (AAAS)**
1333 H Street NW, Washington, DC
20005; (202) 326-6400

**American Business Conference
(ABC)**
1730 K Street NW, Suite 1200,
Washington, DC 20006; (202)
822-9300

**American Society for Training and
Development (ASTD)**
1630 Duke Street, Box 1443,
Alexandria, VA 22313; (703) 683-
8100

The Business Council
888 Seventeenth Street NW,
Washington, DC 20006; (202)
298-7650

The Business Roundtable (BRT)
200 Park Avenue, New York, NY
10166; (212) 682-6370

**Center for Leadership in School
Reform**
950 Breckenridge Lane, Suite 200,
Louisville, KY 40207; (502) 895-
1942

**Committee for Economic
Development (CED)**
477 Madison Avenue, New York,
NY 10022; (212) 688-2063

The Conference Board
845 Third Avenue, New York, NY
10022; (212) 759-0900

Council for Aid to Education, Inc.
51 Madison Avenue, Suite 2200,

New York, NY 10010; (212) 689-
4200

Educate America
310 South Street, Morristown, NJ
07960; (201) 285-5200

**National Alliance of Business—
Center for Excellence in Education**
1201 New York Avenue NW, Suite
700, Washington, DC 20005;
(202) 289-2925

**National Assessment of
Educational Progress (NAEP)**
P.O. Box 6710, Princeton, NJ 08541-
6710; (609) 734-1624

**National Association of Partners
in Education (NAPE)**
209 Madison Street, Alexandria, VA
22314; (703) 836-4880

National Board for Professional Teaching Standards
300 River Place, Suite 3600, Detroit, MI 48207; (313) 259-0830

National Center on Education and the Economy
39 State Street, Suite 500, Rochester, NY 14614; (716) 546-7620

National Center for the Improvement of Science Teaching and Learning (The NETWORK, Inc.)
290 South Main Street, Andover, MA 01810; (617) 470-1080.

National Center for Science Teaching and Learning (NCSTL)
The Ohio State University, Research Center, 1314 Kinnear Road, Columbus, OH 43212; (614) 292-3339.

National Education Goals Panel
1850 M Street NW, Suite 270, Washington, DC 20036; (202) 632-0952

National Science Foundation (NSF)
1800 G Street NW, Washington, DC 20550; (202) 357-7078

National Energy Foundation (NEF)
5160 Wiley Post Way, Suite 200, Salt Lake City, UT 84116; (801) 539-1406

National Science Resources Center (NSRC)
Arts and Industries Building, Room 1201, Smithsonian Institution, Washington, DC 20560; (202) 357-2555

National School Boards Association (NSBA)
1680 Duke Street, Alexandria, VA 22314; (703) 838-6722

Public Education Fund Network
601 13th Street NW, Suite 370 South, Washington, DC 20005-3808; (202) 628-7460

Secretary's Commission on Achieving Necessary Skills (SCANS)
U.S. Department of Labor, 200 Constitution Avenue NW, Washington, DC 20210; (800) 788-SKIL

Triangle Coalition for Science and Technology Education
5112 Berwyn Road, 3d Floor, College Park, MD 20740; (301) 220-0870

United States Chamber of Commerce—Center for Workforce Preparation and Quality Education
1615 H Street NW, Washington, DC 20062; (202) 463-5525

Resource Organizations

American Association of Physics Teachers (AAPT)
5112 Berwyn Road, 2d Floor, College Park, MD 20740; (301) 345-4200

The American Association of Physics Teachers offers professional publications, publications for high school students, a periodic newsletter for students and teachers, activities for students and teachers, curriculum development, and career information.

American Astronomical Society
University of Texas at Austin, Austin, TX 78712-1083; (512) 471-1083

The American Astronomical Society sponsors special meetings for precollege science teachers that are held in conjunction with the association's yearly professional conference. The program introduces teachers to modern research in astronomy through special lectures and activities.

American Chemical Society (ACS)
1155 16th Street NW, Washington, DC 20036; (202) 872-6179

The American Chemical Society resources include *Chem Matters,* a publication for high school teachers and students, *Wonder-Science* for elementary students and their parents, professional publications, curriculum development, and career information.

American Geological Institute (AGI)

National Center for Earth Science Education, 4220 King Street, Alexandria, VA 22302; (703) 379-2480

The American Geological Institute focuses on student and teacher activities, curriculum development, professional publications, and newsletters.

American Geophysical Union

2000 Florida Avenue NW, Washington, DC 20009; (202) 462-6903

The American Geophysical Union promotes educational opportunities through its publications.

American Institute of Aeronautics and Astronautics

370 L'Enfant Promenade SW, Washington, DC 20024; (202) 646-7400

Student activity and career information is provided by the American Institute of Aeronautics and Astronautics.

American Institute of Biological Sciences (AIBS)

College of Natural Sciences, University of Northern Iowa, Cedar Falls, IA 50614-0181; (319) 273-2585

The American Institute of Biological Sciences offers student activities, career information, and professional publications.

American Institute of Chemical Engineers

345 East 47th Street, New York, NY 10017; (212) 705-7370

The American Institute of Chemical Engineers provides student programs and career information.

American Institute of Chemists

Northeast Missouri State University, Kirksville, MO 63701; (816) 785-4620

The American Institute of Chemists sustains teacher activities and professional publications.

American Institute of Physics

335 East 45th Street, New York, NY 10017; (212) 661-9404

The American Institute of Physics produces professional publications, newsletters for students and teachers, activities for students and teachers, curriculum development and career information.

American Meteorological Society

Department of Meteorology, University of Wisconsin, Madison, WI 53706; (608) 262-0776

The American Meteorological Society supports student career information and professional publications.

American Nature Study Society

Pocono Environmental Education Center, R.D.1, Box 268, Dingman's Ferry, PA 18328; (717) 828-2319

The educational products of the American Nature Study Society are student and teacher activities and newsletters.

American Nuclear Society

Department of Mechanical and Energy Engineering, University of Lowell, Lowell, MA 01854; (508) 452-5000

The American Nuclear Society dispenses professional publications, a newsletter for students and teachers, and career information and holds workshops for secondary science and social studies teachers on nuclear technology.

American Physical Society

335 East 45th Street, New York, NY 10017; (212) 682-7341

The American Physical Society provides programs for physics teachers, newsletters, and career information.

American Society for Cell Biology (ASCB)

9650 Rockville Pike, Bethesda, MD 20814; (301) 530-7153

ASCB offers a teacher research fellowship for secondary science teachers through summer research work in the laboratories of ASCB for eight to ten weeks. The purpose of the program is to give science teachers the opportunity to participate in a hands-on research experience in cell biology.

American Society for Engineering Education

11 DuPont Circle #200, Washington, DC 20036; (202) 293-7080

Professional publications, newsletters, and career information can be obtained from the American Society for Engineering Education.

American Society for Microbiology

1913 Eye Street NW, Washington, DC 20006; (202) 833-9680

Student and teacher activities and newsletters are supported by the American Society for Microbiology.

Association for the Education of Teachers in Science (AETS)

5040 Haley Center, Auburn University, Auburn, AL 36849-5212; (205) 844-5785

This association makes presentations of interest to teachers as well as teacher educators at the annual National Science Teachers Association meeting. The presentations include demonstrations, panel discussions, and contributed papers.

Association of Science-Technology Centers
1025 Vermont Avenue NW, Suite 500, Washington, DC 20005-3516; (202) 783-7200

Members of this association offer a variety of programs for science and mathematics teachers. These in-service programs include teacher camp-ins, afternoon courses, and summer institutes. Contact your local center for additional offerings.

Association for Supervision and Curriculum Development (ASCD)
125 North West Street, Alexandria, VA 22314-2798; (703) 549-9110

The Association for Supervision and Curriculum Development recognizes and evaluates educational issues. This organization conducts conferences, publishes newsletters, and provides professional growth opportunities.

Association for Women In Science (AWIS)
2401 Virginia Avenue NW, No. 303, Washington, DC 20037; (202) 833-2998

The Association for Women in Science dispenses career information for women.

Biological Science Curriculum Study (BSCS)
830 N. Tejon Street, Suite 405, Colorado Springs, CO 80903; (719) 578-1136

BSCS is active in the production of curriculum materials for grades K–12. See Appendix A for additional information.

Center for Excellence in Education
7710 Old Springhouse Road, Suite 100, McLean, VA 22102; (703) 448-9062

Lectures, mentor programs, and laboratory experiences for outstanding students and teachers are sustained by Center for Excellence in Education.

The Center for Teaching and Learning
University of North Dakota, Box 8158, University Station, Grand Forks, ND 58202; (701) 777-2674

The Center for Teaching and Learning produces educational monographs.

Coalition for Earth Science Education (CESE)
Geological Society of America, 3300 Penrose Place, P.O. Box 9140, Boulder, CO 80301; (303) 447-2020

CESE was established to promote communication among organizations interested in earth science education. More than thirty organizations have joined the Coalition.

Council for Elementary Science International (CESI)
Department of Curriculum and Instruction, 212 Townsend Hall, University of Missouri, Columbia, MO 65211; (314) 882-7247

The Council for Elementary Science International promotes and produces books related to elementary science teaching.

Council of State Science Supervisors (CSSS)
c/o Michael Lang, Arizona Department of Instruction; (602) 542-3577

This organization composed of state science consultants throughout the United States and its territories develops policy positions and shares information to be disseminated through state education agencies. Each consultant is capable of providing information on science education programs within his or her state. See Appendix B for a complete listing.

The Council of Interracial Books for Children
1841 Broadway, New York, NY 10023; (212) 757-5339

The Council of Interracial Books for Children provides brochures to assist in selection of racially unbiased reading for children.

Educational Products Information Exchange (EPIE)
P.O. Box 839, Water Mill, NY 11976; (516) 283-4922

Educational Products Information Exchange publishes *The Educational Software Selector (TESS)* and newsletters, *Epiegram* and *Microgram*.

Educational Resources Information Center (ERIC)
Educational Resources Information Centers distribute education-related literature published by the Government Printing Office and by other organizations not necessarily under the direction of the federal government. ERIC can be accessed through most libraries. ERIC has several clearinghouses, including:

ERIC Clearinghouse on Elementary and Early Childhood Education
University of Illinois, College of Education, 805 West Pennsylvania Ave., Urbana, IL 61801-4897

ERIC Clearinghouse on Handicapped and Gifted Children
Council for Exceptional Children, 1920 Association Drive, Reston, VA 22091-3660

ERIC Clearinghouse for Science, Mathematics, and Environmental Education
Ohio State University, 1200 Chambers Road, Room 310, Columbus, OH 43212-1792

ERIC Clearinghouse for Social Studies/Social Science Education
Indiana University Social Studies Development Center, 2805 East 10th Street, Suite 120, Bloomington, IN 47405-2373

Environmental Protection Agency (EPA)
Public Information Center and Library, 401 M Street SW, Washington, DC 20460; (202) 260-2090

The Environmental Protection Agency furnishes information and publications relating to environmental concerns.

Fermilab National Accelerator Laboratory Science Education Center
Fermilab MS 777, Box 500, Batavia, IL 60510; (708) 840-2031

The center provides assistance to schools and/or school districts by providing effective instructional materials and basic science content for educators; modeling effective teaching skills and methods; promoting and modeling the effective use of technology as it relates to science instruction; and providing high quality precollege science materials for educators in a collection of trade books, curriculum materials, videos, and other multimedia materials.

Foundation for Science and the Handicapped
West Virginia University, Morgantown, WV 26506-6057; (304) 293-5201

This foundation produces professional publications and newsletters relating to science and the disabled.

Girls Clubs of America, Inc.; Operation SMART
30 East 33rd Street, New York, NY 10016; (212) 689-3700

Career materials and programs designed to encourage girls and minorities in science, mathematics, and technology careers are sustained through the efforts of the Girls Clubs of America, Inc.

Harvard-Smithsonian Center for Astrophysics
Project STAR, 60 Garden Street, Cambridge, MA 02138; (617) 495-9798

The Harvard-Smithsonian Center for Astrophysics's Project STAR includes study modules, software, films, and teacher support materials relating to the role of science and research in astronomy.

International Technology Education Association (ITEA)
1914 Association Drive, Reston, VA 22901-1502; (703) 860-2100

ITEA serves as a clearinghouse for curriculum materials for technology education. The association conducts an annual conference, workshops, and symposia to advance ideas on teaching and learning technology.

Lawrence Hall of Science (LHS)
University of California, Berkeley, CA 94720; (510) 642-7771

The Lawrence Hall of Science has developed several series of materials related to science or the integration of science and mathematics for grades K–6. See Appendix B for curriculum examples.

Mid-Atlantic Equity Center
The American University, School of Education, 5010 Wisconsin Avenue NW, Washington, DC 20016; (202) 885-8517

The Mid-Atlantic Equity Center provides information and materials emphasizing race, sex, and national origin desegregation.

Minority High School Student Research Apprentice Program
National Center for Research Resources, National Institutes of Health, Westwood Building, Room 10A11, Bethesda, MD 20892; (301) 496-6743

This agency-sponsored program offers minority teachers or teachers who reach a significant number of minority students the opportunity to gain hands-on research experience, update their skills in modern research techniques, and broaden their scientific concepts through participation in a summer research project at a local university, health professional school, or research organization.

National Aeronautics and Space Administration (NASA)
NASA Headquarters, CODE XEE, Washington, DC 20546; (202) 453-8396

The National Aeronautics and Space Administration Education Division provides educational programs and materials for teachers and students from the elementary to the university level. See Appendix E for a complete listing of NASA educational centers.

National Association for Research in Science Teaching (NARST)
c/o Dr. William Holliday, 402 Teachers College, University of Cincinnati, Cincinnati, OH 45221; (513) 475-2335

NARST provides presentations on research findings at national and regional meetings of the National Science Teachers Association. These presentations include papers, panel discussions, workshops, and demonstrations on a variety of issues such as teaching science through reading and writing, collaborative learning, and assessment.

National Association for Science, Technology, and Society (NASTS)
The Pennsylvania State University, 128 Willard Building, University Park, PA 16802; (814) 865-9951

The National Association for Science, Technology, and Society conducts annual meetings and publishes newsletters and journals.

National Association of Biology Teachers (NABT)
11250 Roger Bacon Drive #19, Reston, VA 22090; (703) 471-1134

This national organization for biology teachers publishes activities for teachers and students, related journals, and convenes annual conferences.

National Association of Geology Teachers
1041 New Hampshire Street, P.O. Box 368, Lawrence, KS 66044; (913) 843-1234

The National Association of Geology Teachers produces activities for teacher use, newsletters, and career information.

National Audubon Society
613 Riversville Road, Greenwich, CT 06830; (203) 869-5272

The National Audubon Society publishes *Audubon Adventures,* software, and television specials for children and professional growth workshops for teachers.

National Association for the Professional Advancement of Black Chemists and Chemical Engineers
1265 Main Street, W-6, Waltham, MA 02254; (617) 725-2000

Professional publications, Adopt-A-School Program, and career information are sustained by the National Association for the Professional Advancement of Black Chemists and Chemical Engineers.

National Diffusion Network (NDN)
Office of Educational Research and Improvement, U.S. Department of Education, 555 New Jersey Avenue NW, Washington, DC 20208-1525; (202) 357-6134

The National Diffusion Network (NDN) is a system to identify and provide access to exemplary education programs nationwide. The Network provides a listing of programs and state coordinators.

National Earth Science Teachers Association (NESTA)
Department of Geological Sciences,

Michigan State University, East Lansing, MI 48824; (202) 328-5800

The National Earth Science Teachers Association offers activity ideas, background information, and slide sets for earth science.

National Oceanic and Atmospheric Administration (NOAA)
National Weather Service Office of Warning and Forecast, 8060 13th Street, Silver Spring, MD 20910; (301) 443-8910

The National Oceanic and Atmospheric Administration provides pamphlets, booklets, and other information about weather phenomena.

National Science Supervisors Association (NSSA)
Glastonbury Public Schools, 330 Hubbard Street, Glastonbury, CT 06033; (203) 633-5231

NSSA and its Leadership Institute for Science Education (LISE) subsidiary provide programs and publications to improve science education through leadership development. Included are summer leadership institutes, regional workshops, state training programs, directories, handbooks, and other resources.

National Science Teachers Association (NSTA)
1742 Connecticut Avenue NW, Washington, DC 20009; (202) 328-5800

This national professional organization for K–college science educators convenes regional and national conferences and publishes journals, including *Science and Children* (elementary), *Science Scope* (middle school) and *The Science Teacher* (high school). Additional publications can be ordered through its catalog.

National Wildlife Federation
1412 16th Street NW, Washington,

DC 20036; (202) 790-4360

The National Wildlife Federation produces curriculum materials and magazines, including *Ranger Rick* and *Naturescope.*

Native American Science Education Association (NAESA)
1333 H Street NW, Washington, DC 20005; (202) 371-8100

Curriculum materials for teachers and newsletters relating to Native American initiatives can be obtained from the Native American Science Education Association.

Optical Society of America
1816 Jefferson Place NW, Washington, DC 20036; (202) 233-8130

The Optical Society of America provides staff development activities for physics teachers at its annual professional conference.

Oak Ridge Institute of Science and Education (ORISE)
Science Engineering/Education Division, P.O. Box 117, Oak Ridge, TN 37831-0117; (615) 576-6220

ORISE offers a variety of teacher development programs for teachers of various grade levels. Many of the programs are interdisciplinary, combining various physical and life science with mathematics.

Office of Civilian Radioactive Waste Management (OCRWM) Information Center
P.O. Box 44375, Washington, DC 20026; (800-225-6972); in Washington, DC area 488-5513

OCRWM Information Center offers information related to the management of radioactive nuclear waste. The center maintains a toll-free information number Monday through Friday between the hours of 9:00 am and 7:00 pm ET. Information on the curriculum, *Science, Society, and America's Nuclear Waste,* and the national teleconference workshop is available.

Population Association of America

Center for Demographic Studies, U.S. Bureau of the Census, Building 3, Room 3081, Washington, DC 20233; (202) 429-0891

The Population Association of America offers professional publications, newsletters, and career information.

School Science and Mathematics Association (SSMA)

Bowling Green State University, 126 Life Sciences Building, Bowling Green, OH 43403; (419) 372-7393

Professional journals and newsletters are supplied by the School Science and Mathematics Association. This association convenes an annual national conference.

Smithsonian Institution

Arts and Industries Building, Room 1163, Washington, DC 20560; (202) 357-2425

The Smithsonian Institution sponsors educational programs and special events related to education. The National Science Resources Center is supported by Smithsonian Institution.

Society for Social Studies of Science

Department of Sociology, Louisiana State University, Baton Rouge, LA 70803; (504) 388-1645

The Society for Social Studies of Science supports professional publications and newsletters.

The Society for the Advancement of Chicanos and Native Americans in Science

Thinmann Laboratories, University of California, Santa Cruz, CA 95064; (408) 429-2295

The Society for the Advancement of Chicanos and Native Americans in Science furnishes teacher materials and newsletters.

Soil and Water Conservation Society

7515 Northeast Ankeny Road, Ankeny, IA 50021; (515) 289-2831

The Soil and Water Conservation Society produces professional publications, activities for students, curriculum development, career information, regional workshops, and newsletters.

U.S. Department of Education, Eisenhower Program for Mathematics and Science Education, State Program

400 Maryland Avenue SW, Washington, DC 20202; (202) 732-3000

This federal agency is responsible for facilitating the Dwight D. Eisenhower Program for Mathematics and Science Education. This program provides all schools in the nation with funds for staff development in science and mathematics education.

U.S. Geological Survey

Distribution Branch, Box 25286, Federal Center, Denver, CO 80225; (703) 648-6515

The U.S. Geological Survey offers workshops for teachers at three regional centers located in Reston, VA; Denver, CO; and Menlo Park, CA. Teachers participating are usually located within commuting distance, but teachers nationwide are eligible to attend.

U.S. Metric Association

10245 Andasol Avenue, Northridge, CA 91325; (818) 263-5606

Newsletters, activities for students and teachers and curriculum materials can be obtained from the U.S. Metric Society.

The Wildlife Society

5410 Grosvenor Lane, Bethesda, MD 20814; (301) 897-9770

The Wildlife Society provides curriculum materials and programs related to wildlife conservation.

Young Astronaut Council

Box 65432, 1211 Connecticut Avenue NW, Washington, DC 20036; (202) 682-1986

The Young Astronaut Council facilitates a program of enrichment materials through local chapters.

National Aeronautics and Space Administration (NASA) Resources

The National Aeronautics and Space Administration (NASA) Education Division provides educational programs and materials for teachers and students from the elementary to the university level. To help disseminate materials to elementary and secondary educators, the NASA Education Division has established the NASA Teacher Resource Center Network (TRCN). This network is comprised of Teacher Resource Centers (TRCs), Regional Teacher Resource Centers (RTRCs), and the Central Operation of Resources for Educators (CORE).

Located at the nine NASA research centers, TRCs have a variety of NASA-related educational materials in several formats: videotapes, slides, audio tapes, publications, lesson plans and activities. NASA educational materials can be copied at TRCs.

Regional Teacher Resource Centers (RTRCs)

To offer more educators the opportunity to visit the TRCN, NASA forms partnerships with planetariums, universities, museums, and other nonprofit organizations to serve as RTRCs and plans to have RTRCs as broadly distributed geographically as possible. Teachers may preview NASA materials at these RTRCs or copy the materials.

NASA Central Operation Resources for Education (CORE)

Lorain County Joint Vocational School, 15181 Route 58 South, Oberlin, OH 44074; (216) 774-1051 X293/294

Designed for the national and international distribution of aerospace educational materials to enhance the NASA Teacher Resource Center Network, CORE provides educators with another source for NASA educational audiovisual materials. CORE will process teacher requests by mail for a minimal fee. On school letterhead, educators can request a catalogue and order form from Tina Salyer at the address above.

Teacher Resource Centers, Regional Teacher Resource Centers and other NASA program locations are listed by state:

U.S. Space & Rocket Center
NASA Teacher Resource Center
Huntsville, AL 35807
(205) 544-5812

Public Affairs Office (CA21)
NASA Marshall Space Flight
   Center, AL 35812
(205) 544-7391

University of Arkansas-Little Rock
Natural Science Building, Room 215
2801 South University
Little Rock, AK 72204

Lunar and Planetary Lab
NASA Regional Teacher Resource
   Center
University of Arizona
Tucson, AZ 85721

NASA Ames-Dryden Flight
   Research Facility
Public Affairs Office (Trl. 42)
NASA Teacher Resource Center
Edwards AFB, CA 93523
(805) 258-3546

Mail Stop TO-25
NASA Ames Research Center
Moffett Field, CA 94035
(415) 604-5543

Mail Code 180-20 5
Jet Propulsion Laboratory
4800 Oak Grove Drive
Pasadena, CA 91109

U.S. Space Foundation
NASA Regional Teacher Resource
   Center
1525 Vapor Trail
Colorado Springs, CO 80916
(719) 550-1000

Delaware Teacher Center
Claymont Education Campus
NASA Regional Teacher Resource
   Center
3401 Green Street
Claymont, DE 19703
(302) 792-3806

University of the District of
Columbia
NASA Regional Teacher Resource
Center
Mail Stop 4201
4200 Connecticut Avenue NW
Washington, DC 20008
(202) 282-7338

National Air and Space Museum
Smithsonian Institution
Education Resource Center, P-700
Washington, DC 20560
(202) 786-2109

Mail Code PA-EAB
NASA Kennedy Space Center, FL
32899
(407) 867-4444

NASA John F. Kennedy Space
Center
Educators Resources Library
Mail Code ERL
Kennedy Space Center, FL 32899
(407) 867-4090

University of Idaho at Moscow
NASA Regional Teacher Resource
Center
ID Space Grant College Fellowship
Program
College of Education
Moscow, ID 83843
(208) 885-6030

Parks College of St. Louis
University
NASA Regional Teacher Resource
Center
Rt. 157 and Falling Springs Road
Cahokia, IL 62206
(618) 337-7500

Chicago Museum of Science and
Industry
NASA Regional Teacher Resource
Center
57th Street and Lakeshore Drive
Chicago, IL 60637-2093
(312) 684-1414 X429

University of Evansville
NASA Regional Teacher Resource
Center

School of Education
1800 Lincoln Ave.
Evansville, IN 47714
(812) 479-2393

University of Northern Iowa
NASA Regional Teacher Resource
Center
IRTS
Room 222, Schnidler Education
Center
Cedar Falls, IA 50614-0009

Kansas Cosmosphere and Space
Center
NASA Regional Teacher Resource
Center
1100 North Plum
Hutchinson, KS 67501
(316) 662-2305 or (800) 397-0330

Murray State University
NASA Regional Teacher Resource
Center
Waterfield Library
Murray, KY 42071
(502) 762-4420

Bossier Parish Community College
NASA Regional Teacher Resource
Center
2719 Airline Drive
Bossier City, LA 71111
(318) 746-7754

Southern University
NASA Regional Teacher Resource
Center
Downtown Metro Center
610 Texas Street
Shreveport, LA 71101
(318) 674-3444

Public Affairs Office (130)
NASA Goddard Office Space Flight
Center
Greenbelt, MD 20771
(301) 286-7207

NASA Goddard Space Flight
Center
Teacher Resource Laboratory
Mail Code 130.3
Greenbelt, MD 20771
(301) 286-8570

Northern Michigan University
NASA Regional Teacher Resource
Center
Olson Library Media Center
Marquette, MI 49855
(906) 227-2270

Central Michigan University
NASA Regional Teacher Resource
Center
Ronan Hall, Room 101
Mount Pleasant, MI 48859
(517) 774-4387

Oakland University
NASA Regional Teacher Resource
Center
O'Dowd Hall, Room 216
Rochester, MI 48309-4401
(313) 370-2485

Mankato State University
NASA Regional Teacher Resource
Center
Department of Curriculum and
Instruction
MSU Box 52/P.O. Box 8400
Mankato, MN 56002-8400
(507) 389-5710 or 1516

St. Cloud State University
Center for Information Media
NASA Regional Teacher Resource
Center
St. Cloud, MN 56301
(612) 255-2062

Tri-State Learning Center (SSC-
TRC)
NASA Teacher Resource Center
Rt. 72 West Box 508
Iuka, MS 38854
(601) 423-4373

Mississippi Delta Community
College
NASA Regional Teacher Resource
Center
P.O. Box 177
Moorehead, MS 38761
(601) 246-5631

NASA John C. Stennis Space Center
Stennis Space Center, MS 39529
(601) 688-3341

NASA Stennis Space Center
Teacher Resource Center
Building 1200
Stennis Space Center, MS 39529
(601) 688-3338

Rt. 72 West, Box 748
Tishimingo, MS 38852
(601) 423-5055

Western Montana College of the
   University of Montana
NASA Regional Teacher Resource
   Center
Carson Library
Dillon, MT 59725
(406) 683-7011

University of Nebraska State
   Museum
NASA Regional Teacher Resource
   Center
14th & U Streets
P.O. Box 880338
Lincoln, NE 68588-0338
(402) 472-8899

University of New Mexico
NASA Regional Teacher Resource
   Center
Continuing Education and
   Community Service
1634 University NE
Albuquerque, NM 87131
(505) 277-3861

New Mexico State University
NASA Regional Teacher Resource
   Center
New Mexico Space Grant
   Consortium
Box 3001, Department SG
Las Cruces, NM 88003-0001
(505) 646-6414

The City College
NASA Regional Teacher Resource
   Center
NAC Building, Room 5224
Convent Avenue at 138th Street
New York, NY 10031
(212) 690-6993

University of North Carolina,
   Charlotte

NASA Regional Teacher Resource
   Center
J. Murray Atkins Library
Charlotte, NC 28223
(704) 547-2559

University of North Dakota
NASA Regional Teacher Resource
   Center
The Wayne Peterson Room
Earth Systems Science Building
Space Studies Department
P.O. Box 7306, University Station
Grand Forks, ND 58203-7306
(701) 777-4856 or 1-800-828-4274

Mail Stop 7-4
NASA Lewis Research Center
21000 Brookpark Road
Cleveland OH 44135
(216) 433-5583

NASA Lewis Research Center
Teacher Resource Center
Mail Stop 8-1
21000 Brookpark Road
Cleveland, OH 44135
(216) 433-2017

Oklahoma State University
NASA Regional Teacher Resource
   Center
300 North Cordell
Stillwater, OK 74078-0422
(405) 744-7015

Mid-Atlantic Technology
   Application Center
NASA Regional Teacher Resource
   Center

University of Pittsburgh,
823 William Pitt Union
Pittsburgh, PA 15260
(412) 648-7008

Rhode Island College
NASA Regional Teacher Resource
   Center
Aerospace Education
Providence, RI 02908
(401) 456-8567

Dr. Robert W. Fitzmaurice
Center Education Program Officer
Public Affairs Office (AP-4)

NASA Johnson Space Center
Houston, TX 77058
(713) 483-1257

NASA Johnson Space Center
Teacher Resource Center
Mail Code AP-4
Houston, TX 77058
(713) 483-8696

Weber State University
NASA Regional Teacher Resource
   Center
WSU Center for Science Education
Ogden, UT 66048
(801) 626-6160

Mail Stop 154
NASA Langley Research Center
Hampton, VA 23665-5525
(804) 864-3307/3312

NASA Langley Teacher Research
   Center
Virginia Air and Space Center
600 Settler Landing Road
Hampton, VA 23669
(804) 727-0800

Radford University
NASA Regional Teacher Resource
   Center
P.O. Box 6886
Radford, VA 24142
(703) 831-5127

NASA Wallops Flight Facility
Education Complex Visitor Center
NASA Teacher Resource Center
Building J-17, P.O. Box 98
Wallops Island, VA 23337
(804) 824-2295

Norwich University
Vermont College Educational
   Resource Center
NASA Regional Teacher Resource
   Center
Schulman Hall
Montpelier, VT 05602
(802) 828-8845

University of Washington
NASA Regional Teacher Resource
   Center
AK-50, c/o Geophysics Dept.

Seattle, WA 98195
(206) 543-1943

Wheeling Jesuit College
NASA Regional Teacher Resource
Center
220 Washington Ave.
Wheeling, WV 26003
(304) 243-2388

University of Wisconsin at
LaCrosse
NASA Regional Teacher Resource
Center
Morris Hall, Room 200
LaCrosse, WI 54601
(608) 785-8148 or 8650

University of Wyoming
NASA Regional Teacher Resource
Center
Learning Resource Center
P.O. Box 3374 University Station
Laramie, WY 82701-3374
(307) 766-2527

APPENDIX

F

Materials and Resource Sources

Acid Rain Foundation
1630 Blackhawk Hills
St. Paul, MN 55122

AIMS Education Foundation
P.O. Box 7766
Fresno, CA 93747

Allyn & Bacon, Inc.
160 Gould Street
Needham Heights, MA 02194

Arbor Scientific
P.O. Box 2750
Ann Arbor, MI 48106

Associated Microscope, Inc.
P.O. Box 1076
Elon College, NC 27244

Carolina Biological Supply Co.
2700 York Road
Burlington, NC 27215

Children's Press
1224 West Van Buren Street
Chicago, IL 60607

Connecticut Valley Biological
Supply Co., Inc.
82 Valley Road
P.O. Box 326
Southampton, MA 01073

Dale Seymour Publications
P.O. Box 10888
Palo Alto, CA 94303

Delta Education, Inc.
P.O. Box 950
Hudson, NH 03051

Dover Publications, Inc.
180 Varick Street
New York, NY 10014

Edmund Scientific Co.
101 E. Glouster Pike
Barrington, NJ 08007

ERIC Clearinghouse for Science,
Mathematics, and Environmental
Education (ERIC/SMEAC)
1200 Chamber Road, 3rd Floor
Columbus, OH 43212

Flinn Scientific, Inc.
P.O. Box 219
Batavia, IL 60510

Frey Scientific Co.
905 Hickory Lane
Mansfield, OH 44905

Harcourt Brace Jovanovich, Inc.
Five Sampson St.
Saddle Brook, NJ 07662

Harper & Row
10 East 53rd Street
New York, NY 10022

D.C. Heath Company
125 Spring Street
Lexington, MA 02173

Glencoe
383 Madison Avenue
New York, NY 10017

J.B. Lippincott Company
East Washington Square
Philadelphia, PA 19105

Lab-Aids, Inc.
249 Trade Zone Drive
Ronkonkoma, NY 11779

McGraw-Hill, Inc.
1221 Avenue of the Americas
New, York NY 10020

NASCO
901 Janesville Avenue
Fort Atkinson, WI 53538

PASCO Scientific
1876 Sabre Street
Hayward, CA 94545

Sargeant Welch, Inc.
7300 North Linder Avenue
Skokie, IL 60067

Science Kit, Inc.
777 E. Park Drive
Tonawanda, NY 14150-6781

Silver Burdett & Ginn
250 James Street, CN818
Morristown, NJ 07960

Venier Software
2920 SW 89th Street
Portland, OR 97225

APPENDIX **G**   *Out-of-School Resources*

3-2-1 Contact
Children's Television Workshop,
   One Lincoln Plaza, New York,
   NY 10023; (212) 595-3456

Over 220 half-hour award-winning
programs, broadcast over seven seasons, designed to stimulate student
interest in science. 3-2-1 Contact Action Kits are video clips and activities
for use in after-school care facilities.
They are designed to be engaging to
students and require minimal supervision.

Hands-on-Science
Hands-on-Science Outreach, Inc.,
   4910 Macon Road, Rockville,
   MD 20852; (301) 460-5922

Thematically organized materials
provide recreational activities in science for use in after-school settings.
Required leader training sessions facilitate effective discovery of science
by participants at a wide range (K–6)
of age levels. Consumable kits promote ownership and mastery of sci-

entific concepts by participants, especially those from economically disadvantaged backgrounds.

National SERIES Project
300 Lakeside Drive, Oakland, CA
   94612; (510) 987-0119

High school students lead younger
children (ages 9–12) in the discovery
of science. Trained by adult mentors,
teens guide younger students through
six scientific units, addressing such
concepts as chemistry and the environment, agriculture, and recycling.
Each unit culminates in a community
service project, giving students opportunities to apply acquired knowledge to real problems in their own
communities.

**National Urban League Preschool
Science Collaborative**
Education Department, 500 East
   62nd Street, New York, NY
   10021; (212) 310-9214

Materials provide suggestions for

physical science activities for use in
preschool classrooms. Activities are
especially designed to appeal to students from low-income or single-par-
ent households.

Operation SMART
Girls, Inc., 30 E. 33rd Street, New
   York, NY 10016; (212) 689-3700

This program of out-of-school activities emphasizes hands-on experiences
in mathematics, science, and technology for girls ages 6–18. Its activities
are aimed at combating existing barriers to participation in science and
mathematics by girls, through the
creation of positive environments for
learning, special staff awareness training, and bombardment of girls with
information about careers and educational opportunities not traditionally promoted among women.

Reading Rainbow
GNP, P.O. Box 80669, Lincoln, NE
   68501; (800) 228-4630

Books are used as a platform for introducing a wide range of concepts and ideas, including scientific topics, to young viewers (ages 5–9). Videotapes of episodes, booklists, and teacher's guides are available to teachers and librarians across the country to facilitate utilization of the program in schools.

Science-by-Mail
Museum of Science, Science Park, Boston, MA 02114-1099; (800) 729-3300

Three science challenge units per year contain self-explanatory science exploration that may be conducted at home, in community-based activities, or in schools. Solutions to open-ended problems are submitted to scientist mentors, who review and respond to student work.

SuperScience Magazine
Scholastic, Inc., 2931 E. McCarthy Street, P.O. Box 3710, Jefferson City, MO 65102-3710

Student magazines use common scientific topics of interest to students to encourage hands-on activities and discovery of scientific concepts. Activities integrate science learning with reading, mathematics, and social studies. *SuperScience Red:* grades 1–3 and *SuperScience Blue:* grades 4–6.

The Second Voyage of the *Mimi*
Wings for Learning, 1600 Green Hill Road, P.O. Box 660002, Scotts Valley, CA 95067-0002

A voyage into ancient Mayan civilization serves as a vehicle for teaching interdisciplinary science and mathematics. Twelve 15-minute documentary-format episodes, accompanied by student materials and hands-on activities, engage students in the discovery of mathematics and science. Software learning modules whose themes are derived from the video series offer flexible learning opportunities in either science or mathematics to individuals or small groups of students.

Index